Conflict of Laws: A Comparative Approach

To Jan and Julia

Conflict of Laws:
A Comparative Approach

TEXT AND CASES

Gilles Cuniberti

Professor of Comparative and Private International Law, University of Luxembourg

Edward Elgar
PUBLISHING

Cheltenham, UK • Northampton, MA, USA

Published by
Edward Elgar Publishing Limited
The Lypiatts
15 Lansdown Road
Cheltenham
Glos GL50 2JA
UK

Edward Elgar Publishing, Inc.
William Pratt House
9 Dewey Court
Northampton
Massachusetts 01060
USA

A catalogue record for this book
is available from the British Library

Library of Congress Control Number: 2016953925

ISBN 978 1 78536 593 5 (cased)
ISBN 978 1 78536 595 9 (paperback)
ISBN 978 1 78536 594 2 (eBook)

Typeset by Servis Filmsetting Ltd, Stockport, Cheshire
Printed and bound in Great Britain by TJ International Ltd, Padstow

Contents in brief

Full contents

Acknowledgements

I thank Gerald Goldstein, Mary Keyes, Patrick Kinsch, Peter Mankowski, Henry P. Monaghan and Koji Takashi for commenting on drafts or helping me in various ways.

Many thanks as well to Albane Kopf and Chukwuma Okoli for great research assistance.

Finally, I am grateful to Symeon C. Symeonides, T.M.C. Asser Press and Cambridge University Press for permission to excerpt from Symeon C. Symeonides, 'Territoriality and Personality in Tort Conflicts', in T. Einhorn and K. Siehr (eds) *Intercontinental Cooperation Through Private International Law: Essays in Memory of Peter Nygh* 432–3 (T.M.C. Asser Press, 2004), and Gilles Cuniberti, 'The Liberalization of the French Law of Foreign Judgments' (2007) 56 ICLQ 931, 932–3, 936–7.

Table of cases

France

Germany

Ghana

Kenya

Netherlands

Nigeria

Switzerland

United Kingdom

United States

Table of legislation

Model Laws, Restatement and Principles

American Law Institute

Institut de droit international

Introduction

The subject matter

Private international law, which is also traditionally called Conflict of Laws in the English speaking world, is concerned with legal relationships which are connected to more than one legal order. For instance, the parties can be domiciled in different States, or be citizens of different States. They could also be domiciled in the same State, but act in a foreign jurisdiction: marry, enter into a contract, have an accident, and so on. Such legal relationships, and any dispute arising out of such relationships, can be characterized as international, as opposed to a purely domestic relationship or dispute, which is only connected to a single legal order.

International relationships raise a number of issues which do not arise with respect to domestic relationships and which are the focus of private international law.

- The first is the issue of the applicable law. If a German company sells a machine to a US company which subsequently injures a US worker, which law would determine whether the German company would be liable to the worker? It could be the law of the place where the damage occurred, the law of the place where the machine was manufactured, or any other law connected to the relationship.
- The second is the issue of international jurisdiction. In this case, where could the worker initiate proceedings against the German company? In the United States? In Germany? Elsewhere? Courts have rules of *international* jurisdiction, and will only decide a given dispute if it falls within the scope of their international jurisdiction.
- Finally, a third issue is that of the recognition and enforcement of foreign judgments. Suppose that, in this same case, the worker successfully sued the German company in the United States. If the German company only has assets in Germany, or only has sufficient assets to pay the American judgment in Germany, the American judgment could only be enforced there. The issue of enforcing a foreign judgment would thus arise in Germany.

Private international law as national law

Private international law is the body of rules designed to resolve these special issues. These rules are international insofar as they resolve issues which only arise in international disputes: their subject matter is a number of international issues. But this does not mean that the source of private international law is international, and even less that private international law is a branch of (public) international law. Although the issue was debated among scholars in the past, it is now widely accepted that rules of private international law are national rules which vary from one jurisdiction to another (sometimes greatly).

Some efforts to harmonize rules of private international law have been effective. At the international level, they have essentially been conducted by the Hague Conference on Private International Law and have resulted in the conclusion of international conventions (so called Hague Conventions). These conventions, however, have typically been ratified by small numbers of states, originating essentially from Europe, and have not significantly changed the fact that rules of private international law remain essentially national and vary from one country to another.

In the European Union, the Member States granted competence to the Union to legislate in private international law matters in 1997. Since then, the EU has passed a number of Regulations which are gradually harmonizing the field as between the Member States

Federal States

The issues of the applicable law and of international jurisdiction do not only arise in legal relationships involving more than one nation State. They also arise in federal States. The United States is the clearest example. In most fields, private law is not unified, and thus varies from one state to another. Issues of applicable law arise, therefore, in domestic cases involving more than one US state (Texas and Nevada, for instance). Likewise, American courts must determine whether they may retain jurisdiction in cases connected to more than one US state.

Note that, contrary to the EU, many issues of conflict of laws are not unified in the US. This means that, while private international law is being gradually harmonized in the EU, it remains a matter for state law in the US, in particular in the field of choice of law, and will thus vary from one US state to another.

Part I

Choice of law

1

Competing methodologies

While domestic legal relationships are obviously governed by the law of the single State to which they are connected,[1] international relationships raise the special issue of *the applicable law*: it is necessary to determine which law applies to the legal relationship. One might have expected international law to apply. However, (public) international law has traditionally been concerned with the action of States, and has thus traditionally offered rules relevant for their actions (war, status of diplomats, entering into treaties, and so on). There are barely any international rules concerned with private legal relationships. This is the reason why the only option for addressing the issue of the law governing private relationships has traditionally been to choose and apply one national law. The issue of the applicable law is thus also known as the issue of *choice of law*: choosing which national law applies.

The situation has slightly changed in recent years, as States have concluded numerous international conventions harmonizing certain areas of private law. However, despite some significant successes such as the 1980 United Nation Convention on Contracts for International Sales of Goods, most areas of private law remain untouched by the process of international harmonization of private law. International disputes will therefore be settled by the national law which the competent court will declare applicable.

The issue of choice of law can be addressed in different ways. Several methodologies have been proposed by scholars, and used by lawmakers. However, in the last two centuries, one has gradually come to dominate the world and be used throughout Europe, Asia, Africa and South America. In the middle of the 20th century, it was also used in North America, but the American choice of law revolution which started in the 1960s has resulted in a major methodological shift in most of the United States. We shall first focus on what has become the traditional methodology (1), and then present the new American methodology (2). Finally, we shall discuss some advanced issues (3).

---

1 When two Singaporeans living in Singapore marry in Singapore, Singapore law applies.

1   The traditional methodology

In the 21st century, most States approach the issue of choice of law through the same methodology by using multilateral choice of law rules. The first scholar to propose addressing the issue of choice of law through this methodology was a German legal historian named Karl Friedrich von Savigny.[2] In continental Europe, his name has remained associated with the multilateral methodology and is often used to refer to it (in French: *la méthode savignienne*).

The scope of the multilateral methodology is not general, however. It does not apply to public law rules (1.2), and an exception exists for rules which involve the public interest (1.3).

1.1   Multilateral choice of law rules

1.1.1   *Basic principles*

Multilateral choice of law rules address the issue of choice of law by selecting the applicable law through the use of geographical criteria, or pointers. The applicable law is the law of the State designated by the geographical criterion. This geographical criterion, or pointer, is called a 'connecting factor', because it connects the dispute, or the legal relationship, to a legal order, the law of which will be applicable.

> *European Regulation (EC) No 864/2007 of 11 July 2007 on the law applicable to non-contractual obligations (Rome II)*
>
> **Article 4** *General rule*
>
> 1. Unless otherwise provided for in this Regulation, the law applicable to a non-contractual obligation arising out of a tort/delict shall be the law of the country in which the damage occurs irrespective of the country in which the event giving rise to the damage occurred and irrespective of the country or countries in which the indirect consequences of that event occur.
>
> 2. However, where the person claimed to be liable and the person sustaining damage both have their habitual residence in the same country at the time when the damage occurs, the law of that country shall apply. (. . .)

---

2 Karl Friedrich von Savigny (1779–1861). Remarkably, Savigny made his revolutionary proposal in the last volume of his treatise on Roman law in 1849 (*A Treatise on the Conflict of Laws and the Limits of their Operation in Respect of Place and Time*, William Guthrie tr, 2nd edn (T & T Clarke 1880)).

Law of the People's Republic of China on the Laws Applicable to Foreign-Related Civil Relations (2010)

Article 31

Statutory succession is governed by the law of the habitual residence of the deceased when he/she dies. However, statutory succession of immovable property is governed by the law where the immovable property locates.

Japanese Act on the General Rules of Application of Laws (2006)

Article 4 *A Person's Legal Capacity*

(1) The legal capacity of a person shall be governed by his or her national law. (...)

In each of these three examples, the applicable law is determined through the use of a similar rule. The choice of law issue is resolved merely by holding that the law designated by the connecting factor (that is, the territorial pointer) is applicable.

As each of these three choice of law rules, multilateral choice of law rules always have the same structure. They associate a connecting factor with a special category, which is often an entire area of the law. For any legal relationship belonging to this category, the choice of law issue will be resolved in the same way, that is, by applying the same connecting factor. For instance, under Art. 4.1 of the Rome II Regulation, all tort issues are governed by the law of the place of the damage.[3] The relevant category, which is called the 'connecting category', is Tort. The connecting factor is the place where the damage occurs. In the multilateral methodology, therefore, the starting point of the reasoning is the relevant legal relationship. It must be put in the right category, in order to identify the applicable connecting factor, and eventually the applicable law.

Can you identify the connecting categories and factors in the two other rules?

You will also have noticed that two of these three examples come from a particular jurisdiction, Japan and China, and one from a regional ensemble, the European Union. The sources of choice of law rules have traditionally been national. States have sometimes concluded international conventions to harmonize them, in particular under the aegis of the Hague Conference on Private International Law.[4] In Europe, competence was given to the European Union to legislate in the field and thus unify the choice of law rules of the Member States in 1999 (by contrast, in the United States, the field remains a matter of state law). However, harmonization has never been achieved

---

3 This is the general rules. There are special rules for certain torts (see, e.g., 1.1.2 below).

4 For examples, see below p. 437.

beyond a limited number of States. This means that, except in certain regional areas such as the European Union, States apply different choice of law rules: Japanese courts apply Japanese choice of law rules, Brazilian courts apply Brazilian choice of law rules, and so on. The same is true in federal States where the field has not been harmonized, as the United States: New York courts apply New York choice of law rules, California courts apply California choice of law rules. It is therefore not possible to determine 'the' applicable law to a given relationship. One can only determine the law that the courts of a given State would apply. Choice of law is *relative*, and it is always necessary to envisage it from the perspective of one State. This State is called 'the forum': the State the courts of which are seized and confronted to the choice of law issue. The law of this State is referred to as the law of the forum, and all other laws as foreign laws.

1.1.2   Conflicts justice v. substantive justice

The focus of the multilateral methodology is on the geographical proximity between the dispute and the applicable law. Multilateral choice of law rules rely exclusively on connecting factors. By contrast, the substance of the potentially applicable laws is not taken into consideration. The multilateral methodology is substance-neutral, and substance-blind. As we shall see,[5] there is an exception where the content of the law designated by a multilateral choice of law rule is truly outrageous from the perspective of the forum. However, in cases where the laws which could be legitimately considered are merely different, this difference is irrelevant. Multilateral choice of law rules aim at achieving *conflicts justice* rather than *substantive justice*. They should allocate fairly cases between the different jurisdictions, rather than achieve (substantive) justice.

The reasons for focusing on geographical proximity and conflicts justice are twofold.

First, it is argued that the expectations of all interested parties should be that the law which has the closest geographical link with the dispute applies.[6] For example, if an Englishman buys a summer house in France, his intuition should be that the law governing the transaction is probably the law of place where the house is located.

Then, it is unclear whether a system based on substantive justice could work. Substantive justice is relative. The reason why conflicts of laws arise, and

---

5 See below, Ch. 2, Section 5.
6 See, e.g., in France, Batiffol and Lagarde, vol. I, 446.

choice of law rules are necessary, is because different lawmakers have different perceptions of substantive justice and thus lay down different substantive rules. Resolving conflict of laws on the basis of substantive justice would therefore mean to prefer one perception of it over the other. The risk would be high that this would ultimately mean that the forum would always prefer its perception of substantive justice, and thus apply its law, as the 'better law'. Indeed, it could be argued that courts would have to defer to the assessment made by their legislature, and would be thus be required to prefer the view of the forum.

While multilateral choice of law rules are typically substance neutral, it is also possible to create choice of law rules which will favour a certain substantive outcome (substantive choice of law rules). Please consider the two following examples and identify (1) which substantive outcome the lawmaker wants to favour, and (2) the legal technique used to achieve this purpose.

European Regulation (EC) No 593/2008 of 17 June 2008 on the law applicable to contractual obligations (Rome I)

Article 11 *Formal validity*

1. A contract concluded between persons who, or whose agents, are in the same country at the time of its conclusion is formally valid if it satisfies the formal requirements of the law which governs it in substance under this Regulation or of the law of the country where it is concluded. (. . .)

Rome II Regulation (2007)

Article 7 *Environmental damage*

The law applicable to a non-contractual obligation arising out of environmental damage or damage sustained by persons or property as a result of such damage shall be the law determined pursuant to Article 4(1), unless the person seeking compensation for damage chooses to base his or her claim on the law of the country in which the event giving rise to the damage occurred.

1.1.3 *Determining geographical proximity*

The ultimate goal of the multilateral methodology is to hold applicable the law which is the most closely connected to the relevant legal relationship. As we have seen, the typical structure of a multilateral choice of rule is to associate a connecting factor (for example, the place where damage occurred) to a connecting category (for example, tort), and to designate the applicable law to any case belonging to this category by using the connecting factor. The rationale for the choice of a given connecting factor is that it usually points to the legal system which is the most closely connected to the relevant legal relationship. For instance, the place of the country in which the damage occurred was chosen in tort matters because it was considered that this country was usually the most closely connected to the relevant legal relationship, that is, the tort claim.

In international cases, however, legal relationships may be connected to different legal systems from a variety of perspectives: the parties may have different nationalities, they may reside in different countries, one might have been negligent in one country and caused a loss to the other in another country, and so on . . .

In many cases, the parties will reside in two different countries, and will also be citizens of the same countries. If an accident occurs in one of two countries, the law of this country will indeed be the most closely connected to the dispute: it will be the country where one party lives and from which he/she is a citizen, and it will be the country where the accident occurred. However, there could be cases where the connecting factor would designate one law, but all other connections would be with another country. For instance, residents from New York state could drive to Canada for the weekend in the car of one of them, which would be matriculated and insured in New York. If they had an accident in Ontario (with no involvement of any other car), would it make sense to apply Ontario law to a dispute arising out of the accident? Would Ontario law be the most closely connected law? In a famous case of the early 1960s, *Babcock v. Jackson*,[7] the New York Court of Appeals said no, and challenged 'the mechanical formulae of the conflicts of law'.

In the U.S., the case was the starting point of a wider challenge to the multilateral methodology, which would ultimately lead to the American revolution on choice of law (see below 2). In Europe, the case initiated a debate on the narrower issue of whether flexibility should be introduced in the assessment of the law most closely connected to the dispute. Traditional choice of law rules rely on a single connecting factor for all cases belonging to a given connecting category. The closest connection is defined abstractly and rigidly. Please read these provisions and identify the techniques used by the EU and the Swiss lawmakers to address the issue.

Rome II Regulation (2007)

Article 4 *General Rule*

1. Unless otherwise provided for in this Regulation, the law applicable to a

---

7 191 N.E.2d 279 (N.Y. 1963).

non-contractual obligation arising out of a tort/delict shall be the law of the country in which the damage occurs irrespective of the country in which the event giving rise to the damage occurred and irrespective of the country or countries in which the indirect consequences of that event occur.

2. However, where the person claimed to be liable and the person sustaining damage both have their habitual residence in the same country at the time when the damage occurs, the law of that country shall apply.

3. Where it is clear from all the circumstances of the case that the tort/delict is manifestly more closely connected with a country other than that indicated in paragraphs 1 or 2, the law of that other country shall apply. A manifestly closer connection with another country might be based in particular on a pre-existing relationship between the parties, such as a contract, that is closely connected with the tort/delict in question.

Swiss Federal Code of Private International Law (1987)
Article 15 *III. Exception clause*
1 The law designated by this Code shall not be applied in those exceptional situations where, in light of all circumstances, it is manifest that the case has only a very limited connection with that law and has a much closer connection with another law.
2 This article is not applicable in the case of a choice of law by the parties.

? NOTES AND QUESTIONS

1 The provision whereby a court may apply the most closely connected law instead of the law designated by the connecting factor is typically called an exception clause. Why?
2 Does Art. 4.2 of the Rome II Regulation also address the problem?
3 What is the difference in the scope of Art. 4.3 and Art. 15?
4 Note that the general exception clause of the Swiss provision does not apply where the parties may have chosen the law governing their relationship.[8] This is because it would otherwise mislead them: if they chose a given law, their expectation is obviously that this law applies.
5 What is the purpose of this paragraph of Art. 19 of the Belgian Code of Private International Law?

When applying §1 [the general exception clause] special consideration is given to the need of predictability of the applicable law and to the circumstance that the relevant legal relationship was validly established in accordance with the private international law of the States with which the legal relationship was connected when it was created.

Should the application of an 'exception' clause be restricted? If it were applied too often, the connecting factor would arguably become meaningless: it

---

8 A general exception clause with the same exception for cases where the parties chose the applicable law is found in Art. 3082 of the Quebec Civil Code and Art. 19 of the Belgian Code of Private International Law.

would in effect be replaced by a general principle of application of the most closely connected law, to be determined in each particular case. Read the following case and explain whether there is a risk that the connecting factor in Art. 4 of the Rome Convention (today Art. 4 of the Rome I Regulation) might become meaningless because of the operation of the exception clause.

Rome Convention on the Law Applicable to Contractual Obligations (1980)
Article 4 *Applicable law in the absence of choice*
1. To the extent that the law applicable to the contract has not been chosen in accordance with Article 3, the contract shall be governed by the law of the country with which it is most closely connected. (. . .)
2. Subject to the provisions of paragraph 5 of this Article, it shall be presumed that the contract is most closely connected with the country where the party who is to effect the performance which is characteristic of the contract has, at the time of conclusion of the contract, his habitual residence, or, in the case of a body corporate or unincorporate, its central administration. (. . .)
5. (. . .) the presumptions in paragraphs 2 (. . .) shall be disregarded if it appears from the circumstances as a whole that the contract is more closely connected with another country.

 CASE

High Court of England and Wales, 27 March 2001
Definitely Maybe (Touring) Ltd v. Marek Liebererg Konzertagentur GmbH (no 2)[9]

Facts: The claimants who are based in England provide the services of the pop group called Oasis to those who organize live concerts. The defendants are a German-based company which organized two pop festivals in Germany in June, 2000 and contracted with the claimants for live performances by Oasis. Unfortunately, there was apparently a rift between the two Gallagher brothers and Noel, the talented lead guitarist, did not play in Germany. The defendants say that Oasis without Noel Gallagher is not really the group contracted for. Thus, they have refused to pay the full price. The claimants, by these proceedings issued in this jurisdiction, claim the balance of the moneys they say are owing.
Held: German law governs the contract.

Judgment – Morison J.:
5. The answer to the question comes from a proper interpretation of the Rome Convention adopted by both countries. Article 3 of the Convention gives effect to parties' own choice of law. There is no express or implied choice of law clause

9 [2001] 1 W.L.R. 1745.

in this case and, therefore, one must turn to article 4. Paragraph (1) of that article directs that a contract is governed by the law of the country with which it is most closely connected. Paragraph (2) provides, subject to the provisions of paragraph (5), that the country with the closest connection with the contract is to be determined by identifying the place where the party who effects or is to effect the characteristic performance of the contract is 'located' [has its central administration or principal place of business]. Thus, subject to paragraph 5, there are two questions to be answered: which party effects the characteristic performance of the contract, and where is that party located [in the sense used above]. Here, it is common ground that the claimants have the characteristic performance of the contract, in the sense that the substantive obligation under the contract was for Oasis to perform in two concerts in Germany. The claimants are located in England, and hence, by virtue of article 4(2) English law would be the governing law of the contract.

6. But article 4(2) is expressly made subject to the provisions of paragraph (5) of the same article. Paragraph (5) displaces the presumption in paragraph (2): 'if it appears from the circumstances as a whole that the contract is more closely connected with another country.' In such a case, paragraph (5) provides that paragraph (2) shall be disregarded.

7. The real issue between the parties centres on the relationship between these two paragraphs of article 4. While paragraph (2) looks to the location of the principal performer, paragraph (5) looks more widely to a connection between the contract and a country. If there is a divergence between the location of the principal performer and the place of substantial or characteristic performance, what then? On the one hand, were the presumption to be displaced whenever such divergence existed, the presumption would be of little weight or value. Paragraph 2 must have been inserted to provide a 'normal' rule which is simple to apply. Giving wide effect to paragraph (5) will render the presumption of no value and represent a return to the English common law test of ascertaining the proper law, which places much less weight on the location of the performer and much more on the place of performance, and the presumed intention of the parties.

8. Rather than seeking to find an answer to this issue, I turn to those factors which are said to show a closer connection between the contract and Germany than with England. The contract provided for Oasis to perform live in Germany; that was the place of the characteristic or substantial performance of the contract. The defendants were obliged to make arrangements in Germany to enable the performances to take place (for example, marketing and promotion) and to provide facilities such as security and bits of equipment. Thus, the contract required performance of contractual obligations in Germany by both parties. For what it is worth, the defendant company is German and payment was to be made in DMs and subject to deduction for German tax. Apart from the location of the claimants and the group, and the place of payment, there is no other connection between England and the contract.

The centre of gravity of the dispute is, I think, Germany. Therefore, if the test were simply that laid down in paragraph (5), namely, to say with which country was the contract most closely connected, I would have said Germany, rather than England.

9. But I return to the issue of the relationship between paragraphs (2) and (5) of article 4 and the legal effect of the presumption. There are, I think, two schools of thought. The first is to say that the presumption in paragraph (2), which is expressly made subject to paragraph (5), is weak and will more readily be displaced where the place of performance differs from the place of business of the performer. The second, adopts a narrower view of the 'exception' to the presumption in paragraph (5) and gives firm dominance to the presumption.

10. In relation to the first approach, the editors of *Dicey & Morris, The Conflict of Laws* . . . state that 'the presumption may most easily be rebutted in those cases where the place of performance differs from the place of business of the party whose performance is characteristic of the contract'. That is this case. In *Credit Lyonnais v. New Hampshire Insurance Co.*, [1997] 2 Lloyd's Rep. 1 at p. 5, the Court of Appeal noted that art. 4(5) 'formally makes the presumption very weak'.

11. In support of the more restricted view, the claimants rely upon a Dutch case: *Societé Nouvelle des Papéteries de L'Aa S.A. v. B.V. Machinefabriek*, Feb. 25, 1992, unreported where the Court gave a most restrictive interpretation to paragraph (5). It appears that the superior Court in Holland concluded that:

'this exception to the main rule of section 2 [paragraph 2] has to be applied restrictively, to the effect that the main rule should be disregarded only if, in the special circumstances of the case, the place of business of the party who is to effect the characteristic performance has no real significance as a connecting factor' . . .

12. The problem is caused, I think, by the fact that the factor which identifies the governing law in paragraph (2) [namely the location of the principal performer] may well not play an important part in determining the closest connection between country and contract. Thus, the presumption to which it gives rise is likely to be capable of being rebutted in most cases, and as such the presumption may be worthless. Yet, if paragraph (2) has the dominance suggested by the Dutch Court, the presumption becomes a rule of law to which paragraph (5) must be treated as an exception, and that is not the language of the Convention.

(. . .)

16. Here, the defendants have established to my satisfaction that, overall, the contract between the parties has a closer connection with Germany than with England. Even recognizing the Convention's emphasis on England as the place of the performer's business, having regard to the place of performance by both parties and the other factors referred to above, Germany has more attachment to or connection with the contract than England.

QUESTIONS

If the connecting factor used by the choice of law rule had been the place of performance of the contract, do you think the same problem would arise? Do you think the same problem arises with Art. 4 of the Rome II Regulation (see above)?

 CASE

Court of Justice of the European Union, 6 October 2009 *Intercontainer Interfrigo SC (ICF) v. Balkenende Oosthuizen BV* (Case C-133/08)[10]

53 By its fifth question, the national court asks whether the exception in the second clause of Article 4(5) of the Convention must be interpreted in such a way that the presumptions in Article 4(2) to (4) of the Convention do not apply only if it is evident from the circumstances in their totality that the connecting criteria indicated therein do not have any genuine connecting value, or whether the court must also refrain from applying them if it is clear from those circumstances that there is a stronger connection with some other country.

54 As was pointed out in the preliminary observations in paragraphs 24 to 26 of this judgment, Article 4 of the Convention, which sets out the connecting criteria applicable to contractual obligations in the absence of a choice by the parties of the law applicable to the contract, lays down, in Article 4(1), the general principle that the contract is to be governed by the law of the country with which it is most closely connected.

55 In order to ensure a high level of legal certainty in contractual relationships, Article 4(2) to (4) of the Convention provides for a set of criteria on the basis of which it is possible to presume which country the contract is most closely connected with. Those criteria operate like presumptions in the sense that the court before which a case has been brought must take them into consideration in determining the law applicable to the contract.

56 Under the first clause of Article 4(5) of the Convention, the connecting criterion of the place of residence of the party effecting the performance which is characteristic of the contract may be disregarded if that place of residence cannot be determined. Under the second clause of Article 4(5), all the 'presumptions' may be disregarded 'if it appears from the circumstances as a whole that the contract is more closely connected with another country'.

57 In that regard, it is necessary to establish the function and objective of the second clause of Article 4(5) of the Convention.

58 It is apparent from the Giuliano and Lagarde report that the draftsmen of the Convention considered it essential 'to provide for the possibility of applying a law other than those referred to in the presumptions in paragraphs 2, 3 and 4 whenever

---

10 ECLI:EU:C:2009:617.

all the circumstances show the contract to be more closely connected with another country'. It is also apparent from that report that Article 4(5) of the Convention leaves the court 'a margin of discretion as to whether a set of circumstances exists in each specific case justifying the non-application of the presumptions in paragraphs 2, 3 and 4' and that such a provision constitutes 'the inevitable counterpart of a general conflict rule intended to apply to almost all types of contract'.

59 It thus follows from the Giuliano and Lagarde report that the objective of Article 4(5) of the Convention is to counterbalance the set of presumptions stemming from the same article by reconciling the requirements of legal certainty, which are satisfied by Article 4(2) to (4), with the necessity of providing for a certain flexibility in determining the law which is actually most closely connected with the contract in question.

60 Since the primary objective of Article 4 of the Convention is to have applied to the contract the law of the country with which it is most closely connected, Article 4(5) must be interpreted as allowing the court before which a case has been brought to apply, in all cases, the criterion which serves to establish the existence of such connections, by disregarding the 'presumptions' if they do not identify the country with which the contract is most closely connected.

61 It therefore falls to be ascertained whether those presumptions may be disregarded only where they do not have any genuine connecting value or where the court finds that the contract is more closely connected with another country.

62 As is apparent from the wording and the objective of Article 4 of the Convention, the court must always determine the applicable law on the basis of those presumptions, which satisfy the general requirement of foreseeability of the law and thus of legal certainty in contractual relationships.

63 However, where it is clear from the circumstances as a whole that the contract is more closely connected with a country other than that identified on the basis of the presumptions set out in Article 4(2) to (4) of the Convention, it is for that court to refrain from applying Article 4(2) to (4).

64 In the light of those considerations, the answer to the fifth question must be that Article 4(5) of the Convention must be construed as meaning that, where it is clear from the circumstances as a whole that the contract is more closely connected with a country other than that determined on the basis of one of the criteria set out in Article 4(2) to (4) of the Convention, it is for the court to disregard those criteria and apply the law of the country with which the contract is most closely connected.

? **QUESTIONS**

1 Has the European Court of Justice clarified whether the Dutch or the English interpretation of the exception clause should be adopted? Would the English court now reach a different result in the *Definitely Maybe* case?

2 In 2009, the Rome Convention was replaced by the Rome I Regulation. The fundamental structure of Art. 4 was not changed: there is still an exception clause which allows the court to

apply a law more closely connected to the contract. However, Art. 4 was amended in several ways.[11] (1) The general connecting factor applicable to all contracts was replaced by eight more concrete connecting factors applicable to certain special contracts which still use, for the most part, the habitual residence of one party. (2) It is no longer framed in terms of 'presumptions'. (3) The exception clause provides that only a law which is 'manifestly' more closely connected to the contract might be applied (see also Art. 4.3 of the Rome II Regulation above). What do you think the purpose of this last addition is, and its effect will be?

***

In conclusion, the characteristics of multilateral choice of law rules can be summarized as follows.

(1) Multilateral rules start from the relevant legal relationship, to determine which law applies to it. They do not start from the law of any particular State, for the purpose of determining its geographical scope. The question is not 'does Japanese law apply to the capacity of this litigant?' It is rather 'which law applies to the issue of capacity of this litigant?'

(2) Multilateral rules aim at designating the law which is the most closely connected from a geographical point of view to the relevant legal relationship.

(3) Multilateral rules can result in the application of any national law. In particular, they can result in the application of either the law of the forum, or a foreign law. Certain unilateral methodologies, by contrast, would only focus on the territorial reach of one particular law, typically the law of the forum, and would therefore only lead to the application of that law.

(4) Multilateral rules do not favour the application of one law over the other. In particular, they do not favour the application of the law of the forum over the application of foreign laws. The chances of application of the law of a particular State only depend on the chances that the relevant fact, that is, the connecting factor, was located in the territory of that State.

(5) Finally, multilateral rules do not favour one outcome over the other. They designate the applicable law without considering the substance of the laws among which a choice is made.

1.2   Public law

Multilateral choice of law rules are designed to resolve conflicts of private laws. They are not designed to resolve conflicts of public laws. This is because a multilateral choice of law rule assumes that the laws of all countries contain a rule which would address the legal issue at stake in the dispute. It is

---

11 On Art. 4 of the Rome I Regulation, see also below Part 4, Ch. 9.

therefore possible to choose between the laws of the various States which are connected to the dispute: a choice of law is possible.

Public law is different. It is concerned with the State. Not *all* States. *Only* the State which has laid down the rules of public law designed to regulate its own action. A given public law offers rules concerned with one State only. For instance, French tax law is concerned with the taxes that the French State wishes to collect; it is silent on the taxes that Japan, Germany, or any other States may want to collect, from anybody.

As a consequence, if an individual lives in France and works in Germany, the right question to ask is not 'which law applies and determines its income tax?' It is rather 'is he liable to pay taxes to the French State?' and 'is he liable to pay taxes to the German State?' There are as many questions as there are interested States (if that individual is a U.S. national, you should add the 'is he liable to pay taxes to the U.S. State?'). Each question must be asked in isolation from the other. There is no choice to make.

Each State will therefore determine unilaterally the international reach of its public law. It will determine whether and when it wants to tax persons transacting abroad, or whether it will consider that a person is criminally liable for committing a criminal offence abroad. The international reach of public laws is determined by unilateral rules of application.

Of course, if several States have different rules of application, the result will often be that a given action will fall within the territorial scope of the public laws of several States. Private international law does not offer any tool to resolve such a conflict. In principle, therefore, the outcome could, for instance, be double taxation. It will then be for the relevant States to find a solution to this problem. They may want to conclude a treaty to fine tune the unilateral application of their laws: States have traditionally done so in tax law, by concluding conventions aiming at avoiding double taxation. States may also want to unilaterally resolve the problem, through a rule of substantive law taking into account the prior intervention of another State. This is the way the issue is handled in criminal law, through the operation of the rule *non bis in idem*: a delinquent may not be punished twice for the same facts. The conflict of criminal laws is dealt with by the second State, which will take into account the first penalty when trying the delinquent.

A different issue is whether foreign public laws may be applied by the forum.

Institut de droit international, Session de Wiesbaden (1975) Resolution on The Application of Foreign Public Law

II. The so-called principle of the inapplicability a priori of foreign public law, like that of its absolute territoriality, a principle invoked, if not actually applied, in judicial decisions and legal writings of certain countries:

a)   is based on no cogent theoretical or practical reason, and
b)   often duplicates with the principles of public policy,
c)   may entail results that are undesirable and inconsistent with contemporary needs for international co-operation.

III. The same applies for similar reasons to the inapplicability a priori of certain categories of provisions of foreign public law, such as provisions which do not concern the protection of private interests but primarily serve the interests of the State.

IV. The scope of the preceding rule and statements shall in no way be affected by the fact that foreign law which is regarded as public law is still applied less frequently for various reasons, and mainly:

a)   because the question does not arise owing to the nature of the social relationships referred to in the rule of conflict of laws or to the very subject of the foreign provision, or
b)   because the foreign provision is restricted in its scope to the territory of the legislator from whom it originates and because such restriction is in principle respected, or
c)   because authorities of the State of the forum often hold either that they have no jurisdiction to apply certain foreign laws which are regarded as public law, notably in giving administrative or constitutive judgments, or that they need not assist in the application of such provisions in the absence of treaties, of reciprocity or of a convergence of the economic or political interests of the States with which the situation is connected.

Institut de droit international, Session de Oslo (1977) Resolution on Foreign Law Claims Instituted by a Foreign Authority or a Foreign Public Body

I

a) Public law claims instituted in legal proceedings by a foreign authority or a foreign public body should, in principle, be considered inadmissible in so far as, from the viewpoint of the State of the forum, the subject-matter of such claims is related to the exercise of Governmental power.

b) Such claims should nevertheless be considered admissible if, from the viewpoint of the State of the forum and taking account of the right of the defendant to equitable treatment in his relations with the authority or body in question, this is justified by reason of the subject-matter of the claim, the needs of international cooperation or the interests of the States concerned.

II

Public law claims other than those referred to in the preceding Article, instituted in legal proceedings by a foreign authority or a foreign public body, should be considered admissible, as for example claims which from the viewpoint of the State of the forum stem from or are ancillary to private law claims.

❓ NOTES

The traditional position is that courts only apply the public law of their own State, and will not apply foreign public laws. The rationale traditionally put forward is that the forum should not assist foreign States in advancing their own public interest, as the public interest of the forum might be opposite, but it is hard to see why such assistance should be absolutely banned.[12] The resolutions of the Institut de droit international are a welcome attempt to limit the scope of the rule.

While States will not directly apply foreign public laws, in particular revenue and penal laws, they often consider foreign law for the purpose of applying the law of the forum, or the otherwise applicable law. For instance, if foreign criminal law prohibits performance of the contract, the law of the forum may consider it as an excuse for non-performance under the law governing the contract. French scholars explain that foreign public law is not *applied*, but merely *taken into consideration* by the applicable law.[13] English scholars explain that foreign public law is not *enforced*, but simply *recognized*.[14]

1.3 International mandatory rules

Multilateral choice of law rules operate without taking into account the interests of States. As most private law disputes are only concerned with private interests, this typically does not raise any problem. However, certain private law disputes may involve the public interest. In such cases, a conflict arises between the needs of the public interest and the multilateral choice of law methodology, which is designed to serve private interests.

The problem was identified by a number of European scholars[15] who recognized that a State could not be expected to apply a foreign law when

---

12 In France, see Bureau and Muir Watt, para. 111.

13 See, e.g., Mayer & Heuzé, para 144.

14 See, e.g., Briggs, 203.

15 In France, Phocion Francescakis, 'Quelques précisions sur les lois d'application immédiate et leurs rapports avec les règles de conflit de lois' (1966) Rev Crit. DIP 1; in Italy, Giuseppe Sperduti, 'Norme di applicazione

its (public) interest demanded that its own law be applied. These scholars proposed to craft a general exception to the multilateral choice of law methodology allowing the application of the rules of the forum when its crucial interests demanded so.

Those rules serving the most crucial interests of the State would thus apply irrespective of the law designated as applicable by the relevant multilateral choice of law rule. As such they would be *international* mandatory rules, as opposed to domestic mandatory rules, which cannot be derogated from by a contrary agreement of the parties. They are labelled differently across jurisdictions. Yet, they ultimately share a common legal regime, and the different terms used only insist on different features of this regime. The importance of the interest served by international mandatory rules makes their application necessary: they are labelled rules of necessary application in France and Italy (*legge di applicazione necessaria*), or mandatory provisions in Germany (*zwingende Vorschriften*). They are applied directly, as opposed to other substantive rules which only apply if designated by the relevant multilateral choice of law rule: they are sometimes labelled rules of direct application (*loi d'application immédiate*). Finally, they override the otherwise applicable law: the European lawmaker calls them overriding mandatory provisions.[16]

Rome II European Regulation (2007)

Preamble

(32) Considerations of public interest justify giving the courts of the Member States the possibility, in exceptional circumstances, of applying exceptions based on public policy and overriding mandatory provisions. (. . .)

Article 16 *Overriding mandatory provisions*

Nothing in this Regulation shall restrict the application of the provisions of the law of the forum in a situation where they are mandatory irrespective of the law otherwise applicable to the non-contractual obligation.

Law of the People's Republic of China on the Laws Applicable to Foreign-Related Civil Relations (2010)

Article 4 Where a mandatory provision of the law of the People's Republic of China exists with respect to a foreign-related civil relation, that mandatory provision shall be applied directly.

---

necessaria e ordine pubblico' (1976) Riv. Dir. Int. 469; in Germany, Karl Neumeyer, *Internationales Verwaltungsrecht* (Schweitzer 1936) 243.

16 In the francophone world, they are also labelled '*lois de police*', after the term used in Article 3 of the French Civil Code.

1.3.1 Identifying international mandatory rules

Although international mandatory rules could be considered as a competing choice of law methodology, they are better understood as an exception to the multilateral methodology. When a given rule serving a crucial interest of the State can be identified, it must be applied. International mandatory rules have to be assessed on a case-by-case basis. They are not entire statutes or laws, but rather particular rules.

How are these particular rules to be identified?

In rare instances, the lawmaker of the relevant State will expressly provide that a provision should be considered as internationally mandatory and should thus apply irrespective of the otherwise applicable law.

Singapore Unfair Contract Terms Act[17]

S. 27 *Choice of law clauses*

(1) Where the proper law of a contract is the law of Singapore only by choice of the parties (and apart from that choice would be the law of some country outside Singapore) sections 2 to 7 do not operate as part of the proper law.

(2) This Act has effect notwithstanding any contract term which applies or purports to apply the law of some country outside Singapore, where (either or both)

(a) the term appears to the court, or arbitrator or arbiter to have been imposed wholly or mainly for the purpose of enabling the party imposing it to evade the operation of this Act; or

(b) in the making of the contract one of the parties dealt as consumer, and he was then habitually resident in Singapore, and the essential steps necessary for the making of the contract were taken there, whether by him or by others on his behalf.

Directive 93/13/EEC of 5 April 1993 on Unfair Terms in Consumer Contracts

Article 6

2. Member States shall take the necessary measures to ensure that the consumer does not lose the protection granted by this Directive by virtue of the choice of the law of a non-Member country as the law applicable to the contract if the latter has a close connection with the territory of the Member States.

---

17 See also s. 27 of the *Unfair Contract Terms Act 1977* (England, Wales and Northern Ireland).

? NOTES AND QUESTIONS

1 A lawmaker willing to make clear that a particular provision, or statute, is internationally mandatory should not only provide that it applies irrespective of the otherwise applicable law (for instance the law chosen by the parties in contractual matters), but also define the territorial reach of the relevant international mandatory rule. German scholars underscore that a special choice of law rule is associated to the substantive rule (*Sachnorm mit besonderer Kollisionsnorm*).[18] How does the Singapore lawmaker define the territorial reach of its Unfair Contract Terms statute?

2 Contrary to a multilateral choice of law rule, the criteria used will define the geographical scope of the relevant international mandatory rule unilaterally. They will only define the scope of application of the rule of the forum. Which law will apply if a given case falls outside of the geographical scope of the rule?

***

In most cases, however, the lawmaker will not have addressed the issue of the international application of its rules. It will therefore be for courts to assess whether the interests served by a given rule are so important that the rule should be considered as internationally mandatory.

In the 1960s, Phocion Francescakis[19] had proposed a definition of international mandatory rules which inspired the European Court of Justice[20] and later the European lawmaker.

Rome I Regulation (2008)

Article 9 *Overriding mandatory provisions*

1. Overriding mandatory provisions are provisions the respect for which is regarded as crucial by a country for safeguarding its public interests, such as its political, social or economic organisation, to such an extent that they are applicable to any situation falling within their scope, irrespective of the law otherwise applicable to the contract under this Regulation.

2. Nothing in this Regulation shall restrict the application of the overriding mandatory provisions of the law of the forum. (. . .)

Most international mandatory rules are identified by courts on a case-by-case basis after assessing the interests served by the relevant rules. The most common instances of judicial recognition of the existence of such rules include rules of competition law, rules protecting weaker parties (employees, consumers, franchisees, and so on) and rules aiming at sanctioning or preventing corruption.

---

18 von Hoffmann and Thorn, § 10 III 1.
19 N. 15.
20 Cases C-369/96 and C-376/96, *Criminal proceedings against Arblade* [1999] E.C.R. I-08453.

Interpretation of the Supreme People's Court on Issues regarding the Application of the
Law of the PRC on the Laws Applicable to Foreign-Related Civil Relations
(Part 1, 2012)

Article 10

The People's Courts shall consider overriding mandatory provisions, within the meaning of Article 4 of the Act on the Law Applicable to Foreign-related Civil Relations, the provisions of laws and regulations involving public and social interests of the People's Republic of China to the extent that their application cannot be excluded by an agreement of the parties, and that they apply directly to the foreign-related civil relations in question, concerning one of the following issues:

1) the protection of workers' rights;
2) food security and public health;
3) the protection of the environment;
4) the control of foreign exchange and the financial market;
5) anti-trust and anti-dumping;
6) further issues as may be deemed to be governed by overriding mandatory provisions.[21]

 CASE

Court of Justice of the European Communities, 9 November 2000, *Ingmar GB Ltd v. Eaton Leonard Technologies Inc.* (Case C-381/98)[22]

The main proceedings

10 In 1989, Ingmar and Eaton concluded a contract under which Ingmar [a company established in the United Kingdom] was appointed as Eaton's [a company established in California] commercial agent in the United Kingdom. A clause of the contract stipulated that the contract was governed by the law of the State of California.

11 The contract was terminated in 1996. Ingmar instituted proceedings before the High Court of Justice of England and Wales, Queen's Bench Division, seeking payment of commission and, pursuant to Regulation [Art.] 17, compensation for damage suffered as a result of the termination of its relations with Eaton.

12 By judgment of 23 October 1997, the High Court held that the Regulations did not apply, since the contract was governed by the law of the State of California.

13 Ingmar appealed against that judgment to the Court of Appeal of England and

---

21 Translation Ilaria Aquironi (2013), *Diritto del Commercio Internazionale* 891.
22 ECLI:EU:C:2000:605.

Wales (Civil Division), which decided to stay proceedings and to refer the follow-ing question to the Court for a preliminary ruling (. . .)

The question referred for preliminary ruling

14 By its question, the national court seeks to ascertain, essentially, whether Articles 17 and 18 of [Directive 86/653/EEC of 18 December 1986 on the coor-dination of the laws of the Member States relating to self-employed commercial agents], which guarantee certain rights to commercial agents after termination of agency contracts, must be applied where the commercial agent carried on his activity in a Member State although the principal is established in a non-member country and a clause of the contract stipulates that the contract is to be governed by the law of that country.

15 The parties to the main proceedings, the United Kingdom and German Governments and the Commission agree that the freedom of contracting parties to choose the system of law by which they wish their contractual relations to be gov-erned is a basic tenet of private international law and that that freedom is removed only by rules that are mandatory.

16 However, their submissions differ as to the conditions which a legal rule must satisfy in order to be classified as a mandatory rule for the purposes of private inter-national law.

17 Eaton contends that such mandatory rules can arise only in extremely limited circumstances and that, in the present case, there is no reason to apply the Directive, which is intended to harmonise the domestic laws of the Member States, to parties established outside the European Union.

18 Ingmar, the United Kingdom Government and the Commission submit that the question of the territorial scope of the Directive is a question of Community law. In their submission, the objectives pursued by the Directive require that its provisions be applied to all commercial agents established in a Member State, irrespective of the nationality or the place of establishment of their principal.

19 According to the German Government, in the absence of any express provi-sion in the Directive as regards its territorial scope, it is for the court of a Member State seised of a dispute concerning a commercial agent's entitlement to indem-nity or compensation to examine the question whether the applicable national rules are to be regarded as mandatory rules for the purposes of private interna-tional law.

20 In that respect, it should be borne in mind, first, that the Directive is designed to protect commercial agents, as defined in the Directive (Case C-215/97 *Bellone v. Yokohama* [1998] ECR I-2191, paragraph 13).

21 The purpose of Articles 17 to 19 of the Directive, in particular, is to protect the commercial agent after termination of the contract. The regime established by the Directive for that purpose is mandatory in nature. Article 17 requires Member

States to put in place a mechanism for providing reparation to the commercial agent after termination of the contract. Admittedly, that article allows the Member States to choose between indemnification and compensation for damage. However, Articles 17 and 18 prescribe a precise framework within which the Member States may exercise their discretion as to the choice of methods for calculating the indemnity or compensation to be granted.

22 The mandatory nature of those articles is confirmed by the fact that, under Article 19 of the Directive, the parties may not derogate from them to the detriment of the commercial agent before the contract expires. It is also borne out by the fact that, with regard to the United Kingdom, Article 22 of the Directive provides for the immediate application of the national provisions implementing the Directive to contracts in operation.

23 Second, it should be borne in mind that, as is apparent from the second recital in the preamble to the Directive, the harmonising measures laid down by the Directive are intended, inter alia, to eliminate restrictions on the carrying-on of the activities of commercial agents, to make the conditions of competition within the Community uniform and to increase the security of commercial transactions (see, to that effect, *Bellone*, paragraph 17).

24 The purpose of the regime established in Articles 17 to 19 of the Directive is thus to protect, for all commercial agents, freedom of establishment and the operation of undistorted competition in the internal market. Those provisions must therefore be observed throughout the Community if those Treaty objectives are to be attained.

25 It must therefore be held that it is essential for the Community legal order that a principal established in a non-member country, whose commercial agent carries on his activity within the Community, cannot evade those provisions by the simple expedient of a choice-of-law clause. The purpose served by the provisions in question requires that they be applied where the situation is closely connected with the Community, in particular where the commercial agent carries on his activity in the territory of a Member State, irrespective of the law by which the parties intended the contract to be governed.

26 In the light of those considerations, the answer to the question must be that Articles 17 and 18 of the Directive, which guarantee certain rights to commercial agents after termination of agency contracts, must be applied where the commercial agent carried on his activity in a Member State although the principal is established in a non-member country and a clause of the contract stipulates that the contract is to be governed by the law of that country.

? NOTES AND QUESTIONS

1 Which reason does the ECJ give to justify its characterization of the relevant rule as an international mandatory rule? Does it correspond to the definition provided by Art. 9 of the Rome I Regulation? A few days after the *Ingmar* case, the French Supreme court

ruled that the Agency Directive is not an international mandatory rule.[23] Which court is right?

2 When a lawmaker was silent on the international reach of a given rule, courts not only have to decide whether the rule is internationally mandatory, but also, in the affirmative, define its territorial scope by identifying territorial criteria of application. German scholars explain that a hidden choice of law rule (*versteckte Kollisionsnorm*) must be discovered, which is associated to the relevant mandatory rule.[24] Does the ECJ define the territorial scope of the Agency Directive?

3 In 2008, the Rome I Regulation introduced a new rule in Art. 3.4. How does it relate to the *Ingmar* judgment?

Article 3 *Freedom of choice*

4. Where all other elements relevant to the situation at the time of the choice are located in one or more Member States, the parties' choice of applicable law other than that of a Member State shall not prejudice the application of provisions of Community law, where appropriate as implemented in the Member State of the forum, which cannot be derogated from by agreement.

***

The doctrine of international mandatory rules shares similarities with the methodology used to assess the territorial reach of public laws. In both cases, the territorial scope of the rules is determined unilaterally. Both international mandatory rules and rules of public law are concerned with the public interest. Two opposite conclusions could be drawn from these commonalities. First, one could argue that there is no need to use the doctrine of international mandatory rules to justify the international regime of public laws. Conceptual clarity would therefore demand that the concept of international mandatory rules be limited to private law. This view is largely shared among Italian scholars.[25] Second, one could include in the doctrine of international mandatory rules public law, and indeed consider that it should be primarily used for public law rules. This has traditionally been the German view.[26]

1.3.2   Foreign international mandatory rules

The doctrine of international mandatory rules was crafted to allow States to apply their own rules when their public interest so demanded. But what about international mandatory rules of foreign States? Should the forum apply them, or take them into consideration in any way?

---

23 Com. 28 November 2000, *Allium SA v. Alfin Inc. et Groupe Interparfums*, case no. 98-11335.

24 von Hoffmann and Thorn, § 4 IV.

25 See Andrea Bonomi, *Le norme imperative del diritto internazionale privato* (Schulthess 1998) 168; Barel & Armellini, 97.

26 See von Hoffmann and Thorn, § 10–93.

CASE

English Court of Appeal, 26 March 1920 *Ralli Bros*[27]

SCRUTTON L.J.

This is an appeal from the judgment of Bailhache J. on a special case stated by a commercial umpire and raises a question of general importance as to the effect on a contract to be performed in a foreign country of illegality by the law of the place in which it was to be performed.

The question arises as to the freight payable by English charterers to Spanish shipowners for the transit of jute from Calcutta to Spain on a Spanish ship. The umpire finds that in September, 1918, there came into force in Spain a decree having the force of law fixing the maximum freight on jute (imported into Spain) at 875 pesetas per ton. He adds certain exhibits from which it appears that this decree was part of a system for keeping down the price of goods essential for national welfare by, amongst other means, fixing the freight on goods coming to Spain. And the exhibits, together with the full text of that of November 11, 1916, with which we were furnished, show that penal consequences follow infractions of these laws.

It appears from the special case that on July 2, 1918, Messrs. Ralli Bros. sold to Messrs. Godo & Co., of Barcelona, 28,000 bales of jute at various prices from 118l. 10s. to 105l. per ton, to be shipped by the steamer Eretza Mendi from Calcutta to Barcelona. Ralli Bros. were to pay half the freight at Calcutta, Godo & Co. to pay the other half on arrival at Barcelona. The contract document is obscure but the invoice shows that the second half freight was to be paid on account of and as part of the contract price per ton. The Eretza Mendi was a Spanish steamer owned by Compania Naviera Sota y Aznar, a Spanish company with its head office at Bilbao in Spain. Its owners had, on July 3, 1918, chartered the ship to Messrs. Ralli Bros. to load at Calcutta a full cargo of jute, and proceed to Spanish ports as ordered and there deliver the same on being paid freight at the rate of 50l. per ton. Half the freight was to be paid by charterers in London on receipt of telegraphic advice of sailing from Calcutta. The balance of the freight to be paid at the port of discharge by the receivers of the cargo, one half on arrival of the vessel and the remainder concurrent with discharge. The half freight payable at port of discharge was to be paid by cash or approved bills at charterers' option. This half, the freight in question, was payable to Spanish shipowners resident in Spain, for the carriage to

---

27 *Ralli Bros v. Compania Naviera Sota y Aznar* [1920] 2 K.B. 287.

and delivery of goods in Spain by a Spanish ship, in Spanish money at a Spanish port of discharge.

On arrival the receivers alleged that a maximum rate of freight for such goods was fixed by Spanish law, and that they could not legally pay more. They paid or tendered what they alleged to be the right amount of freight at 875 pesetas per ton, the maximum freight fixed by Spanish law. The umpire finds that on their own basis, having regard to the rate of exchange, they tendered too little. Complicated proceedings followed in the Spanish Courts. In April, 1919, 23,084 bales had been delivered by the ship, and 6274 bales were still on board. But I understand these proceedings were not brought to ascertain what was the result, if freight was to be paid at 875 pesetas a ton, but to test the claim by the Spanish shipowners that they were entitled to be paid by the English charterer's freight at the rate of 50l. per ton, without any regard to the Spanish law.

I accept the contention of the shipowners that the charterers remain liable for the freight, in spite of the provision that half of it is to be paid by the receivers.

But I think they remain liable to pay it in Spanish currency at the Spanish port of discharge to a Spanish company resident in Spain. To pay freight in Spain to a Spaniard for goods to be discharged in Spain at a rate in excess of the maximum freight fixed by Spanish law for the carriage of such goods is illegal by the law of Spain. What then is the effect on the contract of illegality by the law of the place where it is to be performed, such law not being British law?

In my opinion the law is correctly stated by Professor Dicey in *Conflict of Laws*, 2nd ed., p. 553, where he says: 'A contract . . . is, in general, invalid in so far as . . . the performance of it is unlawful by the law of the country where the contract is to be performed' – and I reserve liberty to consider whether it is any longer an exception to this proposition that this country will not consider the fact that the contract is obnoxious only to the revenue laws of the foreign country where it is to be performed as an obstacle to enforcing it in the English Courts. The early authorities on this point require reconsideration, in view of the obligations of international comity as now understood.

The argument addressed to us was that illegality by foreign law was only impossibility in fact, which the parties might have provided against by their contract, and for which they must be liable, if they had not expressly relieved themselves from liability. This is the old doctrine of *Paradine v. Jane*: "When the party by his own contract creates a duty or charge upon himself, he is bound to make it good, if he may, notwithstanding any accident by inevitable necessity, because he might have provided against it by his contract.' It was emphasized by Lord Ellenborough in *Atkinson v. Ritchie*, where he said: 'No exception (of a private nature at least) which is not contained in the contract itself, can be engrafted upon it by implication, as an excuse for its non-performance.' And Lord Bowen as late as 1884 in the case of *Jacobs v. Crédit Lyonnais* cited Lord Ellenborough's approval of *Paradine v. Jane* with approval. But the numerous cases, of which *Metropolitan Water Board v. Dick, Kerr & Co.* is a recent example, most of which are cited in McCardie J.'s exhaustive judgment in *Blackburn Bobbin Co. v. Allen & Sons* have made a serious breach in the ancient proposition. It is now quite common for exceptions, or exemptions from liability to be grafted by implication on contracts, if the parties by necessary implication must have treated the continued existence of a specified state of things as essential to liability on the express terms of the contract. If I am asked whether the true intent of the parties is that one has undertaken to do an act though it is illegal by the law of the place in which the act is to be done, and though that law is the law of his own country; or whether their true intent was that the doing of that act is subject to the implied condition that it shall be legal for him to do the act in the place where it has to be done, I have no hesitation in choosing the second alternative. 'I will do it provided I can legally do so' seems to me infinitely preferable to and more likely than 'I will do it, though it is illegal.'

Great reliance was placed by the appellants on the case of *Jacobs v. Crédit Lyonnais*. The headnote in that case speaks of 'the prohibition by the constituted authorities of the export of esparto from Algeria.' I cannot find any authority for this in the case, which only speaks of difficulty from insurrection and Government commands in collecting and transporting cargo to the port of loading. No express exception covered this, and the attempt in the case was to introduce 'force majeure,' which would be a defence by the French law, into the English contract. If it had been illegal to export esparto from Algeria the question in this case would have arisen. In *Blight v. Page* a ship was chartered with fixed lay days to proceed to Libau and load barley. On her arrival there the Russian Government had prohibited the export of barley. Lord Kenyon held the charterer liable for freight, the foreign illegality being no defence to an action for damages. This was followed in *Barker v. Hodgson*, where a charterer who had undertaken to load at Gibraltar in fixed days and who was prevented from doing so by prohibition to load due to plague was held liable on the same principle: 'if he was unable to do the thing, is he not answerable for it upon his covenant?' In sharp contrast with these fixed days cases is the decision in *Ford v. Cotesworth*. That was a charter to discharge at Callao, no fixed time being mentioned and the law implying a reasonable time. Discharge was prevented for a considerable period by prohibition of landing due to the fear of the arrival of the Spanish Fleet. After a long time discharge was finished. When that case was decided, the interpretation of reasonable time as a reasonable time under the existing circumstances, and not the normal time of discharge in normal circumstances, had not been explained as it subsequently was by the House of Lords in *Hick v. Raymond* and *Hulthen v. Stewart & Co.* Lord Blackburn in giving the judgment of the Queen's Bench seems to accept the position that reasonable time means normal time, and that the party prevented from performing his contract by an unforeseen circumstance beyond his control would be liable, but distinguishes the case where the act not done is one in which both parties should concur, and which neither can perform, in which case he says that the obligation on each is to use reasonable diligence, and either is excused by events beyond his control. *Ford v. Cotesworth* would now, under the House of Lords decisions, be decided as a matter of course in favour of the party sued—for the foreign prohibition would be an existing circumstance to be taken into account in fixing the reasonable time in which the act omitted was by implication to be done. Such reasonable time would not now be construed as normal time under normal conditions. In the Exchequer Chamber the case was again put on reasonable time, as distinguished from fixed time, and the ground that a cause of delay affecting both parties must be considered in fixing reasonable time. In *Cunningham v. Dunn* the ship was to proceed to Malta and load dead weight, which both parties knew would be military stores, and then proceed to a Spanish port to load fruit. On arrival at Valencia it was found that the law of Spain did not allow cargo to be loaded on a ship which had military stores on board, and when it was found that permission could not be obtained the vessel sailed away. The charterer sued her, and the Court of Appeal held that both parties being prevented by superior power neither was liable, citing *Ford v. Cotesworth*. The late Mr. Carver forcibly criticises these two cases on the ground that in neither was there really joint disability, but takes the view, in which I concur, that they are both supportable on other grounds, which I take to be that in *Ford v. Cotesworth*, a reasonable time case, the time must be judged by the then existing circumstances, and that in *Cunningham v. Dunn*, the parties must be taken to have contracted on the basis that it should be legally possible to load that ship. At the time the two cases were distinguished from *Barker v. Hodgson* and other fixed lay day cases, on the ground partly of no fixed time partly on joint inability. It may be possible to put the earlier cases on the ground that a contract to load in fixed days, unless prevented by specified causes, excludes implied causes such as foreign illegality. An instance of this class of case is *Braemount Steamship Co. v. Andrew Weir & Co.*, where a clause excusing payment of hire in certain named events was not extended to an unnamed event, strikes, which prevented the vessel being profitably used, though 'strikes' were included in an exception clause. But in my opinion at the present day, in the absence of very special circumstances, cases which decide that a contracting party who has undertaken to do something in a foreign country is not relieved from his obligation by the fact that such an act is, or becomes, illegal in that foreign country are wrongly decided; and this is the true view to be taken of early cases like *Barker v. Hodgson*, decided before the Courts had developed the doctrine of continued validity of contracts being dependent impliedly on the existence or continuance of certain states of fact. Bailhache J. treats the case as one of a joint act to be performed by both parties, paying and receiving a fixed amount of freight, in a country where it is illegal to pay or receive such an amount; and such a joint act prevented by illegality as being within the principle of *Ford v. Cotesworth* and *Cunningham v. Dunn*, which are binding on him. In view of the fact that the recent decisions of the House of Lords would require or enable the results of those decisions to be justified in quite a different way, I should prefer to state the ground of my decision more broadly and to rest it on the ground that where a contract requires an act to be done in a foreign country, it is, in the absence of very special circumstance, an implied term of the continuing validity of such a provision that the act to be done in the foreign country shall not be illegal by the law of that country. This country should not in my opinion assist or sanction the breach of the laws of other independent States. Bailhache J. has arrived at the same result by holding that if there is a contract in spite of its illegality in the place of performance, the charterer is protected by the exception of restraint of princes, rejecting the argument that in this charter the exception clause only protects the shipowner. As the view I have already taken results in the dismissal of the appeal, I prefer to express no opinion on this point. But I may say that as in my experience most charters at the present day avoid the difficulty by using the words 'mutually excepted,' it would be well in future charters to make clear the intention that the exceptions shall protect both parties.

I understand our decision only to settle the point whether the Spanish shipowner can claim freight from the charterer at the rate of 50l. per ton in spite of the law of Spain, and to hold that he cannot. What freight he can claim, in view of the actual facts which are not fully before us, we do not decide.

? QUESTIONS

1 What is the ruling of the court? Does it decide that Spanish law applies because of its particular importance? Does it decide that it applies merely because it is the law of the place of performance of the contract? Does it decide that Spanish law is only considered as a fact, through the operation of a clause of the contract or a concept of the otherwise applicable law?

2 What would happen if the court decided to ignore the Spanish rule holding that the

performance of the contract is illegal? Could the Court order the Spanish party to pay the agreed price? Could such order be enforced?

3 Is it particularly appropriate to apply foreign mandatory rules from the place of performance of the contract?

In 1980, the drafters of the Rome Convention introduced a highly innovative provision granting discretion to the courts of the Contracting States to 'give effect' to any foreign mandatory rule.

> *E.C. Rome Convention of 19 June 1980 on the law applicable to contractual obligations*
> **Article 7** *Mandatory rules*
> 1. When applying under this Convention the law of a country, effect may be given to the mandatory rules of the law of another country with which the situation has a close connection, if and in so far as, under the law of the latter country, those rules must be applied whatever the law applicable to the contract. In considering whether to give effect to these mandatory rules, regard shall be had to their nature and purpose and to the consequences of their application or non-application.
> 2. Nothing in this Convention shall restrict the application of the rules of the law of the forum in a situation where they are mandatory irrespective of the law otherwise applicable to the contract.

However, the application of foreign international mandatory rules had traditionally been rejected in Germany and the United Kingdom. One reason was that this would introduce too much uncertainty in the choice of law process, in particular in contractual matters where the express choice of law of the parties might be overridden. Another was that the same result could be reached by merely taking into account, or recognizing, foreign international mandatory rules rather than by applying or enforcing them, in particular when the foreign rule prevented performance of the contract.[28] Both Germany and the United Kingdom (and Luxembourg and Portugal) declared, as Art. 22 of the Rome Convention allowed them, that they would not apply Art. 7(1) and thus that their courts would only apply (international) mandatory rules of the forum.

> *Rome I Regulation (2008)*
> **Article 9** *Overriding mandatory provisions*
> 1. Overriding mandatory provisions are (. . .) [See *supra*, 1.3.1.]
> 2. Nothing in this Regulation shall restrict the application of the overriding mandatory provisions of the law of the forum.
> 3. Effect may be given to the overriding mandatory provisions of the law of the country where the obligations arising out of the contract have to be or have

---

28 On this distinction, see *supra*, p. 18.

been performed, in so far as those overriding mandatory provisions render the performance of the contract unlawful. In considering whether to give effect to those provisions, regard shall be had to their nature and purpose and to the consequences of their application or non-application.

[?] NOTES AND QUESTIONS

1 In 2008, the European lawmaker severely restricted the power of the courts of the Member States to give effect to foreign international mandatory rules.[29] How does Art. 9.3 compare with the *Ralli Bros* (*supra*)?
   Imagine a U.S. regulation prohibiting any person, wherever situated, to enter into certain transactions with persons associated with certain terrorist organizations (for example, Al Quaida) or with certain States (for example, Iran, Russia). The U.S. regulation has extraterritorial effect and purports to apply to a payment made by a European bank to the targeted person. Should European States assist the United States in their fight against terrorism? Would a court of a Member State have the power to apply or take into consideration such a regulation?
2 Compare Art. 9(2) and Art. 9(3). The first contemplates the *application* of mandatory rules, while the second only refers to *giving effect* to them. What is the content of the distinction? A party could make two different arguments based on a foreign mandatory rule. He could first argue that the foreign rule applies, and that it governs the issue of whether a given action is permitted or not. Alternatively, he could argue that the law chosen by the parties applies, but that the foreign mandatory rule, which makes it illegal to perform the contract, is a fact which could be characterized as a case of frustration, or *force majeure*, under the chosen law. The foreign rule would only be taken into consideration in the context of the application of the chosen law. To which kind of argument does Art. 9(3) apply?
3 In *Nikiforidis*, the European Court of Justice ignored this distinction and held that while Art. 9(3) limits the power of courts to apply foreign mandatory rules, it does not preclude them 'being taken into account as a matter of fact, in so far as this is provided for by a substantive rule of the law that is applicable to the contract pursuant to the regulation.'[30]

Quebec Civil Code

Article 3079

Where legitimate and manifestly preponderant interests so require, effect may be given to a mandatory provision of the law of another State with which the situation is closely connected.

In deciding whether to do so, consideration is given to the purpose of the provision and the consequences of its application.

***

The doctrine of international mandatory rules is useful in the context of a system of private international law based on multilateral choice of law rules.

---

29 'Rumour has it, and reason would corroborate it, that Art. 9(3) was adopted in order to encourage the United Kingdom to exercise its discretion to opt in, rather than remain outside, the Rome I Regulation.' (Briggs, 250).
30 Case C-135/15, *Republik Griechenland v. Grigorios Nikiforidis* ECLI:EU:C:2016:774.

It justifies the direct application of the most crucial rules of the forum despite the operation of the applicable multilateral choice of law rule, which might designate a foreign law as applicable.

The American revolution in choice of law has resulted in a shift from the traditional system based on multilateral choice of law rules to a system based unilateral choice of law rules (*infra*, 2). Furthermore, the criteria of application used in the new American methodology are determined, as in the doctrine of international mandatory rules, by assessing the goal pursued by the relevant lawmaker. In this context, a doctrine of international mandatory rules would be largely redundant.

2 Governmental interest analysis

2.1 The origin: Currie's challenge to the traditional method

In the late 1950s and early 1960s, an American scholar, Brainerd Currie, published a series of articles which revolutionized the field of choice of law. His writings were hugely influential in the United States, and initiated the American revolution of choice of law.

Currie's central insight is that choice of law is essentially a process of interpretation of substantive laws. In Currie's opinion, courts ought to decide whether laws apply by examining their purpose. As a consequence, Currie famously argued that 'we would be better off without choice of law rules'.[31] Courts should only look at the purpose of laws, at the policies that they want to advance, and deduce from these policies whether lawmakers would want to apply them in a particular interstate case.

Here is how he summarized his method:

> *Brainerd Currie, Comments on* Babcock v. Jackson, *63 Colum. L. Rev. 1233, 1242–3 (1963)*
>
> If I were asked to restate the law of conflict of laws I would decline the honor. A descriptive restatement with any sort of internal consistency is impossible. Much of the existing law, or pseudo law, of the subject is irrational; profound changes destructive of the fundamental tenets of the traditional system are gathering momentum. On the assumption that the project admits of a statement of what is reasonable in existing law and what may reasonably be desired for the future,

---

31 Brainerd Currie, 'Notes on Methods and Objectives in the Conflict of Laws', *Selected Essays on the Conflict of Laws* (Duke UP 1963) 183.

however, I volunteer the following as a substitute for all that part of the *Restatement* dealing with choice of law (for the purpose of finding the rule of decision):

§ 1. When a court is asked to apply the law of a foreign state different from the law of the forum, it should inquire into the policies expressed in the respective laws, and into the circumstances in which it is reasonable for the respective states to assert an interest in the application of those policies. In making these determinations the court should employ the ordinary processes of construction and interpretation.

§ 2. If the court finds that one state has an interest in the application of its policy in the circumstances of the case and the other has none, it should apply the law of the only interested state.

§ 3. If the court finds an apparent conflict between the interests of the two states it should reconsider. A more moderate and restrained interpretation of the policy or interest of one state or the other may avoid conflict.

§ 4. If, upon reconsideration, the court finds that a conflict between the legitimate interests of the two states is unavoidable, it should apply the law of the forum.

§ 5. If the forum is disinterested, but an unavoidable conflict exists between the laws of the two other states, and the court cannot with justice decline to adjudicate the case, it should apply the law of the forum—until someone comes along with a better idea.

(. . .)

The explanatory note might run a little longer.

Currie proposed to resolve conflict cases by looking at the policies underlying the potentially applicable laws. His essential contribution to conflict of laws thinking was to show that, in many interstate or international cases, there is no real conflict of laws, because only one state has an actual interest in the application of its law. In what he labeled a 'false conflict', he argued that courts should apply the law of the only interested state.

The first state to follow Currie's doctrine and to take into account states' interests was the state of New York.

 CASE

New York Court of Appeals, 23 April 1969[32] *Tooker v. Lopez*

Facts: On October 16, 1964, Catharina Tooker, a 20-year-old student at Michigan State University, was killed when the Japanese sports car in which she was a passenger overturned

---

32 24 N.Y.2d 569 (1969).

after the driver had lost control of the vehicle while attempting to pass another car. The accident also took the life of the driver of the vehicle, Marcia Lopez, and seriously injured another passenger, Susan Silk. The two girls were classmates of Catharina Tooker at Michigan State University and lived in the same dormitory. They were en route from the university to Detroit, Michigan, to spend the weekend. Catharina Tooker and Marcia Lopez were both New York domiciliaries. The automobile which Miss Lopez was driving belonged to her father who resided in New York, where the sports car he had given his daughter was registered and insured.

Held: New York law governed.

Judgment: This action for wrongful death was commenced by Oliver P. Tooker, Jr., the father of Catharina Tooker, as the administrator of her estate. The defendant asserted as an affirmative defense the Michigan 'guest statute' which permits recovery by guests only by showing willful misconduct or gross negligence of the driver. The plaintiff moved to dismiss the affirmative defense on the ground that under the governing choice-of-law rules it was New York law rather than Michigan law which applied. (. . .)

In *Babcock v. Jackson* the plaintiff was injured when an automobile in which she was a passenger crashed into a stone wall during a weekend trip with her neighbors to Ontario, Canada. The plaintiff as well as her neighbors, who owned and operated the vehicle, were New York domiciliaries and the car was registered and insured in the State. Upon her return to New York the plaintiff commenced an action to recover for her personal injuries. The Ontario 'guest statute', which prohibited suits by guests against negligent hosts, was asserted as a defense.

This court rejected unequivocally the traditional lex loci delictus rule and refused to apply Ontario law. We noted that the traditional rule placed controlling reliance upon one fact which had absolutely no relation to the purpose of the ostensibly conflicting laws and thus resulted in decisions which often frustrated the interests and policies of the State in which the accident had taken place as well as our own State. (. . .)

Viewed in the light of the foregoing discussion, the instant case is one of the simplest in the choice-of-law area. If the facts are examined in light of the policy considerations which underlie the ostensibly conflicting laws it is clear that New York has the only real interest in whether recovery should be granted and that the application of Michigan law 'would defeat a legitimate interest of the forum State without serving a legitimate interest of any other State.'

The policy of this State with respect to all those injured in automobile accidents is reflected in the legislative declaration which prefaces New York's compulsory insurance law: 'The legislature is concerned over the rising toll of motor vehicle accidents and the suffering and loss thereby inflicted. The legislature determines that it is a matter of grave concern that motorists shall be financially able to respond in damages for their negligent acts, so that innocent victims of motor vehicle accidents may be recompensed for the injury and financial loss inflicted upon them.'

Neither this declaration of policy nor the standard required provisions for an auto liability insurance policy make any distinction between guests, pedestrians or other insured parties. New York's 'grave concern' in affording recovery for the injuries suffered by Catharina Tooker, a New York domiciliary, and the loss suffered by her family as a result of her wrongful death, is evident merely in stating the policy which our law reflects. On the other hand, Michigan has no interest in whether a New York plaintiff is denied recovery against a New York defendant where the car is insured here. The fact that the deceased guest and driver were in Michigan for an extended period of time is plainly irrelevant. Indeed, the Legislature, in requiring that insurance policies cover liability for injuries regardless of where the accident takes place has evinced commendable concern not only for residents of this State, but residents of other States who may be injured as a result of the activities of New York residents. Under these circumstances we cannot be concerned with whether Miss Tooker or Miss Lopez were in Michigan for a summer session or for a full college education.

? NOTES AND QUESTIONS

1 The New York court chose to apply New York law over Michigan law after assessing the interests of the two states. Can you explain how the court determined the interests of the two states, and how it used these interests to determine the territorial reach of the laws?

2 In *Tooker*, the rule was a guest statute, that is, a rule making it more difficult for a non-paying passenger in an automobile to recover damages from the driver. American Courts have found that the purpose of such a rule is not to regulate conduct, but rather to allocate loss between the parties, here the driver and her guest. The distinction has become important for choice of law purposes in the United States. Loss allocating rules focus on the parties, by deciding which one will eventually bear the loss. The purpose of states adopting such rules seems to be to allocate losses between persons living within the relevant state. By contrast, conduct regulating rules aim at giving incentives to behave in a certain way. The purpose of states adopting such rules seems to be to regulate conduct within their state. The distinction, therefore, will typically allow to identify different state interests: the state of the common domicile of the parties will be interested in allocating loss between them, while the state of the place of the conduct will be interested in regulating the said conduct (see also *infra* p. 431).

3 What are the differences between the new approach and the traditional method? Is the new approach multilateralist or unilateralist? Is it neutral?

4 Is the new approach closer to the method of international mandatory rules? Does it apply to all rules, or only to the most important ones?

Currie's idea that courts ought to take into account governmental interests in choice-of-law analysis was tremendously influential in the United States. Most U.S. states have rejected the traditional method, and apply new methodologies which, in a way or another, assess state policies to determine the applicable law. No state, however, follows his doctrine entirely. To begin with, governmental interest analysis was only influential in the fields of torts and contracts. Currie, by contrast, would have applied it to all cases. Most importantly, very few states resolve choice of issues solely by reference to states' interests. Most of them use methods which combine various factors, one of which only is states' interests. The best example is the Restatement Second, which is followed by half of U.S. States (*infra*, 2.3).

2.2 Resolving conflicts under the new approach

The new approach mandates courts to assess whether the policies of the states involved in the case would be furthered if their laws were to be applied. This analysis can lead to three different situations.

2.2.1 *False conflicts*

The first is the *false conflict*. There is a false conflict where only one state is interested in the application of its law. In such a case, courts should obviously apply the law of the only interested state. Applying another law instead would hurt the interest of that state without advancing the interest of any other (for instance, applying the law of the place of the accident instead of the law of the common domicile of the parties in *Tooker v. Lopez, supra*, 2.1). The essential contribution of Currie is to have identified this kind of situation, and to have proposed to resolve the choice of law problem by applying the law of the only interested state.

2.2.2 *True conflicts*

There are also, of course, cases where several states will be interested in applying their law. These are *true conflicts*, and they are not easily resolved. Currie advocated systematically applying the law of the forum, especially in cases where the forum was one of the interested states. He explained this solution by arguing that the forum would 'be sure at least that it is consistently advancing the policy of its own state',[33] and also that weighing competing interests was not an option, because 'assessment of the respective values of

---

33 Brainerd Currie, 'Married Women's Contracts: A Study in Conflict-of-laws Method' [1958] U. Chi. L. Rev. 227.

the competing legitimate interests of two sovereign states, in order to determine which is to prevail, is a political function of a very high order (. . .) which should not be committed to courts in a democracy'.[34]

American courts have reacted in a variety of ways when faced with true conflicts. Compare the two following judgments.

 CASE

Supreme Court of Oregon, 30 September 1964[35] *Lilienthal v. Kaufman*

> *Facts:* In an action to collect two promissory notes, the defendant maker argued that he has previously been declared a spendthrift by an Oregon court and placed under a guardianship and that the guardian had declared the obligations void. The plaintiff's counter is that the notes were executed and delivered in California, that the law of California does not recognize the disability of a spendthrift, and that the Oregon court is bound to apply the law of the place of the making of the contract.
>
> *Held:* The spendthrift law of Oregon is applicable and the plaintiff cannot recover.

Judgment: We have, then, two jurisdictions, each with several close connections with the transaction, and each with a substantial interest, which will be served or thwarted, depending upon which law is applied. The interests of neither jurisdiction are clearly more important than those of the other. We are of the opinion that in such a case the public policy of Oregon should prevail and the law of Oregon should be applied; we should apply that choice-of-law rule which will 'advance the policies or interests of' Oregon.

Courts are instruments of state policy. The Oregon Legislature has adopted a policy to avoid possible hardship to an Oregon family of a spendthrift and to avoid possible expenditure of Oregon public funds which might occur if the spendthrift is required to pay his obligations. In litigation Oregon courts are the appropriate instrument to enforce this policy. The mechanical application of choice-of-law rules would be the only apparent reason for an Oregon court advancing the interests of California over the equally valid interests of Oregon. The present principles of conflict of laws are not favorable to such mechanical application.

---

34 Currie, 'Note on Methods and Objectives', n. 31, 182.
35 239 Ore. 1 (1964).

CASE

Supreme Court of California, 2 March 1976[36] *Bernhard v. Harrah's Club*

Facts: On 24 July 1971, Fern and Philip Myers, in response to defendant's advertisements and solicitations, drove from their California residence to defendant's gambling and drinking club in Nevada, where they stayed until the early morning hours of 25 July 1971. During their stay, the Myers were served numerous alcoholic beverages by defendant's employees, progressively reaching a point of obvious intoxication rendering them incapable of safely driving a car. Nonetheless defendant continued to serve and furnish the Myers alcoholic beverages. While still in this intoxicated state, the Myers drove their car back to California, where they collided with Richard Bernhard's motorcycle. Bernhard initiated civil proceedings against the drinking club for serving alcohol to an intoxicated patron. California imposes civil liability on tavern keepers in such circumstances. Nevada does not, but imposes criminal penalties.

Held: California law applied.

Judgment: The search for the proper resolution of a true conflicts case, while proceeding within orthodox parameters of governmental interest analysis, has generated much scholarly examination and discussion. The father of the governmental interest approach, Professor Brainerd Currie, originally took the position that in a true conflicts situation the law of the forum should always be applied. However, upon further reflection, Currie suggested that when under the governmental interest approach a preliminary analysis reveals an apparent conflict of interest upon the forum's assertion of its own rule of decision, the forum should re-examine its policy to determine if a more restrained interpretation of it is more appropriate. '[T]o assert a conflict between the interests of the forum and the foreign state is a serious matter; the mere fact that a suggested broad conception of a local interest will create conflict with that of a foreign state is a sound reason why the conception should be re-examined, with a view to a more moderate and restrained interpretation both of the policy and of the circumstances in which it must be applied to effectuate the forum's legitimate purpose. (. . .) An analysis of this kind (. . .) was brilliantly performed by Justice Traynor in *Bernkrant v. Fowler* (1961)' (. . .)

Once this preliminary analysis has identified a true conflict of the governmental interests involved as applied to the parties under the particular circumstances of the case, the 'comparative impairment' approach to the resolution of such conflict seeks to determine which state's interest would be more

---

36 16 Cal.3d 313.

impaired if its policy were subordinated to the policy of the other state. This analysis proceeds on the principle that true conflicts should be resolved by applying the law of the state whose interest would be the more impaired if its law were not applied. Exponents of this process of analysis emphasize that it is very different from a weighing process. The court does not '"weigh" the conflicting governmental interests in the sense of determining which conflicting law manifested the "better" or the "worthier" social policy on the specific issue. An attempted balancing of conflicting state policies in that sense . . . is difficult to justify in the context of a federal system in which, within constitutional limits, states are empowered to mold their policies as they wish. . . . [The process] can accurately be described as . . . accommodation of conflicting state policies, as a problem of allocating domains of law-making power in multi-state contexts – limitations on the reach of state policies – as distinguished from evaluating the wisdom of those policies. . . . [E]mphasis is placed on the appropriate scope of conflicting state policies rather than on the "quality" of those policies . . .' (Horowitz, *The Law of Choice of Law in California – A Restatement*, 21 UCLA L.Rev. 719, 753; see also Baxter, *Choice of Law and the Federal System*, 16 Stan.L.Rev. 1, 18–19.) (. . .)

Defendant by the course of its chosen commercial practice has put itself at the heart of California's regulatory interest, namely to prevent tavern keepers from selling alcoholic beverages to obviously intoxicated persons who are likely to act in California in the intoxicated state. It seems clear that California cannot reasonably effectuate its policy if it does not extend its regulation to include out-of-state tavern keepers such as defendant who regularly and purposely sell intoxicating beverages to California residents in places and under conditions in which it is reasonably certain these residents will return to California and act therein while still in an intoxicated state. California's interest would be very significantly impaired if its policy were not applied to defendant.

Since the act of selling alcoholic beverages to obviously intoxicated persons is already proscribed in Nevada, the application of California's rule of civil liability would not impose an entirely new duty requiring the ability to distinguish between California residents and other patrons. Rather the imposition of such liability involves an increased economic exposure, which, at least for businesses which actively solicit extensive California patronage, is a foreseeable and coverable business expense. Moreover, Nevada's interest in protecting its tavern keepers from civil liability of a boundless and unrestricted nature will not be significantly impaired when as in the instant case liability is imposed only on those tavern keepers who actively solicit California business.

NOTES AND QUESTIONS

1 Should courts weigh policies? Do you agree with Currie that it is a political function, and should thus be left to the political branches of government? In practice, could courts turn to the political branches each time they are faced with a true conflict? Would the government not always respond that its own policy is to be preferred? Would it attempt to find an agreement with the other interested state?

2 Are you shocked by the California court's attempt to balance state policies? Are you convinced by the distinction between directly weighing policies, and assessing the interest of which state would be more impaired if its law was not applied? Today, California still applies its 'comparative impairment' method to resolve choice of law issues in tort matters.

3 Unilateralist methodologies work well and seem appealing as long as they designate one law only. They typically become much less convincing when hard cases appear, that is, when the methodology designates several laws, and thus must be supplemented by some other doctrine. In applying its comparative impairment method, California is consistent with the tenets of interest analysis, that is, that conflicts should be resolved by assessing the policies of the involved states. An alternative solution would be to come back to the method which would very much look like the traditional one. In New York, courts apply the *lex loci delicti* as a tie-breaker when faced with true-conflicts in tort cases involving loss-allocating rules.[37]

2.2.3 Unprovided-for cases

Finally, there could be cases in which none of the involved states has an interest in applying its law. The Oregon Supreme Court identified one such unprovided-for case in *Erwin*. How did it resolve it?

 CASE

Supreme Court of Oregon, 15 February 1973[38] *Erwin v. Thomas*

Facts: Erwin, a Washington resident, was injured in Washington in a traffic accident by Thomas, an Oregon resident. Erwin's wife sued Thomas in Oregon for loss of consortium. Washington, by court decision, follows the common law rule that no cause of action exists by a wife for loss of consortium. An Oregon statute allows such an action.

Held: Oregon law governs.

Judgment: Let us examine the interests involved in the present case. Washington has decided that the rights of a married woman whose husband

---

37 These are the so-called *Neumeier* Rules: see *Neumeier v. Kuehner*, 31 NY 2d 121 [1972]. In cases involving a loss-allocating rule, there will be a true conflict if the parties are domiciled in two different states (as opposed to the false conflict existing in cases where both parties are domiciled in the same state: see *Tooker v. Lopez*, *supra*, 2.1).

38 264 Ore. 454 (1973).

is injured are not sufficiently important to cause the negligent defendant who is responsible for the injury to pay the wife for her loss. It has weighed the matter in favor of protection of defendants. No Washington defendant is going to have to respond for damages in the present case, since the defendant is an Oregonian. Washington has little concern whether other states require non-Washingtonians to respond to such claims. Washington policy cannot be offended if the court of another state affords rights to a Washington woman which Washington does not afford, so long as a Washington defendant is not required to respond. The state of Washington appears to have no material or urgent policy or interest which would be offended by applying Oregon law.

On the other hand, what is Oregon's interest? Oregon, obviously, is protective of the rights of married women and believes that they should be allowed to recover for negligently inflicted loss of consortium. However, it is stretching the imagination more than a trifle to conceive that the Oregon Legislature was concerned about the rights of all the nonresident married women in the nation whose husbands would be injured outside of the state of Oregon. Even if Oregon were so concerned, it would offend no substantial Washington interest.

It is apparent, therefore, that neither state has a vital interest in the outcome of this litigation and there can be no conceivable material conflict of policies or interests if an Oregon court does what comes naturally and applies Oregon law. Professor Currie expresses it thusly:

> The closest approximation to the renvoi problem that will be encountered under the suggested method is the case in which neither state has an interest in the application of its law and policy; in that event, the forum would apply its own law simply on the ground that that is the more convenient disposition B. Currie, Notes on Methods and Objectives in the Conflict of Laws, SELECTED ESSAYS ON THE CONFLICT OF LAWS 184 (1963).

 NOTES

1 American scholars have proposed different solutions to address the issue of unprovided-for cases. Currie advocated applying the law of the forum. Others argued that the forum should adhere to its own self-restricting self interpretation and thus 'apply the law of the other state even though that law doesn't want to be applied'.[39]

2 Weintraub proposed to resolve unprovided-for cases by re-examining the state interests to

---

39 David Cavers, *The Choice of Law Process* (Univ. Michigan Press 1965) 103. Posnak suggested applying the better law: Bruce Posnak, 'Choice of Law: A very Well-Curried Leflar Approach' [1983] Mercer L. Rev. 777.

find an additional policy which will be advanced by applying the law of one of the states.[40] Experience has indeed shown that American courts have rarely found that they are faced with an unprovided-for case, and that they have typically avoided it by interpreting broadly the forum's interest.[41]

3 Unilateralist methodologies typically create difficult problems when they fail to designate any law. By definition, an alternative methodology is then necessary to resolve the choice of law problem. For unilateralists, this will typically be a problem for two reasons. Firstly, they will have presented their new methodology as a remedy to the irrationality and inconsistency of the old one (for Currie, see *supra*, 2.1), and will thus be reluctant to get back to it. Secondly, they will fear that the problem will be used to denounce the unsoundness of their new methodology all together. On unprovided for cases, Currie observed: '[t]raditionalists may stand aghast at this anomaly, and take it as proof of the unsoundness of the analysis'.[42]

2.3   The U.S. Restatement (Second) on Conflict of Laws

The United States is a federal State. In many fields, especially in private law, the law is not unified, and varies from one state to another. This diversity is mitigated by the work of several institutions. The National Conference of Commissioners on Uniform State Laws (Uniform Law Commission) drafts model laws that states are free to adopt. The American Law Institute (ALI) undertakes scholarly projects aiming at restating a given branch of the law. ALI Restatements are not designed to become laws, but to influence courts which may decide to follow them.

The First Restatement on Conflict of Laws dates back to 1934. It restated the law of the time, and thus follows the traditional method of choice of law. The Second Restatement was essentially drafted during the American choice of law revolution.[43]

> Symeon C. Symeonides, 'A New Conflicts Restatement: Why Not?' [2009]
> J. Priv. Int. L. 383.
>
> The Second Restatement was drafted during the early years of the choice-of-law revolution. It both influenced the revolution and was influenced by it. The drafting began in 1952, while the revolutionary clouds began to gather on the horizon and two years before the New York Court of Appeals decided *Auten v. Auten*. *Auten* replaced the First Restatement's *lex loci contractus* rule with the 'center of gravity' approach and marked the beginning of the choice-of-law revolution in contract conflicts. The task of Reporter was assigned to Professor Willis L. Reese, who was a member of the new school of conflicts thought, although not of its

---

40 Weintraub, 459.
41 Hay, Borchers, Symeonides, 818.
42 B. Currie, *Selected Essays on the Conflict of Laws* (1963) 152.
43 In 2015, the ALI appointed reporters to draft a third restatement.

revolutionary branch. Reese agreed with many of the criticisms levelled against the First Restatement, but, more importantly, he was receptive to the criticisms of his own drafts of the Second Restatement. A cursory look at the successive versions of what eventually became Section 6 of the Second Restatement reveals an evolution in the Reporter's own thinking, as well as the gradual gains of the new school over the old. In 1963, while the Restatement was in draft form, the New York Court of Appeals decided *Babcock v. Jackson*, which abandoned the First Restatement's *lex loci delicti* rule and marked the beginning of the choice-of-law revolution in tort conflicts.

The final version of the Restatement, promulgated in 1969, did not join the revolution, but it was a conscious compromise and synthesis between the old and new schools (and among the various branches of the new schools).

The Second Restatement is important, because it has proved extremely successful. Today, it is the method which is most commonly used by American courts. In almost half of the states, courts have ruled that they would follow the Second Restatement, and ten other states follow very similar methodologies. By contrast, ten states still follow the traditional method (often the First Restatement), and only a couple of states apply a pure interest analysis method.[44]

Restatement (Second) on the Conflict of Laws (1971)
Chapter 1. Introduction

§ **6.** *Choice-Of-Law Principles*

(1) A court, subject to constitutional restrictions, will follow a statutory directive of its own state on choice of law.

(2) When there is no such directive, the factors relevant to the choice of the applicable rule of law include

(a)   the needs of the interstate and international systems,
(b)   the relevant policies of the forum,
(c)   the relevant policies of other interested states and the relative interests of those states in the determination of the particular issue,
(d)   the protection of justified expectations,
(e)   the basic policies underlying the particular field of law,
(f)   certainty, predictability and uniformity of result, and
(g)   ease in the determination and application of the law to be applied.

P. Hay, P.J. Borchers, S.C. Symeonides Conflict of Laws *5th edn (West 2010) 63–4*

---

44 See Hay, Borchers and Symeonides, 93.

From a philosophical perspective, Section 6 is important in that it establishes the ideology of the Restatement in a way that distinguishes it from other rival modern theories such as Leflar's 'better law' approach or Currie's interest analysis . . . Moreover, the list is broader and quantitatively different from the policies relied upon by Currie's, whose analysis disregards, de-emphasizes, or expressly rejects most of § 6 factors other than the policies of the forum or the other involved state(s). The contrast between interest analysis and the Restatement is clearest in their varying degrees of sensitivity towards 'the needs of the interstate and international systems' and the need for 'uniformity of results'. To Currie's ethnocentric attitude toward both of these goals, the Restatement juxtaposes a universalistic perception of private international law reflected in the statement that 'the most important function of choice-of-law rules is to make the interstate system work well[,] . . . to further harmonious relations between states and to facilitate commercial intercourse between them'.

§ 6 is the cornerstone of the Restatement. It articulates the general principles that are designed to guide choice of law. § 6, however, falls short of providing an actual choice of law rule. Its principles are only factors *relevant* to the choice of law process. § 6 is thus meant to be combined with specific provisions of the Restatement.

Restatement (Second) on the Conflict of Laws (1971)
Chapter 7. Wrongs

§ 145. *The General Principle*
(1) The rights and liabilities of the parties with respect to an issue in tort are determined by the local law of the state which, with respect to that issue, has the most significant relationship to the occurrence and the parties under the principles stated in § 6.
(2) Contacts to be taken into account in applying the principles of § 6 to determine the law applicable to an issue include:

(a)   the place where the injury occurred,
(b)   the place where the conduct causing the injury occurred,
(c)   the domicil, residence, nationality, place of incorporation and place of business of the parties, and
(d)   the place where the relationship, if any, between the parties is centered.

These contacts are to be evaluated according to their relative importance with respect to the particular issue.

§ 146. *Personal Injuries*
In an action for a personal injury, the local law of the state where the injury

occurred determines the rights and liabilities of the parties, unless, with respect to the particular issue, some other state has a more significant relationship under the principles stated in § 6 to the occurrence and the parties, in which event the local law of the other state will be applied.

§ 157. *Standard Of Care*

(1) The law selected by application of the rule of § 145 determines the standard of care by which the actor's conduct shall be judged.

(2) The applicable law will usually be the local law of the state where the injury occurred.

? NOTES AND QUESTIONS

Although the Second Restatement includes a few rigid rules in some particular fields (property and successions), it typically offers a much more complex method which combines general and specific provisions. Many of its specific provisions only lay down presumptive rules, providing that the applicable law will 'usually' be the law designated by a particular connecting factor, or that the law designated by the connecting factor will govern except if another law has a 'more significant relationship to the occurrence and the parties'. Such presumptive rules are only designed to facilitate analysis under the most important provision of the restatement, the overarching umbrella provision, § 6.

1 Many provisions of the Restatement rely on the concept of 'the most significant relationship'. In the European conflict of laws, choice of law rules often include an exception clause providing that the applicable law will not be applied if a law is manifestly more closely connected with the dispute (*supra*, 8). How different are the two concepts? Is the answer different depending on whether you look at § 145 or § 146?

2 What is the use of § 145 in the overall scheme of the Restatement? Does it lay down a presumptive rule? Why is it necessary to identify contacts to be taken into account in applying the principles of § 6? Can you imagine how § 6 would work in tort matters without § 145?

3 § 157 refers to § 145, while § 146 does not. Is there a reason? Does it make a difference?

D. Currie, H.H. Kay, L. Kramer, K. Roosevelt, Conflicts of Laws *8th edn (West 2010) 222–3*

The presumptive rules of the Second Restatement are supposed to facilitate analysis under § 6. Do they succeed? Isn't § 6 analysis always required, if only to make sure that no other state has a more significant relationship than the state identified by the rules? Do the presumptive rules simplify this analysis? The Restatement explains that the rules set forth 'the choice of law the courts will "usually" make in given situations. The formulations are cast as empirical appraisals rather than purported rules to indicate how far the statements may be subject to re-evaluation in a concrete instance in light of the more general and open-ended norm [in § 6].' Of what use is the presumption if it has no normative basis and the judge cannot know whether it fits a particular case without doing a full § 6 analysis anyway?

In practice, the difficulty of deciding how much weight to give the presumptive rules has led courts to treat them in one of two ways. Most courts pay lip service to the rules but make their own evaluation under § 6. For these courts, the rules serve little purpose other than to provide a convenient first or last paragraph in an opinion . . . In *Wood Bros. Homes, Inc. v. Walker Adjustment Bureau* (198 Colo. 444 (1979)), for instance, the court ignored the rules explaining why New Mexico law applied under § 6, adding as an afterthought that 'A *fortiori*, the presumption of § 196 that New Mexico law applies has not been rebutted'. For many of these courts, moreover, analysis under § 6 looks an awful lot like interest analysis: as in *Philipps* [*see below*], the other factors are mentioned, but the outcome is determined by the court's examination of state interests. Other courts essentially end their analysis with the rules: little or no attention is paid to § 6, and instead the court makes the presumption effectively irrebuttable. For these courts, the Second Restatement is little more than an updated version of the first.

Read the following case and explain why Montana law applies.

 CASE

Supreme Court of Montana, 7 March 2000 *Phillips v. General Motors Corporation*[45]

Personal representative of estates of accident victims and guardian of surviving accident victim brought federal diversity suit against motor vehicle manufacturer alleging negligence and strict liability in accident on Kansas highway involving Montana residents. The United States District Court for the District of Montana certified three questions to Supreme Court regarding choice of law. Answering questions, the Supreme Court, Regnier, J., held, on matters of first impression, that: (1) most significant relationship test of Restatement (Second) of Conflict of Laws applies in determining choice of law for tort actions; (2) law of Montana applied to suit under most significant relationship test; and (3) considerations of public policy are accounted for under analysis contained in Restatement.

Certified questions answered.

Justice JIM REGNIER delivered the opinion of the Court.

1 The United States District Court for the District of Montana, Missoula Division, has certified the following questions to this Court pursuant to Rule 44, M.R.App.P. 2 1. Whether, in a personal injury/product liability/wrongful death action, where there is a potential conflict of laws, Montana will follow the Restatement (Second)

45 2000 MT 55.

of Conflict of Laws, including the 'most significant relationship' test set forth in §§ 146 and 6, in the determination of which state's substantive law to apply?

3 2. Given the facts of this case, which state's law applies to plaintiff's various tort and damages claims under Montana's choice of law rules?

4 3. Does Montana recognize a 'public policy' exception that would require application of Montana law even where Montana's choice of law rules dictate application of the laws of another state, and would such an exception apply in this case?

Our response to the certified questions can be simply stated. We adopt the Restatement (Second) of Conflict of Laws for tort actions. Under the analysis contained in the Restatement (Second) of Conflict of Laws, we conclude that given the facts as presented in the District Court's Order, the laws of Montana apply. Lastly, considerations of public policy are accounted for under the analysis contained in the Restatement (Second) of Conflict of Laws.

FACTUAL BACKGROUND

6 In its Order certifying these questions to the Supreme Court of Montana, the District Court submitted a statement of agreed facts. We stated in our Order accepting the certified questions that the facts of this case are restricted to those set forth in the certifying order. The following facts have been agreed upon by the parties for purposes of certification:

7 The vehicle which is the subject of this action was a 1985 Chevrolet pickup. The vehicle was originally sold by General Motors in North Carolina. Darrell Byrd subsequently purchased the pickup in or about February 1995 from Mike's Wholesale Cars in Newton, North Carolina. In doing so, he supplied a North Carolina address. The 1985 Chevrolet pickup truck was designed, tested, manufactured, and distributed by General Motors. The subject vehicle had fuel tanks mounted outside the frame rail.

8 On December 22, 1997, Darrell Byrd was driving with his family in the 1985 Chevrolet pickup truck from their home near Fortine, Montana, where Darrell Byrd was employed and where Timothy and Samuel Byrd attended school. The purpose of the trip was to spend Christmas vacation with family in North Carolina. The Byrds were domiciled in Montana before and at the time of the 1997 accident.

9 The wreck and fire which form the basis of this action occurred on December 22, 1997, on Interstate 70 near Russell, Kansas. A 1997 International semi-tractor trailer driven by Betty J. Kendall collided with the subject 1985 Chevrolet pickup truck driven by Darrell Byrd. A fire ensued. Darrell, Angela, and Timothy Byrd died. Samuel Byrd sustained personal injuries which required emergency treatment and hospitalization. (. . .)

12 In these product liability cases, in which Plaintiffs raise claims of negligence and

strict liability, Plaintiffs seek compensatory and punitive damages related to the deaths of Darrell, Angela, and Timothy Byrd and the personal injuries sustained by Samuel Byrd. General Motors denies all liability.

13 According to the District Court's Order, the parties disagree about the substantive law that should be applied to this case. 'To determine the applicable law, a federal district court is to apply the choice of law rules of the state in which it sits.' *Federal Ins. Co. v. Scarsella Bros., Inc.* (9th Cir.1991), 931 F.2d 599, 602. Montana does not have a statutory provision governing choice of law nor has this Court reached a choice of law issue in a case involving conflicting tort rules. See In re Mower, 1999 MT 73, ¶ 27. Absent a definitive determination of Montana's choice of law rule in tort cases, federal judges for the District of Montana have applied the 'most significant relationship' test of the Restatement (Second) of Conflict of Laws. See, e.g., *O'Neal v. Koehring Bomag* (J. Battin, 1995), 19 Mont. F. Rptr. 366.

14 The District Court observed that the instant case raised significant policy questions involving Montana's choice of law rules, that choice of law questions in tort cases are frequent in diversity litigation in federal court, and that it would be helpful in resolving this case and others to have a definitive determination of what the Montana choice of law rule is.

QUESTION ONE

15 Whether, in a personal injury/product liability/wrongful death action, where there is a potential conflict of laws, Montana will follow the Restatement (Second) of Conflict of Laws, including the 'most significant relationship' test set forth in §§ 146 and 6, in the determination of which state's substantive law to apply?

16 The traditional choice of law rule, known as lex loci delicti commissi (or the law of place where the wrong was committed), provides that the infliction of injury is actionable under the law of the state in which it was received. See *Alabama Great S. R.R. Co. v. Carroll* (Ala. 1892), 97 Ala. 126. In Carroll, the plaintiff, a resident of Alabama employed by the Alabama Great Southern Railroad Company, an Alabama corporation, was injured when, because of the negligence of his fellow employees occurring in Alabama, a link between two freight cars broke in Mississippi. Carroll brought suit in Alabama. Although Alabama law recognized a cause of action for injuries caused by the negligence of fellow employees, Mississippi did not. Following the traditional rule, the Supreme Court of Alabama applied the law of the place of injury, Mississippi, despite the fact that the conduct giving rise to Carroll's injury occurred in Alabama, both Carroll and his employer were from Alabama, and the relationship between the parties was based on an employment contract entered into in Alabama.

17 The theoretical basis for the traditional rule was the 'vested rights' theory propounded by Joseph H. Beale. The theory explained the forum's use of foreign legal rules in terms of the creation and enforcement of vested rights. According

to Professor Beale's theory, the only law that can operate in a foreign territory is the law of the foreign sovereign. When an event occurred in a foreign territory (an injury caused by a defective product, for example), and under the laws of that territory that event gave rise to a right (damages), a right 'vested' under that territory's law. The role of the forum court was simply to enforce the right which had vested in the foreign territory according to that territory's law. Crucial to this theory was a determination of where and when a right vested, because the law in place where the right vested would control the existence and content of the right. As evidenced by the decision in Carroll, courts have held that for tort claims a right vested where and when an injury occurred. See William M. Richman & David Riley, The First Restatement of Conflict of Laws on the Twenty-fifth Anniversary of its Successor: Contemporary Practice in Traditional Courts, 56 Md. L.Rev. 1196, 1197 (1997).

18 Traditional practice depends on a few broad, single-contact, jurisdiction-selecting rules. Traditionalist courts find the location of the last event necessary for a right to vest and apply the law of that location. As a result, courts following the traditional approach often choose the law of a state with no interest in the resolution of the dispute, like the choice of Mississippi law in Carroll. See Richman & Riley, *supra*, at 1198.

19 The traditional rule has largely been justified on the basis of the practical advantages that it offers: certainty, predictability, and forum neutrality. See Richman & Riley, *supra*, at 1200. However, problems inherent in its application as well as escape devices used to avoid results perceived to be arbitrary or unfair have greatly diminished the advantages the traditional rule supposedly provides. For example, the explicit public policy exception to the lex loci rule allows courts to avoid the law of the place of injury by concluding that it violates the public policy of the forum. Use of the public policy escape device by lex loci courts continues today. Observers have noted:

> It is impossible to predict which issues will prompt a court to use the public policy escape. Surprisingly, courts in both Tennessee and Georgia, for instance, held that the failure to adopt strict liability in tort by the state in which the injury occurred (relying instead on negligence and warranty) was sufficiently crucial as to violate fundamental forum public policy. (Richman & Riley, *supra*, at 1228).

20 The traditional rule also no longer affords consistency and predictability across jurisdictions. While some jurisdictions still cling to the traditional rule, the vast majority of states have rejected it. At the end of 1998, only 11 states still adhered to the lex loci rule, and their continued adherence is questionable. See Symeon C. Symeonides, Choice of Law in the American Courts in 1998: Twelfth Annual Survey, 47 Am. J. Comp. L. 327, 331. Professor Symeonides observes:

As the century draws to a close, the traditional theory in tort and contract conflicts in the United States finds itself in a very precarious state. This assessment is based not simply on the relatively low number of states that still adhere to that theory, but also on the shallowness of their commitment to it. Although the degree of commitment varies from state to state, it is fair to say that very few of these states are philosophically committed to the traditional theory. . . . More often, these rules remain in place only because court is able to find a way to evade them by using one of the traditional escapes, such as characterization, substance versus procedure, renvoi, or, more often, the [public policy] exception.(Symeonides, *supra*, at 345).

21 The Restatement (Second) of Conflict of Laws largely abandoned the traditional rule in favor of an approach which seeks to apply the law of the state with the 'most significant relationship to the occurrence and the parties.' Restatement (Second) of Conflict of Laws § 145(1)(1971) (hereinafter 'Restatement (Second)'). In adopting a policy analysis approach, the drafters noted that '[e]xperience has shown that the last event rule does not always work well. Situations arise where the state of the last event (place of injury) bears only a slight relationship to the occurrence and the parties with respect to the particular issue.' Restatement (Second), Introductory Note to Ch. 7, at 412.

22 In abandoning the lex loci rule in favor of the most significant relationship test, one court observed:

> The majority of courts which have considered the question have abandoned the lex loci rule in favor of a more flexible approach which permits analysis of the policies and interests underlying the particular issue before the court. Additionally, the commentators are overwhelmingly opposed to its retention and, although they disagree as to a substitute approach, all advocate a method which allows Courts to focus on the policies underlying the conflicting laws . . . and the governmental interests which would be advanced by their application. *In re Air Crash Disaster at Boston, Mass. on July 31, 1973* (D.Mass.1975), 399 F.Supp. 1106, 1110.

23 In determining the choice of law rules for contract disputes, we adopted the approach contained in the Restatement (Second) of Conflict of Laws. We see no reason to have one choice of law approach for contracts and another for torts. For the reasons set forth above, we now hereby adopt the 'most significant relationship' approach to determine the applicable substantive law for issues of tort.

QUESTION TWO

24 Given the facts of this case, which state's law applies to plaintiff's various tort and damages claims under Montana's choice of law rules?

25 The Byrds claim that under the most significant relationship test Montana law applies. General Motors contends that under this same test, the law of Kansas applies. We agree with the Byrds.

26 At the outset, we note that many appellate courts that have analyzed the most significant relationship test have done so in a fairly conclusory fashion. Although the analysis that follows appears somewhat tedious, our attempt is to comply with the procedures set forth in the Restatement (Second) of Conflict of Laws. We also raise an additional caveat. Any analysis under the Restatement approach is necessarily driven by the unique facts, issues, applicable law, and jurisdictions implicated in a particular case.

27 A. Relevant Restatement Provisions.

28 Any conflict of law analysis under the Restatement must begin with § 6. Section 6 provides: see *supra*, p. 44.

29 Since we have no statutory directive regarding choice of law, we turn to the specific section that relates to tort and personal injury actions. Section 145 of the Restatement (Second) of Conflict of Laws provides: see *supra*, p. 45. These contacts are to be evaluated according to their relative importance with respect to the particular issue.

30 The Restatement also has more specific sections relating to personal injury and wrongful death actions. Sections 146 and 175 provide that the rights and liabilities of the parties are to be determined in accordance with the law of the state where the injury occurred unless, with respect to a particular issue, another state has a more significant relationship. Whether another state has a more significant relationship is determined under § 145(2). We further note that issues such as the tortious character of conduct, available defenses, contributory fault, and damages are all to be determined by applying the most significant relationship rule of § 145. See, e.g., Restatement (Second) §§ 156 ('Tortious Character of Conduct'), 157 ('Standard of Care'), 161 ('Defenses'), 164 ('Contributory Fault'), and 171 ('Damages').

31 B. Most Significant Relationship Analysis.

32 Under the Restatement (Second) approach, the local law of the place of injury, Kansas, is presumptively applicable in a product liability and wrongful death action unless, with respect to a particular issue, a different state has a more significant relationship. See Restatement (Second) §§ 146 and 175. In order to determine whether a state other than the place of injury has a more significant relationship, the contacts listed under § 145(2) 'are to be taken into account in applying the principles of § 6.' Restatement (Second) § 145(2). Accordingly, we shall address each of the factors enumerated under § 6(2), taking into account, when appropriate, the contacts of § 145(2).

33 1. Needs of the Interstate and International System.

34 The first factor we must consider under § 6(2) is the needs of the interstate and international system. Restatement (Second) § 6(2)(a). The drafters stated,

> Choice-of-law rules, among other things, should seek to further harmonious relations between states and to facilitate commercial intercourse between them.

In formulating rules of choice of law, a state should have regard for the needs and policies of other states and of the community of states. Rules of choice of law formulated with regard for such needs and policies are likely to commend themselves to other states and to be adopted by these states (Restatement § 6 cmt. D).

35 On the facts of this case, this factor does not point toward the importance of applying any particular state's law. Rather, this factor supports the application of the Restatement approach, namely the law of the state with the most significant relationship to an issue. We believe the Restatement approach fosters harmonious relationship between states by respecting the substantive law of other states when those states have a greater interest in the determination of a particular issue litigated in a foreign jurisdiction. The Restatement approach is preferable, in our view, to the traditional lex loci rule which applies the law of the place of the accident which may be fortuitous in tort actions. We further conclude that there is no need to evaluate the contacts listed in § 145 to this issue.

36 2. The Policies of Interested States.

37 The second and third factors we must consider are the relevant policies of the forum state and other interested states. See Restatement (Second) § 6(2)(b) and (c). In the case sub judice, these are the most important factors in our analysis. The drafters stated,

Every Rule of Law, whether embodied in a statute or in a common law rule, was designed to achieve one or more purposes. A court should have regard for these purposes in determining whether to apply its own rule or the rule of another state in the decision of a particular issue. If the purposes sought to be achieved by a local statute or common law rule would be furthered by its application to out-of-state facts, this is a weighty reason why such application should be made. Restatement (Second) § 6 cmt. e.

This principle requires us to consider whether applying the law of a state with a relevant contact would further the purpose that law was designed to achieve. Upon consideration of this principle, it is clear that Montana has the more significant relationship to the issues raised by this dispute for the reasons set forth below.

38 a. Place of Injury.

39 As noted above, in product liability and wrongful death actions, the law of the place of injury is presumptively applicable unless another state has a more significant relationship. See Restatement (Second) §§ 146 and 175. The injury here occurred in Kansas. Kansas law provides for a cause of action against a manufacturer whose product causes harm as a result of its defective design. See Kan. Stat. Ann. § 60–3302. The purpose of a state's product liability statute is to regulate the sale of products in that state and to prevent injuries incurred by that state's residents due to defective products. See *Thornton v. Sea Quest, Inc.* (N.D.Ind.1998),

999 F.Supp. 1219, 1223–24 (noting that a state has an interest in compensating its citizens who are victims of torts and preventing the sale of supposedly defective products within its borders). Any conduct the state of Kansas may have been attempting to regulate through § 60–3302 could not be implicated by the facts of this case as it involves neither a sale in Kansas nor an injury to a Kansas resident.

40 Kansas law provides for multiple defenses to a product liability claim. For example, Kansas law bars recovery for injuries occurring after 'the time during which the product would be normally likely to perform or be stored in a safe manner.' Kan. Stat. Ann. § 60–3303(a)(1). Kansas law also allows a party defending a product liability claim to assert that the injury causing aspect of the product was in compliance with the regulatory standards relating to design or performance at the time of manufacture. See Kan. Stat. Ann. § 60–3304(a). Once again, the overriding purpose of Kansas's product liability laws is to establish the level of safety of products sold either in Kansas or to a Kansas resident. Clearly, these rules regarding defenses were not enacted in order to grant a defense to a manufacturer when a non-Kansas resident is injured by a product not purchased in Kansas.

41 Under Kansas law, an award of damages for product liability may be diminished in proportion to the amount of negligence attributed to the plaintiff or decedent. General Motors asserts that the issue of comparative negligence turns upon conduct that occurred in Kansas and therefore Kansas law should apply because Kansas has an interest in regulating conduct which occurred within its borders. However, the record before us does not contain the substance of General Motors' allegations regarding the Byrds' allegedly negligent conduct. Therefore, there is no evidence that General Motors' allegations concerning the comparative negligence of the Byrds are limited to conduct occurring solely within Kansas.

42 Moreover, even if General Motors' allegations concerned conduct occurring solely in Kansas, the Kansas Supreme Court did not extend Kansas's comparative negligence statute to product liability causes of action in order to regulate conduct occurring in Kansas. In concluding that the comparative negligence statute applied to product liability actions, the Kansas Supreme Court stated:

> Comparative liability provides a system for allocating responsibility for an injury while still serving the social policy of not allowing a manufacturer or seller to escape liability for defective products merely because of slight culpability on the part of the product user in bringing about the injury. *Kennedy*, 618 P.2d at 796 (emphasis added).

43 It is clear from the Kennedy decision that the Kansas Supreme Court extended Kansas's comparative negligence standard to product liability cases in order to 'allocate responsibility for an injury' due to a defective product, disallowing defenses such as 'assumption of the risk,' 'product misuse,' or 'unreasonable use' from completely precluding recovery under Kansas product liability law. See Kennedy, 618 P.2d at 796. Kansas has no interest in allocating responsibility for

the injuries suffered by Montana residents and caused by a product purchased in North Carolina. Again, the purpose of a state's product liability laws is to protect and provide compensation to its residents and regulate the sale of products within its borders.

44 Kansas law limits the total amount recoverable for 'noneconomic loss' in a personal injury action to $250,000, and limits 'nonpecuniary' damages in wrongful death actions to $100,000. Kan. Stat. Ann. §§ 60–19a02, 1903. Section 60–1903 was enacted in an effort to alleviate a perceived crisis in the availability and affordability of liability insurance. The purpose of these limitations would be furthered if any damage award issued would affect the availability or affordability of liability insurance for Kansas residents. The purpose of these limitations would not be furthered by applying them to the instant case because an award of damages against General Motors which exceeded Kansas's statutory damage limitations would not affect the availability or affordability of liability insurance for Kansas residents.

45 Lastly, Kansas law allows for punitive damages, but limits them to the lesser of $5 million or the defendant's highest gross annual income earned during any one of the five years immediately before the act for which such damages are awarded. The purpose of the availability and extent of punitive damage awards is to punish or deter conduct deemed wrongful when the availability of a cause of action and compensatory damages are considered an insufficient punishment or deterrence. See, e.g., *Tillett v. Lippert* (1996), 275 Mont. 1, 8, 909 P.2d 1158, 1162 ('The decisions of this Court further support the conclusion that punitive damages serve not only to punish, but also to set an example to the public for purposes of deterrence.'). Accordingly, the purpose of Kansas's punitive damage provisions would only be furthered on a particular set of facts if it had an interest in punishing or deterring the conduct at issue. As noted above, the purpose of Kansas's cause of action for product liability would not be furthered by its application to these facts because the pickup was not sold in Kansas nor were the Byrds Kansas residents. Correspondingly, this case does not involve conduct which Kansas was attempting to punish or deter through its punitive damage provisions.

46 b. Place of Conduct.

47 The Byrds purchased the vehicle in North Carolina. General Motors has made a general assertion that North Carolina might have an interest in having its law applied, but has not briefed us on which North Carolina laws might be applicable. Accordingly, our discussion will be somewhat general in nature. General Motors has argued that North Carolina has an interest because General Motors initially sold the truck in North Carolina, the Byrds subsequently purchased the truck in North Carolina, and the Byrds may have been North Carolina residents when they made this purchase.

48 The fact that the Byrds purchased the truck in North Carolina while residing there indicates that one of the purposes of North Carolina product liability law—the regulation of products sold within its borders—might be implicated by

the facts of this case. However, we think it significant that a North Carolina court would not apply North Carolina law to these facts, even if the Byrds had remained in North Carolina; North Carolina still adheres to the traditional place of injury rule in tort cases. On the facts of this case, a North Carolina court would apply the law of Kansas because they still adhere to the 'vested rights' theory that any right created by an injury is solely a product of the law of the territory in which that injury occurred. See *Terry v. Pullman Trailmobile, Inc.* (1989), 92 N.C.App. 687, 376 S.E.2d 47, 49 ('If no right exists at the [place of injury], there is none to enforce anywhere.'). Accordingly, the scope of North Carolina product liability law does not include causes of action for products purchased in North Carolina by North Carolina residents which cause injury outside of North Carolina. This belies the significance of North Carolina's interest in having its law applied. We note, however, that the place of purchase may have had greater significance if North Carolina followed the Restatement's approach rather than the traditional place of injury rule.

49 General Motors asserts that Michigan has an interest in regulating conduct occurring in Michigan. We note that evidence of where the pickup truck was designed and manufactured is not in the record nor has General Motors briefed us on the content of the precise laws which it claims might be applicable to these facts. However, we do not believe that the purpose of any potentially applicable Michigan product liability law would be to regulate the design and manufacture of products within its borders. Cf. *Crisman v. Cooper Indus.* (Tex.App.1988), 748 S.W.2d 273, 277 ('[T]he mere design or manufacture of a defective product is not actionable. To invoke the doctrine of strict liability in tort, the product producing the injury must enter the stream of commerce.'). The purpose of product liability law is to regulate in-state sales or sales to residents and to set the level of compensation when residents are injured.

50 Significantly, Michigan courts have recognized that it would not further the purpose of Michigan product liability law to apply it to a similar set of facts. Michigan courts have not applied Michigan law under similar circumstances because Michigan has little interest in applying its law when its only contact with the dispute is the location of the manufacturer.

51 Other courts have observed that applying the law of the place of manufacture would be unfair because it would tend to leave victims under compensated as states wishing to attract and hold manufacturing companies would raise the threshold of liability and reduce compensation. We agree that stressing the importance of the place of manufacture for choice of law purposes in a product liability case would be unfair. The conclusion that the place of manufacture is a relatively unimportant factor in a product liability case is obvious when we consider a hypothetical case in which all of the relevant contacts are in the forum state except the location of the manufacturer (most likely the fact pattern for the vast majority of product liability cases). Applying the law of the place of manufacture to that case simply because

the product was manufactured out-of-state would allow a state with a high concentration of industry to capture all of the benefits of a high threshold of liability and a low level of compensation. Specifically, the manufacturing state could enjoy the benefits associated with liability laws which favored manufacturers in order to attract and retain manufacturing firms and encourage business within its borders while placing the costs of its legislative decision, in the form of less tort compensation, on the shoulders of nonresidents injured by its manufacturers' products. This seems inherently unfair.

52 c. Residence of Parties.

53 The Plaintiffs were residents of Montana at the time they were injured. Unlike the laws of the other states with relevant contacts under § 145(2), the purposes sought to be achieved by Montana's product liability laws would be furthered by their application to this set of facts.[FN1] One of the central purposes of Montana's product liability scheme is to prevent injuries to Montana residents caused by defectively designed products. In contrast to Kansas, Montana has a direct interest in the application of its product liability laws because its residents were injured in this accident. Montana adopted a strict liability standard in order to afford 'maximum protection for consumers against dangerous defects in manufactured products with the focus on the condition of the product, and not on the manufacturer's conduct or knowledge.' See *Sternhagen v. Dow Co.* (1997), 282 Mont. 168, 176, 935 P.2d 1139, 1144 (emphasis added).

> FN1. In analyzing the place of manufacture, we fully addressed the relative significance of General Motors' principal place of business under this principle. Neither party asserts that Delaware, General Motors' place of incorporation, has any interest in having its product liability or wrongful death statutes apply to this case.

54 As is clear from Sternhagen, the focus of Montana law is not only on the regulation of products sold in Montana, but also on providing the maximum protection and compensation to Montana residents with the focus on the condition of the product and not on the conduct of the manufacturer. Applying Montana's provisions guaranteeing strict liability and full compensation to a cause of action involving a Montana domiciliary injured by a defective product would further the purposes of Montana law by insuring that the costs to Montana residents due to injuries from defective products are fully borne by the responsible parties. It will also have the salutary effect of deterring future sales of defective products in Montana and encouraging manufacturers to warn Montana residents about defects in their products as quickly and as thoroughly as possible.

55 Likewise, the purposes of Montana's laws regarding the availability and extent of punitive damages in product liability actions would also be furthered by their application to these facts. This is because, as described more fully above, punitive damages serve to punish and deter conduct deemed wrongful—in

this case, placing a defective product into the stream of commerce which subsequently injured a Montana resident. See Tillett, 275 Mont. at 8, 909 P.2d at 1162 (the purpose of punitive damages is to punish and deter culpable conduct). (. . .)

58 d. The place where the relationship, if any, between the parties is centered.

59 It doesn't appear that there is a place where the relationship, if any, between General Motors and the Byrds is centered. As one court described in similar circumstances:

> [P]roducts liability arises out of the most casual 'relationship' imaginable, the one-time purchase and sale of the product, and the plaintiff, as here, may have had no connection with it. The only 'relationship' between the parties here is that of injured victim and alleged tortfeasor. Ness, 1993 U.S. Dist. LEXIS 9938.

60 In sum, upon an analysis of the principle requiring us to consider the policies of interested states, it appears that Montana, as the domicile of the Byrds, has a significant relationship to the issues raised by this dispute. This is because, in general, the purpose of a state's product liability law is to regulate purchases made within its borders and to protect and compensate its residents. The policies underlying Montana product liability law would be furthered on these facts because the Byrds were Montana domiciliaries at the time they were injured. The policies underlying Kansas and Michigan law would not be furthered by their application to these facts because the product was not sold in either state, nor were the Plaintiffs domiciled in either state at the time they were injured. The purposes underlying North Carolina product liability law would not be furthered on these facts because, under North Carolina's vested rights approach to conflict of laws, North Carolina would apply the law of the jurisdiction where the injury occurred, whatever that law may be.

61 3. Justified Expectations.

62 Although we are to consider the justified expectations of the parties, tort cases generally do not involve justified expectations. Particularly in the area of negligence, when parties act without giving thought to the legal consequences of their conduct or to the law to be applied, they have no justified expectations. See Restatement (Second) § 6 cmt. g.

63 Automobile manufacturers do presumably give advance thought to the legal consequences of their conduct when designing and manufacturing their products. However, we note that the law of any state could potentially apply in a product liability action involving an automobile. For example, because North Carolina employs the traditional place of injury rule for choice of law purposes, if a North Carolina resident receives an injury from a defective vehicle while driving out-of-state, the law of the place of injury would govern that dispute. Accordingly, any expectation General Motors had that the law of North Carolina would govern a product liability suit involving a pickup truck it sold in North Carolina would not be justified. Furthermore, as noted by the court in Ness, automobiles are moveable and

frequently resold and the maintenance of a product liability action does not require privity. For example, the pickup could have been subsequently resold by the initial purchaser in a state which does not adhere to the traditional lex loci rule. Therefore, any expectation General Motors had that a dispute concerning this pickup truck would be governed by North Carolina's place of injury rule would not be justified.

64 4. Basic Policies Underlying Particular Field of Law.

65 We must also consider the relevant contacts in regard to the basic policies underlying the particular field of law. See Restatement (Second) § 6(2)(e). The drafters state that:

> This factor is of particular importance in situations where the policies of the interested states are largely the same but there are nevertheless minor differences between their relevant local law rules. In such instances, there is good reason for the court to apply the local law of the state which will best achieve the basic policy, or policies, underlying the particular field of law involved. Restat. (Second) § 6(2) cmt. h.

66 This is not a case in which the policies of interested states are basically the same except for minor differences in their local rules. For example, although under Kansas and Montana law, manufacturers of defective products are strictly liable for injuries, North Carolina law does not permit strict liability in tort in product liability actions. Instead, it appears that the various interested states have reached different conclusions concerning the right level of compensation and deterrence for injuries caused by defective products. Therefore, we need go no further in addressing this contact.

67 5. Certainty, Predictability, Uniformity, Ease.

68 We are also instructed to give consideration to the certainty, predictability and uniformity of result as well as the ease in the determination and application of the law to be applied. See Restatement (Second) § 6(2)(f) and (g). The comments state:

> Predictability and uniformity of result are of particular importance in areas where parties are likely to give advance thought to *457 the legal consequences of their transactions. It is partly on account of these factors that the parties are permitted within broad limits to choose the law that will determine the validity and effect of their contract. . . . Restatement (Second) § 6(2) cmt. i.

69 A consideration of this principle does not indicate that any one state has a more significant relationship than any other. Applying the law of the place of injury would not increase certainty or predictability any more than applying the law of the plaintiff's residence at the time of accident.

70 C. Conclusion.

71 Under the most significant relationship approach of the Restatement (Second), the local law of the place of injury, Kansas, governs the rights and liabilities of

the parties to a product liability and wrongful death action unless, with respect to a particular issue, a different state has a more significant relationship. See Restatement (Second) §§ 146 and 175. In order to determine whether a state other than the place of injury has a more significant relationship, the contacts listed under § 145(2) must be analyzed in relation to the principles enumerated under § 6(2). However, the principles of § 6(2) need not be given equal consideration in each case. Varying weight must be given to a particular factor, or group of factors, in different areas of choice of law. See Restatement (Second) § 6 cmt. c. On the facts before us, we give most weight to the principles requiring us to consider the relevant policies of interested states. Restatement (Second) § 6(2)(b) and (c). The other principles do not indicate the significance of any one contact. 72 Upon an analysis of the policies of interested states, it appears that the purposes of both Montana and North Carolina product liability law would presumably be furthered by their application to these facts. The place of purchase has an interest in regulating the safety of products sold within its borders; the place of the plaintiff's residence has an interest in deterring injuries to its residents and setting the level of compensation. Significantly, however, North Carolina law would not apply its own law to these facts, even if the Byrds had been North Carolina residents at the time of injury.

73 The purpose behind Montana product liability laws is clearly implicated by these facts. The following factors all point toward applying Montana law: the Byrds resided in Montana at the time of the accident, General Motors does business in Montana, Montana has a direct interest in preventing defective products from causing injuries to Montana residents as well as punishing and deterring manufacturers whose products injure Montana residents, and finally Montana is interested in fully compensating Montana residents. All of these factors would be furthered by applying Montana product liability, defenses, damages, and wrongful death statutes to the facts of this case.

? QUESTIONS

1 Why does the court consider the applicability of the laws of Kansas, North Carolina and Montana?
2 Why does the court conclude that the law of the place of the injury should not apply?
3 How important were the factors other than the policies of the interested states?
4 If the purpose of punitive damages is to punish and deter conduct, should the law of the place of conduct or the place of residence of the victims be applicable?

CASE

Court of Appeals of Washington, 28 March 2011 *Hillcrest Media, LLC v. Fisher Communications, Inc., et al.*[46]

Spearman, J.

1 At issue in this case is whether Washington law applies, and therefore, whether Hillcrest Media, LLC was precluded by former RCW 18.85.100 (2008) from suing for a commission for a real estate transaction where Hillcrest was not a licensed real estate broker in Washington. Because the state 'having the most significant relationship with the contract' at issue here was Washington, the trial court correctly concluded Washington law applies and properly dismissed Hillcrest's claims. We affirm.

FACTS

2 Hillcrest Media is an Arkansas limited liability company, and its agent, Larry Morton, is an Arkansas resident and Arkansas-licensed real estate broker. Neither Hillcrest nor Morton is a licensed real estate broker in Washington. Fisher Broadcasting Company and its parent corporation, Fisher Communications (hereinafter collectively 'Fisher'), are both Washington corporations whose principal places of business are in Washington state.

3 Fisher sought to purchase KWOG, a Bellevue, Washington television station. KWOG was owned by African-American Broadcasting of Bellevue, Inc. ('AAB'), a Washington corporation. Hillcrest alleges that in a letter dated March 24, 2006, Fisher authorized Hillcrest to act as its agent in negotiating this purchase. (. . .)

DISCUSSION

6 Hillcrest concedes that if Washington law applies, former RCW 18.85.100 would preclude him from suing for a commission under the March 24, 2006 letter agreement. That statute expressly barred suits by an unlicensed broker seeking compensation:

> No suit or action shall be brought for the collection of compensation as a real estate broker . . . without alleging and proving that the plaintiff was a duly licensed real estate broker . . . prior to the time of offering to perform any such act or service or procuring any promise or contract for the payment of compensation for any such contemplated act or service. Former RCW 18.85.100.

---

46 2011 Wash. App. LEXIS 727.

9 Thus, if Washington laws applies, Hillcrest must be a real estate broker licensed in Washington before it can sue in a Washington court to collect compensation on its agreement with Fisher. Hillcrest does not contend otherwise, but it argues that on the facts of this case, Arkansas law should apply. We reject this argument for the reasons described herein.

10 Since 1967, Washington courts have applied the 'most significant relationship test' to contract choice of law issues. "'In the absence of an effective choice of law by the parties, the validity and effect of a contract are governed by the law of the state having the most significant relationship with the contract.'" RESTATEMENT OF LAW (SECOND) § 188 (1971) (hereinafter 'Restatement').

11 Section 188 of the Restatement sets forth the factors courts consider as part of the 'most significant relationship' test:

> (1) The rights and duties of the parties with respect to an issue in contract are determined by the local law of the state which, with respect to that issue, has the most significant relationship to the transaction and the parties under the principles stated in § 6.
>
> (2) In the absence of an effective choice of law by the parties (see § 187), the contacts to be taken into account in applying the principles of § 6 to determine the law applicable to an issue include:
>
> > (a) the place of contracting,
> > (b) the place of negotiation of the contract,
> > (c) the place of performance,
> > (d) the location of the subject matter of the contract, and
> > (e) the domicil, residence, nationality, place of incorporation and place of business of the parties.
>
> These contacts are to be evaluated according to their relative importance with respect to the particular issue.

In determining the weight to be given to these factors, '[t]he approach is *not* to count contacts, but rather to consider which contacts are most significant[.]' Hillcrest contends an analysis of the factors shows Arkansas law should apply. We disagree.

12 *Place of contracting.* Contrary to Hillcrest's argument, the place of contracting did not occur solely within Arkansas. Indeed, although the letter was signed by Morton in Arkansas, it was drafted and signed by Fisher in Washington. Moreover, '[s]tanding alone, the place of contracting is a relatively insignificant contact.' RESTATEMENT § 188 cmt. e. As such, this factor does not weigh in favor of application of Arkansas law.

13 *Place of negotiation.* As was the case with the place of contracting, negotiations for the contract occurred in both Washington and Arkansas, as representatives for Fisher communicated with Morton from Washington, and Morton communicated with Fisher from Arkansas. Hillcrest alleged in its complaint that the negotiations occurred 'in substantial part' in Arkansas. Even assuming this is true, the place of negotiation 'is of less importance when there is no one single place of negotiation and agreement, as, for example, when the parties do not meet but rather conduct their negotiations from separate states by mail or telephone.' RESTATEMENT § 188 cmt. e. As such, this factor is not dispositive, and does not weigh in favor of application of Arkansas law.

14 *Place of performance.* Hillcrest contends the place of performance factor weighs toward application of Arkansas law. Hillcrest reaches this conclusion, however, only by entirely omitting Fisher's required performance under the contract, and by claiming that Morton 'could have' plausibly carried out all of his duties in Arkansas. Performance of the contract, however, contemplated communication with two Washington corporations to complete a transfer of Washington-based assets (including real estate used in the operation of a Washington television station) from one Washington corporation to another Washington corporation. The contract called for a due diligence examination of the Washington corporation that owned the Washington television station, and it required the Washington-based Fisher to draft the asset purchase agreement. The 'place of performance' factor thus weighs heavily in favor of application of Washington law.

15 Moreover, where the contract is for the rendition of services, the most significant contact is the location where the contract requires performance. Under section 196 of the Restatement, 'in personal service contracts the local law of the place of performance should be applied "unless, with respect to a particular issue, some other state has a more significant relationship[.]"' *Nelson*, 19 Wn. App. at 897 (quoting RESTATEMENT § 196).

16 Citing *Nelson*, Hillcrest contends Arkansas has a greater policy interest in regulating the type of transaction entered into by Hillcrest and Fisher. We disagree. In *Nelson*, Kaanapali Properties, which was a joint venture between a Washington corporation and a Hawaiian corporation, contracted with Nordic Tile, a Washington corporation, to provide flooring in condominiums being built in Maui. The King County Superior Court dismissed on grounds that although Nordic Tile was a licensed contractor in Washington, it was not a licensed contractor in Hawaii. This court reversed, holding that, given both Hawaii and Washington have similar interests in protecting the public from unlicensed contractors, the Washington policy of 'providing Washington residents a forum for the resolution of an adjudicable issue' was a more important consideration. *Nelson*, 19 Wn. App. at 899. In other words, given both states had similar public policy interests, the law of the forum applied. Here, unlike *Nelson*, the trial court did not seek to improperly apply Arkansas law; rather, it properly applied the law of the forum: Washington law.

17 *Location of subject matter.* As was the case with place of performance, the location of subject matter of the contract strongly favors application of Washington law. Again, the subject matter of the contract was entirely about Washington corporations. The contract required Hillcrest to communicate with two Washington corporations to complete a transfer of Washington-based assets from one Washington corporation to another Washington corporation.

18 *Domicile of the parties.* Hillcrest is an Arkansas company, whereas Fisher is a Washington corporation. This factor is thus neutral and does not weigh in favor of application of Arkansas law.

19 In sum, the location of negotiation and contracting, and the domicile of the parties are neutral and do not weigh in favor of application of Arkansas law. Place of performance and location of subject matter, however, weigh heavily in favor of application of Washington law. Where, as here, the contract is for the rendition of services, the most significant contact is the location where the contract requires performance. The most significant contacts at issue in this case thus were with Washington State. As such, the trial court properly applied Washington law in dismissing Hillcrest's claims.

 **QUESTIONS**

1 How much attention does the court pay to the policies underlying the rules in conflict? Is the analysis actually conducted by the court very different from the traditional multilateral choice of law analysis?

2 The Court explains that it does not count the factors, but conduct a qualitative analysis. Does it?

3 Does the Court consider that certain factors are more important than others? How different is the analysis applied by the court from Article 4 of the Rome I Regulation?

3 Advanced issues

3.1 Fundamental rights

Choice of law rules must, as any other rule, comport with fundamental rights. One obvious issue has been that of choice of law rules favouring one sex over the other, for instance rules providing for the application of the law of the nationality of one parent to determine parenthood, or the law of the nationality of the husband to govern marriage. But besides issues of discrimination, it seemed that the substance neutrality of the traditional choice of law methodology would shield this field of the law from the scrutiny of human rights law.

Read the following case and assess whether the U.S. Constitution imposes limitations on choice of law.

CASE

U.S. Supreme Court *Phillips Petroleum v. Shutts*[47]

Facts: During the 1970s, petitioner produced or purchased natural gas from leased land located in 11 States. Respondents, royalty owners possessing rights to leases from which petitioner produced the gas, brought a class action against petitioner in a Kansas state court, seeking to recover interest on royalty payments that had been delayed by petitioner. The trial court certified a class consisting of 33,000 royalty owners. Respondents provided each class member with a notice by first-class mail describing the action and informing each member that he could appear in person or by counsel, that otherwise he would be represented by respondents, and that class members would be included in the class and bound by the judgment unless they 'opted out' of the action by returning a 'request for exclusion.' The final class consisted of some 28,000 members, who reside in all 50 States, the District of Columbia, and several foreign countries. Notwithstanding that over 99% of the gas leases in question and some 97% of the plaintiff class members had no apparent connection to Kansas except for the lawsuit, Kansas courts applied Kansas contract and equity law to every claim, and found petitioner liable for interest on the suspended royalties to all class members.

Held: The application of Kansas law to all claims was unconstitutional.

JUSTICE REHNQUIST

The Kansas courts applied Kansas contract and Kansas equity law to every claim in this case, notwithstanding that over 99% of the gas leases and some 97% of the plaintiffs in the case had no apparent connection to the State of Kansas except for this lawsuit. Petitioner protested that the Kansas courts should apply the laws of the States where the leases were located, or at least apply Texas and Oklahoma law because so many of the leases came from those States. The Kansas courts disregarded this contention and found petitioner liable for interest on the suspended royalties as a matter of Kansas law, and set the interest rates under Kansas equity principles.

Petitioner contends that total application of Kansas substantive law violated the constitutional limitations on choice of law mandated by the Due Process Clause of the Fourteenth Amendment and the Full Faith and Credit Clause of Article IV, § 1. (. . .)

Four Terms ago we addressed a similar situation in *Allstate Ins. Co. v. Hague*,

---

47 472 U.S. 797 (1985).

449 U. S. 302 (1981). In that case we were confronted with two conflicting rules of state insurance law. Minnesota permitted the 'stacking' of separate uninsured motorist policies while Wisconsin did not. Although the decedent lived in Wisconsin, took out insurance policies and was killed there, he was employed in Minnesota, and after his death his widow moved to Minnesota for reasons unrelated to the litigation, and was appointed personal representative of his estate. She filed suit in Minnesota courts, which applied the Minnesota stacking rule.

The plurality in *Allstate* noted that a particular set of facts giving rise to litigation could justify, constitutionally, the application of more than one jurisdiction's laws. The plurality recognized, however, that the Due Process Clause and the Full Faith and Credit Clause provided modest restrictions on the application of forum law. These restrictions required

> that for a State's substantive law to be selected in a constitutionally permissible manner, that State must have a significant contact or significant aggregation of contacts, creating state interests, such that choice of its law is neither arbitrary nor fundamentally unfair. *Id.* at 312–313.

The dissenting Justices were in substantial agreement with this principle. *Id.* at 332 (opinion of POWELL, J., joined by BURGER, C.J., and REHNQUIST, J.). The dissent stressed that the Due Process Clause prohibited the application of law which was only casually or slightly related to the litigation, while the Full Faith and Credit Clause required the forum to respect the laws and judgments of other States, subject to the forum's own interests in furthering its public policy. *Id.* at 335–336.

The plurality in *Allstate* affirmed the application of Minnesota law because of the forum's significant contacts to the litigation which supported the State's interest in applying its law. *See id.* at 313–329. Kansas' contacts to this litigation, as explained by the Kansas Supreme Court, can be gleaned from the opinion below.

Petitioner owns property and conducts substantial business in the State, so Kansas certainly has an interest in regulating petitioner's conduct in Kansas. Moreover, oil and gas extraction is an important business to Kansas, and although only a few leases in issue are located in Kansas, hundreds of Kansas plaintiffs were affected by petitioner's suspension of royalties; thus the court held that the State has a real interest in protecting 'the rights of these royalty owners both as individual residents of [Kansas] and as members of this particular class of plaintiffs.' The Kansas Supreme Court pointed out that Kansas courts are quite familiar with this type of lawsuit, and '[t]he plaintiff class members have indicated their desire to have this action determined under the laws of Kansas.' Finally, the Kansas court buttressed its use of Kansas law by stating that this lawsuit was analogous to a suit against a 'common fund' located in Kansas. (. . .)

We also give little credence to the idea that Kansas law should apply to all claims because the plaintiffs, by failing to opt out, evinced their desire to be bound by Kansas law. Even if one could say that the plaintiffs 'consented' to the application of Kansas law by not opting out, plaintiff's desire for forum law is rarely, if ever controlling. In most cases, the plaintiff shows his obvious wish for forum law by filing there.

> If a plaintiff could choose the substantive rules to be applied to an action . . . the invitation to forum shopping would be irresistible. *Allstate, supra,* at 337.

Even if a plaintiff evidences his desire for forum law by moving to the forum, we have generally accorded such a move little or no significance. *John Hancock Mut. Life Ins. Co. v. Yates,* 299 U. S. 178, 182 (1936); *Home Ins. Co. v. Dick,* 281 U. S. 397, 408 (1930). In *Allstate,* the plaintiff's move to the forum was only relevant because it was unrelated and prior to the litigation. Thus, the plaintiffs' desire for Kansas law, manifested by their participation in this Kansas lawsuit, bears little relevance. (. . .)

Kansas must have a 'significant contact or significant aggregation of contacts' to the claims asserted by each member of the plaintiff class, contacts 'creating state interests,' in order to ensure that the choice of Kansas law is not arbitrary or unfair. *Allstate,* at 312–313. Given Kansas' lack of 'interest' in claims unrelated to that State, and the substantive conflict with jurisdictions such as Texas, we conclude that application of Kansas law to every claim in this case is sufficiently arbitrary and unfair as to exceed constitutional limits.

When considering fairness in this context, an important element is the expectation of the parties. *See Allstate, supra,* at 333. There is no indication that, when the leases involving land and royalty owners outside of Kansas were executed, the parties had any idea that Kansas law would control. Neither the Due Process Clause nor the Full Faith and Credit Clause requires Kansas 'to substitute for its own [laws], applicable to persons and events within it, the conflicting statute of another state,' *Pacific Employees Ins. Co. v. Industrial Accident Comm'n,* 306 U. S. 493, 502 (1939), but Kansas 'may not abrogate the rights of parties beyond its borders having no relation to anything done or to be done within them.' *Home Ins. Co. v. Dick, supra,* at 410.

Here the Supreme Court of Kansas took the view that in a nationwide class action where procedural due process guarantees of notice and adequate representation were met, 'the law of the forum should be applied unless compelling reasons exist for applying a different law.' Whatever practical reasons may have commended this rule to the Supreme Court of Kansas, for the reasons already stated we do not believe that it is consistent with the decisions of this Court. We make no effort to determine for ourselves which law must apply to the various transactions involved in this lawsuit, and we reaffirm our observation in *Allstate* that in many situations a state court may be free to apply one of several choices of law. But the constitutional limitations laid down in cases such as *Allstate* and *Home Ins. Co. v. Dick, supra,* must be respected even in a nationwide class action.

? NOTES AND QUESTIONS

1 What is the extent of the constitutional limitation on choice of law in this case? Could Kansas courts apply Kansas law to certain claims? Which one?
2 The U.S. Supreme Court has consistently ruled since *Allstate* that both the Due Process and the Full Faith and Credit Clauses are relevant in this context. This explains why the focus is not only on the rights of parties to the litigation, but also on state interests to regulate a given activity.
3 In Europe, the European Court of Human Rights has long recognized that certain fundamental rights can demand the application of the norms of the place where a person acquired a given status. The issue was typically that of the recognition of a foreign judgment which had constituted the status of one of the litigants, for instance by ruling that one party was the adoptive child of the other. The Court held several times that the right to a family life afforded by Art. 8 of the European Convention on Human Rights demanded that such judgment be recognized in contracting States, irrespective of the requirements of the law of foreign judgments of the relevant State.[48] The rationale and reasons of these judgments have made it clear that the court would, when confronted with such a case, rule that a choice of law rule providing for a law other than the law of origin of the litigants violate the fundamental right of the plaintiff to see their status recognized abroad.

3.2   Federalism

Conflicts of laws arise not only in cases connected to several nation States, but also within federal systems where the law of the different states is not unified. In principle, the issue of the applicable law is addressed in the same way in international and inter-state cases. However, certain fundamental principles of federalism can influence, and sometimes even command, the solution to the choice of law problem.

One of the essential goals of federal systems is to maintain or build an internal market where residents of the different states can circulate and trade freely.

---

48 See, e.g., *Wagner v. Luxembourg*, App. no. 76240/01 (ECHR 28 June 2007).

Any obstacle which might hinder the exercise of such rights, including rules and indeed choice of law rules, is thus to be eliminated.

In the following case, what is the impact of European federalism on the resolution of the choice of law problem?

 CASE

European Court of Justice, 14 October 2008 *Grunkin and Paul* (Case C–353/06)[49]

> 5 Leonhard Matthias Grunkin-Paul was born on 27 June 1998 in Denmark to Dr Paul and Mr Grunkin, who were at that time married and who are both of German nationality. Their child also has German nationality and has lived in Denmark since he was born.
>
> 6 In accordance with a certificate issued by the competent Danish authority attesting to that name ('navnebevis'), the child was given, pursuant to Danish law, the surname Grunkin-Paul, which was also entered on his Danish birth certificate.
>
> 7 The German registry office refused to recognise the surname of the child as it had been determined in Denmark on the ground that, under Article 10 of the EGBGB, the surname of a person falls to be determined by the law of the State of his or her nationality, and that German law does not allow a child to bear a double-barrelled surname composed of the surnames of both the father and mother. The appeals brought by Leonhard Matthias' parents against that refusal were dismissed. (. . .)
>
> 14 By its question, the national court asks essentially whether Articles 12 EC (*Treaty establishing the European Community*) and 18 EC preclude the competent authorities of a Member State from refusing to recognise a child's surname, as determined and registered in a second Member State in which the child – who, like his parents, has only the nationality of the first Member State – was born and has been resident since birth.

> *The scope of the EC Treaty*
>
> 15 It must be pointed out at the outset that the situation of the child Leonhard Matthias falls within the scope of the EC Treaty.
>
> 16 Although, as Community law stands at present, the rules governing a person's surname are matters coming within the competence of the Member States, the latter must none the less, when exercising that competence, comply with

---

49 ECLI:EU:C:2008:559.

Community law unless what is involved is an internal situation which has no link with Community law (see Case C-148/02 *Garcia Avello* [2003] ECR I-11613, paragraphs 25 and 26, and the case-law cited).

17 The Court has already held that such a link with Community law does exist in regard to children who are nationals of one Member State and are lawfully resident in the territory of another Member State (see *Garcia Avello*, paragraph 27).

18 Therefore, the child Leonhard Matthias can rely, in principle, as regards the Member State of which he is a national, on the right conferred by Article 12 EC not to be discriminated against on grounds of nationality and on the right, established in Article 18 EC, to move and reside freely within the territory of the Member States.

Article 12 EC

19 With regard to Article 12 EC, the Court would, however, point out that, as was submitted by all the Member States which made observations to the Court and by the Commission of the European Communities, the child Leonhard Matthias is not, in Germany, being discriminated against on grounds of nationality.

20 Since the child and his parents have only German nationality and, in respect of the conferring of a surname, the German conflicts rule refers to the German substantive law on surnames, the determination of that child's surname in Germany in accordance with German legislation cannot constitute discrimination on grounds of nationality.

Article 18 EC

21 National legislation which places certain of the nationals of the Member State concerned at a disadvantage simply because they have exercised their freedom to move and to reside in another Member State is a restriction on the freedoms conferred by Article 18(1) EC on every citizen of the Union.

22 Having to use a surname, in the Member State of which the person concerned is a national, that is different from that conferred and registered in the Member State of birth and residence is liable to hamper the exercise of the right, established in Article 18 EC, to move and reside freely within the territory of the Member States.

23 The Court has already held, as regards children with the nationality of two Member States, that a discrepancy in surnames is liable to cause serious inconvenience for those concerned at both professional and private levels resulting from, inter alia, difficulties in benefiting, in the Member State of which they are nationals, from the legal effects of diplomas or documents drawn up in the surname recognised in another Member State of which they are also nationals. (*Garcia Avello*, point 36). (. . .)

29 An obstacle to freedom of movement such as that resulting from the serious

inconvenience described in paragraphs 23 to 28 of this judgment could be justified only if it was based on objective considerations and was proportionate to the legitimate aim pursued.

30 In order to justify using nationality as the sole connecting factor for the determination of surnames, the German Government and some of the other Governments that submitted observations to the Court maintain inter alia that that connecting factor constitutes an objective criterion which makes it possible to determine a person's surname with certainty and continuity, to ensure that siblings have the same surname and to preserve relationships between members of an extended family. Moreover, that criterion is intended to ensure that all persons of a particular nationality are treated in the same way and that the surnames of persons of the same nationality are determined in an identical manner.

31 None of the grounds put forward in support of the connecting factor of nationality for determination of a person's surname, however legitimate those grounds may be in themselves, warrants having such importance attached to it as to justify, in circumstances such as those of the case in the main proceedings, a refusal by the competent authorities of a Member State to recognise the surname of a child as already determined and registered in another Member State in which that child was born and has been resident since birth.

32 In so far as the connecting factor of nationality seeks to ensure that a person's surname may be determined with continuity and stability, in circumstances such as those in the main proceedings, as was pointed out by the Commission, that connecting factor will result in an outcome contrary to that sought. Every time the child crosses the border between Denmark and Germany, he will bear a different name. (. . .)

34 It should further be noted that the connecting factor of nationality under German private international law for the determination of a person's surname is not without exception. It is not disputed that the German conflict rules relating to the determination of a child's surname permit the connecting factor of the habitual residence of one of the parents where that habitual residence is in Germany. Therefore, a child who, like his parents, does not have German nationality may nevertheless have conferred on him in Germany a surname formed in accordance with German legislation if one of his parents has his habitual residence there. A situation similar to that of the child Leonhard Matthias could therefore also arise in Germany. (. . .)

39 In view of the foregoing considerations, the answer to the question referred to the Court must be that, in circumstances such as those of the case in the main proceedings, Article 18 EC precludes the authorities of a Member State, in applying national law, from refusing to recognise a child's surname, as determined and registered in a second Member State in which the child – who, like his parents, has only the nationality of the first Member State – was born and has been resident since birth.

QUESTIONS

1 The Court rules that the application of the German choice of law rule would not be compliant with the freedom of movement of the child. What is the applicable law, then? Does the court lay down a new choice of law rule? Which one? If Denmark had applied the law of nationality to determine the name of the child, what would it be in Germany?

2 While the German government framed the issue as one of choice of law, the Court answered that Germany had to recognize the name of the child. What was there to recognize in this case? A judgment from Denmark? There was none. Danish law? But it was not applicable. So maybe it was the actual application of Danish law by a Danish official, who had issued an official document mentioning the name of the child. This official document had created expectations for the child and his family about the name of the child.

The following case shows how a different type of choice of law rules could raise a similar issue.

CASE

United States Court of Appeals for the Seventh Circuit, 28 January 2010 *Midwest Title Loans, Inc., v. David Mills*[50]

Facts: Plaintiff Midwest Title is an Illinois business corporation licensed in Illinois as a consumer installment loan company. It issues consumer loans, which are secured by the borrower's motor vehicle, and operates exclusively from 23 separate locations throughout the state of Illinois. It has no business locations within Indiana. It does not own or lease property in Indiana and does not hold a certificate of authority or license to do business in Indiana. No Midwest Title agent or employee solicits business *in person* in Indiana, and all reminder and collection calls to Indiana borrowers are made from Plaintiff's Illinois-based offices. However, Plaintiff does solicit business from Indiana consumers via other means. It engaged in advertising and solicitation activities targeting Indiana customers. Plaintiff made annual mailings to Indiana residents who had previously used its services, with the effect of soliciting repeat business from those customers. Plaintiff further admits to advertising on television stations in Indianapolis and Terre Haute, Indiana, and on Chicago-based television and radio stations that reached Indiana residents.

Midwest brought action against director of the Indiana Department of Financial Institutions, seeking to enjoin him from enforcing the Indiana Uniform Consumer Credit Code against it.

Posner, Circuit Judge.

A provision added to the Indiana version of the model [Consumer Credit]

---

50 593 F.3d 660.

code in 2007 and aptly termed the 'territorial application' provision states that a loan is deemed to occur in Indiana if a resident of the state 'enters into a consumer sale, lease or loan transaction with a creditor . . . in another state and the creditor . . . has advertised or solicited sales, leases, or loans in Indiana by any means, including by mail, brochure, telephone, print, radio, television, the Internet, or electronic means.' § 24-4.5-1-201(1)(d). If the territorial-application provision is triggered, the lender becomes subject to the code and must therefore get a license from the state to make consumer loans and is bound by a variety of restrictions that include a ceiling on the annual interest rate that a lender may charge. (. . .)

Article I, § 8, cl. 8 of the Constitution, which provides so far as bears on this case that 'Congress shall have Power . . . to regulate Commerce . . . among the several States,' has been interpreted to bar states from establishing tariff walls or other harmful barriers to trade across state lines. (references omitted). (. . .)

Tariffs seek to protect local producers from competition. Indiana, however, isn't trying to protect its title lenders from the competition of title lenders in other states. The territorial-application provision does not make Indiana law treat a title lender located in another state, such as Midwest, any worse than it treats Indiana lenders. All are subject to the same interest-rate ceilings and other strictures of the consumer credit code. But as the case law has long recognized, the commerce clause can be violated even when there is no outright discrimination in favor of local business. An earlier case of ours gave the example of 'a severance tax on a raw material, such as oil or coal, of which the state (perhaps in conjunction with other states) has a monopoly or near monopoly and which is almost entirely exported rather than consumed locally. The incidence of the tax will fall on the consumers in other states, who have no voice in the politics of the producing state, and the result may be a level of taxation and resulting price to consumers that greatly exceeds the cost of the services that the state provides to producers of the raw material and that by doing so burdens the export of the raw material to other states.' *Cavel Int'l, Inc. v. Madigan*, 500 F.3d 551, 555 (7th Cir. 2007). In such a case, however, where the regulation is local but the consequences felt elsewhere, we explained that a plaintiff 'has a steep hill to climb.' 'Where the statute regulates even-handedly to effectuate a legitimate local public interest, and its effects on interstate commerce are only incidental, it will be upheld unless the burden imposed on such commerce is *clearly* excessive in relation to the putative local benefits.'

But another class of nondiscriminatory local regulations is invalidated without a balancing of local benefit against out-of-state burden, and that is where states actually attempt to regulate activities in other states. 'The Commerce Clause dictates that no State may force an out-of-state merchant to seek regulatory approval in one State before undertaking a transaction in another.' *Healy v. Beer Institute*, 491 U.S. 324, 337, 1 (1989) (. . .)

'Generally speaking,' the Supreme Court said in *Healy*, 'the Commerce Clause protects against inconsistent legislation arising from the projection of one state regulatory regime into the jurisdiction of another State.' (. . .)

The concerns behind the due process and commerce clauses are different. The former protects persons from unreasonable burdens imposed by government, including extraterritorial regulation that is disproportionate to the governmental interest. The latter protects interstate commerce from being impeded by extraterritorial regulation. And imposing a state's law on transactions in another state has a greater extraterritorial effect (and greater effect on commerce) than the state's applying its own law to suits in its courts. (. . .)

The interference was with a commercial activity that occurred in another state. Each title loan that Midwest made to a Hoosier was in the form of a check, drawn on an Illinois bank, that was handed to the borrower at Midwest's loan office and could be cashed there. Illinois was also where the conditional transfer of title to the collateral was made (the handing over of the keys – the 'pawn') and where the payments required by the loan agreement were received by Midwest. The contract was, in short, made and executed in Illinois, and that is enough to show that the territorial-application provision violates the commerce clause. (. . .)

Our conclusion is not altered by the fact that Midwest advertises in Indiana. If Indiana cannot prevent Midwest from lending money to Hoosiers in Illinois, it cannot prevent Midwest from truthfully advising them of this opportunity. A state may not 'take the commercial speech that is vital to interstate commerce and use it as a basis to allow the extraterritorial regulation that is destructive of such commerce.' *Carolina Trucks & Equipment, Inc. v. Volvo Trucks of North America, Inc.*, 492 F.3d at 491 (4th Cir. 2007) (. . .)

❓ NOTES AND QUESTIONS

1 Why is the Indiana choice of law rule impeding interstate commerce? How should the 'territorial application' provision of the Indiana code be drafted to be constitutional? What are the constitutionally acceptable connecting factors that the Indiana lawmaker could use?

2 The Court distinguishes the Due Process from the Commerce clause. The Due Process clause

has a limited influence on choice of law: see *supra* 3.1. It has a much stronger influence on jurisdiction: see *infra* Ch. 3.

3 In Europe, the European Court of Justice has held that overriding mandatory provisions could impede the freedom of service of European businesses. In several cases[51] where French businesses had deployed workers on Belgium sites to carry out temporary work and where Belgian authorities demanded the application of Belgian labour law provisions that they deemed overriding mandatory provisions, the court ruled that overriding mandatory provisions could potentially be illegal restrictions to the fundamental freedom to provide services in other Member States. However, it also ruled that such a restriction could be justified if necessary in order to safeguard the public interest, and if the litigious provision were non-discriminatory, and actually necessary to safeguard the public interest. The protection of social workers was found to belong to this category, and certain Belgian rules to be unjustified for not being necessary and proportionate to the purpose of protecting the workers concerned.

4 Article 6 of the Rome I Regulation provides for the application of the mandatory rules of the law of the residence of the consumer where the professional directed his activities to that country (see *infra* p. 407). Is Art. 6 compatible with the freedom to provide services? To avoid the risk of displacing the protective mechanism of Art. 6, some European legislation expressly insulate 'contractual obligations concerning consumer contacts' and party autonomy from the scope of the freedom to provide services.[52]

---

51 See, e.g., Joined Cases C-369/96 and C-376/96 *Criminal Proceedings against Arblade* [1999] E.C.R. I-8453; Case C-165/98 *Mazzoleni v. Inter Surveillance Assistance SARL* [2001] E.C.R. I-2189.
52 See Annex to the Directive 2000/31/EC of 8 June 2000 on certain legal aspects of information society services, in particular electronic commerce, in the Internal Market ('Directive on electronic commerce').

2

The choice of law process

1 Characterization

The determination of the applicable law requires identifying the applicable choice of law rule. In most cases, this is obvious, and no problem arises. In some cases, however, it is less easy to determine whether the legal relationship falls within the scope of one or another choice of law rule. It is necessary to characterize the legal relationship to identify the applicable choice of law rule.

While characterization is not an exercise peculiar to choice of law, it is more complex in this field because of the number of legal systems involved. The same issue could be characterized differently in the different systems. In such a case, it becomes necessary to choose which characterization will be relied on. As the problem was first identified at the end of the 19th century almost simultaneously by Etienne Bartin, a French scholar, and Franz Kahn, a German scholar, their names have remained associated with the problem in the civil law tradition.

1.1 Multilateral methodology

In this American case which dates back before the American Revolution on choice of law, the court was confronted with a characterization problem. In order to determine which law it would apply, it had to decide which choice of law rule it would apply and, for that purpose, characterize the issue.

Read the judgment and identify which choice of law rules were considered in this case, and which law would apply depending on the characterization.

CASE

Supreme Court of Errors of Connecticut, 28 September 1928 *Levy v. Daniels' U–Drive Auto Renting Co., Inc. et al.*[1]

WHEELER, C.J.

The complaint alleged these facts: The defendant, Daniels' U–Drive Auto Renting Company, Incorporated, rented in Hartford to Sack an automobile, which he operated, and in which Levy, the plaintiff, was a passenger. During the time the automobile was rented and operated, the defendant renting company was subject to section 21 of chapter 195 of the Public Acts of Connecticut, 1925, which provides:

> 'Any person renting or leasing to another any motor vehicle owned by him shall be liable for any damage to any person or property caused by the operation of such motor vehicle while so rented or leased.'

While the plaintiff was a passenger, Sack brought the car to a stop on the main highway at Longmeadow, Mass., and negligently allowed it to stand directly in the path of automobiles proceeding southerly in the same direction his automobile was headed, without giving sufficient warning to automobiles approaching from his rear, and without having a tail light in operation, and when, due to inclement weather, the visibility was reduced to an exceedingly low degree. At this time the defendant Maginn negligently ran into and upon the rear end of the car Sack was operating, and threw plaintiff forcibly forward, causing him serious injuries. The specific acts of Maginn's negligence are set up at length in the complaint; it is not essential at this time to recite them. The plaintiff suffered his severe injuries in consequence of the concurrent negligence of both defendants.

The defendant demurred to the complaint upon several grounds, upon only one of which the trial court rested its decision; namely, that the liability of the defendant must be determined by the law of Massachusetts, which did not impose upon persons renting automobiles any such obligation as the Connecticut act did. This is the only ground of demurrer which was presented in the argument of the appeal. Since all of the grounds of demurrer were raised by the appeal, we have examined the others, and deem it sufficient in disposing of them to say that none is well taken.

---

1 108 Conn. 333.

It is the defendant's contention in support of this ground of demurrer that the action set forth in the complaint is one of tort, and, since Massachusetts has no statute like, or substantially like, the Connecticut act, it must be determined by the common law of that state, under which the plaintiff must prove, to prevail, the negligence of the defendant in renting a defective motor vehicle and in failing to disclose the defect. If this were the true theory of the complaint, the conclusion thus reached must have followed. 'The locus delicti determined the existence of the cause of action.' *Orr v. Ahern*, 107 Conn. 174, 176; *Commonwealth Fuel Co. v. McNeil*, 103 Conn. 390. Under the law of Massachusetts, the plaintiff concededly would have a cause of action against Sack and Maginn for their tortious conduct in the operation of the cars they were driving. The plaintiff concedes the correctness of this. His counsel, however, construe the complaint as one in its nature contractual. The act makes him who rents or leases any motor vehicle to another liable for any damage to any person or property caused by the operation of the motor vehicle while so rented or leased. Liability for 'damage caused by the opera-tion of such motor vehicle' means caused by its tortious operation. This was undoubtedly the legislative intent; otherwise the act would be invalid. The plaintiff concedes this to be the true construction of these words, and the defendant acquiesces in this construction.

The complaint alleges a tortious operation of the automobile rented to Sack by the defendant, causing the injuries to the plaintiff as alleged, and consti-tuting an action ex delicto. The statute gives, in terms, the injured person a right of action against the defendant which rented the automobile to Sack, though the injury occurred in Massachusetts. It was a right which the statute gave directly, not derivatively, to the injured person as a consequence of the contract of hiring. The purpose of the statute was not primarily to give the injured person a right of recovery against the tortious operator of the car, but to protect the safety of the traffic upon highways by providing an incentive to him who rented motor vehicles to rent them to competent and careful operators, by making him liable for damage resulting from the tor-tious operation of the rented vehicles. The common law would not hold the defendant liable upon the facts recited in the complaint for the negligence of Sack in the operation of this automobile. Huddy on Automobiles (8th Ed.) § 200, and cases cited. The rental of motor vehicles to any but competent and careful operators, or to persons of unknown responsibility, would be liable to result in injury to the public upon or near highways, and this imminent danger justified, as a reasonable excercise of the police power, this statute, which requires all who engage in this business to become responsible for any injury inflicted upon the public by the tortious operation of the rented motor vehicle. Blashfield, in Cyclopedia of Automobile Law, vol. 2, p. 1313, expresses the opinion that 'of late there has been a tendency on the part of the courts to break away from the rigid limitation of the liability of the owner of the automobile to the strict application of the doctrine of respondeat superior.' 'Thus,' he continues, 'in some states, there are statutes providing, in effect, that every owner of a motor vehicle operated upon the public highway shall be liable for injuries resulting from negligence in the operation of such motor vehicle in the business of such owner or otherwise, by any person legally using or operating the same, with the permission, express or implied, of such owner, and such statutes are within the police power of the state.' He cites a number of authorities in support of his statement. Statutes of this character are so clearly within the reasonable exercise of the police power that we do not deem it necessary to fortify his opinion, or the opinion we have already expressed, by detailed reference to the cases.

The statute made the liability of the person renting motor vehicles a part of every contract of hiring a motor vehicle in Connecticut. A liability ex delicto is created by the law of the place of the delict. *Orr v. Ahern, supra*; *Commonwealth Fuel Co. v. McNeil, supra.* A liability arising out of a contract depends upon the law of the place of contract, 'unless the contract is to be performed or to have its beneficial operation and effect elsewhere, or it is made with reference to the law of another place.' *Illustrated Postal Card & Novelty Co. v. Holt*, 85 Conn. 140, 143. We will enforce rights of action on contracts arising in other jurisdictions unless these contravene our own law, or our own fundamental and important public policy imperatively requires their nonenforcement. *Maisch v. Maisch*, 87 Conn. 377, 381; *Dennick v. Railroad Co.*, 103 U. S. 11, 17; *Flash v. Conn*, 109 U. S. 371, 377. It is a general rule, subject to the exceptions we have noted, that rights ex contractu may be enforced anywhere. *Maisch v. Maisch, supra; Tuttle v. Jockmus*, 106 Conn. 683; Goodrich on Conflict of Laws, § 103.

If the liability of this defendant under this statute is contractual, no question can arise as to the plaintiff's right to enforce this contract, provided the obligation imposed upon this defendant was for the 'direct, sole and exclusive benefit' of the plaintiff. The contract was made in Connecticut; at the instant of its making the statute made a part of the contract of hiring the liability of the defendant which the plaintiff seeks to enforce. The law inserted in the contract this provision. The statute did not create the liability; it imposed it in case the defendant voluntarily rented the automobile. Whether the defendant entered into this contract of hiring was his own voluntary act; if he did he must accept the condition upon which the law permitted the making of the contract. The contract was for the 'direct, sole, and exclusive benefit' of the plaintiff, who is alleged to have been injured through the tortious operation of the automobile rented by the defendant to Sack. The right of the plaintiff as a beneficiary of this contract to maintain this action is no longer an open question in this state. *Baurer v. Devenis*, 99 Conn. 203; *Tuttle v. Jockmus, supra*. The contract was made for him and every other member of the public. That the beneficiary was undisturbed because each member of the public was a beneficiary is of no consequence. His injury determines his identity and right of action. *Whitehead v. Burgess*, 61 N. J. Law, 75; *Smead v. Stearns*, 173 Iowa, 174; Williston on Contracts (1924 Ed.) § 378; Page on Contracts, §§ 2391, 2392. The assent of the beneficiary, if required, is manifested in his action upon the contract. The demurrer should have been overruled.

There is error, the judgment of the superior court is reversed, and the cause remanded to be proceeded with according to law.

This case predates the American Revolution on choice of law. It is still relevant in U.S. states which follow the traditional multilateral methodology, but the issue arises differently in unilateral methodologies: see below 1.2.

 QUESTIONS

What is the subject-matter of the characterization? Is it facts? Is it a legal rule? Is it a legal issue, or question? What does the court focus on?

There is wide agreement today, both in the civil law[2] and in the common law[3] worlds, that the subject matter of characterization should be the relevant legal issue, not the relevant rules. The first reason is that multilateral choice of law rules connect categories of legal issues with a choice of law, not rules. The second is that a particular dispute will raise only one issue, but potentially involve several rules, belonging to different laws.

 CASE

French Cour de cassation, 22 June 1955 *Caraslanis*

Facts: On September 12th, 1931, Dimitri Caraslanis and Maria-Richarde Dumoulin were married in Paris by an official of the city of Paris. Caraslanis was a Greek national and a member of the orthodox Church. When his wife, who was a French national, sued for divorce in a French court, Caraslanis argued that the marriage was void for lack of an orthodox religious ceremony as required by Greek law. According to him, Greek law applied to the determination of the substantive validity of marriage of a Greek national. The Paris Court

---

2 See in France, Mayer and Heuzé, para. 157; Bertrand Ancel, *Les conflits de qualification à l'épreuve de la donation entre époux* (Dalloz 1977).
3 See in England, Briggs, 18; Rogerson, 269.

of appeal held that the requirement that the marriage be celebrated in a religious form was an issue of formal validity which was governed by the law of the place of celebration of the marriage. Caraslanis appealed to the French supreme court.

Judgment: Whether an aspect of the celebration of a marriage belongs to the category of rules of form or rules of substance is to be decided in accordance with French conceptions, which are that whether a marriage must be religious is an issue of form. As a consequence, the civil marriage performed in France by Caraslanis and Dumoulin is valid under the rule *locus regit actum*.
For these reasons: — the appeal is dismissed.

NOTES AND QUESTIONS

1 Greece and France share the same choice of law rules: formal requirements of marriage are governed by the law of the place where the marriage was celebrated, while substantive requirements are governed by the national law of the spouses. Under Greek law, such a celebration was necessary; Greek law would therefore characterize the celebration as a substantive requirement. By contrast, under French law, a religious celebration was not required, and French law thus characterized it as a formal requirement. The *Caraslanis* case is an excellent example why courts should characterize legal issues rather than rules. How many issues were there in this case? How many rules? Which law would be held applicable should the court characterize rules? Which rule would it characterize?

2 A separate question is whether the relevant issue should be characterized according to the conceptions of the forum or of another law, for instance the law which will eventually be found to govern the issue (the *lex causae*). This question was the main focus of Kahn and Bartin when they studied the topic at the end of the 19th century. In *Caraslanis*, the court eventually decided to follow French conceptions and to characterize the requirement (or lack thereof) of a religious celebration accordingly. The case is considered in France as the leading authority for the proposition that, for choice of law purposes, courts should always characterize issues according to the conceptions of the forum. Two reasons were identified to support that conclusion. First, a choice of law rule is a rule of the forum, laid down by a lawmaker of the forum. It should thus be interpreted in accordance with the conceptions of the forum, because it is these conceptions that the lawmaker likely had in mind. Second, there is no alternative, because the applicable law is not known: it is the purpose of the whole exercise to designate it. In other words, applying the *lex causae* for the purpose of determining whether it applies is arguing in circle.

As these two provisions appearing in recent codifications demonstrate, the application of the *lex fori* to the interpretation of the forum's choice of law rules is widely accepted in comparative private international law.[4]

Romanian Civil Code (2009)

Article 2.558 *Characterization*

1) When determining the applicable law depends on the characterization which will be given to a legal institution or a legal relationship, it is the legal characterization adopted by Romanian law which will be followed.

---

4 See also, in England, Briggs, p. 15; in Germany, von Hoffmann and Thorn, § 6–12, in Tunisia: Art. 27 of the Code of Private International Law; in Russia, Art. 1187 of the Civil Code.

2) In case of *renvoi*, characterization is made according to the foreign law referring to Romanian law.

3) The movable or immovable nature of property shall be determined in accordance with the law of the place where it is located or, where applicable, of where it is localized.

4) If Romanian law does not know a foreign legal institution or knows it under a different designation or with a different content, the legal characterization made by the foreign law may be taken into consideration.

5) However, where the parties themselves have determined the meaning of concepts in a legal act, the characterization of these concepts will be made according to the will of the parties.

Quebec Civil Code

Article 3078

Characterization is made according to the legal system of the court seised of the matter; however, characterization of property as movable or immovable is made according to the law of the place where it is situated.

Where a legal institution is unknown to the court or known to it under a different designation or with a different content, foreign law may be taken into account.

? NOTES AND QUESTIONS

1 Should characterization be made differently for property? Why? Is it because, as *in rem* rights will be enforced at the place where the relevant property is situated, its views cannot be ignored?[5] But, as we shall see later, a judgment deciding a dispute relating to moveable property would not necessarily be denied recognition in the country of the place of the property for the sole reason that it would have applied a different law.[6]

2 While it is widely admitted that characterization for the purpose of determining the applicable law should be made in accordance with the concepts of the forum, this does not exclude taking into account foreign law for the purpose of understanding the object of characterization. This will be the case where the parties will have acted on the basis of a foreign legal institution which does not exist in the substantive law of the forum.

A traditional example is trusts. In the civil law world, trusts are unknown, as there is no distinction between equity and common law in civil law jurisdictions. In order to understand common law trusts and to decide how to characterize them, it was necessary for civil law courts to understand the function and purpose of trusts under the relevant common law system.

In this Swiss case, can you explain the respective roles of the foreign law and of the law of the forum?

---

5 *Compare* the scope of *renvoi* in the common law jurisdiction *infra* 3.1.
6 *Infra*, Part III.

CASE

Swiss Federal Tribunal, 12 June 1980 *S. et consorts v. Département de justice du canton du Tessin*[7]

III.1. The child Stuart Marshall has dual citizenship: British iure sanguinis, by his father, and iure soli, being born in London; Swiss iure sanguinis, by his mother (art. 1er para. 1 lettera b Law on Nationality and art. 271 para. 2 Civil Code 'CC'). It is necessary to examine under what name it should be registered in the Swiss civil status registers.

III.2. Recognized by his father before the registrar of English civil status, a British citizen, the child has, according to English law, the father's surname. But he can only be entered under this surname in Switzerland if English law appears to be applicable by virtue of a rule of Swiss private international law. Indeed, the application of Swiss substantive law excludes that the child acquires the father's surname: under the old law, because the English declaration of paternity cannot be equated to the recognition under former art. 303 and 325 CC; under the new law, because the child of unmarried parents bears, even in case of recognition by the father, the name of the mother (art. 270 para. 2 CC). (. . .)

III.5.b) The application of art. 8 of the Act on Relationships of Civil Law ('LRDC') does not mean that the present case is subject to English law.

aa) When the acquisition of the name is the effect of a parent child relationship, it is governed by the law applicable to parentage, that is to say by the national law of the father if paternity is in question (art. 8 para. 2 LRDC). It would thus be for English law to determine whether and how a parent-child relationship has been created between the child Stuart Marshall and S., and what are the effects of this relationship, including with respect to the name.

bb) However, Art. 8 LRDC did not cover only parent-child relationship and their effects. He embraced all elements of the status of a person (ATF 86 II 444 para. 5 and references) – including the name (ATF 102 Ib 246/247 para. 2), especially change of name (ATF 60 II 388 /389 and references) – and subjected them to personal law, which was national law (ATF 92 II 132 consid. 3). There must be a connection to the personal law of the person concerned when the issue of the right to the name arises independently of the family relationships of the name holder.

---

7 ATF 106 II 236.

cc) The declaration of paternity of English law does not create a relationship of filiation, but simply grants a name. Certainly, it normally presupposes the existence of a natural birth relationship and thus belongs to family law; However, to characterize an institution and attribute it to personal status or family relationships, we must first consider the legal effects it produces. An institution whose main legal effect is to give a child the name of a third party, without creating family relationship with that third party, belongs to the child's personal status, not to his family relationships. It must therefore be characterized as belonging to the status of persons, that is to say, the personal law of the child. In this regard, a decision of the *Bundesgerichtshof* [*Federal Civil Court*] of the German Federal Republic on the 'Einbenennung' of § 1618 BGB [*German Civil Code*] will be noted, which allows the giving of a name without establishing a relationship of filiation (cf. GÖTZ, Namenserteilung nach deutschem Recht Review Vital 1971 6/7 p.): the Bundesgerichtshof characterized this institution as belonging to the personal law of the child, not to the law applicable to his family relationships (decision of 28 September 1972 BGHZ 59 No. 46).

Thus, the very application of art. 8 LRDC leads to the national law of the child Stuart Marshall, that is Swiss law.

? QUESTIONS

The Swiss Federal Court eventually rules that Swiss law applies. Why does the Court look at the legal regime of the declaration of paternity under English law? According to which law does it characterize the legal issue: Swiss or English law?

1.2 Unilateral methodology

As we have seen, the fundamental principle is that rules should be interpreted in accordance with the conceptions of the legal system from which they originate, because it is those conceptions that the lawmaker which produced them likely had in mind.

In the multilateral methodology, the forum applies its own choice of law rules, which were made by the lawmaker of the forum. Courts should therefore always characterize issues according to the conceptions of the forum. This is different in unilateral methodologies where the first step of the choice of law process is to assess which foreign laws want to be applied. The assessment of whether a foreign law wants to apply should be made in accordance with its own conceptions and characterizations. By doing such assessment, the forum seeks to assess the will of the foreign lawmaker. This should be done by respecting faithfully such views.

Thus, in governmental interest analysis,[8] the interests of the foreign state to apply its law should be determined by assessing them in accordance with the views of the foreign lawmaker.

2   Evasion of the law

In the multilateral choice of law methodology, the applicable law is determined by using a connecting factor which will designate a legal order. If one party was able to manipulate the connecting factor, she could change the applicable law and thus avoid its application. Would it be acceptable?

In this French case, a party attempted to manipulate a connecting factor. Can you identify which one, and for which purpose?

 CASE

French Cour de cassation, 18 March 1878 *Princess of Bauffremont v. Prince of Bauffremont*

Facts: On August 1, 1874, the Court of Appeal of Paris pronounced the legal separation of Prince of Bauffremont, a French citizen, from his wife, who was originally Belgian but had become French by marriage. At that time, French law did not allow divorce. As legal separation made her free to choose a separate home, the Princess travelled to the duchy of Saxe-Altenburg (Germany) and obtained its nationality on May 3, 1875. In both France and Germany, the law of nationality applied to personal status. Under German law, separated Catholics were deemed divorced. On October 24, 1875, the princess could thus remarry in Berlin with Romanian prince Bibesco, who had travelled with her to Germany.

However, Prince of Bauffremont was still French and still married to a woman who now claimed to be the wife of another. He initiated proceedings before a Paris Court seeking cancellation 1) of the naturalization obtained without his authorization and, 2) of the second marriage contracted in violation of French law.

Held: the second marriage, made in fraud of French law, could not be opposed to Prince of Bauffremont.

On the second argument, taken in its second limb.

Whereas the plaintiff, of Belgian origin, became French through her marriage with Prince Bauffremont, a French national; that separated from bed

8 *Supra*, Ch.1.

and board, according to the judgment of 1 August 1874, she nevertheless remained the wife of Prince Bauffremont and French, the effect of the separation being only to relax the marriage bond without dissolving it; thus, she was French and married in France, when she contracted marriage with Prince Bibesco in Berlin, following the naturalization she had obtained in the duchy of Saxe-Altenburg; the lower court did not rule and did not have to rule on the regularity and legal value, in Germany and under German law, of these acts resulting from the sole will of the plaintiff; taking only the point of view of French law, which indeed dominates the debate and is binding on the parties, the court held that, even had she been authorized by her husband, the plaintiff could not be admitted to invoke the law of the State where she has obtained a new nationality, thanks to which, transforming her status of a separated woman into that of a divorced woman, she would evade French law, which rules alone the effects of marriage of its nationals, and provides that such bond is unbreakable. Endorsing the reasons of the first instance court, the judgment further noted in fact that, moreover, the plaintiff sought and obtained this new nationality, not in order to exercise rights and fulfill the duties thereunder, by establishing her residence in the State of Saxe-Altenburg, but simply to escape the prohibitions of French law by contracting a second marriage, and to alienate her new nationality as soon as it was gained. By ruling, in these circumstances, that acts made in fraud of French law and in defiance of commitments contracted earlier in France could not be opposed to Prince of Bauffremont, the judgment under scrutiny ruled in conformity with the principle of French law on the indissolubility of marriage and did not violate any of the provisions of the law put forward by the appellant;

For these reasons: dismisses the appeal.

? QUESTIONS

1 Why did the French court sanction the behavior of Princess of Bauffremont? Could she not decide to live in another country? If so, was she not obliged to follow local rules?
2 A French court may not set aside a foreign public act granting nationality. Which remedy is Prince of Bauffremont granted? What is its impact on the validity of the second marriage of his wife?

Tunisian Code of Private International Law (1998)

Article 30

Evasion of law is constituted by the artificial change in one of the connecting factors related to the actual legal situation with the intention of avoiding the application of Tunisian or foreign law designated by the applicable choice of law rule.

When the conditions of evasion of the law are met, the change in the connecting factor will not be taken into account.

Belgian Code of Private International Law (2004)

Article 18 *Evasion of the law*

For the determination of the applicable law in a matter where parties may not freely dispose of their rights, facts and acts committed for the sole purpose of evading the application of the law designated by the present statute [*code*] are not taken into account.

Interpretation of the Supreme People's Court on Issues regarding the Application of the Law of the PRC on the Laws Applicable to Foreign-Related Civil Relations (Part 1, 2012)

Article 11

If a party intentionally manipulates the connecting factor for a foreign-related civil relation with a view to circumventing the mandatory provisions of laws or regulations of the People's Republic of China, the People's Courts shall disregard the effects of any designated foreign law.[9]

? NOTES AND QUESTIONS

1 These provisions lay down a similar test. The first prong is that a party must have manipulated, or changed artificially, the connecting factor. In practical terms, the doctrine can only play a role if the connecting factor of the applicable law can be manipulated. Can you identify connecting factors which can easily be manipulated, and others which cannot be?

2 The second prong is that the manipulator must have done so for the purpose of evading the application of mandatory provisions. The Belgian statute adds that the sole purpose of the manipulation should have been the evasion of the applicable law. How easy is it to assess what the purpose of a change in a connecting factor was? What about a change of domicile associated with a genuine relocation in the chosen country? How can you assess what the purpose of the change was?

3 The Chinese and Tunisian provisions focus on the manipulation of a connecting factor. But it is also conceivable to manipulate the connecting category. For instance, one could turn an immoveable asset into a moveable asset by transferring the ownership of the property to a company. This might have an impact on the applicable law if different choice of law rules apply to immoveable and moveable property (for instance in succession matters): the French supreme court applied the doctrine of the evasion of law in exactly such a case.[10] Would the Belgian rule cover such a case?

There is no general doctrine of evasion of law in the common law world. But there can be special provisions aiming at avoiding certain instances of evasion of law. One of them is the Uniform Marriage Evasion Act, a model law which

---

9 Translation Ilaria Aquironi, (2013) Diritto del Commercio Internazionale 891.
10 Cass. Civ. 1ere, 20 March 1985, *Caron*, case no. 82-15033 (1986) Rev. Crit. DIP 66.

was adopted by only a few American states, including Massachusetts. It was later withdrawn by the Uniform Law Commission, but it remains in force in states which adopted it at the beginning of the 20th century.

 CASE

Supreme Judicial Court of Massachusetts, 30 March 2006
Sandra Cote-Whitacre & others v. Department of Public Health & others[11]

Spina, J. (concurring, with whom Cowin and Sosman, JJ., join).

In these companion cases, eight nonresident same-sex couples[FN1] (couples) and thirteen municipal clerks (clerks) (collectively, plaintiffs) have challenged the constitutionality of General Laws c. 207, §§ 11 and 12, as well as the interpretation and enforcement of these statutory provisions to prohibit the issuance of Massachusetts marriage licenses to nonresident same-sex couples. The backdrop for their challenges is our decision in *Goodridge v. Department of Pub. Health*, 440 Mass. 309 (2003). A judge in the Superior Court denied the plaintiffs' motions for preliminary injunctions to bar the ongoing enforcement of §§ 11 and 12, and we allowed the defendants' application for direct appellate review.[FN2] For the reasons that follow, I conclude that the plaintiffs' motions for preliminary injunctions were properly denied.

> FN1. The couples live in Vermont, New York, Connecticut, Rhode Island, Maine, and New Hampshire.
>
> FN2. Amicus briefs have been filed by the Massachusetts Bar Association and the Boston Bar Association; nine professors of United States constitutional law; twenty-three professors of conflict of laws and family law; thirty-nine civil rights organizations and university professors; George I. Goverman; and Raymond Flynn and Thomas Shields.

1. *Statutory framework.* General Laws c. 207, the marriage licensing statute, controls entry into civil marriage in this Commonwealth. As a preliminary matter, I set forth those statutory provisions that will be pertinent to the ensuing discussion. Sections 11 and 12, were first enacted by St.1913, c. 360, as part of the Uniform Marriage Evasion Act.[FN3]

> FN3. In 1912, the National Conference of Commissioners on Uniform State Laws approved the Uniform Marriage Evasion Act. Although the Commissioners

---

11 446 Mass. 350.

ultimately withdrew their approval of the Act in 1943, Massachusetts was one of the few States that had already enacted its provisions, which remain in effect. See Handbook of the National Conference of Commissioners on Uniform State Laws and Proceedings 64 (1943).

General Laws c. 207, § 11, directed at who may not marry in Massachusetts, provides as follows:

'No marriage shall be contracted in this commonwealth by a party residing and intending to continue to reside in another jurisdiction if such marriage would be void if contracted in such other jurisdiction, and every marriage contracted in this commonwealth in violation hereof shall be null and void.'

General Laws c. 207, § 12, directed at the responsibilities of municipal clerks, provides as follows:

'Before issuing a license to marry a person who resides and intends to continue to reside in another state, the officer having authority to issue the license shall satisfy himself, by requiring affidavits or otherwise, that such person is not prohibited from intermarrying by the laws of the jurisdiction where he or she resides.'

General Laws c. 207, § 13, directed at the construction of §§ 11 and 12, provides as follows:

'The . . . preceding sections shall be so interpreted and construed as to effectuate their general purpose to make uniform the law of those states which enact like legislation.'

2. *Factual and procedural background.* To marry in Massachusetts, all applicants for a certificate of intention of marriage commonly known as a marriage license, must complete a written notice of intention of marriage (notice) on forms provided by the registrar of vital records and statistics (registrar), and submit it to the clerk or registrar of any city or town in the Commonwealth, along with the appropriate fee. See G.L. c. 207, §§ 19, 20. The notice shall include 'a statement of absence of any legal impediment to the marriage, to be given before such town clerk under oath by both of the parties to the intended marriage.' *Id.* at § 20. The applicants also shall provide the clerk with the residence address of both parties. See *id.*

On or after the third day from the filing of the notice (or sooner if the time period has been waived by a judge), the clerk shall deliver the marriage license to the parties. See *id.* at §§ 19, 28, 30. Then, an authorized officiant may solemnize the marriage. See *id.* at §§ 28, 38–39. After solemnization, the officiant completes the portion of the license setting forth the time and place of the ceremony, signs it, and returns it to the clerk who issued it. See *id.* at § 40. The clerk records the marriage in the appropriate registry, transmits the original record of the marriage and all documentary evidence to the registrar, and retains a certified copy of the license. See G.L. c. 46, §§ 1–2, 17A. The Commissioner of Public Health (commissioner) binds the marriage records with indexes thereto and retains their custody. See G.L. c. 111, § 2.

To provide guidance to applicants as to what constitutes a 'legal impediment' to marriage, clerks must display, in a conspicuous location, a printed notice of the prohibitions to marriage in Massachusetts, provided to them by the commissioner and the registrar. See G.L. c. 207, § 37. See also G.L. c. 17, § 4 (pertaining to responsibilities of registrar). The notice specifically incorporates the language of G.L. c. 207, § 11. The registrar has also issued to clerks a guide setting forth legal impediments to marriage in the fifty States, the District of Columbia, and various territories of the United States. The clerks were informed by the registrar that they should not issue a marriage license to an applicant if, based on a comparison between the factual information set forth on the notice and the list of legal impediments to marriage, there is an impediment to the applicant marrying in Massachusetts or in the applicant's home State.

Beginning on May 17, 2004, the date this court's decision in *Goodridge v. Department of Pub. Health, supra,* became effective, municipal clerks in several cities and towns began to receive notices of intention of marriage from non-resident same-sex couples. Five of the couples herein received licenses and had their marriages solemnized. Three of the couples were denied marriage licenses. The office of the Attorney General contacted those cities and towns where the marriage licenses had been issued, instructed them to cease and desist from issuing such licenses, and directed their attention to G.L. c. 207, § 50, setting forth the penalties for noncompliance with G.L. c. 207, §§ 11 and 12. In response, the clerks at issue stopped accepting notices from nonresident same-sex couples.

On June 18, 2004, the couples brought an action against the Department of Public Health, the commissioner, the registry of vital records and statistics, and the registrar (collectively, the defendants), seeking declaratory and injunctive relief and relief in the nature of mandamus. The couples claimed that the defendants' enforcement of §§ 11 and 12 to deny marriage licenses to nonresident same-sex couples violated the due process and equal protection provisions of the Massachusetts Constitution and violated the privileges and immunities clause of the United States Constitution, art. IV, § 2. (. . .)

Massachusetts follows the general rule that the validity of a marriage is governed by the law of the State where the marriage is contracted.[FN7] See *Damaskinos v. Damaskinos*, 325 Mass. 217, 219 (1950). When a person domiciled in another State comes to Massachusetts with the intent to marry, that person's ability to enter into a valid marriage contract, in the first instance, is governed by G.L. c. 207, §§ 11 and 12, which, in turn, mandate that the Commonwealth look to the marriage laws of the person's domiciliary State. The language of § 12 is plain and unambiguous that a municipal clerk, who is vested with the authority to issue or deny a marriage license, see G.L. c. 207, §§ 20, 28, 35, must be satisfied that the applicant 'is not prohibited from intermarrying' by the laws of the applicant's home State.

> FN7. A significant exception to this general rule is set forth in G.L. c. 207, § 10, which provides: 'If any person residing and intending to continue to reside in this commonwealth is disabled or prohibited from contracting marriage under the laws of this commonwealth and goes into another jurisdiction and there contracts a marriage prohibited and declared void by the laws of this commonwealth, such marriage shall be null and void for all purposes in this commonwealth with the same effect as though such prohibited marriage had been entered into in this commonwealth.'

One such prohibition is described in the narrow and specific language of § 11. The applicant is a nonresident who plans to continue residing outside Massachusetts, and the marriage would be 'void' if contracted in the applicant's home State. See, e.g., Me. Rev. Stat. Ann. tit. 19–A, §§ 701, 751 (West 1998) (persons of same sex may not contract marriage and such marriage, if solemnized in Maine, is void). In other words, the relevant statutory language of the applicant's home State explicitly provides that particular marriages are 'void.' Under Massachusetts law, not only are such marriages not to be contracted in the first place, but to the extent that such marriages may be erroneously contracted, either intentionally or unintentionally, they are considered 'null and void' in Massachusetts and everywhere else. G.L. c. 207, § 11.

A marriage that would be 'void' if contracted in the applicant's home State is not, however, the only prohibition that would preclude the issuance of a Massachusetts marriage license to a nonresident. An applicant may be prohibited from intermarrying by the laws of the applicant's home State because of a variety of other statutory legal impediments to marriage, including age, consanguinity or affinity, mental incompetence, or the fact that both parties are the same sex.[FN9] In essence, marriages that are defined by State statutes as 'void' constitute a specific category of marriages that are prohibited under G.L. c. 207.

FN9. General Laws c. 207, § 37, provides that '[t]he commissioner of public health shall furnish to the clerk or registrar of every town a printed list of all legal impediments to marriage, and the clerk or registrar shall forthwith post and thereafter maintain it in a conspicuous place in his office.' In Massachusetts, the legal impediments to marriage include (1) consanguinity or affinity; (2) polygamy (except as specifically provided); (3) age (except as specifically provided); and (4) the presence of communicable syphilis in one of the parties. See G.L. c. 207, §§ 1, 2, 4, 6, 7. In Vermont, the legal impediments to marriage include (1) consanguinity or affinity; (2) bigamy; (3) sex; (4) age (except as specifically provided); (5) lack of sound mind; and (6) need for a guardian (except as specifically provided). See Vt. Stat. Ann. tit. 15, §§ 1–4, 8 (LexisNexis 2002); Vt. Stat. Ann. tit. 18, § 5142 (Lexis 2000). In New York, the legal impediments to marriage include (1) consanguinity or affinity; (2) bigamy (except as specifically provided); (3) age (except as specifically provided); (4) lack of consent for want of understanding; (5) physical cause; (6) consent secured by reason of force, duress, or fraud; and (7) mental illness for five or more years. See N.Y. Dom. Rel. Law §§ 5, 6, 7 (McKinney 1999). In Connecticut, the legal impediments to marriage include (1) consanguinity or affinity; (2) need for a conservator (except as specifically provided); (3) age (except as specifically provided); and (4) bigamy (except as specifically provided). See Conn. Gen.Stat. Ann. §§ 46b–21, 46b–29, 46b–30 (West 2004); Conn. Gen.Stat. Ann. § 53a–190 (West 2001). Cf. *Rosengarten v. Downes*, 71 Conn.App. 372, 378 (2002) (concluding that, in action to dissolve civil union entered into in Vermont by Connecticut resident, such union not a 'marriage' recognized under Connecticut statutes because not entered into by one man and one woman). In Rhode Island, the legal impediments to marriage include (1) consanguinity or affinity (except as specifically provided); (2) bigamy; (3) lack of mental competence; and (4) age (except as specifically provided). See R.I. Gen. Laws §§ 15–1–1, 15–1–2, 15–1–4, 15–1–5, 15–2–11 (LexisNexis 2003). In Maine, the legal impediments to marriage include (1) age (except as specifically provided); (2) consanguinity (except as specifically provided); (3) mental illness or mental retardation; (4) polygamy; and (5) sex. See Me. Rev. Stat. Ann. tit. 19–A, §§ 652, 701 (West 1998). In New Hampshire, the legal impediments to marriage include (1) consanguinity; (2) sex; and (3) age (except as specifically provided). See N.H.Rev.Stat. Ann. §§ 457:1, 457:2, 457:4, 457:6 (1992). (. . .)

When §§ 11 and 12 were enacted in 1913, same-sex marriage was not visible on the horizon of our jurisprudence, suggesting that the Legislature did not, in fact, promulgate these statutes for the express purpose of discriminating against same-sex couples. (. . .) Rather, the focus of §§ 11 and 12 was on the status of all nonresidents who were prohibited from entering into marriage contracts in this Commonwealth where precluded from doing so in their home States. This focus originated from the enactment of the

Uniform Marriage Evasion Act in 1912, which was intended to promote general uniformity in the prohibitory laws of every State. See note 3, *supra*. Now, in the aftermath of the *Goodridge* decision, §§ 11 and 12 have found renewed application as nonresident same-sex couples have sought to secure marriage licenses in Massachusetts. The couples have not challenged the Commonwealth's right to revive a statute that they had long thought moribund. The registrar has acknowledged in his affidavit that, before the *Goodridge* case, 'detailed enforcement of G.L. c. 207, §§ 11 and 12 was not a stated priority for [the registry of vital records and statistics].' Nonetheless, a lack of detailed statutory enforcement in the past, to the extent that it was necessary, does not preclude more vigorous statutory enforcement in the present. See *Doris v. Police Comm'r of Boston*, 374 Mass. 443, 449 (1978). (. . .)

Here, it is likely that the couples will be unable to demonstrate that the enforcement of G.L. c. 207, §§ 11 and 12, denies them a fundamental right solely on the basis of their nonresidency. Rather than differentiating between all residents and all nonresidents, §§ 11 and 12 differentiate between two types of nonresidents, those who can receive a marriage license in this Commonwealth because there are no legal impediments to their marriages, and those who cannot receive a license because their marriages would be prohibited under the laws of their home States. At a fundamental level, and in accordance with the underlying purpose of the privileges and immunities clause, §§ 11 and 12 promote interstate harmony by mandating respect for the laws of other jurisdictions. Moreover, Massachusetts residents will, in fact, be treated in a similar fashion as nonresidents. General Laws c. 207, § 10, states that if a Massachusetts resident 'goes into another jurisdiction and there contracts a marriage prohibited and declared void by the laws of this commonwealth, such marriage shall be null and void for all purposes in this commonwealth.' Thus, pursuant to the Massachusetts marriage laws, both residents and nonresidents alike are precluded from going out of their home States and securing a marriage license in another jurisdiction where they would be prohibited from obtaining such a license in their home States. Because residents are essentially subject to the same types of rights and restrictions as nonresidents under the challenged statutes, there is no violation of the privileges and immunities clause.

8. *Conclusion.* The judge in the Superior Court did not err in denying the plaintiffs' motions for preliminary injunctions.

QUESTIONS

Contrary to the civil law doctrine of evasion of law, there is no requirement under the Uniform Marriage Evasion Act that the parties acted for the purpose of evading the law of their domicile. Is the rule a tool to resist evasion of law, or rather a sophisticated choice of law rule? What is the law governing validity of marriage in Massachusetts? How many laws is it necessary to consult for the purpose of assessing whether a marriage is valid?[12]

3   Renvoi

As choice of law rules are typically national they may, and often do, vary from one jurisdiction to another. As a result, the choice of law rule of the forum could provide for the application of a foreign law, but the choice of law rule of this foreign country could provide for the application of another law, and indeed possibly the law of the forum.

Should the forum take into account foreign choice of law rules and, as the case may be, apply the law designated by the foreign choice of law rule as opposed to the law designated by its own choice of law rule? This is the problem of *renvoi*. *Renvoi* is a French word meaning 'return' or 'referral'. Remarkably, the word is used widely in the English-speaking world, as well as in Germany, to refer to this particular issue.

3.1   Common law jurisdictions

In Re Schneider Estate is the most famous American case on *renvoi*. Did the American court apply the choice of law rule of the forum, or a foreign choice of law rule?

CASE

Surrogate's Court, New York County, New York, 10 April 1950 *In re Schneider estate*[13]

Proceeding in the matter of the estate of Chico Schneider, deceased. The Surrogate's Court, Frankenthaler, S., held that reference was required to be made to the law of Switzerland in determining whether proceeds of sale of deceased's Swiss realty should be distributed to the devisee of the realty under the terms of the will, that the *renvoi* principle was applicable, that under Swiss law the proceeds of the sale of the realty would be distributed

---

12 See, *infra*, Part VI.
13 96 N.Y.S.2d 652 (1950).

pursuant to directions contained in the will, and that administratrix' account should be settled in accordance with opinion.

Decree settling account.

Frankenthaler, Surrogate.

This case presents a novel question in this State in the realm of the conflict of laws. Deceased, a naturalized American citizen of Swiss origin, died domiciled in New York County, leaving as an asset of his estate certain real property located in Switzerland. In his will he attempted to dispose of his property, including the parcel of Swiss realty, in a manner which is said to be contrary to the provisions of Swiss internal law. That law confers upon one's legitimate heirs a so-called *legitime*, i.e., a right to specified fractions of a decedent's property, which right cannot be divested by testamentary act. The precise issue, therefore, is whether this deceased had the power to dispose of the realty in the manner here attempted.

Ordinarily, the courts of a country not the situs of an immovable are without jurisdiction to adjudicate questions pertaining to the ownership of that property. *Knox v. Jones*, 47 N.Y. 389; *British South Africa Co. v. Companhia de Mocambique* [1893] A.C. 602. Actions concerning realty are properly litigable only before the courts of the situs. However, in this case the administratrix appointed prior to the probate of the will has liquidated the foreign realty and transmitted the proceeds to this State. She is now accounting for the assets of the estate including the fund representing that realty. As a consequence this court is called upon to direct the administration and distribution of the substituted fund and to determine the property rights therein. *Butler v. Green*, 65 Hun 99. In doing so, however, reference must be made to the law of the situs, as the question of whether the fund shall be distributed to the devisee of the realty under the terms of the will is dependent upon the validity of the original devise thereof, *Butler v. Green, supra* which must be determined under the law of the situs of the land itself. *Monypeny v. Monypeny*, 202 N.Y. 90, 95 N.E. 1.

The court is confronted at the outset with a preliminary question as to the meaning of the term 'law of the situs'—whether it means only the internal or municipal law of the country in which the property is situated or whether it also includes the conflict of laws rules to which the courts of that jurisdiction would resort in making the same determination. If the latter is the proper construction to be placed upon that term, then this court must, in effect, place itself in the position of the foreign court and decide the matter as would that court in an identical case.

The meaning of the term 'law of the situs' can be ascertained best from a consideration of the reasons underlying the existence of the rule which requires the application thereof. The primary reason for its existence lies in the fact that the law-making and law-enforcing agencies of the country in which land is situated have exclusive control over such land. *Watts v. Waddle*, 6 Pet. 389; 1 Wharton, Conflict of Laws, sections 276b, 278. As only the courts of that country are ultimately capable of rendering enforceable judgments affecting the land, the legislative authorities thereof have the exclusive power to promulgate the law which shall regulate its ownership and transfer. When the land itself formed the estate asset upon which the will was intended to operate, the power of sovereign to enforce such laws created rights therein between the parties in interest. If an instrument which was intended to transfer that land did not meet the standards set by that law or violated some provision thereof regarding the land, the courts had the physical power to deny it effect and enforce instead the rights decreed by the law of that country or the law of any other country which the law-making agencies deemed appropriate in a particular case.

Hence, the rights which were created in that land are those which existed under the whole law of the situs and as would be enforced by those courts which normally would possess exclusive judicial jurisdiction. Griswold, Renvoi Revisited, 51 Harvard L.R. 1165, 1186; cf. Schreiber, The Doctrine of Renvoi in Anglo-American Law, 31 Harvard L.R. 523, 559. If another court, in this case our own, is thrust into a position where it is obliged to adjudicate the same questions concerning title to that land, or a substitute therefor, it should be guided by the methods which would be employed in the country of situs. The purely fortuitous transfer of the problem to the courts of another state by virtue of a post-mortuary conversion of the land, effected for the purpose of administering the entire estate in the country of domicile, ought not to alter the character of the legal relations which existed with respect to the land at the date of death and which continued to exist until its sale. Consequently, this court, in making a determination of ownership, must ascertain the body of local law to which the courts of the situs would refer if the matter were brought before them.

It has been urged, however, that a reference to the conflict of laws rules of the situs may involve an application of the principle of *renvoi*, and if so it would place the court in a perpetually-enclosed circle from which it could never emerge and that it would never find a suitable body of substantive rules to apply to the particular case. This objection is based upon the assumption that if the forum must look to the whole law of the situs, and that law refers the matter to the law of the domicile, this latter reference must be considered to be the whole law of the latter country also, which would refer the matter back to the law of the situs, which process would continue without end. That reasoning is based upon a false premise, for as has been said by Dean Griswold, Renvoi Revisited, op. cit. *supra*, p. 1190: 'Recognition of the foreign conflict of laws rule will not lead us into an endless chain of references if it is clear for any reason that the particular foreign conflicts rule (or any rule along the line of reference) is one which refers to the internal law alone * * *.'

The precise question here considered, namely whether there shall be a reference to the entire law of the situs to determine the ownership of the proceeds of foreign realty, is one of first impression in this State. Nevertheless, the above stated principles, together with the rule enunciated in the Restatement of the Conflict of Laws, in the English authorities on the subject and in analogous cases in courts of this State and others, require us to accept it as a part of our law and to hold that a reference to the law of the situs necessarily entails a reference to the whole law of that country, including its conflict of laws rules.

The rule as formulated in the Restatement is as follows: 'Section 8. Rule in questions of title to land or divorce. (1) All questions of title to land are decided in accordance with the law of the state where the land is, including the Conflict of Laws rules of that State. (2) All questions concerning the validity of a decree of divorce are decided in accordance with the law of the domicile of the parties, including the Conflict of Laws rules of that State.' In all other cases the Restatement rejects the *renvoi* principle and provides that where a reference is made to foreign law that law should be held to mean only the internal law of the foreign country. Section 7.

The English rule as to *renvoi* in the field of immovables has been established and defined in two leading decisions. In re Baines, unreported, stated in Dicey, Conflict of Laws, 5th Ed., p. 877 and In re Ross [1930] 1 Ch. 377; see also In re Askew [1930] 2 Ch. 259. In both cases the English courts were confronted with the precise question here involved. In the Baines case, the decedent, an English national died leaving land in Egypt which was sold subsequent to his death and the proceeds transmitted to England. The will, although valid under English law, would have been invalid under the local law of Egypt. However, under the Egyptian conflict of law rules the succession to land is governed by the internal law of the country of which the decedent was a national. Accordingly, the will was upheld.

Similarly, in the Ross case, a question arose concerning title to an Italian estate which the testatrix had owned at her death. A claim was made by her son, similar to that interposed in this case, that he was entitled to a 'legitima portio' under local Italian law, which right, it was asserted, should attach to the proceeds of a sale of the land. In answer to this contention, the court declared that the 'lex situs must * * * be considered in the way the Courts of a country where the immovables are situate would themselves determine. On this basis, the expert evidence is clear that the Italian courts would decide the succession to the immovable property in the same manner as the English Court could determine it if the immovable property in question belonged to an Englishman and was situated in England.' In both of these cases, the courts employed the law which would have been enforced in the courts of the situs. Cf. *Kotia v. Nahas* [1941] 3 All E.R. 20; *Ross v. Ross*, 25 Can. S.C. 307.

The decisions in this State also indicate the applicability of the doctrine of *renvoi* in this field. In the early case of *Dupuy v. Wurtz*, 53 N.Y. 556, which involved personal property, there appears the first reference to the doctrine. The Court there said, by way of dictum, 53 N.Y. at page 573: '[W]hen we speak of the law of domicil as applied to the law of succession, we mean not the general law, but the law which the country of the domicil applies to the particular case under consideration (*Maltass v. Maltass*, 1 Rob.Ecc.R. 72, per Dr. Lushington).' If the word 'situs' is substituted therein for 'domicil' the language becomes appropriate to a case involving real property. (. . .)

Thus it is now necessary to ascertain the whole of the applicable Swiss law and apply it to this case. (. . .).

? NOTES AND QUESTIONS

1   In the common law tradition, *renvoi* is accepted in certain particular fields. In the United States, these are title to land and divorce. In England, its scope is limited to succession and to certain questions related to marriage.[14] In other fields, it does not apply.

2   What is the rationale given by the court for applying foreign choice of law rules in immoveable matters? What is its relationship with the issue of the international jurisdiction of the court? Does this rationale also justify the application of the *renvoi* doctrine in divorce cases?

3   The doctrine of *renvoi* allows courts to take into consideration foreign choice of law rules. It is useful in a context where the applicable choice of law methodology does not consider foreign choice of law rules in the first place, that is, the multilateral methodology. The American choice of law revolution has resulted in a shift to a unilateral methodology which requires the consideration of the rules of application of the laws of all interested states. Some American scholars have called it *renvoi*,[15] but it has very little in common with the traditional doctrine of *renvoi* discussed here.

---

14   Dicey, Morris and Collins, para. 4–21. The rule is also followed in other common law jurisdictions such as Ghana (*Akoto v. Akoto* (2011) 1 SCGLR 533).

15   See e.g. Larry Kramer, 'Return of *Renvoi*' (1991) 66 NYU L. Rev. 979.

The New York court referred to a number of English authorities. While *renvoi* has also long been admitted in England, it has been for the peculiar reason that the English court ought to rule as the foreign court would have. As a consequence, an English court might not only apply foreign choice of law rules, but also other foreign doctrines of private international law.

CASE

High Court of England and Wales, 30 May 1930 *In Re Askew*[16]

Facts: By an indenture of settlement dated 30 June 1893, on the marriage of John Bertram Askew, a British subject, with his wife Frederica Louisa Dallas, the husband's trust fund was settled on the usual trusts for him and his wife and children if any, and it contained a power of revocation as to one-half of the fund in the event of the wife's death and the husband marrying again in favour of such second wife and any children by her as he should appoint. In January 1911, a child, Margarete, was born to Ana Wengels, a single woman, of which child JB Askew was the father. Later in 1911, JB Askew, who had acquired a domicil in Germany, obtained from a German court a decree of divorce from Frederica Louisa. In April 1912, JB Askew married Ana, in Germany. In 1913, Askew by deed poll exercised the power of revocation in the settlement and appointed the part of the fund to which it extended after his death in favour of his second wife and the child, Margarete. Evidence was given that under German law the question of legitimation per subsequens matrimonium was governed by the law of the country of which at the time of the marriage the father was a national, and that in the present case the German court, in deciding the question, would apply, not only the municipal law of England, but also the rules of international law as interpreted by the English courts, and would hold that Margarete was legitimated by the marriage of her parents.

Held: In accordance with the doctrine of renvoi in a case concerning status, the lex domicilii must apply, and Margarete must be regarded as the legitimate child of JB Askew; and, therefore, the appointment in her favour was good.

Maugham J:

The trustees are naturally desirous of the protection of the court in relation to the question whether the power of appointment in question was validly exercised by the deed poll, and for this purpose it is necessary to determine whether the defendant Margarete Askew, though born out of wedlock, during the continuance of a previous marriage, is, having regard to her father's domicil, legitimate. The Legitimacy Act, 1926, I may point out, would not have had that effect, having regard to the fact that J B Askew was married to his first wife when the defendant M Askew was born.

The question of legitimation of a child by the subsequent marriage of its parents in a foreign country, apart from the provisions of the Legitimacy Act, 1926, s 1(2) and s 8, appears at first sight to be well settled. DICEY (Rule 137, case I, in his CONFLICT of LAWS) states the result of the decisions thus:

> If both the law of the father's domicil at the time of the birth of the child and the law of the father's domicil at the time of the subsequent marriage allow of legitimatio per subsequens matrimonium, the child becomes or may become legitimate on the marriage of the parents.

The authorities cited are: *Udny v Udny*; *Re Wrights' Trust*; *Re Grove, Vaucher v Treasury Solicitor*; and they bear out the proposition. J B Askew was admittedly domiciled in Germany both at the date of the birth and at the time of the subsequent marriage. But what is the meaning of the phrase 'the law of the father's domicil'? Does it refer to the municipal law or local law of Germany or does it refer to the whole of the laws applicable in Germany, including the views entertained in Germany as to the rules of private international law? There is no doubt that DICEY means the latter – see his INTERPRETATION OF TERMS, DEFINITION 11 – but, in my opinion, it is much more doubtful whether the courts who have dealt with the matter did not mean the former.

(. . .)

I will now return to the present case which, if I am right in the views expressed above, will present little difficulty. There is, fortunately, no contest as to the German law, for the affidavit of Dr Hellmut Rost, a doctor of laws of the University of Erlangen, was accepted by all parties as being correct, another affidavit being withdrawn. Dr Rost deposed as follows:

> The child Margarete Askew is according to German law legitimated by the subsequent marriage of John Bertram Askew and Anna Wengels. I have come to this conclusion on the following grounds: The German Civil Code and the Introductory Act do not contain any specific rule as to the effect of a subsequent marriage of the parents of an illegitimate child where the father of the child is not a German national, but only provides that where the father is a German national the question is to be decided by German law (art 1719 of the Civil Code combined with art 22

of the Introductory Act). A general principle of the German law is, however, that the law of the country of which the father at the time of the marriage is a national governs the question of legitimation *per subsequens matrimonium*. I am informed and believe that J B Askew was an Englishman. Therefore, English law would be applied by the German court in deciding the question. (I am informed that the English law refers the question back to the law of the domicil, in the present case German law.) The German court would in these circumstances first have to decide whether to apply the municipal law of England only or also the principles of international private law as interpreted by the English courts. The rule followed by the German court is that both the municipal law and the rules of international law as interpreted by the English court are to be applied. The German court, therefore, accepts the renvoi. There is no general statutory rule of German law as to which municipal law in the case of renvoi as in the present case is to be ultimately applied. The question has, however, been decided by numerous decisions of the Reichsgericht, the court of the highest instance in Germany (Confer Reports, vol 62, p 404; vol 64, p 393; vol 78, p 28; and others). These decisions are to the effect that in a case where the German law provides that the law of nationality is to govern a question and the law of nationality refers to the law of domicil and the domicil is German, the German court is to apply German municipal law. I am, therefore, of the opinion that the German court would hold that according to German law Margarete Askew was legitimated by the marriage of her parents notwithstanding the fact that her father at the time of her birth was still married to a woman other than her mother, and that by reason of the legitimation of the child Margarete Askew has become issue of the marriage between John Bertram Askew and Anna Askew, née Wengels.

I take this deposition as proving as a fact that the defendant Margarete Askew acquired in Germany the status of legitimacy. For the reasons given above I hold that in an English court the lex domicilii in the wide sense must prima facie apply, and this being a law which the English courts will recognize, the conclusion is that the defendant M Askew is a legitimate child of J B Askew and that the power of appointment was effectively exercised in her favour.

I think it proper to add that, in my opinion, it is unsatisfactory to find that upon the evidence adduced in *Re Annesley, Davidson v. Annesley* and *Re Ross, Ross v. Waterfield* the courts were bound to hold that, although both in France and in Italy the national law of the de cujus is held to prevail, yet owing to a divergence on the theoretical question of renvoi, the property and capacity of an Englishman domiciled in Italy is held to be a matter of (local) English law, whilst the property and capacity of an Englishman domiciled in France is held to be a matter of (local) French law. Nor is there any certainty that a contrary result will not be reached upon the evidence adduced in the next two cases which arise as to persons dying in France and Italy respectively. Those who have any acquaintance with the extensive literature that has appeared on the continent on the subject of renvoi and the great diversity of view that exists would not be surprised to find that the legal decisions in France and Italy, where legal decisions are not binding as authorities to be followed, had changed in their effect. An Englishman domiciled de facto in France cannot be certain that his personal law is the municipal law of France, nor that, if he crosses the border and becomes domiciled de facto in Italy, his personal law will become the municipal law of England. It may be added that views which seem strange to an English lawyer are entertained in these matters in some eastern countries and also in some of the States in South America; and in those countries the result of acquiring a domicil must be very doubtful. I cannot refrain from expressing the opinion that it is desirable that the position of British subjects who acquire domicils in countries which do not agree with our view as to the effect of a foreign domicil should be made clear by a very short statute. There is much to be said for the 'simple and rational solution' suggested by RUSSELL, J, in *Re Annesley, Davidson v. Annesley*; but whether the municipal law of the foreign country or the municipal law of England is to be held applicable in British courts in these cases, it is clearly desirable that the matter should be certain and should not be held ultimately to depend on the doubtful and conflicting evidence of foreign experts.

? QUESTIONS

1 Under the English doctrine of *renvoi*, the forum should rule as the foreign court would have. In *Re Askew*, what did this entail? The English doctrine of *renvoi* is sometimes called the 'foreign court theory' or 'double *renvoi*'. Can you explain why?

2 In *Re Schneider*, the New York court noted that the foreign choice of law rule provided for the application of New York law, and thus applied New York law. By contrast, in *Re Askew*, the English court noted that the foreign choice of law rule provided for the application of English law, but eventually applied German law. Can these two cases be reconciled?

3.2 Civil law jurisdictions

Renvoi is widely accepted in the civil law world. In France, it was accepted by the French supreme court as early as 1878 in the *Forgo* case.[17] Unlike common law jurisdictions, most civil law jurisdictions do not limit the scope of *renvoi* to certain particular fields. It is a doctrine of general application.[18]

Civil law jurisdictions typically distinguish between two instances of *renvoi*.

---

17 Cass. Civ. 24 June 1878, (1879) JDI 285.
18 Exceptions include Switzerland (see Article 14 of the Swiss PIL Act).

The first is *renvoi* to the law of the forum. This was also the case in *In re Schneider estate*. Such cases are the most common, and can be called cases of simple *renvoi*. The second instance of *renvoi* is considered by Article 13(1)(a) of the Italian Law or Article 4(1) of the German Law: *renvoi* to the law of a third State.

Reform of the Italian System of Private International Law (1995)

Article 13 *Renvoi*

1. Whenever reference is made to a foreign law in the following articles, account shall be taken of the *renvoi* made by foreign private international law to the law in force in another State if:

   a) *renvoi* is accepted under the law of that State.
   b) *renvoi* is made to Italian law.

2. Paragraph 1 shall not apply:

   a) to those cases in which the provisions of this law make the foreign law applicable according to the choice of law made by the parties concerned;
   b) with respect to the statutory form of acts;
   c) as related to the provisions of Chapter XI of this Title.

3. In the cases referred to in Articles 33, 34 and 35, account shall be taken of the *renvoi* only if the latter refers to a law allowing filiation to be established.
4. Where this law makes an international convention applicable in any event, the solution adopted in the convention in matters of *renvoi* shall always apply.

Article 34 *Legitimation*

1. Legitimation by subsequent marriage shall be governed either by the child's national law at the time when the legitimation occurs, or by the national law of either parent at that time.
2. In the remaining cases, legitimation shall be governed by the law of the State of which, at the time of the application, the parent requesting legitimation is a national. With respect to legitimation to be effective after the decease of the legitimating parent, account shall be taken of the latter's nationality at the time of his/her decease.

Article 35 *Recognition of a natural child*

1. Conditions for the recognition of a natural child shall be governed either by the child's national law at the time of birth or, if this is more favourable, by the national law of the person recognizing the natural child at the time when recognition occurs.
2. The capacity of a parent to recognize a natural child shall be governed by the parent's national law.

3. As to form, recognition shall be governed either by the law of the State where it occurs or by the law governing its substance.

Introductory Act to the German Civil Code

Art. 4 *Renvoi; split law*

(1) If referral is made to the law of another country, the private international law of that country shall also be applied, insofar as this is not incompatible with the meaning of the referral. If the law of another country refers back to German law, the German substantive provisions shall apply.

(2) Where the parties can choose the law of a certain country, that choice may only relate to the substantive provisions.

(3) If referral is made to the law of a country having several partial legal systems, without indicating the applicable one, then the law of that country will determine which partial legal system shall be applicable. Failing any such rules, the partial legal system to which the connection of the subject matter is closest shall be applied.

 NOTES AND QUESTIONS

1 Article 13(1)(a) of the Italian Law contemplates *renvoi* to the law of a third State which is accepted under this law. In this second case of *renvoi*, the law eventually applied is not the law of the forum (law of State 1), nor the law designated by the choice of law rule of the forum (law of State 2), but the law of a third State (law of State 3) which is designated by the choice of law rule of State 2. That law will only be applied if the *renvoi* is 'accepted' by State 3, which means that its choice of law rule also designates the law of State 3 (i.e. its own law).

State 1 (forum) ☛ State 2 ☛ State 3 ☛ State 3.

This second instance of *renvoi* is very different from simple *renvoi*. The French call it 'second degree *renvoi*', as opposed to 'first degree *renvoi*'. The Germans call it 'further referral' (*Weiterverweisung*), as opposed to 'referral back' (*Rückverweisung*).

2 What is the rationale for *renvoi*? In the common law tradition, the rationale is field specific, and explains why *renvoi* is only accepted in certain fields. By contrast, in the civil law tradition, *renvoi* is a doctrine of general application. Its rationale must therefore be general as well.

For second degree or further *renvoi*, the rationale is that the doctrine creates international harmony.[19] *Renvoi* only operates where the relevant States have different choice of law rules. In the absence of *renvoi*, these differences would lead to different outcomes depending on the jurisdiction where the case is brought. By contrast, should the *renvoi* doctrine be applied by the courts of all relevant States, they would all apply the same choice of law rule (that is, the rule of the last State, accepting *renvoi*) and thus the same substantive law.

For simple *renvoi*, the rationale is more pragmatic. The forum considers that foreign law applies. The foreign legal system considers that the law of the forum should apply. As identifying the most appropriate connecting factor is not always easy, the fact that the foreign legal system considers that the law of the forum applies probably means that the law of the forum has a serious connection with the dispute (that is, the connecting factor used by the foreign choice of law rule). Given the important practical advantages of applying the law of the forum (saving the costs

---

19 In France, see Mayer and Heuzé, para. 229; in Germany, see von Hoffmann and Thorn, § 6–87.

of determining its content, avoiding the risk of misunderstanding it), and the fact that the forum has a serious connection with the dispute, it is more efficient to apply the law of the forum.[20]

3 However, even civil law jurisdictions consider that there are exceptional cases where the doctrine of *renvoi* is inappropriate. Why do you think *renvoi* is excluded in Article 4(2) of the German Act and Article 13(2)(a) of the Italian Law?

4 In certain particular cases, the doctrine of *renvoi* might have a special rationale. What is the purpose of Article 13(3) of the Italian law? (French courts have used *renvoi* in similar circumstances).

Japanese Act on the General Rules of Application of Laws (2006)
Article 41 [*Renvoi*]
Where a case should be governed by a person's national law and pursuant to the rules of that law the case should be governed by Japanese law, the case shall be governed by Japanese law. However, this shall not apply where the person's national law should govern pursuant to Article 25 (including its application *mutatis mutandis* in Article 26, paragraph 1 and Article 27) or Article 32.

Article 25 [*Effect of Marriage*]
The effect of a marriage shall be governed by the spouses' national law when it is the same, or where that is not the case, by the law of the spouses' habitual residence when that is the same, or where neither of these is the case, by the law of the place with which the spouses are most closely connected.

Article 32 [*The Legal Relationship Between Parents and Child*]
The legal relationship between parents and their child shall be governed by the child's national law where that is the same as the national law of either the mother or father (or the national law of the other parent in the case where one parent has died or is unknown), or in all other cases by the law of the child's habitual residence.

 NOTES AND QUESTIONS

1 Article 41 does not appear in the general part of the law, but in the section on family law.
2 Why is *renvoi* excluded where Art. 25 or 32 apply?

European Regulation (EC) No 864/2007 of 11 July 2007 on the law applicable to non-contractual obligations (Rome II)
Article 24 *Exclusion of* renvoi
The application of the law of any country specified by this Regulation means the application of the rules of law in force in that country other than its rules of private international law.

---

20 In France, see Muir Watt and Bureau, para. 498; in Germany, see von Hoffmann and Thorn, § 6–91.

NOTES AND QUESTIONS

1 Article 20 of the Rome I Regulation and Article 11 of the Rome III Regulation also exclude *renvoi*. So do many Hague Conventions, by providing that the uniform choice of law rules they lay down designate the internal law of the relevant legal system.

2 The reason why so many international and European instruments exclude *renvoi* seems to be that the drafters are afraid that *renvoi* might jeopardize the uniform application of their rules. Are you convinced?

3 One exception is the 2012 Succession Regulation (no 650/2012), which allows first and second degree *renvoi* where the Regulation leads to the application of the law of a third State (art. 34).

Russian Civil Code (2013)

Article 1190 *Renvoi*

1. Any reference to a foreign law pursuant to the provisions of the present Title [on private international law] shall be deemed a reference to substantive law rather than conflict rules of the relevant country, except for the cases specified in paragraph 2 of the present article.

2. A *renvoi* of a foreign law may be accepted in cases concerned with the legal status of a natural person where the reference is to Russian law.

Law of the People's Republic of China on the Laws Applicable to Foreign-Related Civil Relations (2010)

Article 9

The foreign law applicable to a foreign-related civil relation does not include the conflict rules of that country.

 NOTES AND QUESTIONS

1 The purpose of the reference to the internal law of the designated legal order, or of excluding conflict rules of that legal order, is to exclude *renvoi*.

2 Is *renvoi* simply too complicated? *Renvoi* obliges lawyers and courts to investigate into foreign choice of law rules. Do the costs outweigh the benefits? Compare the choices made by the Russian and the Chinese lawmakers.

4 Incidental question

Many cases do not raise one single issue, but several. These issues might be independent from each other, but they could also be interrelated. For instance, it might be necessary to resolve a preliminary issue before addressing the main issue arising in a case. One common example is the need to assess the validity of a marriage for the purpose of deciding whether a woman has a right to inherit from her alleged husband.

In private international law, each of these issues might fall within the scope of different choice of law rules, and thus be governed by different laws. Is it an acceptable outcome? If two issues are interrelated, should they be governed by one single law, for instance the law governing the main issue?

In this Australian case, the main issue was one of inheritance, and the preliminary issue the validity of a polygamous marriage. Under Australian private international law, inheritance issues are governed by the law of the domicile of the deceased for moveable property, and by the law of the place of the property for immoveable property. In the 1950s, issues relating to the substantive validity of a marriage were governed by the personal law of the spouses, namely the law of their ante nuptial domiciles.[21] However, a polygamous marriage celebrated in Australia would not be recognized irrespective of the domicile of the spouses. Did the court decide the issue of the validity of the marriage differently because it was preliminary to the issue of inheritance?

 CASE

High Court of Australia, 2 August 1962 *Haque v. Haque*[22]

Facts: Abdul Haque's father had come to Western Australia in 1870 and established a business in that State. He had returned at regular intervals to his family home in India where Abdul Haque was born in 1912. In 1925 Abdul married Kulsum Bibi and two years later came out to Western Australia to join his father in the business which he subsequently managed until it was sold in 1955. Kulsum Bibi remained in India. In 1937 Abdul returned to India where in 1938 and in 1939 two daughters were born. He returned to Western Australia in 1940. In 1951, in Western Australia, he went through a Muslim form of marriage with Azra Bux. Immediately prior to the marriage a deed was executed by Abdul and Azra which provided that she and the issue of the marriage should be considered for all intents and purposes Abdul's lawful wife and children and that as such they should be entitled to all the rights and claims to Abdul's present and future property as the Muslim law allowed them irrespective of any contrary testamentary or other disposition Abdul might make with reference to such property. A son was born of the second marriage in Western Australia in 1952 and a daughter was born in India in 1954.

In 1954 Abdul Haque divorced Azra by triple talaq. In 1956 he went through another Muslim form of marriage with Azra; but by Muslim law that marriage was irregular. Abdul died in Western Australia in 1956. By his will he purported to give all his estate to his brother Nural Haque absolutely. By Muslim law the provisions of the will were void

---

21 The rule was superseded by legislation in 1961, but the new rule only took effect in 1986. The validity of marriages celebrated after 1986 is governed by the law of the place of celebration of the marriage.
22 36 ALJR 179.

as they would otherwise have excluded the heirs. The estate of the testator in Western Australia consisted almost entirely of interests in two family partnerships the assets of which primarily comprised land. At no time had the testator owned a home in Western Australia in his own right. Throughout his life he had remained a Muslim. It was admitted on the pleadings that the deceased was domiciled in India until 1927. Azra and her son and daughter claimed to be entitled to share in the distribution of the testator's estate pursuant to the provisions of the deed. Kulsum Bibi and her two daughters claimed to be entitled to share in the distribution of the testator's estate by virtue of the rules of Muslim law.

Held: (1) That the testator was domiciled at the date of his death in India.

(2) That to entitle Azra to benefit under the deed she had to answer the description of a wife; but this she failed to do because the testator had divorced her in accordance with Muslim law and had not validly remarried her.

(3) That the testator's movable estate should be distributed in accordance with Muslim law between Kulsum Bibi, the two daughters by his first marriage and the son and the daughter by his second marriage.

Dixon C.J., Kitto, Menzies and Owen JJ.

[Chief Justice *Wolff* in the lower court] decided that the domicil of the deceased was India and held that the distribution of his property (presumably movables) was accordingly governed by Muslim law. He found that Azra had for the purposes of Muslim law been married to Abdul and that she was later validly divorced under that law and that under Muslim law the divorce meant that she could not share and his Honour construed the deed as giving her no greater right. He held that the dispositions of the will in favour of Nural were under Muslim law void. The judgment or decree declared accordingly that the will was totally void in its dispositions and that the persons entitled in the distribution and the proportions in which they were so entitled were as follows: Saiful, the son of the deceased Abdul by Azra (fourteen-fortieths), next Farida, the daughter of Azra, and Sufia Ahmed and Jabonessa Begum, the two daughters of Bibi (each seven-fortieths) and the widow Bibi (five-fortieths). From this decree the defendant, the original defendant that is to say, Nural Haque, appealed on the ground that the domicil of his deceased brother Abdul was in Western Australia and that the will operated in his favour according to its terms: for various reasons the deed did not confer any superior right on Azra or her children Saiful and Farida. The plaintiff Azra cross-appealed against her exclusion from the distribution. If her cross-appeal succeeded and otherwise the decree stood it would mean that she would share with Bibi the widow's portion of five-fortieths, each taking a share amounting to five-eightieths. It is to be noted that the decree does not distinguish between immovables situated in Western Australia and movables. It seems to be thought by the parties, however, that the decree was not intended to include immovables situated in Western Australia. But attention does not appear to have been directed to the question of the classification or characterization of certain assets as movable or immovable, it being assumed perhaps that they were movable and accordingly that the distinction was of little practical importance.

(. . .) Then was Abdul domiciled at his death in Western Australia? If the case is stated simply as one in which a father came here in 1870, remained building up a business and returned to his native land only at the end of his life, leaving a son to carry on the business until in all eighty years passed, it seems astonishing that the son should be domiciled elsewhere. But if you take the close association always maintained with the family in the Valley of the Ganges and the village of Milky, the visits there, the formation of partnerships with relatives there, the constant intercourse with what they evidently regarded as the base and home, the existence of wives there, the birth and education of children like Abdul and Nural there, it begins to seem that they all regarded the business in Fremantle as a station—trading station perhaps—to which some of them went for unlimited periods perhaps but not as persons taking up a permanent home. Evidently they did not put off in the least degree their Mohammedanism and the ways of life it involved and they did not identify themselves with the Australian community or share in its life or manner of living. All this attitude must be counted against mere length of time, prolonged as it was. (. . .)

On all the facts the conclusion adopted by *Wolff* C.J. that the domicil of Abdul was his domicil of origin, viz. India, appears to be correct. That means that Muslim law as administered in India forms his personal law. His will, which was made on 7th May 1954, could not under Muslim law dispose of his property inconsistently with the rights of his children and his widow or widows. Muslim law recognizes the marriage celebrated in Fremantle between Abdul and Azra on 23rd September 1951 as a union the issue of which would be legitimate, whatever the law of Western Australia might say. The children Saiful and Farida are therefore entitled to share in the distribution of movables situated in Australia notwithstanding the dispositions of the will. But as to immovables in Western Australia the will must prevail, that is unless in some way the children can make a claim arising under the deed. That question was not argued before us and ought not in our present state of information on the whole subject of immovables to be dealt with by the Court.

It is only necessary to add that in the view expressed above an argument advanced against the effectiveness of the deed does not arise. The argument was that the deed was unenforceable in our Courts because it contemplated cohabitation between man and woman without lawful marriage, for the polygamous marriage celebrated within Western Australia had no effect as a marriage under our law. In the circumstances of this case it is by no means certain that a court would adopt such a position: for it was an attempt by Muslims honestly and genuinely to establish a relation which Muslim law would recognize although the ceremony was performed in Australia where the law would not recognize a polygamous marriage entered into within Australia.

? NOTES AND QUESTIONS

1 In *Haque*, Australian courts applied the choice of law rule of the forum with respect to the inheritance issue and ruled that Indian law applied, and thus invalidated in part the validity of the will of Abdul Haque. Under Indian law, the wife and children of the deceased were thus to share his property. But was Azra the wife of the deceased, and Saiful and Farida his legitimate children? The issue was one of personal status and thus to be addressed separately from a private international law perspective. In order to answer the main issue raised in the case – who will inherit? – it was necessary to first address another issue – are Azra, Saiful and Farida the wife and legitimate children of the deceased? In private international law, the first issue is labelled a *preliminary*, or *incidental* question.

2 How does the court address the incidental question in *Haque*? Does it apply its own choice of law rule? Which law is applied to the issue of the validity of the first marriage of Azra and Abdul Haque? Why?

***

The issue raised by incidental questions was identified in the 1930s by two German scholars, Melchior and Wengler. They argued that a problem arises when the choice of law rule of the forum with respect to the main question designates a foreign law, and the forum and the foreign legal system would resolve differently the incidental question, for instance because they have different choice of law rules with respect to the incidental question. This was the case in *Haque*: the Australian choice of law rule designated Indian law to govern the main issue, and Australia and India would resolve differently the incidental issue. This situation raises several difficulties. First, the conflict of laws, and thus the dispute, is resolved differently depending on the forum before which the action is brought. Second, the integrity of the foreign legal system is hurt if its views on the resolution of the incidental question are ignored. The solution advocated by Melchior and Wengler was for the forum to apply its own choice of law rule to the main question, but to apply the foreign choice of law rule to the incidental question. By doing so, the forum would decide the (entire) dispute exactly as the foreign court would.

QUESTIONS

1 Is *Haque* consistent with the analysis of Melchior and Wengler? Did the Australian court apply foreign substantive law or foreign private international law to the incidental question? What is the best solution?

2 Is there a relation between *renvoi* and incidental questions? Some English scholars argue that foreign choice of law rules should be applied to incidental questions only in matters where *renvoi* is accepted.[23] Do you see the logic behind this proposition? Do you agree?

Dutch Civil Code Book 10 Private International Law

Article 10:4 *Preliminary question to be answered first*

If the question which legal effects arise from a fact has to be answered as a preliminary question in connection with another question which is governed by foreign law, then that preliminary question shall be regarded as a self-dependant question.

Regulation (EU) No 1259/2010 of 20 December 2010 implementing enhanced cooperation in the area of the law applicable to divorce and legal separation (Rome III Regulation)

Preamble

(10) . . .

This Regulation should apply only to the dissolution or loosening of marriage ties. The law determined by the conflict-of-laws rules of this Regulation should apply to the grounds for divorce and legal separation.

Preliminary questions such as legal capacity and the validity of the marriage, and matters such as the effects of divorce or legal separation on property, name, parental responsibility, maintenance obligations or any other ancillary measures should be determined by the conflict-of-laws rules applicable in the participating Member State concerned.

Interpretation of the Supreme People's Court on Issues regarding the Application of the Law of the PRC on the Laws Applicable to Foreign-Related Civil Relations (Part 1, 2012)

Article 12

When, in order to decide an issue concerning a foreign-related civil relation, a different issue has to be decided in the first place as a preliminary issue, the People's Courts shall determine the law applicable to the latter issue as if it were considered in isolation.

Article 13

If a case involves two or more foreign related civil relations, the People's Courts shall determine the applicable law separately for each relation.[24]

---

23 See Briggs, 25.
24 Translation Ilaria Aquironi, (2013) Diritto del Commercio Internazionale 891.

NOTES

1 In the civil law world, the proposition that incidental questions should be treated differently has typically been rejected. In France, it was rejected by the supreme court for civil and criminal matters in 1986.[25] Even in Germany, the Federal Supreme Court ruled against it in 1964.[26]

2 There are several arguments against the incidental question doctrine. The first is that it prefers the coherence of the foreign legal system over the coherence of the legal system of the forum. The choice of law rules of the forum are a coherent set of rules which interact with each other. By applying a foreign choice of law rule, it is the coherence of the legal system of the forum which is hurt. The second argument is that the rationale for the application of foreign law is not that the dispute should be resolved in the exact same way as the foreign court would resolve it. It is simply that the forum has deemed it more adequate to borrow the solution of foreign law on a particular issue. Indeed, whether or not foreign law agrees to govern the main question is not considered.

5   Foreign law

5.1   Applying choice of law rules

5.1.1   *Ex officio application*

All legal systems distinguish between law and fact. In the civil law tradition, an important consequence of the distinction concerns the respective roles of the court and the parties. While it is for the parties to allege the existence of facts and adduce evidence in support of such allegations, it is for the court to say what the law is: *da mihi factum, dabo tibi jus*. As a result, civil law courts should apply the right rule of law irrespective of the legal arguments developed by the parties and, as the case may be, correct the analysis offered by all parties: *iura novit curia*.

It is therefore unsurprising that, in the vast majority of civil law jurisdictions, courts have duty to apply the right choice of law rule and, as the case may be, declare foreign law applicable, even if the parties ignored the international aspect of the dispute and the choice of law issue.

> *Dutch Civil Code Book 10 Private International Law*
> **Article 10:2** *Application ex officio*
> The rules of private international law and the law designated by those rules shall be applied ex officio (i.e. applied by the court of its own motion).

---

25 Cass. Civ. 1ere, 22 April 1986, *Djenangi*, case no. 85-11666, (1988) Rev. Crit. DIP 302.
26 BGH, 22 January 1965, BGHZ 43, 213.

5.1.2 *Permissive application*

Contrary to the civil law tradition, courts in the common law tradition have traditionally relied on lawyers not only to adduce evidence of facts, but also to research the law and assess the applicable legal principles.

In England, the application of choice of law rules must therefore be pleaded. If it is not, the court will apply English law.[27] The application of choice of law rules is not mandatory, and it is for the parties to decide whether they have an interest to plead foreign law.

The result of the English view on choice of law rules is that international cases can be treated as domestic cases if the parties so choose. This means that, in all fields, the parties always have the choice between applying foreign law or English law. If foreign law contains a mandatory rule, and English substantive law is permissive, is it not a way to bypass the foreign mandatory rule? Is it acceptable?

The situation in the United States is intermediate.

U.S. Federal Rules of Civil Procedure

Rule 44.1 *Determining Foreign Law*

A party who intends to raise an issue about a foreign country's law must give notice by a pleading or other writing. In determining foreign law, the court may consider any relevant material or source, including testimony, whether or not submitted by a party or admissible under the Federal Rules of Evidence. The court's determination must be treated as a ruling on a question of law.

 CASE

U.S. Court of Appeals, Second Circuit, 29 September 1981
Vishipco Line, Ha Nam Cong Ty and others v. The Chase Manhattan Bank, N.A.[28]

Mansfield, Circuit Judge:

Plaintiffs appeal from a judgment of the United States District Court for the Southern District of New York entered after a non-jury trial by Judge Robert L. Carter on December 5, 1980, dismissing their claims against Chase Manhattan

---

27 There are some rare exceptions: see *Shaker v. Al-Bedrawi* [2002] EWCA Civ 1452.
28 660 F.2d 854 (2d Cir. 1981).

Bank, N.A. ('Chase'), for breach of contract. The ten corporate plaintiffs Vishipco Line, Ha Nam Cong Ty, Dai Nam Hang Hai C.T., Rang Dong Hang Hai C.T., Mekong Ship Co. Sarl, Vishipco Sarl, Thai Binh C.T., VN Tau Bien C.T., Van An Hang Hai C.T., and Cong Ty U Tau Sao Mai are Vietnamese corporations which maintained piastre demand deposit accounts at Chase's Saigon branch in 1975. Invoking diversity jurisdiction, they claim that Chase breached its deposit contracts with them when it closed the doors of its Saigon branch on April 24, 1975, to escape from the Communist insurgents and subsequently refused to make payment in New York of the amount owed.

We reverse. Chase was clearly obligated to pay plaintiffs the amounts it owed them. None of the affirmative defenses raised by Chase to its conceded obligations to plaintiffs can be sustained. Under Rule 44.1, plaintiffs' failure to introduce evidence of their right to recovery under Vietnamese law governing deposit obligations is not a ground for dismissal of their claims. (. . .)

DISCUSSION

Chase here first contends that plaintiffs' claims were dismissible for failure to prove that under Vietnamese law they were entitled to recover. We disagree. The district court largely agreed with Chase's contention, stating:

> When foreign law is an issue in a case, that law must be proved as a fact. Plaintiffs, however, presented no evidence concerning the law of Vietnam. Such failure has resulted in dismissal of a plaintiff's claims. However, since defendant has shouldered plaintiffs' burden and offered proof of Vietnamese law, there is no need to dismiss for lack of evidence on which to determine Vietnamese law.

Although this statement reflects the law as it existed prior to the adoption of Rule 44.1 F.R.Civ.P. in 1966, it no longer governs the manner in which questions of foreign law are to be dealt with in the federal courts. Prior to 1966 foreign law questions were regarded as questions of fact, 9 C. Wright & A. Miller, Federal Practice and Procedure s 2441 (1971), and, as the district court's citations indicate, a number of courts took the position that a failure to prove foreign law was fatal to a claim, even if the parties had not raised the issue of the applicability of foreign law on their own. Even in this state of the law, however, federal courts frequently refused to dismiss where they were sitting in a state which provided for judicial notice of foreign law.

Rule 44.1 of the Federal Rules of Civil Procedure, which became effective in 1966, put to rest the idea that foreign law is a question of fact which has to be proven by the claimant in order to recover. It declared that '(t)he court's determination shall be treated as a ruling on a question of law.'

Chase nevertheless contends that even under the more liberal standards of Rule 44.1, plaintiffs' claims should have been dismissed for failure to provide evidence of foreign law after it became clear that under New York's choice of law rules the entire case would normally be governed by Vietnamese law.

This assumes that the forum's choice of law rules are mandatory rather than permissive. See generally Sass, Foreign Law in Federal Courts, 29 Am.J.Comp.L. 97, 103–07 (1981). However, with the decline of the vested rights theory (. . .), the movement has been away from a mandatory application of the forum's choice of law rules and toward the adoption of a discretionary rule. While, as the Advisory Committee's notes to Rule 44.1 make clear, a court is still permitted to apply foreign law even if not requested by a party, we believe that the law of the forum may be applied here, where the parties did not at trial take the position that plaintiffs were required to prove their claims under Vietnamese law, even though the forum's choice of law rules would have called for the application of foreign law. This reflects the view adopted by ourselves and other federal courts since 1966.

While Chase invoked foreign law under Rule 44.1 with respect to its own affirmative defenses only, neither party invoked foreign law with respect to Chase's basic obligations to its depositors and holders of certificates of deposit. Nor did Chase ever suggest that under Vietnamese law those obligations would not have formed a basis for recovery. Therefore, while Vietnamese law as invoked by Chase will be applied to those affirmative defenses which rest on Vietnamese law, the parties' failure to invoke foreign law with respect to the underlying obligations themselves would not mandate dismissal of the claims. Under New York law it is clear that, unless relieved of liability under one or more of the affirmative defenses asserted by it, Chase was obligated under its contracts with plaintiffs to pay them the amounts deposited with it. (. . .)

? NOTES AND QUESTIONS

1 In the common law world, foreign law was traditionally treated as a fact. As a consequence, it had to be pleaded and proven. In the United States, this characterization had further consequences: foreign law was an issue to be decided by the trier of fact, often a jury, and it was essentially unreviewable on appeal, as appeals are only allowed on points of law in the United States.[29] But the most dramatic consequence was that if a plaintiff failed to prove the content

---

29 Hay, Borchers and Symeonides, § 12–15.

of foreign law, his claim would be dismissed for that reason alone: the plaintiff had not proven all the facts required for his claim to be allowed.[30] The status of foreign law in U.S. courts today is different. It is to be 'treated' as law, and thus an issue for the judge rather than for the jury. It needs not be proven as a fact (on proof of foreign law, see *infra* 5.2).

2 The United States is a federal system where federal courts (U.S. courts) coexist with state courts (courts of the state of Texas, courts of the state of California, and so on . . .). Rule 44.1 is a rule of federal civil procedure, and thus applies in federal courts. State courts apply their own rules of civil procedure, which may be different.

3 Could a U.S. court decide to apply choice of law rules of its own motion?

4 If none of the parties plead the application of the choice of law rule and of foreign law, the law of the forum (that is, the relevant U.S. state) should be applied instead. Contrary to England where such a result is uncontroversial, American lawyers have tried to find an acceptable justification for such outcome. Some courts have held that the parties should be deemed to have chosen the law of the forum, but the U.S. has traditionally limited the power of parties to choose the applicable law by establishing a connection requirement. An alternative doctrine is to use a presumption that foreign law is similar to the forum's law.[31]

5.1.3 Mixed systems

In France as in most civil law systems, it is for the court to say what the law is, and French courts will correct the legal arguments of all parties if necessary. Yet, the French supreme court has been reluctant to impose on French courts a full duty to apply choice of law rules.

 CASE

French Cour de cassation, 26 May 1999[32] *Belaid*

Having regard to Article 311-14 of the Civil Code, together with Article 3 of the Civil Code;

According to the first of these provisions, parenthood is governed by the personal law of the mother on the day of birth of the child; according to the second, it is for French courts, where rights that the parties may not dispose of are concerned, to apply choice of law rules and to designate the applicable foreign law.

Ms Y. . . gave birth on May 7, 1991, to a child called Samy Z. . . ; she initiated proceedings against M. X. . . for the purpose of ascertaining fatherhood on the ground of Article 340 of the French Civil Code; the Court of Appeal allowed her claim;

---

30 A famous example is *Walton v. Arabian Oil. Co.*, 233 F.2d 541 (2d Cir. 1956).

31 Hay, Borchers and Symeonides, § 12–19.

32 Civ. 1ère, 26 May 1999, case no. 97-16684.

By ruling so, without assessing, ex officio, whether to allow the claim under the personal law of the mother who, according to documents produced in the procedure, held a resident card, the Court of appeal has violated the requirements of the abovementioned provisions;

For these reasons: the appeal is allowed and the judgment of the Court of appeal is set aside.

NOTES

1   This judgment is one of two which hopefully put an end to a period of 40 years during which the French supreme court varied considerably on the issue of whether choice of law rules ought to be mandatory or permissive. In *Belaid*, the court ruled that in matters where the parties may not dispose of their rights, French courts ought to apply choice of law rules ex officio. In the *Mutuelle du Mans IARD* case of the same day,[33] the court ruled that in matters where the parties may dispose of their rights, French courts have no obligation to apply choice of law rules if none of the parties raised their application or the application of foreign law. The system is mixed: some choice of law rules must be applied ex officio, others need not.

2   The distinction is between rights that the parties may dispose of, and rights that parties may not dispose of. The origin of the distinction is to be found in the writings of the most influential scholar in French private international law in the last decades, Pierre Mayer.[34] Mayer argued that, while in principle foreign law should be considered as law and thus applied ex officio, an exception should be made for those rights which the parties could modify, and indeed waive. This is because they could decide to settle their dispute at any time, under any terms. Thus, a pragmatic solution should be to allow them to argue their case under French law if they so wish. Just as they could have ignored the content of the applicable law to reach a settlement, they should be allowed to implicitly designate another law. The *Mutuelle du Mans IARD* case was concerned with rights arising out of an international sale of goods. In commercial law, most rights may be waived. The *Belaid* case was concerned with parenthood. Rights in this context may not be waived.

CASE

French Cour de cassation, 6 May 1997[35] *Société Hannover International*

Whereas the Belgian company Anglo Belgian Corporation NV (ABC), which had provided Mr. X a mechanical set of propulsion for the equipment of a trawler, criticizes, with its insurer, society Hannover International, the judgment (Court of Appeal of Poitiers, 18 January 1995), for ordering them to compensate Mr. X for the loss sustained due to a defect of the equipment

---

33   Civ. 1ère, 26 May 1999, case no. 96-16361.
34   Mayer and Heuzé, para. 148.
35   Civ. 1ère, 6 May 1997, case no. 95-15309.

sold, based on the implied warranty of Article 1641 of the Civil Code, in violation both of the Hague Convention of 15 June 1955 on the law applicable to international sales of goods, which imposed to determine the applicable law, concerning the guarantee due by a Belgian seller to French buyer, and the agreement of the parties, which submitted the contract to the Belgian law of the seller and contractually fixed the period of the warranty

But whereas, for the rights they may freely dispose of, the parties may agree on the application of the French law of the forum despite the existence of an international treaty or a contractual clause designating the applicable law; that such an agreement can result from submissions of the parties invoking a law other than the one designated by treaty or by the contract (. . .)

For these reasons: the appeal is dismissed.

? NOTE AND QUESTION

Where parties are entitled not to plead foreign law, the issue arises as to whether they could be entitled to change their mind at a late stage of the proceedings. It could then become a delaying tactic. How do French courts address the issue?

Tunisian Code of Private International Law (1998)

Article 28
Choice of law rules are of mandatory application where their subject matter is a category of rights that the parties may not freely dispose of.
In other cases, the rule is mandatory for the court, unless the parties explicitly expressed their will to derogate from its application.

? QUESTION

How does Article 28, para. 2, differ from the French rule in *Société Hannover International*?

5.2 Proof of foreign law

Once a court has ruled that foreign law is applicable, its content must be determined to the satisfaction of the court.

5.2.1 Role of courts and parties in determining foreign law

A first issue is whether the burden of establishing the content of foreign law should lie with the court or with the parties. The answer to this question is logically dependent on the answer given to the question of whether courts should apply choice of law rules ex officio. When this is the case, courts are also typically supposed to make efforts to establish the content of foreign law themselves.

Swiss Federal Code of Private International Law (1987)
Article 16 *IV. Establishment of foreign law*
1 The content of the applicable foreign law shall be established ex officio. The assistance of the parties may be requested. In the case of pecuniary claims, the burden of proof on the content of the foreign law may be imposed on the parties.
2 Swiss law shall apply if the content of the foreign law cannot be established.

Reform of the Italian System of Private International Law (1995)
Article 14 *Ascertainment of the applicable foreign law*
1. The judge shall ascertain the applicable foreign law *ex officio.* To that effect, he may use, in addition to the instruments referred to in international conventions, information obtained through the Ministry of Justice, or from experts or specialized institutions. (...)

Belgian Code of Private International Law (2004)
Art. 15. *Application of foreign law*
§ 1. The judge establishes the content of the foreign law designated by the present statute. That law is applied in accordance with the interpretation given to it in the foreign country.
§ 2. The judge may require the cooperation of the parties if he cannot establish the content. When it is clear that the content of the foreign law cannot be established timely, Belgian law is applied.

Of course, the rule cannot mean that courts are under an obligation to succeed in establishing the content of foreign law. They must make efforts in that direction, and may not simply rely on the evidence adduced by the parties.[36] As the Swiss and Belgian laws indicate, this does not exclude the possibility of requesting the assistance of the parties.[37]

In cases where choice of law rules are permissive and foreign law must be pleaded, the burden of proof is typically on the party pleading a particular content of foreign law. In England, courts must rely exclusively on the evidence adduced by the parties (see *infra* the *Bumper Development* case). In the United States, courts will often expect from the parties that they adduce evidence of foreign law, but may take a more active role if they wish (see *infra* the *Bodum*

---

36 See, in France, Civ. 1ère, 28 June 2005, case no. 00-15734.
37 This is also the rule under French law: see Civ. 1ère, 28 June 2005, *supra*.

case). Finally, in France, the burden of determining the content of foreign law still lies primarily with the court even where the choice of law rule was not applicable *ex officio*, but foreign law was pleaded by one of the parties.[38]

5.2.2 Means to determine foreign law

There are essentially two ways to establish the content of foreign law. The first is to use directly primary sources such as statutory provisions, judicial decisions and scholarly writing. The second is to ask an expert in the foreign legal system to report to the court.

In legal systems where the court has primarily the burden of establishing the content of foreign law, this obligation is typically understood as an invitation to follow the first way and to consult foreign primary materials when they can be found by the court. However, a court could also fulfil its obligation by appointing a judicial expert and entrusting him with the task of writing a report to the court. Although judicial experts are appointed on a daily basis in many civil law jurisdictions to make factual assessments, it is rare that courts make such appointments for the purpose of establishing the content of foreign law. The only exceptions are Austria and Germany where it is a common practice. The experts appointed by German courts are typically German law professors specializing in comparative law. The system works well because of the great resources enjoyed by German universities and research institutes which can afford to establish rich libraries containing a wealth of comparative legal materials and to permanently employ scholars specialized in foreign legal systems.

However, in most countries, courts simply do not have the resources to establish the content of foreign law. For instance, while the French supreme court has imposed on French courts a duty to make efforts to establish the content of foreign law themselves, their resources are very limited, and so are the resources of French universities and comparative law institutes. As a result, it is for the parties to adduce evidence of foreign law. In many countries (France, for instance), the parties may either identify and produce primary materials of foreign law, or hire an expert, who will typically be a foreign lawyer or academic.

Read the two following cases and determine which means can be used to determine the content of foreign law in England and in the United States.

---

38 See Civ. 1ère, 28 June 2005, *supra*.

CASE

English Court of Appeal, 13 February 1991 *Bumper Development Corp v. Commissioner of Police of the Metropolis*[39]

Purchas L.J.:

Proof of foreign law

It is clear that the true status in Hindu law of the third, fourth and fifth claimants (. . .) is central to the issues raised. (. . .)

Ian Kennedy J. reviewed at length the evidence of Hindu law not only as set out by textbook writers and in judgments delivered in the Indian courts, but also the oral evidence given before him by the expert witnesses before reaching his conclusions as to which claimants would be acceptable as juristic entities in the courts of Tamil Nadu, and whether, and if so, what circumstances such a party could claim a title to the Nataraja. However, before coming to consider the evidence on this aspect of the case, it is convenient to consider the position in the English courts. It is trite law that foreign law in our courts is treated as a question of fact which must be proved in evidence. In the absence of any evidence to the contrary, it is to be assumed to be the same as English law. It is however the duty of the judge when faced with conflicting evidence from witnesses about a foreign law to resolve those differences in the same way as he must in the case of other conflicting evidence as to facts.

What is not so plain, however, is how he should deal with documentary evidence in the form of textbooks and reports of judgments and decisions in foreign courts. Ian Kennedy J. expressed a firm view when rejecting the evidence upon one issue over which both expert witnesses were agreed. This was to the effect that the third claimant did not have a sufficient continuity of association with the temple to qualify as a 'de facto' trustee:

> I think they are both mistaken and have failed to read in their true import of the judgments Vemareddi Ramaraghava v. Konduru Seshu A.I.R. 1967 S.C. 436 and Vikrama Das Mahant v. Daulat Ram Asthana A.I.R. 1956 S.C. 382 to which I have just referred. It is well settled that the English court will take the exposition of its

---

own law by the Supreme Court of another jurisdiction as wholly authoritative and an opinion to be preferred to that of any witness; that I do.

Unfortunately, the judge did not refer to any authority for this proposition, nor were we in argument referred to any such authority. Mr. Calcutt attacked this part of the judgment and in our view rightly so. This proposition as stated without qualification does not find any support in *Dicey & Morris, The Conflict of Laws*, 11th ed. (1987), vol. 1, p. 217:

> (1) In any case to which foreign law applies, that law must be pleaded and proved as a fact to the satisfaction of the judge by expert evidence or sometimes by certain other means.
> (2) In the absence of satisfactory evidence of foreign law, the court will apply English law to such a case.

The propositions in the notes to this rule, so far as relevant to this appeal, are based on well established authority, especially the judgment of Lord Langdale M.R. in *Earl Nelson v. Lord Bridport* (1845) 8 Beav. 527. In our judgment the following extracts from the notes in *Dicey & Morris* accurately set out the relevant aspects of English law in regard to the proof of a foreign law.

(1) An English court will not conduct its own researches into foreign law:' *Dicey & Morris*, vol. 1, p. 222. See *Duchess Di Sora v. Phillipps* (1863) 10 H.L.Cas. 624, 640, *per* Lord Chelmsford:

> It seems, however, rather questionable whether the judge has a right to resort to the foreign law itself for information, when the evidence of the witnesses is not satisfactory to his mind. The witnesses are at liberty to adduce, in support or confirmation of their testimony, text books, decisions of the foreign courts, or rather authorities, which, becoming a part of their evidence, may enable the judge to form his own opinion upon the particular text of foreign law thus laid before him. But it seems contrary to the nature of the proof required in these cases, that the judge should be at liberty to search for himself into the sources of knowledge from which the witnesses have drawn, and produce for himself the fact which is required to be proved as a part of the case before him. As my noble and learned friend, Lord Brougham, said in the Sussex Peerage Case (1844) 11 Cl. & Fin. 85, 115, 'the judge has not organs to know and to deal with the text of the foreign law, and therefore requires the assistance of a lawyer who knows how to interpret it.'

(2) 'If the evidence of several expert witnesses conflicts as to the effect of foreign sources, the court is entitled, and indeed bound, to look at those

sources in order itself to decide between the conflicting testimony:' *Dicey &*
Morris, vol. 1, p. 223. See *Earl Nelson v. Lord Bridport*, 8 Beav. 527, 537, *per*
Lord Langdale M.R.:

> Such I conceive to be the general rule; but the cases to which it is applicable admit
> of great variety. Though a knowledge of foreign law is not to be imputed to the
> judge, you may impute to him such a knowledge of the general art of reasoning,
> as will enable him, with the assistance of the bar, to discover where fallacies are
> probably concealed, and in what cases he ought to require testimony more or less
> strict. If the utmost strictness were required in every case, justice might often have
> to stand still; and I am not disposed to say, that there may not be cases, in which
> the judge may, without impropriety, take upon himself to construe the words of a
> foreign law, and determine their application to the case in question, especially, if
> there should be a variance or want of clearness in the testimony.

This was the approach made by Scarman J. to a mass of conflicting expert
evidence on German private international law in In the Estate of Fuld, decd.
(No. 3) [1968] P. 675, 700–703.

(3) The Court of Appeal, whilst slow to interfere as in all cases where the
decision involves findings of fact, may in appropriate cases be somewhat
more ready to question the trial judge's conclusions than in normal cases
(. . .)

With these authorities in mind we have come to the conclusion that the
judge was not entitled to reject the evidence of the experts to the effect
that Sadogopan did not have a sufficient continuity of association with
the temple to qualify as a 'de facto' trustee. Furthermore, we have also
come to the conclusion that Mr. Calcutt was correct in submitting that Ian
Kennedy J. was not entitled to rely upon his own researches based on pas-
sages from *B. K. Mukherjea on The Hindu Law of Religious and Charitable
Trust*, 5th ed. (1983) without having the assistance of the expert witnesses and the submissions of counsel. However, when the transcript of
Mr. Vadivelu's evidence is considered, it is clear that the paragraphs to
which the judge referred had already been referred to by Mr. Vadivelu
in his reports and were adopted by him in evidence. There is therefore
admissible evidence in support of the paragraphs in the textbook upon
which the judge's research was based. Mr. Calcutt's submission therefore
becomes largely academic.

United States Court of Appeals, Seventh Circuit, 2 September 2010 *Bodum USA, Inc. v. La Cafetière, Inc.*[40]

Posner, Circuit Judge, concurring.

I join the majority opinion, and write separately merely to express emphatic support for, and modestly to amplify, the court's criticism of a common and authorized but unsound judicial practice. That is the practice of trying to establish the meaning of a law of a foreign country by testimony or affidavits of expert witnesses, usually lawyers or law professors, often from the country in question. For earlier criticism, see *Sunstar, Inc. v. Alberto–Culver Co.*, 586 F.3d 487, 495–96 (7th Cir.2009). (. . .)

Rule 44.1 of the Federal Rules of Civil Procedure provides that a federal court, 'in determining foreign law, . . . may consider any relevant material or source, including testimony, whether or not submitted by a party or admissible under the Federal Rules of Evidence.' The committee note explains that the court 'may engage in its own research and consider any relevant material thus found. The court may have at its disposal better foreign law materials than counsel have presented, or may wish to re-examine and amplify material that has been presented by counsel in partisan fashion or in insufficient detail.' Thus the court doesn't *have* to rely on testimony; and in only a few cases, I believe, is it justified in doing so. This case is not one of them.

The only evidence of the meaning of French law that was presented to the district court or is found in the appellate record is an English translation of brief excerpts from the French Civil Code and affidavits by three French law professors. The district court did no research of its own, but relied on the parties' submissions.

When a court in one state applies the law of another, or when a federal court applies state law (or a state court federal law), the court does not permit expert testimony on the meaning of the 'foreign' law that it has to apply. This is true even when it's the law of Louisiana, which is based to a significant degree on the *Code Napoléon* (curiously, adopted by Louisiana after the United States acquired Louisiana from France).

Yet if the law to be applied is the law of a foreign country, even a country such

---

40 621 F.3D 624 (7th. Cir. 2010).

as the United Kingdom, Canada, or Australia in which the official language is English and the legal system derives from the same source as ours, namely the English common law, our courts routinely rely on lawyers' testimony about the meaning of the foreign law. (. . .) Not only rely but sometimes suggest, incorrectly in light of Rule 44.1, that testimony is *required* for establishing foreign law.

Lawyers who testify to the meaning of foreign law, whether they are practitioners or professors, are paid for their testimony and selected on the basis of the convergence of their views with the litigating position of the client, or their willingness to fall in with the views urged upon them by the client. These are the banes of expert testimony. When the testimony concerns a scientific or other technical issue, it may be unreasonable to expect a judge to resolve the issue without the aid of such testimony. But judges are experts on law, and there is an abundance of published materials, in the form of treatises, law review articles, statutes, and cases, all in English (if English is the foreign country's official language), to provide neutral illumination of issues of foreign law. I cannot fathom why in dealing with the meaning of laws of English-speaking countries that share our legal origins judges should prefer paid affidavits and testimony to published materials.

It is only a little less perverse for judges to rely on testimony to ascertain the law of a country whose official language is not English, at least if is a major country and has a modern legal system. Although most Americans are monolingual, including most judges, there are both official translations of French statutes into English, Legifrance, 'Codes and Texts,' http:// 195. 83. 177. 9/ code/ index. phtml? lang= uk (visited Aug. 4, 2010), and abundant secondary material on French law, including French contract and procedural law, published in English. Neither party cited *any* such material, except translations of statutory provisions; beyond that they relied on the affidavits of their expert witnesses.

Because English has become the international *lingua franca*, it is unsurprising that most Americans, even when otherwise educated, make little investment in acquiring even a reading knowledge of a foreign language. But our linguistic provincialism does not excuse intellectual provincialism. It does not justify our judges in relying on paid witnesses to spoon feed them foreign law that can be found well explained in English-language treatises and articles. I do not criticize the district judge in this case, because he was following the common practice. But it is a bad practice, followed like so many legal practices out of habit rather than reflection. It is excusable only when the foreign law is the law of a country with such an obscure or poorly developed legal system that there are no secondary materials to which the judge could turn. The French legal system is obviously not of that character. The district court could (. . .) have based his interpretation of French contract law on published writings as distinct from paid testimony.

Of course often the most authoritative literature will be in the language of the foreign country. But often too there will be official, or reputable unofficial, translations and when there are not the parties can have the relevant portions translated into English. Translations figure prominently in a variety of cases tried in American courts, such as drug-trafficking and immigration cases; why not in cases involving foreign law? (. . .)

The parties' reliance on affidavits to establish the standard for interpreting their contract has produced only confusion. They should have relied on published analyses of French commercial law.

 NOTES AND QUESTIONS

1 In England, expert evidence is required to prove foreign law. How is it explained by the English court? In some countries of the commonwealth, the rule was actually codified, such as in Nigeria.[41]

   As already underscored (see *supra*, 5.1), the reform of the U.S. Rules of Civil Procedure led to treating foreign law as 'law' rather than fact. As explained by Judge Posner, one consequence was that U.S. evidentiary rules need not be applied anymore, and that providing expert evidence ceased to be required. However, as noted by Judge Posner, it is still the practice of the vast majority of U.S. courts in cases involving the law of foreign nations.

2 What is the best rule? Is it a good idea to rely exclusively on literature on the foreign legal system to assess the content of its law? What about a change in the foreign law (a recent case, a recent statutory amendment)? How can you check that the literature on foreign law is up to date?

   Is the American rule more efficient? Expert witnesses must be paid. However, an American lawyer engaging in an exercise of comparative law to select materials on French law to be produced to the court will also charge his client. Who will charge more?

3 As Judge Posner explains, expert witnesses, unless appointed by the court (which virtually never happens outside of the Germanic world), are paid by the party who hired them. Their impartiality, therefore, can be doubted. In the common law tradition, however, they can be cross-examined in court, and cross-examination is a very powerful tool to reveal bias and partiality.

   The worst possible system is one where experts file written reports and will never be asked to give any explanation as to their statements. This will likely happen in civil law jurisdictions where there is no tradition to interrogate experts in civil proceedings. France is one of them: experts are never asked to appear in court to justify what they wrote in their reports (*certificat de coutume*).[42]

---

41 See section 68 and 69 of the Nigerian *Evidence Act* 2011.
42 Mayer and Heuzé, para. 193.

4 In American state courts, Rule 44.1 of the Federal Rules of Civil Procedure does not apply. Foreign law might thus still be regarded as a fact. However, many state lawmakers have limited the consequences of such characterization by allowing their courts to take judicial notice of the law of other jurisdictions. In the American law of evidence, the rule is that a court may not rely on a fact which was not proven by the parties in accordance with the law of evidence of the forum. An exception exists if the court is authorized to take judicial notice of a fact, typically because the truth of that fact is so notorious that it cannot reasonably be doubted. The fact may then be admitted without being formally introduced by a witness or any other admissible evidence.

New York – Civil Practice Law and Rules

Rule 4511. *Judicial notice of law.*

(a) *When judicial notice shall be taken without request.*

Every court shall take judicial notice without request of the common law, constitutions and public statutes of the United States and of every state, territory and jurisdiction of the United States and of the official compilation of codes, rules and regulations of the state except those that relate solely to the organization or internal management of an agency of the state and of all local laws and county acts.

(b) *When judicial notice may be taken without request; when it shall be taken on request.*

Every court may take judicial notice without request of private acts and resolutions of the congress of the United States and of the legislature of the state; ordinances and regulations of officers, agencies or governmental subdivisions of the state or of the United States; and the laws of foreign countries or their political subdivisions. Judicial notice shall be taken of matters specified in this subdivision if a party requests it, furnishes the court sufficient information to enable it to comply with the request, and has given each adverse party notice of his intention to request it. Notice shall be given in the pleadings or prior to the presentation of any evidence at the trial, but a court may require or permit other notice.

(c) *Determination by court; review as matter of law.*

Whether a matter is judicially noticed or proof is taken, every matter specified in this section shall be determined by the judge or referee, and included in his findings or charged to the jury. Such findings or charge shall be subject to review on appeal as a finding or charge on a matter of law.

(d) *Evidence to be received on matter to be judicially noticed.*

In considering whether a matter of law should be judicially noticed and in determining the matter of law to be judicially noticed, the court may consider any testimony, document, information or argument on the subject, whether offered by a party or discovered through its own research. Whether or not judicial notice is taken, a printed copy of a statute or other written law or a proclamation, edict, decree or ordinance by an executive contained in a book or publication, purporting to have been published by a government or commonly admitted as evidence of the existing law in the judicial tribunals of the jurisdiction where it is in force, is prima facie evidence of such law and the unwritten or common law of a jurisdiction may be proved by witnesses or printed reports of cases of the courts of the jurisdiction.

(a) Judicial notice can be permissive or mandatory. Can you identify which judicial notice is permissive or mandatory in these provisions? Can you explain this difference?
(b) What are the legal consequences of judicial notice of foreign law in New York?
(c) Other federal States compel courts to take judicial notice of the various laws in force within the federal system. In Nigeria, this applies to any custom certified and recorded by a Nigerian court.[43]

Could the proof of foreign law be facilitated by the conclusion of an international treaty to that effect? The 1968 London Convention, which was adopted under the aegis of the Council of Europe, was ratified by over 40 States member of the Council of Europe and a few non member States (including Morocco and Mexico). How does it mean to improve the proof of foreign law?

European Convention on Information on Foreign Law London, 7 June 1968
Article 1 – *Scope of the Convention*

1. The Contracting Parties undertake to supply one another, in accordance with the provisions of the present Convention, with information on their law and procedure in civil and commercial fields as well as on their judicial organisation.
2. However, two or more Contracting Parties may decide to extend as between themselves the scope of the present Convention to fields other than those mentioned in the preceding paragraph. The text of such agreements shall be communicated to the Secretary General of the Council of Europe.

Article 2 – *National liaison bodies*

1. In order to carry out the provisions of the present Convention each Contracting Party shall set up or appoint a single body (hereinafter referred to as the 'receiving agency'):

---

43 See section 122 of the Nigerian *Evidence Act* 2011.

    a.   to receive requests for the information referred to in Article 1, paragraph 1, of the present Convention from another Contracting Party;

    b.   to take action on these requests in accordance with Article 6.

    The receiving agency may be either a ministerial department or other State body. (. . .)

Article 3 – *Authorities entitled to make a request for information*

1.   A request for information shall always emanate from a judicial authority, even when it has not been drawn up by that authority. The request may be made only where proceedings have actually been instituted.

Article 7 – *Content of the reply*

The object of the reply shall be to give information in an objective and impartial manner on the law of the requested State to the judicial authority from which the request emanated. The reply shall contain, as appropriate, relevant legal texts and relevant judicial decisions. It shall be accompanied, to the extent deemed necessary for the proper information of the requesting authority, by any additional documents, such as extracts from doctrinal works and *travaux préparatoires*. It may also be accompanied by explanatory commentaries.

Article 8 – *Effects of the reply*

The information given in the reply shall not bind the judicial authority from which the request emanated.

Article 14 – *Languages*

1.   The request for information and annexes shall be in the language or in one of the official languages of the requested State or be accompanied by a translation into that language. The reply shall be in the language of the requested State.

? NOTES

1 In theory, the system established by the London Convention could have been a remarkably efficient tool for ascertaining the content of foreign law in Europe. In practice, it is very little used.[44] The main criticism is that it takes too long to receive replies. It also seems that the usefulness of the replies varies a great deal, with some replies only mentioning the relevant legal provisions with no further detail, in particular on how it was interpreted by local courts.

2 A number of courts in the common law world have signed bilateral memoranda of understanding on reference of questions of law (e.g. Memorandum Of Understanding Between The

---

44 See, e.g., Swiss Institute for Comparative Law, *The Application of Foreign Law in Civil Matters in EU Member States and its Perspective for the Future* (2011) 14.

Supreme Court Of Singapore And The Supreme Court Of New South Wales On References Of Questions Of Law of 2010). The goal is to establish procedures whereby, in cases where the law of one court would govern a dispute pending in the other, the latter could refer questions of law to the former.

5.2.3 Failure to determine the content of foreign law

A third issue is what the forum should do in case the content of the foreign law could not be established to the satisfaction of the court. As you could see, the rule in the vast majority of countries is that the law of the forum should apply instead. The result is either fully assumed as in most countries of the civil law tradition (see, e.g., Art. 15 of the Belgian Code, Art. 16 of the Swiss law, *supra* 5.2.1), or hidden behind an assumption of similarity of the foreign law with the forum (see, e.g., the *Bumper Development* case, *supra* 5.2.2, for England and Wales).

A few legal systems provide for a different solution, including Italy.

> *Reform of the Italian System of Private International Law (1995)*
> **Article 14** *Ascertainment of the applicable foreign law*
> 2. Should the judge be unable to ascertain the foreign law to which reference is made, even with the co-operation of the parties, he shall apply the law that can be determined on the basis of other connecting factors as possibly provided for with respect to the same matter. In the absence of other connecting factors, Italian law applies.

? QUESTIONS

Article 14 provides that where other connecting factors are available, they should be applied to identify another law. Where would these other connecting factors come from? From Art. 34 of the Italian law (*supra*, 3)? Why would it be better to use them instead of applying Italian law directly?

5.2.4 The subject matter of proof

The last issue is whether the purpose of the establishment of foreign law should merely be to identify the main sources and rules in the foreign law (for instance, applicable statutes and/or leading precedents), or the precise outcome that the foreign court would reach. All legal systems require that the precise and actual outcome that the foreign court would reach be assessed. German scholars explain that courts must determine the 'legal reality' of foreign law.

Russian Civil Code (2013)
Article 1191 *Establishing the content of foreign law*
1. Where foreign law is applicable, the court shall establish its content in accordance with official interpretation, practices adopted and scholarship existing in the relevant foreign State. (. . .)

Reform of the Italian System of Private International Law (1995)
Article 15 *Interpretation and application of foreign law*
Foreign law shall be applied pursuant to its own criteria of interpretation and application.

6 Public policy

One of the most common rules in comparative private international law is that the forum will not apply foreign law if its application would infringe its public policy.

Rome I Regulation (2008)
Article 21 *Public policy of the forum*
The application of a provision of the law of any country specified by this Regulation may be refused only if such application is manifestly incompatible with the public policy (*ordre public*) of the forum.

 NOTE

The same provision is found in all European regulations on choice of law.[45]

Japanese Act on the General Rules of Application of Laws (2006)
Article 42 [Public Policy (*Ordre Public*)]
Where a case should be governed by a foreign law but application of those provisions would contravene public policy (*ordre public*), those provisions shall not apply.

6.1 Defining public policy

While the multilateral methodology essentially focuses on conflict justice and is thus substance-neutral (*supra*, Ch. 1, 1.1.2), the public policy exception allows the forum to avoid the application of foreign law on the ground that it is contrary to a 'policy' of the forum. How is public policy to be

---

45 See e.g. Art. 26 of the Rome II Regulation, Art. 12 of the Rome III Regulation, Art. 35 of the Succession Regulation.

defined? Does it refer to all policies underlying the rules of the forum? Or, by contrast, is it limited to its most fundamental principles and values?

 CASE

Court of Appeals of New York, 12 July 1918 *Loucks et al. v. Standard Oil Co. of New York*[46]

Cardozo, J.

The action is brought to recover damages for injuries resulting in death. The plaintiffs are the administrators of the estate of Everett A. Loucks. Their intestate, while traveling on a highway in the state of Massachusetts, was run down and killed through the negligence of the defendant's servants then engaged in its business. He left a wife and two children, residents of New York. A statute of Massachusetts (R. L. c. 171, § 2, as amended by L. 1907, c. 375) provides that:

> If a person or corporation by his or its negligence, or by the negligence of his or its agents or servants while engaged in his or its business, causes the death of a person who is in the exercise of due care, and not in his or its employment or service, he or it shall be liable in damages in the sum of not less than $500, nor more than $10,000, to be assessed with reference to the degree of his or its culpability, or . . . that of his or its . . . servants, to be recovered in an action of tort commenced within two years after the injury which caused the death, by the executor or administrator of the deceased, one-half thereof to the use of the widow and one-half to the use of the children of the deceased, or, if there are no children, the whole to the use of the widow, or, if there is no widow, the whole to the use of the next of kin.

The question is whether a right of action under that statute may be enforced in our courts.

1. 'The courts of no country execute the penal laws of another.' The Antelope, 10 Wheat. [23 U.S.] 66, 123. The defendant invokes that principle as applicable here. (. . .)

2. Another question remains. Even though the statute is not penal, it differs from our own. We must determine whether the difference is a sufficient reason for declining jurisdiction. A tort committed in one state creates a right of action that may be sued upon in another unless public policy forbids. That

---

46 120 N.E. 198.

is the generally accepted rule in the United States. (. . .). It is not the rule in every jurisdiction where the common law prevails. In England it has been held that the foreign tort must be also one by English law (. . .), which then becomes the source and measure of the resulting cause of action (. . .). That is certainly not the rule with us. (. . .).

A foreign statute is not law in this state, but it gives rise to an obligation, which, if transitory, 'follows the person and may be enforced wherever the person may be found.' (. . .) 'No law can exist as such except the law of the land; but . . . it is a principle of every civilized law that vested rights shall be protected.' (. . .). The plaintiff owns something, and we help him to get it. (. . .). We do this unless some sound reason of public policy makes it unwise for us to lend our aid. 'The law of the forum is material only as setting a limit of policy beyond which such obligations will not be enforced there.' (. . .) Sometimes we refuse to act where all the parties are nonresidents. (. . .). That restriction need not detain us; in this case all are residents. If did is to be withheld here, it must be because the cause of action in its nature offends our sense of justice or menaces the public welfare. (. . .).

Our own scheme of legislation may be different. We may even have no legislation on the subject. That is not enough to show that public policy forbids us to enforce the foreign right. A right of action is property. If a foreign statute gives the right, the mere fact that we do not give a like right is no reason for refusing to help the plaintiff in getting what belongs to him. We are not so provincial as to say that every solution of a problem is wrong because we deal with it otherwise at home. Similarity of legislation has indeed this importance; its presence shows beyond question that the foreign statute does not offend the local policy. But its absence does not prove the contrary. It is not to be exalted into an indispensable condition. The misleading word 'comity' has been responsible for much of the trouble. It has been fertile in suggesting a discretion unregulated by general principles. (. . .).

The sovereign in its discretion may refuse its aid to the foreign right. (. . .). From this it has been an easy step to the conclusion that a like freedom of choice has been confided to the courts. But that, of course, is a false view. (. . .) The courts are not free to refuse to enforce a foreign right at the pleasure of the judges, to suit the individual notion of expediency or fairness. They do not close their doors, unless help would violate some fundamental principle of justice, some prevalent conception of good morals, some deeprooted tradition of the common weal.

This test applied, there is nothing in the Massachusetts statute that outrages the public policy of New York. We have a statute which gives a civil remedy where death is caused in our own state. We have though it so important that we have now imbedded it in the Constitution. Const. art. 1, § 18. The fundamental policy is that there shall be some atonement for the wrong. Through the defendant's negligence, a resident of New York has been killed in Massachusetts. He has left a widow and children, who are also residents. The law of Massachusetts gives them a recompense for his death. It cannot be that public policy forbids our courts to help in collecting what belongs to them. We cannot give them the same judgment that our law would give if the wrong had been done here. Very likely we cannot give them as much. But that is no reason for refusing to give them what we can. We shall not make things better by sending them to another state, where the defendant may not be found, and where suit may be impossible. Nor is there anything to shock our sense of justice in the possibility of a punitive recovery. The penalty is not extravagant. It conveys no hint of arbitrary confiscation. (...). It varies between moderate limits according to the defendant's guilt. We shall not feel the pricks of conscience, if the offender pays the survivors in proportion to the measure of his offense.

We have no public policy that prohibits exemplary damages or civil penalties. We give them for many wrongs. To exclude all penal actions would be to wipe out the distinction between the penalties of public justice and the remedies of private law. Finally, there are no difficulties of procedure that stand in the way. We have a statute authorizing the triers of the facts, when statutory penalties are sued for, to fit the award to the offense. Code Civ. Proc. § 1898. The case is not one where special remedies established by the foreign law are incapable of adequate enforcement except in the home tribunals. (...).

We hold, then, that public policy does not prohibit the assumption of jurisdiction by our courts and that this being so, mere differences of remedy do not count. For many years the courts have been feeling their way in the enforcement of these statutes. A civil remedy for another's death was something strange and new, and it did not find at once the fitting niche, the proper category, in the legal scheme. We need not be surprised, therefore, if some of the things said, as distinguished from those decided, must be rejected to-day. But the truth, of course, is that there is nothing sui generis about these death statutes in their relation to the general body of private international law. We must apply the same rules that are applicable to other torts; and the tendency of those rules to-day is toward a larger comity, if we must cling to the traditional term. (...). The fundamental public policy is perceived to be that rights lawfully vested shall be everywhere maintained. At least, that is so among the states of the Union. (...). There is a growing conviction that only exceptional circumstances should lead one of the states to refuse to enforce a right acquired in another. The evidences of this tendency are many. One typical instance will suffice. For many years Massachusetts closed her courts to actions of this order based on foreign statutes. (. . .). The test of similarity has been abandoned there. If it has ever been accepted here, we think it should be abandoned now.

The judgment of the Appellate Division should be reversed, and the order of the Special Term affirmed, with costs in the Appellate Division and in this court.

 CASE

House of Lords, 16 May 2002 *Kuwait Airways Corporation v. Iraqi Airways Co. and others*[47]

Lord Nicholls of Birkenhead

15. Conflict of laws jurisprudence is concerned essentially with the just disposal of proceedings having a foreign element. The jurisprudence is founded on the recognition that in proceedings having connections with more than one country an issue brought before a court in one country may be more appropriately decided by reference to the laws of another country even though those laws are different from the law of the forum court. The laws of the other country may have adopted solutions, or even basic principles, rejected by the law of the forum country. These differences do not in themselves furnish reason why the forum court should decline to apply the foreign law. On the contrary, the existence of differences is the very reason why it may be appropriate for the forum court to have recourse to the foreign law. If the laws of all countries were uniform there would be no 'conflict' of laws.

16. This, overwhelmingly, is the normal position. But, as noted by Scarman J in *In the Estate of Fuld, decd (No 3)* [1968] P 675, 698, blind adherence to foreign law can never be required of an English court. Exceptionally and rarely, a provision of foreign law will be disregarded when it would lead to a result wholly alien to fundamental requirements of justice as administered by an English court. A result of this character would not be acceptable to an English court. In the conventional phraseology, such a result would be contrary to public policy. Then the court will decline to enforce or recognise the foreign decree to whatever extent is required in the circumstances.

17. This public policy principle eludes more precise definition. Its flavour is

---

47 [2002] 2 A.C. 883.

captured by the much repeated words of Judge Cardozo that the court will exclude the foreign decree only when it 'would violate some fundamental principle of justice, some prevalent conception of good morals, some deep-rooted tradition of the common weal': see *Loucks v. Standard Oil Co of New York* (1918) 120 NE 198, 202

18. Despite its lack of precision, this exception to the normal rule is well established in English law. This imprecision, even vagueness, does not invalidate the principle. Indeed, a similar principle is a common feature of all systems of conflicts of laws. The leading example in this country, always cited in this context, is the 1941 decree of the National Socialist Government of Germany depriving Jewish émigrés of their German nationality and, consequentially, leading to the confiscation of their property. Surely Lord Cross of Chelsea was indubitably right when he said that a racially discriminatory and confiscatory law of this sort was so grave an infringement of human rights that the courts of this country ought to refuse to recognise it as a law at all: *Oppenheimer v. Cattermole* [1976] AC 249, 277–278. When deciding an issue by reference to foreign law, the courts of this country must have a residual power, to be exercised exceptionally and with the greatest circumspection, to disregard a provision in the foreign law when to do otherwise would affront basic principles of justice and fairness which the courts seek to apply in the administration of justice in this country. Gross infringements of human rights are one instance, and an important instance, of such a provision. But the principle cannot be confined to one particular category of unacceptable laws. That would be neither sensible nor logical. Laws may be fundamentally unacceptable for reasons other than human rights violations. (. . .) [see *infra*, p. 138].

Introductory Act to the German Civil Code

Article 6 *Public policy* (ordre public)

A provision of the law of another country shall not be applied where its application would lead to a result which is manifestly incompatible with the fundamental principles of German law. In particular, inapplicability ensues, if its application would be incompatible with fundamental rights.

Tunisian Code of Private International Law (1998)

Article 36 (para. 1)

The public policy exception may only be raised by the court if the provisions of the designated foreign law are contrary to the fundamental choices of the Tunisian legal system. (. . .)

Quebec Civil Code

Article 3081 The provisions of the law of a foreign State do not apply if their application would be manifestly inconsistent with public order as understood in international relations.

? NOTES

1 The term 'public policy' is misleading. It seems to refer to the policies underlying the rules of the forum. All rules, however, were laid down by a lawmaker to advance a (public) policy. The reason why foreign rules will be different is because foreign lawmakers seek to advance different policies. If foreign law could only be applied in cases where it would advance the same policy as the forum, this would mean that foreign law would only be applied where it would be the same as the law of the forum. In choice of law theory, public policy has been understood as being a very different and much narrower concept. That might explain why the English speaking world often qualifies the term by associating it with its French equivalent *ordre public*. In French, however, the term is equally misleading. French courts and scholars call it 'international public order' (*ordre public international*) to underscore that the concept is different from domestic concepts.

2 In the context of choice of law, public policy or *ordre public (international)* refers to a small number of core values and fundamental principles of the forum. The dictum of Cardozo J. in *Loucks* is widely accepted in the English speaking world. Foreign law should not only be different, it should 'violate some fundamental principle of justice, some prevalent conception of good morals, some deep-rooted tradition of the common weal'. Certain statutory provisions in the civil law world also insist that public policy is composed of the fundamental principles of the forum. How are these core values to be identified? It is for courts to do so on a case-by-case basis. However, in jurisdictions where a hierarchy of norms will exist, courts will logically use such hierarchy to identify domestic rules or values to be considered as the most important in the relevant jurisdiction. This is the reason why rights afforded by constitutional charters or bills of fundamental rights will often be used for the purpose of defining public policy, as Article 6 of the Introductory Act to the German Civil Code expressly provides. But public policy is not limited to human rights and may include any norm that the forum considers as essential, irrespective of its blessing by human right authorities.

3 *Loucks* dates back before the American Revolution on choice of law. In the context of governmental interest analysis, the public policy exception makes little sense, because the new American choice of law methodology is not substance neutral. Today, the relevance of *Loucks* and the public policy doctrine is limited to those U.S. states which still follow the traditional methodology.

 CASE

Supreme Court of Montana, March 7, 2000 *Phillips v. General Motors Corporation*[48]

74 Does Montana recognize a 'public policy' exception that would require application of Montana law even where Montana's choice of law rules dictate application of the laws of another state, and would such an exception apply in this case?

75 For choice of law purposes, the public policy of a state is simply the rules, as expressed in its legislative enactments and judicial decisions, that it uses to decide controversies. See *Casarotto*, 268 Mont. at 375; *see also Rothwell v. Allstate Ins. Co.*, 1999 MT 50, ¶ 24 (Gray, J., dissenting) ('It can—and should—be said that every statute duly enacted by the Legislature is an expression of public policy with

---

48 2000 MT 55. The first part of the judgment is reproduced *supra*, p. 47.

regard to its subject matter.'). The purpose of a choice of law rule is to resolve conflicts between competing policies. Considerations of public policy are expressly subsumed within the most significant relationship approach. *See* Restatement (Second) § 6(2)(b) and (c) (mandating consideration of the relevant policies of the forum state and other interested states). In order to determine which state has the more significant relationship, the public policies of all interested states must be considered. A 'public policy' exception to the most significant relationship test would be redundant.

4   Would a foreign law be contrary to public policy for the sole reason to it does not comport with international law?

 CASE

House of Lords, 16 May 2002 *Kuwait Airways Corporation v. Iraqi Airways Co. and others*[49]

Lord Nicholls of Birkenhead

1. On 2 August 1990 military forces of Iraq forcibly invaded and occupied Kuwait. They completed the occupation in the space of two or three days. The Revolutionary Command Council of Iraq then adopted resolutions proclaiming the sovereignty of Iraq over Kuwait and its annexation to Iraq. Kuwait was designated a 'governate' within Iraq.

2. When the Iraqi forces took over the airport at Kuwait they seized ten commercial aircraft belonging to Kuwait Airways Corporation (KAC): two Boeing 767s, three A300 Airbuses, and five A310 Airbuses. They lost no time in removing these aircraft to Iraq. By 9 August nine of the aircraft had been flown back to Basra, in Iraq. The tenth aircraft, undergoing repair at the time of the invasion, was flown direct to Baghdad a fortnight later. On 9 September the Revolutionary Command Council of Iraq adopted a resolution dissolving KAC and transferring all its property worldwide, including the ten aircraft, to the state-owned Iraqi Airways Co (IAC). This resolution, resolution 369, came into force upon publication in the official gazette on 17 September. On the same day IAC's board passed resolutions implementing RCC resolution 369.

3. On 11 January 1991 KAC commenced these proceedings against the Republic of Iraq and IAC, claiming the return of its ten aircraft or payment of their value, and damages. The aircraft were valued by KAC at US$630 million. The damages claimed at the trial exceeded $800 million. (. . .) [para. 15 to 18 are reproduced above, p. 135.]

---

49 [2002] 2 A.C. 883.

19. The question raised in the present proceedings is whether resolution 369 of the Revolutionary Command Council of Iraq is [contrary to public policy]. This decree was one of the RCC resolutions issued with a view to giving effect to the integration of Kuwait into Iraq following the invasion. It was part and parcel of the Iraqi seizure of Kuwait and its assets and the assimilation of these assets into the political, social and economic structure of Iraq.

20. That this seizure and assimilation were flagrant violations of rules of international law of fundamental importance is plain beyond argument. (. . .)

24. On behalf of IAC Mr Donaldson submitted that the public policy exception to the recognition of provisions of foreign law is limited to infringements of human rights. The allegation in the present action is breach of international law by Iraq. But breach of international law by a state is not, and should not be, a ground for refusing to recognise a foreign decree. An English court will not sit in judgment on the sovereign acts of a foreign government or state. It will not adjudicate upon the legality, validity or acceptability of such acts, either under domestic law or international law. For a court to do so would offend against the principle that the courts will not adjudicate upon the transactions of foreign sovereign states. This principle is not discretionary. It is inherent in the very nature of the judicial process: see *Buttes Gas and Oil Co v Hammer (No 3)* [1982] AC 888, 932. KAC's argument, this submission by IAC continued, invites the court to determine whether the invasion of Kuwait by Iraq, followed by the removal of the ten aircraft from Kuwait to Iraq and their transfer to IAC, was unlawful under international law. The courts below were wrong to accede to this invitation.

25. My Lords, this submission seeks to press the non-justiciability principle too far. (. . .)

28. The acceptability of a provision of foreign law must be judged by contemporary standards. Lord Wilberforce, in a different context, noted that conceptions of public policy should move with the times: see *Blathwayt v Baron Cawley* [1976] AC 397, 426. In *Oppenheimer v Cattermole* [1976] AC 249, 278, Lord Cross said that the courts of this country should give effect to clearly established rules of international law. This is increasingly true today. As nations become ever more interdependent, the need to recognise and adhere to standards of conduct set by international law becomes ever more important. RCC resolution 369 was not simply a governmental expropriation of property within its territory. Having forcibly invaded Kuwait, seized its assets, and taken KAC's aircraft from Kuwait to its own territory, Iraq adopted this decree as part of its attempt to extinguish every vestige of Kuwait's existence as a separate state. An expropriatory decree made in these circumstances and for this purpose is simply not acceptable today.

29. I have already noted that Iraq's invasion of Kuwait and seizure of its assets were a gross violation of established rules of international law of fundamental importance. A breach of international law of this seriousness is a matter of deep

concern to the world-wide community of nations. This is evidenced by the urgency with which the UN Security Council considered this incident and by its successive resolutions. Such a fundamental breach of international law can properly cause the courts of this country to say that, like the confiscatory decree of the Nazi government of Germany in 1941, a law depriving those whose property has been plundered of the ownership of their property in favour of the aggressor's own citizens will not be enforced or recognised in proceedings in this country. Enforcement or recognition of this law would be manifestly contrary to the public policy of English law. For good measure, enforcement or recognition would also be contrary to this country's obligations under the UN Charter. Further, it would sit uneasily with the almost universal condemnation of Iraq's behaviour and with the military action, in which this country participated, taken against Iraq to compel its withdrawal from Kuwait. International law, for its part, recognises that a national court may properly decline to give effect to legislative and other acts of foreign states which are in violation of international law: see the discussion in *Oppenheim's International Law*, 9th ed (1992), vol 1, (ed Jennings and Watts) pages 371–376, paragraph 113. (. . .)

What is relevant to determine whether international law defines the public policy of the forum: that it is binding on all states, including the forum and the foreign lawmaker, or the importance of the relevant rule that the foreign lawmaker violated?

5 Will China develop a different, more expansive, view of public policy?
Law of the People's Republic of China on the Laws Applicable to Foreign-Related Civil Relations (2010)
Article 5 Where the application of a foreign law will be prejudicial to the social and public interest of the PRC, the PRC law shall be applied.

6.2   Limiting the scope of the public policy exception

A fundamental assumption of the multilateral methodology is that choice of law should be neutral and that the applicable law should be identified without considering the substance of the potentially applicable laws. As a consequence, a number of limits have been put on the operation of the public policy exception in order to ensure that it would only be used only in those cases where it is absolutely necessary.

The first limit is that whether public policy is violated in a given case should not be assessed by examining the foreign *rule*, but rather the *result* to which its *application* would lead in the case at hand. The public policy exception does not call for an abstract evaluation of foreign law, but rather a concrete assessment of the outcome that the forum would reach in application of the foreign rule.

Belgian Code of Private International Law (2004)
Article 21. *Public policy exception* (para. 1)
The application of a provision of the foreign law designated by the present statute
is refused in so far as it would lead to a result that would be manifestly incompatible
with public policy. (. . .)

The second limit is that the finding that the application of one particular
rule of foreign law would be contrary to public policy should not lead to the
exclusion of foreign law generally, but only to the exclusion of that particular
rule. Other rules of foreign law should be applied.

Tunisian Code of Private International Law (1998)
Article 36 (para. 4 and 5)
Only the provisions of foreign law which are contrary to public policy in the
meaning of Tunisian private international law are disregarded.
The court applies provisions of Tunisian law instead of the provisions of foreign
law which were disregarded.

The third limit, which is found in certain civil law jurisdictions only, is that
the operation of the public policy of the forum should be limited to those
cases which are closely connected to the forum. By contrast, if all parties
involved are foreigners, refusing to apply their law on the ground that it is
incompatible with the values of the forum where the parties might all be
happy with the foreign rule and its underlying values could be considered as
judgmental.

Belgian Code of Private International Law (2004)
Article 21. *Public policy exception* (para. 2)
In determining this incompatibility, special consideration is given to the degree
in which the situation is connected with the Belgian legal order and to the significance of the consequences produced by the application of the foreign law. (. . .)

 CASE

French Cour de cassation, 6 July 1988 *Baaziz*[50]

Given the principles of French private international law and Article 29 of
the General Convention on social security concluded on 19 January 1965
between France and Algeria, applicable in the case;

---

50 Civ. 1ère, 6 July 1988, case no. 85-12743 (1989) Rev. Crit. DIP 70.

Whereas Mr. Rabah Baaziz and Miss Marinette Arthaud, both of French nationality, were married in Lyon August 9, 1954; after the accession of Algeria to independence, Mr Baaziz acquired Algerian nationality and contracted a second marriage in Algeria with Mrs Fethita M'djahri, in accordance with Algerian law; he died in France on 11 May 1978 in a work related accident; by judgment of 10 July 1980, which has become final, the court of appeal of Lyon ruled that the second marriage could only produce effect in France to the extent that it would not infringe the French conception of international public order and, similarly, Mrs. M'djahri could make use on the French territory of her status of widow of Mr Baaziz only insofar as it would not be contrary to public order; Whereas the judgment said, on the basis of Article 29 of the aforementioned Convention that the surviving spouse's pension due to the death of Mr. Rabah Baaziz must be split equally between Ms Arthaud and Ms M'djahri;

Whereas, however, that unless otherwise specified, international conventions reserve the application of the French conception of international public order; that this conception does not allow that a polygamous marriage contracted abroad by a man who is still married to a French woman produce effects against her; thus, in ruling as it did, the Court of Appeal violated the aforementioned principles and text;

For these reasons: the appeal is allowed and the judgment of the Court of appeal is set aside.

NOTES AND QUESTIONS

1 In a similar case involving two Algerian wives, the French supreme court had held a few years earlier that the second (polygamous) marriage contracted in Algeria could be recognized in France, and that both wives could therefore receive an equal share in the French estate of the deceased husband.[51] As both marriages had been celebrated in Algeria, and all parties were Algerian nationals, it did not appear as legitimate for a French court to apply French law and hold the second marriage invalid. Furthermore, the only issue was one of succession, and, while the foreign rule might have been shocking, the result of its application in a succession case was not highly controversial. Why does the court reach a different result in *Baaziz*?

2 The result of *Baaziz* is that French wives will be treated better by French courts than Algerian or Moroccan wives. The purpose of the rule is to ensure that the operation of French public policy is limited to cases closely connected to France. Still, is the ruling discriminatory? Subsequent judgments limiting the operation of French public policy in family law (parenthood) have identified two relevant connecting factors: nationality and residence.[52] Could you rephrase the rule in *Baaziz* in a more acceptable way?

---

51 Civ. 1ère, 3 January 1980, case no. 78-13762, *Bendeddouche v. Boumaza* (1980) Rev. Crit. DIP 331.
52 Civ. 1ère, 10 February 1993, case no. 89-21.997.

3 Some lawmakers have expressly rejected the proposition that the operation of public policy should depend on the connections between the dispute and the forum.

Tunisian Code of Private International Law (1998)

Article 36 (para. 3)

The public policy exception does not depend on the intensity of the connection between the Tunisian legal order and the dispute.

6.3 Limiting the consequences of the public policy exception

Finding that the application of a rule of foreign law would be contrary to the public policy of the forum has far reaching consequences. The law that the forum considered to be the most closely connected may not be applied. The dispute, however, must be decided. The vast majority of jurisdictions would thus apply the substantive law of the forum instead of the foreign law. This result, however, has been regarded as unsatisfactory by a number of lawmakers, as the law of the forum might not be closely connected to the dispute.

Reform of the Italian System of Private International Law (1995)

Article 16 *Public policy*

1. No foreign law shall be applied whose effects are incompatible with public policy (*ordre public*).

2. In that case, the applicable law shall be determined on the basis of other connecting factors possibly provided for with respect to the same matter. In the absence of other connecting factors, Italian law applies.

Belgian Code of Private International Law (2004)

Article 21. *Public policy exception* (para. 3)

If a provision of the foreign law is not applied because of this incompatibility, another relevant provision of that law or, if necessary, of Belgian law applies.

? **QUESTIONS**

1 Art. 16 of the Italian law mandates Italian courts to apply other connecting factors before resorting to Italian law? Which are these other factors? Why would it be a better solution than applying directly Italian law?

2 How does Art. 21 of the Belgian Code address the issue? What could be another 'relevant provision' of the foreign law?

Part II

Jurisdiction

3

General rules

Rules of international jurisdiction determine when a given court has the power to decide a dispute having a foreign element. They are distinct from choice of law rules, which are concerned with the rules that the competent court will apply to decide the dispute on the merits (*supra*, Part I). As we have seen, courts do not necessarily apply their own law. If two different courts were to have the same choice of law rules, whichever would be seized and retain jurisdiction would apply the same law to decide the dispute. But different courts could also have different choice of law rules; while being distinct from the choice of law rules, the rules of international jurisdiction of each court would indirectly impact the determination of the applicable law, as choice of law would depend indirectly on which court would retain jurisdiction.

While some scholars claim that public international law constrains States with respect to the international jurisdiction of their courts, States have always determined freely the international jurisdiction of their courts. Of course, they could not possibly determine the jurisdiction of a foreign court: this would be a clear infringement on the sovereignty of the foreign State. As a result, all rules of international jurisdiction are unilateral. States only determine the international jurisdiction of the courts which they have established, and never attempt to determine the jurisdiction of a foreign court.[1] If a court does not have jurisdiction under its own rules of international jurisdiction, it will simply decline jurisdiction, but it will neither direct the parties to another court, nor even indicate them which court is 'the right' one. It will be for the plaintiff to look for another court which would accept to retain jurisdiction.

---

1 They sometimes indirectly interfere in the jurisdiction of foreign courts by issuing anti-suit injunctions: see *infra*, Ch. 4.

1   Foundational assumptions

Private international law, in both its legislative and jurisdictional dimensions, was long essentially perceived as an exercise of state power. By retaining jurisdiction in a particular case, States are indeed exercising (adjudicatory) power over the litigants. As international cases are connected to more than one nation or State, States cared to exercise their power without infringing the sovereignty of a foreign State. For that purpose, various theories were crafted which offered a foundation for international jurisdiction in public law terms.[2]

The first was to insist on the personal bond existing between a ruler and its subjects. The origin of the theory lies in medieval Europe, where the lord had a personal and inescapable duty to render justice to his tenants. While societies evolved in Europe, the idea remained, and became that justice was a right afforded by a given State to its nationals. The French Civil Code only contains provisions granting jurisdiction to French courts for disputes involving at least one national,[3] and, until the 1950s, French courts would only entertain disputes involving a French national.

A second theory offered a justification for adjudicatory authority by focusing on the power that could be actually exercised on the parties. Since the concern was to exercise power on the parties without infringing on the sovereignty of other States, the theory posited that adjudicatory jurisdiction could be justified when physical power could be exercised on the defendant within the territory of the forum. The focus was on the defendant, because he was the one compelled to litigate in a court that he had not chosen. Such a power theory lead to the development of jurisdictional grounds relying on physical presence in the territory of the relevant State, whether habitual (domicile) or temporary. In the common law world generally and in England more specifically, the fundamental rule of international jurisdiction is that service of the document initiating the proceedings on the defendant within the jurisdiction of the court grants jurisdiction (tag or transient jurisdiction). As service on a party requires only a few moments, this means that, in principle, physical presence for a few moments in England (for instance in transit in an English airport) suffices to grant international jurisdiction to an English court.

A shift in paradigm occurred in the middle of the 20th century, first in the United States, and then in Europe. Instead of analyzing jurisdiction solely

---

2 See generally Arthur T. von Merhen, 'Adjudicatory Jurisdiction: General Theories Compared and Evaluated' (1983) 63 Boston U.L.R. 279.

3 See *infra*, 3.3.

through a public law lens, courts and scholars started to take into account the private interests of the parties.

1.1   Minimum contacts and appropriateness of jurisdiction

1.1.1   United States

The foundational assumption in the United States is that jurisdiction should be based on certain minimum contacts between the dispute and the forum. The purpose is to afford a fair treatment to the defendant, which is guaranteed by the Fourteenth Amendment to the U.S. Constitution (also known as the Due Process Clause). It is therefore a constitutional right of the defendant. It is his interest which has become the sole focus of the fairness theory that the U.S. Supreme Court has developed since 1945.

 CASE

U.S. Supreme Court, 14 January 2014 *Daimler A.G. v. Bauman*[4]

III

In *Pennoyer v. Neff*, 95 U.S. 714 (1878), decided shortly after the enactment of the Fourteenth Amendment, the Court held that a tribunal's jurisdiction over persons reaches no farther than the geographic bounds of the forum. See *id.*, at 720 ('The authority of every tribunal is necessarily restricted by the territorial limits of the State in which it is established.'). See also *Shaffer v. Heitner*, 433 U.S. 186, 197 (1977) (Under *Pennoyer*, 'any attempt "directly" to assert extraterritorial jurisdiction over persons or property would offend sister States and exceed the inherent limits of the State's power.'). In time, however, that strict territorial approach yielded to a less rigid understanding, spurred by 'changes in the technology of transportation and communication, and the tremendous growth of interstate business activity.' *Burnham v. Superior Court of Cal., County of Marin*, 495 U.S. 604, 617, (1990) (opinion of SCALIA, J.).

'The canonical opinion in this area remains *International Shoe*, in which we held that a State may authorize its courts to exercise personal jurisdiction over an out-of-state defendant if the defendant has "certain minimum contacts with [the State] such that the maintenance of the suit does not offend 'traditional notions of fair play and substantial justice.'" *Goodyear*, 564 U.S., at __. Following *International Shoe*, 'the relationship among the defendant, the

---

4   134 S.Ct. 746.

forum, and the litigation, rather than the mutually exclusive sovereignty of the States on which the rules of *Pennoyer* rest, became the central concern of the inquiry into personal jurisdiction.' *Shaffer*, at 204.

International Shoe's conception of 'fair play and substantial justice' presaged the development of two categories of personal jurisdiction. The first category is represented by *International Shoe* itself, a case in which the in-state activities of the corporate defendant 'ha[d] not only been continuous and systematic, but also gve rise to the liabilities sued on.' 326 U.S., at 317. *International Shoe* recognized, as well, that 'the commission of some single or occasional acts of the corporate agent in a state' may sometimes be enough to subject the corporation to jurisdiction in that State's tribunals with respect to suits relating to that in-state activity. *Id.*, at 318. Adjudicatory authority of this order, in which the suit 'aris[es] out of or relate[s] to the defendant's contacts with the forum,' *Helicopteros Nacionales de Colombia, S.A. v. Hall*, 466 U.S. 408, 414, n. 8 (1984), is today called 'specific jurisdiction.' See *Goodyear* (citing von Mehren & Trautman, Jurisdiction to Adjudicate: A Suggested Analysis, 79 Harv. L.Rev. 1121, 1144–1163 (1966) (hereinafter von Mehren & Trautman)).

International Shoe distinguished between, on the one hand, exercises of specific jurisdiction, as just described, and on the other, situations where a foreign corporation's 'continuous corporate operations within a state [are] so substantial and of such a nature as to justify suit against it on causes of action arising from dealings entirely distinct from those activities.' 326 U.S., at 318. As we have since explained, 'court may assert general jurisdiction over foreign (sister-state or foreign-country) corporations to hear any and all claims against them when their affiliations with the State are so 'continuous and systematic' as to render them essentially at home in the forum State.' *Goodyear*; see *Helicopteros*, at 414, n. 9. (. . .)

 CASE

U.S. Supreme Court, 27 June 2011 *J. McIntyre Machinery Ltd v. Nicastro*[5]

II

The Due Process Clause protects an individual's right to be deprived of life, liberty, or property only by the exercise of lawful power. Cf. *Giaccio v. Pennsylvania*, 382 U. S. 399, 403 (1966) (The Clause 'protect[s] a person

---

5 131 S.Ct. 2780.

against having the Government impose burdens upon him except in accordance with the valid laws of the land'). This is no less true with respect to
the power of a sovereign to resolve disputes through judicial process than
with respect to the power of a sovereign to prescribe rules of conduct for
those within its sphere. See *Steel Co. v. Citizens for Better Environment*, 523
U. S. 83, 94 (1998) ('Jurisdiction is power to declare the law'). As a general
rule, neither statute nor judicial decree may bind strangers to the State. Cf.
Burnham v. Superior Court of Cal., County of Marin, 495 U. S. 604, 608–609
(1990) (opinion of SCALIA, J.) (invoking 'the phrase *coram non judice*,
"before a person not a judge"—meaning, in effect, that the proceeding in
question was not a *judicial* proceeding because lawful judicial authority was
not present, and could therefore not yield a *judgment*')

A court may subject a defendant to judgment only when the defendant has
sufficient contacts with the sovereign 'such that the maintenance of the suit
does not offend "traditional notions of fair play and substantial justice."'
International Shoe Co. v. Washington, 326 U. S. 310, 316 (1945)). Freeform
notions of fundamental fairness divorced from traditional practice cannot
transform a judgment rendered in the absence of authority into law. As a
general rule, the sovereign's exercise of power requires some act by which
the defendant 'purposefully avails itself of the privilege of conducting activities within the forum State, thus invoking the benefits and protections of its
laws, '*Hanson*, 357 U. S., at 253, though in some cases, as with an intentional
tort, the defendant might well fall within the State's authority by reason of
his attempt to obstruct its laws. In products-liability cases like this one, it is
the defendant's purposeful availment that makes jurisdiction consistent with
'traditional notions of fair play and substantial justice.'

A person may submit to a State's authority in a number of ways. There is,
of course, explicit consent. *See, e.g., Insurance Corp. of Ireland v. Compagnie
des Bauxites de Guinee*, 456 U. S. 694, 703 (1982). Presence within a State at
the time suit commences through service of process is another example. See
Burnham. Citizenship or domicile—or, by analogy, incorporation or principal place of business for corporations—also indicates general submission to
a State's powers. *Goodyear Dunlop Tires Operations, S. A. v. Brown*, p. __. Each
of these examples reveals circumstances, or a course of conduct, from which
it is proper to infer an intention to benefit from and thus an intention to
submit to the laws of the forum State. Cf. *Burger King Corp. v. Rudzewicz*, 471
U. S. 462, 476 (1985). These examples support exercise of the general jurisdiction of the State's courts and allow the State to resolve both matters that
originate within the State and those based on activities and events elsewhere.
Helicopteros Nacionales de Colombia, S. A. v. Hall, 466 U. S. 408, and n. 9

(1984). By contrast, those who live or operate primarily outside a State have a due process right not to be subjected to judgment in its courts as a general matter.

There is also a more limited form of submission to a State's authority for disputes that 'arise out of or are connected with the activities within the state.' *International Shoe Co.*, at 319. Where a defendant 'purposefully avails itself of the privilege of conducting activities within the forum State, thus invoking the benefits and protections of its laws,' *Hanson*, at 253, it submits to the judicial power of an otherwise foreign sovereign to the extent that power is exercised in connection with the defendant's activities touching on the State. In other words, submission through contact with and activity directed at a sovereign may justify specific jurisdiction 'in a suit arising out of or related to the defendant's contacts with the forum.' *Helicopteros*, at 414, n. 8; see also *Goodyear*, at 2.

As most aspects of the conflict of laws, international jurisdiction is a matter governed by state law in the United States. It varies, therefore, from one state to the other. All states, however, are bound by the federal Constitution. The minimum contacts doctrine developed by the Supreme Court is based on the Due Process Clause of the federal Constitution. The doctrine only sets a constitutional limit beyond which states may not go. It does not, however, directly lay down precise rules of jurisdiction. The lawmaker of each state remains free to lay down any rule of international jurisdiction, as long as it comports with the constitutional requirement of the Due Process clause. In this case, Justice Ginsburg gave the two following examples:

> When industrial accidents happen, a long-arm statute in the State where the injury occurs generally permits assertion of jurisdiction, upon giving proper notice, over the foreign manufacturer. For example, the State's statute might provide, as does New York's long-arm statute, for the 'exercise [of] personal jurisdiction over any non-domiciliary . . . who . . . "commits a tortious act without the state causing injury to person or property within the state, . . . if he . . . expects or should reasonably expect the act to have consequences in the state and derives substantial revenue from interstate or international commerce".' N. Y. Civ. Prac. Law Ann. §302(a)(3)(ii) (West 2008).
> Or, the State might simply provide, as New Jersey does, for the exercise of jurisdiction 'consistent with due process of law.' N. J. Ct. Rule 4:4–4(b)(1) (2011).

Until 2011, the Supreme Court had laid down a test in two parts. The first was that there should be sufficient contacts between the forum and the defendant. The second was that the exercise of jurisdiction should be reasonable.

CASE

U.S. Supreme Court, 24 February 1987 *Asahi Metal Industry Co. v. Superior Court of Cal., Solano Cty*[6]

The strictures of the Due Process Clause forbid a state court to exercise personal jurisdiction over Asahi under circumstances that would offend 'traditional notions of fair play and substantial justice.' *International Shoe Co. v. Washington, 326 U.S. at 316, quoting Milliken v. Meyer, 311 U.S. at 463.*

We have previously explained that the determination of the reasonableness of the exercise of jurisdiction in each case will depend on an evaluation of several factors. A court must consider the burden on the defendant, the interests of the forum State, and the plaintiff's interest in obtaining relief. It must also weigh in its determination 'the interstate judicial system's interest in obtaining the most efficient resolution of controversies; and the shared interest of the several States in furthering fundamental substantive social policies.' *World-Wide Volkswagen, 444 U.S. at 292* (citations omitted).

A consideration of these factors in the present case clearly reveals the unreasonableness of the assertion of jurisdiction over Asahi, even apart from the question of the placement of goods in the stream of commerce.

Certainly the burden on the defendant in this case is severe. Asahi has been commanded by the Supreme Court of California not only to traverse the distance between Asahi's headquarters in Japan and the Superior Court of California in and for the County of Solano, but also to submit its dispute with Cheng Shin to a foreign nation's judicial system. The unique burdens placed upon one who must defend oneself in a foreign legal system should have significant weight in assessing the reasonableness of stretching the long arm of personal jurisdiction over national borders.

When minimum contacts have been established, often the interests of the plaintiff and the forum in the exercise of jurisdiction will justify even the serious burdens placed on the alien defendant. In the present case, however, the interests of the plaintiff and the forum in California's assertion of jurisdiction over Asahi are slight. All that remains is a claim for indemnification asserted by Cheng Shin, a Taiwanese corporation, against Asahi. The transaction on which the indemnification claim is based took place in Taiwan; Asahi's components were shipped from Japan to Taiwan. Cheng Shin has not

---

6 480 U.S. 102.

demonstrated that it is more convenient for it to litigate its indemnification claim against Asahi in California, rather than in Taiwan or Japan.

Because the plaintiff is not a California resident, California's legitimate interests in the dispute have considerably diminished. The Supreme Court of California argued that the State had an interest in 'protecting its consumers by ensuring that foreign manufacturers comply with the state's safety standards.' 39 Cal.3d at 49. The State Supreme Court's definition of California's interest, however, was overly broad. The dispute between Cheng Shin and Asahi is primarily about indemnification, rather than safety standards. Moreover, it is not at all clear at this point that California law should govern the question whether a Japanese corporation should indemnify a Taiwanese corporation on the basis of a sale made in Taiwan and a shipment of goods from Japan to Taiwan. *Phillips Petroleum Co. v. Shutts*, 472 U.S. 797, 821–822 (1985); *Allstate Insurance Co. v. Hague*, 449 U.S. 302, 312–313 (1981). The possibility of being haled into a California court as a result of an accident involving Asahi's components undoubtedly creates an additional deterrent to the manufacture of unsafe components; however, similar pressures will be placed on Asahi by the purchasers of its components as long as those who use Asahi components in their final products, and sell those products in California, are subject to the application of California tort law.

World-Wide Volkswagen also admonished courts to take into consideration the interests of the 'several States,' in addition to the forum State, in the efficient judicial resolution of the dispute and the advancement of substantive policies. In the present case, this advice calls for a court to consider the procedural and substantive policies of other *nations* whose interests are affected by the assertion of jurisdiction by the California court. The procedural and substantive interests of other nations in a state court's assertion of jurisdiction over an alien defendant will differ from case to case. In every case, however, those interests, as well as the Federal Government's interest in its foreign relations policies, will be best served by a careful inquiry into the reasonableness of the assertion of jurisdiction in the particular case, and an unwillingness to find the serious burdens on an alien defendant outweighed by minimal interests on the part of the plaintiff or the forum State. 'Great care and reserve should be exercised when extending our notions of personal jurisdiction into the international field.' *United States v. First National City Bank*, 379 U.S. 378, 404 (1965) (Harlan, J., dissenting).

Considering the international context, the heavy burden on the alien defendant, and the slight interests of the plaintiff and the forum State, the exercise of personal jurisdiction by a California court over Asahi in this instance would be unreasonable and unfair.

In *J. McIntyre Machinery Ltd v. Nicastro*, none of the justices referred to the second prong of the test, that is, reasonableness. U.S. scholars wonder whether it remains, or whether the test focuses today on minimum contacts only. Some courts continue to evaluate the reasonableness of their jurisdiction separately.[7]

1.1.2 European Union

The foundational assumption in the European Union is also that jurisdictional rules should be based on a close connection existing between the dispute and the forum. While the 'close connection' requirement could appear as similar to the U.S. 'minimum contacts' requirement, it has a different purpose. The interest of the defendant is only part of the equation.

European Regulation (EU) No 1215/2012 of 12 December 2012 on jurisdiction and on the enforcement and recognition of judgments in civil and commercial matters (Brussels Ibis)

PREAMBLE

(15) The rules of jurisdiction should be highly predictable and founded on the principle that jurisdiction is generally based on the defendant's domicile. Jurisdiction should always be available on this ground save in a few well-defined situations in which the subject-matter of the dispute or the autonomy of the parties warrants a different connecting factor. The domicile of a legal person must be defined autonomously so as to make the common rules more transparent and avoid conflicts of jurisdiction.

(16) In addition to the defendant's domicile, there should be alternative grounds of jurisdiction based on a close connection between the court and the action or in order to facilitate the sound administration of justice. The existence of a close connection should ensure legal certainty and avoid the possibility of the defendant being sued in a court of a Member State which he could not reasonably have foreseen. This is important, particularly in disputes concerning non-contractual obligations arising out of violations of privacy and rights relating to personality, including defamation.

CHAPTER II JURISDICTION

Section 1 General provisions
Article 4

---

7 For an example, see *infra* Ch. 8.

1. Subject to this Regulation, persons domiciled in a Member State shall, whatever their nationality, be sued in the courts of that Member State.

2. Persons who are not nationals of the Member State in which they are domiciled shall be governed by the rules of jurisdiction applicable to nationals of that Member State.

Article 5

1. Persons domiciled in a Member State may be sued in the courts of another Member State only by virtue of the rules set out in Sections 2 to 7 of this Chapter.

(...)

Article 6

1. If the defendant is not domiciled in a Member State, the jurisdiction of the courts of each Member State shall, subject to Article 18(1), Article 21(2) and Articles 24 and 25, be determined by the law of that Member State.

(...)

SECTION 2 Special jurisdiction

Article 7

A person domiciled in a Member State may be sued in another Member State:

(1) (a) in matters relating to a contract, in the courts for the place of performance of the obligation in question;

(b) for the purpose of this provision and unless otherwise agreed, the place of performance of the obligation in question shall be:

— in the case of the sale of goods, the place in a Member State where, under the contract, the goods were delivered or should have been delivered,

— in the case of the provision of services, the place in a Member State where, under the contract, the services were provided or should have been provided;

(c) if point (b) does not apply then point (a) applies;

(2) in matters relating to tort, delict or quasi-delict, in the courts for the place where the harmful event occurred or may occur;

(...)

The Brussels Ibis Regulation is a European piece of legislation which attempts to unify the law of international jurisdiction of the Member States of the European Union. It therefore lays down precise rules which the Member States must apply.[8]

The European lawmaker, however, has essentially unified the law of international jurisdiction in intra-European disputes. The principle is that the

---

8 The Lugano Convention of 30 October 2007, which was drafted on the model of the 2001 Brussels I Regulation, contains similar rules which apply in Switzerland, Norway and Iceland.

Brussels Ibis Regulation (and Lugano Convention) only applies to cases where the defendant is domiciled within a Member State of the European Union (see Art. 5(1)). It does not apply to proceedings initiated in the court of a Member State against a defendant domiciled in a third State: the national rules of the relevant Member State apply then (Art. 6(1)).[9]

1.1.3   Commonwealth

The members of the British Commonwealth largely follow English traditional rules. So does England (and Wales) where the European Union law of jurisdiction does not apply.

 CASE

House of Lords, 11 November 1919 *Johnson v. Taylor Brothers and Co Ltd*[10]

Lord Dunedin:

I think it is legitimate to begin by considering the genesis of the rule. I understand that jurisdiction according to English law is based on the act of personal service and that if this is effected the English law does not feel bound by the Roman maxim Actor sequitur forum rei. It is far otherwise in other systems where service is in no sense a foundation of jurisdiction but merely a sine qua non before effective action is allowed. Now service being the foundation of jurisdiction, it follows that that service naturally and normally would be service within the jurisdiction. But there is an exception to this normal rule and that is service out of the jurisdiction. This, however, is not allowed as a right but is granted in the discretion of the judge as a privilege, and the rule in question here prescribes the limits within which that discretion should be exercised. The spirit of the rule I take to be that when what the plaintiff wishes really to complain of is the non-performance of something which the defendant ought to have performed within the jurisdiction according to the proper interpretation of the contract, he should be allowed to try that question here, notwithstanding that there might be some other acts which the defendant ought to have performed abroad. It seems to me to follow that there must be substance in the breach.

---

9 Art. 6(1) provides for a few exceptions, which include rules of exclusive jurisdiction (*infra*, 2) and choice of court agreements (*infra*, Ch. 5).
10 [1918–1919] All E.R. Rep. Ext. 1210.

> Lord Lindley said in the case of *Rein v Stein* ([1892] 1 Q B 753; 66 L T 469), quoting with approval an earlier dictum of Cotton, LJ, that you must look at the whole circumstances to determine whether the contract was one that ought, according to the terms thereof, to be performed within the jurisdiction. In like manner I think we must look at the circumstances to see what is the breach alleged, and whether that breach is substantial.

? **NOTES**

1 The traditional English rule is that the foundation of personal jurisdiction is service of process. Jurisdiction exists where there can be lawful service of process. By contrast, in the civil law tradition, jurisdiction and service of process are typically examined separately, lawful service being a condition for the admissibility of the claim rather than the jurisdiction of the court.

2 All persons present within the jurisdiction of an English or commonwealth court may be served. The origin of the rule lies in the territorial theory of jurisdiction whereby persons present within the jurisdiction owed at least partial allegiance to the king. As a result, service is available as of right against them, and, if effected lawfully on them, entails jurisdiction. English courts, therefore, essentially have jurisdiction over defendants who could be served in England. The only exceptions are actions related to foreign land and to rights registered in a foreign State (*infra*, 2).

3 In a system where service is coextensive with jurisdiction, it was necessary to allow service outside of the jurisdiction to extend the jurisdiction of courts to cases where the defendant was not present within the jurisdiction. This was done by legislation in England and in a number of Commonwealth countries (Australia, Canada, Singapore, Nigeria, Ghana, and so on . . .).

English Practice Direction 6B Service Out of the Jurisdiction

Service out of the jurisdiction where permission is required

3.1 The claimant may serve a claim form out of the jurisdiction with the permission of the court under rule 6.36 where –

General Grounds

(1) A claim is made for a remedy against a person domiciled within the jurisdiction.

(. . .)

Claims in relation to contracts

(6) A claim is made in respect of a contract where the contract –

(a)   was made within the jurisdiction;

(b)   was made by or through an agent trading or residing within the jurisdiction;

(c)   is governed by English law; or

(d)   contains a term to the effect that the court shall have jurisdiction to determine any claim in respect of the contract.

(7) A claim is made in respect of a breach of contract committed within the jurisdiction.

(8) A claim is made for a declaration that no contract exists where, if the contract was found to exist, it would comply with the conditions set out in paragraph (6).

Claims in tort

(9) A claim is made in tort where –

(a)   damage was sustained, or will be sustained, within the jurisdiction; or

(b)   damage which has been or will be sustained results from an act committed, or likely to be committed, within the jurisdiction.

(...)

QUESTION

How do the grounds for serving out of the jurisdiction compare with the jurisdictional grounds under Art. 7 (1) and (2) of the Brussels Ibis Regulation?

Service outside of the jurisdiction is essentially regarded as exorbitant by Commonwealth lawyers, because it has appeared to them that it might infringe the sovereignty of foreign States. It is therefore subject to stringent conditions.

CASE

Judicial Committee of the Privy Council, 10 March 2011
AK Investment CJSC v. Kyrgyz Mobil Tel Ltd & Ors (Isle of Man) (Rev 1)[11]

Lord Collins:

71. On an application for permission to serve a foreign defendant (including an additional defendant to counterclaim) out of the jurisdiction, the claimant (or counterclaimant) has to satisfy three requirements: *Seaconsar Far East Ltd. v. Bank Markazi Jomhouri Islami Iran* [1994] 1 AC 438, 453–457. First, the claimant must satisfy the court that in relation to the foreign defendant there is a serious issue to be tried on the merits, i.e. a substantial question of fact or law, or both. The current practice in England is that this is the same test as for summary judgment, namely whether there is a real (as opposed to a fanciful) prospect of success: e.g., *Carvill America Inc v. Camperdown UK Ltd* [2005] EWCA Civ 645, at [24]. Second, the claimant must satisfy the court that there is a good arguable case that the claim falls within one or more classes of case in which permission to serve out may be given. In this context 'good arguable case' connotes that one side has a much better argument than the other: see *Canada Trust Co v. Stolzenberg (No 2)* [1998] 1 WLR 547, 555–7 per Waller LJ, affd [2002] 1 AC 1; *Bols Distilleries BV v. Superior Yacht Services* [2006] UKPC 45, [26]-[28]. Third, the claimant must satisfy the court

---

11 [2011] UKPC 7.

that in all the circumstances the Isle of Man [*the forum*] is clearly or distinctly the appropriate forum for the trial of the dispute, and that in all the circumstances the court ought to exercise its discretion to permit service of the proceedings out of the jurisdiction.

 CASE

U.K. Supreme Court, 6 February 2013 *VTB Capital Plc v. Nutritek International Corp & Ors (Rev 1)*[12]

Lord Mance:

12. The *locus classicus* in relation to issues of appropriate forum at common law is *Spiliada Maritime Corpn v. Cansulex Ltd* [1987] AC 460, where Lord Goff of Chieveley gave the leading speech. He identified as the underlying aim in all cases of disputed forum, 'to identify the forum in which the case can be suitably tried for the interests of all the parties and for the ends of justice'. But he also identified the important distinction in the starting point and onus of proof between cases where permission is required to serve proceedings out of the jurisdiction and situations where service is possible without permission. The present case falls into the former category. In cases within that category, permission was not to be granted under the former rules of court 'unless it shall be made sufficiently to appear to the court that the case is a proper one for service out' (RSC Ord 11, r 4(2)), and, as Lord Goff noted, the jurisdiction being exercised 'may be "exorbitant"'. On this basis, Lord Goff concluded that:

> The effect is, not merely that the burden of proof rests on the plaintiff to persuade the court that England is the appropriate forum for the trial of the action, but that he has to show that this is clearly so.

13. Lord Goff went on to explain that caution was necessary in respect of the word 'exorbitant' – caution that explains his statement that the jurisdiction to serve out 'may' be exorbitant. He noted that the circumstances in which permission to serve out may be granted:

> are of great variety, ranging from cases where, one would have thought, the discretion would normally be exercised in favour of granting leave (e.g., where the relief sought is an injunction ordering the defendant to do or refrain from doing something within the jurisdiction) to cases where the grant of leave is far more problematical. In addition, the importance to be attached to any particular ground invoked by the plaintiff may vary from case to case. For example, the fact that English law

---

12 [2013] UKSC 5.

is the putative proper law of the contract may be of very great importance . . .; or it may be of little importance as seen in the context of the whole case. In these circumstances, it is, in my judgment, necessary to include both the residence or place of business of the defendant and the relevant ground invoked by the plaintiff as factors to be considered by the court when deciding whether to exercise its discretion to grant leave; but, in so doing, the court should give to such factors the weight which, in all the circumstances of the case, it considers to be appropriate.

The modern rules reflect more precisely Lord Goff's statement of general principle, in providing that permission is not to be given unless the court is 'satisfied that England and Wales is the proper place in which to bring the claim': CPR, rule 6.37(3).

? NOTES

1   The first requirement for service out of the jurisdiction is procedural: the plaintiff should apply for leave to do so. The application is made *ex parte* (that is, unilaterally, in the defendant's absence), but the plaintiff must demonstrate that the applicable requirements are satisfied. In certain cases, legislation may expressly authorize service outside the jurisdiction without the need to apply for permission. This is rare in England, but it has become the rule in certain Commonwealth countries, such as (common law) Canada and some Australian states.

2   The different Commonwealth countries follow to varying extents the requirements listed by Lord Collins. Many Australian and Canadian jurisdictions have abandoned the requirement that there be a serious issue to be tried and thus focus on the two other requirements. The third requirement that the forum be the proper place in which to bring the claim is also applied differently in jurisdictions which have adopted a different doctrine of *forum non conveniens*, such as Australia.

3   The third requirement for service outside of the jurisdiction is that the forum should be the proper place in which to bring the action. The requirement is construed as meaning that the forum should be clearly the most appropriate forum for the trial of the dispute. For the purpose of making such assessment, the forum should take into account a variety of factors which include not only the geographical connections of the dispute with the forum, but also practical considerations such as the availability of the evidence and the costs of the trial (the test is the same as under the doctrine of *forum non conveniens*: see *infra*, Ch. 4). The fairness of the jurisdiction of Commonwealth courts is thus tested in each case involving serving outside of the jurisdiction. Contrary to other models, it is not limited to the existence of a close connection between the forum and the dispute, but incorporates a number of other variables.

1.2   A special focus on product liability cases

> *Ronald Brand, Access-to-Justice Analysis on a Due Process Platform*[13]
> The major difference between the United States and other countries (particularly civil law countries) on jurisdictional analysis comes in how courts conceptualize jurisdiction itself.

---

13 (2012) 112 Columbia L.R. Sidebar 76, 78–9.

In the United States, the jurisdictional question has been, since *Pennoyer v. Neff* in 1877, a constitutional matter based on the right of a defendant to 'due process of law' in any question involving life, liberty, or property (i.e., any question that arises in litigation). Thus, the analysis of jurisdiction depends on the due process rights of the defendant, and requires a three-way nexus among the court, the defendant, and the claim.

In civil law countries, questions of jurisdiction are not so much questions of a defendant's rights as they are questions of what court is 'competent' to hear the case. Thus, for example, the rules of special jurisdiction found in the Brussels I Regulation of the European Union rely on a two-way nexus between the court and the claim. The resulting rules allow jurisdiction that would be held to violate due process in the United States.

The result of this distinction between the United States and the rest of the world is that the United States focuses on the due process rights of the defendant, while the rest of the world focuses on access to justice—the plaintiffs right to have his or her day in court. The former is a clear defendant-protection approach, and the latter is a clear plaintiff-protection approach. The difference is fundamental (. . .)

Does the difference between the concept of jurisdiction in the U.S. and in the civil law world produce different results? Let us compare U.S. and civil law rules of international jurisdiction in product liability cases.

Please read the following case and identify the courts where victims of defective products may initiate proceedings in the European Union.

 CASE

European Court of Justice, 16 July 2009 *Zuid-Chemie BV v. Philippo's Mineralenfabriek NV/SA*, Case C-189/08[14]

The dispute in the main proceedings and the questions referred for a preliminary ruling

6 Zuid-Chemie is an undertaking manufacturing fertiliser which, in July 2000, purchased two consignments of a product called 'micromix' from HCI Chemicals Benelux BV ('HCI'), an undertaking established in Rotterdam (Netherlands).

7 HCI, which is itself unable to manufacture micromix, ordered it from Philippo's and provided the latter with all the raw materials – except for one – necessary for

---

14 ECLI:EU:C:2009:475, [2009] E.C.R. I-06917.

the manufacture of that product. In consultation with HCI, Philippo's purchased the outstanding raw material, namely zinc sulphate, from G.J. de Poorter, trading under the name Poortershaven, in Rotterdam.

8 Philippo's manufactured the micromix in its factory in Belgium, to which Zuid-Chemie came to take delivery of that product.

9 Zuid-Chemie processed the micromix in its factory in the Netherlands in order to produce various consignments of fertiliser. It sold and dispatched a number of those consignments to its customers.

10 It subsequently transpired that the cadmium content of the zinc sulphate purchased from Poortershaven was too high, with the result that the fertiliser was rendered unusable or of limited utility. Zuid-Chemie claims that this has caused it to suffer loss.

11 On 17 January 2003, Zuid-Chemie instituted proceedings against Philippo's before the Rechtbank (Local Court) Middleburg (Netherlands) in which it sought a declaration that Philippo's was liable for the damage which Zuid-Chemie had sustained and an order requiring that undertaking to pay it various sums in respect of the loss which it claimed to have suffered, in addition to payment of compensation plus interest and costs. (. . .)

The questions referred for a preliminary ruling

The first question

16 By its first question, the referring court seeks essentially to ascertain whether Article 5(3) [*now Art. 7(2)*][15] of Regulation No 44/2001 must be interpreted as meaning that, in the context of a dispute such as that in the main proceedings, the words 'place where the harmful event occurred' designate the place where the defective product was delivered to the purchaser or whether they refer to the place where the initial damage occurred following normal use of the product for the purpose for which it was intended. (. . .)

20 Thus, it is necessary to bear in mind that the Court has already held, when interpreting Article 5(3) of the Brussels Convention, that the system of common rules of conferment of jurisdiction laid down in Title II of that convention is based on the general rule, set out in the first paragraph of Article 2, that persons domiciled in a Contracting State are to be sued in the courts of that State, irrespective of the nationality of the parties (Case C-168/02 *Kronhofer* [2004] ECR I-6009, paragraph 12).

21 It is only by way of derogation from that fundamental principle attributing jurisdiction to the courts of the defendant's domicile that Section 2 of Title II of the Brussels Convention makes provision for certain special jurisdictional

---

15 See text *supra* 1.1.2.

rules, such as that laid down in Article 5(3) of the Convention (*Kronhofer*, paragraph 13).

22 The Court has also held that those rules of special jurisdiction must be interpreted restrictively and cannot give rise to an interpretation going beyond the cases expressly envisaged by that convention (see Case 189/87 *Kalfelis* [1988] ECR 5565, paragraph 19; . . .).

23 Nevertheless, it is settled case-law that, where the place in which the event which may give rise to liability in tort, delict or quasi-delict occurs and the place where that event results in damage are not identical, the expression 'place where the harmful event occurred' in Article 5(3) of the Brussels Convention must be understood as being intended to cover both the place where the damage occurred and the place of the event giving rise to it, so that the defendant may be sued, at the option of the claimant, in the courts for either of those places (see, inter alia, Case 21/76 Bier ('*Mines de potasse d'Alsace*') [1976] ECR 1735, paragraphs 24 and 25; . . .).

24 In that connection, the Court has stated that the rule of special jurisdiction laid down in Article 5(3) of the Brussels Convention is based on the existence of a particularly close connecting factor between the dispute and the courts of the place where the harmful event occurred, which justifies the attribution of jurisdiction to those courts for reasons relating to the sound administration of justice and the efficacious conduct of proceedings (see to that effect, inter alia, *Mines de Potasse d'Alsace*, paragraph 11; . . .). The courts for the place where the harmful event occurred are usually the most appropriate for deciding the case, in particular on the grounds of proximity and ease of taking evidence (see *Henkel*, paragraph 46).

25 Although it is common ground between the parties to the main proceedings, as stated in paragraph 13 of the present judgment, that Essen is the place of the event giving rise to the damage ('Handlungsort'), they disagree as regards the determination of the place where the damage occurred ('Erfolgsort').

26 The place where the damage occurred is, according to the case-law cited in paragraph 23 of the present judgment, the place where the event which may give rise to liability in tort, delict or quasi-delict resulted in damage.

27 The place where the damage occurred must not, however, be confused with the place where the event which damaged the product itself occurred, the latter being the place of the event giving rise to the damage. By contrast, the 'place where the damage occurred' (see *Mines de potasse d'Alsace*, paragraph 15, and *Shevill and Others*, paragraph 21) is the place where the event which gave rise to the damage produces its harmful effects, that is to say, the place where the damage caused by the defective product actually manifests itself.

28 It must be recalled that the case-law distinguishes clearly between the damage and the event which is the cause of that damage, stating, in that connection, that liability in tort, delict or quasi-delict can arise only on condition that a causal

connection can be established between those two elements (see *Mines de potasse d'Alsace*, paragraph 16).

29 Regard being had to the foregoing, the place where the damage occurred cannot be any other than Zuid-Chemie's factory in the Netherlands where the micromix, which is the defective product, was processed into fertiliser, causing substantial damage to that fertiliser which was suffered by Zuid-Chemie and which went beyond the damage to the micromix itself.

30 It must also be observed that the choice of the Netherlands courts which is thereby available to Zuid-Chemie makes it possible, in particular for the reasons laid down in paragraph 24 of the present judgment, for the court which is most appropriate to deal with the case and, therefore, enables the rule of special jurisdiction laid down in Article 5(3) of Regulation No 44/2001 to have practical effect.

31 In that connection, it is worth pointing out that the Court has held, by its interpretation of Article 5(3) of the Brussels Convention to the effect that that provision covers not only the place of the event giving rise to the damage, but also the place where the damage occurred, and that to decide in favour only of the place of the event giving rise to the damage would, in a significant number of cases, cause confusion between the heads of jurisdiction laid down by Articles 2 and 5(3) of that convention, with the result that the latter provision would, to that extent, lose its effectiveness (see *Mines de potasse d'Alsace*, paragraphs 15 and 20, . . .). Such a consideration relating to confusion between the heads of jurisdiction is likely to apply in the same way with regard to the failure to take account, where appropriate, of a place where damage occurred which differs from the place of the event which gave rise to that damage.

32 It follows from the foregoing that Article 5(3) of Regulation No 44/2001 must be interpreted as meaning that, in the context of a dispute such as that in the main proceedings, the words 'place where the harmful event occurred' designate the place where the initial damage occurred as a result of the normal use of the product for the purpose for which it was intended.

? NOTES AND QUESTIONS

1 The Court has always insisted that only the initial damage is relevant for the purpose of Art. 5(3). In *Dumez*,[16] the European Court of Justice held that the court of the place where secondary victims suffered from damage as a consequence of the damage suffered by the primary victim does not have jurisdiction under Art. 5(3). In *Marinari*, it further held that the place of the damage 'does not, on proper interpretation, cover the place where the victim claims to have suffered financial damage following upon initial damage arising and suffered by him in another Contracting State'.[17]

---

16 Case C-220/88 *Dumez France v. Hessische Landesbank* ECLI:EU:C:1990:8, [1990] E.C.R. I-00049.
17 Case C-364/93 *Marinari v. Lloyds Bank* ECLI:EU:C:1995:289, [1995] E.C.R. I-02719.

2 In *Kainz v. Pantherwerke*, the European Court of Justice held that 'in the case where a manufacturer faces a claim of liability for a defective product, the place of the event giving rise to the damage is the place where the product in question was manufactured'.[18] Does *Kainz* contradict or complement *Zuid-Chemie*?

3 In the European Union, which of the following courts have jurisdiction in a product liability case: the court of the place where the product was sold to the end purchaser? The court of the place where the product caused damage? The court of the place where the product was manufactured? The court of the domicile of the manufacturer? Why?

4 The E.U. law of jurisdiction only applies where the defendant is domiciled in a Member State (see Brussels Ibis Reg., Art. 6, *supra* 1.1.2). If the defendant, i.e. the manufacturer, is domiciled in a third State, for instance in the United States, the courts of the Member States apply their national rules of jurisdiction. They include exorbitant rules of jurisdiction (*infra*, 3).

Are the rules in Japan different?

Japanese Code of Civil Procedure

Article 3–3

The actions set out in each sub-paragraph below may be filed with the courts of Japan in the circumstances described in each of them.

(viii) An action relating to a tort: in the circumstances where the tort occurred in Japan (except where the result of a harmful act committed abroad has occurred in Japan and the occurrence of that result in Japan would have been normally unforeseeable).

 NOTES AND QUESTIONS

1 Article 3–3 was introduced by a 2011 statute which largely codified rules laid down by Japanese courts. According to a Japanese scholar, 'in the cases where the place of a harmful act and the place of the result of the act differ, it is sufficient if either the act or the result took place in Japan except in the case mentioned in the bracket'.[19]

2 What is the impact of the unforeseeable damage exclusion in the context of product liability cases?

Now read this American case and identify the courts where victims of defective products may initiate proceedings in the United States.

---

18 Case C-45/13 *A. Kainz v. Pantherwerke AG* ECLI:EU:C:2014:7.
19 Koji Takahashi, *Japan's New Act on International Jurisdiction* (Smashwords 2011).

CASE

U.S. Supreme Court, 27 June 2011 *J. McIntyre Machinery Ltd v. Nicastro*[20]

Justice Kennedy announced the judgment of the Court and delivered an opinion, in which *the Chief Justice, Justice Scalia*, and *Justice Thomas* join.

I

This case arises from a products-liability suit filed in New Jersey state court. Robert Nicastro seriously injured his hand while using a metal-shearing machine manufactured by J. McIntyre Machinery, Ltd. (J. McIntyre). The accident occurred in New Jersey, but the machine was manufactured in England, where J. McIntyre is incorporated and operates. The question here is whether the New Jersey courts have jurisdiction over J. McIntyre, notwithstanding the fact that the company at no time either marketed goods in the State or shipped them there. (...)

II

See excerpts above at p. 150.

III

In this case, petitioner directed marketing and sales efforts at the United States. (...) Here the question concerns the authority of a New Jersey state court to exercise jurisdiction, so it is petitioner's purposeful contacts with New Jersey, not with the United States, that alone are relevant.

Respondent has not established that J. McIntyre engaged in conduct purposefully directed at New Jersey. Recall that respondent's claim of jurisdiction centers on three facts: The distributor agreed to sell J. McIntyre's machines in the United States; J. McIntyre officials attended trade shows in several States but not in New Jersey; and up to four machines ended up in New Jersey. The British manufacturer had no office in New Jersey; it neither paid taxes nor owned property there; and it neither advertised in, nor sent any employees to, the State. Indeed, after discovery the trial court found that the 'defendant does not have a single contact with New Jersey short of the machine in question ending up in this state.' These facts may reveal an intent to serve the U. S. market, but they do not show that J. McIntyre purposefully availed itself of the New Jersey market.

---

20 131 S.Ct. 2780.

It is notable that the New Jersey Supreme Court appears to agree, for it could 'not find that J. McIntyre had a presence or minimum contacts in this State– in any jurisprudential sense–that would justify a New Jersey court to exercise jurisdiction in this case.' The court nonetheless held that petitioner could be sued in New Jersey based on a 'stream-of-commerce theory of jurisdiction.' As discussed, however, the stream-of-commerce metaphor cannot supersede either the mandate of the Due Process Clause or the limits on judicial author- ity that Clause ensures. The New Jersey Supreme Court also cited 'significant policy reasons' to justify its holding, including the State's 'strong interest in protecting its citizens from defective products.' That interest is doubtless strong, but the Constitution commands restraint before discarding liberty in the name of expediency.

***

Due process protects petitioner's right to be subject only to lawful authority. At no time did petitioner engage in any activities in New Jersey that reveal an intent to invoke or benefit from the protection of its laws. New Jersey is without power to adjudge the rights and liabilities of J. McIntyre, and its exercise of jurisdiction would violate due process.

Justice Breyer, with whom *Justice Alito* joins, concurring in the judgment.

In asserting jurisdiction over the British Manufacturer, the Supreme Court of New Jersey relied most heavily on three primary facts as providing constitutionally sufficient 'contacts' with New Jersey, thereby making it fundamentally fair to hale the British Manufacturer before its courts: (1) The American Distributor on one occasion sold and shipped one machine to a New Jersey customer, namely, Mr. Nicastro's employer, Mr. Curcio; (2) the British Manufacturer permitted, indeed wanted, its independent American Distributor to sell its machines to anyone in America willing to buy them; and (3) representatives of the British Manufacturer attended trade shows in 'such cities as Chicago, Las Vegas, New Orleans, Orlando, San Diego, and San Francisco.' In my view, these facts do not provide contacts between the British firm and the State of New Jersey constitutionally sufficient to support New Jersey's assertion of jurisdiction in this case.

None of our precedents finds that a single isolated sale, even if accompanied by the kind of sales effort indicated here, is sufficient. Rather, this Court's previous holdings suggest the contrary. The Court has held that a single sale to a customer who takes an accident-causing product to a different State (where the accident takes place) is not a sufficient basis for asserting jurisdiction. See *World-Wide Volkswagen Corp. v. Woodson*, 444 U. S. 286 (1980). And the Court, in separate opinions, has strongly suggested that a single sale of a product in a State does not constitute an adequate basis for asserting jurisdiction over an out-of-state defendant, even if that defendant places his goods in the stream of commerce, fully aware (and hoping) that such a sale will take place. See *Asahi Metal Industry Co. v. Superior Court of Cal., Solano Cty.*, 480 U. S. 102, 111, 112 (1987) (opinion of O'Connor, J.) (requiring 'something more' than simply placing 'a product into the stream of commerce,' even if defendant is 'awar[e]' that the stream 'may or will sweep the product into the forum State'); *id.*, at 117 (Brennan, J., concurring in part and concurring in judgment) (jurisdiction should lie where a sale in a State is part of 'the regular and anticipated flow' of commerce into the State, but not where that sale is only an 'edd[y],' *i.e.*, an isolated occurrence); *id.*, at 122 (Stevens, J., concurring in part and concurring in judgment) (indicating that 'the volume, the value, and the hazardous character' of a good may affect the jurisdictional inquiry and emphasizing Asahi's 'regular course of dealing').

Here, the relevant facts found by the New Jersey Supreme Court show no 'regular . . . flow' or 'regular course' of sales in New Jersey; and there is no 'something more,' such as special state-related design, advertising, advice, marketing, or anything else. Mr. Nicastro, who here bears the burden of proving jurisdiction, has shown no specific effort by the British Manufacturer to sell in New Jersey. He has introduced no list of potential New Jersey customers who might, for example, have regularly attended trade shows. And he has not otherwise shown that the British Manufacturer 'purposefully avail[ed] itself of the privilege of conducting activities' within New Jersey, or that it delivered its goods in the stream of commerce 'with the expectation that they will be purchased' by New Jersey users. *World-Wide Volkswagen*, *supra*, at 297–298 (internal quotation marks omitted).

There may well have been other facts that Mr. Nicastro could have demonstrated in support of jurisdiction. And the dissent considers some of those facts. See *post*, at 3 (opinion of *Ginsburg, J.*) (describing the size and scope of New Jersey's scrap-metal business). But the plaintiff bears the burden of establishing jurisdiction, and here I would take the facts precisely as the New Jersey Supreme Court stated them. (. . .)

Accordingly, on the record present here, resolving this case requires no more than adhering to our precedents.

NOTES AND QUESTIONS

1 This case and these two opinions are concerned with the specific jurisdiction of U.S. and American courts. American courts may also have general jurisdiction in tort cases. Is this the case here?

2 In *Nicastro*, only three justices supported the opinion for the court. This means that, while a majority supported the outcome, no majority could be found with respect to the reasons explaining it. As a consequence, many U.S. scholars consider that the Supreme Court failed to clarify the law of personal jurisdiction in general, and the law of specific jurisdiction in particular.

3 The Supreme Court held that New Jersey courts did not have jurisdiction. Would the courts of other U.S. states have jurisdiction?

4 In this case, the constitutional protection afforded by the Due Process Clause benefits an English corporation. In the European Union, by contrast, exorbitant heads of jurisdiction only apply against defendants from third States.

5 Foreign manufacturers may be worried that selling products on the U.S. market creates the risk to be sued in the United States and to be subjected to the peculiarities of its tort law: jury trial, contingency fees, punitive damages, class actions. After *Nicastro*, what is the risk?

Finally, how would a court following traditional English rules on service out of the jurisdiction decide similar cases? The following case is not a product liability case, but a personal injury case. Read it and wonder how an English court would have decided *Nicastro* if the manufacturer had been American and the accident had occurred in England?

 CASE

English High Court of Justice, 19 December 2013 *Pike & Doyle v. The Indian Hotels Company Ltd*[21]

Mr Justice Stewart:

1 On 26 November 2008 the Taj Mahal Palace, Mumbai, India was the subject of a terrorist attack. On that night the Claimants were British guests at the hotel. They had just spent 15 days backpacking around Goa and, as a treat, the 2nd Claimant had booked a one night stay before they were due to fly home from Mumbai. Shortly after the attack began the Claimants returned to their room, locked the door and turned off the lights. Some hours later they tried to escape through the window. Their room was on the third floor of the tower part of the hotel. They tied together sheets, curtains and towels to make a rope. They hung it outside their room and the First Claimant went first. The 'rope' came apart and he fell to the ground suffering serious spinal injuries which have left him paraplegic. The Second

---

21 [2013] EWHC 4096 (QB).

Claimant was rescued subsequently. She did not suffer physical injuries but claims for continuing psychiatric consequences.

2 The Defendants are the company which operate the hotel. They are an Indian company. (. . .)

The Issues for Determination

5 There are three main issues for determination. These are:

- (i) Does the English Court have jurisdiction to hear the Claimants' claim in accordance with CPR 6.36, 6.37 and Practice Direction 6B? (. . .)
- (iii) Are the English Courts the forum conveniens for this claim?

Jurisdiction

6 The relevant provisions of the Civil Procedural Rules provide:

In any proceedings to which rule 6.32 or 6.33 does not apply, the Claimant may serve a claim form out of the jurisdiction with the permission of the court if any of the grounds set out in paragraph 3.1 of Practice Direction 6B apply.

(1) An application for permission under rule 6.36 must set out –

(a) which ground in paragraph 3.1 of Practice Direction 6B is relied on;

(b) that the claimant believes that the claim has a reasonable prospect of success; and

(c) the defendant's address or, if not known, in what place the defendant is, or is likely, to be found.

. . .

(3) The court will not give permission unless satisfied that England and Wales is the proper place in which to bring the claim.

Practice Direction 6B provides:

3.1 The claimant may serve a claim form out of the jurisdiction with the permission of the court under rule 6.36 where –

. . . .

(9) A claim is made in tort where:

(a) damage was sustained within the jurisdiction; or

(b) the damage sustained resulted from an act committed within the jurisdiction.

7 In respect of the first issue there are two questions to be answered:

- (i) Can the Claimants satisfy the Court that in relation to the Defendants there is a serious issue to be tried on the merits?
- (ii) Can the Claimants satisfy the Court that there is a good arguable case that the Claimant falls within paragraph 3.1(9)(a) of Practice Direction 6B? A 'good arguable case' means that one side has a much better argument than the other.

The Defendants concede for the purposes of this hearing that the Claimants satisfy the first test, namely a serious issue is to be tried on the merits. Thus the only question for the court to determine is the second one.

8 The First Claimant suffers continuing pain and loss of amenity and substantial economic losses caused by his injuries. The Second Claimant sustained loss of earnings in England and Wales and has a continuing loss in the form of counselling. On that basis both Claimants have suffered indirect or secondary damage as a result of the Defendants alleged negligence in Mumbai. The Claimants' submission is that this is sufficient to found jurisdiction. The Defendants challenge this.

9 The question as to whether indirect or secondary damage is sufficient to give jurisdiction to the English and Welsh courts is by no means tabula rasa so far as the present type of case is concerned. Indeed four High Court decisions have all answered in the affirmative. (. . .)

14 The High Court cases have determined that the ordinary natural meaning of 'damage' includes physical and economic damage. (. . .).

16 (. . .) As Haddon-Cave J said in Wink at paragraph 33 'there are no limiting words in sub paragraph (a) which would justify such a narrow meaning and exclude indirect damage. The word "damage" is not modified or trammelled in any way. The ordinary and natural meaning of the word "damage". . .is any damage flowing from the Tort. In the words of Teare J at paragraph [37] in Booth, "damage" in this context means any "physical or economic" harm, ie. direct or indirect.'

(. . .)

Are the English Courts the Forum Conveniens for this Claim?

30 The relevant rule is CPR 6.37(3) which provides: 'The court will not give permission unless satisfied that England and Wales is the proper place in which to bring the claim.'

31 The leading authority is *Spiliada Maritime Corporation v. Cansulex Limited* [1987] 1A.C. 460. The Claimants concede that the '*natural forum*' ie. that with which the action had the most real and substantial connection is India. In those circumstances the court 'will ordinarily grant a stay unless there are circumstances' by reason of which justice requires that a stay should nevertheless not be granted. In this enquiry, the court will consider all the circumstances of the case, including circumstances which go beyond those taken into account when

considering connecting factors with other jurisdictions. One such factor can be the fact, if established objectively by cogent evidence, that the Plaintiff will not obtain justice in the foreign jurisdiction. . .on this enquiry the burden of proof shifts to the Plaintiff. Lord Goff in *Spiliada* at 477G-478 E.

32 I should cite a further passage from Lord Goff's speech in *Spiliada*. He said:

> A second, and more fundamental, point of distinction. . .is that in the Order 11 cases the plaintiff is seeking to persuade the court to exercise its discretionary power to permit service on the defendant outside the jurisdiction. Statutory authority has specified the particular circumstances in which that power *may be* exercised, but leaves it to the court to decide whether to exercise its discretionary power in a particular case, while providing that leave shall not be granted 'unless it shall be made sufficiently to appear to the court that the case is a proper one for service out of the jurisdiction' (see R.S.C., Ord. 11, r.4(2)).

Third, it is at this point that special regard must be had for the fact stressed by Lord Diplock in the Amin Rasheed case . . . the jurisdiction exercised under Order 11 may be 'exorbitant'. (. . .)

36 The applicable law, whether the case is tried in England or in India will be Indian law. The Indian and English law contain similar rules on substantive law of negligence. Nevertheless the Defendants make the following points:

- (i) Breach of duty would have to be tested against local standards. (. . .)
- Thus the English courts will have to determine the case by reference to the Indian standards. I regard this as a matter of some, but not a very strong, significance which I need to weigh in the balance. English courts are well used to determining such cases.
- (ii) There is not so much personal injury litigation brought in the Mumbai High Court. The gist of the expert evidence was that English law is more developed in the Tort of negligence. The present case requires a court to scrutinise the duty of an occupier to visitors injured by acts of war/terrorism perpetrated by third parties.

Neither Indian expert professed to be able to deal with this point in detail. It is right to say that there is some risk that an English court will be required to determine what the law of India would be to cover the Claimants' claim against the Defendants, in circumstances where there is no clear authority in the Indian courts. However, I can put it no higher than that. Again this is a factor which I take into account but I do not give it a great deal of weight.

37 I must consider on the one hand the practicalities of a trial in India for the Claimants and the Claimants' witnesses and on the other the practicalities for the Defendants and the Defendant's witnesses.

38 As far as the First Claimant is concerned, he is now paraplegic and suffers from

ongoing problems managing his bowels and bladder. It would be extremely difficult for him to travel to and stay in India, apart from the obvious psychological difficulties in returning to Mumbai. The last point also is of relevance for the Second Claimant. If the claim was heard in England, both could attend a trial with relatively little difficulty. They both attended the three day hearing of the present application.

39 As to the Defendants' witnesses, it is correct that the majority of them are likely to be Indian residents. The Defendants submit that many will have no passports and would require visas to come to England. The witness evidence served by the Defendants shows that travel to England for trial would be onerous for many of them. The Defendants do not know how many witnesses they would wish to call. However, they suggested, upon questioning from me, perhaps 10 to 20 staff with evidence from other hotels, local police and security services in addition. I accept that the Defendants may wish some central witnesses to give evidence live in England. To a substantial extent, a number of witnesses could give evidence by video link (there is approximately a six hour time difference I am told). Also (a) some evidence of witnesses might be given on commission (b) there is a real possibility that evidence as to what happened during the attack may not be contested. It has already been exhaustively investigated in the criminal trial of the attacker who was captured and in a (non adversarial) enquiry carried out by the State. (. . .)

41 I now turn to a major contention between the parties, namely delay in the Bombay High Court. I shall subsequently consider the further effect of appeals and the possible effect of expedition. The first matter is an estimation of the time it will take for a first instance (what in Mumbai is called 'original jurisdiction') case would take to come to trial, absent expedition.

42 I was told by Mr Block QC, in his final submission, that the Defendants undertake to cooperate to move proceedings along as quickly as possible if the case takes place in Mumbai. For example they would support expedition. Whilst no doubt a worthy and sincere expression, I am not persuaded that this would have a significant effect on the timetable of a case in Mumbai.

43 It was not disputed that until recently the situation illustrated in the Indian statistics applied to the Bombay High Court. Indeed the Bombay High Court historically has been in about the third worst position so far as delay in the Indian courts is concerned. (. . .)

58 In summary, my estimation is that the time this case would take to reach the probable end stage in India is some 20 years ie. about 15 years in High Court plus 5 years on first appeal. There is the possibility of an appeal to the Supreme Court delaying the claim for another 3–4 years and of interlocutory appeals from the original jurisdiction adding to that total period. There is also the possibility that reform will reduce the time span. Overall, I remain with the bracket of 15 to 20 years.

59 Mr Havers QC estimation of the likely procedure in England is that there would be a split trial within 2 to 3 years. The court would then have power, if the Claimants succeeded, to award substantial interim payments pending the hearing of (or agreement in respect of) quantum issues. (. . .)

62 Finally I turn to the issue of funding. (. . .)

64 (. . .) The Claimants assert that they cannot fund this case in India. The Indian experts agree that public funding, conditional and contingency fee arrangements are absent in India and there is no funding available for the costs of experts in India. In England the Claimants have the benefit of conditional fee agreements and after the event insurance, all entered into before the 1 April 2013. This is a significant benefit to any Claimant. The Claimants will be able therefore to litigate their claims in England.

65 There is no doubt that, in order to run the litigation properly, the Claimants need experienced lawyers and reliance on expert evidence, not just on quantum but also on liability. It would be impossible for them to litigate without expert evidence and almost impossible for them to litigate without experienced lawyers.

66 The evidence tends to show that trial costs of litigating in India would be in the region of £200,000–£300,000. Given the number of witnesses, it is perhaps more likely that the top end of that bracket would be applicable. In addition, if the Claimants succeeded, there would almost certainly be an appeal which would require further costs. Also there would be the Claimants' costs of travel/accommodation in India. (. . .)

Conclusion on the Third Issue

70 I have reviewed the factors which I consider to be relevant to my decision. I have made findings of fact and referred to the leading authorities. I remind myself of the caution which the court must exercise having regard to Lord Goff's speech in Spiliada at pages 480–481 and particularly that the burden of proof rests on the Claimants to persuade the court that England is the appropriate forum for the trial of the action and they have to show that this is clearly so.

71 I have come to the conclusion that there are, in this case, circumstances by reason of which justice requires that a stay should not be granted. I am persuaded that it is clearly the case that England is the appropriate forum for the trial of this action. I have had regard to the interests of all the parties and the ends of justice. I have taken into account the fact that there are factors in favour of a trial in India, including that Indian law is the applicable law, that the breach of duty has to be tested against local standards in India and the fact that there will be certain evidential difficulties for the Defendants if the case proceeds in England. I have noted and taken account of the fact that the Defendants have sought to smooth the path of the Claimants bringing proceedings in India by (i)

stating that they will not raise any limitation defence in any proceedings brought in India, (ii) offering the undertaking to pay the Claimants' reasonable costs if they succeed in India and (iii) expressing a willingness to cooperate in trying to move the proceedings in India along as quickly as possible. (. . .) Nevertheless, in the balancing exercise I come down firmly in favour of the Claimants because, in my judgment, the Claimants have clearly demonstrated and proved that granting a stay in English proceedings and requiring proceedings to be commenced in India would amount to a denial of justice. If proceedings are commenced in India then the delay which I have found would result cannot possibly be said to be proper access to justice. This factor alone I regard as sufficient. However it is given extra force by my finding that the Claimants will not even get that far because of their inability to litigate in India through lack of funding. In short, the reality is that their claims would come to a juddering halt if the stay was granted. Even if that were not so, they would be pending for some 15 to 20 further years in the Bombay High Court. I exercise my discretion in their favour for those reasons.

? QUESTIONS

1 If the victims of the bombings had been American citizens and residents, would an American court have jurisdiction?

2 If the bombings had occurred in a French hotel and the victims had been Luxembourg citizens and residents, would a Luxembourg court have jurisdiction?

2 Exclusive jurisdiction

In the modern paradigm of minimum contacts/proximity, it is perfectly acceptable that the courts of several States have jurisdiction over a given dispute in cases which are connected to several States. It follows that, if the court of a foreign State is closely connected to the dispute, the forum would typically recognize its judgment even though it would also have had jurisdiction over the same dispute (*infra*, Ch. 6).

Yet, in certain areas of the law, States consider that their courts have exclusive jurisdiction and that they should be the only ones to decide the dispute. Of course, they could not force foreign courts to decline jurisdiction, but they would deny recognition to any foreign judgment rendered in such circumstances. In any case, States often agree on the areas of the law where the courts of one single State should have exclusive jurisdiction, and there is typically no need to sanction foreign States for unacceptable exercise of jurisdiction.

What could be the reason why a private dispute, despite being international and connected to several States, would belong only to one and be out of reach of the jurisdiction of all other courts?[22]

2.1 Immoveable property

Real property disputes are certainly the oldest and most widely shared instance of exclusive jurisdiction. It seems to be universally accepted that the courts of the place of a given immoveable (land, homes) should have exclusive jurisdiction over any dispute related to such property. As a consequence, even if all parties are domiciled in another State, any issue relating to the property should be litigated locally.

Why? Read the two following excerpts and identify the rationale put forward by each court.

 CASE

House of Lords, 8 September 1893 *British South Africa Co v. Companhia de Mocambique*[23]

Lord Herschell L.C.:

My Lords, the principal question raised by this appeal is whether the Supreme Court of Judicature has jurisdiction to try an action to recover damages for a trespass to lands situate in a foreign country. (...)

The distinction between matters which are transitory or personal and those which are local in their nature, and the refusal to exercise jurisdiction as regards the latter where they occur outside territorial limits, is not confined to the jurisprudence of this country. Story, in his work on the Conflict of Laws (s. 551), after stating that by the Roman law a suit might in many cases be brought, either where property was situate or where the party sued had his domicil, proceeds to say that 'even in countries acknowledging the Roman law it has become a very general principle that suits in rem should be brought where the property is situate; and this principle is applied with almost universal approbation in regard to immovable property. The same rule is applied to mixed actions, and to all suits which touch the realty.'

---

22 Disputes involving States, by contrast, may typically only be litigated in one forum, as States enjoy sovereign immunities which prevent the courts of any other State from exercising adjudicatory jurisdiction over them. These immunities from jurisdiction, however, are typically limited to cases where the relevant State acted as a Sovereign, as opposed to cases where it acted as a private person (e.g., commercial activities).
23 [1893] A.C. 602.

In section 553, Story quotes the following language of Vattel: 'The defendant's judge' (that is, the competent judge) says he, 'is the judge of the place where the defendant has his settled abode, or the judge of the place where the defendant is when any sudden difficulty arises, provided it does not relate to an estate in land, or to a right annexed to such an estate. In such a case, as property of this kind is to be held according to the laws of the country where it is situated, and as the right of granting it is vested in the ruler of the country, controversies relating to such property can only be decided in the state in which it depends.' He adds, in the next section:

> It will be perceived that in many respects the doctrine here laid down coincides with that of the common law. It has been already stated that by the common law personal actions, being transitory, may be brought in any place where the party defendant can be found; that real actions must be brought in the forum rei sitæ; and that mixed actions are properly referable to the same jurisdiction. Among the latter are actions for trespasses and injuries to real property which are deemed local; so that they will not lie elsewhere than in the place rei sitæ. (. . .)

The question what jurisdiction can be exercised by the Courts of any country according to its municipal law cannot, I think, be conclusively determined by a reference to principles of international law. No nation can execute its judgments, whether against persons or movables or real property, in the country of another. On the other hand, if the Courts of a country were to claim, as against a person resident there, jurisdiction to adjudicate upon the title to land in a foreign country, and to enforce its adjudication in personam, it is by no means certain that any rule of international law would be violated. But in considering what jurisdiction our Courts possess, and have claimed to exercise in relation to matters arising out of the country, the principles which have found general acceptance amongst civilised nations as defining the limits of jurisdiction are of great weight. (. . .)

 CASE

U.S. Supreme Court, 24 June 1977 *Shaffer v. Heitner*[24]

The case for applying to jurisdiction in rem the same test of 'fair play and substantial justice' as governs assertions of jurisdiction in personam is simple and straightforward. It is premised on recognition that '(t)he phrase, "judicial jurisdiction over a thing", is a customary elliptical way of referring to

---

24 433 U.S. 186.

jurisdiction over the interests of persons in a thing.' Restatement (Second) of Conflict of Laws s 56, Introductory Note (1971) (hereafter Restatement). This recognition leads to the conclusion that in order to justify an exercise of jurisdiction in rem, the basis for jurisdiction must be sufficient to justify exercising 'jurisdiction over the interests of persons in a thing.' The standard for determining whether an exercise of jurisdiction over the interests of persons is consistent with the Due Process Clause is the minimum-contacts standard elucidated in *International Shoe*.

This argument, of course, does not ignore the fact that the presence of property in a State may bear on the existence of jurisdiction by providing contacts among the forum State, the defendant, and the litigation. For example, when claims to the property itself are the source of the underlying controversy between the plaintiff and the defendant, it would be unusual for the State where the property is located not to have jurisdiction. In such cases, the defendant's claim to property located in the State would normally indicate that he expected to benefit from the State's protection of his interest. The State's strong interests in assuring the marketability of property within its borders and in providing a procedure for peaceful resolution of disputes about the possession of that property would also support jurisdiction, as would the likelihood that important records and witnesses will be found in the State. The presence of property may also favor jurisdiction in cases such as suits for injury suffered on the land of an absentee owner, where the defendant's ownership of the property is conceded but the cause of action is otherwise related to rights and duties growing out of that ownership.

It appears, therefore, that jurisdiction over many types of actions which now are or might be brought in rem would not be affected by a holding that any assertion of state-court jurisdiction must satisfy the *International Shoe* standard. For the type of quasi in rem action typified by *Harris v. Balk* and the present case, however, accepting the proposed analysis would result in significant change. (. . .)[25]

? QUESTION

Disputes related to real property are private disputes. Do they, however, involve the public interest? Is the rationale for the exclusive jurisdiction of the local court simply that States consider that land is an essential dimension of their sovereignty, and that it should therefore only be regulated by local courts?

---

25 See below p. 185 for the part of the opinion discussing quasi-in rem jurisdiction.

Article 24 of the Brussels Ibis Regulation (*infra*, 2.2) also provides for the exclusive jurisdiction of the court of the place of the immoveable property. How does the European Court of Justice explain it?

 CASE

European Court of Justice 15 January 1985 *Rösler v. Rottwinkel* (Case C-241/83)[26]

19. The raison d'être of the exclusive jurisdiction conferred by Article 16(1) [*now Art. 24(1)*] on the courts of the Contracting State in which the property is situated is the fact that tenancies are closely bound up with the law of immovable property and with the provisions, generally of a mandatory character, governing its use, such as legislation controlling the level of rents and protecting the rights of tenants, including tenant farmers.

20. Article 16(1) seeks to ensure a rational allocation of jurisdiction by opting for a solution whereby the court having jurisdiction is determined on the basis of its proximity to the property since that court is in a better position to obtain first-hand knowledge of the facts relating to the creation of tenancies and to the performance of the terms thereof.

21. The question submitted by the Bundesgerichtshof is designed to ascertain whether exceptions may be made to the general rule laid down in Article 16 owing to the special character of certain tenancies, such as short-term lettings of holiday homes, even though the wording of that Article provides no indication in that respect.

22. It must be emphasized in this regard that, as the Italian government has rightly pointed out, inherent in any exception to the general rule laid down in Article 16(1) is the risk of further extensions which might call in question the application of national legislation governing the use of immovable property.

23. Account must also be taken of the uncertainty which would be created if the courts allowed exceptions to be made to the general rule laid down in Article 16(1), which has the advantage of providing for a clear and certain attribution of jurisdiction covering all circumstances, thus fulfilling the purpose of the Convention, which is to assign jurisdiction in a certain and predictable way.

24. It follows that the provision in question applies to all tenancies of immovable property irrespective of their special characteristics.

25. The reply to the first question must therefore be that Article 16(1) of the Convention applies to all lettings of immovable property, even for a short term and even where they relate only to the use and occupation of a holiday home.

---

26 ECLI:EU:C:1985:6.

? **QUESTIONS**

1   The Court insists that the law relating to immovable property is 'generally of a mandatory character'. Are there mandatory rules also in family law? In contract law?

2   Disputes relating to immovable property can involve legislation aiming at protecting tenants. Is it enough of a reason to create an exclusive head of jurisdiction? Jurisdiction over employment contracts is not exclusive under the Brussels Ibis Regulation. Furthermore, disputes relating to real property can also arise out of sales of lands or homes. Should they fall out of the scope of Art. 24(1)?

3   Is the reasoning of the Court based on the proximity principle? If all the parties are domiciled in another Member State, which court would be the most closely connected to the dispute? Article 16(1) of the Brussels Convention was eventually amended to allow parties to short term rental contract to litigate in the State of their common domicile: see below Art. 24(1) of the Brussels Ibis Regulation.

2.2   Public registers

Below is the statutory basis of cases of exclusive jurisdiction in Japan and in the European Union. Can you identify the rationale(s) for their inclusion in the list?

Japanese Code of Civil Procedure

Article 3–5 *Exclusivity of Jurisdiction*

(1) Actions provided in Chapter II (except those provided in Sections 4 and 6) of Part VII of the Companies Act, actions provided in Section 2 of Chapter VI of the Act on General Incorporated Associations and General Incorporated Foundations (Act No. 48 of 2006) and analogous actions relating to associations or foundations incorporated under other Japanese legislation shall be subject to the exclusive jurisdiction of the Japanese courts.

(2) An action with respect to registration shall be subject to the exclusive jurisdiction of the Japanese courts if the place of registration is located in Japan.

(3) An action with respect to the existence and effect of an intellectual property right (*viz.* the right as defined by Article 2(2) of the Basic Act of Intellectual Property (Act No. 122 of 2002)) which comes into existence by registration shall be subject to the exclusive jurisdiction of the Japanese courts if the registration was effected in Japan.

Article 3–10 *Exclusion of Application in the Case of Exclusive Jurisdiction*

The provisions contained in Article 3–2 to Article 3–4 and those contained in Article 3–6 to the preceding Article shall have no application where, with respect to the action in question, the exclusive jurisdiction of the Japanese courts is pre-scribed by legislation.

Jurisdiction over actions relating to real property is not exclusive in Japan. It falls within the scope of Art. 3–3(xi). However, actions relating to the registration of immoveable property fall within the scope of Art. 3–5(2).[27] Can you explain this distinction?

Brussels Ibis Regulation (2012)

Section 6 Exclusive jurisdiction

Article 24

The following courts of a Member State shall have exclusive jurisdiction, regardless of the domicile of the parties:

(1) in proceedings which have as their object rights *in rem* in immovable property or tenancies of immovable property, the courts of the Member State in which the property is situated.

However, in proceedings which have as their object tenancies of immovable property concluded for temporary private use for a maximum period of six consecutive months, the courts of the Member State in which the defendant is domiciled shall also have jurisdiction, provided that the tenant is a natural person and that the landlord and the tenant are domiciled in the same Member State;

(2) in proceedings which have as their object the validity of the constitution, the nullity or the dissolution of companies or other legal persons or associations of natural or legal persons, or the validity of the decisions of their organs, the courts of the Member State in which the company, legal person or association has its seat. In order to determine that seat, the court shall apply its rules of private international law;

(3) in proceedings which have as their object the validity of entries in public registers, the courts of the Member State in which the register is kept;

(4) in proceedings concerned with the registration or validity of patents, trade marks, designs, or other similar rights required to be deposited or registered, irrespective of whether the issue is raised by way of an action or as a defence, the courts of the Member State in which the deposit or registration has been applied for, has taken place or is under the terms of an instrument of the Union or an international convention deemed to have taken place.

Without prejudice to the jurisdiction of the European Patent Office under the Convention on the Grant of European Patents, signed at Munich on 5 October 1973, the courts of each Member State shall have exclusive jurisdiction in proceedings concerned with the registration or validity of any European patent granted for that Member State;

(5) in proceedings concerned with the enforcement of judgments, the courts of the Member State in which the judgment has been or is to be enforced.

---

27 See Koji Takahashi, *Japan's New Act on International Jurisdiction* (Smashwords 2011).

1 Is there a common rationale for the Japanese heads of exclusive jurisdiction and Art 24(2) to (4)?

2 Article 24(5) is concerned with enforcement of judgments. It may involve use for force (for instance for attaching and ultimately selling land). There is no doubt that, under public international law, States have exclusive jurisdiction to use force within their territory.

3 Contrary to the general principle that jurisdictional rules of the Brussels Ibis Regulation only apply where the defendant has its domicile in the European Union, Art. 24 applies irrespective of the domicile of the parties. It suffices that the relevant criterion (place of the immoveable, place of the enforcement) be within the European Union.

3 Exorbitant jurisdiction

Modern theories of jurisdiction require that a close connection, or relationship, exist between the dispute and the forum (European Union), or the defendant, the dispute and the forum (United States). The logical result has been to condemn jurisdictional rules based on weak connecting factors. Such rules could be found in the laws of most States. They were often very old, as they had been crafted in times where jurisdiction was conceptualized differently (allegiance, power theories).

When they unified their rules of jurisdiction in 1968, the Member States of the European Union decided to establish a 'black' list of such national rules of jurisdiction existing in the Member States which should not be used in intra-European litigation.

Brussels Ibis Regulation (2012)

Section 1 General provisions

Article 5

1. Persons domiciled in a Member State may be sued in the courts of another Member State only by virtue of the rules set out in Sections 2 to 7 of this Chapter.

2. In particular, the rules of national jurisdiction of which the Member States are to notify the Commission pursuant to point (a) of Article 76(1) shall not be applicable as against the persons referred to in paragraph 1.

Article 6

1. If the defendant is not domiciled in a Member State, the jurisdiction of the courts of each Member State shall, subject to Article 18(1), Article 21(2) and Articles 24 and 25, be determined by the law of that Member State.

2. As against such a defendant, any person domiciled in a Member State may, whatever his nationality, avail himself in that Member State of the rules of jurisdiction there in force, and in particular those of which the Member States are to notify the

Commission pursuant to point (a) of Article 76(1), in the same way as nationals of that Member State.

Rules of jurisdiction referred to in Article 5(2) and Article 6(2)

The rules of jurisdiction referred to in Article 5(2) and Article 6(2) are the following:

- in Germany: Article 23 of the Code of Civil Procedure (*Zivilprozessordnung*),
- in France: Articles 14 and 15 of the Civil Code (Code civil),
- in Ireland: the rules which enable jurisdiction to be founded on the document instituting the proceedings having been served on the defendant during his temporary presence in Ireland,
- in Italy: Articles 3 and 4 of Act 218 of 31 May 1995,
- in Luxembourg: Articles 14 and 15 of the Civil Code (Code civil),
- in the United Kingdom: rules which enable jurisdiction to be founded on:
- (a) the document instituting the proceedings having been served on the defendant during his temporary presence in the United Kingdom; or
- (b) the presence within the United Kingdom of property belonging to the defendant; or
- (c) the seizure by the plaintiff of property situated in the United Kingdom.

(. . .)

? NOTES AND QUESTIONS

1 What is the use of this list? Article 5(1) provides that all national jurisdictional rules are inapplicable when the European Regulation applies, and Art. 5(2) repeats it for the rules appearing in the list, which are all national rules and are thus inapplicable in any case.

2 A possible purpose of the establishment of such a list of inadmissible exorbitant rules of jurisdiction could have been to extend the scope of the prohibition to relations with third States. But Art. 6(1) provides that the Regulation does not apply in such a case, and that all national rules do, including exorbitant rules appearing on the list. This means that the Member States have decided to improve the fairness of jurisdictional rules for European based defendants, but not for defendants based outside of Europe. By contrast, American courts afford the protection of the Due Process clause to all defendants, irrespective of their origin, and American scholars can thus legitimately regret that European law discriminates against them[28] (and all other defendants based in third States). Indeed, Art. 6(2) extends the scope of certain exorbitant rules of jurisdiction. Should States unilaterally disarm and abandon their exorbitant rules of jurisdiction? Or should they instead only do it on a reciprocal basis?

Despite the wide understanding that exorbitant heads of jurisdiction are unfair, many States have kept theirs. One reason is that they essentially benefit their own citizens, and thus offer them protection by allowing them

---

28 See, e.g., Friedrich Juenger, 'La Convention de Bruxelles du 27 septembre 1968 et la courtoisie internationale – Réflexions d'un américain' (1983) 72 Rev. Crit. DIP 37.

to sue in their own courts. Another reason is that abandoning them unilaterally can be perceived as limiting the incentives of other States to enter into reciprocal agreements to that end.[29]

3.1   Property-based jurisdiction

Is it fair to assert jurisdiction over a defendant for the sole reason that he has assets locally? An important distinction should certainly be made between claims relating to the relevant asset, for instance a claim for restitution of a stolen property, and claims which are unrelated to the relevant property. In the first case scenario, the subject matter of the dispute would be the relevant property, and it has long been regarded as legitimate to use the place of the property to locate such disputes for private international law purposes. For instance, the law of the place of a property (*lex situs*) typically governs rights related to that property (*in rem* rights). In the second case scenario, however, the place of the property does not seem to be a relevant connecting factor. Yet, many countries have used the presence of property on their territory as a ground for retaining jurisdiction in any dispute, including the United States, Germany, Japan and France.[30]

Read the following case and identify the reasons in favour and against such rule.

 CASE

U.S. Supreme Court, 24 June 1977 *Shaffer v. Heitner*[31]

It appears, therefore, that jurisdiction over many types of actions which now are or might be brought in rem would not be affected by a holding that any assertion of state-court jurisdiction must satisfy the *International Shoe* standard. For the type of quasi in rem action typified by *Harris v. Balk* and the present case, however, accepting the proposed analysis would result in significant change. These are cases where the property which now serves as the basis for state-court jurisdiction is completely unrelated to the plaintiff's cause of action. Thus, although the presence of the defendant's property in a State might suggest the existence of other ties among the defendant, the State, and the litigation, the presence of the property alone would not support the State's jurisdiction. If those other ties did not exist, cases over

---

29 See *infra*, p. 195.
30 The French supreme court introduced property based jurisdiction in 1979. It abandoned it in 1997: Cass. Civ. 1ère, 11 February 1997, *Soc. Strojexport c. Banque centrale de Syrie*, case no. 94-21500.
31 433 U.S. 186.

which the State is now thought to have jurisdiction could not be brought in that forum.

Since acceptance of the *International Shoe* test would most affect this class of cases, we examine the arguments against adopting that standard as they relate to this category of litigation.[FN31] Before doing so, however, we note that this type of case also presents the clearest illustration of the argument in favor of assessing assertions of jurisdiction by a single standard. For in cases such as Harris and this one, the only role played by the property is to provide the basis for bringing the defendant into court.[FN32] Indeed, the express purpose of the Delaware sequestration procedure is to compel the defendant to enter a personal appearance. In such cases, if a direct assertion of personal jurisdiction over the defendant would violate the Constitution, it would seem that an indirect assertion of that jurisdiction should be equally impermissible.

> FN31. Concentrating on this category of cases is also appropriate because in the other categories, to the extent that presence of property in the State indicates the existence of sufficient contacts under International Shoe, there is no need to rely on the property as justifying jurisdiction regardless of the existence of those contacts.

> FN32. The value of the property seized does serve to limit the extent of possible liability, but that limitation does not provide support for the assertion of jurisdiction.

The primary rationale for treating the presence of property as a sufficient basis for jurisdiction to adjudicate claims over which the State would not have jurisdiction if *International Shoe* applied is that a wrongdoer 'should not be able to avoid payment of his obligations by the expedient of removing his assets to a place where he is not subject to an in personam suit.' Restatement s 66, Comment a. Accord, Developments 955. This justification, however, does not explain why jurisdiction should be recognized without regard to whether the property is present in the State because of an effort to avoid the owner's obligations. Nor does it support jurisdiction to adjudicate the underlying claim. At most, it suggests that a State in which property is located should have jurisdiction to attach that property, by use of proper procedures, as security for a judgment being sought in a forum where the litigation can be maintained consistently with International Shoe. Moreover, we know of nothing to justify the assumption that a debtor can avoid paying his obligations by removing his property to a State in which his creditor cannot obtain personal jurisdiction over him. The Full Faith and Credit Clause, after all, makes the valid in personam judgment of one State enforceable in all other States.

It might also be suggested that allowing in rem jurisdiction avoids the uncertainty inherent in the *International Shoe* standard and assures a plaintiff of a forum. We believe, however, that the fairness standard of *International Shoe* can be easily applied in the vast majority of cases. Moreover, when the existence of jurisdiction in a particular forum under International Shoe is unclear, the cost of simplifying the litigation by avoiding the jurisdictional question may be the sacrifice of 'fair play and substantial justice.' That cost is too high.

We are left, then, to consider the significance of the long history of jurisdiction based solely on the presence of property in a State. Although the theory that territorial power is both essential to and sufficient for jurisdiction has been undermined, we have never held that the presence of property in a State does not automatically confer jurisdiction over the owner's interest in that property. This history must be considered as supporting the proposition that jurisdiction based solely on the presence of property satisfies the demands of due process, cf. *Ownbey v. Morgan*, 256 U.S. 94, 111 (1921), but it is not decisive. '(T)raditional notions of fair play and substantial justice' can be as readily offended by the perpetuation of ancient forms that are no longer justified as by the adoption of new procedures that are inconsistent with the basic values of our constitutional heritage. Cf. *Sniadach v. Family Finance Corp.*, 395 U.S., at 340; *Wolf v. Colorado*, 338 U.S. 25, 27 (1949). The fiction that an assertion of jurisdiction over property is anything but an assertion of jurisdiction over the owner of the property supports an ancient form without substantial modern justification. Its continued acceptance would serve only to allow state-court jurisdiction that is fundamentally unfair to the defendant. (. . .)

The Delaware courts based their assertion of jurisdiction in this case solely on the statutory presence of appellants' property in Delaware. Yet that property is not the subject matter of this litigation, nor is the underlying cause of action related to the property. Appellants' holdings in Greyhound do not, therefore, provide contacts with Delaware sufficient to support the jurisdiction of that State's courts over appellants. If it exists, that jurisdiction must have some other foundation.

? NOTES AND QUESTIONS

1 What is the difference between *in rem* and *quasi in rem* actions? Do they both violate the U.S. Constitution?

2 Property based jurisdiction often starts with the attachment (seizure) of local assets. Yet, the

purpose of property-based jurisdiction is to grant jurisdiction to decide the dispute on the merits. A different issue is whether a property situated in a given state could be frozen by some protective measure so that a future judgment on the merits, rendered in another state, could eventually be enforced. It is widely accepted that such protective measures are always available locally in support of foreign proceedings on the merits. What do you think, then, of the argument that property-based jurisdiction should be available to prevent debtors from removing their assets in other states?

3 Property-based jurisdiction can be limited by the value of the attached property, or unlimited. In this case, the local court had jurisdiction to issue a judgment for an amount which could not be more than the value of the property. Is this form of property based jurisdiction more legitimate?

4 The Due Process clause protects defendants against unfair assertions of jurisdiction. What about the interests of the plaintiff? Are they neglected by the court?

Article 23 of the German Code of Civil Procedure is probably the most famous rule granting international jurisdiction on the basis of location of property in the forum. However, the German federal court severely limited its effect in the following judgment.

German Code of Civil Procedure

Art. 23 *Specific jurisdiction of assets and of an object*

Jurisdiction for actions for pecuniary claims against persons who have no residence in Germany shall lie with the court of the place where assets belonging to that person are located, or the place where the property which is the subject matter of the claim is located. Claims shall be deemed to be located at the place of the residence of the debtor and, in cases in which a tangible asset was given as a security for payment of the claims, the place where this tangible asset is located.

 CASE

German Federal Court, 2 July 1991[32]

Facts: A Cyprus construction company had entered into a contract to build a port facility in Libya. A Turkish bank provided the Libyan party with a guarantee of USD 20 million in case of non performance by the construction company which, for that purpose, deposited the same sum with the bank. After the contract was terminated, the Libyan party called the guarantee, which the bank paid. The construction company denied that the bank was entitled to pay under the guarantee and sought reimbursement of the deposit before English courts, which eventually stayed the proceedings on the ground of *forum non conveniens*. As the bank had a branch in Germany (and thus assets), the same action was brought in German courts.

---

32 XI ZR 206/90.

Held: German courts did not have jurisdiction in the absence of an additional connection with the forum.

11. The lower court was right to decline jurisdiction in this case.

12. Art. 23 sentence 1 alternative 1 provides that for actions for pecuniary claims against a person who has no residence in Germany, the court has territorial and thus international jurisdiction, where property can be found in the forum. The fact that the wording of the provision is not limited either by the value of the assets or by the requirement of a connection with the forum has lead courts to adopt a broad interpretation and scope which were criticized in the legal literature. As an exception to the principle that the action should be introduced before the court of the defendant (*actor sequitur forum rei*), Art. 23 was used to retain international jurisdiction in cases where the defendant had left trading book or abandoned fruit baskets, without requiring a connection between the claim and the forum. This has resulted in the so-understood property based jurisdiction being labelled, inter alia, undesirable, exorbitant and martial jurisdiction.

13. This purely literal interpretation of Art. 23 is indeed neither unconstitutional, nor contrary to international law, but its rationale is disputed. As requested by the federal constitutional court, it also requires to be interpreted by courts appropriately in conformity with international law. (. . .)

18. Limitations to the previous interpretation are established in so far as property based jurisdiction may only be relied on if the dispute has a sufficient connection with the forum. The court endorses the increasingly held view that the jurisdiction of German courts on the ground of Art. 23 sentence 1 alternative 1 can only be justified where the dispute reveals a connection between the location of the property and the forum. (. . .)

29. The genesis of the provision shows that it should not be used as a provision protecting residents of the forum by granting jurisdiction over foreigners for settling disputes that originate exclusively abroad and are to be decided under foreign law. It would contradict such legislative intent to interpret § 23 ZPO in a purely literal manner so that the presence of assets of the defendant in the forum would suffice to establish the international jurisdiction of German courts for any dispute between parties who are not resident in Germany and therefore incentivize to a large extent 'forum shopping', i.e. afford a calculated choice of venue. This would deprive the otherwise competent foreign courts from such disputes – at least from the perspective of enforcement in Germany – at the same time. The jurisdictional arrogance of German courts that the use of unjustifiable requirements would reveal, would lead to foreign trade and foreign policy pressures. The Federal Constitutional Court already underlined such risks in the aforementioned decision of 12 April 1983 (BVerfGE 64, 1, 18). Contrary to the opinion of the lower court, it has underlined that addressing the risk that 'German rules of international jurisdiction be perceived as undesirable from a legal or political and

> economic perspective' should not be considered as the sole responsibility of the legislator, but rather called expressly for courts to carry out this legislative task within the limits allowed by an interpretation in conformity with international law (ibid p.20). (. . .)

? NOTES AND QUESTIONS

1 What is the ruling of the German federal court? Does it find that Art. 23 is invalid for lack of compliance with the German Constitution or international law? What is the law in Germany after this ruling?

2 Which reasons did German courts give to amend Art. 23? Did they consider, as did the U.S. Supreme Court, that property-based jurisdiction was a violation of the rights of the defendant? Were they more concerned with possible retaliation from foreign countries?

3 In this case, the plaintiff had first brought proceedings in England before suing in Germany. Each time, the action was dismissed for lack of jurisdiction. The plaintiff might have been looking for a jurisdiction which would have given him a decisive advantage, and the German federal court warns against the risks of forum shopping. But it could also be that the plaintiff feared that he would not have been treated fairly in more closely connected fora such as Turkey or Libya. As already alluded to, one of the reasons why exorbitant heads of jurisdiction are not easily abolished is that they can represent the only chance for citizens to find a neutral forum to adjudicate their claims. Certain exorbitant rules, however, could benefit both citizens and outsiders, as this case also demonstrates (by contrast, nationality based jurisdiction only benefits citizens: *infra*, 3.3). Furthermore, if the only acceptable rationale for exorbitant rules of jurisdiction was to afford protection against denial of justice, a better tailored rule could be to grant jurisdiction on this very ground. A number of countries have a special rule granting jurisdiction to their courts where no other court is effectively available, including where it would be unreasonable to expect the plaintiff to litigate in available foreign courts (*forum necessitatis*).[33]

4 What could be this additional connection between the dispute and the forum? It seems clear that it could be the traditional connecting factors used for private international law purposes such as the place of performance of the contract or the place where the tort occurred. However, in 2012, the German Federal court accepted that the domicile of the plaintiff could be such connection.[34] By doing so, it arguably turned Art. 23 into another exorbitant rule benefiting German residents.

Japanese Code of Civil Procedure

Article 3–3 *Jurisdiction over Actions Relating to, inter alia, Contractual Obligations*
The actions set out in each sub-paragraph below may be filed with the courts of Japan in the circumstances described in each of them. (. . .)
(iii) An action relating to a property right:

---

33 See, e.g., Art. 3 of the 1987 Swiss Statute of private international law. A similar rule is also found in some specialized EU regulations such as the 2009 Maintenance Regulation (Art. 7) or the 2012 Succession Regulation (Art. 11).

34 BGH, 13 December 2012 – III ZR 282/11, *IPRax* 2014.312 with note Koechel.

> – in the circumstances where the object of the claim is located in Japan; or
> – if the action is for the payment of money, in the circumstances where the defendant's asset capable of being seized is located in Japan (except where the value of the asset is extremely low).

NOTES AND QUESTIONS

1 Is Art. 3–3(iii) an exorbitant head of jurisdiction? The first prong is not: it relies on the subject matter of the dispute. The second prong, however, grants jurisdiction for the sole reason that property of the defendant can be found in Japan. Some Japanese scholars argue that the exclusion of assets of an extremely low value make it less unpalatable.[35] Do you agree?

2 The Japanese lawmaker introduced a corrective device granting discretion to Japanese courts to dismiss proceedings in 'special circumstances' which should allow them to restrict the exercise of jurisdiction under Art. 3–3(iii): see *infra*, p. 232.

3.2   Jurisdiction based on physical presence

CASE

U.S. Supreme Court, 29 May 1990 *Burnham v. Superior Court of California, County of Marin*[36]

Justice SCALIA, with the Chief Justice and two other justices joining:

The question presented is whether the Due Process Clause of the Fourteenth Amendment denies California courts jurisdiction over a nonresident, who was personally served with process while temporarily in that State, in a suit unrelated to his activities in the State. (. . .)

Among the most firmly established principles of personal jurisdiction in American tradition is that the courts of a State have jurisdiction over nonresidents who are physically present in the State. The view developed early that each State had the power to hale before its courts any individual who could be found within its borders, and that once having acquired jurisdiction over such a person by properly serving him with process, the State could retain jurisdiction to enter judgment against him, no matter how fleeting his visit. See, e.g., *Potter v. Allin*, 2 Root 63, 67 (Conn.1793) . . . That view had antecedents in English common-law practice, which sometimes allowed 'transi-

---

35 See, e.g., Koji Takahashi, 'The Jurisdiction of Japanese Courts in a Comparative Context' (2015) 11 JPIL 103, 120.
36 495 U.S. 604.

tory' actions, arising out of events outside the country, to be maintained against seemingly nonresident defendants who were present in England. See, e.g., *Mostyn v. Fabrigas*, 98 Eng.Rep. 1021 (K.B.1774) (. . .). Justice Story believed the principle, which he traced to Roman origins, to be firmly grounded in English tradition: '[B]y the common law[,] personal actions, being transitory, may be brought in any place, where the party defendant may be found,' for 'every nation may . . . rightfully exercise jurisdiction over all persons within its domains.' J. Story, Commentaries on the Conflict of Laws §§ 554, 543 (1846).

Recent scholarship has suggested that English tradition was not as clear as Story thought, see Hazard, A General Theory of State–Court Jurisdiction, 1965 S.Ct.Rev. 241, 253–260; Ehrenzweig, The Transient Rule of Personal Jurisdiction: The 'Power' Myth and Forum Conveniens, 65 Yale L.J. 289 (1956). Accurate or not, however, judging by the evidence of contemporaneous or near-contemporaneous decisions, one must conclude that Story's understanding was shared by American courts at the crucial time for present purposes: 1868, when the Fourteenth Amendment was adopted. (. . .)

Decisions in the courts of many States in the 19th and early 20th centuries held that personal service upon a physically present defendant sufficed to confer jurisdiction, without regard to whether the defendant was only briefly in the State or whether the cause of action was related to his activities there. (. . .)

This American jurisdictional practice is, moreover, not merely old; it is continuing. It remains the practice of, not only a substantial number of the States, but as far as we are aware *all* the States and the Federal Government (. . .)

Nothing in *International Shoe* or the cases that have followed it, however, offers support for the very different proposition petitioner seeks to establish today: that a defendant's presence in the forum is not only unnecessary to validate novel, nontraditional assertions of jurisdiction, but is itself no longer sufficient to establish jurisdiction. That proposition is unfaithful to both elementary logic and the foundations of our due process jurisprudence. The distinction between what is needed to support novel procedures and what is needed to sustain traditional ones is fundamental, as we observed over a century ago:

> [A] process of law, which is not otherwise forbidden, must be taken to be due process of law, if it can show the sanction of settled usage both in England and in this country; but it by no means follows that nothing else can be due

process of law . . . [That which], in substance, has been immemorially the actual law of the land . . . therefor[e] is due process of law. But to hold that such a characteristic is essential to due process of law, would be to deny every quality of the law but its age, and to render it incapable of progress or improvement. It would be to stamp upon our jurisprudence the unchangeableness attributed to the laws of the Medes and Persians. *Hurtado v. California*, 110 U.S. 516, 528–529 (1884).

The short of the matter is that jurisdiction based on physical presence alone constitutes due process because it is one of the continuing traditions of our legal system that define the due process standard of 'traditional notions of fair play and substantial justice.' That standard was developed by *analogy* to 'physical presence,' and it would be perverse to say it could now be turned against that touchstone of jurisdiction.

Justice BRENNAN, with three other justices joining:

I agree with Justice SCALIA that the Due Process Clause of the Fourteenth Amendment generally permits a state court to exercise jurisdiction over a defendant if he is served with process while voluntarily present in the forum State. I do not perceive the need, however, to decide that a jurisdictional rule that 'has been immemorially the actual law of the land' automatically comports with due process simply by virtue of its 'pedigree.' Although I agree that history is an important factor in establishing whether a jurisdictional rule satisfies due process requirements, I cannot agree that it is the *only* factor such that all traditional rules of jurisdiction are, *ipso facto*, forever constitutional. Unlike Justice SCALIA, I would undertake an 'independent inquiry into the . . . fairness of the prevailing in-state service rule.' I therefore concur only in the judgment. (. . .)

While our *holding* in *Shaffer* may have been limited to *quasi in rem* jurisdiction, our mode of analysis was not. Indeed, that we were willing in *Shaffer* to examine anew the appropriateness of the *quasi in rem* rule—until that time dutifully accepted by American courts for at least a century—demonstrates that we did not believe that the 'pedigree' of a jurisdictional practice was dispositive in deciding whether it was consistent with due process. We later characterized *Shaffer* as 'abandon[ing] the outworn rule of *Harris v. Balk*, 198 U.S. 215 (1905), that the interest of a creditor in a debt could be extinguished or otherwise affected by any State having transitory jurisdiction over the debtor.' *World–Wide Volkswagen Corp. v. Woodson*, 444 U.S. 286, 296 (1980). If we could discard an 'ancient form without substantial modern justification' in *Shaffer*, at 212, we can do so again.

By visiting the forum State, a transient defendant actually 'avail[s]' himself, *Burger King*, at 476, of significant benefits provided by the State. His health and safety are guaranteed by the State's police, fire, and emergency medical services; he is free to travel on the State's roads and waterways; he likely enjoys the fruits of the State's economy as well. Moreover, the Privileges and Immunities Clause of Article IV prevents a state government from discriminating against a transient defendant by denying him the protections of its law or the right of access to its courts. See *Supreme Court of New Hampshire v. Piper*, 470 U.S. 274, 281, n. 10 (1985) (...). Subject only to the doctrine of *forum non conveniens*, an out-of-state plaintiff may use state courts in all circumstances in which those courts would be available to state citizens. Without transient jurisdiction, an asymmetry would arise: A transient would have the full benefit of the power of the forum State's courts as a plaintiff while retaining immunity from their authority as a defendant. See Maltz, Sovereign Authority, Fairness, and Personal Jurisdiction: The Case for the Doctrine of Transient Jurisdiction, 66 Wash.U.L.Q. 671, 698–699 (1988).

The potential burdens on a transient defendant are slight. '[M]odern transportation and communications have made it much less burdensome for a party sued to defend himself' in a State outside his place of residence. *Burger King*, at 474. That the defendant has already journeyed at least once before to the forum—as evidenced by the fact that he was served with process there—is an indication that suit in the forum likely would not be prohibitively inconvenient. Finally, any burdens that do arise can be ameliorated by a variety of procedural devices. For these reasons, as a rule the exercise of personal jurisdiction over a defendant based on his voluntary presence in the forum will satisfy the requirements of due process.

[?] **QUESTIONS**

Do you agree with Scalia or with Brennan? Is transient jurisdiction an exorbitant head of jurisdiction, or does it comport with basic notions of fairness?

3.3 Jurisdiction based on nationality

French Civil Code

Art. 14

An alien, even if not residing in France, may be cited before French courts for the performance of obligations contracted by him in France with a French person; he may be called before the courts of France for obligations contracted by him in a foreign country towards French persons.

Art. 15

French persons may be called before a court of France for obligations contracted by them in a foreign country, even with an alien.

NOTES AND QUESTIONS

1 Articles 14 and 15 date back to the 1804 Napoleonic Code. At that time, French courts would only retain jurisdiction for disputes involving one national. Jurisdiction was therefore perceived as a right granted by a Nation to its nationals.[37]

2 Although Arts. 14 and 15 only refer to contractual obligations, the material scope was extended by the French Supreme Court to all disputes involving French nationals. The only exceptions are real property and enforcement matters, which have traditionally been regarded in France as falling within the exclusive jurisdiction of the place where the property is situated, or where the enforcement must be carried out.[38]

3 Today, Arts. 14 and 15 of the French (and Luxembourg) Civil Code are widely known as exorbitant rules of jurisdiction. Why? Do you think it is so irrespective of the subject matter of the dispute?

4 Belgium abolished the same Arts. 14 and 15 of its Civil Code respectively in 1948 and 2004. A Belgian commentator noted:

> the [2004 Belgian Code of Private International Law] brings Belgium into the category of states that retain a purely privatist concept of international jurisdiction. It is now focused not on considerations of sovereignty and allegiance but on procedural fairness and proximity, the criterion of nationality being only used in matters of personal status where it is an objective connection with the forum.[39]

5 While exorbitant rules of jurisdiction might not be fair to defendants, they are very helpful to plaintiffs, who are typically local residents and indeed nationals. Exorbitant rules of jurisdiction are therefore a favor granted to local residents. If other States also grant similar favours to their own residents, why should a given state give up unilaterally its own rules and disfavor its people? A number of French senior judges have explained that they thought that French courts should ensure that Arts. 14 and 15 remain fully effective in order to give incentive to foreign states to enter into bilateral agreements resolving in a mutually acceptable way the issue.

In 2004, in a divorce case between an American husband and a Franco-American wife, the French Supreme Court explained:

> absent a treaty of judicial cooperation between the United States and France in civil matters, the favor benefiting [the wife] arising under the exclusive jurisdictional rule of Art. 15 was not more exorbitant than the one arising under the rule

---

37 *Supra*, p. 148.
38 Cass. Civ. 1ère, 27 May 1970, *Weiss* (1971) Rev. Crit. DIP 113.
39 Arnaud Nuyts, 'Le Nouveau droit international privé belge – Compétence judiciaire' (2005) Journal des Tribunaux 177.

of Florida law granting jurisdiction on the ground of temporary presence of the plaintiff in that State[40].

6   As a more extensive procedure for challenging the constitutionality of statutes was introduced in France in 2010, the question constitutionality of nationality based jurisdiction was eventually introduced before the French Supreme Court in 2012.

 CASE

French Cour de cassation, 29 February 2012 Case no 11-40101

Whereas the transmitted question is worded as follows:

'Does the nationality-based jurisdictional privilege benefiting French plaintiffs established by Article 14 of the Civil Code infringe the right to a fair trial, as a right guaranteed by the Constitution?'

'Does the nationality-based jurisdictional privilege benefiting French plaintiffs established by Article 14 of the Civil Code infringe the principle of equality enshrined in Article 6 of the 1789 Declaration of Human and Civil Rights?'

(. . .) whereas (. . .) Article 14 of the Civil Code does not grant exclusive, but subsidiary jurisdiction to French courts, the exercise of which is optional for the parties; it has no effect where its beneficiary waived it or an international treaty or Community regulation providing for a different solution applies; it does not preclude the operation of international *lis pendens* and is no ground for denying recognition to foreign judgments; therefore, it cannot be regarded as infringing the principle of equality and the right to a fair trial, so that the question is not serious under the requirements of the constitutionally guaranteed principles invoked (. . .)

FOR THESE REASONS: FINDS that the issue of constitutionality needs not be referred to the Constitutional Council;

Are you convinced by the reasons given by the court? Article 14 grants subsidiary jurisdiction insofar as it may only be relied upon where no other head of jurisdiction is available. But if the issue is that Art. 14 grants jurisdiction precisely where there is no other connection between the dispute and

---

40 Cass. Civ. 1ère, 30 March 2004, case no 02-17974.

France, is whether Art 14 is available in other cases really relevant? A French national may waive his right to rely on Art. 14, for instance by starting proceedings in a foreign court. But again, isn't the issue the operation of the rule in absence of such waiver?

4

Parallel litigation

In international litigation, the parties often wish the case to be handled by different courts. One reason is often only psychological: each party feels more comfortable litigating in a familiar environment, that is, in its home court. But there can also be more tangible reasons. The courts of different jurisdictions could have different choice of law rules and would thus apply different laws to the merits of the case. Courts will always follow their own procedural rules, and some of these rules can give an important, sometimes decisive, advantage to one of the parties. For instance, under American civil procedure, a combination of unique procedural tools (class actions, contingency fees) make it much easier for certain plaintiffs (groups of consumers, shareholders) to access justice, as they will not need to pay their lawyers unless they eventually win the case. It is therefore understandable that parties compare the different courts and legal systems to assess where it would be more advantageous to sue. This is typically referred to as 'forum shopping': shopping for the best forum, that is, court.

Forum shopping is possible because States are free to adopt whichever rules of international jurisdiction they prefer. Experience has shown that States typically adopt numerous rules of jurisdiction, which often overlap. The result is that, in any given international dispute, there will virtually always be several courts which could retain jurisdiction. Some will be strongly connected to the dispute (court of the domicile of the parties, of the place of performance of the contract, and so on). Others will not, but will have the power to retain jurisdiction on the ground of exorbitant heads of jurisdictions.

The issue of parallel litigation has traditionally been handled very differently in the civil law and in the common law traditions.

1   *Lis pendens*

The traditional tool to address the issue of parallel litigation in the civil law tradition is the doctrine of *lis alibi pendens*. Under this doctrine, the issue of parallel litigation is resolved through the application of a mere chronological factor: the court seised first is preferred, and the court seised second must decline jurisdiction once it becomes clear that the first court will exercise jurisdiction.

Lis pendens only applies where the two courts are seised of the same dispute. In most civil law jurisdictions, a dispute will be considered as being the same if it is identical in three respects (triple identity): the parties to the proceedings before each court should be the same, the legal ground of the action should be the same, and the remedies sought should be the same.

Lis pendens was initially a doctrine developed in the domestic civil procedure of civil law jurisdictions. The goal, therefore, was to decide which of two courts of the same country should be preferred. By definition, these courts were identical in most respects: they would apply the same civil procedure, they were staffed with judges who had received the same training, and so on. As it would not have been acceptable to actually compare those courts (is a judge in city X known to be less competent than a judge in city Y?), a tool was developed which would only rely on a neutral factor: time. Is the situation the same in international litigation? Are courts of different jurisdictions fungible, interchangeable? And even if they are not, should they be considered so? The answer to this question might be different depending on whether parallel litigation develops in a truly international environment (1.1) or in a federal ensemble (1.2).

1.1   With respect to litigation in foreign nations

In most civil law jurisdictions, the doctrine of *lis pendens* also applies to international parallel litigation.[1] This has a number of consequences. The most obvious one is that a civil law court may only decline jurisdiction on the ground that proceedings were also brought before a foreign court if the foreign court was seised first. Another important consequence is that both courts must be seised of the dispute. This means that proceedings must be pending in both courts. The *lis pendens* doctrine is designed to resolve actual conflict of proceedings. It does not apply at any earlier stage. It is thus not possible to challenge the international jurisdiction of a civil law court on the ground that a foreign court, if seised, would be a more appropriate forum: as long as a second court has not been seised, there is no '*lis pendens* situation', and thus no problem to address.

---

1 See, e.g., in France, Civ. 1ère, 26 Nov. 1974, *Société Miniera di Fragne*, (1975) Rev Crit DIP 491; in Italy, Art. 7 of the 1995 PIL Law; in Belgium, see Art. 14 of the 2004 Code of PIL.

The *lis pendens* doctrine posits that courts are interchangeable, and that each court could equally resolve the dispute. An important difference between domestic and international *lis pendens*, however, is that the contemplated judgments will not automatically produce the same effects. While two domestic judgments are indeed interchangeable, a foreign judgment will only produce effect in the forum if it satisfies the test for being recognized and declared enforceable in the forum. This is the reason why civil law jurisdictions add a requirement that the foreign judgment be capable of recognition in the forum.[2] It would indeed be unacceptable that the forum declines jurisdiction on the ground that a foreign court was seised first if its judgment could not be recognized: this would mean that no judgment producing effect in the forum would resolve the dispute and grant a remedy to the judgment creditor.

If these requirements are met, is the forum under an obligation to decline jurisdiction, and does it only have discretion to do so?

Swiss Law of Private International Law (1987)

Article 9 – *Lis pendens*

1 If the same parties are engaged in proceedings abroad based on the same causes of action, the Swiss court shall stay the proceeding if it may be expected that the foreign court will, within a reasonable time, render a decision that will be recognizable in Switzerland.

2 To determine when a court in Switzerland is seized, the date of the first act necessary to institute the action shall be decisive. The initiation of conciliation proceedings shall suffice.

3 The Swiss court shall dismiss the action as soon as a foreign decision is submitted to it which can be recognized in Switzerland.

European Regulation (EU) No 1215/2012 of 12 December 2012 on jurisdiction and on the enforcement and recognition of judgments in civil and commercial matters (Brussels Ibis)

PREAMBLE

(23) This Regulation should provide for a flexible mechanism allowing the courts of the Member States to take into account proceedings pending before the courts of third States, considering in particular whether a judgment of a third State will be capable of recognition and enforcement in the Member State concerned under the law of that Member State and the proper administration of justice.

---

2 See all the laws and cases cited in the previous note.

(24) When taking into account the proper administration of justice, the court of the Member State concerned should assess all the circumstances of the case before it. Such circumstances may include connections between the facts of the case and the parties and the third State concerned, the stage to which the proceedings in the third State have progressed by the time proceedings are initiated in the court of the Member State and whether or not the court of the third State can be expected to give a judgment within a reasonable time

SECTION 9 *Lis pendens* — related actions

Article 33

1. Where jurisdiction is based on Article 4 or on Articles 7, 8 or 9 and proceedings are pending before a court of a third State at the time when a court in a Member State is seised of an action involving the same cause of action and between the same parties as the proceedings in the court of the third State, the court of the Member State may stay the proceedings if:

(a) it is expected that the court of the third State will give a judgment capable of recognition and, where applicable, of enforcement in that Member State; and

(b) the court of the Member State is satisfied that a stay is necessary for the proper administration of justice.

2. The court of the Member State may continue the proceedings at any time if:

(a) the proceedings in the court of the third State are themselves stayed or discontinued;

(b) it appears to the court of the Member State that the proceedings in the court of the third State are unlikely to be concluded within a reasonable time; or

(c) the continuation of the proceedings is required for the proper administration of justice.

3. The court of the Member State shall dismiss the proceedings if the proceedings in the court of the third State are concluded and have resulted in a judgment capable of recognition and, where applicable, of enforcement in that Member State.

4. The court of the Member State shall apply this Article on the application of one of the parties or, where possible under national law, of its own motion

? | NOTES AND QUESTIONS

1 The EU law of jurisdiction has traditionally been concerned with intra-European disputes. However, in 2012, the EU lawmaker introduced a new provision dealing with parallel litigation with third States. A different rule applies to *lis pendens* between courts of Member States (see *infra* 1.2).

2 In a domestic context, the *lis pendens* doctrine operates mechanically. If another court was seised first, the court seised second must decline jurisdiction. It is an obligation, and the court has not discretion in this respect. Should the doctrine operate as automatically in an

international context? Article 9 of the Swiss Law of Private International Law provides so, and imposes an obligation on the Swiss court seised second to stay proceedings and eventually decline jurisdiction. In many other civil law countries, however, the doctrine of *lis pendens* operates differently in an international context. The forum may decline jurisdiction if it is seised second, but it is under no obligation to do so.[3] Certain legislations expressly provide a test for exercising this discretion. Article 33 of the Brussels Ibis Regulation provides that a stay should be necessary for the proper administration of justice. By granting discretion to the forum to retain jurisdiction irrespective of when it was seised, these countries recognize that courts of different countries are not always interchangeable, and that it might be necessary to take into account other considerations before declining jurisdiction. What do you think these other considerations should be?

3 Besides the *lis pendens* rule, civil law jurisdictions often also provide for the possibility to stay proceedings where the actions are not identical, but merely related: see, for instance, Art. 34 of the Brussels Ibis Regulation.

1.2 With respect to litigation in sister states

Brussels Ibis Regulation (2012)

PREAMBLE

(21) In the interests of the harmonious administration of justice it is necessary to minimise the possibility of concurrent proceedings and to ensure that irreconcilable judgments will not be given in different Member States. There should be a clear and effective mechanism for resolving cases of *lis pendens* and related actions, and for obviating problems flowing from national differences as to the determination of the time when a case is regarded as pending. For the purposes of this Regulation, that time should be defined autonomously

SECTION 9 *Lis pendens* — related actions

Article 29

1. Without prejudice to Article 31(2), where proceedings involving the same cause of action and between the same parties are brought in the courts of different Member States, any court other than the court first seised shall of its own motion stay its proceedings until such time as the jurisdiction of the court first seised is established.

2. In cases referred to in paragraph 1, upon request by a court seised of the dispute, any other court seised shall without delay inform the former court of the date when it was seised in accordance with Article 32.

3. Where the jurisdiction of the court first seised is established, any court other than the court first seised shall decline jurisdiction in favour of that court.

---

3 This is the case in France, Italy and Belgium, for instance: see all the laws and cases cited in the previous note.

Article 30

1. Where related actions are pending in the courts of different Member States, any court other than the court first seised may stay its proceedings.

2. Where the action in the court first seised is pending at first instance, any other court may also, on the application of one of the parties, decline jurisdiction if the court first seised has jurisdiction over the actions in question and its law permits the consolidation thereof.

3. For the purposes of this Article, actions are deemed to be related where they are so closely connected that it is expedient to hear and determine them together to avoid the risk of irreconcilable judgments resulting from separate proceedings.

Article 32

1. For the purposes of this Section, a court shall be deemed to be seised:

(a)   at the time when the document instituting the proceedings or an equiva-lent document is lodged with the court, provided that the claimant has not subsequently failed to take the steps he was required to take to have service effected on the defendant; or

(b)   if the document has to be served before being lodged with the court, at the time when it is received by the authority responsible for service, pro-vided that the claimant has not subsequently failed to take the steps he was required to take to have the document lodged with the court.

The authority responsible for service referred to in point (b) shall be the first authority receiving the documents to be served.

2. The court, or the authority responsible for service, referred to in paragraph 1, shall note, respectively, the date of the lodging of the document instituting the pro-ceedings or the equivalent document, or the date of receipt of the documents to be served.

 NOTE AND QUESTION

In the context of litigation within the European Union, the Brussels Ibis Regulation provides for a different *lis pendens* rule. Contrary to the rule applying to litigation involving third States,[4] it is not necessary to assess whether the judgment that the foreign court would eventually deliver would be capable of recognition in the forum. This is because under the Brussels Ibis Regulation, the grounds for denying recognition to a judgment made by the court of another Member State are extremely limited.[5] The recognition of the foreign judgment is presumed.

Additionally, Article 29 does not grant any discretion to the court seised second, which must decline jurisdiction once the jurisdiction of the court first seised has been established. Should it be the case even if the process in the court first seised would be wholly inappropriate?

---

4 See Art. 33, *supra*, 1.1.
5 See *infra*, Ch. 7.

European Court of Justice, 9 December 2003 *Eric Gasser Gmbh v. MISAT srl* (Case C-116/02)[6]

55 By its third question, the national court seeks in essence to ascertain whether Article 21 of the Brussels Convention [*now Art. 29 of the Brussels Ibis Regulation*] must be interpreted as meaning that it may be derogated from where, in general, the duration of proceedings before the courts of the Contracting State in which the court first seised is established is excessively long. (. . .)

68 It is not compatible with the philosophy and the objectives of the Brussels Convention for national courts to be under an obligation to respect rules on *lis pendens* only if they consider that the court first seised will give judgment within a reasonable period. Nowhere does the Convention provide that courts may use the pretext of delays in procedure in other contracting States to excuse themselves from applying its provisions.

69 Moreover, the point from which the duration of proceedings becomes excessively long, to such an extent that the interests of a party may be seriously affected, can be determined only on the basis of an appraisal taking account of all the circumstances of the case. That is an issue which cannot be settled in the context of the Brussels Convention. It is for the European Court of Human Rights to examine the issue and the national courts cannot substitute themselves for it by recourse to Article 21 of the Convention.

Findings of the Court

70 As has been observed by the Commission and by the Advocate General in points 88 and 89 of his Opinion, an interpretation of Article 21 of the Brussels Convention whereby the application of that article should be set aside where the court first seised belongs to a Member State in whose courts there are, in general, excessive delays in dealing with cases would be manifestly contrary both to the letter and spirit and to the aim of the Convention.

71 First, the Convention contains no provision under which its articles, and in particular Article 21, cease to apply because of the length of proceedings before the courts of the Contracting State concerned.

72 Second, it must be borne in mind that the Brussels Convention is necessarily based on the trust which the Contracting States accord to each other's legal systems and judicial institutions. It is that mutual trust which has enabled a compulsory system of jurisdiction to be established, which all the courts within the purview of the Convention are required to respect, and as a corollary the waiver by those States of the right to apply their internal rules on recognition and enforcement of

---

6 ECLI:EU:C:2003:657, [2003] E.C.R. I-14693.

foreign judgments in favour of a simplified mechanism for the recognition and enforcement of judgments. It is also common ground that the Convention thereby seeks to ensure legal certainty by allowing individuals to foresee with sufficient certainty which court will have jurisdiction.

73 In view of the foregoing, the answer to the third question must be that Article 21 of the Brussels Convention must be interpreted as meaning that it cannot be derogated from where, in general, the duration of proceedings before the courts of the Contracting State in which the court first seised is established is excessively long.

NOTES AND QUESTIONS

1 A fundamental principle of E.U. law is mutual trust in other Member States. In judicial matters, the principle means that the courts of the Member States must trust the judicial systems of all other Member States, and thus consider that there is no difference between a foreign court and a local court. Under such principle and assumptions, the use of a strict doctrine of *lis pendens* is logical.

2 One rationale for mutual trust in judicial matters is that all Member States are parties to the European Convention on Human Rights. But what if a Member State is regularly found in breach of its obligations under this Convention, such as Italy for the delays in its proceedings? Should other Member States still trust the Italian legal system?

As the *lis pendens* rule creates an obligation for any court in Europe seised second to stay proceedings, it has the potential of being used strategically. Could a potential defendant, who knows, suspects or fears that he might be sued, use the rule to secure the jurisdiction of its preferred court? Read the following case and assess whether it could be useful for a defendant to seek first a declaration that he is not liable for a particular loss.

CASE

European Court of Justice, 6 December 1994 *The ship 'Tatry'* (Case C-406/92)[7]

The first question

28 The national court's first question is essentially whether, on a proper construction, Article 21 of the Convention [*now Art. 29 of the Brussels Ibis Regulation*] is applicable in the case of two sets of proceedings involving the same cause of action where some but not all of the parties are the same, at least one of the plaintiffs and one of the defendants to the proceedings first commenced also being among the plaintiffs and defendants in the second proceedings, or vice versa.

---

7 *Tatry v. Maciej Rataj* ECLI:EU:C:1994:400, [1994] E.C.R.I-05439.

29 The question refers to the term 'the same parties' mentioned in Article 21, which requires as a condition for its application that the two sets of proceedings be between the same parties. As the Court held in Case 144/86 *Gubisch Maschinenfabrik v Palumbo* [1987] ECR 4861, the terms used in Article 21 in order to determine whether a situation of *lis pendens* arises must be regarded as independent (paragraph 11 of the judgment).

30 Moreover, as the Advocate General noted in his Opinion (paragraph 14), it follows by implication from that judgment that the question whether the parties are the same cannot depend on the procedural position of each of them in the two actions, and that the plaintiff in the first action may be the defendant in the second.

31 The Court stressed in that judgment (paragraph 8) that Article 21, together with Article 22 on related actions, is contained in Section 8 of Title II of the Convention, a section intended, in the interests of the proper administration of justice within the Community, to prevent parallel proceedings before the courts of different Contracting States and to avoid conflicts between decisions which might result therefrom. Those rules are therefore designed to preclude, in so far as is possible and from the outset, the possibility of a situation arising such as that referred to in Article 27(3), that is to say the non-recognition of a judgment on account of its irreconcilability with a judgment given in a dispute between the same parties in the State in which recognition is sought.

32 In the light of the wording of Article 21 of the Convention and the objective set out above, that article must be understood as requiring, as a condition of the obligation of the second court seised to decline jurisdiction, that the parties to the two actions be identical.

33 Consequently, where some of the parties are the same as the parties to an action which has already been started, Article 21 requires the second court seised to decline jurisdiction only to the extent to which the parties to the proceedings pending before it are also parties to the action previously started before the court of another Contracting State; it does not prevent the proceedings from continuing between the other parties.

34 Admittedly, that interpretation of Article 21 involves fragmenting the proceedings. However, Article 22 mitigates that disadvantage. That article allows the second court seised to stay proceedings or to decline jurisdiction on the ground that the actions are related, if the conditions there set out are satisfied.

35 Accordingly, the answer to the first question is that, on a proper construction of Article 21 of the Convention, where two actions involve the same cause of action and some but not all of the parties to the second action are the same as the parties to the action commenced earlier in another Contracting State, the second court seised is required to decline jurisdiction only to the extent to which the parties to the proceedings before it are also parties to the action previously commenced; it does not prevent the proceedings from continuing between the other parties.

The fifth question

36 The national court's fifth question is essentially whether, on a proper construction of Article 21 of the Convention, an action seeking to have the defendant held liable for causing loss and ordered to pay damages has the same cause of action and the same object as earlier proceedings brought by that defendant seeking a declaration that he is not liable for that loss.

37 It should be noted at the outset that the English version of Article 21 does not expressly distinguish between the concepts of 'object' and 'cause' of action. That language version must however be construed in the same manner as the majority of the other language versions in which that distinction is made (see the judgment in *Gubisch Maschinenfabrik v Palumbo*, cited above, paragraph 14).

38 For the purposes of Article 21 of the Convention, the 'cause of action' comprises the facts and the rule of law relied on as the basis of the action.

39 Consequently, an action for a declaration of non-liability, such as that brought in the main proceedings in this case by the shipowners, and another action, such as that brought subsequently by the cargo owners on the basis of shipping contracts which are separate but in identical terms, concerning the same cargo transported in bulk and damaged in the same circumstances, have the same cause of action.

40 The 'object of the action' for the purposes of Article 21 means the end the action has in view.

41 The question accordingly arises whether two actions have the same object when the first seeks a declaration that the plaintiff is not liable for damage as claimed by the defendants, while the second, commenced subsequently by those defendants, seeks on the contrary to have the plaintiff in the first action held liable for causing loss and ordered to pay damages.

42 As to liability, the second action has the same object as the first, since the issue of liability is central to both actions. The fact that the plaintiff's pleadings are couched in negative terms in the first action whereas in the second action they are couched in positive terms by the defendant, who has become plaintiff, does not make the object of the dispute different.

43 As to damages, the pleas in the second action are the natural consequence of those relating to the finding of liability and thus do not alter the principal object of the action. Furthermore, the fact that a party seeks a declaration that he is not liable for loss implies that he disputes any obligation to pay damages.

44 In those circumstances, the answer to the fifth question is that, on a proper construction of Article 21 of the Convention, an action seeking to have the defendant held liable for causing loss and ordered to pay damages has the same cause of action and the same object as earlier proceedings brought by that defendant seeking a declaration that he is not liable for that loss. (. . .)

? **NOTES**

1 The European Court adopts a broad definition of the object of the action, and accepts that an action in damages has the same object as an action seeking a declaration that the alleged tort-feasor is not liable. The result is that if a court of Member State is seised first of such a negative declaration, all other courts in the European Union would be bound to decline jurisdiction if they were subsequently seised by the other party of an action in damages.

2 Granting the right to initiate proceedings to the party who should logically be the defendant has been largely criticized in Europe as being artificial and an abuse of process. Yet, one must wonder why a choice as important as that of the court should be reserved to plaintiffs only. Certainly, plaintiffs should not receive such a tremendous advantage for the reason that they are victims: before judgment, this is only an allegation which remains to be demonstrated. The European Court of Human Rights has repeatedly held that equality of arms is a fundamental procedural right, and it is hard to see why this should not result in defendants being equally able to secure the jurisdiction of their preferred court.

3 If one accepts that any party may seise a court first for the purpose of *lis pendens*, the danger is obviously that the rule will result in a race to court. As soon as a potential dispute arises, both parties might rush to seise their preferred court in order to secure its jurisdiction. This in turn might give them an advantage in any negotiation that they might start to resolve 'amicably' the dispute with other party.

4 In such a context, the definition of seizure for the purpose of *lis pendens* becomes crucial. See Article 32 of the Brussels Ibis Regulation *supra*.

2 Forum non conveniens

The doctrine of *forum non conveniens* was originally developed by the Scottish courts in the 19th century. It was later adopted not only in England, but throughout the common law world (Australia, Singapore, Nigeria, Ghana, and so on). The main purpose of the doctrine is not to handle parallel litigation, but rather to regulate the jurisdiction of the (common law) forum. Contrary to *lis pendens, forum non conveniens* can apply and, as the case may be, result in a common law court staying proceedings initiated in the forum, even if no foreign court was seised of the same dispute. However, the main ground for staying proceedings under the doctrine of *forum non conveniens* is that there be a foreign court which is clearly more appropriate than the forum for the resolution of the dispute. Indirectly, therefore, *forum non conveniens* resolves an issue of parallel litigation. The conflict can be only potential, however, as the foreign court might not yet have been seised. But the defendant in the common law forum is asking the common law court to rule that the foreign court is a more appropriate forum, and should be preferred.

The most fundamental difference between *forum non conveniens* and *lis pendens*, however, is the test used to decide which court should be preferred.

CASE

House of Lords, 19 November 1986 *Spiliada Maritime Corporation Appellants v. Cansulex Ltd Respondents*[8]

LORD GOFF OF CHIEVELEY

The fundamental principle

In cases where jurisdiction has been founded as of right, i.e. where in this country the defendant has been served with proceedings within the jurisdiction, the defendant may now apply to the court to exercise its discretion to stay the proceedings on the ground which is usually called forum non conveniens. That principle has for long been recognised in Scots law; but it has only been recognised comparatively recently in this country. In *The Abidin Daver* [1984] A.C. 398, 411, Lord Diplock stated that, on this point, English law and Scots law may now be regarded as indistinguishable. It is proper therefore to regard the classic statement of Lord Kinnear in *Sim v. Robinow* (1892) 19 R. 665 as expressing the principle now applicable in both jurisdictions. He said, at p. 668:

> the plea can never be sustained unless the court is satisfied that there is some other tribunal, having competent jurisdiction, in which the case may be tried more suitably for the interests of all the parties and for the ends of justice.

I feel bound to say that I doubt whether the Latin tag forum non conveniens is apt to describe this principle. For the question is not one of convenience, but of the suitability or appropriateness of the relevant jurisdiction. However the Latin tag (sometimes expressed as forum non conveniens and sometimes as forum conveniens) is so widely used to describe the principle, not only in England and Scotland, but in other Commonwealth jurisdictions and in the United States, that it is probably sensible to retain it. But it is most important not to allow it to mislead us into thinking that the question at issue is one of 'mere practical convenience.' Such a suggestion was emphatically rejected by Lord Kinnear in *Sim v. Robinow*, 668, and by Lord Dunedin, Lord Shaw of Dunfermline and Lord Sumner in the *Société du Gaz* case, 1926 S.C. (H.L.) 13, 18, 19, and 22 respectively. Lord Dunedin, with reference to the expressions forum non competens and forum non conveniens, said, at p. 18:

> In my view, 'competent' is just as bad a translation for 'competens' as 'convenient' is for 'conveniens.' The proper translation for these Latin words, so far as this plea is concerned, is 'appropriate.'

---

8 [1987] A.C. 460.

Lord Sumner referred to a phrase used by Lord Cowan in *Clements v. Macaulay* (1866) 4 Macph. 583, 594, viz. 'more convenient and preferable for securing the ends of justice,' and said, at p. 22:

> one cannot think of convenience apart from the convenience of the pursuer or the defender or the court, and the convenience of all these three, as the cases show, is of little, if any, importance. If you read it as 'more convenient, that is to say, preferable, for securing the ends of justice,' I think the true meaning of the doctrine is arrived at. The object, under the words 'forum non conveniens' is to find that *forum* which is the more suitable for the ends of justice, and is preferable because pursuit of the litigation in that *forum* is more likely to secure those ends.

In the light of these authoritative statements of the Scottish doctrine, I cannot help thinking that it is wiser to avoid use of the word 'convenience' and to refer rather, as Lord Dunedin did, to the *appropriate* forum.

How the principle is applied in cases of stay of proceedings

In my opinion, having regard to the authorities (including in particular the Scottish authorities), the law can at present be summarised as follows.

(a) The basic principle is that a stay will only be granted on the ground of forum non conveniens where the court is satisfied that there is some other available forum, having competent jurisdiction, which is the appropriate forum for the trial of the action, i.e. in which the case may be tried more suitably for the interests of all the parties and the ends of justice.

(b) As Lord Kinnear's formulation of the principle indicates, in general the burden of proof rests on the defendant to persuade the court to exercise its discretion to grant a stay (see, e.g., the *Société du Gaz* case, 21; and Anton, *Private International Law* (1967) p. 150). It is however of importance to remember that each party will seek to establish the existence of certain matters which will assist him in persuading the court to exercise its discretion in his favour, and that in respect of any such matter the evidential burden will rest on the party who asserts its existence. Furthermore, if the court is satisfied that there is another available forum which is prima facie the appropriate forum for the trial of the action, the burden will then shift to the plaintiff to show that there are special circumstances by reason of which justice requires that the trial should nevertheless take place in this country (see (f), below).

(c) The question being whether there is some other forum which is the appropriate forum for the trial of the action, it is pertinent to ask whether the fact that the plaintiff has, ex hypothesi, founded jurisdiction as of right in accordance with the law of this country, of itself gives the plaintiff an advantage in the sense that the English court will not lightly disturb jurisdiction so established. Such indeed appears to be the law in the United States, where 'the court hesitates to disturb the plaintiff's choice of forum and will not do so unless the balance of factors is strongly in favor of the defendant': see Scoles and Hay, Conflict of Laws (1982), p. 366, and cases there cited; and also in Canada, where it has been stated (see Castel, *Conflict of Laws* (1974), p. 282) that 'unless the balance is strongly in favor of the defendant, the plaintiff's choice of forum should rarely be disturbed.' This is strong language. However, the United States and Canada are both federal states; and, where the choice is between competing jurisdictions within a federal state, it is readily understandable that a strong preference should be given to the forum chosen by the plaintiff upon which jurisdiction has been conferred by the constitution of the country which includes both alternative jurisdictions. (. . .)

(d) Since the question is whether there exists some other forum which is clearly more appropriate for the trial of the action, the court will look first to see what factors there are which point in the direction of another forum. These are the factors which Lord Diplock described, in *MacShannon's* case [1978] A.C. 795, 812, as indicating that justice can be done in the other forum at 'substantially less inconvenience or expense.' Having regard to the anxiety expressed in your Lordships' House in the *Société du Gaz* case, 13 concerning the use of the word 'convenience' in this context, I respectfully consider that it may be more desirable, now that the English and Scottish principles are regarded as being the same, to adopt the expression used by my noble and learned friend, Lord Keith of Kinkel, in *The Abidin Daver*, 415, when he referred to the 'natural forum' as being 'that with which the action had the most real and substantial connection.' So it is for connecting factors in this sense that the court must first look; and these will include not only factors affecting convenience or expense (such as availability of witnesses), but also other factors such as the law governing the relevant transaction, and the places where the parties respectively reside or carry on business.

(e) If the court concludes at that stage that there is no other available forum which is clearly more appropriate for the trial of the action, it will ordinarily refuse a stay; see, e.g., the decision of the Court of Appeal in *European Asian Bank A.G. v. Punjab and Sind Bank* [1982] 2 Lloyd's Rep. 356. It is difficult to imagine circumstances where, in such a case, a stay may be granted.

(f) If however the court concludes at that stage that there is some other available forum which prima facie is clearly more appropriate for the trial of the action, it will ordinarily grant a stay unless there are circumstances by reason of which justice requires that a stay should nevertheless not be granted. In this inquiry, the court will consider all the circumstances of the case, including circumstances which go beyond those taken into account when considering connecting factors with other jurisdictions. One such factor can be the fact, if established objectively by cogent evidence, that the plaintiff will not obtain justice in the foreign jurisdiction; see *The Abidin Daver*, 411, a passage which now makes plain that, on this inquiry, the burden of proof shifts to the plaintiff. (. . .)

Treatment of 'a legitimate personal or juridical advantage'

Clearly, the mere fact that the plaintiff has such an advantage in proceedings in England cannot be decisive. (. . .)

Indeed, as Oliver L.J. [1985] 2 Lloyd's Rep. 116, 135, pointed out in his judgment in the present case, an advantage to the plaintiff will ordinarily give rise to a comparable disadvantage to the defendant; and simply to give the plaintiff his advantage at the expense of the defendant is not consistent with the objective approach inherent in Lord Kinnear's statement of principle in *Sim v. Robinow*, 668.

The key to the solution of this problem lies, in my judgment, in the underlying fundamental principle. We have to consider where the case may be tried 'suitably for the interests of all the parties and for the ends of justice.' Let me consider the application of that principle in relation to advantages which the plaintiff may derive from invoking the English jurisdiction. Typical examples are: damages awarded on a higher scale; a more complete procedure of discovery; a power to award interest; a more generous limitation period. Now, as a general rule, I do not think that the court should be deterred from granting a stay of proceedings, or from exercising its discretion against granting leave under R.S.C. Ord. 11, simply because the plaintiff will be deprived of such an advantage, provided that the court is satisfied that substantial justice will be done in the available appropriate forum. Take, for example, discovery. We know that there is a spectrum of systems of discovery applicable in various jurisdictions, ranging from the limited discovery available in civil law countries on the continent of Europe to the very generous pre-trial oral discovery procedure applicable in the United States of America. Our procedure lies somewhere in the middle of this spectrum. No doubt each of these systems has its virtues and vices; but, generally speaking, I cannot see that, objectively, injustice can be said to have been done if a party is, in effect, compelled to accept one of these well-recognised systems applicable in the appropriate forum overseas. In this, I recognise that we appear to be differing from the approach presently prevailing in the United States: see, e.g., the recent opinion of Judge Keenan in *Re Union Carbide Corp.* (1986) 634 F.Supp. 842 in the District Court for the Southern District of New York, where a stay of proceedings in New York, commenced on behalf of Indian plaintiffs against Union Carbide arising out of the tragic disaster in Bhopal, was stayed subject to, inter alia, the condition that Union Carbide was subject to discovery under the model of the United States Federal Rules of Civil Procedure after appropriate demand by the plaintiff. But in the *Trendtex* case [1982] A.C. 679, this House thought it right that a stay of proceedings in this country should be granted where the appropriate forum was Switzerland, even though the plaintiffs were thereby deprived of the advantage of the more extensive English procedure of discovery of documents in a case of fraud. Then take the scale on which damages are awarded. Suppose that two parties have been involved in a road accident in a foreign country, where both were resident, and where damages are awarded on a scale substantially lower than those awarded in this country. I do not think that an English court would, in ordinary circumstances, hesitate to stay proceedings brought by one of them against the other in this country merely because he would be deprived of a higher award of damages here.

But the underlying principle requires that regard must be had to the interests of all the parties and the ends of justice; and these considerations may lead to a different conclusion in other cases. (. . .) Again, take the example of cases concerned with time bars. Let me consider how the principle of forum non conveniens should be applied in a case in which the plaintiff has started proceedings in England where his claim was not time barred, but there is some other jurisdiction which, in the opinion of the court, is clearly more appropriate for the trial of the action, but where the plaintiff has not commenced proceedings and where his claim is now time barred. Now, to take some extreme examples, suppose that the plaintiff allowed the limitation period to elapse in the appropriate jurisdiction, and came here simply because he wanted to take advantage of a more generous time bar applicable in this country; or suppose that it was obvious that the plaintiff should have commenced proceedings in the appropriate jurisdiction, and yet he did not trouble to issue a protective writ there; in cases such as these, I cannot see that the court should hesitate to stay the proceedings in this country, even though the effect would be that the plaintiff's claim would inevitably be defeated by a plea of the time bar in the appropriate jurisdiction. Indeed a strong theoretical argument can be advanced for the proposition that, if there is another clearly more appropriate forum for the trial of the action, a stay should generally be granted even though the plaintiff's action would be time barred there. But, in my opinion, this is a case where practical justice should be done, and practical justice demands that, if the court considers that the plaintiff acted reasonably in commencing proceedings in this country, and that, although it appears that (putting on one side the time bar point) the appropriate forum for the trial of the action is elsewhere than England, the plaintiff did not act unreasonably in failing to commence proceedings (for example, by issuing a protective writ) in that jurisdiction within the limitation period applicable there, it would not, I think, be just to deprive the plaintiff of the benefit of having started proceedings within the limitation period applicable in this country. This approach is consistent with that of Sheen J. in *The Blue Wave* [1982] 1 Lloyd's Rep. 151. It is not to be forgotten that, by making its jurisdiction available to the plaintiff – even the discretionary jurisdiction under R.S.C., Ord. 11 – the courts of this country have provided the plaintiff with an opportunity to start proceedings here; accordingly, if justice demands, the court should not deprive the plaintiff of the benefit of having complied with the time bar in this country. Furthermore, as the applicable principles become more clearly established and better known, it will, I suspect, become increasingly difficult for plaintiffs to prove lack of negligence in this respect. The fact that the court has been asked to exercise its discretion under R.S.C., Ord. 11, rather than that the plaintiff has served proceedings upon the defendant in this country as of right, is, I consider, only relevant to consideration of the plaintiff's conduct in failing to save the time bar in the other relevant alternative jurisdiction. The appropriate order, where the application of the time bar in the foreign jurisdiction is dependent upon its invocation by the defendant, may well be to make it a condition of the grant of a stay, or the exercise of discretion against giving leave to serve out of the jurisdiction, that the defendant should waive the time bar in the foreign jurisdiction; this is apparently the practice in the United States of America.

? NOTES

1 Contrary to the doctrine of *lis pendens*, which is solely based on a chronological factor, the doctrine of *forum non conveniens* empowers common law courts to decide whether to exercise jurisdiction by comparing the appropriateness of the forum and of the foreign court to decide the particular case. Whether one court is more appropriate than the other will be assessed by taking into account a number of factors, which vary from one common law jurisdiction to another.

Ronald Brand, Access-to-Justice Analysis on a Due Process Platform[9]

The doctrine of forum non conveniens, developed in common law jurisdictions, favors equitable analysis over efficient rules and gives courts discretion in determining the most appropriate forum for a dispute. By contrast, civil law states generally address the 'problem' of parallel litigation through predictable rules found in code-type instruments. The ordinary rule is the concept of lis alibi pendens, by which the first court seised retains jurisdiction and all subsequent courts in which an action involving the same issues and parties is brought dismiss the case.

Neither approach to parallel litigation is wholly satisfactory. The civil law approach (*lis pendens*) favors efficiency and predictability (values focused on societal interests) over equity and fairness (values focused on individual interests). The result is a race to the courthouse that can interrupt (and perhaps prevent) rational negotiated resolution of disputes before tensions are raised by formal legal proceedings. The common law approach (forum non conveniens) requires that courts be given discretion (something disfavored in civil law systems) and brings with it significant uncertainty.

2   Crucially, none of the factors taken into account include an assessment of the respective quality of the contemplated courts. The point is not to assess which is the better court, but rather which would be the most appropriate one for the parties in the particular case. The most important factors relate to the costs of the litigation. If the witnesses live in one of the two countries, litigating in the other would be much more expensive as the witnesses would have to travel to give testimony. If the law of one of the two courts is applicable, additional costs would be incurred should the dispute be litigated in the other court, where the applicable law would be foreign and would thus have to be proven.

3   Lord Goff distinguishes between cases where the defendant was sued in England as of right and cases where leave to serve out of the jurisdiction was granted. Recall that, in the latter, the plaintiff had to convince the court that England was the *forum conveniens* (*supra*, Ch. 3). The purpose of the doctrine of *forum non conveniens* is to enable the defendant to raise the issue of the appropriateness of the jurisdiction of the English court in cases where he was served within the jurisdiction.

4   The English test is twofold. At the first stage of the test, the defendant must convince the forum that a foreign court is clearly more appropriate and is therefore the natural forum. At a second stage, however, the plaintiff may show that the stay should not be granted, because substantial justice would not be done abroad. In this context, 'substantial justice' does not mean that the plaintiff would lose on the merits, or even that he could not enjoy procedural tools available in the English legal process such as pre-trial discovery. It means that the foreign court would be dysfunctional in some fundamental way. Examples include a foreign court biased against the plaintiff due to racial or political motivation, or a foreign court unable to handle a very complex commercial case due to its lack of experience.

---

9 (2012) 112 Columbia L.R. Sidebar 76, 80.

In the United States, there is no autonomous requirement that justice could be done abroad. But the first prong of the *forum non conveniens* test is that there be an 'adequate available forum'.

 CASE

U.S. District Court, C.D. California,Western Division, 28 June 2005 *Gambra v. International Lease Finance Corp, Boeing and Honeywell International, Inc.*[10]

SNYDER, District Judge.

I. BACKGROUND

This case arises out of the crash of Flash Airlines ('Flash') Flight 604 in the Red Sea off the coast of Egypt while en route from Sharm el-Sheikh, Egypt, to Paris, France, on January 3, 2004. All 148 aboard Flight 604 were killed in the crash. Pursuant to Annex 13 to the Convention on International Civil Aviation, the Egyptian Ministry of Civil Aviation ('the MCA') is conducting the official investigation of the crash of Flight 604. France's Bureau d'Enquête et d'Analyses ('BEA') and the United States National Transportation Safety Board ('NTSB') are also participating in the MCA's investigation.

The 150 plaintiffs in the 56 consolidated cases before the Court are the heirs and beneficiaries of the estates of those who perished on Flight 604. These plaintiffs are suing based on the deaths of 122 decedents. The plaintiffs are 145 individuals who are citizens or residents of France. All but two, *i.e.* 120 out of 122, of the decedents who are the subject of this litigation are citizens or residents of France. Included in the plaintiffs before this Court are 139 plaintiffs who have also sued Flash and its insurer Al Chark Insurance Company ('Al Chark') in French courts, namely the Tribunal de Grande Instance ('TGI') of Bobigny, France. At least 121 of the 143 potential heirs and beneficiaries of the estates of the decedents are citizens or residents of France. It appears undisputed that the Warsaw Convention mandates that plaintiffs' claims against Flash be brought in France or Egypt but not in the United States.

Defendant International Lease Finance Corporation ('ILFC') is a corporation 'engaged in the leasing of commercial aircraft, which activity it conducts primarily from its California headquarters.' ILFC leased to Flash the Boeing 737–300 aircraft involved in the crash of Flight 604 which bore the serial

---

10 377 F.Supp.2d 810.

number 26283 and Egyptian registration number SU–ZCF ('the subject air-craft'). Defendant The Boeing Company ('Boeing') manufactured the subject aircraft, except for certain component parts that were manufactured by sub-contractors or suppliers. Boeing sold the subject aircraft to ILFC in 1992 and ILFC leased the subject aircraft to Flash in 2001. Defendant Parker Hannifin Corporation ('Parker Hannifin') manufactured certain component parts of the subject aircraft. Parker Hannifin Answer to Gambra First Amended Complaint. Defendant Honeywell International Inc. ('Honeywell') manu-factured certain component parts of the flight management system for the subject aircraft. Honeywell Answer to Gambra Complaint at 2. Plaintiffs allege strict liability, negligence and breach of warranty claims against all defendants. (. . .)

II. DISCUSSION

Defendants seek to dismiss this case on grounds of *forum non conveniens*. Plaintiffs argue that this Court is the most appropriate forum for this litigation.

'The *forum non conveniens* determination is committed to the sound discre-tion of the trial court.' *Piper Aircraft Co. v. Reyno*, 454 U.S. 235, 257 (1981). 'A party moving to dismiss based on *forum non conveniens* bears the burden of showing (1) that there is an adequate alternative forum, and (2) that the balance of private and public interest factors favors dismissal.' *Dole Food Co., Inc. v. Watts*, 303 F.3d 1104, 1118 (9th Cir.2002). 'The plaintiff's choice of forum will not be disturbed unless the "private interest" and "public interest" factors strongly favor trial in the foreign country.' *Id.* The Ninth Circuit has recognized that 'the standard to be applied to a motion for dismissal on the ground of *forum non conveniens* is whether . . . defendants have made a clear showing of facts which . . . establish such oppression and vexation of a defendant as to be out of proportion to plaintiff's convenience, which may be shown to be slight or nonexistent.' *Id.* (internal brackets omitted). While there is a strong presumption in favor of plaintiff's choice of forum, 'a foreign plaintiff's choice deserves less deference.' *Piper*, at 256. Nevertheless, '[f]orum non conveniens is "an exceptional tool to be employed sparingly, not a . . . doctrine that compels plaintiffs to choose the optimal forum for their claim."' *Dole* at 1118 (internal brackets omitted).

A. Adequate Alternative Forum

'To satisfy the adequacy requirement, this Court must find that (1) defend-ants are amenable to process in the alternative forum, and (2) the subject matter of the lawsuit is cognizable in the alternative forum so as to provide plaintiff[s] appropriate redress.' *Bodner v. Banque Paribas*, 114 F.Supp.2d 117, 132 (E.D.N.Y.2000).

(1) Subject to Jurisdiction and Amenable to Service of Process

If defendants are amenable to service of process, an alternative forum ordinarily exists. *Piper*, 454 U.S. at 254 n. 22. 'A defendant's agreement to submit to personal jurisdiction of the foreign country satisfies this requirement.' Judge William W. Schwarzer *et al.*, California Practice Guide: Federal Civil Procedure Before Trial § 4:315 (The Rutter Group 2004) (additional citation omitted).

Defendants argue that France is an available alternative forum because 'defendants are willing to submit, as a condition to forum non conveniens dismissal of these actions, to the jurisdiction of a French court in actions refiled by plaintiffs there and to toll any statute of limitations that might apply to such refiled actions for 120 days after dismissal by this Court.' Defendants contend that consent to jurisdiction in the French courts is permitted under French law and that '[w]hen a defendant voluntarily appears before a French court and participates in the proceedings, that tribunal has no power to decline to exercise its jurisdiction where, as here, no other country's courts have exclusive jurisdiction over the case.' In support of this argument, defendants proffer portions of the Delebecque Decl. Professor Delebecque opines that if defendants consent to the jurisdiction of a French court, by participating in proceedings or demonstrating a willingness to be subject to such jurisdiction, a French court would not refuse to exercise jurisdiction over plaintiffs' claims. Professor Delebecque opines that Article 46 of the Noveau code de procédure civile ('N.C.P.C.') permits defendants to choose to refer the case to the location where the injury was suffered, which in this case might be the residence of the relatives and beneficiaries of decedents. Further, according to Professor Delebecque, Article 14 of the French Civil Code would also justify French jurisdiction because it provides for jurisdiction in France when a plaintiff is a French citizen or resident. Although Professor Delebecque notes that a French plaintiff waives the ability to assert jurisdiction based on Article 14 if he 'voluntarily serves a writ on a foreigner abroad,' he opines that plaintiffs may reverse the waiver by demonstrating that this Court rejected jurisdiction and that no case is currently pending in the United States. Professor Delebecque further suggests that Article 42(2) of the N.C.P.C. may provide a basis for jurisdiction based on the French court's jurisdiction over Flash in a related case.

Defendants contend that, based on two Cour de Cassation cases, Article 14 would permit non-French plaintiffs like the five in the present case to join their claims with those of French citizens such that a French court could exercise jurisdiction over all plaintiffs' claims. Defendants refer to these cases as decided by the 'French Supreme Court.' It appears that this is a reference to the Cour de Cassation.

Nevertheless, plaintiffs dispute that France provides an alternative forum. Plaintiffs argue that France is not an adequate alternative forum because the French courts do not have jurisdiction over claims by non-French plaintiffs. Plaintiffs also proffer the declarations of their experts, who opine that a French court could determine *sua sponte* that French plaintiffs have waived their Article 14 privileges. Moreover, plaintiffs' experts opine that jurisdiction pursuant to Article 42 of the N.C.P.C. would not exist because the statute provides for jurisdiction in the domicile of a co-defendant with a related case and none of the defendants or Flash is domiciled in France. In addition, according to plaintiffs' experts, Article 46 of the N.C.P.C. does not provide a basis for jurisdiction because the harm in this case, namely the crash, did not occur in France.

Defendants respond that Articles 331 and 333 of N.C.P.C. would allow plaintiffs to implead any third party necessary to the resolution of the case against Flash and that the Cour de Cassation has permitted non-French plaintiffs to join their claims with French plaintiffs' claims pursuant to Article 14 of the French Civil Code. Moreover, defendants argue that if the Court has any doubts about whether French courts will accept jurisdiction, the Court may condition its dismissal on the acceptance of jurisdiction by the French courts over the claims asserted in these cases.

First, defendants' agreement as a condition of dismissal 'to submit. . .to the jurisdiction of a French court in actions refiled by plaintiffs there and to toll any statute of limitations that might apply to such refiled actions for 120 days after dismissal by this Court' supports a finding that defendants are amenable to personal jurisdiction in France. As to whether French courts will assume jurisdiction over plaintiffs' claims, both parties submit evidence in support of their respective positions. It appears that there is a reasonable basis for concluding that French courts will be able to exercise jurisdiction over plaintiffs' claims. To the extent that the possibility remains that French courts will refuse to assert jurisdiction over plaintiffs' claims, any order of dismissal based on *forum non conveniens* grounds will be conditioned on the French court's assumption of jurisdiction over plaintiffs' claims. *See Contact Lumber v. P.T. Moges Shipping Co. Ltd.*, 918 F.2d 1446, 1450 (9th Cir.1990).

(2) Adequacy of Forum

Defendants maintain that France is an adequate forum for this litigation. Plaintiffs do not appear to dispute that France would be an adequate forum once all necessary parties are subject to its jurisdiction.

(a) Subject Matter and Remedies

'A foreign forum is adequate when it provides the plaintiff with a sufficient remedy for his wrong.' *Dole*, 303 F.3d at 1118 (citation omitted). However, '[i]f the remedy provided by the alternative forum is so clearly inadequate or unsatisfactory that it is no remedy at all, the unfavorable change in law may be given substantial weight; the district court may conclude that dismissal would not be in the interests of justice.' *Piper*, 454 U.S. at 254.

Defendants argue that the plaintiffs in this case have already conceded that France is an adequate forum by filing their cases against Flash in France. Although plaintiffs assert that the action against Flash in France was involuntarily dismissed on February 22, 2005, defendants maintain that the French action against Flash has been 'temporarily halted' and 'can be resumed at any time.' Moreover, defendants assert that France provides remedies for negligence and product liability claims and permits plaintiffs to recover losses on behalf of the deceased passengers as well as economic and non-economic damages on behalf of themselves as 'indirect victims.' Defendants have proffered expert testimony demonstrating that French law provides substantial remedies for product liability claims like those brought by plaintiffs. Although the parties do not agree that French substantive law necessarily governs plaintiffs' claims, plaintiffs do not argue that a French forum would refuse to recognize plaintiffs' claims or provide adequate remedies for plaintiffs.

(b) Procedural Safeguards

Defendants contend that the judicial system in France would provide a fair and thorough proceeding and the opportunity to appeal to an intermediate as well as the highest court. Defendants have proffered expert testimony demonstrating that French courts have a rigorous judicial system that seeks to promote fair proceedings and debate. Plaintiffs do not dispute the adequacy of judicial procedure in France. Accordingly, potentially inadequate procedural safeguards do not counsel against litigation in France.

Because the Court concludes that an adequate alternative forum exists in

France, the Court finds that defendants have satisfied the first prong of the *forum non conveniens* analysis. *See Gschwind v. Cessna Aircraft Co.*, 161 F.3d 602 (10th Cir.1998), 606–08 (holding France is adequate alternative forum in litigation involving airplane crash), *Magnin v. Teledyne Continental Motors*, 91 F.3d 1424, 1429 (11th Cir.1996) (same). The Court next considers whether the public and private interest factors weigh in favor of dismissal on *forum non conveniens* grounds.

B. Private Interest Factors

'Private interest factors include: ease of access to sources of proof; compulsory process to obtain the attendance of hostile witnesses, and the cost of transporting friendly witnesses; and other problems that interfere with an expeditious trial.' *Contact Lumber*, 918 F.2d at 1451 (citing *Gulf Oil v. Gilbert*, 330 U.S. 501, 508 (1947), *superseded by statute on other grounds as recognized in Hartford Fire Ins. Co. v. Westinghouse Elec. Corp.*, 725 F.Supp. 317 (S.D.Miss.1989)).[FN9] Defendants argue that the private interest factors favor dismissal.

> FN9. The Ninth Circuit has also stated that these factors include: '(1) the residence of the parties and the witnesses; (2) the forum's convenience to the litigants; (3) access to physical evidence and other sources of proof; (4) whether unwilling witnesses can be compelled to testify; (5) the cost of bringing witnesses to trial; (6) the enforceability of the judgment; and (7) "all other practical problems that make trial of a case easy, expeditious and inexpensive."' *Lueck* at 1145 (citing *Gulf Oil*, 330 U.S. at 508).

(1) Ease of Access to Sources of Proof

Defendants contend that only a French court will have access to all of the necessary evidence, which is currently located in France, Egypt, and the United States. First, defendants maintain that nearly all of the evidence supporting plaintiffs' damages, including documents and witnesses establishing financial losses and witnesses with knowledge of the health and life expectancy of the numerous decedents, is presently located in France. Second, defendants contend that documents regarding Flash Airlines, civilian aviation oversight, and the Egyptian MCA investigation, which are located in Egypt, would be available in France from Flash by compulsory process and from parties located in Egypt pursuant to a bilateral convention permitting French courts to obtain evidence located in Egypt. Defendants assert that, by contrast, Flash's evidence cannot be compelled in this Court and that evidence in Egypt will be difficult, if not impossible, to obtain because it is unlikely that an Egyptian court would enforce an international letter rogatory from this Court asking for assistance in obtaining evidence located in Egypt. Defendants argue that if plaintiffs were to proceed in the French courts, they would have access to defendants' documents pursuant to defendants' agreement to produce them as a condition of dismissal. Moreover, defendants contend that only a small portion of the necessary evidence is located in California, while most of the evidence in the United States is located outside of California.

Plaintiffs argue that France cannot rely on its bilateral treaties with Egypt to obtain evidence from Egypt because the Convention between the United States of America and Other Governments Respecting International Civil Aviation 'controls every aspect of an aircraft accident investigation, including the sharing of information generated during the course of an investigation,' and thus supersedes any subsequent conventions between France and Egypt. Plaintiffs also contend that Egyptian authorities have not cooperated with French requests for information in the criminal investigation of the crash and are not likely to be more cooperative in the future. Notwithstanding potential problems obtaining evidence from Egypt, plaintiffs maintain that all necessary evidence of liability is currently available in the United States, including engineering documents and data. In particular, plaintiffs argue that '[w]hile parts of the wreckage [located in Egypt] are relevant to Plaintiffs' proof, a total wreckage inspection is not required.' As to the relevant parts of the wreckage, plaintiffs assert that the MCA has already relinquished custody of the aileron power control unit to NTSB and has demonstrated that they are likely to cooperate with the NTSB in the future. Plaintiffs argue that damages evidence consists mainly of documents which are easily transportable and a few willing witnesses who will travel to California at plaintiffs' expense. Finally, plaintiffs contend that French discovery rules would result in defendants being required to produce less evidence than would be required in the United States.

Defendants respond that much of the critical evidence they need is not located in Egypt, but rather is under the control of Flash. Reply at 20. In addition, defendants assert that Egyptian authorities have at least partially complied with French requests for evidence and that evidence gathered by the MCA will be available pursuant to the Egypt–France treaty once the MCA's investigation of the crash is complete.

Only one piece of the wreckage of Flight 604 is located in the United States. The evidence to be supplied by California-based ILFC appears minimal and easily transportable to France. ('ILFC has approximately 600–700 pages of documents relating to the accident aircraft. All of these documents are located in California. There are four to six ILFC current and former employees with relevant knowledge regarding the accident or the accident aircraft, most of whom are located in California with one in Alabama and one former employee in New York City.'). Moreover, it appears that at least a substantial portion of defendants' evidence regarding aircraft design, manufacture, assembly, testing, certification, and customer support services is located outside California. Even so, defendants have agreed to produce such evidence in any action before a French court.

As to the evidence located outside the United States, the Court finds that such evidence is more easily accessible in France. As defendants note, most of the documents and witnesses concerning damages, such as the tax returns, pay stubs, employment records, health records, and family members of decedents are overwhelmingly located in France, where the majority of decedents resided. *See Taiwan Straits*, 331 F.Supp.2d at 1196 ('While the parties dispute the location of the relevant liability proof, there is no question that damages proof is overwhelmingly located in Taiwan. Given the number of decedents, the volume of this evidence is substantial.'). In addition, it appears that it will be easier for all parties to obtain evidence from Flash in France than in California, where Flash is likely beyond this Court's subpoena power. Finally, although France and Egypt are parties to a bilateral treaty relating to judicial cooperation, the parties disagree about the extent of assistance that Egyptian officials will provide to French courts attempting to obtain evidence from Egypt. Because the Court finds that this factor strongly favors dismissal, the relative ease by which the United States or France could obtain evidence from Egypt does not change the Court's conclusion regarding this factor. Given that a large volume of relevant evidence is either located in France now or can be made available there by agreement, while much of the evidence located in France would be difficult, if not impossible, to obtain in California, the Court finds that this factor favors dismissal.

(2) Compulsory Process to Obtain the Attendance of Hostile Witnesses, and the Cost of Transporting Friendly Witnesses

Defendants contend that witnesses critical to this case are beyond the reach of this Court's compulsory processes because they are located in foreign countries. However, defendants contend that these witnesses would be available in France because they reside in France or have brought claims against Flash and its insurer, Al Chark, in France. Moreover, cooperation between France and Egypt pursuant to their bilateral convention would also likely result in important witnesses located in Egypt being available in France. As already discussed above, there appear to be a large number of damages witnesses located in France. Even if they were willing to testify voluntarily, the cost of their traveling to this district would be great. If these French witnesses were to refuse to testify, it is unlikely that this Court would be able to compel them to do so. Conversely, defendants have agreed to make witnesses and other evidence available in France as a condition to dismissal. Accordingly, the Court concludes that this factor weighs in favor of dismissal.

(3) Other Problems that Interfere with an Expeditious Trial

Defendants argue that the fact that many of the plaintiffs are already pursuing an action against Flash and its insurer in France also weighs in favor of dismissal. Defendants contend that permitting concurrent actions to proceed in France and the United States would be inefficient and duplicative and may result in inconsistent results. *Id.* at 18–19. Defendants note that the Warsaw Convention prohibits plaintiffs from bringing their claims against Flash in the United States, but that plaintiffs' claims against the instant defendants can be brought in France. *Id.* Finally, defendants argue that the absence of Flash from the present actions creates the potential for incomplete relief, prejudice to defendants with respect to the allocation of liability, and conflicting results.

Plaintiffs further argue that the parties' expectation that the litigation will proceed in California weighs in favor of denying defendants' motion. A forum selection clause in the ILFC–Flash lease provides as follows:

> *Waiver.* LESSEE AND LESSOR HEREBY WAIVE THE RIGHT TO A TRIAL BY JURY. LESSEE AND LESSOR HEREBY IRREVOCABLY WAIVE ANY OBJECTION WHICH IT MAY NOW OR HEREAFTER HAVE TO THE LAYING OF THE VENUE OF ANY SUIT, ACTION OR PROCEEDING ARISING OUT OF OR RELATED TO THE LEASE BROUGHT IN ANY OF THE COURTS REFERRED TO IN ARTICLE 27.2, AND HEREBY FURTHER IRREVOCABLY WAIVE ANY CLAIM THAT ANY SUCH SUIT, ACTION OR PROCEEDING BROUGHT IN ANY SUCH COURT HAS BEEN BROUGHT IN AN INCONVENIENT FORUM.

Plaintiffs assert that ILFC and Flash agreed that California law governs their lease agreement and that the parties 'selected ILFC's home district as the proper forum for disputes involving the leased aircraft, and clearly agreed that neither would challenge the contractually selected forum as inconvenient.' Accordingly, plaintiffs contend that the Court must enforce this forum selection clause pursuant to *M/S Bremen v. Zapata Off–Shore Co.*, 407 U.S.

1 (1972). Plaintiffs contend that they are entitled to rely upon the forum selection clause in the lease between ILFC and Flash because they are intended third party beneficiaries of the lease agreement.[FN12]

> FN12. For reasons discussed in connection with the public interest factor regarding the preference for having a forum apply a law with which it is familiar, plaintiffs argue that even if a French court were to hear this case, the application of French choice-of-law rules would result in further inconvenience and difficulty.

Defendants respond that the lease between ILFC and Flash does not make plaintiffs third party beneficiaries. More specifically, defendants argue that the insurance and aircraft maintenance provisions of the lease upon which plaintiffs rely to demonstrate that they are intended beneficiaries were not intended to be invoked by plaintiffs or other third parties. Defendants point to Article 8.5 of the lease as demonstrating that the lease was not intended to apply to claims involving the condition of the subject aircraft.

In addition, defendants argue that plaintiffs are not seeking to enforce any particular provision of the lease besides the forum selection clause and are not asserting claims arising out of or related to the lease.

The Court concludes that the lease between ILFC and Flash does not weigh in favor of retaining the case. First, the forum selection clause does not govern the claims of plaintiffs against the defendants in these cases. The lease governs the obligations of ILFC and Flash with respect to the subject aircraft, not the liability of either of them to those passengers and crew aboard the subject aircraft. In fact, Article 8.5 of the lease explicitly provides that it does not cover losses to anyone arising out of the condition of the aircraft. Accordingly, the Court finds that the claims asserted in these cases are not governed by the express terms of the forum selection clause.

Second, even if the Court were to conclude that these actions arise out of or are related to the lease, plaintiffs are not third party beneficiaries who are entitled to enforce all provisions of the lease, including the forum selection clause. (. . .)

Finally, the Court concludes that the fact that Flash cannot be compelled to appear as a defendant in the United States is a substantial consideration weighing in favor of dismissal. In *Piper*, the Supreme Court addressed a similar situation in which potential third-party defendants could not be impleaded into an action in the United States, but could appear as defendants in a trial in Scotland. *Piper*, 454 U.S. at 258. The Court reasoned as follows:

> Joinder of the pilot's estate, Air Navigation, and McDonald is crucial to the presentation of petitioners' defense. If Piper and Hartzell can show that the accident was caused not by a design defect, but rather by the negligence of the pilot, the plane's owners, or the charter company, they will be relieved of all liability. It is true, of course, that if Hartzell and Piper were found liable after a trial in the United States, they could institute an action for indemnity or contribution against these parties in Scotland. It would be far more convenient, however, to resolve all claims in one trial. *Piper*, at 259.

Similarly, in this case, not only would an inability to compel Flash to appear hinder defendants' ability to present a complete case, but it would also be more convenient to resolve all claims involving defendants in litigation in France. Accordingly, because the lease between ILFC and Flash does not require the present actions to proceed in this Court and because Flash's absence from these actions would pose significant problems and inconvenience, the Court finds that this factor weighs in favor of dismissal.

C. Public Interest Factors

'Public interest factors encompass court congestion, the local interest in resolving the controversy, and the preference for having a forum apply a law with which it is familiar.' *Contact Lumber*, 918 F.2d at 1452; *see also Gulf Oil*, 330 U.S. at 508 ('Important considerations are the relative ease of access to sources of proof; availability of compulsory process for attendance of unwilling, and the cost of obtaining attendance of willing, witnesses; possibility of view of premises, if view would be appropriate to the action; and all other practical problems that make trial of a case easy, expeditious and inexpensive.').

(1) Court Congestion

In considering court congestion, '[t]he real issue is not whether a dismissal will reduce a court's congestion but whether a trial may well be speedier in another court because of its less crowded docket.' *Gates Learjet Corp. v. Jensen*, 743 F.2d 1325, 1337 (9th Cir.1984). Neither party appears to discuss this factor specifically. However, this Court has noted:

> The Central District of California . . . is one of the busiest districts in the country. In 2003, 14,720 cases were filed in the Central District. The median time from

filing to disposition is 7.5 months. For civil cases proceeding to trial, however, the median time from filing to trial is 21.2 months. *Taiwan Straits*, at 1202.

Further, defendants' expert states the following:

> The average length of proceedings before the *TGI*, from the time the summons is filed through the end of trial, varies from nine months to two years. Before the Court of Appeal, the average length of the proceedings is two years. Before the *Cour de Cassation*, the average length of proceedings is from two to three years. In any event, the length of the proceedings must be 'reasonable' in accordance with article 6 § 1 of the *European Convention for the Protection of Human Rights and Fundamental Freedoms* dated November 4, 1950.

Based on the present record, the Court finds that the factor is neutral and does not favor dismissal.

(2) Local Interest in Resolving the Controversy

Defendants argue that France has a compelling interest in this litigation for the following reasons: the crash at issue killed over 100 French residents; the subject aircraft was transporting French tourists on tour packages offered by French travel agencies; over 500 French claimants, including many of the plaintiffs in this case, are already involved in French court proceedings related to the crash; a criminal investigation into the crash has commenced in France; litigation involving the crash is already underway in France; the BEA has been involved in the investigation of the crash, including search and recovery efforts; the crash has been covered extensively in the French media; and French officials have been in contact with and assisted the crash victims' families. Defendants argue that California's interest in the litigation, in contrast, is extremely limited and consists solely of the fact that ILFC, a California corporation, leased the subject aircraft to Flash approximately two years before the crash. Accordingly, defendants argue that litigating the case before this Court would 'impose a considerable and unwarranted burden on this Court and on the citizens of this jurisdiction, whose tax dollars would have to support the expense of trying this case and whose time would be taken up by sitting as jurors.'

Plaintiffs argue that the United States has an interest in 'judging the products of its own manufacturers against standards established and described under United States law,' while French law favors 'adjudicating cases in the forum of the defendant's domicile.'

Defendants respond that even if this case were to proceed in France, the

United States' interests in promoting air safety are served by the services and involvement of the NTSB and FAA and will also be served by adjudication before French courts.

The Court finds that France has a greater interest in hearing this case and thus concludes that this factor weighs in favor of dismissal. Of the 122 decedents whose deaths are the subject of the 57 consolidated cases, 120 were citizens or residents of France. In comparison, four United States citizens perished in the crash. The Court finds that France's interest in ensuring that the heirs and beneficiaries of the majority of those on Flight 604 are compensated and treated fairly is great. The United States has an interest in ensuring that products produced by United States companies in the United States are safe. However California's interest in these actions is minimal. A substantial portion of defendants' evidence regarding liability is located outside of California. In addition, California's interest in enforcing the terms of the lease between ILFC and Flash is minimal in light of the Court's rejection of plaintiffs' argument that they are third party beneficiaries of the lease.

(3) Preference for Having a Forum Apply Law with Which It Is Familiar

Generally, the need to apply foreign law favors dismissal. *Piper*, 454 U.S. at 260 (citing *Gilbert*). 'This court has held that before dismissing a case for forum non conveniens, a district court must first make a choice of law determination.' *Lueck* at 1148 (internal citations and quotation marks omitted). 'However, the choice of law analysis is only determinative when the case involves a United States statute requiring venue in the United States, such as the Jones Act or the Federal Employers' Liability Act.' *Id.* 'The purpose of a choice of law inquiry in a forum non conveniens analysis is to determine if one of these statutes would apply.' *Id.*, *Taiwan Straits*, 331 F.Supp.2d at 1207.

Defendants argue that the Court need not engage in a complex choice of law analysis because such analysis is only determinative of *forum non conveniens* motions when 'the case involves a United States statute requiring venue in the United States.' Because these actions would be governed by the Death on the High Seas Act, 46 U.S.C. app. §§ 761–767 ('DOHSA'), if the law of the United States were to apply at all, and DOHSA does not mandate venue in the United States, defendants argue that a choice of law analysis is not mandatory. *Id.*

Plaintiffs assert that it is likely that United States substantive law will apply whether or not the litigation occurs in France or this Court. Plaintiffs contend that a French court hearing these cases and applying French choice of law rules would be compelled to apply the law of defendants' home jurisdiction, resulting in a foreign court being required to interpret the laws of several different states.

Defendants respond that plaintiffs' conclusions regarding applicable law are incorrect in that a choice of law analysis based on the law of France could result in the application of foreign law, most likely the law of Egypt, or possibly the law of France.

The Court presently declines to undertake a lengthy choice of law analysis. However, insofar as it has been suggested that if United States law were to apply at all, DOHSA would govern the present claims, the Court agrees that DOHSA would appear to apply to the present claims and finds the discussion of choice of law in *Taiwan Straits* to be persuasive. *See Taiwan Straits*, 331 F.Supp.2d at 1206–11; 46 U.S.C. app. § 761 ('[W]henever the death of a person shall be caused by wrongful act, neglect, or default occurring on the high seas beyond a marine league from the shore of any State, or the District of Columbia, or the Territories or dependencies of the United States, the personal representative of the decedent may maintain a suit for damages in the district courts of the United States, in admiralty, for the exclusive benefit of the decedent's wife, husband, parent, child, or dependent relative against the vessel, person, or corporation which would have been liable if death had not ensued.').[FN16] In *Taiwan Straits*, after concluding that DOHSA does not mandate venue in the United States over cases arising out of the crash in Taiwan of a Boeing aircraft operated by China Airlines, the court considered whether admiralty law or federal common law would provide the appropriate choice of law rules under DOHSA. *Taiwan Straits* at 1208–09. The court concluded that Taiwan law would apply to plaintiffs' claims under either admiralty choice of law rules or federal common law choice of law rules. *Id.* at 1211. Accordingly, the Court held that its lack of familiarity with Taiwanese law weighed in favor of dismissal. Similarly, in this case, in light of the Court's conclusion that the ILFC–Flash lease's forum selection clause does not mandate the application of California law, the possibility that DOHSA could apply, and the possibility that either French or Egyptian law could apply to all or part of this case, it appears that the French forum should be favored in the interests of justice. Therefore, because the Court would be compelled to apply foreign law, the Court finds that this factor weighs in favor of dismissal.

FN16. The Court does not definitively decide at this time whether DOHSA would be applicable.

III. CONCLUSION

For the reasons discussed herein, the Court GRANTS defendants' motion to dismiss on grounds of *forum non conveniens*. The Court's dismissal is subject to the following conditions:

(1) Defendants' agreement to

(a) submit to the jurisdiction of a French court in actions refiled by plaintiffs there;

(b) toll any statute of limitations that might apply to such refiled actions for 120 days after dismissal by this Court;

(c) make available in such refiled actions in the courts of France any evidence and witnesses in their possession, custody, or control in the United States that the French courts properly deem discoverable and relevant to the resolution of any issue before them; and

(d) pay any damages awarded by the French courts in such refiled actions, subject to any right to appeal; and

(2) A French court's acceptance of jurisdiction over the claims of all plaintiffs presently before this Court.

[?] NOTES AND QUESTIONS

1 The U.S. doctrine of *forum non conveniens* is critically different from other common law doctrines in one respect: it does not only take into account private interest factors, but also public interest factors.[11] Public interest factors are concerned with the impact of deciding the dispute for the United States. They compare the interests of the relevant States to adjudicate the dispute. These interests include the burden that the dispute would represent for judicial resources. They also include the interest to address the policy issues raised by the case and to resolve them by laying down rules which will then regulate society in the future.

2 The unique features of American civil procedure (for example, class actions, contingency fees) coupled with certain unique features of substantive law (for example, punitive damages) are strong incentives for foreign plaintiffs to seek to enter into American courts. In the words of a leading English judge, '[a]s a moth is drawn to the light, so is a litigant drawn to the United States.'[12] U.S. courts have long held, however, that the nationality of the plaintiff plays a role, and

---

11 The House of Lords specifically declined to incorporate public interest factors into its test of *forum non conveniens* in *Lubbe v. Cape Plc* [2000] 1 W.L.R. 1545.

12 *Per* Lord Denning, in *Smith Kline & French Labs v. Bloch* [1983] 2 All E.R. 72, 74.

that the choice of foreign plaintiffs to sue in the United States deserves less deference. This is consistent with the focus on public interest factors. By initiating proceedings, plaintiffs decide to use judicial resources which are financed by local taxpayers. Foreign nationals and residents typically do not pay taxes in the United States, and are thus less legitimate to trigger the use of American public resources, including judicial resources.

These actions could also have been perceived as additional business brought to the U.S. legal community, which would result in additional taxes for the U.S. government, and could justify dedicating it judicial resources. England has never been reluctant to welcome foreign plaintiffs looking for a suitable forum:

> But we in England think differently. If a plaintiff considers that the procedure of our courts, or the substantive law of England, may hold advantages for him superior to that of any other country, he is entitled to bring his action here – provided always that he can serve the defendant, or arrest his ship, within the jurisdiction of these courts – and provided also that his action is not vexatious or oppressive. (. . .) This right to come here is not confined to Englishmen. It extends to any friendly foreigner. He can seek the aid of our courts if he desires to do so. You may call this 'forum-shopping' if you please, but if the forum is England, it is a good place to shop in, both for the quality of the goods and the speed of service.[13]

3 Initially, the doctrine could not be opposed to U.S. plaintiffs. The rule evolved and nowadays, although their choice deserves more deference, 'there is no rigid rule of decision protecting U.S. citizen or resident plaintiffs from dismissal for *forum non conveniens*'.[14]

4 Parties to international litigation often prefer to litigate in their home courts. However, American law is so clearly more plaintiff friendly than the laws of most other States that American defendants will typically argue in favour of a dismissal on *forum non conveniens* grounds to avoid their own courts. To improve their chance to obtain such dismissal, they will often offer to undertake to cooperate in the foreign proceedings should such stay be granted. These offers will in turn facilitate the decision of the U.S. court by cancelling certain of the factors against dismissal. Did this happen in the *Flashairlines* case?

5 Foreign plaintiffs may also try to influence the decision of the U.S. court by attempting to create conditions where a dismissal would not be available. The requirement which they can impact is the jurisdiction of the foreign court. A U.S. court will only dismiss an action if another forum is available. This would not be the case if the foreign court would not retain jurisdiction in the case. In the *Flashairlines* case, after their action was conditionally dismissed by the U.S., the French plaintiffs brought an action in France seeking a declaration that French courts did *not* have jurisdiction over the dispute.[15] In Panama, the following provision was added to the Judicial Code in 2006:

Chapter IV – Special Procedure for the Resolution of International Disputes in
Matters of Private Law

Art. 1421-J. In cases referred to in this chapter, national judges lack jurisdiction if the claim or the action filed in the country has been previously rejected or

---

13 *Per* Lord Denning, in *The Atlantic Star* [1973] Q.B. 364, 382 (CA).

14 *Iragorri v. United Technologies Corp.* 274 F.3d 65 (2d Cir. 2001). See generally Gary Born and Peter Rutledge, *International Civil Litigation in US Courts* (Aspen 2011) 397.

15 The Paris Court of Appeal ruled so in 2008 (CA Paris, 6 March 2008, (2009) JDI 180), but the ruling was set aside by the *Cour de cassation* on a procedural ground.

dismissed by a foreign judge applying *forum non conveniens*. In these cases, national judges must reject hearing the lawsuit or the action due to reasons of a constitutional or preventive jurisdiction nature.

Similar statutes can be found in other Latin American countries. What do you think their effect on the jurisdiction of a U.S. court might be?

6 In order to obtain a dismissal on the ground of *forum non conveniens*, an American defendant should argue that the foreign court is an adequate forum, and in particular that it would handle the dispute fairly to all parties. If the foreign plaintiffs do initiate proceedings in the foreign court and win, they will then likely seek to enforce the judgment in the U.S. over the assets of the American party. Could the American party then resist enforcement on the ground that he was treated unfairly or inadequately in the foreign court?

7 In a resolution prepared by a leading English scholar and judge, the *Institut de droit international* summarized the test of *forum non conveniens* as follows:

2. In deciding whether the courts of another country are clearly more appropriate, the court seised may take into account (in particular): (a) the adequacy of the alternative forum; (b) the residence of the parties; (c) the location of the evidence (witnesses and documents) and the procedures for obtaining such evidence; (d) the law applicable to the issues; (e) the effect of applicable limitation or prescription periods; (f) the effectiveness and enforceability of any resulting judgment.[16]

How does it compare with the English and the U.S. tests?

Japanese Code of Civil Procedure

Article 3–9 *Dismissal of Action under Special Circumstances*

Even where the Japanese courts have jurisdiction over an action (except where the action has been brought on the basis of an exclusive jurisdiction agreement in favour of the Japanese courts), the court may dismiss whole or part of it if, taking into account the nature of the case, the burden of the defendant to answer the claim, the location of evidence and any other factors, the court finds that there are special circumstances under which hearing and determining the case in Japan would impair fairness between the parties or hinder the proper and efficient conduct of hearing.

 NOTES

1 Article 3–9 is the only provision included in the 2011 Japanese Act on International Jurisdiction which can be relied upon to deal with parallel litigation. No consensus emerged among the drafters of the Act as to how best address such situation.[17]

2 The essential purpose of Art. 3–9 is to avoid the risks arising out of the rules of the new act granting excessively broad jurisdiction to Japanese courts. Instead of restricting such grounds

---

16 Institut de droit international, Resolution on the principles for determining when the use of the doctrine of forum non conveniens and anti-suit injunctions is appropriate, Session de Bruges (2003).

17 See Koji Takahashi, *Japan's New Act on International Jurisdiction* (Smashwords, 2011).

of jurisdiction, the Japanese lawmaker preferred to adopt a tool to correct any excess in the exercise of such jurisdiction. Examples of rules which might require the use of the corrective device include Art. 3–3(iii), *supra*, p. 190, where the sum of money claimed in the action is disproportionate compared to the value of the defendant's seizable asset or where the location of the asset in Japan is fortuitous or transient (as in the case of the defendant's ship calling temporarily at a port in Japan). [18]

3   Anti-suit injunctions

Anti-suit injunctions are a controversial tool used by common law courts to resolve certain cases of parallel litigation. They are judicial orders whereby a common law court restrains a party from instituting or continuing proceedings in a foreign court. If the party disobeys the injunction, he will be in contempt of court and will face sanctions in the common law jurisdiction where the injunction was issued.

In accordance with the doctrine of equitable injunctions, an anti-suit injunction only acts *in personam*. It is addressed to the party who initiated the proceedings abroad. It is not addressed to the foreign court. However, if the plaintiff discontinues his action, the proceedings will almost certainly stop (by definition, the defendant will not insist on maintaining them, since it is he who sought the injunction to stop them). Thus, an anti-suit injunction indirectly interferes with the foreign judicial process, and it could be regarded as an infringement of the sovereignty of the foreign state. [19] English and U.S. courts are aware of the problem, but believe that anti suit injunctions are necessary in certain categories of cases.

Lis pendens and *forum non conveniens* are clearly less conflictual doctrines than anti suit injunctions. They aim, however, at addressing a certain category of cases of parallel litigation. Under each of these doctrines, the forum accepts that the jurisdiction of the foreign court is legitimate. The question for the court is therefore which of two courts having legitimate jurisdiction should be preferred. But there are also cases where each of the two courts considers that the jurisdiction of the other is illegitimate. The result is that none of the two courts will unilaterally decide to decline jurisdiction in favour of the other, because each court has come to the conclusion that it is the only legitimate forum for the action. In such cases, there are only two possible outcomes. The first, which is the only one contemplated by civil law jurisdictions, is that two sets of proceedings will develop in parallel,

---

18 *Id.*

19 The French Cour de cassation ruled so in 2004, for instance (Cass. Civ. 1ère, 30 June 2004, case no 01-03248).

and two judgments will eventually be rendered, which might be contradictory. The second is to attempt to indirectly force the other court to stop its proceedings.

3.1 With respect to litigation in foreign nations

The first use of anti-suit injunctions is to protect and enforce jurisdiction clauses. Where a choice of court agreement grants exclusive jurisdiction to an English court, the English court will logically consider that it is the only legitimate court to decide the dispute, and that all other courts, which by definition were not designated by the agreement, should enforce the agreement and decline jurisdiction. However, a non-designated court could find that jurisdiction clauses are illegal in general, or that the particular clause is not applicable in the case at hand, and may conclude that the jurisdiction of the English court is illegitimate. If the English court disagrees, the conflict cannot be resolved, except if one court imposes its views indirectly by forcing the defendant in the English action to discontinue the foreign proceedings. In which other cases are anti-suit injunctions available in England?

 CASE

Court of Appeal of England and Wales, 20 January 2012
Star Reefers Pool Inc. v. JFC Group Co. Ltd.[20]

Lord Justice Rix:

Jurisprudence

25 There was no dispute about the basic principles applicable to the power to grant an anti-suit injunction. What was needed was *either* an agreement for exclusive English jurisdiction or, its equivalent, an agreement for arbitration in England, in which case the court would ordinarily enforce the parties agreement by granting an anti-suit injunction in the absence of strong reason not to do so; *or* else two other conditions had to be satisfied, namely England had to be the natural forum for the resolution of the dispute and the conduct of the party to be injuncted had to be unconscionable: see *South Carolina Co v. Maatshappij 'De Zeven Provincien' NV* [1987] AC 24, *SNIA v. Lee Kui Jak* [1987] AC 871, *Airbus Industrie GIE v. Patel* [1999] 1 AC 119. In the present case, there was no agreement for English jurisdiction or arbitration in the guarantees, and therefore it was the second of the alternatives which was in issue.

---

20 [2012] EWCA Civ 14.

26 I ventured to summarise the relevant authorities in *Glencore International AG v. Exter Shipping Ltd* [2002] 2 All ER (Comm) 1 at paras 42/43 as follows:

42 . . .However, jurisprudence has limited the conditions under which such an injunction may be regarded as 'just and convenient'. The following conditions are necessary. First, the threatened conduct must be 'unconscionable'. It is only such conduct which founds the right, legal or equitable but here equitable, for the protection of which an injunction can be granted. What is unconscionable cannot be defined exhaustively, but it includes conduct which is 'oppressive or vexatious or which interferes with the due process of the court' (see the *South Carolina* case [1987] AC 24 at 41 per Lord Brandon of Oakbrook). The underlying principle is one of justice in support of the 'ends of justice' (see the *SNI Aerospatiale* case [1987] AC 871 at 892, 893 per Lord Goff of Chieveley). It is analogous to 'abuse of process'; it is related to matters which should affect a person's conscience (see *Turner v. Grovit* [2002] 1 WLR 107 at [24] per Lord Hobhouse of Woodborough). Secondly, to reflect the interests of comity and in recognition of the possibility that an injunction, although directed against the respondent personally, may be regarded as an (albeit indirect) interference in the foreign proceedings, an injunction must be necessary to protect the applicant's legitimate interest in English proceedings; he must be a party to litigation in this country at which the unconscionable conduct of the party to be restrained is directed, and so there must be a clear need to protect existing English proceedings ([2002] 1 WLR 107 at [27]–[28]); the *Airbus Industrie* case). It follows that the natural forum for the litigation must be in England, but this, while necessary, is not a sufficient condition.

43 While these are the conditions (and in this sense may be said to go to jurisdiction) for the grant of an anti-suit injunction, at a secondary stage, that of the exercise of discretion, the court will always exercise caution before granting an injunction (but cf *Aggeliki Charis Cia Maritima v. Pagnan SpA, The Angelic Grace* [1995] 1 Lloyd's Rep 87 in cases dealing with contractual arbitration and jurisdiction clauses). Moreover, because the court is concerned with the ends of justice, the respondent will always be entitled to show why it would nevertheless be unjust for the injunction to be granted (see the *SNI Aerospatiale* case [1987] AC 871 at 896; *Dicey and Morris on the Conflict of Laws* (13th edn, 2000) para 12-064).

27 To similar effect is this summary by Toulson LJ from *Deutsche Bank AG v. Highland Crusader Offshore Partners LP* [2010] 1 WLR 1023 at [50]:

(1) Under English law the court may restrain a defendant over whom it has personal jurisdiction from instituting or continuing proceedings in a foreign court when it is necessary in the interests of justice to do.

(2) It is too narrow to say that such an injunction may be granted only on the

grounds of vexation or oppression, but, where a matter is justiciable in England and a foreign court, the party seeking an anti-suit injunction must generally show that proceeding before the foreign court is or would be vexatious or oppressive.

(3) The courts have refrained from attempting a comprehensive definition of vexation or oppression, but in order to establish that proceeding in a foreign court is or would be vexatious or oppressive on grounds of forum non conveniens, it is generally necessary to show that (a) England is clearly the more appropriate forum ('the natural forum'), and (b) justice requires that the claimant in the foreign court should be restrained from proceeding there.

(4) If the English court considers England to be the natural forum and can see no legitimate personal or juridical advantage in the claimant in the foreign proceedings being allowed to pursue them, it does not automatically follow that an anti-suit injunction should be granted. For that would be to overlook the important restraining influence of considerations of comity.

(5) An anti-suit injunction always requires caution because by definition it involves interference with the process or potential process of a foreign court. An injunction to enforce an exclusive jurisdiction clause governed by English law is not regarded as a breach of comity, because it merely requires a party to honour his contract. In other cases, the principle of comity requires the court to recognise that, in deciding questions of weight to be attached to various factors, different judges operating under different legal systems with different legal policies may legitimately arrive at different answers, without occasioning a breach of customary international law or manifest injustice, and that in such circumstances it is not for an English court to arrogate to itself the decision how a foreign court should determine the matter. The stronger the connection of the foreign court with the parties and the subject matter of the dispute, the stronger the argument against intervention.

(6) The prosecution of parallel proceedings in different jurisdictions is undesirable but not necessarily vexatious or oppressive.

 QUESTIONS

In which cases is there a need for such a robust remedy? Do you think anti suit injunctions are appropriate to avoid vexatious and oppressive proceedings? To protect the jurisdiction of the forum in such matters as the administration of estates and insolvency?

Read the following case and identify differences between English and U.S. law.

CASE

U.S. Court of Appeals for the 8th Circuit, 18 June 2007
Goss International Corp. v. Tokyo Kikai Seisakusho and others[21]

Riley, Circuit Judge.

On December 3, 2003, a jury found Japanese-based Tokyo Kikai Seisakusho, Ltd. (TKS), liable to Goss International Corporation (Goss), under the Antidumping Act of 1916 (the 1916 Act), 15 U.S.C. § 72 (repealed 2004), which made it unlawful for foreign persons to sell imported articles within the United States at a price substantially less than the actual market value or wholesale price at the time of exportation, with the intent of destroying or injuring an industry in the United States. The judgment, inclusive of statutory treble damages, attorney fees, and costs, amounted to more than $ 35,000,000.

During the pendency of TKS's appeal, Congress prospectively repealed the 1916 Act. See Miscellaneous Trade & Technical Corrections Act of 2004, Pub. L. No. 108–429, § 2006, 118 Stat. 2434, 2597 (2004). Shortly thereafter, the Japanese government passed 'The Special Measures Law concerning the Obligation to Return Profits Obtained pursuant to the Antidumping Act of 1916 of the United States, etc., Law No. 162, 2004'[FN1] (Special Measures Law), a clawback statute[FN2] allowing Japanese nationals to sue for the recovery of any judgment entered against them under the 1916 Act.

> FN1 Amerika gasshuukoku no 1916 nen no han futou renbai hou ni motoduki uketa rieki no henkan gimu tou ni kansuru tokubetsu sochi hou [Special Measures Law], Law No. 162 of 2004.
> FN2 A clawback statute is a countermeasure that enables defendants who have paid a multiple damage judgment in a foreign country to recover the multiple portion of that judgment from the plaintiff. See generally, Joseph E. Neuhaus, Note, Power to Reverse Foreign Judgments: The British Clawback Statute Under International Law, 81 Colum. L. Rev. 1097, 1097-98 (1981) (citing the Protection of Trading Interests Act, 1980, c.11, § 5 (U.K.)); Joseph P. Griffin, United States Antitrust Laws and Transnational Business Transactions: An Introduction, 21 Int'l Law. 307, 327 (1987) (discussing clawback legislation enacted by the United Kingdom, Australia, and Canada that allows companies which have paid treble damages under United States antitrust law judgments to 'sue the successful plaintiff in the local courts for a return of all or a portion of the damages').

On June 15, 2006, the district court granted Goss's motion for preliminary injunction, prohibiting TKS from filing suit in Japan under the Special Measures Law. On June 19, 2006, TKS paid the judgment in full, and the district court entered a satisfaction of judgment on June 21, 2006. On June 23, 2006, TKS filed this interlocutory appeal. In light of the changed circumstances since the district court entered its preliminary injunction, we vacate the district court's preliminary injunction. (. . .)

II. DISCUSSION

A. Proper Standard for Issuance of a Foreign Antisuit Injunction

The propriety of issuing a foreign antisuit injunction is a matter of first impression for our circuit. Other circuits having decided the issue agree that 'federal courts have the power to enjoin persons subject to their jurisdiction from prosecuting foreign suits.' *Kaepa, Inc. v. Achilles Corp.*, 76 F.3d 624, 626 (5th Cir. 1996); see *Laker Airways Ltd. v. Sabena, Belgian World Airlines*, 731 F.2d 909, 926 (D.C. Cir. 1984). The circuits are split, however, on the level of deference afforded to international comity in determining whether a foreign antisuit injunction should issue.

The First, Second, Third, Sixth, and District of Columbia Circuits have adopted the 'conservative approach,' under which a foreign antisuit injunction will issue only if the movant demonstrates (1) an action in a foreign jurisdiction would prevent United States jurisdiction or threaten a vital United States policy, and (2) the domestic interests outweigh concerns of international comity. See *Quaak v. Klynveld Peat Marwick Goerdeler Bedrijfsrevisoren*, 361 F.3d 11, 17 (1st Cir. 2004) (adopting the 'conservative approach,' which questions 'whether the foreign action either imperils the jurisdiction of the forum court or threatens some strong national policy' and 'accords appreciably greater weight to considerations of international comity'). Under the conservative approach, '[c]omity dictates that foreign antisuit injunctions be issued sparingly and only in the rarest of cases.' Gau Shan Co., 956 F.2d at 1354 (citing Laker Airways, 731 F.2d at 927); see also China Trade, 837 F.2d at 35–36 (holding an antisuit injunction 'effectively restricts the jurisdiction of the court of a foreign sovereign,' thus, such orders 'should be used sparingly, and should be granted only with care and great restraint' (internal quotation marks and citations omitted)).

In contrast, the Fifth and Ninth Circuits follow the 'liberal approach,' which places only modest emphasis on international comity and approves the issuance of an antisuit injunction when necessary to prevent duplicative and vexatious foreign litigation and to avoid inconsistent judgments. See Kaepa, Inc. at 627–28 (concluding a district court does not abuse its discretion by issuing an antisuit injunction when litigation of the same action in a foreign forum 'would result in inequitable hardship and tend to frustrate and delay the speedy and efficient determination of the cause' (internal quotations omitted)); see also E. & J. Gallo Winery v. Andina Licores S.A., 446 F.3d 984, 989-91 (9th Cir. 2006) (applying the Fifth Circuit's standard for issuance of an antisuit injunction). The Seventh Circuit similarly has indicated its agreement with the liberal approach. See Allendale Mut. Ins. Co. v. Bull Data Sys., Inc., 10 F.3d 425, 430-31 (7th Cir. 1993).

Under either the conservative or liberal approach, '[w]hen a preliminary injunction takes the form of a foreign antisuit injunction, [courts] are required to balance domestic judicial interests against concerns of international comity.' Karaha Bodas Co., 335 F.3d at 366. We agree with the observations of the First Circuit that the conservative approach (1) 'recognizes the rebuttable presumption against issuing international antisuit injunctions,' (2) 'is more respectful of principles of international comity,' (3) 'compels an inquiring court to balance competing policy considerations,' and (4) acknowledges that 'issuing an international antisuit injunction is a step that should "be taken only with care and great restraint" and with the recognition that international comity is a fundamental principle deserving of substantial deference.' Quaak, 361 F.3d at 18 (quoting Canadian Filters (Harwich) Ltd. v. Lear-Siegler, Inc., 412 F.2d 577, 578 (1st Cir. 1969)). Likewise, we agree with the Sixth Circuit's observation the liberal approach 'conveys the message, intended or not, that the issuing court has so little confidence in the foreign court's ability to adjudicate a given dispute fairly and efficiently that it is unwilling even to allow the possibility.' Gau Shan Co. at 1355.

Although comity eludes a precise definition, its importance in our globalized economy cannot be overstated. Compare Hilton v. Guyot, 159 U.S. 113, 164 (1895) (defining comity as 'the recognition which one nation allows within its territory to the legislative, executive or judicial acts of another nation'), with Turner Entm't Co. v. Degeto Film GmbH, 25 F.3d 1512, 1519 n.10 (11th Cir. 1994) (noting commentators have defined comity using terms such as, 'courtesy, politeness, convenience or goodwill between sovereigns, a moral necessity, expediency, reciprocity or consideration of high international politics concerned with maintaining amicable and workable relationships between nations' (internal quotation marks omitted)). Indeed, the 'world economic interdependence has highlighted the importance of comity, as international commerce depends to a large extent on "the ability of merchants to predict the likely consequences of their conduct in overseas markets."'

(See Quaak at 19). We also note that the Congress and the President possess greater experience with, knowledge of, and expertise in international trade and economics than does the Judiciary. The two other branches, not the Judiciary, bear the constitutional duties related to foreign affairs. For these reasons, we join the majority of our sister circuits and adopt the conservative approach in determining whether a foreign antisuit injunction should issue.

B. Application of the Standard

3. Goss's Antisuit Injunction

At the outset of our review, we acknowledge the district court's unenviable task to navigate the uncharted waters of foreign antisuit injunctions. We begin our review with a discussion of the instructive Laker Airways case relied upon by the district court. Laker Airways (Laker) brought an antitrust action against four foreign airlines and four domestic corporations in the United States District Court for the District of Columbia. Laker Airways, 731 F.2d at 917. Shortly after Laker filed the lawsuit, the foreign defendants filed an action in the United Kingdom's High Court of Justice, requesting a declaration of non-liability and an injunction to prevent Laker from pursuing remedies in the United States courts under United States antitrust laws. *Id.* at 918. The requested relief stemmed from the alleged incompatibility between United States antitrust laws with their consequent treble damages on the one hand, and the Bermuda II Treaty and the British Protection of Trading Interests Act on the other. *Id.* The United Kingdom's High Court of Justice granted the injunction, which effectively terminated Laker's pending United States litigation as to the four foreign defendants. *Id.* In the district court. Laker successfully enjoined the remaining domestic defendants and two foreign airline defendants in a second antitrust action from filing any action in a foreign court that 'would interfere with the district court's jurisdiction over the matters alleged in the complaint.' *Id.* at 918–19.

On appeal, the Laker Airways defendants argued 'the injunction was unnecessary to protect the district court's jurisdiction and violate[d] their right to take part in the "parallel" actions commenced in the English courts.' *Id.* at 921. A divided panel affirmed the decision, concluding an injunction by the United Kingdom's High Court of Justice would have stripped the United States court of control over Laker's pending litigation. *Id.* at 955–56. The court did not reach this conclusion without much deliberation, first recognizing 'the fundamental corollary to concurrent jurisdiction must ordinarily be respected: parallel proceedings on the same in personam claim should ordinarily be allowed to proceed simultaneously, at least until a judgment is reached in one which can be pled as res judicata in the other.' *Id.* at 926–27. The court cautioned that while foreign antisuit injunctions only operate on the parties within the court's jurisdiction, 'they effectively restrict the foreign court's ability to exercise its jurisdiction.' *Id.* at 927.

In deciding the propriety of issuing an antisuit injunction, the Laker Airways court established factors to be considered, which included protecting United States jurisdiction, preserving important United States public policies, and balancing domestic interests with the principles of international comity. *Id.* at 926–45. The court recognized the futility of an interest balancing test in determining prescriptive jurisdiction because the 'courts are forced to choose between a domestic law which is designed to protect domestic interests, and a foreign law which is calculated to thwart the implementation of the domestic law in order to protect foreign interests allegedly threatened by the objectives of the domestic law.' *Id.* at 948. While acknowledging the domestic courts' obligation 'to apply international law and foster comity,' the court conceded that, when in doubt, 'national interests will tend to be favored over foreign interests.' *Id.* at 951. The court concluded, to protect properly the jurisdiction of the United States over the prescriptive jurisdiction of its United States antitrust laws, the district court acted within its discretion by enjoining the defendants from pursuing an injunction in the United Kingdom's High Court of Justice. *Id.* at 955–56. The court recognized, however, along with this act of preserving its own jurisdiction ran 'the risk that counterinjunctions or other sanctions will eventually preclude Laker from achieving any remedy, if it is ultimately entitled to one under United States law. In either case the policies of both countries are likely to be frustrated at the cost of substantial prejudice to the litigants' rights.' *Id.* at 953.

As in Laker Airways, most cases dealing with foreign antisuit injunctions involve simultaneous litigation in both United States and foreign courts. In *Gau Shan Co. v. Bankers Trust Co.*, for example, a borrower brought an action in a United States district court against its lender for fraud in connection with a loan note. Gau Shan at 1352. When the lender tried to file an action in Hong Kong against the borrower for failure to pay the loan note, the United States court granted the borrower's motion for a foreign antisuit injunction. *Id.* The Sixth Circuit reversed, holding a parallel suit did not threaten United States jurisdiction and international comity precluded the issuance of an antisuit injunction. *Id.* at 1355-59. The court reasoned, 'The possibility that a holding of a Hong Kong court might permit [the lender] to gain control of [the borrower] is not a threat to the jurisdiction of the United States courts; rather, it is merely a threat to [the borrower]'s interest in prosecuting its lawsuit.' *Id.* at 1356. Similarly, in *China Trade & Dev. Corp. v. M.V. Choong*

Yong, the Second Circuit reversed the issuance of an antisuit injunction, concluding parallel litigation in the United States and Korea concerning a Korean corporation's liability did not frustrate an important United States policy or threaten the jurisdiction of the United States courts. China Trade at 34.

Other courts have upheld the issuance of a foreign antisuit injunction in the face of parallel litigation. For example, in *Quaak v. Klynveld Peat Marwick Goerdeler Bedrijfsrevisoren*, when investors filed a securities fraud class action lawsuit in a United States district court against Klynveld Peat Marwick Goerdeler Bedrijfsrevisoren (KPMG-B), KPMG-B was also a defendant in a contemporaneous criminal action in Belgium. Quaak, at 14. The class action plaintiffs sought documents from KPMG-B, but KPMG-B claimed Belgian law prohibited KPMG-B from releasing the information. *Id.* at 14–15. Thereafter, KPMG-B instituted an action in the Belgian judicial system seeking to enjoin the class action plaintiffs from 'taking any step' toward the discovery requests and to impose substantial penalties on parties pursuing discovery procedures. *Id.* The class action plaintiffs countered this move by filing a motion in the United States action and obtaining a foreign antisuit injunction against KPMG-B to prevent KPMG-B from pursuing the Belgian injunctive action. *Id.* On appeal, the First Circuit affirmed the injunction, agreeing with the district court that the character of the foreign action, the public policy of protecting investors against fraud, and the need to protect the court's jurisdiction all counterbalanced comity concerns under the peculiar circumstances of the case. *Id.* at 20.

The case before us does not fit within the category of cases in which foreign antisuit injunctions have been considered. We do not believe the rationale of those cases compels an injunction in the present case. (. . .)

Second, in cases involving parallel litigation in foreign countries, once one court reaches a final judgment, the role of comity for antisuit injunction purposes essentially is moot because there is no longer tension with the foreign country over *concurrent* jurisdiction. Instead, the doctrine of res judicata should apply as a defense to further litigation of the same issues. As the Laker Airways court explained, 'Comity ordinarily requires that courts of a separate sovereign not interfere with concurrent proceedings based on the same transitory claim, at least until a judgment is reached in one action, allowing res judicata to be pled in defense.' Laker Airways, at 939.

The issues previously decided below in the district court are different from the issues sought to be litigated in the foreign jurisdiction. TKS now seeks to litigate in Japan a cause of action solely available in Japan and not previously litigated in the antidumping litigation. The issues are not the same simply because TKS's cause of action under the Special Measures Law rests on the imposition of an adverse judgment against TKS under the 1916 Act.

Third, we disagree with the district court's assertion that Congress's decision to repeal the 1916 Act prospectively, rather than retroactively, may play a role in the decision to grant a foreign antisuit injunction to protect the court's jurisdiction or an important United States policy. (. . .)

The district court also placed too much emphasis on the impact of the Special Measures Law on United States public policy. The Special Measures Law has a onetime application: There is no pending litigation under the now-defunct 1916 Act; Goss received the only judgment ever granted under the Act; thus, the only lawsuit possible under the Special Measures Law can be brought against Goss alone. Our consideration of international comity must allow the Japanese courts, in the first instance, to determine the enforceability of the Special Measures Law, which will undoubtedly involve application of Japanese precedent and domestic policy, and the Japanese courts' own consideration of international comity. If the Japanese judiciary upholds the enforceability of the Special Measures Law, it must next determine whether jurisdiction over Goss exists to maintain the lawsuit. International comity requires us to give deference to the Japanese courts to interpret Japanese laws. Goss is not precluded from seeking affirmative defenses under Japanese law in defending itself from the countermeasure. Furthermore, the United States representative to the WTO may seek to enforce provisions of the WTO Agreement to prevent TKS from enforcing the Special Measures Law as a suspension of obligations. (. . .)

As in Laker Airways, the matter before us did not begin as an international jurisdictional standoff.[FN8] Rather, it arose out of the legislative policies of the United States and Japan, which resulted in 'a head-on collision between the diametrically opposed antitrust policies of the United States and [Japan].' Laker Airways at 916, 948. Unlike Laker Airways, however, the present case involves no pending litigation between the parties (other than the present appeal) in the United States courts. Consequently, regardless of our approval or disapproval of clawback litigation in a particular foreign court, given the present posture of this case, it is beyond our limited jurisdiction and contrary to principles of comity to prevent TKS from seeking an action under the Special Measures Law in Japan. See *Neighborhood Transp. Network, Inc. v. Pena*, 42 F.3d 1169, 1172 (8th Cir. 1994) (noting federal courts 'can only hear actual "cases or controversies" as defined by Article III of the Constitution,' and '[w]hen a case on appeal no longer presents an actual, ongoing case or controversy, the case is moot and the federal court no longer has jurisdiction to hear it').

FN8 The Laker Airways court discussed the tension between the antitrust laws of the United States and the United Kingdom, and the potential ramifications under the Protection of Trading Interests Act, 1980, c.11, § 5 (U.K.), a British clawback statute, which provides protection from multiple damage awards imposed under the laws of countries outside the United Kingdom. See Laker Airways at 943; see also *Laker Airways Ltd. v. Pan Am. World Airways*, 559 F. Supp. 1124, 1137 (D.D.C. 1983) ('The Protection of Trading Interests Act of 1980 directs British courts not to enforce treble damage awards against British firms, and . . . [its] "clawback" provision allows non-United States firms doing business in the United Kingdom to sue there to recover two-thirds of treble damage awards levied against them in the United States.').

Although the Special Measures Law, like other clawback or blocking provisions, can be regarded as an affront to the laws and judicial rules of the United States, see, e.g., *Societe Nationale Industrielle Aerospatiale v. United States Dist. Court for Southern Dist.*, 482 U.S. 522, 542–44 & n.29 (1987) (discussing France's blocking statute aimed at frustrating the disfavored United States antitrust discovery rules, and concluding the Hague Convention did not deprive the district court of jurisdiction it otherwise possessed to order a foreign national to produce evidence physically located within a foreign signatory nation), the United States Executive and Legislative Branches, not the Judiciary, are the governmental bodies to address those diplomatic tensions, see, e.g., *Dames & Moore v. Regan*, 453 U.S. 654, 686–87 (1981) (concluding, under the specific facts of the case, the district court properly denied injunctive relief because the President acted within his executive powers in nullifying claims pending in the United States court against Iranian assets); Karaha Bodas Co. at 373 (concluding the district court acted in contravention of a treaty – the United Nations Convention on the Recognition and Enforcement of Foreign Arbitral Awards – by enjoining a party from seeking an action to annul an arbitration award). (. . .)

? QUESTIONS

1 Do you think that the liberal or the conservative approach is more appropriate for the issuance of anti-suit injunctions?

2 In *Goss* and *Lakers*, the essential disagreement between the two courts was not so much on their respective jurisdiction than on the application of their own mandatory laws. Is such a conflict an appropriate ground for issuing an anti-suit injunction? Should anti-suit injunctions be tools for resolving conflict of laws and protecting vital interests of the forum?

3 When the two courts belong to common law jurisdictions, they may both issue an anti-suit injunction ordering the party who initiated proceedings in the foreign forum to terminate them. This happened in the *Lakers* case. What is the solution to such a conflict of injunctions?

CASE

French Cour de cassation, 14 October 2009, *In Zone Brands International Inc* Case no 08-16369

On the sole ground of appeal:

Whereas American company In Zone Brand International Inc. entered into an exclusive distribution agreement relating to the sale of drinks in Europe with French company In Zone Brands Europe, which became In Beverage International, the chairman of which was M. X; that agreement, which was governed by the laws of the State of Georgia (United States of America), included a clause granting jurisdiction to the courts of that state; after the American company terminated the agreement, In Beverage International and M. X initiated proceedings in the Nanterre Commercial Court the jurisdiction of which the defendant disputed invoking the jurisdiction clause; in parallel, In Zone Brand International Inc started proceedings in the United States and that, by decision of 3 March 2006, the *Superior Court* of the County of Cobb (Georgia) granted, on the one hand, a final permanent injunction ('*anti-suit injunction*') forbidding the French parties from continuing the proceedings started before the Nanterre Commercial Court, and, on the other hand, recognised that the American company had a good arguable case; the latter sought to declare enforceable in France the judgment of the *Superior Court*.

Whereas the appellant criticizes the judgment appealed against (Versailles Court of Appeal, April 17, 2008) for declaring the American judgment enforceable in France on the ground that, in refusing to find that a decision of a foreign court issuing an injunction known as 'anti-suit' violated French international public order, although the injunction forbad a party to initiate or continue proceedings before a French court, without the French court being able to decide on its jurisdiction, and affects the sovereignty of the French State as well as the right of access to court of the party who seised a French court or intended to do so, the Court of Appeal violated Art. 509 of the Code of Civil Procedure, and Art.6 of the Convention for the Protection of Human Rights and Fundamental Freedoms.

But whereas the judgment correctly ruled, firstly, that concerning a jurisdiction clause freely agreed by the parties, no strategic behavior [*fraude*] could result from the American company initiating proceedings before the court expressly designated as having jurisdiction; and, secondly, that there could not be any deprivation of the right of access to a court, since the aim of the decision of the

Georgian judge was precisely to rule on its own jurisdiction and to ensure that the jurisdiction clause undertaken by the parties was enforced;

An '*anti-suit injunction*' does not violate international public order where its aim, as in the present case, is solely to sanction the violation of a pre-existing contractual obligation, outside the scope of international conventions or European community law; (. . .)

FOR THESE REASONS, the Court: Dismisses the appeal.

 NOTES AND QUESTIONS

1   Remarkably, a foreign court indirectly injuncted to decline jurisdiction by a common law court can consider that an anti-suit injunction is not an unacceptable interference in the process of its courts. In truth, French courts had not yet ruled on their own jurisdiction, and it seems clear that they would have declined jurisdiction irrespective of the U.S. injunction to do so.

2   The French ruling limits the scope of its decision to cases where the aim of the injunction is to protect a jurisdiction clause. This confirms that this is the most widely accepted case for the use of anti-suit injunctions. Do you think the ruling also applies to violations of arbitration agreements?

3   The *Cour de cassation* expressly excludes from the scope of its ruling injunctions falling within the field of application of European law. This recognizes the existence of the special regime designed by the European Court of Justice for disputes falling within the scope of the European law of jurisdiction.

3.2   With respect to litigation in sister states

Anti-suit injunctions are even more controversial in federal ensembles.

 CASE

European Court of Justice, 27 April 2004 *Turner v. Grovit* (Case C-159/02)[22]

The dispute in the main proceedings

3 Mr Turner, a British citizen domiciled in the United Kingdom, was recruited in 1990 as solicitor to a group of undertakings by one of the companies belonging to that group.

4 The group, known as Chequepoint Group, is directed by Mr Grovit and its main business is running *bureaux de change*. It comprises several companies established in different countries, one being China Security Ltd, which initially recruited Mr

---

22 ECLI:EU:C:2004:228, [2004] E.C.R. I-03565.

Turner, Chequepoint UK Ltd, which took over Mr Turner's contract at the end of 1990, Harada, established in the United Kingdom, and Changepoint, established in Spain.

5 Mr Turner carried out his work in London (United Kingdom). However, in May 1997, at his request, his employer allowed him to transfer his office to Madrid (Spain).

6 Mr Turner started working in Madrid in November 1997. On 16 November 1998, he submitted his resignation to Harada, the company to which he had been transferred on 31 December 1997.

7 On 2 March 1998 Mr Turner brought an action in London against Harada before the Employment Tribunal. He claimed that he had been the victim of efforts to implicate him in illegal conduct, which, in his opinion, were tantamount to unfair dismissal.

8 The Employment Tribunal dismissed the objection of lack of jurisdiction raised by Harada. Its decision was confirmed on appeal. Giving judgment on the substance, it awarded damages to Mr Turner.

9 On 29 July 1998, Changepoint brought an action against Mr Turner before a court of first instance in Madrid. The summons was served on Mr Turner around 15 December 1998. Mr Turner did not accept service and protested the jurisdiction of the Spanish court.

10 In the course of the proceedings in Spain, Changepoint claimed damages of ESP 85 million from Mr Turner as compensation for losses allegedly resulting from Mr Turner's professional conduct.

11 On 18 December 1998 Mr Turner asked the High Court of Justice of England and Wales to issue an injunction under section 37(1) of the Supreme Court Act 1981, backed by a penalty, restraining Mr Grovit, Harada and Changepoint from pursuing the proceedings commenced in Spain. An interlocutory injunction was issued in those terms on 22 December 1998. On 24 February 1999, the High Court refused to extend the injunction.

12 On appeal by Mr Turner, the Court of Appeal (England and Wales) on 28 May 1999 issued an injunction ordering the defendants not to continue the proceedings commenced in Spain and to refrain from commencing further proceedings in Spain or elsewhere against Mr Turner in respect of his contract of employment. In the grounds of its judgment, the Court of Appeal stated, in particular, that the proceedings in Spain had been brought in bad faith in order to vex Mr Turner in the pursuit of his application before the Employment Tribunal.

13 On 28 June 1999, in compliance with that injunction, Changepoint discontinued the proceedings pending before the Spanish court.

14 Mr Grovit, Harada and Changepoint then appealed to the House of Lords, claiming in essence that the English courts did not have the power to make restraining orders preventing the continuation of proceedings in foreign jurisdictions covered by the Convention. (. . .)

The question referred to the Court

19 By its question, the national court seeks in essence to ascertain whether the Convention precludes the grant of an injunction by which a court of a Contracting State prohibits a party to proceedings pending before it from commencing or continuing legal proceedings before a court in another Contracting State even where that party is acting in bad faith in order to frustrate the existing proceedings. (. . .)

Findings of the Court

24 At the outset, it must be borne in mind that the Convention is necessarily based on the trust which the Contracting States accord to one another's legal systems and judicial institutions. It is that mutual trust which has enabled a compulsory system of jurisdiction to be established, which all the courts within the purview of the Convention are required to respect, and as a corollary the waiver by those States of the right to apply their internal rules on recognition and enforcement of foreign judgments in favour of a simplified mechanism for the recognition and enforcement of judgments (Case C-116/02 *Gasser* [2003] ECR I-0000, paragraph 72).

25 It is inherent in that principle of mutual trust that, within the scope of the Convention, the rules on jurisdiction that it lays down, which are common to all the courts of the Contracting States, may be interpreted and applied with the same authority by each of them (see, to that effect, Case C-351/89 *Overseas Union Insurance and Others* [1991] ECR I-3317, paragraph 23, and *Gasser*, paragraph 48).

26 Similarly, otherwise than in a small number of exceptional cases listed in the first paragraph of Article 28 of the Convention, which are limited to the stage of recognition or enforcement and relate only to certain rules of special or exclusive jurisdiction that are not relevant here, the Convention does not permit the jurisdiction of a court to be reviewed by a court in another Contracting State (see, to that effect, *Overseas Union Insurance and Others*, paragraph 24).

27 However, a prohibition imposed by a court, backed by a penalty, restraining a party from commencing or continuing proceedings before a foreign court undermines the latter court's jurisdiction to determine the dispute. Any injunction prohibiting a claimant from bringing such an action must be seen as constituting interference with the jurisdiction of the foreign court which, as such, is incompatible with the system of the Convention.

28 Notwithstanding the explanations given by the referring court and contrary to the view put forward by Mr Turner and the United Kingdom Government, such interference cannot be justified by the fact that it is only indirect and is intended to prevent an abuse of process by the defendant in the proceedings in the forum State.

In so far as the conduct for which the defendant is criticised consists in recourse to the jurisdiction of the court of another Member State, the judgment made as to the abusive nature of that conduct implies an assessment of the appropriateness of bringing proceedings before a court of another Member State. Such an assessment runs counter to the principle of mutual trust which, as pointed out in paragraphs 24 to 26 of this judgment, underpins the Convention and prohibits a court, except in special circumstances which are not applicable in this case, from reviewing the jurisdiction of the court of another Member State.

29 Even if it were assumed, as has been contended, that an injunction could be regarded as a measure of a procedural nature intended to safeguard the integrity of the proceedings pending before the court which issues it, and therefore as being a matter of national law alone, it need merely be borne in mind that the application of national procedural rules may not impair the effectiveness of the Convention (Case C-365/88 *Hagen* [1990] ECR I-1845, paragraph 20). However, that result would follow from the grant of an injunction of the kind at issue which, as has been established in paragraph 27 of this judgment, has the effect of limiting the application of the rules on jurisdiction laid down by the Convention.

30 The argument that the grant of injunctions may contribute to attainment of the objective of the Convention, which is to minimise the risk of conflicting decisions and to avoid a multiplicity of proceedings, cannot be accepted. First, recourse to such measures renders ineffective the specific mechanisms provided for by the Convention for cases of *lis alibi pendens* and of related actions. Second, it is liable to give rise to situations involving conflicts for which the Convention contains no rules. The possibility cannot be excluded that, even if an injunction had been issued in one Contracting State, a decision might nevertheless be given by a court of another Contracting state. Similarly, the possibility cannot be excluded that the courts of two Contracting States that allowed such measures might issue contradictory injunctions.

31 Consequently, the answer to be given to the national court must be that the Convention is to be interpreted as precluding the grant of an injunction whereby a court of a Contracting State prohibits a party to proceedings pending before it from commencing or continuing legal proceedings before a court of another Contracting State, even where that party is acting in bad faith with a view to frustrating the existing proceedings.

❓ NOTES AND QUESTIONS

1 In *Turner*, the European Court of Justice excluded that a court of a Member State issues an anti-suit injunction against proceedings initiated in another Member State in a dispute governed by the European law of jurisdiction (then the Brussels Convention). One of the main grounds for the decision is that the European law of jurisdiction is based on a principle of mutual trust between the Member States' legal systems and institutions. The Member States of the European Union have built a federal ensemble, and a founding principle of European integration is mutual trust between the Member States.

2   In *West Tankers*,[23] the European Court of Justice went even farther and held that anti-suit injunctions were also prohibited in a field, arbitration, which is outside of the scope of the European law of jurisdiction. In this case, the purpose of the injunction was to protect the jurisdiction of an arbitral tribunal sitting in London. Proceedings had been initiated before an Italian court. The Court held that an anti-suit injunction against the party suing in Italy might prevent the Italian court from retaining jurisdiction under the Brussels Convention, should it rule first that the arbitration agreement was invalid or did not apply.

3   Anti-suit injunctions, however, are tools which were designed by common law courts to address certain particular problems such as the initiation of vexatious and oppressive proceedings by one party against the other. What is the remedy that the *Turner* court offers to address this issue? The court rules that the specific mechanisms provided to address parallel litigation by the Convention (now Regulation) should not be rendered ineffective by the development of others. But are those mechanisms designed to address the same issues? How efficient had those mechanisms been in this particular case?

4   As an alternative to anti-suit injunctions, it has been suggested that the violation of a choice of court agreement could be protected by allowing the aggrieved party to sue for damages in the court designated by the clause.[24] Do you think that such mechanism would be compatible with the Brussels Regulation?

5   Most Member States belong to the civil law tradition. As a consequence, most of the members of the European Court of Justice are lawyers trained in the civil law tradition. The Brussels Convention was negotiated in 1968 when there were only six Member States which all belong to the civil law tradition. A member of the European court, who was to become its president, explained:

> (. . .) inspired by civil law systems, the Brussels I Regulation (the Brussels Convention) seeks to guarantee the predictability and inviolability of rules on jurisdiction. Consequently, a balancing approach such as that traditionally followed by common law systems in the context of conflict of laws was discarded by the Union legislator. This legislative choice explains why the ECJ has held the principle of legal certainty excludes anti-suit injunctions. Since anti-suit injunctions would require a case-by-case assessment, they seem incompatible with a clear and predictable *lis pendens* rule.[25]

6   Would the situation be different in a federal ensemble dominated by states belonging to the common law tradition, or is it simply inconceivable to allow anti suit injunctions as between sister states? We now turn to the United States.

Anti-Injunction Act
(28 U.S.C. § 2283, formerly Section 5 of the Judiciary Act of 1793)

---

23 Case C-185/07 *Allianz SpA, & Generali Assicurazioni Generali SpA v West Tankers Inc.* ECLI:EU:C:2009:69, [2009] E.C.R. I-00663.

24 See Adrian Briggs, *Agreements on Jurisdiction and Choice of Law* (OUP, 2008) 8.14; Koji Takahashi, 'Damages for Breach of a Choice-of-Court Agreement' (2008) X YPIL 57.

25 Koen Lenaerts, 'The Contribution of the European Court of Justice to the Area of Freedom, Security and Justice' (2010) 59 ICLQ 287.

A court of the United States may not grant an injunction to stay proceedings in a state court except as expressly authorized by Act of Congress, or where necessary in aid of its jurisdiction, or to protect or effectuate its judgments.

 CASE

U.S. Supreme Court, 21 Aug 2012 *Vendo Co. v. Lektro-Vend Corp.*[26]

III

The Anti-Injunction Act, 28 U.S.C. s 2283, provides:

> A court of the United States may not grant an injunction to stay proceedings in a State court except as expressly authorized by Act of Congress, or where necessary in aid of its jurisdiction, or to protect or effectuate its judgments.

The origins and development of the present Act, and of the statutes which preceded it, have been amply described in our prior opinions and need not be restated here. The most recent of these opinions are *Mitchum v. Foster*, 407 U.S. 225 (1972), and *Atlantic Coast Line R. Co. v. Brotherhood of Locomotive Engineers*, 398 U.S. 281 (1970). Suffice it to say that the Act is an absolute prohibition against any injunction of any state-court proceedings, unless the injunction falls within one of the three specifically defined exceptions in the Act. The Act's purpose is to forestall the inevitable friction between the state and federal courts that ensues from the injunction of state judicial proceedings by a federal court. *Oklahoma Packing Co. v. Oklahoma Gas & Electric Co.*, 309 U.S. 4, 9 (1940). Respondents' principal contention is that, as the Court of Appeals held, s 16 of the Clayton Act, which authorizes a private action to redress violations of the antitrust laws, comes within the 'expressly authorized' exception to s 2283. (. . .)

Our inquiry, of course, begins with the language of s 16 of the Clayton Act, which is the statute claimed to 'expressly authorize' the injunction issued here. It provides, in pertinent part:

> (A)ny person . . . shall be entitled to sue for and have injunctive relief, in any court of the United States having jurisdiction over the parties, against threatened loss or damage by violation of the antitrust laws . . . when and under the same conditions and principles as injunctive relief against threatened conduct that will cause

---

26 433 U.S. 623.

loss or damage is granted by courts of equity, under the rules governing such proceedings . . . 38 Stat. 737, 5 U.S.C. s 26.

On its face, the language merely authorizes private injunctive relief for anti-trust violations. Not only does the statute not mention s 2283 or the enjoining of state-court proceedings, but the granting of injunctive relief under s 16 is by the terms of that section limited to 'the same conditions and principles' employed by courts of equity, and by 'the rules governing such proceedings.' In 1793 the predecessor to s 2283 was enacted specifically to limit the general equity powers of a federal court. *Smith v. Apple*, 264 U.S. 274, 279 (1924). When s 16 was enacted in 1914 the bar of the Anti-Injunction Act had long constrained the equitable power of federal courts to issue injunctions. Thus, on its face, s 16 is far from an express exception to the Anti-Injunction Act, and may be fairly read as virtually incorporating the prohibitions of the Anti-Injunction Act with restrictive language not found, for example, in 42 U.S.C. s 1983. See discussion of *Mitchum v. Foster*, infra.

Respondents rely, as did the Court of Appeals and the District Court, on the following language from Mitchum:

> . . . (I)t is clear that, in order to qualify as an 'expressly authorized' exception to the anti-injunction statute, an Act of Congress must have created a specific and uniquely federal right or remedy, enforceable in a federal court of equity, that could be frustrated if the federal court were not empowered to enjoin a state court proceeding. This is not to say that in order to come within the exception an Act of Congress must, on its face and in every one of its provisions, be totally incompatible with the prohibition of the anti-injunction statute. The test, rather, is whether an Act of Congress, clearly creating a federal right or remedy enforceable in a federal court of equity, could be given its intended scope only by the stay of a state court proceeding. 407 U.S., at 237–238. (Emphasis added, footnote omitted.)

But we think it is clear that neither this language from Mitchum nor Mitchum's ratio decidendi supports the result contended for by respondents.

The private action for damages conferred by the Clayton Act is a 'uniquely federal right or remedy,' in that actions based upon it may be brought only in the federal courts. See *General Investment Company v. Lake Shore & Mich. So. R. Co.*, 260 U.S. 261, 287 (1922). It thus meets the first part of the test laid down in the language quoted from Mitchum.

But that authorization for private actions does not meet the second part of the Mitchum test; it is not an 'Act of Congress . . . (which) could be given its intended scope only by the stay of a state court proceeding,' 407 U.S., at 238. Crucial to our determination in Mitchum that 42 U.C.S. s 1983 fulfilled this requirement but wholly lacking here was our recognition that one of the clear congressional concerns underlying the enactment of s 1983 was the possibility that state courts, as well as other branches of state government, might be used as instrument to deny citizens their rights under the Federal Constitution. This determination was based on our review of the legislative history of s 1983; similar review of the legislative history underlying s 16 demonstrates that that section does not meet this aspect of the Mitchum test.

Section 1983 on its face, of course, contains no reference to s 2283, nor does it expressly authorize injunctions against state-court proceedings. But, as Mitchum recognized, such language need not invariably be present in order for a statute to come within the 'expressly authorized' exception if there exists sufficient evidence in the legislative history demonstrating that Congress recognized and intended the statute to authorize injunction of state-court proceedings. In Part IV of our opinion in Mitchum we examined in extenso the purpose and legislative history underlying s 1983, originally s 1 of the Civil Rights Act of 1871. We recounted in detail that statute's history which made it abundantly clear that by its enactment Congress demonstrated its direct and explicit concern to make the federal courts available to protect civil rights against unconstitutional actions of state courts.

We summarized our conclusion in these words:

> This legislative history makes evident that Congress clearly conceived that it was altering the relationship between the States and the Nation with respect to the protection of federally created rights; it was concerned that state instrumentalities could not protect those rights; it realized that state officers might, in fact, be antipathetic to the vindication of those rights; and it believed that these failings extended to the state courts. 407 U.S., at 242.

Thus, in Mitchum, absence of express language authorization for enjoining state-court proceedings in s 1983 actions was cured by the presence of relevant legislative history. In this case, however, neither the respondents nor the courts below have called to our attention any similar legislative history in connection with the enactment of s 16 of the Clayton Act. It is not suggested that Congress was concerned with the possibility that state-court proceedings would be used to violate the Sherman or Clayton Acts. Indeed, it seems safe to say that of the many and varied anticompetitive schemes which s 16 was intended to combat, Congress in no way focused upon a scheme using litigation in the state courts. The relevant legislative history of s 16 simply suggests that in enacting s 16 Congress was interested in extending the right to enjoin antitrust violations to private citizens. The critical aspects of the legislative history recounted in Mitchum which led us to conclude that s 1983 was within the 'expressly authorized' exception to s 2283 are wholly absent from the relevant history of s 16 of the Clayton Act. (. . .)

IV

Although the Court of Appeals did not reach the issue, the District Court found that, in addition to being 'expressly authorized,' the injunction was 'necessary in aid of its jurisdiction,' a separate exception to s 2283. (. . .)

In *Toucey v. New York Life Insurance Company*, 314 U.S., at 134–135, we acknowledged the existence of an historical exception to the Anti-Injunction Act in cases where the federal court has obtained jurisdiction over the res, prior to the state-court action. Although the 'necessary in aid of' exception to s 2283 may be fairly read as incorporating this historical in rem exception, see C. Wright, Law of Federal Courts s 47, p. 204 (3d ed. 1976), the federal and state actions here are simply in personam. The traditional notion is that in personam actions in federal and state court may proceed concurrently, without interference from either court, and there is no evidence that the exception to s 2283 was intended to alter this balance. We have never viewed parallel in personam actions as interfering with the jurisdiction of either court; as we stated in *Kline v. Burke Construction Co.*, 260 U.S. 226 (1922):

> (A)n action brought to enforce (a personal liability) *does not tend to impair or defeat the jurisdiction* of the court in which a prior action for the same cause is pending. Each court is free to proceed in its own way and in its own time, without reference to the proceedings in the other court. 'Whenever a judgment is rendered in one of the courts and pleaded in the other, the effect of that judgment is to be determined by the application of the principles of res adjudicata . . ..' *Id.*, at 230, (emphasis added).

No case of this Court has ever held that an injunction to 'preserve' a case or controversy fits within the 'necessary in aid of its jurisdiction' exception; neither have the parties directed us to any other federal court decisions so holding.

 NOTE

The *Anti Injunction Act* addresses an issue which does not arise in other federal systems: the relationship between federal and state courts. The issue is different from the relationship between sister states, as federal courts are ultimately in a higher hierarchical position than state courts. This explains why, while the principle is that anti-suit injunctions are illegal, it is open to Congress to create any exception it may wish to ensure the enforcement of federal rights. This also explains why state courts are clearly without power to issue antisuit injunctions against federal proceedings: *Donovan v. City of Dallas*, 377 U.S. 408 (1964).

CASE

U.S. Supreme Court, 13 January 1998 *Baker v. General Motors Corp.*[27]

Facts: For 15 of the years Ronald Elwell worked for respondent General Motors Corporation (GM), he was assigned to a group that studied the performance of GM vehicles. Elwell's studies and research concentrated on vehicular fires, and he frequently aided GM lawyers defending against product liability actions. The Elwell-GM employment relationship soured in 1987, and Elwell agreed to retire after serving as a consultant for two years. Disagreement surfaced again when Elwell's retirement time neared and continued into 1991. That year, plaintiffs in a Georgia product liability action deposed Elwell. The Georgia case involved a GM pickup truck fuel tank that burst into flames just after a collision. Over GM's objection, Elwell testified that the truck's fuel system was inferior to competing products. This testimony differed markedly from testimony Elwell had given as GM's in-house expert witness. A month later, Elwell sued GM in a Michigan County Court, alleging wrongful discharge and other tort and contract claims. GM counterclaimed, contending that Elwell had breached his fiduciary duty to GM. In settlement, GM paid Elwell an undisclosed sum of money, and the parties stipulated to the entry of a permanent injunction barring Elwell from testifying as a witness in any litigation involving GM without GM's consent, but providing that the injunction 'shall not operate to *interfere with the jurisdiction of the Court in . . . Georgia* [where the litigation involving the fuel tank was still pending].' (Emphasis added.) In addition, the parties entered into a separate settlement agreement, which provided that GM would not institute contempt or breach-of-contract proceedings against Elwell for giving subpoenaed testimony in another court or tribunal. Thereafter, the Bakers, petitioners here, subpoenaed Elwell to testify in their product liability action against GM, commenced in Missouri state court and removed by GM to federal court, in which the Bakers alleged that a faulty GM fuel pump caused the vehicle fire that killed their mother. GM asserted that the Michigan injunction barred Elwell's testimony.

Held: Elwell may testify in the Missouri action without offense to the national full faith and credit command.

---

27 522 U.S. 222 (1998).

JUSTICE GINSBURG.

The Court has never placed equity decrees outside the full faith and credit domain. Equity decrees for the payment of money have long been considered equivalent to judgments at law entitled to nationwide recognition. See, e.g., *Barber v. Barber*, 323 U. S. 77 (1944) (unconditional adjudication of petitioner's right to recover a sum of money is entitled to full faith and credit . . .). We see no reason why the preclusive effects of an adjudication on parties and those 'in privity' with them, i.e., claim preclusion and issue preclusion (res judicata and collateral estoppel), should differ depending solely upon the type of relief sought in a civil action. Cf. *Barber*, 323 U.S., at 87 (Jackson, J., concurring) (Full Faith and Credit Clause and its implementing statute speak not of 'judgments' but of '"judicial proceedings" without limitation').

Full faith and credit, however, does not mean that States must adopt the practices of other States regarding the time, manner, and mechanisms for enforcing judgments. Enforcement measures do not travel with the sister state judgment as preclusive effects do; such measures remain subject to the evenhanded control of forum law. (. . .)

Orders commanding action or inaction have been denied enforcement in a sister State when they purported to accomplish an official act within the exclusive province of that other State or interfered with litigation over which the ordering State had no authority. Thus, a sister State's decree concerning land ownership in another State has been held ineffective *to transfer title*, see *Fall v. Eastin*, 215 U. S. 1 (1909), although such a decree may indeed preclusively adjudicate the rights and obligations running between the *parties* to the foreign litigation, see, e.g., *Robertson v. Howard*, 229 U. S. 254, 261 (1913) ('[I]t may not be doubted that a court of equity in one State in a proper case could compel a defendant before it to convey property situated in another State.'). And anti suit injunctions regarding litigation elsewhere, even if compatible with due process as a direction constraining parties to the decree, see *Cole v. Cunningham*, 133 U. S. 107 (1890), in fact have not controlled the second court's actions regarding litigation in that court. See, e.g., *James v. Grand Trunk Western R. Co.*, 14 Ill. 2d 356, 372 (1958); see also E. Scoles & P. Hay, Conflict of Laws § 24.21, p. 981 (2d ed. 1992) (observing that anti suit injunction 'does not address, and thus has no preclusive effect on, the merits of the litigation [in the second forum]').[FN9] Sanctions for violations of an injunction, in any event, are generally administered by the court that issued the injunction. See, e.g., *Stiller v. Hardman*, 324 F.2d 626, 628 (CA2 1963) (nonrendition forum enforces monetary relief portion of a judgment but leaves enforcement of injunctive portion to rendition forum).

FN9: This Court has held it impermissible for a state court to enjoin a party from proceeding in a federal court, see *Donovan* v. *Dallas*, 377 U. S. 408 (1964), but has not yet ruled on the credit due to a state-court injunction barring a party from maintaining litigation in another State, see Ginsburg, Judgments in Search of Full Faith and Credit: The Last-in-Time Rule for Conflicting Judgments, 82 Harv. L. Rev. 798, 823 (1969); see also Reese, Full Faith and Credit to Foreign Equity Decrees, 42 Iowa L. Rev. 183, 198 (1957) (urging that, although this Court 'has not yet had occasion to determine [the issue], . . . full faith and credit does not require dismissal of an action whose prosecution has been enjoined,' for to hold otherwise 'would mean in effect that the courts of one state can control what goes on in the courts of another'). State courts that have dealt with the question have, in the main, regarded antisuit injunctions as outside the full faith and credit ambit. See Ginsburg, 82 Harv. L. Rev., at 823, and n. 99; see also *id.*, at 828–829 ('The current state of the law, permitting [an antisuit] injunction to issue but not compelling any deference outside the rendering state, may be the most reasonable compromise between . . . extreme alternatives,' i.e., ' general rule of respect for antisuit injunctions running between state courts,' or 'a general rule denying the states authority to issue injunctions directed at proceedings in other states').

 NOTES AND QUESTIONS

1 While Justice Ginsburg does discuss the issue in *Baker v. General Motors Corporation*, many American scholars do not consider the opinion as direct authority on whether a state court may issue an anti-suit injunction with respect to proceedings initiated in another state court.[28] Justice Ginsburg seems to acknowledge it in footnote 9 of her decision.

2 The focus of *Baker* is on recognition and enforcement (which is governed in the United States by the Full Faith and Credit Clause of the Constitution)[29] of equitable decrees, including injunctions, issued by the court of one U.S. state in another one. It is not on the power to issue such injunctions. Nowhere in the opinion does Justice Ginsburg suggest that a state court would lack power to do so. Indeed, she envisages that the issuing court could sanction violations of the injunctions, which suggests that issuing it is permissible.

3 In the United States, therefore, the issue is whether the Full Faith and Credit Clause mandates the recognition and enforcement of antisuit injunction issued by sister states. Justice Ginsburg lays down a distinction between recognition and enforcement. Does it apply to anti-suit injunctions? What is the effect of an anti-suit injunction in another sister state?

---

28 See Currie, Kay, Kramer and Roosevelt, 593.
29 See *infra*, Ch. 7.

5

Choice of court agreements

States have freely defined the international jurisdiction of their courts. Such rules typically include reasonable rules based on minimum contacts and close connections, but also exorbitant rules (*supra*, Ch. 3). As a result, in any given international dispute, a variety of courts will typically be available to the parties. If the parties have incentives to sue in different courts, parallel litigation may follow. The consequence will be uncertainty and additional costs.

Allowing the parties to agree in advance on a single court having jurisdiction to resolve their disputes (exclusive jurisdiction clauses) is a solution to many of these problems. This explains why choice of court agreements, or forum selection clauses, have widely been favoured by States in recent times.

An alternative could have been to conclude an international treaty unifying the rules of international jurisdiction of most nations. A number of States, including the United States and the European Union, conducted negotiations to this effect for years under the aegis of the Hague Conference of Private International Law, but the negotiations eventually failed, in particular because international jurisdiction is conceptualized so differently in Europe and the United States. However, the negotiators did reach an agreement on choice of court agreements, and concluded the 2005 Hague Convention on Choice of Court Agreements.[1]

1   General rules

1.1   Enforceability of agreement

1.1.1   *Validity of agreement*

Choice of court agreements allow the parties to derogate from rules of jurisdiction, either by stripping jurisdiction from courts which might otherwise

---

1 As of October 2016, the Convention was in force in Mexico, Singapore and the European Union (except Denmark). The United States has signed, but not ratified the Convention.

have had jurisdiction, or by granting jurisdiction to a court which might not have had jurisdiction otherwise. Is it acceptable at all? How did the U.S. Supreme Court answer in the following case?

 CASE

U.S. Supreme Court, 12 June 1972 *M/S Bremen v. Zapata Off-Shore Co.*[2]

Chief Justice BURGER

Forum-selection clauses have historically not been favored by American courts. Many courts, federal and state, have declined to enforce such clauses on the ground that they were 'contrary to public policy,' or that their effect was to 'oust the jurisdiction' of the court. Although this view apparently still has considerable acceptance, other courts are tending to adopt a more hospitable attitude toward forum-selection clauses. This view, advanced in the well-reasoned dissenting opinion in the instant case, is that such clauses are prima facie valid and should be enforced unless enforcement is shown by the resisting party to be 'unreasonable' under the circumstances. We believe this is the correct doctrine to be followed by federal district courts sitting in admiralty. It is merely the other side of the proposition recognized by this Court in *National Equipment Rental, Ltd. v. Szukhent*, 375 U.S. 311 (1964), holding that in federal courts a party may validly consent to be sued in a jurisdiction where he cannot be found for service of process through contractual designation of an 'agent' for receipt of process in that jurisdiction. In so holding, the Court stated:

> (I)t is settled . . . that parties to a contract may agree in advance to submit to the jurisdiction of a given court to permit notice to be served by the opposing party, or even to waive notice altogether. *Id.*, at 315–316, 84 S.Ct., at 414.

This approach is substantially that followed in other common-law countries including England. It is the view advanced by noted scholars and that adopted by the Restatement of the Conflict of Laws. It accords with ancient concepts of freedom of contract and reflects an appreciation of the expanding horizons of American contractors who seek business in all parts of the world. Not surprisingly, foreign businessmen prefer, as do we, to have disputes resolved in their own courts, but if that choice is not available, then in a neutral forum with expertise in the subject matter. Plainly, the courts of

---

2 407 U.S. 1.

England meet the standards of neutrality and long experience in admiralty litigation. The choice of that forum was made in an arm's-length negotiation by experienced and sophisticated businessmen, and absent some compelling and countervailing reason it should be honored by the parties and enforced by the courts.

The argument that such clauses are improper because they tend to 'oust' a court of jurisdiction is hardly more than a vestigial legal fiction. It appears to rest at core on historical judicial resistance to any attempt to reduce the power and business of a particular court and has little place in an era when all courts are overloaded and when businesses once essentially local now operate in world markets. It reflects something of a provincial attitude regarding the fairness of other tribunals. No one seriously contends in this case that the forum selection clause 'ousted' the District Court of jurisdiction over Zapata's action. The threshold question is whether that court should have exercised its jurisdiction to do more than give effect to the legitimate expectations of the parties, manifested in their freely negotiated agreement, by specifically enforcing the forum clause.

There are compelling reasons why a freely negotiated private international agreement, unaffected by fraud, undue influence, or overweening bargaining power, such as that involved here, should be given full effect. In this case, for example, we are concerned with a far from routine transaction between companies of two different nations contemplating the tow of an extremely costly piece of equipment from Louisiana across the Gulf of Mexico and the Atlantic Ocean, through the Mediterranean Sea to its final destination in the Adriatic Sea. In the course of its voyage, it was to traverse the waters of many jurisdictions. The Chaparral could have been damaged at any point along the route, and there were countless possible ports of refuge. That the accident occurred in the Gulf of Mexico and the barge was towed to Tampa in an emergency were mere fortuities. It cannot be doubted for a moment that the parties sought to provide for a neutral forum for the resolution of any disputes arising during the tow. Manifestly much uncertainty and possibly great inconvenience to both parties could arise if a suit could be maintained in any jurisdiction in which an accident might occur or if jurisdiction were left to any place where the Bremen or Unterweser might happen to be found. The elimination of all such uncertainties by agreeing in advance on a forum acceptable to both parties is an indispensable element in international trade, commerce, and contracting. There is strong evidence that the forum clause was a vital part of the agreement, and it would be unrealistic to think that the parties did not conduct their negotiations, including fixing the monetary terms, with the consequences of the forum clause figuring prominently in their calculations. Under these circumstances, as Justice Karminski reasoned in sustaining jurisdiction over Zapata in the High Court of Justice, '(t)he force of an agreement for litigation in this country, freely entered into between two competent parties, seems to me to be very powerful.'

Thus, in the light of present-day commercial realities and expanding international trade we conclude that the forum clause should control absent a strong showing that it should be set aside. Although their opinions are not altogether explicit, it seems reasonably clear that the District Court and the Court of Appeals placed the burden on Unterweser to show that London would be a more convenient forum than Tampa, although the contract expressly resolved that issue. The correct approach would have been to enforce the forum clause specifically unless Zapata could clearly show that enforcement would be unreasonable and unjust, or that the clause was invalid for such reasons as fraud or overreaching. Accordingly, the case must be remanded for reconsideration.

The enforceability of choice of court agreements is widely accepted today, at least between parties with equivalent bargaining power. There are, however, a few validity requirements. Please read the following three rules and identify under which conditions choice of court agreements are valid.

Brussels Ibis Regulation (2012)

SECTION 7 Prorogation of jurisdiction

Article 25

1. If the parties, regardless of their domicile, have agreed that a court or the courts of a Member State are to have jurisdiction to settle any disputes which have arisen or which may arise in connection with a particular legal relationship, that court or those courts shall have jurisdiction, unless the agreement is null and void as to its substantive validity under the law of that Member State. Such jurisdiction shall be exclusive unless the parties have agreed otherwise. The agreement conferring jurisdiction shall be either:

(a) in writing or evidenced in writing;

(b) in a form which accords with practices which the parties have established between themselves; or

(c) in international trade or commerce, in a form which accords with a usage of which the parties are or ought to have been aware and which in such trade or commerce is widely known to, and regularly observed by, parties to contracts of the type involved in the particular trade or commerce concerned.

2. Any communication by electronic means which provides a durable record of the agreement shall be equivalent to 'writing'.

3. The court or courts of a Member State on which a trust instrument has

conferred jurisdiction shall have exclusive jurisdiction in any proceedings brought against a settlor, trustee or beneficiary, if relations between those persons or their rights or obligations under the trust are involved.

4. Agreements or provisions of a trust instrument conferring jurisdiction shall have no legal force if they are contrary to Articles 15, 19 or 23, or if the courts whose jurisdiction they purport to exclude have exclusive jurisdiction by virtue of Article 24.

5. An agreement conferring jurisdiction which forms part of a contract shall be treated as an agreement independent of the other terms of the contract.

The validity of the agreement conferring jurisdiction cannot be contested solely on the ground that the contract is not valid.

Article 26

1. Apart from jurisdiction derived from other provisions of this Regulation, a court of a Member State before which a defendant enters an appearance shall have jurisdiction. This rule shall not apply where appearance was entered to contest the jurisdiction, or where another court has exclusive jurisdiction by virtue of Article 24.

2. In matters referred to in Sections 3, 4 or 5 where the policyholder, the insured, a beneficiary of the insurance contract, the injured party, the consumer or the employee is the defendant, the court shall, before assuming jurisdiction under paragraph 1, ensure that the defendant is informed of his right to contest the jurisdiction of the court and of the consequences of entering or not entering an appearance.

2005 Hague Convention on Choice of Court Agreements

Article 3 *Exclusive choice of court agreements*

For the purposes of this Convention –

a) 'exclusive choice of court agreement' means an agreement concluded by two or more parties that meets the requirements of paragraph *c)* and designates, for the purpose of deciding disputes which have arisen or may arise in connection with a particular legal relationship, the courts of one Contracting State or one or more specific courts of one Contracting State to the exclusion of the jurisdiction of any other courts;

b) a choice of court agreement which designates the courts of one Contracting State or one or more specific courts of one Contracting State shall be deemed to be exclusive unless the parties have expressly provided otherwise;

c) an exclusive choice of court agreement must be concluded or documented –

i) in writing; or

ii) by any other means of communication which renders information accessible so as to be usable for subsequent reference;

d) an exclusive choice of court agreement that forms part of a contract shall be treated as an agreement independent of the other terms of the contract. The validity of the exclusive choice of court agreement cannot be contested solely on the ground that the contract is not valid.

Article 5 *Jurisdiction of the chosen court*

(1) The court or courts of a Contracting State designated in an exclusive choice of court agreement shall have jurisdiction to decide a dispute to which the agreement applies, unless the agreement is null and void under the law of that State.

(2) A court that has jurisdiction under paragraph 1 shall not decline to exercise jurisdiction on the ground that the dispute should be decided in a court of another State.

(3) The preceding paragraphs shall not affect rules –

a)   on jurisdiction related to subject matter or to the value of the claim;

b)   on the internal allocation of jurisdiction among the courts of a Contracting State. However, where the chosen court has discretion as to whether to transfer a case, due consideration should be given to the choice of the parties.

The respective territorial scopes of regional instruments such as the Brussels Ibis Regulation and the Hague Convention are delineated as follows: the Hague Convention only applies where one of the parties to the choice of court agreement is a resident in a Contracting State (to the Convention) which is not a member of the regional organization (Art. 26(6)(a) of the Hague Convention). This means that the regional instrument applies to purely regional cases (for instance, all parties to the choice of court agreement are resident in the European Union) or to cases involving parties based in Member States of the regional organization and third States (to both the regional organization and the Convention).

Japanese Code of Civil Procedure

Article 3–7 *Jurisdiction Agreement*

(1) The parties may decide by agreement the country in which they may file an action.

(2) The agreement provided in the preceding paragraph shall have no effect unless it is in writing and is concerned with an action arising from specific legal relationships.

(3) For the purpose of the preceding paragraph, an agreement is deemed to be in writing if it is recorded in an electromagnetic record (viz. a record made in an electronic form, a magnetic form, or any other form unrecognizable to human perception, which is used for information processing by computers).

(4) An agreement to file an action exclusively with the courts of a particular foreign country may not be invoked if those courts are legally or factually unable to exercise jurisdiction.

(. . .) *[see infra, p. 281.]*

Article 3–8 *Jurisdiction by Submission*
The courts shall have jurisdiction in the circumstances where the defendant, without objecting to the jurisdiction, made an oral argument on the merits or made a statement in preparatory proceedings.

? NOTES AND QUESTIONS

1 Are there any formal requirements for choice of court agreements? Is it, for instance, required that they be in writing? *Compare* Art. 25 of the Brussels Ibis Regulation and Art. 3–7 of the Japanese Code of Civil Procedure. Can choice of court agreements be entered into by email?

2 Choice of court agreements are contracts which must meet a number of requirements common to all contracts. Where are the rules applicable to this issue to be found?

3 Does the chosen court have jurisdiction to decide whether the choice of court agreement was validly concluded? But if the court concludes that the contract was void or inexistent under the applicable law, could you not argue that it never was granted jurisdiction, including to rule on the validity of the clause? How do the Brussels Ibis Regulation and the 2005 Hague Convention resolve the issue?

1.1.2 Is a connection between the dispute and the chosen jurisdiction required?

Should the parties be allowed to grant jurisdiction to whichever court, irrespective of whether the chosen court is connected with the dispute? This very much depends on the rationale for allowing forum selection clauses in the first place. If the rationale is to enable them to clarify which of the available courts should decide the dispute, a logical consequence would be to limit the parties' freedom accordingly.

One such example is the following rule of Chinese law:

Chinese Law on Civil Procedure (1991, as amended)

Article 34
The parties to a contract or to any dispute regarding other property rights and interests may agree to choose in their written contract the people's court in the place where the defendant has his domicile, where the contract is performed, where the contract is signed, where the plaintiff has his domicile or where the object of the action is located or other locations which have material connection to this dispute, to exercise jurisdiction over the case, provided that the provisions of this Law regarding jurisdiction by level and exclusive jurisdiction are not violated.

Please read the following case and assess whether there is a connection requirement under American law.

CASE

U.S. Supreme Court, 12 June 1972 *M/S Bremen v. Zapata Off-Shore Co.*[3]

Courts have also suggested that a forum clause, even though it is freely bargained for and contravenes no important public policy of the forum, may nevertheless be 'unreasonable' and unenforceable if the chosen forum is seriously inconvenient for the trial of the action. Of course, where it can be said with reasonable assurance that at the time they entered the contract, the parties to a freely negotiated private international commercial agreement contemplated the claimed inconvenience, it is difficult to see why any such claim of inconvenience should be heard to render the forum clause unenforceable. We are not here dealing with an agreement between two Americans to resolve their essentially local disputes in a remote alien forum. In such a case, the serious inconvenience of the contractual forum to one or both of the parties might carry greater weight in determining the reasonableness of the forum clause. The remoteness of the forum might suggest that the agreement was an adhesive one, or that the parties did not have the particular controversy in mind when they made their agreement; yet even there the party claiming should bear a heavy burden of proof. Similarly, selection of a remote forum to apply differing foreign law to an essentially American controversy might contravene an important public policy of the forum. For example, so long as *Bisso* governs American courts with respect to the towage business in American waters, it would quite arguably be improper to permit an American tower to avoid that policy by providing a foreign forum for resolution of his disputes with an American towee.

This case, however, involves a freely negotiated international commercial transaction between a German and an American corporation for towage of a vessel from the Gulf of Mexico to the Adriatic Sea. As noted, selection of a London forum was clearly a reasonable effort to bring vital certainty to this international transaction and to provide a neutral forum experienced and capable in the resolution of admiralty litigation. Whatever 'inconvenience' Zapata would suffer by being forced to litigate in the contractual forum as it agreed to do was clearly foreseeable at the time of contracting. In such circumstances it should be incumbent on the party seeking to escape his contract to show that trial in the contractual forum will be so gravely difficult and inconvenient that he will for all practical purposes be deprived of his day in court. Absent that, there is no basis for concluding that it would be unfair, unjust, or unreasonable to hold that party to his bargain.

---

3 407 U.S. 1.

CASE

Court of Appeal, First District, Division 2, California, 21 June 2001 *America Online, Inc. (AOL) v. Superior Court of Alameda County*[4]

AOL correctly posits that California favors contractual forum selection clauses so long as they are entered into freely and voluntarily, and their enforcement would not be unreasonable. (*Smith Valentino*, 17 Cal.3d at pp. 495–496.) This favorable treatment is attributed to our law's devotion to the concept of one's free right to contract, and flows from the important practical effect such contractual rights have on commerce generally. This division has characterized forum selection clauses as 'play[ing] an important role in both national and international commerce.' (*Lu*, 11 Cal.App.4th at p. 1493.) The *Wimsatt* court similarly exhorted that '[f]orum selection clauses *are* important in facilitating national and international commerce, and as a general rule should be welcomed.' (*Wimsatt*, 32 Cal.App.4th at p. 1523, original italics.)

We agree with these sentiments, and view such clauses as likely to become even more ubiquitous as this state and nation become acculturated to electronic commerce. (See *Carnival Cruise Lines, Inc. v. Shute* (1991) 499 U.S. 585.) Moreover, there are strong economic arguments in support of these agreements, favoring both merchants and consumers, including reduction in the costs of goods and services and the stimulation of e-commerce.

But this encomium is not boundless. Our law favors forum selection agreements only so long as they are procured freely and voluntarily, with the place chosen having some logical nexus to one of the parties of the dispute, and so long as California consumers will not find their substantial legal rights significantly impaired by their enforcement. Therefore, to be enforceable, the selected jurisdiction must be 'suitable,' 'available,' and able to 'accomplish substantial justice.' (*The Bremen v. Zapata Off–Shore Co.* (1972) 407 U.S. 1, 17; *Smith Valentino*, 17 Cal.3d at p. 494.)

NOTES AND QUESTIONS

1 Is *AOL* consistent with the *Bremen*? Did the *Bremen* court mean that there should be a connection between the chosen court and the dispute or the parties? Could reasonableness be defined differently? The *AOL* court requires that the chosen court have 'some logical nexus' to the dispute. Is it different from a material connection in the meaning of Art. 34 of the Chinese law above?

---

4 90 Cal.App.4th 1.

2 *AOL* was a consumer case. Does the California court establish a requirement for consumer cases only, or is the scope of its ruling more general?

3 In the context of choice of law, U.S. law does require that there be either a connection between the dispute and the law chosen by the parties or a reasonable basis for the choice: see *infra*, Ch. 9.

 CASE

European Court of Justice, 17 January 1980 *Zelger v. Salinitri* (Case C-56/79)[5]

Article 17 [*now 25*], which occurs in Section 6 of the Convention entitled 'prorogation of jurisdiction' and which provides for the exclusive jurisdiction of the court designated by the parties in accordance with the prescribed form, puts aside both the rule of general jurisdiction – provided for in Article 2 – and the rules of special jurisdiction – provided for in Article 5 [*now 7*] – and dispenses with any objective connexion between the legal relationship in dispute and the court designated.

 NOTES AND QUESTIONS

1 Neither the Brussels Ibis Regulation, nor the 2005 Hague Convention limits the freedom of the parties to choose the competent court.

2 Is unlimited freedom dangerous? As underlined by the Supreme Court in the *Bremen*,[6] parties to international contract, if they cannot litigate in their home courts, would rather agree on the jurisdiction of a neutral forum, which should be unconnected to the dispute.

3 Is there, however, a danger of evasion of the jurisdiction of the competent courts, or of rules of civil procedure which might be common to them, but unknown in the chosen forum?

1.1.3 *Effect of applicability of mandatory rules of the forum*

Because international mandatory rules serve their most crucial interests, States derogate from the multilateral choice of law methodology and apply them directly.[7] However, instances where courts have applied foreign mandatory rules are few, and, in many jurisdictions, courts have a limited power to do so. This could give incentives to parties willing to avoid the application of the mandatory rules of a given State to provide for the jurisdiction of a court (and the application of the law) of another State which would not apply foreign mandatory rules (and which would not have any similar local mandatory rule).

---

5 ECLI:EU:C:1980:15.
6 *Supra*, 1.1.1.
7 *Supra*, Ch. 1.

The question arises, therefore, whether the existence of international mandatory rules should be a ground for denying effect to a choice of court agreement granting jurisdiction to a foreign court. In practical terms, the issue would be raised by a party who would benefit from the application of the mandatory rule, and would therefore bring proceedings in the jurisdiction of the rule, in violation of the choice of court agreement. If the forum chose to enforce the choice of court agreement and to decline jurisdiction, the crucial interest served by its mandatory rule would not be served. However, this would open the door for challenges throughout the world of the enforceability of choice of court agreements on the ground of the existence of local mandatory rules, and undermine the legal certainty that choice of court agreements are meant to bring to international trade.

Read the two following cases and identify the cases where an American court would deny enforcement to a jurisdiction clause on the ground that the law of the forum applies.

 CASE

U.S. Supreme Court, 12 June 1972 *M/S Bremen v. Zapata Off-Shore Co.*[8]

Thus, in the light of present-day commercial realities and expanding international trade we conclude that the forum clause should control absent a strong showing that it should be set aside. Although their opinions are not altogether explicit, it seems reasonably clear that the District Court and the Court of Appeals placed the burden on Unterweser to show that London would be a more convenient forum than Tampa, although the contract expressly resolved that issue. The correct approach would have been to enforce the forum clause specifically unless Zapata could clearly show that enforcement would be unreasonable and unjust, or that the clause was invalid for such reasons as fraud or overreaching. Accordingly, the case must be remanded for reconsideration.

We note, however, that there is nothing in the record presently before us that would support a refusal to enforce the forum clause. The Court of Appeals suggested that enforcement would be contrary to the public policy of the forum under *Bisso v. Inland Waterways Corp.*, 349 U.S. 85 (1955), because of the prospect that the English courts would enforce the clauses of the towage contract purporting to exculpate Unterweser from liability for damages to the Chaparral. A contractual choice-of-forum clause should

---

8 407 U.S. 1.

be held unenforceable if enforcement would contravene a strong public policy of the forum in which suit is brought, whether declared by statute or by judicial decision. See, e.g., *Boyd v. Grand Trunk W.R. Co.*, 338 U.S. 263 (1949). It is clear, however, that whatever the proper scope of the policy expressed in Bisso, it does not reach this case. Bisso rested on considerations with respect to the towage business strictly in American waters, and those considerations are not controlling in an international commercial agreement. Speaking for the dissenting judges in the Court of Appeals, Judge Wisdom pointed out:

> (W)e should be careful not to overemphasize the strength of the (Bisso) policy . . . (T)wo concerns underlie the rejection of exculpatory agreements: that they may be produced by overweening bargaining power; and that they do not sufficiently discourage negligence . . . Here the conduct in question is that of a foreign party occurring in international waters outside our jurisdiction. The evidence disputes any notion of overreaching in the contractual agreement. And for all we know, the uncertainties and dangers in the new field of transoceanic towage of oil rigs were so great that the tower was unwilling to take financial responsibility for the risks, and the parties thus allocated responsibility for the voyage to the tow. It is equally possible that the contract price took this factor into account. I conclude that we should not invalidate the forum selection clause here unless we are firmly convinced that we would thereby significantly encourage negligent conduct within the boundaries of the United States. 428 F.2d, at 907—908. (Footnotes omitted.)

 CASE

Court of Appeal, First District, Division 2, California, 21 June 2001 *America Online, Inc. (AOL) v. Superior Court of Alameda County*[9]

California courts will refuse to defer to the selected forum if to do so would substantially diminish the rights of California residents in a way that violates our state's public policy. For example, in *CQL Original Products, Inc. v. National Hockey League Players' Assn.* (1995) 39 Cal.App.4th 1347 (CQL), a dispute arose following the termination of a merchandise licensing agreement between CQL Original Products, Inc. and the National Hockey League (NHL). The merchandiser's breach of contract suit in California was met with a motion filed by the NHL to dismiss based on a forum selection clause contained in the licensing agreement. (*Id.* at p. 1353.) The trial court granted

---

9 90 Cal.App.4th 1.

the NHL's motion. In affirming the trial court's ruling, the appellate court noted that 'a forum selection clause will not be enforced if to do so will bring about a result contrary to the public policy of the forum . . . .' (*Id.* at p. 1354) After reviewing the agreement in question, the court concluded there was no public policy reason to deny enforcement of the provision. (*Id.* at p. 1356)

In *Hall v. Superior Court* (1983) 150 Cal.App.3d 411 (*Hall*), two California investors exchanged their interests in an oil and gas limited partnership in return for stock in one of their co-investors, Imperial Petroleum, Inc., a Utah corporation. Closer to the facts of this case, the contract embodying their exchange agreement contained *both* forum selection and choice of law provisions identifying Nevada as the selected forum and governing law. A dispute arose, and the two investors sued Imperial in California. (*Id.* at pp. 413–415) Imperial asserted the forum selection clause, and the trial court found the forum selection clause was enforceable.

In reversing the lower court's decision, the appellate court undertook an examination of both the choice of law clause as well as the forum selection clause noting that the enforceability of these clauses were 'inextricably bound up' in one another. (*Hall*, at p. 416.) The reason for considering them together was that absent a choice of law clause, the selected forum could apply California law to the dispute under the selected forum's conflict of laws principles. If so, there would be no risk that substantive law might be employed which would materially diminish rights of California residents in violation of California public policy. (*Ibid.*) However, where the effect of the transfer would be otherwise, the forum selection clause would not be enforced: 'While "California does not have any public policy against a choice of law provision, where it is otherwise appropriate" [citation] and "choice of law provisions are usually respected by California courts . . ." [citing *Smith Valentino,* 17 Cal.3d at p. 494] "an agreement designating [a foreign] law will not be given effect if it would violate a strong California public policy . . ." [or] "result in an evasion of . . . a statute of the forum protecting its citizens." [Citation.]' (*Hall* at pp. 416–417)

The *Hall* court determined that if the pending securities litigation were transferred to Nevada where Nevada law would be applied, the plaintiffs would lose the benefit of California's Corporate Securities Law of 1968 which would otherwise govern the transaction in question. This California law was designed to protect the public from fraud and deception in securities matters, by providing statutory remedies for violations of the California Corporations Code. (*Hall*, at p. 417.) For this reason, the remedial scheme, like the CRLA involved in this case, contains an anti-waiver provision. (Corp Code, § 25701; *Hall*, at pp. 417–418.) The court concluded: '[W]e believe the right of a buyer of securities in California to have California law and its concomitant nuances apply to any future dispute arising out of the transaction is a "provision" within the meaning of [Corporations Code] section 25701 which cannot be waived or evaded by stipulation of the parties to a securities transaction. Consequently, we hold the choice of Nevada law provision in this agreement violates section 25701 and the public policy of this state [citation] and for that reason deny enforcement of the forum selection clause as unreasonable.' (*Id.* at p. 418.)

 QUESTIONS

1 Is *AOL* consistent with the *Bremen*?
2 *AOL* was a consumer case. Is the scope of the rule laid down by the court limited to consumer cases, or to cases where the legislation of the forum aims at protecting a weaker party?

2005 Hague Convention on Choice of Court Agreements
Article 6 *Obligations of a court not chosen*
A court of a Contracting State other than that of the chosen court shall suspend or dismiss proceedings to which an exclusive choice of court agreement applies unless –
c) giving effect to the agreement would lead to a manifest injustice or would be manifestly contrary to the public policy of the State of the court seised;

Trevor Hartley and Masato Dogauchi
Explanatory Report on the 2005 Hague Choice of Court Agreements Convention[10]

153. The third exception (second limb): public policy. The phrase 'manifestly contrary to the public policy of the State of the court seised' is intended to set a high threshold. It refers to basic norms or principles of that State; it does not permit the court seised to hear the case simply because the chosen court might violate, in some technical way, a mandatory rule of the State of the court seised (fn: Here 'public policy' includes the international public policy of the State concerned: [citations]). As in the case of manifest injustice, the standard is intended to be high: the provision does not permit a court to disregard a choice of court agreement simply because it would not be binding under domestic law.

 QUESTIONS

1 How does Art. 6(c) compare with American law? Is the concept of public policy the same in each context? Why do you think Art 6(c) refers to 'manifest' violations of public policy?
2 May a court deny enforcement to a choice of court agreement on the ground that foreign public policy would be manifestly violated otherwise?

---

10 Hague Conference on Private International Law 2013.

Is there a case for enforcing jurisdiction clauses despite the applicability of a mandatory rule of the forum? Is the certainty that jurisdiction clauses bring with respect to the forum an important value?

 CASE

French Cour de cassation, 22 October 2008, *Monster Cable Products Inc v. Audio Marketing Services* Case no 07-15.823

Having regard to art. 3 of the Civil Code and the general principles of private international law;

Whereas, on 22 October 1986, and then on 18 September 1995, American company Monster Cable Products Inc. (hereinafter 'Monster Cable') entered into an exclusive distribution agreement of its products on French territory with French company Audio Marketing Services (hereinafter 'AMS'). Article 7.5 of the second agreement provided for the jurisdiction of San Francisco courts over any action arising out of the agreement. Monster Cable terminated the agreement on 2 August 2002. On 3 January 2003, AMS brought proceedings against Monster Cable in the Bobigny Commercial Court pursuant to Art. L 442–6 of the Commercial Code for abuse of economic dependency.

Whereas the Court of Appeal disregarded the jurisdiction clause and ruled that French courts had jurisdiction on the ground that the dispute involved applying mandatory provisions belonging to economic public policy which are international mandatory rules (*lois de police*), and sanctioning discriminatory practices assimilated to civil torts which were committed on national territory.

By ruling as it did, although the jurisdiction clause included in that agreement was aimed to cover any dispute arising out of the agreement, and therefore had to be enforced, even if international mandatory rules might be applicable to the merits of the dispute, the Court of Appeal violated the abovementioned provision and the principles.

FOR THESE REASONS: allows the appeal and sets aside the judgment of the Paris Court of Appeal.

 NOTES AND QUESTIONS

1 What is the scope of the ruling of the court? Does the judgment suggest that a French court might be entitled to deny enforcement to jurisdiction clauses for certain mandatory rules only?

2 Contrary to the position in the United States, there are special rules under French law protecting certain categories of parties deemed weaker (consumers and employees, in particular). Such rules typically limit the power of parties to enter into choice of court agreements and thus, indirectly, to evade the laws that might be protecting them.

3 In this case, the European law of jurisdiction was not applicable. Contrary to Art 6(c) of the Hague Convention, Art 25 of the Brussels Ibis Regulation does not allow a court of a Member State to decline jurisdiction on the ground that an overriding mandatory provision of the forum applies.

4 In a judgment of 5 September 2012, the German Federal Court denied enforcement to a clause providing for the jurisdiction of an American court on the ground that a European overriding mandatory provision governed.[11] The plaintiff was a German commercial agent who sought payment of an indemnity after termination of the contract by his American principal. The contract provided for the application of Virginia law, which does not recognize such indemnity. However, the European Court of Justice has ruled the 1986 Directive on Self Employed Commercial Agents is an overriding mandatory provision which protects European agents irrespective of the law governing the contract.[12] The German Court held that the purpose of the ruling of the ECJ was to ensure the application of the Directive, and that the rationale also demanded that the forum selection clause be denied enforcement.

1.2 Effectiveness of agreement

1.2.1 *Parallel litigation*

Exclusive choice of court agreements grant jurisdiction to a single court and exclude the jurisdiction of all others. Thus, they should be the perfect recipe for avoiding parallel litigation: none of the parties should attempt to initiate proceedings in another court, as this court should have the obligation to decline jurisdiction.

There are, however, several reasons why parties bring proceedings in courts other than the chosen court. The most important one is that the parties may disagree on whether an agreement on jurisdiction was actually reached: the agreement is alleged, but its existence has not yet been proven to the satisfaction of any court. Likewise, the parties may disagree on whether the agreement is valid. In both cases, the party who argues either that no agreement was reached, or that the agreement was invalid also believes that he is entitled to initiate proceedings in any court having jurisdiction under its default rules, for instance the court of the place of performance of the contract.

In certain cases, a party might have an incentive to initiate proceedings in another court for purely tactical reasons. This could be the case if this other

---

11 BGH, VII ZR 25/12.
12 *Supra*, p. 22.

court was known to be very slow. Even if it were to eventually decline jurisdiction in favour of the chosen court, it might be several years later, and the resolution of the dispute would have been disrupted accordingly. The tactic would work especially well if the chosen court had to wait for the other court to decline jurisdiction before being able to proceed, which was the case within the European Union under the Brussels Regulation. As Italian courts are notoriously slow, this tactic was known in Europe as the Italian Torpedo.[13] The European lawmaker tried to address the issue in the Brussels Ibis Regulation.

Brussels Ibis Regulation (2012)

PREAMBLE

(21) In the interests of the harmonious administration of justice it is necessary to minimise the possibility of concurrent proceedings and to ensure that irreconcilable judgments will not be given in different Member States. There should be a clear and effective mechanism for resolving cases of lis pendens and related actions, and for obviating problems flowing from national differences as to the determination of the time when a case is regarded as pending. For the purposes of this Regulation, that time should be defined autonomously.

(22) However, in order to enhance the effectiveness of exclusive choice-of-court agreements and to avoid abusive litigation tactics, it is necessary to provide for an exception to the general lis pendens rule in order to deal satisfactorily with a particular situation in which concurrent proceedings may arise. This is the situation where a court not designated in an exclusive choice-of-court agreement has been seised of proceedings and the designated court is seised subsequently of proceedings involving the same cause of action and between the same parties. In such a case, the court first seised should be required to stay its proceedings as soon as the designated court has been seised and until such time as the latter court declares that it has no jurisdiction under the exclusive choice-of-court agreement. This is to ensure that, in such a situation, the designated court has priority to decide on the validity of the agreement and on the extent to which the agreement applies to the dispute pending before it. The designated court should be able to proceed irrespective of whether the non- designated court has already decided on the stay of proceedings.

This exception should not cover situations where the parties have entered into conflicting exclusive choice-of- court agreements or where a court designated in an exclusive choice-of-court agreement has been seised first. In such cases, the general lis pendens rule of this Regulation should apply.

---

13 Mario Franzosi, 'Worldwide Patent Litigation and the Italian Torpedo' (1997) 19 *European Intellectual Property Review* 382.

Section 9 *Lis pendens* — related actions

Article 31

1. Where actions come within the exclusive jurisdiction of several courts, any court other than the court first seised shall decline jurisdiction in favour of that court.

2. Without prejudice to Article 26, where a court of a Member State on which an agreement as referred to in Article 25 confers exclusive jurisdiction is seised, any court of another Member State shall stay the proceedings until such time as the court seised on the basis of the agreement declares that it has no jurisdiction under the agreement.

3. Where the court designated in the agreement has established jurisdiction in accordance with the agreement, any court of another Member State shall decline jurisdiction in favour of that court.

4. Paragraphs 2 and 3 shall not apply to matters referred to in Sections 3, 4 or 5 where the policyholder, the insured, a beneficiary of the insurance contract, the injured party, the consumer or the employee is the claimant and the agreement is not valid under a provision contained within those Sections.

QUESTIONS

1 How would the general *lis pendens* rule favour abusive litigation tactics undermining the effectiveness of choice of court agreements? What is the remedy introduced to fight such tactics?
2 Article 31 gives priority to the designated court to rule on its own jurisdiction. Why? If one of the parties challenges the existence of a choice of court agreement, why should the allegedly chosen court be given any priority to settle the issue?

2005 Hague Convention on Choice of Court Agreements

Article 5 *Jurisdiction of the chosen court*

(2) A court that has jurisdiction under paragraph 1 shall not decline to exercise jurisdiction on the ground that the dispute should be decided in a court of another State. (. . .)

Article 6 *Obligations of a court not chosen*

A court of a Contracting State other than that of the chosen court shall suspend or dismiss proceedings to which an exclusive choice of court agreement applies unless –

a)   the agreement is null and void under the law of the State of the chosen court;
b)   a party lacked the capacity to conclude the agreement under the law of the State of the court seised;
c)   giving effect to the agreement would lead to a manifest injustice or would be manifestly contrary to the public policy of the State of the court seised;
d)   for exceptional reasons beyond the control of the parties, the agreement cannot reasonably be performed; or
e)   the chosen court has decided not to hear the case.

QUESTIONS

1 How does the Hague Convention handle parallel litigation? If a party challenges the validity of a choice of court agreement, may he initiate proceedings before another court of competent jurisdiction? What about cases where he challenges the existence of the agreement?

2 Where a court is designated by a valid choice of court agreement, should it have the power to decline jurisdiction? On which grounds? To which doctrines does Art. 5(2) refer?[14]

In the United States, parallel litigation is essentially handled through the doctrine of *forum non conveniens*. Is the doctrine applicable where the parties agreed on the U.S. forum?

CASE

U.S. Supreme Court, 3 December 2013 *Atlantic Marine Const. Co., Inc. v. U.S. Dist. Court for Western Dist. of Texas*[15]

Justice ALITO.

(. . .)

In the typical case not involving a forum-selection clause, a district court considering a § 1404(a) motion (or a *forum non conveniens* motion) must evaluate both the convenience of the parties and various public-interest considerations.[FN6] Ordinarily, the district court would weigh the relevant factors and decide whether, on balance, a transfer would serve 'the convenience of parties and witnesses' and otherwise promote 'the interest of justice.' § 1404(a).

> FN6. Factors relating to the parties' private interests include 'relative ease of access to sources of proof; availability of compulsory process for attendance of unwilling, and the cost of obtaining attendance of willing, witnesses; possibility of view of premises, if view would be appropriate to the action; and all other practical problems that make trial of a case easy, expeditious and inexpensive.' *Piper Aircraft Co. v. Reyno*, 454 U.S. 235, 241, n. 6 (1981) (internal quotation marks omitted). Public-interest factors may include 'the administrative difficulties flowing from court congestion; the local interest in having localized controversies decided at home; [and] the interest in having the trial of a diversity case in a forum that is at home with the law.' Ibid. (internal quotation marks omitted). The Court must also give some weight to the plaintiffs' choice of forum. See *Norwood v. Kirkpatrick*, 349 U.S. 29, 32 (1955).

---

14 See Trevor Hartley and Masato Dogauchi, *Explanatory Report on the 2005 Hague Choice of Court Agreements Convention* (Hague Conference on Private International Law 2013) paras. 132–134.

15 134 S.Ct. 568.

The calculus changes, however, when the parties' contract contains a valid forum-selection clause, which 'represents the parties' agreement as to the most proper forum.' *Stewart*, 487 U.S., at 31. The 'enforcement of valid forum-selection clauses, bargained for by the parties, protects their legitimate expectations and furthers vital interests of the justice system.' *Id.*, at 33 (KENNEDY, J., concurring). For that reason, and because the overarching consideration under § 1404(a) is whether a transfer would promote 'the interest of justice,' 'a valid forum-selection clause [should be] given controlling weight in all but the most exceptional cases.' *Id.*, at 33, (same). The presence of a valid forum-selection clause requires district courts to adjust their usual § 1404(a) analysis in three ways.

First, the plaintiff's choice of forum merits no weight. Rather, as the party defying the forum-selection clause, the plaintiff bears the burden of establishing that transfer to the forum for which the parties bargained is unwarranted. Because plaintiffs are ordinarily allowed to select whatever forum they consider most advantageous (consistent with jurisdictional and venue limitations), we have termed their selection the 'plaintiff's venue privilege.' *Van Dusen*, 376 U.S., at 635. But when a plaintiff agrees by contract to bring suit only in a specified forum—presumably in exchange for other binding promises by the defendant—the plaintiff has effectively exercised its 'venue privilege' before a dispute arises. Only that initial choice deserves deference, and the plaintiff must bear the burden of showing why the court should not transfer the case to the forum to which the parties agreed.

Second, a court evaluating a defendant's § 1404(a) motion to transfer based on a forum-selection clause should not consider arguments about the parties' private interests. When parties agree to a forum-selection clause, they waive the right to challenge the preselected forum as inconvenient or less convenient for themselves or their witnesses, or for their pursuit of the litigation. A court accordingly must deem the private-interest factors to weigh entirely in favor of the preselected forum. As we have explained in a different but 'instructive' context, *Stewart, supra*, at 28, '[w]hatever "inconvenience" [the parties] would suffer by being forced to litigate in the contractual forum as [they] agreed to do was clearly foreseeable at the time of contracting.' *The Bremen v. Zapata Off–Shore Co.*, 407 U.S. 1, 17–18 (1972); see also *Stewart, supra*, at 33 (KENNEDY, J., concurring) (stating that *Bremen's* 'reasoning applies with much force to federal courts sitting in diversity').

As a consequence, a district court may consider arguments about public-interest factors only. See n. 6, *supra*. Because those factors will rarely defeat a transfer motion, the practical result is that forum-selection clauses should control except in unusual cases. Although it is 'conceivable in a particular case' that the district court 'would refuse to transfer a case notwithstanding the counterweight of a forum-selection clause,' *Stewart, supra*, at 30–31, such cases will not be common.

Third, when a party bound by a forum-selection clause flouts its contractual obligation and files suit in a different forum, a § 1404(a) transfer of venue will not carry with it the original venue's choice-of-law rules—a factor that in some circumstances may affect public-interest considerations. See *Piper Aircraft Co. v. Reyno*, 454 U.S. 235, 241, n. 6 (1981) (listing a court's familiarity with the 'law that must govern the action' as a potential factor). A federal court sitting in diversity ordinarily must follow the choice-of-law rules of the State in which it sits. See *Klaxon Co. v. Stentor Elec. Mfg. Co.*, 313 U.S. 487, 494–496 (1941). However, we previously identified an exception to that principle for § 1404(a) transfers, requiring that the state law applicable in the original court also apply in the transferee court. See *Van Dusen*, 376 U.S., at 639. We deemed that exception necessary to prevent 'defendants, properly subjected to suit in the transferor State,' from 'invok[ing] § 1404(a) to gain the benefits of the laws of another jurisdiction . . .' *Id.*, at 638; see *Ferens v. John Deere Co.*, 494 U.S. 516, 522 (1990) (extending the *Van Dusen* rule to § 1404(a) motions by plaintiffs).

The policies motivating our exception to the *Klaxon* rule for § 1404(a) transfers, however, do not support an extension to cases where a defendant's motion is premised on enforcement of a valid forum-selection clause. See *Ferens, supra*, at 523. To the contrary, those considerations lead us to reject the rule that the law of the court in which the plaintiff inappropriately filed suit should follow the case to the forum contractually selected by the parties. In *Van Dusen*, we were concerned that, through a § 1404(a) transfer, a defendant could 'defeat the state-law advantages that might accrue from the exercise of [the plaintiff's] venue privilege.' 376 U.S., at 635. But as discussed above, a plaintiff who files suit in violation of a forum-selection clause enjoys no such 'privilege' with respect to its choice of forum, and therefore it is entitled to no concomitant 'state-law advantages.' Not only would it be inequitable to allow the plaintiff to fasten its choice of substantive law to the venue transfer, but it would also encourage gamesmanship. Because '§ 1404(a) should not create or multiply opportunities for forum shopping,' *Ferens, supra*, at 523, we will not apply the *Van Dusen* rule when a transfer stems from enforcement of a forum-selection clause: The court in the contractually selected venue should not apply the law of the transferor venue to which the parties waived their right.[FN8]

FN8. For the reasons detailed above, see Part II–B, *supra*, the same standards should apply to motions to dismiss for *forum non conveniens* in cases involving valid forum-selection clauses pointing to state or foreign forums. We have noted in contexts unrelated to forum-selection clauses that a defendant 'invoking *forum non conveniens* ordinarily bears a heavy burden in opposing the plaintiff's chosen forum.' *Sinochem Int'l Co. v. Malaysia Int'l Shipping Co.*, 549 U.S. 422, 430. That is because of the 'hars[h] result' of that doctrine: Unlike a § 1404(a) motion, a successful motion under *forum non conveniens* requires dismissal of the case. *Norwood*, 349 U.S., at 32. That inconveniences plaintiffs in several respects and even 'makes it possible for [plaintiffs] to lose out completely, through the running of the statute of limitations in the forum finally deemed appropriate.' *Id.*, at 31 (internal quotation marks omitted). Such caution is not warranted, however, when the plaintiff has violated a contractual obligation by filing suit in a forum other than the one specified in a valid forum-selection clause. In such a case, dismissal would work no injustice on the plaintiff.

When parties have contracted in advance to litigate disputes in a particular forum, courts should not unnecessarily disrupt the parties' settled expectations. A forum-selection clause, after all, may have figured centrally in the parties' negotiations and may have affected how they set monetary and other contractual terms; it may, in fact, have been a critical factor in their agreement to do business together in the first place. In all but the most unusual cases, therefore, 'the interest of justice' is served by holding parties to their bargain. (...)

? QUESTION

In which circumstances could a U.S. court decline jurisdiction on conveniens grounds despite being the court chosen by the parties?

1.2.2 Scope of choice

The parties are free to agree on the court having jurisdiction to decide any dispute arising out of their contract. They may also, and often do, define the jurisdiction that they intend to grant to this court in a number of ways.

1. They may grant non-exclusive jurisdiction to the chosen court. This means that their agreement grants jurisdiction to the chosen court, but does not exclude the jurisdiction of courts which would otherwise have had jurisdiction.
2. The parties may want to make different provisions depending on the

party initiating the proceedings. Asymmetric clauses grant jurisdiction to different courts depending on who is the plaintiff. A number of banking contracts, for instance, contain clauses obliging the customer to sue in one court, but allowing the bank to sue in any court of competent jurisdiction. These clauses have typically been validated in the common law world, but a number of civil law courts have invalidated them, including the French Supreme Court in a highly controversial judgment.[16]

3. The parties are also free to grant jurisdiction to the chosen court for certain kinds of disputes, and not for others. For instance, they could grant jurisdiction to the chosen court to decide disputes concerning interpretation and performance of the contract, and not the validity of the contract. This would mean that a defense based on the invalidity of the contract might have to be entertained by another court, which would not be very efficient. This is the reason why it is wiser to provide that the chosen court would have exclusive jurisdiction to decide all disputes 'arising out' of the relevant contract.

4. But even such a clause might be regarded as too narrow. Should it be considered as applying to actions which might be related to the contract, but would not be contractual in nature (actions in tort, actions in restitution)? A broader clause could provide that it applies to all disputes 'arising out of, or in connection with' the relevant contract.

But would a jurisdiction clause purporting to apply to actions in tort be valid? Does the language of Art. 25 of the Brussels Ibis Regulation or Art. 3–7 of the Japanese Code of Civil Procedure (*supra*, 1.1.1) suggest an answer?

2 Protecting weaker parties

While the advantages of choice of court agreements are clear, they could also be abused by parties with high bargaining power. The issue of the protection of weaker parties such as consumers or employees was therefore raised in most countries.

The 2005 Hague Convention avoids the issue by expressly excluding from its scope consumer and employment contracts (Art. 2).

---

16 Cass., Civ. 1ère 26 September 2012, case no. 11-26022.

2.1   European Union

Brussels Ibis Regulation (2012)

SECTION 4 Jurisdiction over consumer contracts

Article 19

The provisions of this Section may be departed from only by an agreement:

(1) which is entered into after the dispute has arisen;

(2) which allows the consumer to bring proceedings in courts other than those indicated in this Section; or

(3) which is entered into by the consumer and the other party to the contract, both of whom are at the time of conclusion of the contract domiciled or habitually resident in the same Member State, and which confers jurisdiction on the courts of that Member State, provided that such an agreement is not contrary to the law of that Member State.

SECTION 5 Jurisdiction over individual contracts of employment

Article 23

The provisions of this Section may be departed from only by an agreement:

(1) which is entered into after the dispute has arisen; or

(2) which allows the employee to bring proceedings in courts other than those indicated in this Section.

❓ NOTES AND QUESTIONS

1   Articles 19 and 23 provide for the enforcement of choice of court agreements entered into after the dispute has arisen. Why does it make a difference for a weaker party whether the agreement is reached before or after the dispute arises?

2   What does the requirement in Art. 19(2) and Art. 23(2) mean?

3   The Brussels Ibis Regulation also affords a similar protection to the insured litigating against his insurer: see Art. 15.

2.2   Japan

The Japanese Parliament introduced provisions protecting consumers and employees in 2011.

Japanese Code of Civil Procedure

Article 3–7 *Jurisdiction Agreement*

(. . .) see *supra*, p. 263.

(5) The agreement provided in Paragraph (1) having as its object a future dispute arising in connection with a consumer contract shall have effect only in the circumstances set forth below:

(i)   where it is an agreement which allows an action to be filed in the country where the consumer was domiciled at the time of the conclusion of the contract (If the agreement purports to allow an action to be filed exclusively in that country, it shall be without prejudice to the right to file in other countries except in the cases provided in the following sub-paragraph.); or

(ii)   where the consumer filed an action in the country specified by the agreement or where the consumer invoked the agreement in response to an action brought by the business operator in Japan or in a foreign country.

(6) The agreement provided in Paragraph (1) having as its object a future civil dispute over individual employment relations shall have effect only in the circumstances set forth below:

(i)   where it is an agreement which was concluded when the employment contract was terminated and stipulates that an action may be brought in the country in which the labor was being supplied at the time of the conclusion of the agreement (If the agreement purports to allow an action to be filed exclusively in that country, it shall be without prejudice to the right to file in other countries except in the cases provided in the following sub-paragraph.); or

(ii)   where the employee filed an action in the country specified by the agreement or where the employee invoked the agreement in response to an action brought by the employer in Japan or in a foreign country.

? QUESTIONS

1   Art 3–7(5) and (6) only apply to agreements with respect to future disputes. They do not limit the freedom of the parties where the dispute has already arisen. Does this distinction also exist under EU law?

2   Under Art 3–4 of the Code, Japanese courts have jurisdiction to entertain actions initiated by consumers if the consumer has his domicile in Japan, and actions initiated by employees if the place of supply of labour is located in Japan. In this context, what is the purpose of Art 3–7(5)(i) and (6)(ii)?

3   Japanese law uses an additional technique to protect weaker parties. The agreement is enforceable when it is relied on by the consumer or the employee. By contrast, the Brussels Ibis Regulation does not take this circumstance into account. What is the better rule?

2.3   United States

 CASE

U.S. Supreme Court, 17 April 1991 *Carnival Cruise Lines, Inc. v. Shute*[17]

Facts: After the respondents Shute, a Washington State couple, purchased passage on a ship owned by petitioner, a Florida-based cruise line, petitioner sent them tickets containing a clause designating courts in Florida as the agreed-upon fora for the resolution of disputes. The Shutes boarded the ship in Los Angeles, and, while in international waters off the Mexican coast, Mrs. Shute suffered injuries when she slipped on a deck mat. The Shutes filed suit in a Washington Federal District Court, which granted summary judgment for petitioner. The Court of Appeals reversed, holding, inter alia, that the forum-selection clause should not be enforced under *The Bremen v. Zapata Off-Shore Co.*, 407 U.S. 1, because it was not 'freely bargained for,' and because its enforcement would operate to deprive the Shutes of their day in court in light of evidence indicating that they were physically and financially incapable of pursuing the litigation in Florida.

Held: The Court of Appeals erred in refusing to enforce the forum-selection clause.

Justice BLACKMUN

(. . .)

In contrast, respondents' passage contract was purely routine and doubtless nearly identical to every commercial passage contract issued by petitioner and most other cruise lines. See, e.g., *Hodes v. S.N.C. Achille Lauro ed Altri-Gestione*, 858 F.2d 905, 910 (CA3 1988). In this context, it would be entirely unreasonable for us to assume that respondents–or any other cruise passenger–would negotiate with petitioner the terms of a forum-selection clause in an ordinary commercial cruise ticket. Common sense dictates that a ticket of this kind will be a form contract the terms of which are not subject to negotiation, and that an individual purchasing the ticket will not have bargaining parity with the cruise line. But by ignoring the crucial differences in the business contexts in which the respective contracts were executed, the Court of Appeals' analysis seems to us to have distorted somewhat this Court's holding in *The Bremen*.

---

17   499 U.S. 585 (1991).

In evaluating the reasonableness of the forum clause at issue in this case, we must refine the analysis of *The Bremen* to account for the realities of form passage contracts. As an initial matter, we do not adopt the Court of Appeals' determination that a nonnegotiated forum-selection clause in a form ticket contract is never enforceable simply because it is not the subject of bargaining. Including a reasonable forum clause in a form contract of this kind well may be permissible for several reasons: First, a cruise line has a special interest in limiting the fora in which it potentially could be subject to suit. Because a cruise ship typically carries passengers from many locales, it is not unlikely that a mishap on a cruise could subject the cruise line to litigation in several different fora. See *The Bremen*, 407 U.S., at 13, and n. 15; *Hodes*, 858 F.2d, at 913. Additionally, a clause establishing *ex ante* the forum for dispute resolution has the salutary effect of dispelling any confusion about where suits arising from the contract must be brought and defended, sparing litigants the time and expense of pretrial motions to determine the correct forum and conserving judicial resources that otherwise would be devoted to deciding those motions. See *Stewart Organization*, 487 U.S., at 33 (concurring opinion). Finally, it stands to reason that passengers who purchase tickets containing a forum clause like that at issue in this case benefit in the form of reduced fares reflecting the savings that the cruise line enjoys by limiting the fora in which it may be sued. Cf. *Northwestern Nat. Ins. Co. v. Donovan*, 916 F.2d 372, 378 (CA7 1990).

We also do not accept the Court of Appeals' 'independent justification' for its conclusion that *The Bremen* dictates that the clause should not be enforced because '[t]here is evidence in the record to indicate that the Shutes are physically and financially incapable of pursuing this litigation in Florida.' 897 F.2d, at 389. We do not defer to the Court of Appeals' findings of fact. In dismissing the case for lack of personal jurisdiction over petitioner, the District Court made no finding regarding the physical and financial impediments to the Shutes' pursuing their case in Florida. The Court of Appeals' conclusory reference to the record provides no basis for this Court to validate the finding of inconvenience. Furthermore, the Court of Appeals did not place in proper context this Court's statement in *The Bremen* that 'the serious inconvenience of the contractual forum to one or both of the parties might carry greater weight in determining the reasonableness of the forum clause.' 407 U.S., at 17. The Court made this statement in evaluating a hypothetical 'agreement between two Americans to resolve their essentially local disputes in a remote alien forum.' *Ibid.* In the present case, Florida is not a 'remote alien forum,' nor-given the fact that Mrs. Shute's accident occurred off the coast of Mexico–is this dispute an essentially local one inherently more suited to resolution in the State of Washington than in Florida. In light of these distinctions, and because respondents do not claim lack of notice of the forum clause, we conclude that they have not satisfied the 'heavy burden of proof,' *ibid.*, required to set aside the clause on grounds of inconvenience.

It bears emphasis that forum-selection clauses contained in form passage contracts are subject to judicial scrutiny for fundamental fairness. In this case, there is no indication that petitioner set Florida as the forum in which disputes were to be resolved as a means of discouraging cruise passengers from pursuing legitimate claims. Any suggestion of such a bad-faith motive is belied by two facts: Petitioner has its principal place of business in Florida, and many of its cruises depart from and return to Florida ports. Similarly, there is no evidence that petitioner obtained respondents' accession to the forum clause by fraud or overreaching. Finally, respondents have conceded that they were given notice of the forum provision and, therefore, presumably retained the option of rejecting the contract with impunity. In the case before us, therefore, we conclude that the Court of Appeals erred in refusing to enforce the forum-selection clause. (. . .)

Justice STEVENS, with whom Justice MARSHALL joins, dissenting.

The Court prefaces its legal analysis with a factual statement that implies that a purchaser of a Carnival Cruise Lines passenger ticket is fully and fairly notified about the existence of the choice of forum clause in the fine print on the back of the ticket. Even if this implication were accurate, I would disagree with the Court's analysis. But, given the Court's preface, I begin my dissent by noting that only the most meticulous passenger is likely to become aware of the forum-selection provision. I have therefore appended to this opinion a facsimile of the relevant text, using the type size that actually appears in the ticket itself. A careful reader will find the forum-selection clause in the 8th of the 25 numbered paragraphs.

Of course, many passengers, like the respondents in this case, will not have an opportunity to read paragraph 8 until they have actually purchased their tickets. By this point, the passengers will already have accepted the condition set forth in paragraph 16(a), which provides that '[t]he Carrier shall not be liable to make any refund to passengers in respect of . . . tickets wholly or partly not used by a passenger.' Not knowing whether or not that provision is legally enforceable, I assume that the average passenger would accept the risk of having to file suit in Florida in the event of an injury, rather than canceling–without a refund–a planned vacation at the last minute. The fact that the cruise line can reduce its litigation costs, and therefore its liability insurance premiums, by forcing this choice on its passengers does not, in my opinion, suffice to render the provision reasonable. Cf. *Steven v. Fidelity & Casualty Co. of New York,* 58 Cal.2d 862, 883 (1962) (refusing to enforce limitation on liability in insurance policy because insured 'must purchase the policy before he even knows its provisions').

Even if passengers received prominent notice of the forum-selection clause before they committed the cost of the cruise, I would remain persuaded that the clause was unenforceable under traditional principles of federal admiralty law and is 'null and void' under the terms of Limitation of Vessel Owners Liability Act, ch. 521, 49 Stat. 1480, 46 U.S.C.App. § 183c, which was enacted in 1936 to invalidate expressly stipulations limiting shipowners' liability for negligence. (. . .)

 NOTES AND QUESTIONS

1   Do you agree with the arguments of Justice Brennan in favour of the enforceability of jurisdiction clause in consumer contracts? What do you think consumers prefer: a cheaper product or the possibility to sue the professional at home?

2   The United States are not only more liberal with respect to jurisdiction clauses, but also with respect to arbitration clauses. In the United States, arbitration is not perceived as a luxurious alternative dispute resolution mechanism fit for commercial disputes, but as a cheaper mode of dispute resolution which allows to bypass costly court procedures.

3   The Supreme Court rules that the clause granting jurisdiction to Florida courts is enforceable. Do you think it would have reached the same conclusion had the clause designated the courts of Wyoming? Mexico? China?

4   The majority opinion relies on the fact that the consumers had not claimed lack of notice of the clause. This leaves open the issue as to whether forum clauses should be enforced in cases where the consumer did not read the clause at the time of conclusion of the contract. Many U.S. courts have held that forum and choice of law clauses written in small and undistinguishable print were unenforceable,[18] but others have been more liberal. In the context of arbitration clauses, a much noticed opinion held:

> A contract need not be read to be effective; people who accept take the risk that the unread terms may in retrospect prove unwelcome. Terms inside Gateway's box stand or fall together. If they constitute the parties' contract because the Hills had an opportunity to return the computer after reading them, then all must be enforced. (. . .) *[the court discusses and relies on, among other cases, Carnival Cruise v. Shute]* Practical considerations support allowing vendors to enclose the full legal terms with their products. Cashiers cannot be expected to read legal documents to customers before ringing up sales. If the staff at the other end of the phone for direct-sales operations such as Gateway's had to read the four-page statement of terms before taking the buyer's credit card number, the droning voice would anes-

18 See, e.g., *Oxman v. Amoroso,* 659 N.Y.S.2d 963, 967 (City Ct 1997).

thetize rather than enlighten many potential buyers. Others would hang up in a rage over the waste of their time. And oral recitation would not avoid customers' assertions (whether true or feigned) that the clerk did not read term X to them, or that they did not remember or understand it. Writing provides benefits for both sides of commercial transactions. Customers as a group are better off when vendors skip costly and ineffectual steps such as telephonic recitation, and use instead a simple approve-or-return device. Competent adults are bound by such documents, read or unread.[19]

Is the reference to the opportunity to return the computer, and to cancel the contract without penalty consistent with *Carnival Cruise*? Is it a good criterion to decide whether to enforce a jurisdiction clause in a consumer contract?

 CASE

Court of Appeal, First District, Division 2, California, 21 June 2001 *America Online, Inc. (AOL) v. Superior Court of Alameda County*[20]

This petition (. . .) was filed by petitioner America Online, Inc. (AOL) following the denial of its motion to stay or dismiss a putative consumer class-action lawsuit. The motion was based on a claim that California is an inconvenient forum in which to litigate the dispute concerning AOL's proprietary Internet service. In support of its motion, AOL exclusively relied on a forum selection clause in its contracts with real parties in interest, Al Mendoza, Jr. (Mendoza) and the potential class members, which designated Virginia as the jurisdiction in which all disputes arising out of the relationship would be litigated. The agreement also included a choice of law provision requiring that Virginia law be applied to any such dispute. (. . .)

C. Enforcement of the Forum Selection Clause Violates Strong California Public Policy

California courts will refuse to defer to the selected forum if to do so would substantially diminish the rights of California residents in a way that violates our state's public policy. (. . .) [*see supra, p. 269.*]

The CLRA [Consumers Legal Remedies Act] is a legislative embodiment of a desire to protect California consumers and furthers a strong public policy

---

19 *Hill v. Gateway 2000*, 105 F.3d 1147 (7th Cir 1997), per Judge Easterbrook.
20 90 Cal.App.4th 1.

of this state. 'The CLRA was enacted in an attempt to alleviate social and economic problems stemming from deceptive business practices, which were identified in the 1969 Report of the National Advisory Commission on Civil Disorders (i.e., the Kerner Commission). [Citation.] Section 1760 contains an express statement of legislative intent: "This title shall be liberally construed and applied to promote its underlying purposes, which are to protect consumers against unfair and deceptive business practices and to provide efficient and economical procedures to secure such protection."' (*Broughton*, 21 Cal.4th at p. 1077.)

Certainly, the CLRA provides remedial protections *at least* as important as those under the Corporate Securities Law of 1968. Therefore, by parity of reasoning, enforcement of AOL's forum selection clause, which is also accompanied by a choice of law provision favoring Virginia, would necessitate a waiver of the statutory remedies of the CLRA, in violation of that law's antiwaiver provision (Civ.Code, § 1751) and California public policy. For this reason alone, we affirm the trial court's ruling.

This conclusion is reinforced by a statutory comparison of California and Virginia consumer protection laws, which reveals Virginia's law provides significantly less consumer protection to its citizens than California law provides for our own. Consumers who prove violations of the CLRA within the three-year limitations period may be entitled to a minimum recovery of $1000, restitution or property, power of injunctive relief, and punitive damages. Attorney fees and costs are also recoverable if the plaintiffs prevail on their claim under the act. In addition to these extraordinary remedies, if the complaining consumer is a senior citizen or disabled person, up to $5000 may be awarded for substantial physical, emotional distress, or economic damage. Of course, the CLRA specifies that actions under that act may be prosecuted as class actions.

Of greater importance is the absence of any provision in the VCPA [Virginia Consumer Protection Act of 1977] that allows suits under the Act to proceed as class actions. Unless specifically allowed by statute, class action relief is not generally available in Virginia in actions at law. In contrast to Virginia consumer law's ostensible hostility to class actions, the right to seek class action relief in consumer cases has been extolled by California courts. (. . .)

That this view has endured over the last 30 years is of little surprise given the importance class action consumer litigation has come to play in this state. In light of that history, we cannot accept AOL's assertion that the elimination of class actions for consumer remedies if the forum selection clause is enforced is a matter of insubstantial moment. The unavailability of class action relief in this context is sufficient in and by itself to preclude enforcement of the TOS forum selection clause.

In addition to the unavailability of class actions and the apparent limitation in injunctive relief, neither punitive damages, nor enhanced remedies for disabled and senior citizens are recoverable under Virginia's law. More nuanced differences are the reduced recovery under the VCPA for 'unintentional' acts, a shorter period of limitations, and Virginia's use of a Lodestar formula alone to calculate attorney fees recovery. (*Holmes v. L.G. Marion Corp.* (1999) 258 Va. 473, 521) Quite apart from the remedial limitations under Virginia law relating to injunctive and class action relief, the cumulative importance of even these less significant differences is substantial. Enforcement of a forum selection clause, which would impair these aggregate rights, would itself violate important California public policy.

NOTES

1 Is *AOL* consistent with *Carnival Cruise*? While *Carnival Cruise* addressed the issue of whether choice of court clauses included in consumer contracts are valid, *AOL* addresses the issue of the impact of mandatory rules of the enforceability of forum selection clauses.

2 Given that the protection of consumers is based on the particular mandatory rules of the forum, it will vary from one U.S. state to another.

3 In the context of choice of law, U.S. states also protect weaker parties through the use of general doctrines of the conflict of laws rather than by the application of special rules: see *infra*, Ch. 9.

Part III

Foreign judgments

Judgments produce many different effects. They decide disputes and rule on the rights and obligations of the parties. After being judicially recognized, such rights and obligations are to be considered as finally declared (for example, the contract is and always was valid) or granted (for example, the divorce is granted). Judgments also grant affirmative remedies such as orders to pay damages or injunctions to perform or to abstain.

The law of foreign judgments is concerned with the issue of whether the effects of foreign judgments should be extended in the forum. A distinction is generally made between *recognition* and *enforcement* of foreign judgments. Recognition means that the rights and obligations declared or granted by the foreign court are considered as having the same legal value in the forum. For instance, a person who was divorced abroad is considered as divorced in the forum. Recognition has a positive effect: the status obtained abroad is also valid in the forum. But it also has a negative effect. The rights and obligations cannot be relitigated: recognition entails a *res judicata* effect. Enforcement means that the remedies granted by the foreign court not only are recognized, but can be equally granted in the forum. The enforcement authorities of the forum may be requested to intervene in order to compel the judgment debtor to satisfy the judgment, typically by attaching his local assets.[1]

---

1 Foreign judgments can also produce non-normative effects. For instance, they can be used as evidence of the existence of a given fact (recognized by the foreign court). Foreign judgments could also be considered as a fact excusing non-performance of a contract. See for instance the Belgian Code of Private International Law (2004):

Article 26. *Foreign judgments as evidence*

§ 1. A foreign judgment is evidence in Belgium of the findings of fact made by the judge if it meets the conditions required for the authenticity of judgments according to the law of the State where it was rendered.

The findings of fact made by the foreign judge are not taken into account to the extent that they would produce an effect manifestly incompatible with the public policy.

§ 2. Evidence to the contrary relating to facts established by the foreign judge can be brought by any legal means.

Article 29. *Factual effect of foreign judgments and authentic instruments*

In Belgium consideration is given to the existence of a foreign judgment or authentic instrument without verification of the conditions required for recognition, enforcement or its value as evidence.

In this Part, we shall study the requirements for the recognition and enforcement of foreign judgments. In many federal systems, these requirements have been lowered for judgments originating from states from within the system (sister states). We shall therefore distinguish between foreign nation judgments (Chapter 6) and sister states judgments (Chapter 7).

6

Foreign nation judgments

1 Why recognize foreign judgments?

The highest courts of common law jurisdictions have long discussed the
foundation of the recognition and the enforcement of foreign judgments.
Read the following cases and identify the rationale for extending the effect of
foreign judgments in the forum.

 CASE

U.S. Supreme Court, 3 June 1895 *Hilton v. Guyot*[1]

No law has any effect, of its own force, beyond the limits of the sovereignty
from which its authority is derived. The extent to which the law of one nation,
as put in force within its territory, whether by executive order, by legislative
act, or by judicial decree, shall be allowed to operate within the dominion of
another nation, depends upon what our greatest jurists have been content to
call 'the comity of nations.' Although the phrase has been often criticised, no
satisfactory substitute has been suggested.

'Comity,' in the legal sense, is neither a matter of absolute obligation, on
the one hand, nor of mere courtesy and good will, upon the other. But it is
the recognition which one nation allows within its territory to the legislative, executive, or judicial acts of another nation, having due regard both to
international duty and convenience, and to the rights of its own citizens, or of
other persons was are under the protection of its laws. (. . .)

---

1 159 U.S. 113.

CASE

Court of Appeal of England and Wales, 27 July 1989
Adams v. Cape Industries Plc[2]

(. . .) at common law in this country foreign judgments are enforced, if at all, not through considerations of comity but upon the basis of a principle explained thus by Parke B. in *Williams v. Jones* (1845) 13 M. & W. at p. 133:

> Where a court of competent jurisdiction has adjudicated a certain sum to be due from one person to another, a legal obligation arises to pay that sum, on which an action of debt to enforce the judgment may be maintained. It is in this way that the judgments of foreign and colonial courts are supported and enforced.

Blackburn J. stated and followed the same principle in delivering the judgment of himself and Mellor J. in *Godard v. Gray* (1870) L.R. 6 Q.B. 139 at p. 146 and the judgment of the Court of Queen's Bench in *Schibsby v. Westenholz & Others* (1870) L.R. 6 Q.B. 139 at p. 159. In the latter case he said (at p. 159):

> It is unnecessary to repeat again what we have already said in *Godard v. Gray*.

> We think that, for the reasons there given, the true principle on which the judgments of foreign tribunals are enforced in England is that stated by Parke, B. in *Russell v. Smyth*, and again repeated by him in *Williams v. Jones*, that the judgment of a court of competent jurisdiction over the defendant imposes a duty or obligation on the defendant to pay the sum for which judgment is given, which the courts in this country are bound to enforce; and consequently that anything which negatives that duty, or forms a legal excuse for not performing it, is a defence to the action.

 CASE

Supreme Court of Canada, 20 Dec 1990 *Morguard Investments Ltd. v. De Savoye*[3]

La Forest J.:

31. For my part, I much prefer the more complete formulation of the idea of comity adopted by the Supreme Court of the United States in *Hilton v. Guyot*:

---

2 [1990] 2 W.L.R. 657.
3 [1990] 3 S.C.R. 1077.

[see supra, 2nd paragraph of the extract]

As Dickson J. in *Zingre v. R.*, [1981] 2 S.C.R. 392 at 400, citing Marshall C.J. in *The Exchange v. M'Faddon*, 11 U.S. (7 Cranch) 116 (1812), stated, 'common interest impels sovereigns to mutual intercourse' between sovereign states. In a word, the rules of private international law are grounded in the need in modern times to facilitate the flow of wealth, skills and people across state lines in a fair and orderly manner. Von Mehren and Trautman have observed in 'Recognition of Foreign Adjudications: A Survey and A Suggested Approach' (1968), 81 Harvard L. Rev. 1601, at p. 1603:

> The ultimate justification for according some degree of recognition is that if in our highly complex and interrelated world each community exhausted every possibility of insisting on its parochial interests, injustice would result and the normal patterns of life would be disrupted.

32. Hessel E. Yntema, in 'The Objectives of Private International Law' (1957), 35 Can. Bar Rev. 721 (though speaking more specifically there about choice of law), caught the spirit in which private international law, or conflict of laws, should be approached when he stated at p. 741:

> In a highly integrated world economy, politically organized in a diversity of more or less autonomous legal systems, the function of conflict rules is to select, interpret and apply in each case the particular local law that will best promote suitable conditions of interstate and international commerce, or, in other words, to mediate in the questions arising from such commerce in the application of the local laws.

As is evident throughout his article, what must underlie a modern system of private international law are principles of order and fairness, principles that ensure security of transactions with justice.

? NOTES

1   The oldest theory justifying the recognition of foreign judgments, which is still dominant in the United States, is that international law is founded upon reciprocity and mutuality, and that, if a country is courteous to others, others will reciprocate the courtesy shown to them. The doctrine of comity posits that, although States are under no international obligation to recognize and enforce foreign judgments, they may not ignore the existence of each other. Recognizing foreign judgments would therefore be in the interest of States, but none of them would actually be obliged to do so.

A logical consequence of a theory of foreign judgments based on the mutual interests of States rather than on actual obligations should be to make the recognition of foreign judgments conditional upon foreign States recognizing the judgments of the forum. In *Hilton*, the U.S. Supreme Court insisted that the French judgment under scrutiny should not be recognized if evidence had been provided that French courts would not recognize a U.S. judgment. The reciprocity requirement of *Hilton*, however, has lost considerable ground in the United States. But it is still followed in some states (Massachusetts, Florida), and foreign judgments have been denied recognition for lack of reciprocity.[4]

2   England abandoned the doctrine of comity in the 19th century, and replaced it with a theory of obligation.[5] The theory doctrine posits that a foreign judgment ruling that a debtor owes a sum of money to a creditor imposes a legal obligation on this debtor to pay this sum of money. English courts are ready to recognize this obligation and to enforce it in England. They therefore rule that the foundation of the enforcement of foreign judgments in England is the obligation created by the foreign court and imposed *on the debtor*. It is not an obligation imposed *on English courts* to recognize foreign judgments. It is not, for instance, an obligation arising under public international law to enforce foreign judgments. It is an obligation created by a foreign court that English courts (want to) recognize.

An important consequence of the English theory is that foreign judgments are not, as a matter of principle, enforced by English courts. Foreign substantive legal obligations are. The purpose of an action before an English court relying on a foreign judgment is therefore to obtain an English judgment on the merits enforcing the obligation and ordering the debtor to pay, rather than an English judgment extending the effect of the foreign judgment in England.[6]

3   There are certainly good policy reasons to recognize and enforce foreign judgments. As underscored by the Canadian Supreme Court, the development of international private relations demand that rights and obligations be recognized across the borders. In France, the law of foreign judgments initially developed to avoid that people have different family status in different jurisdictions. French courts first allowed the recognition of foreign divorce decrees.[7] Today, the focus might be more on the needs of international commerce, but the importance of international family law issues remains.

These policy reasons could be phrased or refined in a number of ways. A number of scholars have used game theory analysis in this context,[8] and interesting insights might be offered by other approaches. Insisting on the policy justifications to recognize foreign judgments is all the more important when legal doctrines afford an important amount of discretion. The Canadian Supreme Court put forward policy considerations after endorsing a comity doctrine which entails little constrain.

2   Requirements for recognition of foreign judgments

While it is widely accepted that foreign judgments should in principle be recognized, this is only so if certain requirements are met. These requirements are laid down by the enforcing State, and are thus essential to understand its policy with respect to foreign judgments. They vary from one

---

4   See, e.g., *Evans Cabinet Corp. v. Kitchen Int'l, Inc.*, 593 F.3d, 135, 142 (1st Cir) and more generally Little, 960.
5   The doctrine was also adopted in a number of jurisdictions of the Commonwealth such as Nigeria: see *Alfred C. Toepfer Inc v. Edokpolor* (1965) NCLR 89, 91–2 (Biramian J.S.C).
6   See Adrian Briggs, 'Recognition of Foreign Judgments: A Matter of Obligation' (2013) 129 LQR 87, 89.
7   Cass. Ch. Civ. 28 Feb. 1860, *Bulkley v. Defresne*, (1860) Sirey 1.210.
8   See Michael Whincop, 'The Recognition Scene: Game Theoretic Issues in the Recognition of Foreign Judgments' (1999) 23 Melb. U. L. Rev. 416.

jurisdiction to another, but two are extremely common and arguably the most important: the foreign court ought to have jurisdiction, and the foreign judgment should comport with public policy.

2.1 Jurisdiction of the foreign court

The requirements that the foreign court has jurisdiction is found in the law of foreign judgments of most jurisdictions. At the outset, it is important to understand that the purpose of this requirement is not to enable the forum, that is, the enforcing State, to decide whether its courts should retain jurisdiction to decide the dispute. The dispute has already been decided by the foreign court. The purpose is therefore to assess whether the decision of the *foreign court* to retain jurisdiction was appropriate. In order to distinguish these two different appreciations of international jurisdiction, continental scholars give them different names. Rules on the jurisdiction of the forum to decide the dispute can be labeled rules of *direct* international jurisdiction (France) or rules of jurisdiction to *adjudicate* (Germany), while rules on the jurisdiction of the foreign court can be labeled rules of *indirect* international jurisdiction (France, Japan) or rules of jurisdiction to *recognize* (Germany).

Why should the enforcing State assess the jurisdiction of the foreign court? We have already underlined the fact that States freely decide on the jurisdiction of their courts.[9] The foreign court, therefore, retained jurisdiction by applying its own jurisdictional criteria. Should the enforcing court verify that the foreign court properly applied its own law? Which legitimacy would it have to do so? Foreign courts know best what their own law is.

The purpose of the assessment of the jurisdiction of the foreign court is different. It is to assess whether, from the perspective of the enforcing State, it was appropriate to retain jurisdiction in the relevant dispute. The result will be that some foreign judgments will be denied recognition on the ground that it was inappropriate for the foreign court to retain jurisdiction, and that other foreign judgments, other things being equal, will be recognized. The rule, therefore, is essential, as it reveals the policy of the enforcing state with respect to the recognition and enforcement of foreign judgments. The purpose is not to check that the foreign court applied properly its law, but to identify foreign judgments which deserve recognition in the enforcing State, and foreign judgments which do not.

---

9 *Supra*, Part II.

As will be discussed in the next section, it is generally accepted that the appropriateness of the foreign judgment should not be appreciated by looking at its content. Thus, enforcing courts essentially assess whether the foreign court relied on an appropriate head of jurisdiction, that is an appropriate geographical connection with the dispute.

The appropriateness of the geographical connection between the foreign court and the dispute can be assessed in different ways. A basic distinction is between derivative and non-derivative theories. Derivative theories take the position that the content of jurisdictional tests for recognition purposes must, in principle and as a matter of logic, stem from the basis on which jurisdiction to adjudicate is asserted. Non-derivative theories posit that rules of recognition of foreign judgment should be developed independently as they implicate different policies and purposes.[10]

1995 Italian Private International Law Act

Title IV – Effects of Foreign Acts and Judgments

Article 64 *Recognition of foreign judgments*

A judgment rendered by a foreign authority shall be recognized in Italy without requiring any further proceedings if:

a) the authority rendering the judgment had jurisdiction pursuant to the criteria of jurisdiction in force under Italian law; (. . .)

German Code of Civil Procedure

Section 328 *Recognition of foreign judgments*

(1) Recognition of a judgment handed down by a foreign court shall be ruled out if:

1. The courts of the state to which the foreign court belongs do not have jurisdiction according to German law; (. . .)

[?] NOTES

A first way to assess the jurisdiction of foreign courts is to consider that the issue can be addressed by resorting to the criteria of jurisdiction that the forum would use to retain jurisdiction. The result is that the same rules of jurisdiction are used both to define the jurisdiction of the courts of the forum and to assess the appropriateness of the taking of jurisdiction of foreign courts. This is a derivative theory.

1 Article 64 of the Italian Act provides that the jurisdiction of foreign courts is assessed in Italy by applying the criteria of jurisdiction in force in Italy. The criteria are those used by Italian courts to retain jurisdiction. This means that Art. 64 assigns them a second function, namely to assess the appropriateness of the jurisdiction of the foreign court. Italian scholars explain that the

---

10 See generally Arthur T. von Mehren, 'Recognition and Enforcement of Foreign Judgments – General Theory and the Role of Jurisdictional Requirements' (1980) 167 *Collected Courses of the Hague Academy of International Law* 56.

rules have been made 'bilateral',[11] or multilateral: they do not only define unilaterally the jurisdiction of Italian courts, but also, from the perspective of the Italian legal order, the jurisdiction of foreign courts.

For instance, Art. 3 of the 1995 Italian Act provides that Italian courts have jurisdiction when the defendant is domiciled or resides in Italy. Article 32 of the same Act provides that Italian courts also have jurisdiction over invalidity, nullity, separation and dissolution of marriage when one of the spouses is an Italian citizen. Italian courts will consider that foreign courts have jurisdiction in divorce proceedings if the defendant either was domiciled or resided in the foreign jurisdiction, or was a national of the foreign jurisdiction.[12] This will be irrespective of the head of jurisdiction actually used by the foreign court, if the preferred criteria of the Italian law are met.

2   The same derivate theory is applied by German courts pursuant to Section 328(1) of the German Code of Civil Procedure. This is the so-called Mirror Image Principle (*Spiegelbildprinzip*).[13] While German scholars distinguish conceptually jurisdiction to adjudicate and jurisdiction to recognize, they apply the same test for both purposes.[14]

3   Article 118 of the Japanese Code of Civil Procedure provides that the jurisdiction of the foreign court is assessed pursuant to Japanese rules of international jurisdiction. Japanese scholars debate whether a judgment of the Japanese Supreme Court of 1998 allows for some flexibility.

4   Using the same rules of jurisdiction in these two different contexts amounts to demanding that foreign courts have the same jurisdictional rules as the forum. The forum may, like Italy does, pretend to be ready to recognize foreign judgments. However, by using the same jurisdictional criteria to assess the jurisdiction of the foreign court, the forum in effect accepts to recognize foreign judgments only where made pursuant to the same rules. Foreign judgments, by definition, will be made according to different procedures. If one only accepts to recognize foreign judgments which are the same as local ones, one is not serious about recognition.

5   A rationale for the conservative Italian model could be the view that only certain rules of jurisdiction are acceptable and can thus be tolerated. In accordance with this view, lawmakers of the forum might have felt constrained to adopt the local rules of jurisdiction. They might then be of the opinion that not only they, but also foreign lawmakers should be equally constrained, and thus deny recognition to any judgments infringing their view of the global allocation of jurisdiction. Where could such constrain come from? Public international law? Compare the discussion *supra* 1 on comity.

6   If the forum is not constrained and has discretion to adopt the most appropriate jurisdictional rules, the issue becomes whether the same policies are at stake for both problems. Arthur T. von Mehren made the following comment on derivative theories:

> Although there are important similarities between the policies relevant for these two problems, significant differences also exist. In particular, recognition practice involves situations in which at least one party (in the case of default judgments) and more often both parties have participated in, and relied on, a given legal order's administration of justice. Especially where both parties have so relied, the issue is no longer the abstract fairness and convenience of litigating in the given forum. The issue becomes instead, at least when viewed from the parties' perspective,

---

11   See Barel and Armellini, p. 304.
12   See Ballarino and Milan, p. 111.
13   See von Hoffmann and Thorn, § 3 III 2 b.
14   *Id.*

whether there are compelling reasons to ignore in whole or in part what has taken place.

When the jurisdictional question is seen in policy terms, it is evident that standards for recognition practice cannot be logically derived from the bases on which jurisdiction to adjudicate is assumed unless the policies that inform these two topics are identical.[15]

An alternative position is to define the jurisdiction of foreign courts with autonomous criteria. What are these criteria in England? Do you agree with the critique of the Canadian Supreme court?

 CASE

Court of Appeal of England and Wales, 27 July 1989
Adams v. Cape Industries Plc[16]

Provision has been made by statute for the enforcement in this country of the judgments of the courts of Commonwealth and foreign countries in a number of different circumstances: (see in particular section 9 of the Administration of Justice Act 1920; section 4 of the Foreign Judgments (Reciprocal Enforcement) Act 1933 and the Civil Jurisdiction and Judgments Act 1982). However, none of these statutory provisions applies in the present case. We are concerned solely with the common law (. . .).

We will begin by mentioning some of the leading cases relating to judgments given against individuals.

(. . .) in deciding whether the foreign court was one of competent jurisdiction, our courts will apply not the law of the foreign court itself but our own rules of private international law. As Lindley M.R. put it in *Pemberton v. Hughes* (1899) 1 Ch. 781:

> There is no doubt that the Courts of this country will not enforce the decisions of foreign Courts which have no jurisdiction in the sense above explained – i.e., over the subject-matter or over the persons brought before them . . . But the jurisdiction which alone is important in these matters is the competence of the Court in an international sense – i.e., its territorial competence over the subject-matter and over the defendant. Its competence or jurisdiction in any other sense is not regarded as material by the Courts of this country.

---

15 von Mehren, n 10, 58.
16 [1990] 2 W.L.R. 657.

Subsequent references in this section of this judgment to the competence of a foreign court are intended as references to its competence under our principles of private international law, which will by no means necessarily coincide with the rules applied by the foreign court itself as governing its own jurisdiction. As the decision in *Pemberton v. Hughes* shows, our courts are generally not concerned with those rules.

Under the plaintiffs' case as pleaded, the obligation of the defendants to obey the judgment of the Tyler Court is said to arise because 'the defendants were resident in the United States of America at the time the plaintiffs' proceedings were commenced in the Tyler Court'. The jurisdiction of the Tyler Court is thus said to be founded on territorial factors.

Nearly 120 years ago in *Schibsby v. Westenholz* the 'residence' of an individual in a foreign country at time of commencement of suit was recognised by the Court of Queen's Bench as conferring jurisdiction on the court of that country to give a judgment in personam against him. In that case the court declined to enforce a judgment of a French tribunal obtained in default of appearance against defendants who at the time when the suit was brought in France were not subjects of nor resident in France. On these facts the court decided (at p. 163) that 'there existed nothing in the present case imposing on the defendants any duty to obey the judgment of the French tribunal'. However, it regarded certain points as clear on principle (at p. 161):

> If the defendants had been at the time of the judgment subjects of the country whose judgment is sought to be enforced against them, we think that its laws would have bound them. Again, if the defendants had been at the time when the suit commenced resident in the country, so as to have the benefit of its laws protecting them, or, as it is sometimes expressed, owing temporary allegiance to that country, we think that its laws would have bound them.

In *Roussillon v. Roussillon* (1880) 14 Ch. D. 351, Fry J., after referring to *Schibsby v. Westenholz* and in enumerating the cases where the courts of this country regard the judgment of a foreign court as imposing on the defendant the duty to obey it, (at p. 371) similarly referred to one such case as being 'where he was resident in the foreign country when the action began'.

In *Emanuel v. Symon* (1908) 1 K.B. 302, this court had to consider whether the fact of possessing property situate in Western Australia or the fact of entering into a contract of partnership in that country was sufficient to give a Western Australian court jurisdiction (in the private international law sense) over a British subject not resident in Western Australia at the start of the action, who had neither appeared to the process nor expressly agreed to submit to the jurisdiction of that court. This question was answered in the negative. Buckley L.J. said (at p. 309):

> In actions in personam there are five cases in which the courts of this country will enforce a foreign judgment: (1) Where the defendant is a subject of the foreign country in which the judgment has been obtained; (2) where he was resident in the foreign country when the action began; (3) where the defendant in the character of plaintiff has selected the forum in which he is afterwards sued; (4) where he has voluntarily appeared; and (5) where he has contracted to submit himself to the forum in which the judgment was obtained. The question in the present case is whether there is yet another and a sixth case.

After referring to the principles established by (inter alia) *Godard v. Gray* and *Schibsby v. Westenholz*, Buckley L.J. observed (at p. 310):

> In other words, the Courts of this country enforce foreign judgments because those judgments impose a duty or obligation which is recognised in this country and leads to judgment here also.

In agreement with the rest of the court, he considered that the factors relied on by the plaintiff mentioned above did not suffice to impose a duty on the defendant to obey the Western Australian judgment which should be recognised in this country.

We pause to observe that Buckley L.J.'s second, third, fourth and fifth cases mentioned in his statement broadly correspond with Dicey & Morris' respective four cases. It is doubtful whether the first case mentioned in his statement would still be held to give rise to jurisdiction: (see Dicey & Morris Vol. 1 at pp. 447–448 and the cases there cited). With this point we are not concerned.

Residence will much more often than not import physical presence. On the facts of the four cases last mentioned, any distinction between residence and presence would have been irrelevant. However, the brief statements of principle contained in the judgments left at least three questions unanswered. First, does the temporary presence of a defendant in a foreign country render the court of that country competent (in the private international law sense) to assume jurisdiction over him? Secondly, what is the relevant time for the purpose of ascertaining such competence? Thirdly, what is to be regarded as the 'country' in the case of a political country, such as the U.S.A. comprising different states which have different rules of law and legal procedure? (...)

From the three last-mentioned authorities read together, the following principles can, in our judgment, be extracted. First, in determining the jurisdiction of the foreign court in such cases, our court is directing its mind to the competence or otherwise of the foreign court 'to summon the defendant before it and to decide such matters as it has decided': (see *Pemberton v. Hughes* (1899) 1 Ch. at p. 790 per Lindley M.R.). Secondly, in the absence of any form of submission to the foreign court, such competence depends on the physical presence of the defendant in the country concerned at the time of suit. (We leave open the question whether residence without presence will suffice). From the last sentence of the dictum of Lord Parmoor cited above, and from a dictum of Collins M.R. in *Dunlop Pneumatic Tyre Company v. Actiengesselschaft fur Motor Und Motorfahr-Zeugbau Vorm, Cudell & Co.* (1902) 1 K.B. 342 at p. 346 it would appear that the date of service of process rather than the date of issue of proceedings is to be treated as 'the time of suit' for these purposes. But nothing turns on this point in the present case and we express no final view on it. Thirdly, we accept the submission of Sir Godfray Le Quesne (not accepted by Mr. Morison) that the temporary presence of a defendant in the foreign country will suffice provided at least that it is voluntary (i.e. not induced by compulsion, fraud or duress). Some further support for this submission is to be found in dicta of Parke B. in *The General Steam Navigation Company v. Guillou* (1843) 11 M. & W. 877.

The decision in *Carrick v. Hancock* has been the subject of criticism in Cheshire & North's *Private International Law* (11th Edition) at p. 342 ('Cheshire & North'), and in Dicey & Morris where it is said (at pp. 439–440):

> It may be doubted, however, whether casual presence, as distinct from residence, is a desirable basis of jurisdiction if the parties are strangers and the cause of action arose outside the country concerned. For the court is not likely to be the forum conveniens, in the sense of the appropriate court most adequately equipped to deal with the facts or the law. Moreover, the English case referred to above is open to the comment that the jurisdiction of the foreign court might just as well have been based on the defendant's submission as on his presence.

Our own courts regard the temporary presence of a foreigner in England at the time of service of process as justifying the assumption of jurisdiction over him: (see *Colt Industries Inc. v. Sarlie* (1966) 1 A.E.R. 673 and *H.R.H. Maharanee Seethaderi of Baroda v. Wildenstein* (1972) 2 Q.B. 283. However, Cheshire & North comment (at p. 342)):

> Any analogy based on the jurisdiction of the English courts is not particularly convincing, since the rules on jurisdiction are operated in conjunction with a

discretion to stay the proceedings, and the exercise of the discretion is likely to be an issue when jurisdiction is founded on mere presence.

We see the force of these points. They highlight the possible desirability of a further extension of reciprocal arrangements for the enforcement (or non-enforcement) of foreign judgments by Convention. Nevertheless, while the use of the particular phrase 'temporary allegiance' may be a misleading one in this context, we would, on the basis of the authorities referred to above, regard the source of the territorial jurisdiction of the court of a foreign country to summon a defendant to appear before it as being his obligation for the time being to abide by its laws and accept the jurisdiction of its courts while present in its territory. So long as he remains physically present in that country, he has the benefit of its laws, and must take the rough with the smooth, by accepting his amenability to the process of its courts. In the absence of authority compelling a contrary conclusion, we would conclude that the voluntary presence of an individual in a foreign country, whether permanent or temporary and whether or not accompanied by residence, is sufficient to give the courts of that country territorial jurisdiction over him under our rules of private international law.

 CASE

Supreme Court of Canada, 20 Dec 1990 *Morguard Investments Ltd. v. De Savoye*[17]

La Forest J.:

14. (. . .) The law on the matter has remained remarkably constant for many years. It originated in England during the 19th century and, while it has been subjected to considerable refinement, its general structure has not substantially changed. The two cases most commonly relied on, *Singh v. Faridkote (Rajah)*, [1894] A.C. 670 (P.C.) [Punjab], and *Emanuel v. Symon, supra*, date from the turn of the century. I shall confine myself to a discussion of the latter because it is the more frequently cited.

15. In *Symon*, the defendant, while residing and carrying on business in Western Australia, entered into a partnership in 1895 for the working of a gold mine situated in the colony and owned by the partnership. He later ceased to carry on business there, and moved permanently to England in 1899. Two years later, other members of the partnership brought an action in the colony for the dissolution of the partnership, sale of the mine, and an accounting. The writ was served on the

---

17 1990] 3 S.C.R. 1077.

defendant in England, but he took no step to defend the action. The colonial court decreed a dissolution of the partnership and sale of the mine, and in taking the accounts found a sum due from the partnership. The plaintiffs paid the sum and brought action in England to recover the portion which they alleged was owed by the defendant. Channell J. gave judgment for the plaintiffs, but a unanimous Court of Appeal reversed the judgment.

16. Buckley L.J.'s summary of the law in that case bears a remarkable resemblance to a code and has been cited repeatedly ever since. He stated, at p. 309:

> In actions in personam there are five cases in which the Courts of this country will enforce a foreign judgment: (1.) Where the defendant is a subject of the foreign country in which the judgment has been obtained; (2.) where he was resident in the foreign country when the action began; (3.) where the defendant in the character of plaintiff has selected the forum in which he is afterwards sued; (4.) where he has voluntarily appeared; and (5.) where he has contracted to submit himself to the forum in which the judgment was obtained.

Though the first of these propositions may now be open to doubt (see Robert J. Sharpe, 'The Enforcement of Foreign Judgments', in M.A. Springman and E. Gertner (eds.), *Debtor-Creditor Law: Practice and Doctrine* (1985), at p. 645), Buckley L.J.'s statement of the law, with one qualification to be noted, otherwise accurately represents the common law in England to this day. (. . .)

28 The common law regarding the recognition and enforcement of foreign judgments is firmly anchored in the principle of territoriality as interpreted and applied by the English courts in the 19th century: see *Faridkote, supra*. This principle reflects the fact, one of the basic tenets of international law, that sovereign states have exclusive jurisdiction in their own territory. As a concomitant to this, states are hesitant to exercise jurisdiction over matters that may take place in the territory of other states. Jurisdiction being territorial, it follows that a state's law has no binding effect outside its jurisdiction. Great Britain, and specifically its courts, applied that doctrine more rigorously than other states: see *Libman v. R.*, [1985] 2 S.C.R. 178, which deals with the question in its criminal aspect. The English approach, we saw, was unthinkingly adopted by the courts of this country, even in relation to judgments given in sister provinces.

29. Modern states, however, cannot live in splendid isolation, and do give effect to judgments given in other countries in certain circumstances. Thus a judgment in rem, such as a decree of divorce granted by the courts of one state to persons domiciled there, will be recognized by the courts of other states. In certain circumstances, as well, our courts will enforce personal judgments given in other states. Thus, we saw, our courts will enforce an action for breach of contract given by the courts of another country if the defendant was present there at the time of the action or has agreed to the foreign court's exercise of jurisdiction. This, it was thought, was in conformity with the requirements of comity, the informing

principle of private international law, which has been stated to be the deference and respect due by other states to the actions of a state legitimately taken within its territory. Since the state where the judgment was given had power over the litigants, the judgments of its courts should be respected.

30. But a state was under no obligation to enforce judgments it deemed to fall outside the jurisdiction of the foreign court. In particular, the English courts refused to enforce judgments on contracts, wherever made, unless the defendant was within the jurisdiction of the foreign court at the time of the action or had submitted to its jurisdiction. And this was so, we saw, even on actions that could most appropriately be tried in the foreign jurisdiction, such as a case like the present, where the personal obligation undertaken in the foreign country was in respect of property located there. Even in the 19th century this approach gave difficulty, a difficulty in my view resulting from a misapprehension of the real nature of the idea of comity, an idea based not simply on respect for the dictates of a foreign sovereign, but on the convenience, nay necessity, in a world where legal authority is divided among sovereign states, of adopting a doctrine of this kind. (. . .)

41. A similar approach should, in my view, be adopted in relation to the recognition and enforcement of judgments within Canada. As I see it, the courts in one province should give full faith and credit, to use the language of the United States Constitution, to the judgments given by a court in another province or a territory, so long as that court has properly, or appropriately, exercised jurisdiction in the action. I referred earlier to the principles of order and fairness that should obtain in this area of the law. Both order and justice militate in favour of the security of transactions. It seems anarchic and unfair that a person should be able to avoid legal obligations arising in one province simply by moving to another province. Why should a plaintiff be compelled to begin an action in the province where the defendant now resides whatever the inconvenience and costs this may bring and whatever degree of connection the relevant transaction may have with another province? And why should the availability of local enforcement be the decisive element in the plaintiff's choice of forum?

42. These concerns, however, must be weighed against fairness to the defendant. I noted earlier that the taking of jurisdiction by a court in one province and its recognition in another must be viewed as correlatives, and I added that recognition in other provinces should be dependent on the fact that the court giving judgment 'properly' or 'appropriately' exercised jurisdiction. It may meet the demands of order and fairness to recognize a judgment given in a jurisdiction that had the greatest, or at least significant, contacts with the subject matter of the action. But it hardly accords with principles of order and fairness to permit a person to sue another in any jurisdiction, without regard to the contacts that jurisdiction may have to the defendant or the subject matter of the suit: see Joost Blom, 'Conflict of Laws — Enforcement of Extraprovincial Default Judgment — Reciprocity of Jurisdiction: *Morguard Investments Ltd. v. De Savoye*' (1989), 68 Can. Bar Rev. 359,

at p. 360. Thus fairness to the defendant requires that the judgment be issued by a court acting through fair process and with properly-restrained jurisdiction.

43. As discussed, fair process is not an issue within the Canadian federation. The question that remains, then, is: When has a court exercised its jurisdiction appropriately for the purposes of recognition by a court in another province? This poses no difficulty where the court has acted on the basis of the accepted grounds traditionally accepted by courts as permitting the recognition and enforcement of foreign judgments — in the case of judgments in personam, where the defendant was within the jurisdiction at the time of the action or when he submitted to its judgment, whether by agreement of by attornment. In the first case, the court had jurisdiction over the person, and in the second case by virtue of the agreement. No injustice results.

44. The difficulty, of course, arises where, as here, the defendant was outside the jurisdiction of that court and he was served ex juris. To what extent may a court of a province properly exercise jurisdiction over a defendant in another province? The rules for service ex juris in all the provinces are broad — in some provinces, Nova Scotia and Prince Edward Island, very broad indeed. It is clear, however, that, if the courts of one province are to be expected to give effect to judgments given in another province, there must be some limits to the exercise of jurisdiction against persons outside the province. (. . .)

51. I am aware, of course, that the possibility of being sued outside the province of his residence may pose a problem for a defendant. But that can occur in relation to actions in rem now. In any event, this consideration must be weighed against the fact that the plaintiff, under the English rules, may often find himself subjected to the inconvenience of having to pursue his debtor to another province, however just, efficient or convenient it may be to pursue an action where the contract took place or the damage occurred. It seems to me that the approach of permitting suit where there is a real and substantial connection with the action provides a reasonable balance between the rights of the parties. It affords some protection against being pursued in jurisdictions having little or no connection with the transaction or the parties. In a world where even the most familiar things we buy and sell originate or are manufactured elsewhere, and where people are constantly moving from province to province, it is simply anachronistic to uphold a 'power theory' or a single situs for torts or contracts for the proper exercise of jurisdiction.

? | **NOTES AND QUESTIONS**

In *Emanuel v. Symon*, Buckley L.J. established a list of five cases where English courts would consider that a foreign court has jurisdiction over an individual. While the list might have changed since 1908, and may change in the future, the methodological approach remains. Foreign courts will only be found to have jurisdiction if one of the criteria on the list is met.

1   Interestingly enough, the list is shorter than the cases where an English court may directly retain jurisdiction to decide a dispute.[18] This means that, in certain cases, an English court would find that the jurisdiction of a foreign court is inappropriate although it would have retained jurisdiction if the same claim had been brought in England. Should it not be the case that when a foreign court relies on a jurisdictional criterion which is also used in the forum, its jurisdiction should automatically be considered as appropriate? Or are there heads of jurisdiction that States use to retain jurisdiction while knowing that they are not really appropriate? In his Hague Lectures, Professor von Mehren commented:

> Lord Hodson stated the general approach and suggested its basis in *Travers v. Holley* [1953]: 'it must surely be that what entitles an English court to assume jurisdiction must be equally effective in the case of a foreign court'. This proposition would be acceptable, at least in principle, if all jurisdictional bases asserted by a State were universalistic, that is to say, generally appropriate and not self-regarding. However, the equivalence theory is problematical at least to the extent that States assert jurisdiction to advance particular forum interests even at the possible expense of standards of fairness considered applicable in the absence of these special concerns.[19]

2   How can the five cases of the *Emanuel* list be justified? Is it that they are perceived by English courts as the most appropriate jurisdictional criteria? Is it that they reveal the theory underlying the English law of foreign judgments? What is this theory, and is it appropriately served by this list, and more generally by the list method?

3   In *De Savoye*, the Canadian Supreme Court rejected the rigid list method and adopted a flexible test. The test was laid down for the recognition of judgments made in other Canadian provinces, but it was later extended to foreign judgments in *Beals v. Saldanha*.[20]

France also adopted a flexible test in 1985.

> *Gilles Cuniberti, The Liberalization of the French Law of Foreign Judgments*[21]
> The origin of the modern French law on the recognition and enforcement of judgments is the 1964 *Munzer* decision. In *Munzer v. Munzer* [1964] Rev Crit DIP 344, the *Cour de cassation* abandoned the 150-year-old judicial practice of *révision au fond*. The *révision au fond* was the power of French courts to recognize foreign judgments on condition that such judgments were right on the merits. In other words, French courts could verify whether the foreign court had properly assessed the facts and properly applied the law. In *Munzer*, the *Cour de cassation* held that

---

18 Rogerson, p. 237.

19 von Mehren, n 10, 59. Compare the discussion on exorbitant fora *supra* Part II.

20 [2003] 3 S.C.R. 416. The UK Supreme Court rejected the new Canadian approach in *Rubin v. Eurofinance* [2012] UKSC 46.

21 (2007) 56 I.C.L.Q. 931, 932–3, 936–7.

revision au fond was prohibited. French courts could not any more assess whether foreign judgments were right in order to declare them enforceable in France. Instead, they would have to verify whether they met a number of newly laid-down conditions. The French law of judgments was moving into a new era. In theory at least, it was accepted that it was no longer a condition that foreign judgments be the same as French judgments to be recognized in France. Foreign judgments would be truly recognized as such, ie judgments made by a foreign court, and thus potentially different.

Since *Munzer*, the *Cour de cassation* and French commentators have been discussing what the conditions of the recognition of foreign judgments should be. In *Munzer*, the *Cour de cassation* held that the newly laid-down conditions would suffice to 'ensure the protection of the French legal order and interests'. This is the tension of the modern law of judgments: being open to foreign legal and judicial cultures, but only to the extent that the French legal order is not hurt.

The *Cour de cassation* initially laid down five conditions. First, the foreign court ought to have jurisdiction to hear the dispute. (. . .) *[See below p. 328].*

After some hesitation, the condition of the jurisdiction of the foreign court was interpreted along the same lines. For years, there was much debate as to what the condition actually meant. It was wondered whether the jurisdiction of the foreign court should be appreciated pursuant to the law of jurisdiction of the forum or of the foreign court. The first solution seemed too conservative, as it did not accept that foreign courts could retain jurisdiction on different grounds than those used by French courts. The second solution seemed too liberal as it allowed the recognition of judgments made by courts retaining jurisdiction on any ground as long as the foreign law allowed. In 1985, the *Cour de cassation* chose a third way. In *Simitch v. Fairhurst* [1985] Rev Crit DIP 369, the court held that foreign courts would be regarded as having jurisdiction for the purpose of the recognition of foreign judgments if French enforcing courts could be satisfied that there was 'an actual connection between the dispute and the country of the foreign court'. This flexible text would enable French courts to allow the recognition of foreign judgments made by courts retaining jurisdiction on grounds unknown to French jurisdiction rules, as long as these grounds could be regarded as serious. But it would also allow French courts to deny recognition when the jurisdiction of the foreign court would not be founded on a serious or acceptable connection to the dispute. When the jurisdiction of the foreign court would be exorbitant, it would fail the test. The test seemed to reveal an enlightened judiciary which did not fear the world and was open to cultural differences. (. . .)

In addition to the jurisdiction of the foreign court and the compatibility with public policy, the *Munzer-Bachir* line of authorities had laid down two final conditions which related to the law applied by the foreign court.

The first remaining condition is *fraude à la loi*. It is quite different from the common law concept of fraud. It sanctions a specific strategic behaviour. The foreign judgment should not have been obtained with the sole purpose of avoiding the application of the law that a French court would have applied. *Fraude* is a general doctrine of French private law. In all fields, it purports to sanction any strategic behaviour resulting in the avoidance of the application of rules which would have otherwise applied. The test for *fraude* is twofold. First, the action of a party must result in the application of one rule instead of another. Secondly, the sole purpose for the action must have been the avoidance of the application of the rule which does not apply as a consequence of the said action. The sanction is that the action is then ignored and the defrauded rule is declared applicable. The most famous application of the doctrine has been in choice of law, when parties would change nationalities in order to have a court apply another law and thus, for instance, to be entitled to divorce. In the context of foreign judgments, French courts want to prevent parties from seeking the application of another law by suing abroad. The doctrine of *fraude*, however, raises an important evidentiary issue. In practice, showing that a party sued abroad for the sole reason of avoiding the application of the law that a French court would have applied, is extremely difficult. The parties could have chosen to litigate abroad for a variety of reasons. And even more so when there is a serious connection between the dispute and the foreign court. For instance, when two Algerian spouses live in France, the husband could be tempted to seek divorce in Algeria for the sole purpose of avoiding the application of French law by a French court. Yet, he is an Algerian citizen, and so is his wife. Furthermore, he typically travels to Algeria each summer. Algerian courts are thus seriously connected to the dispute. They have jurisdiction from the French perspective. The initiation of the Algerian proceedings may be *a fraude*, but the truth of the matter is that, the difference between French and Algerian laws aside, it is almost as reasonable for the husband to sue in Algeria as it is to sue in France. Thus, except when the husband has brought proceedings in Algeria immediately after his wife initiated proceedings in France, it will be hard to prove that *a fraude* actually took place. (. . .)

CASE

Cour de cassation, 20 February 2007, *Cornelissen* Case 05-14082

Whereas, by judgment of 27 August 1993, the District Court of the District of Columbia (United States) ordered Mr X, of Colombian nationality, to pay US companies North American Air Service company INC and Avianca INC, as well as Colombian companies Avianca SA, Helicopteros Nacionales of Columbia and Aeronautico Medellin Consolida (the 'companies') the sum of US\$ 3,987,916.66, plus interest; Mr X having relocated to France, the companies applied for a declaration of enforceability (*exequatur*) of the decision; by judgment of 1 February 2000, the first instance court dismissed their application on the grounds that there was no link between the facts at issue and U.S. territory and that furthermore Colombian law applied;

On the first argument:

Whereas Mr X criticizes the judgment under scrutiny (Court of Appeal of Aix-en-Provence, 11 January 2005) for declaring enforceable the judgment delivered on 27 August 1993 by the District Court of the District of Columbia in civil Action no 85-3277 on the ground that both the main plaintiffs and the defendant, Mr X, were domiciled in Colombia, and that by considering that the only signing in the District of Columbia of an agreement with a company headed by Mr X, allegedly in breach of its obligations towards Avianca, was a sufficient link between the dispute and that district, the court of appeal disregarded the principles governing international jurisdiction;

But whereas the judgment explains that in a previous judgment of 31 May 1991, ruling on the objection to jurisdiction raised by Mr X, the U.S. District Court retained international jurisdiction pursuant to the federal rules of civil procedure which granted it jurisdiction over the claims brought against citizens of a foreign state who were 'additional party'; such was the case insofar as Mr X was co-defendant in the proceedings against the companies, the main defendant being himself domiciled in Washington; 'indictment grounds' directed against Mr X were for acts committed in the context of his Washington business relationships with the main defendant and two of the five plaintiff companies were American and domiciled in the US; the court of appeal could conclude that the dispute had an actual connection with the United States of America so that the U.S. court had jurisdiction to decide it; the argument is unfounded;

On the second argument:

Whereas Mr X further criticizes the judgment under scrutiny to have so ruled, while, according to the appellant, the exequatur of a foreign judgment may be granted only if the foreign court has applied the law designated by the French choice of law rule or a law leading to an equivalent result; thus in granting exequatur to an American judgment which had applied American law, without inquiring, as it was invited to, whether, concerning the assessment of the liability of a company director, the applicable law was not the Colombian law of the seat of the company, which ignored triple damages as found in American law which the U.S. District court applied, the court of appeal did not give legal foundation to its decision;

But whereas for the purpose of granting exequatur outside the scope of any international treaty, French courts must ensure that three conditions are met, namely the indirect jurisdiction of the foreign court based on the existence of an actual connection between the dispute and the foreign court, compliance with international substantive and procedural public policy and absence of evasion of the law; exequatur courts do not have to verify whether the law applied by the foreign court is that designated by the French choice of law rule;

On these grounds: Dismisses the appeal . . .

 NOTES

1 The French and the Canadian tests both call for an inquiry into the significance of the connections between the dispute and the foreign court. The purpose is to assess whether there were sufficient geographical connections when the foreign court retained jurisdiction. If the connections were real and substantial, the jurisdiction of the foreign court will be considered as appropriate.

The tests are flexible insofar as any appropriate connection will do. There is no prior list of acceptable grounds for jurisdiction. This is because, if the forum is serious about recognizing foreign judgments, it should accept that foreign courts may legitimately have used grounds of jurisdiction other than those chosen and preferred by the forum. In a liberal and open-minded doctrine of recognition of foreign judgments, it should be accepted that foreign courts might use a number of different grounds of jurisdiction which may well be unknown in the forum. If these grounds are appropriate, they should in principle be accepted, unless the forum believes all foreign solutions are inferior to its own. This is the main reason why a flexible test should be used to assess the jurisdiction of foreign courts. Lists will always be incomplete, and often culturally biased.

The purpose of a liberal test should not be to define appropriate heads of jurisdiction, but to exclude inappropriate ones. Inappropriate heads of jurisdiction are all those based on criteria which are not real and substantial connections between the foreign country and the dispute. In this context, inappropriate should therefore be understood as meaning lacking a substantial connection. The consequence is that the test will essentially exclude cases where foreign courts relied on exorbitant heads of jurisdiction (*supra*, Chapter 3).

Under a liberal doctrine of foreign judgments, it is accepted that judgments rendered by any foreign court with a substantial connection with the dispute will be recognised, and would therefore prevent relitigation in the forum. This is to say that it is acceptable and legitimate for the parties to choose among all available courts with such connection. It therefore becomes difficult to sanction strategic behaviour, as the unsatisfactory French doctrine of *fraude* demonstrates.

Finally, States may want to craft exceptions to their liberal doctrine by using a list of cases where only one ground of jurisdiction will be considered as appropriate, and thus where any other one will be deemed inappropriate. The most common example is jurisdiction in real property matters, which is considered to belong exclusively to the court of the *situs* of the property. In the civil law tradition, such cases are labeled exclusive heads of jurisdiction.

2 While *Hilton* is authority for the proposition that foreign judgments will only be recognised if the foreign court has jurisdiction over the defendant, the U.S. Supreme Court has never clarified which test should be used for that purpose. Lower courts sometimes apply the law of the foreign court, sometimes U.S. law, sometimes both.[22]

The U.S. Supreme Court has developed a standard for assessing whether the exercise of jurisdiction of American courts comports with the Due Process Clause of the US Constitution. This same test is also often used for the purpose of assessing the jurisdiction of foreign courts.

 CASE

U.S. Court of Appeals, Seventh Circuit, 3 Feb. 1981
Hendrik Koster v. Automark Industries, Inc.[23]

Facts: Hendrik Koster, a citizen of the Netherlands obtained a default judgment in district court in Amsterdam against Automark Industries, Inc. ('Automark'), a corporation doing business in Illinois, in a case brought on a claimed breach of contract. Koster then sought to enforce the Dutch judgment in the United States.

Held: Automark did not have sufficient contact with the Netherlands to vest U.S. courts with personal jurisdiction over Automark so as to permit enforcement of the default judgment in United States courts. The Dutch judgment may not be enforced in the United States.

HARLINGTON WOOD, Jr., Circuit Judge.

2. Whether a court may, under American law, assert jurisdiction over a foreign defendant-company depends upon whether the company 'purposefully avails itself of the privilege of conducting activities within the forum State.' *Shaffer v. Heitner*, 433 U.S. 186, 216 (1977). This means that the company must pass a threshold of minimum contacts with the forum state so that it is fair to subject it to the jurisdiction of that state's courts. *World-Wide Volkswagen Corp. v. Woodson*, 444 U.S. 286, 292, (1980); *International Shoe v. Washington*, 326 U.S. 310 (1945).

---

22 *Evans Cabinet Corp. v. Kitchen Int'l, Inc.*, 593 F.3d, 135, 142 (1st Cir).
23 640 F.2d 77 (7th Cir. 1981).

3. The parties agree that the document alleged to be Automark's contract to purchase up to 600,000 units of Koster's valve cap gauges was executed in Milan, Italy. The Milan meeting between Koster and Automark followed preliminary inquiry and discussion between the two parties during a period of five months. The discussion was carried on via mail between Koster's Amsterdam office and Automark's Illinois address. Automark began the exchange of letters in June, 1970 with a one-sentence request for 'descriptive material and prices' of Koster's product. Automark subsequently expressed interest in marketing the tire gauges, but stated that it needed to know the details of such important factors as Koster's relationship with the Swiss factory that produced the gauges, Koster's present patent rights, and his rights to worldwide distribution of the total output of the Swiss factory. Automark expressly disclaimed willingness to negotiate and conclude a contract through the mail. In early November, 1970, Automark's vice-president, J. L. Bohmrich, wrote that he would like to meet with Koster in Amsterdam or at the Swiss factory during a European trip Bohmrich planned to take later in the month. Koster replied that he would instead be willing to meet in Milan, and would telephone Bohmrich's Illinois office to make arrangements. As noted, the Milan meeting resulted in execution of the document involved in this case. So far as the record shows, Automark never ordered Koster's gauges, and Koster never shipped any gauges.

4. The business contacts described above are insufficient to reach the minimum level needed to satisfy due process requirements prerequisite to enforcement of the Dutch default judgment. A recent opinion of this court, *Lakeside Bridge & Steel Co. v. Mountain State Construction Co.*, 597 F.2d 596 (7th Cir. 1979), thoroughly analyzed the due process requirements of minimum contacts in concluding that a federal court sitting in a diversity case arising in Wisconsin did not have personal jurisdiction of a West Virginia defendant. Whether it be Wisconsin or the Netherlands, the standard of minimum contacts is the same. See generally *Somportex Limited v. Philadelphia Chewing Gum Corp.*, 453 F.2d 435, 440 (3d Cir. 1971). The facts in the Lakeside case were similar to those involved here, and if anything, presented a more compelling case for recognizing personal jurisdiction.

5. In Lakeside, the defendant construction company had ordered structural assemblies from plaintiff Lakeside, a Wisconsin company. Several letters and telephone calls had been exchanged between the two businesses, and a contract concluded by mail. The assemblies were delivered, and Lakeside sued when the defendant withheld part of the purchase price. The court assumed that the defendant believed that Lakeside would perform the contract in Wisconsin, the forum state. Focusing on the nature and quality of the contacts between the two companies, the court nevertheless concluded that Wisconsin could not assert jurisdiction over the West Virginia company because the defendant's Wisconsin contacts did not show that it 'purposefully avail(ed) itself of the privilege of conducting activities within the forum state.' 597 F.2d at 603.

6. The document at issue in the case before us was executed in Italy and involved the purchase of goods manufactured in Switzerland. While the document contains language that might be construed as an agreement to pay, which payment Koster claims was to take place in the Netherlands, such a promise even if so interpreted is not sufficient contact to confer personal jurisdiction. *Kulko v. California Superior Court*, 436 U.S. 84, 93 n.6, (1978) (child-support payments required under separation agreement to spouse living in California insufficient contact to confer jurisdiction on that state).

7. In comparison to the facts in the Lakeside case, Automark's only contacts with the Netherlands were eight letters, and possibly a telegram and a transatlantic telephone call all preliminary to the meeting in Italy. In Lakeside, 597 F.2d at 604, the court notes that such contacts cannot be held to satisfy jurisdictional requirements, otherwise '(u)se of the interstate telephone and mail service to communicate with (an out-of-state) plaintiff, if constituting contacts supporting jurisdiction, would give jurisdiction to any state into which communications were directed.' Such a result would make virtually every business subject to suit in any state with which it happened to communicate in some manner. That clearly would not satisfy the demands of due process.

8. Lakeside emphasizes that 'the best interests of the international and state systems' of commerce should be considered when making determinations about minimum contacts in individual cases. 597 F.2d at 603, quoting Restatement (Second) of Conflict of Laws § 37, Comment a (1971). This consideration weighs in favor of Automark, since it 'is based on the proposition that "(a) state should not improperly impinge upon the interests of other states by trying in its courts a case with which it has no adequate relationship."' *Id.*, quoting Restatement, *supra*, § 24, Comment b. The Netherlands lacks an adequate relationship to defendant's presence and conduct to justify trial of the case in that country. The interests of international business are better served by protecting potential international purchasers from being unreasonably called to defend suits commenced in foreign courts which lack jurisdiction according to our recognized standards of due process. See at 603 n.12.

9. Moreover, the Lakeside opinion stresses that where the nature of a defendant's business contact in the forum state does not involve activities dangerous to persons and property, the propriety of vesting personal jurisdiction in that state must be considered in light of its relationship with the defendant other than that at issue in the lawsuit. At 603. The purchase and shipment of valve gauges is not a dangerous activity. And here, there are no allegations that Automark had any relationship with the Netherlands beyond the letters, telegram and telephone call involved in its business contact with Koster.

10. On these facts, Automark did not have the minimum contacts necessary to show that it purposefully utilized the privilege to conduct business activities in the Netherlands sufficient to confer on that country's courts personal jurisdiction

over Automark. The district court concluded that cases decided under the Illinois long-arm statute, Ill.Rev.Stat.Ch. 110, § 17(a), supported his finding that Automark satisfied the requirement of minimum contacts to support the Dutch court's jurisdiction. We disagree. We note that the Illinois courts have held that the state long-arm statute is intended to assert jurisdiction over non-resident defendants only 'to the extent permitted by the due process clause.' *Colony Press, Inc. v. Fleeman*, 17 Ill.App.3d 14, 19 (1974). The Lakeside court's discussion of the application of Wisconsin's long-arm statute to a decision on the basis of federal due process rights is pertinent. The court noted that the Wisconsin law 'was intended by the state legislature to reach only so far as permitted by the due process clause . . . In these circumstances we are interpreting the statute, not ruling on its constitutionality, when we decide the due process question; yet we are of course not bound by the (state courts') determination of that federal question'. At 599. Likewise, in the case before us we are not bound by Illinois judicial determinations on the requirements of due process to support personal jurisdiction. This is especially true where we are considering the powers of a court in a jurisdiction other than Illinois.

11. At any rate, the cases relied upon by the district court for its determination that the Dutch court was vested with personal jurisdiction do not detract from our holding here. Thus, in Colony Press, *supra*, the state court noted that the 'essential points' for purposes of its determination that an Ohio corporation was subject to a suit brought in Illinois courts by an Illinois company were that the contract was accepted in Illinois and performance thereunder was expected to occur wholly within that state. 17 Ill.App.3d at 18. As our discussion indicates, the document involved in this case was executed in Italy, and the goods to which it related were to be produced in Switzerland: the Netherlands was not the situs of either activity.

12. And the other case relied upon by the district judge, *Cook Associates, Inc. v. Colonial Broach & Machine Co.*, 14 Ill.App.3d 965 (1973), dealt with a service contract involving an out-of-state company that had used the services of an Illinois employment agency via a single telephone call. This satisfied the requirements for minimum contacts under the circumstances of that case since 'that call was all that was necessary for defendant to achieve its (business) purpose', i.e., obtaining the names of prospective employees. At 970. The conclusion and performance of the contract were carried out in Illinois via that telephone call, unlike the situation before us where neither activity occurred in the Netherlands.

13. Absent personal jurisdiction over Automark in the Dutch case that resulted in a default judgment, the courts of this country lack jurisdiction to enforce the foreign default judgment. The decision of the district court accordingly is reversed and the case is remanded with directions to dismiss the complaint.

NOTE

In this case, the U.S. court used a test designed to control the taking of jurisdiction by American courts to the different issue of assessing whether a foreign court had jurisdiction. At first sight, this could appear as a sign of parochialism and narrow mindedness. This would be wrong. The test used is not a rule of jurisdiction, but a constitutional limit. The purpose is not to lay down precise rules of jurisdiction. It is to assess when a rule of jurisdiction is fair and thus acceptable. Once such a constitutional standard exists, it seems logical to use it not only for defining the jurisdiction of the courts of the forum, but also for appreciating the jurisdiction of foreign courts.

Indeed, the Due Process jurisdictional standard is very close to the test developed by French and Canadian courts in the context of law of foreign judgments.

2.2   Public policy

The second essential requirement for the recognition of foreign judgments is that they comport with the public policy of the forum. As in the context of choice of law, the term 'public policy' is misleading. The requirement is not that foreign judgments respect the public policies of the forum. There are policies behind all rules and, if foreign judgments could be attacked on the ground that they do not follow the policies of the forum, this would amount to a review of the foreign judgment on the merits. The public policy exception is universally understood as being much narrower. Foreign judgments might be denied recognition on this ground only if they violate the *most fundamental* policies of the forum. Logically, such fundamental policies will often be expressed in the fundamental norms of the forum, that is, its constitution or its bill of rights.

 CASE

U.S. District Court for the Northern District of California, 7 November 2001 *Yahoo! Inc. v. La Ligue contre le Racisme et l'Antisémitisme*[24]

Facts: Yahoo! Inc., a California Internet service provider, sued French parties who had obtained order from French court requiring Yahoo! to block French citizens' access to Nazi material displayed or offered for sale on Yahoo!'s United States site, seeking declaration that order was unenforceable in United States.

Held: French order presented a real and immediate threat to ISP's First Amendment rights, and would thus not be recognized.

---

24 169 F.Supp.2d 1181.

II. Overview

As this Court and others have observed, the instant case presents novel and important issues arising from the global reach of the Internet. Indeed, the specific facts of this case implicate issues of policy, politics, and culture that are beyond the purview of one nation's judiciary. Thus it is critical that the Court define at the outset what is and is not at stake in the present proceeding.

This case is *not* about the moral acceptability of promoting the symbols or propaganda of Nazism. Most would agree that such acts are profoundly offensive. By any reasonable standard of morality, the Nazis were responsible for one of the worst displays of inhumanity in recorded history. This Court is acutely mindful of the emotional pain reminders of the Nazi era cause to Holocaust survivors and deeply respectful of the motivations of the French Republic in enacting the underlying statutes and of the defendant organizations in seeking relief under those statutes. Vigilance is the key to preventing atrocities such as the Holocaust from occurring again.

Nor is this case about the right of France or any other nation to determine its own law and social policies. A basic function of a sovereign state is to determine by law what forms of speech and conduct are acceptable within its borders. In this instance, as a nation whose citizens suffered the effects of Nazism in ways that are incomprehensible to most Americans, France clearly has the right to enact and enforce laws such as those relied upon by the French Court here.[FN6]

> FN6. In particular, there is no doubt that France may and will continue to ban the purchase and possession within its borders of Nazi and Third Reich related matter and to seek criminal sanctions against those who violate the law.

What *is* at issue here is whether it is consistent with the Constitution and laws of the United States for another nation to regulate speech by a United States resident within the United States on the basis that such speech can be accessed by Internet users in that nation. In a world in which ideas and information transcend borders and the Internet in particular renders the physical distance between speaker and audience virtually meaningless, the implications of this question go far beyond the facts of this case. The modern world is home to widely varied cultures with radically divergent value systems. There is little doubt that Internet users in the United States routinely engage in speech that violates, for example, China's laws against religious expression, the laws of various nations against advocacy of gender equality or homosexuality, or even the United Kingdom's restrictions on freedom of the press. If the government or another party in one of these sovereign nations were to seek enforcement of such laws against Yahoo! or another U.S.-based Internet service provider, what principles should guide the court's analysis?

The Court has stated that it must and will decide this case in accordance with the Constitution and laws of the United States. It recognizes that in so doing, it necessarily adopts certain value judgments embedded in those enactments, including the fundamental judgment expressed in the First Amendment that it is preferable to permit the non-violent expression of offensive viewpoints rather than to impose viewpoint-based governmental regulation upon speech. The government and people of France have made a different judgment based upon their own experience. In undertaking its inquiry as to the proper application of the laws of the United States, the Court intends no disrespect for that judgment or for the experience that has informed it. (. . .)

IV. LEGAL ISSUES

4. Comity

No legal judgment has any effect, of its own force, beyond the limits of the sovereignty from which its authority is derived. However, the United States Constitution and implementing legislation require that full faith and credit be given to judgments of sister states, territories, and possessions of the United States. U.S. CONST. art. IV, §§ 1, cl. 1. The extent to which the United States, or any state, honors the judicial decrees of foreign nations is a matter of choice, governed by 'the comity of nations.' *Hilton v. Guyot*, 159 U.S. 113, 163 (1895). Comity 'is neither a matter of absolute obligation, on the one hand, nor of mere courtesy and good will, upon the other.' *Hilton*, at 163–64. United States courts generally recognize foreign judgments and decrees unless enforcement would be prejudicial or contrary to the country's interests. *Laker Airways v. Sabena Belgian World Airlines*, 731 F.2d 909, 931 (D.C.Cir.1984) ('[T]he court is not required to give effect to foreign judicial proceedings grounded on policies which do violence to its own fundamental interests.'); *Tahan v. Hodgson*, 662 F.2d 862, 864 (D.C.Cir.1981) ('[R]equirements for enforcement of a foreign judgment expressed in *Hilton* are that . . . the original claim not violate American public policy . . . that it not be repugnant to fundamental notions of what is decent and just in the State where enforcement is sought.').

As discussed previously, the French order's content and viewpoint-based regulation of the web pages and auction site on Yahoo.com, while entitled to great deference as an articulation of French law, clearly would be inconsistent with the First Amendment if mandated by a court in the United States.

What makes this case uniquely challenging is that the Internet in effect allows one to speak in more than one place at the same time. Although France has the sovereign right to regulate what speech is permissible in France, this Court may not enforce a foreign order that violates the protections of the United States Constitution by chilling protected speech that occurs simultaneously within our borders. See, e.g., *Matusevitch v. Telnikoff*, 877 F.Supp. 1, 4 (D.D.C.1995) (declining to enforce British libel judgment because British libel standards 'deprive the plaintiff of his constitutional rights'); *Bachchan v. India Abroad Publications, Inc.*, 154 Misc.2d 228 (Sup.Ct.1992) (declining to enforce a British libel judgment because of its 'chilling effect' on the First Amendment); *see also, Abdullah v. Sheridan Square Press, Inc.*, No. 93 Civ. 2515, 1994 WL 419847 (S.D.N.Y. May 4, 1994) (dismissing a libel claim brought under English law because 'establishment of a claim for libel under the British law of defamation would be antithetical to the First Amendment protection accorded to the defendants.'). The reason for limiting comity in this area is sound. 'The protection to free speech and the press embodied in [the First] amendment would be seriously jeopardized by the entry of foreign [ ] judgments granted pursuant to standards deemed appropriate in [another country] but considered antithetical to the protections afforded the press by the U.S. Constitution.' *Bachchan*, 585 N.Y.S.2d at 665. Absent a body of law that establishes international standards with respect to speech on the Internet and an appropriate treaty or legislation addressing enforcement of such standards to speech originating within the United States, the principle of comity is outweighed by the Court's obligation to uphold the First Amendment.

 CASE

U.S. Court of Appeals, Ninth Circuit, 12 January 2006 *Yahoo! Inc. v. La Ligue contre le Racisme et l'Antisémitisme*[25]

The legal question presented by this case is whether the two interim orders of the French court are enforceable in this country. (. . .) We are asked to decide whether enforcement of these interim orders would be 'repugnant' to California public policy.

There is currently no federal statute governing recognition of foreign judgments in the federal courts. *See* American Law Institute, *Recognition and Enforcement of Foreign Judgments: Analysis and Proposed Federal Statute*

---

25 433 F.3d 1199, 1206 (9th Cir.2006).

(April 11, 2005) (proposed final draft). The federal full faith and credit statute, 28 U.S.C. § 1738, governs only judgments rendered by courts of states within the United States. (. . .)

California, along with many other states, has adopted the Uniform Foreign Money-Judgments Recognition Act ('Uniform Act' or 'Act'). Cal.Civ.Proc. Code §§ 1713–1713.8. The relevant standard for enforceability under the Act is whether 'the cause of action or defense on which the judgment is based is *repugnant to the public policy* of this state.' *Id.* § 1713.4(b)(3) (emphasis added). However, the Act is not directly applicable to this case, for it does not authorize enforcement of injunctions. *See id.* § 1713.1(2) ('"Foreign judgment" means any judgment of a foreign state granting or denying recovery of a sum of money, other than . . . a fine or other penalty[.]') But neither does the Uniform Act prevent enforcement of injunctions, for its savings clause specifies that the Act does not foreclose enforcement of foreign judgments 'in situations not covered by [the Act].' *Id.* § 1713.7.

Because the Uniform Act does not cover injunctions, we look to general principles of comity followed by the California courts. We may appropriately consult the Restatement (Third) of the Foreign Relations Law of the United States ('Third Restatement' or 'Restatement'), given that California courts frequently cite the Restatement, as well as earlier Restatements, as sources of law. (. . .) The general principle of enforceability under the Third Restatement is the same as under California's Uniform Act. That is, an American court will not enforce a judgment if 'the cause of action on which the judgment was based, or the judgment itself, is *repugnant to the public policy* of the United States or of the State where recognition is sought[.]' Restatement § 482(2)(d) (emphasis added); *see also* Restatement (Second) of the Conflict of Laws § 117 cmt. c (1971) ('[E]nforcement will usually be accorded judgment [of a foreign court] except in situations where the original claim is *repugnant to fundamental notions of what is decent and just* in the State where enforcement is sought.') (emphasis added).

There is very little case law in California dealing with enforceability of foreign country injunctions under general principles of comity, but that law is consistent with the repugnancy standard of the Restatement. We have found only one case in which a California court has ruled on the enforceability of an injunction granted in another country. In *In re Stephanie M.,* 7 Cal.4th 295 (1994), a Mexican court had entered a guardianship decree purporting to authorize the named guardian to take immediate custody of a child and to return her to Mexico. The California Supreme Court recognized that an injunction could be enforced by the California courts as a matter of comity, but it declined to order enforcement in this particular case because the Mexican decree conflicted with California public policy. (. . .)

Under the repugnancy standard, American courts sometimes enforce judgments that conflict with American public policy or are based on foreign law that differs substantially from American state or federal law. See, e.g., *In re Hashim*, 213 F.3d 1169, 1172 (9th Cir.2000) (reversing bankruptcy court's refusal to enforce English court's award of $10 million in costs against debtors whose assets had been frozen by Saddam Hussein); *Milhoux v. Linder*, 902 P.2d 856, 861–62 (Colo.Ct.App.1995) (affirming recognition of Belgian judgment as a matter of comity, even though it was based on a 30-year Belgian statute of limitations). Inconsistency with American law is not necessarily enough to prevent recognition and enforcement of a foreign judgment in the United States. The foreign judgment must be, in addition, repugnant to public policy. (. . .)

The dissent repeatedly states that the French court's interim orders are facially unconstitutional. It writes, 'The French orders on their face . . . violate the First Amendment and are plainly contrary to one of America's, and by extension California's, most cherished public policies.' (Dissent at 1239.) It later refers to the French court's orders as 'foreign court orders that so obviously violate the First Amendment.' (*Id.* at 1239-40.) It writes further, '[T]he absence of a discernible line between the permitted and the unpermitted . . . makes the orders facially unconstitutional.' (*Id.* at 1244.)

The dissent is able to conclude that the French court's interim orders are facially unconstitutional only by ignoring what they say. The dissent appears to assume that the orders, on their face, require Yahoo! to block access by United States users. It writes, '[T]he question we face in this federal lawsuit is whether our own country's fundamental constitutional guarantee of freedom of speech protects Yahoo! (and, derivatively, at least its users in the United States) against some or all of the restraints the French defendants have deliberately imposed upon it *within the United States*.' (*Id.* at 1234–1235) (emphasis in original). Further, 'Yahoo! confront[s] the dilemma of whether or not to stand by its United States constitutional rights or constrain its speech and that of its user[.]' (*Id.* at 1238.) 'Legions of cases permit First Amendment challenges to governmental actions or decrees that on their face are vague, overbroad and threaten to chill protected speech. Indeed, the sweeping injunction here presents just such a paradigmatic case.' (*Id.* at 1238.) Still further, 'Under the principles articulated today, a foreign party can use a foreign court decree to censor free speech here in the United States[.]' (*Id.* at 1240.)

If it were true that the French court's orders by their terms require Yahoo! to block access by users in the United States, this would be a different and much easier case. In that event, we would be inclined to agree with the dissent. See, e.g., *Sarl Louis Feraud Int'l v. Viewfinder Inc.*, No. 04 Civ. 9760, 2005 WL 2420525 (S.D.N.Y. Sept. 29, 2005) (holding unenforceable as contrary to the First Amendment a French damage judgment based on photographs posted on the Internet freely accessible to American viewers). But this is not the case. The French court's orders, by their terms, require only that Yahoo! restrict access by users in France. The boundary line between what is permitted and not permitted is somewhat uncertain for users in France. But there is no uncertainty about whether the orders apply to access by users in the United States. They do not. They say nothing whatsoever about restricting access by users in the United States.

The dissent's conclusion that the French court's orders are unconstitutional may be based in part on an assumption that a necessary consequence of compliance with the French court's orders will be restricted access by users in the United States. But if this is the basis for the dissent's conclusion, it could hardly say that the orders are unconstitutional 'on their face.' Whether restricted access by users in the United States is a necessary consequence of the French court's orders is a factual question that we cannot answer on the current record.

If the only consequence of compliance with the French court's orders is to restrict access by Internet users in France, Yahoo!'s only argument is that the First Amendment has extraterritorial effect. The dissent fails to acknowledge that this is inescapably a central part of Yahoo!'s argument, let alone acknowledge that it may be Yahoo!'s *only* argument. (. . .)

Conclusion

First Amendment issues arising out of international Internet use are new, important and difficult. We should not rush to decide such issues based on an inadequate, incomplete or unclear record. We should proceed carefully, with awareness of the limitations of our judicial competence, in this undeveloped area of the law. Precisely because of the novelty, importance and difficulty of the First Amendment issues Yahoo! seeks to litigate, we should scrupulously observe the prudential limitations on the exercise of our power.

Yahoo! wants a decision providing broad First Amendment protection for speech and speech-related activities on the Internet that might violate the laws or offend the sensibilities of other countries. As currently framed, however, Yahoo!'s suit comes perilously close to a request for a forbidden advisory opinion. There was a live dispute when Yahoo! first filed suit in federal district court, but Yahoo! soon thereafter voluntarily changed its policy to comply, at least in part, with the commands of the French court's interim orders. This change in policy may or may not have mooted Yahoo!'s federal suit, but it has at least come close. Unless and until Yahoo! changes its policy again, and thereby more clearly violates the French court's orders, it is unclear how much is now actually in dispute.

It is possible that because of Yahoo!'s voluntary change of policy it has now complied 'in large measure' with the French court's orders. It is also possible that Yahoo! has not yet complied 'in large measure.' If further compliance is required, Yahoo! will have to impose further restrictions on access by French users. The necessary consequence of such further restrictions on French users may or may not be that Yahoo! will have to impose restrictions on access by American users. Until we know whether further restrictions on access by French, and possibly American, users are required, we cannot decide whether or to what degree the First Amendment might be violated by enforcement of the French court's orders, and whether such enforcement would be repugnant to California public policy. We do not know whether further restrictions are required, and what they might be, because Yahoo! has chosen not to ask the French court. Instead, it has chosen to come home to ask for a declaratory judgment that the French court's orders – whatever they may or may not require, and whatever First Amendment questions they may or may not present – are unenforceable in the United States. (. . .)

? NOTE

The public policy exception is not a tool for comparing laws in the abstract and for underlying dramatic differences which could potentially be problematic. It is a narrow exception, which should only be used when the foreign judgment actually hurts a fundamental value of the forum. In France, scholars insist that only 'actual' (*concrète*) violations of public policy should be sanctioned. Is it different in California?

CASE

European Court of Human Rights, 20 July 2001 *Pellegrini v. Italy*[26]

Facts: In 1962, Ms M. Pellegrini married Mr A. Gigliozzi in a religious ceremony which was also valid in the eyes of the law. On 23 February 1987, she petitioned the Rome District Court for judicial separation. In 1990, the Italian Court granted her petition and ordered Mr Gigliozzi to pay the applicant maintenance.

In the meantime, on 20 November 1987, Ms Pellegrini was summoned to appear before the Lazio Regional Ecclesiastical Court of the Rome Vicariate on 1 December 1987 'to answer questions in the Gigliozzi-Pellegrini matrimonial case'. On this date, she went alone to the Ecclesiastical Court without knowing why she had been summoned to appear. She was informed that on 6 November 1987 her husband had sought to have the marriage annulled on the ground of consanguinity (her mother and Mr Gigliozzi's father being cousins). She was questioned by the judge and stated that she had known of her consanguineous relationship with Mr Gigliozzi but did not know whether, at the time of her marriage, the priest had requested a special dispensation. In a judgment delivered on 10 December 1987, the Ecclesiastical Court annulled the marriage on the ground of consanguinity. Ms Pellegrini lodged an appeal with a superior Ecclesiastical body, the Roman *Rota*, against the Ecclesiastical Court's judgment, which was eventually dismissed.

The Rota then informed her and her ex-husband that its judgment, which had become enforceable by a decision of the superior ecclesiastical review body, had been referred to the Florence Court of Appeal for a declaration that it could be enforced under Italian law. Ms Pellegrini requested the Florence court to refuse to declare the Rota's judgment enforceable on the ground that her defence rights were infringed in the Vatican proceedings. The Florence Court declared the Vatican judgment enforceable.

Held: Italy violated Article 6 of the European Convention on Human Rights by enforcing the foreign judgment without verifying whether the Vatican proceedings had comported with Article 6. Italy is ordered to pay Ms Pellegrini €5,000, plus costs and expenses.

---

26 App no 30882/96.

Judgment:

I. Alleged Violation of Article 6 § 1 of the Convention

33. The applicant complained of a violation of Article 6 of the Convention on the ground that the Italian courts declared the decision of the ecclesiastical courts annulling her marriage enforceable at the end of proceedings in which her defence rights had been breached.

34. The relevant part of Article 6 of the Convention provides:

> 1. In the determination of his civil rights and obligations . . . everyone is entitled to a fair . . . hearing . . . by . . . court . . .

35. The applicant submitted that, in proceedings under canon law, the respondent is not informed before being questioned by the court either of the identity of the petitioner or of the grounds on which they allege that the marriage should be annulled. The respondent is not informed of the possibility of securing the assistance of a defence lawyer (a possibility which some legal writers, moreover, claim does not exist) or of requesting copies of the case file. Consequently, their defence rights are greatly reduced. In the instant case the applicant was not informed in advance of the reasons for summoning her to appear; nor was she informed of the possibility of instructing a lawyer, either on the summons to appear or when being questioned. She was thus prevented from making a properly considered answer to her ex-husband's requests. She could, for example, have not attended for questioning or have chosen not to reply. Furthermore, without the assistance of a lawyer, she had been intimidated by the fact that the judge was a religious figure.

36. The applicant's defence rights were therefore irremediably compromised after she had appeared before the Ecclesiastical Court and the Italian courts should have refused to ratify the result of such unfair proceedings instead of confining themselves to asserting – without examining the matter thoroughly – that the proceedings before the ecclesiastical courts had been adversarial and fair. (. . .)

40. The Court notes at the outset that the applicant's marriage was annulled by a decision of the Vatican courts which was declared enforceable by the Italian courts. The Vatican has not ratified the Convention and, furthermore, the application was lodged against Italy. The Court's task therefore consists not in examining whether the proceedings before the ecclesiastical courts complied with Article 6 of the Convention, but whether the Italian courts, before authorising enforcement of the decision annulling the marriage, duly satisfied themselves that the relevant proceedings fulfilled the guarantees of Article 6. A review of that kind is required where a decision in respect of which enforcement is requested emanates from the courts of a country which does not apply the Convention. Such a review is

especially necessary where the implications of a declaration of enforceability are of capital importance for the parties.

41. The Court must examine the reasons given by the Florence Court of Appeal and the Court of Cassation for dismissing the applicant's complaints about the proceedings before the ecclesiastical courts.

42. The applicant had complained of an infringement of the adversarial principle. She had not been informed in detail of her ex-husband's application to have the marriage annulled and had not had access to the case file. She was therefore unaware, in particular, of the contents of the statements made by the three witnesses who had apparently given evidence in favour of her ex-husband and of the observations of the defensor vinculis. Furthermore, she was not assisted by a lawyer.

43. The Florence Court of Appeal held that the circumstances in which the applicant had appeared before the Ecclesiastical Court and the fact that she had subsequently lodged an appeal against that court's judgment were sufficient to conclude that she had had the benefit of an adversarial trial. The Court of Cassation held that, in the main, ecclesiastical court proceedings complied with the adversarial principle.

44. The Court is not satisfied by these reasons. The Italian courts do not appear to have attached importance to the fact that the applicant had not had the possibility of examining the evidence produced by her ex-husband and by the 'so-called witnesses'. However, the Court reiterates in that connection that the right to adversarial proceedings, which is one of the elements of a fair hearing within the meaning of Article 6 § 1, means that each party to a trial, be it criminal or civil, must in principle have the opportunity to have knowledge of and comment on all evidence adduced or observations filed with a view to influencing the court's decision . . .

45. It is irrelevant that, in the Government's opinion, as the nullity of the marriage derived from an objective and undisputed fact the applicant would not in any event have been able to challenge it. It is for the parties to a dispute alone to decide whether a document produced by the other party or by witnesses calls for their comments. What is particularly at stake here is litigants' confidence in the workings of justice, which is based on, inter alia, the knowledge that they have had the opportunity to express their views on every document in the file . . .

46. The position is no different with regard to the assistance of a lawyer. Since such assistance was possible, according to the Court of Cassation, even in the context of the summary procedure before the Ecclesiastical Court, the applicant should have been put in a position enabling her to secure the assistance of a lawyer if she wished. The Court is not satisfied by the Court of Cassation's argument that the applicant should have been familiar with the case-law on the subject: the ecclesiastical courts could have presumed that the applicant, who

was not assisted by a lawyer, was unaware of that case-law. In the Court's opinion, given that the applicant had been summoned to appear before the Ecclesiastical Court without knowing what the case was about, that court had a duty to inform her that she could seek the assistance of a lawyer before she attended for questioning.

47. In these circumstances the Court considers that the Italian courts breached their duty of satisfying themselves, before authorising enforcement of the Roman Rota's judgment, that the applicant had had a fair trial in the proceedings under canon law.

48. There has therefore been a violation of Article 6 § 1 of the Convention. (. . .)

 NOTES AND QUESTIONS

1 As public policy is constituted of the fundamental values of the forum, it was only logical that fundamental rights afforded by constitutions or autonomous charters of fundamental rights would become its essential source. Conversely, violations of public policy will often amount to violations of human rights and thus trigger remedies available under human rights law. In *Pellegrini*, the applicant sought remedies under European human rights law: the declaration that Italy had violated the European Convention, and an award in damages. However, the European Court of Human Rights did not have the power to set aside any national judgment, or to declare the Vatican judgment unenforceable in Italy. It can be predicted that Italian courts, and indeed the courts of all European States will take notice of the *Pellegrini* decision and will verify that foreign judgments comport with human rights before declaring them enforceable, but they are not legally bound to do so.

2 The Vatican is not a party to the European Convention on Human Rights, and it has thus no obligation to respect the rights that it affords. This makes a review of the compatibility of judgments rendered by Vatican courts with Convention rights meaningful. Is it different for judgments originating from other contracting States? Should there simply be no review of judgments coming from sister states? See infra Ch. 7.

3 As the *Pellegrini* case shows, public policy does not only consist of substantive values such as the freedom of expression or non-discrimination on sexual grounds (see below), but also in procedural fundamental values. It is traditional to distinguish between substantive and proce-dural public policy.

Gilles Cuniberti, The Liberalization of the French Law of Foreign Judgments[27]

The origin of the modern French law on the recognition and enforcement of judg-ments is the 1964 *Munzer* decision. In *Munzer v. Munzer*, the *Cour de cassation* abandoned the 150-year-old judicial practice of *révision au fond*. The *révision au fond* was the power of French courts to recognize foreign judgments on condition that such judgments were right on the merits. In other words, French courts could verify whether the foreign court had properly assessed the facts and properly

---

27 (2007) 56 ICLQ 931, 932–3.

applied the law. In *Munzer*, the *Cour de cassation* held that *révision au fond* was prohibited. French courts could not anymore assess whether foreign judgments were right in order to declare them enforceable in France. Instead, they would have to verify whether they met a number of newly laid-down conditions. The French law of judgments was moving into a new era. In theory at least, it was accepted that it was no longer a condition that foreign judgments be the same as French judgments to be recognized in France. Foreign judgments would be truly recognized as such, i.e. judgments made by a foreign court, and thus potentially different.

Since *Munzer*, the *Cour de cassation* and French commentators have been discussing what the conditions of the recognition of foreign judgments should be. In *Munzer*, the *Cour de cassation* held that the newly laid-down conditions would suffice to 'ensure the protection of the French legal order and interests'. This is the tension of the modern law of judgments: being open to foreign legal and judicial cultures, but only to the extent that the French legal order is not hurt.

The *Cour de cassation* initially laid down five conditions. First, the foreign court ought to have jurisdiction to hear the dispute. Secondly, the foreign court ought to have properly applied its rules of procedure. Thirdly, the foreign court ought to have applied the law that the French choice-of-law rule would have designated. Fourthly, the foreign judgment should not be contrary to public policy. Fifthly, the foreign judgment should not have been obtained for the sole purpose of avoiding the application of the applicable law (*fraude à la loi*). These conditions were soon reduced to four. Three years after *Munzer*, in *Bachir v. Bachir* [1968], the *Cour de cassation* dropped the second condition. It held that the procedure followed by the foreign court could only be appreciated through the condition of public policy. If the initial idea had been that the forum could generally verify that the foreign court had properly applied its own rules of procedure, it quickly became clear that such a condition did not make sense. In practice, this was giving the power to French courts to criticize the application made by foreign judges of their own law. In theory, this was allowing them to revise the foreign judgment. This was not exactly *revision au fond*, since the revision would have been conducted in the light of the foreign law, but it was arguably much worse. It was not consistent with the liberal turn of the French law of judgments.

The new paradigm is best illustrated by the condition of public policy. In principle, French law now accepts that foreign judgments can be recognized irrespective of whether a French court would have reached the same solution if it had decided the dispute. French courts will not verify whether the foreign court assessed the facts properly. They will not verify either whether they applied the law properly, be it its rules of procedure or the *lex causae*. It is accepted that the foreign judgment can be different, as it is the product of a different legal culture. Yet, there is a limit to the acceptance of the differences of foreign legal cultures. If a foreign solution or practice is not only different but shocking to a French lawyer, it will be held as contrary to French public policy. In 40 years, the *Cour de cassation* has shown a remarkable openness to foreign legal cultures. The public policy condition has been interpreted narrowly. It is mainly used in family law to deny recognition to North African Islamic divorces, which are held to be contrary to the principle of equality between men and women. It is also sometimes used in civil procedure. But in other fields such as commercial law, it is simply never used. It is easy to understand why. One can imagine how a foreign legal order could have different rules of commercial law, but not really truly shocking ones, except in the most extreme instances. (. . .)

 CASE

Cour of Cassation, 23 October 2013 Case no 12-21344

Facts: M. Abdelhak X . . . and Mme Fairouz Y . . . who were both Algerian nationals, married in Algeria where they first lived together before moving to France where their two last children were born. In 2005, the husband applied to an Algerian court for termination of the marriage under Article 48 of the Algerian Family Code, which was granted. In 2010, as the wife sought divorce in France, the husband relied on the *res judicata* effect of the Algerian decision to request that the French proceedings be dismissed.

Held: the recognition of the 2005 Algerian judgment is denied for violation of French public policy.

Judgment:

(. . .) Whereas, under Article 1, d), of the Franco-Algerian Convention of 27 August 1964, judgments rendered by Algerian courts are *res judicata* only if they do not violate public policy and, under Article 5 of Protocol of 22 November 1984 No. 7 to the Convention for the Protection of Human Rights and Fundamental Freedoms, spouses shall enjoy equality of rights and responsibilities in the dissolution of marriage.

Whereas, in order to rule that the Algerian judgment did not violate the French conception of international public order, the Court of Appeal of Orléans first insisted that the wife had been duly called to the conciliation hearing. It then explained that the Algerian Family Code provides for three different divorce procedures: the first may be initiated by the husband, the second may be initiated jointly by the spouses, and the third may be initiated by the wife where a fault was committed or where there is a persisting disagreement between the spouses. The Court concluded that as the wife was entitled to initiate divorce proceedings and to present her case under Algerian law, she had not suffered a sexual discrimination in the Algerian proceedings.

Whereas, by ruling as it did, the Court of appeal violated the above mentioned provisions on the grounds that the Algerian judgment rendered under Article 48 of the Algerian Family Code (which was left untouched by the 2005 reform) was the result of a unilateral and discretionary repudiation based on the sole will of the husband, for reasons that he was neither required to give, nor to justify; the wife might have been duly called in the proceedings, but her opposition to the claim would be irrelevant and could not produce any legal effect; as the domicile of the wife was in France, the Algerian judgment thus violated the principle of equality of spouses in the dissolution of marriage, irrespective of the right of the wife to initiate proceedings herself.

On these grounds: the judgment of the Court of Appeal of Orléans is set aside.

Belgian Code of Private International Law (2004)
Article 57. *Foreign divorce based on the will of the husband*
§ 1. A foreign deed establishing the intent of the husband to dissolve the marriage without the wife having the same right cannot be recognized in Belgium.
§ 2. Such deed can however be recognized in Belgium after verifying whether the following cumulative conditions are satisfied:

1   the deed has been sanctioned by a judge in the State of origin,
2   neither of the spouses had at the time of the certification the nationality of a State of which the law does not know this manner of dissolution of the marriage;
3   neither of the spouses had at the time of the certification their habitual residence in a State of which the law does not know this manner of dissolution of the marriage;
4   the wife has accepted the dissolution in an unambiguous manner and without any coercion.
5   none of the grounds of refusal provided for in article 25 prohibits the recognition.

NOTES AND QUESTIONS

1 France has concluded a number of bilateral conventions mandating the recognition and enforcement of foreign judgments with its former colonies. These conventions, however, typically maintain a public order exception which expressly refers to the national conception of public order of the enforcing state. In other words, these conventions are essentially transparent.

2 The two most important immigrant communities in France in the last decades have been Moroccans and Algerians. When Algerian or Moroccan couples living in France divorce, husbands are tempted to travel back to their country of origin to seek an Islamic divorce which they are entitled to obtain. They then seek its recognition in France in order to terminate divorce proceedings initiated by their wives. As France recognizes nationality as the connecting factor in family matters,[28] it can barely criticize an Algerian party for seeking a remedy in Algeria in a family dispute. The French supreme court has thus relied on the public policy exception. In the first cases, husbands did not even care for calling their wives in the foreign proceedings: after all, they were entitled to divorce under Islamic law, and wives had no say in the procedure. From the French perspective, this made the cases easy, as French courts could simply underline the breach of a fundamental procedural right of the wife and rule that the foreign judgment violated French procedural public order.

Husbands changed strategies and began calling their wives in the foreign proceedings. This compelled the French Supreme Court to change its own strategy and to open the door of the assessment of the compatibility of Islamic substantive law with fundamental rights. As there are several schools in Islamic law, and as States might have adopted laws which were only inspired from religion, the French Supreme Court had to identify which particular features of Islamic divorce law are unacceptable and thus repugnant to French public policy. Can you summarize these features after reading the judgment above? Has the Belgian lawmaker identified the same features?

3 This exercise of assessing the compatibility of Islamic divorce law to fundamental rights was carried out by the French court alone, without outside influences. In order to legitimize its ruling, the court has long relied on a particular provision of European human rights law. But this is not to say that it felt bound to do so as a consequence of some ruling of the European Court of Human Rights. The reference to the European norm only aims at increasing the legitimacy of its decision.

4 The French Supreme Court limits the application of the public policy exception to cases where both parties, or at least wives, live in France. What about Art. 57 of the Belgian Code? As in choice of law,[29] the infringement of public policy can be considered more severe when the dispute has a strong connection to France. Conversely, when such connection is absent, it can appear unnecessary and disruptive to deny recognition to a foreign judgment which will in any case govern the rights and duties of the parties in their country of origin.

---

28 *Infra*, Part VI.
29 *Supra*, p. 141.

2.3   Other requirements

National statutes typically afford additional grounds for denying recognition and enforcement to foreign judgments.

A common requirement is that the foreign judgment would not conflict with an existing judgment in the forum. The purpose of this requirement is to avoid contradictory judgments coexisting in the same legal order and giving opposite commands to the parties and enforcement authorities. Such requirement is found in the laws of the many U.S. states (over 30) which have adopted the 1962 *Uniform Foreign Money Judgments Recognition Act* (Section 4(b)(4)), as well as in the German and Italian provisions on foreign judgments.[30] Under French or Japanese law, the requirement is not autonomous, and a foreign judgment conflicting with an existing judgment in the forum would be found to violate public policy.

Many national statutes also insist on certain specific violations of the fundamental rights of the defendant. The most common one is lack of notice of the proceedings in sufficient time to enable the defendant to defend, which is found in the *Uniform Foreign Money Judgments Recognition Act* (Section 4(b)(1)) and in the national laws of Japan and several European States.[31] Other States consider that the general public policy exception suffices to sanction such violations.

Common law jurisdictions typically afford a special ground for denying recognition to judgments obtained by fraud.[32] In this context, fraud does not mean evasion of the law (*fraude*), but rather any act whereby one of the parties misleads or deceives the foreign court, for instance by bribing a witness.

Finally, a few states have a reciprocity requirement, and would only recognize judgments originating from states which recognize their own judgments.[33] This is the most important requirement in the Chinese law of foreign

---

30 See § 328(1)3 of the German Code of Civil Procedure (ZPO), Art. 64(e) of the Italian 1995 Private International Law Act.

31 See Art. 118(2) of the Japanese Code of Civil Procedure, Art. 64(e) of the Italian 1995 Private International Law Act. See also § 328(1)2 of the German Code of Civil Procedure (ZPO), which only applies if the defendant did not enter into appearance.

32 In the U.S., see Section 4(b)(2) of the 1962 Uniform Foreign Money Judgments Recognition Act. In England, see *Jet Holdings Inc. v. Patel* [1990] 1 QB 335.

33 See Art. 118(4) of the Japanese Code of Civil Procedure, § 328(1)5 of the German Code of Civil Procedure (ZPO). The requirement is also found in a few U.S. states (Massachusetts and Texas, for instance).

judgments,[34] and judgments originating from the United States, Japan, Germany or England have been denied recognition on the ground that there is no reciprocal relationship with China.[35]

---

34 See Art. 281 of the Civil Procedure Law 1991.

35 See Wenliang Zhang, 'Recognition of Foreign Judgments in China: The Essentials and Strategies' (2013–2014) 15 Yearbook Pr. Int. L. 319. An exception exists for divorce judgments involving Chinese citizens, which are routinely recognized in China: see Regulation of the Supreme People's Court of Procedural Issues on Chinese Citizen's Applications for the Recognition of Foreign Divorce Judgments of 5 July 1991.

7

Sister states judgments

In many parts of the world, groups of sovereign States have joined together to form a common entity to which they have transferred parts of their sovereignty. In North America, the 13 original colonies established a federal State, the United States of America, in 1776. In Europe, the six original Member States established several international organizations in 1958 (the most famous of which being the European Economic Communities) which eventually became the European Union.

A central project common to all such organizations of states is that judgments made by the courts of one member of the organization should easily circulate in other states of the organization. One important reason is that, by joining the organization, members accept that they have a common destiny. They also agree to share common values, which are typically expressed in documents binding on all members such as the U.S. Constitution, the Charter of Fundamental Rights of the European Union or the European Convention on Human Rights. States members of such organizations accept, thus, that other members are not truly foreign. They are, in American parlance, *sister states*. They should therefore be trusted, and their judgments recognised.

1   Faith and trust in sister states

Both in the United States and in the European Union, the principle is that judgments of sister states should be recognized and enforced. This is mandated by federal law in the United States, and by E.U. law in the European Union.

CASE

U.S. Supreme Court, 13 January 1998 *Baker v. General Motors Corp.*[1]

JUSTICE GINSBURG.

(. . .) The Constitution's Full Faith and Credit Clause provides:

> Full Faith and Credit shall be given in each State to the public Acts, Records, and judicial Proceedings of every other State. And the Congress may by general Laws prescribe the Manner in which such Acts, Records and Proceedings shall be proved, and the Effect thereof. Art. IV; § 1.3

Pursuant to that Clause, Congress has prescribed:

> Such Acts, records and judicial proceedings or copies thereof, so authenticated, shall have the same full faith and credit in every court within the United States and its Territories and Possessions as they have by law or usage in the courts of such State, Territory or Possession from which they are taken. 28 U. S. C. § 1738.4

The animating purpose of the full faith and credit command, as this Court explained in *Milwaukee County* v. *M. E. White Co.*, 296 U. S. 268 (1935),

> was to alter the status of the several states as independent foreign sovereignties, each free to ignore obligations created under the laws or by the judicial proceedings of the others, and to make them integral parts of a single nation throughout which a remedy upon a just obligation might be demanded as of right, irrespective of the state of its origin. *Id.*, at 277.

See also *Estin* v. *Estin*, 334 U. S. 541, 546 (1948) (the Full Faith and Credit Clause 'substituted a command for the earlier principles of comity and thus basically altered the status of the States as independent sovereigns').

Our precedent differentiates the credit owed to laws (legislative measures and common law) and to judgments. 'In numerous cases this Court has held that credit must be given to the judgment of another state although the forum would not be required to entertain the suit on which the judgment was founded.' *Milwaukee County*, at 277. The Full Faith and Credit Clause does not compel 'a state to substitute the statutes of other states for its own statutes dealing with a

---

1 522 U.S. 222 (1998).

subject matter concerning which it is competent to legislate.' *Pacific Employers Ins. Co. v. Industrial Accident Comm'n*, 306 U.S. 493, 501 (1939); see *Phillips Petroleum Co. v. Shutts*, 472 U.S. 797, 818–819 (1985). Regarding judgments, however, the full faith and credit obligation is exacting. A final judgment in one State, if rendered by a court with adjudicatory authority over the subject matter and persons governed by the judgment, qualifies for recognition throughout the land. For claim and issue preclusion (res judicata) purposes, in other words, the judgment of the rendering State gains nationwide force. (. . .)

European Regulation (EU) No 1215/2012 of 12 December 2012 on jurisdiction and on the enforcement and recognition of judgments in civil and commercial matters (Brussels Ibis)

PREAMBLE

(26) Mutual trust in the administration of justice in the Union justifies the principle that judgments given in a Member State should be recognised in all Member States without the need for any special procedure. In addition, the aim of making cross-border litigation less time-consuming and costly justifies the abolition of the declaration of enforceability prior to enforcement in the Member State addressed. As a result, a judgment given by the courts of a Member State should be treated as if it had been given in the Member State addressed.

(27) For the purposes of the free circulation of judgments, a judgment given in a Member State should be recognised and enforced in another Member State even if it is given against a person not domiciled in a Member State. (. . .)

CHAPTER III RECOGNITION AND ENFORCEMENT

Section 1 Recognition

Article 36

1. A judgment given in a Member State shall be recognised in the other Member States without any special procedure being required.

2. Any interested party may, in accordance with the procedure provided for in Subsection 2 of Section 3, apply for a decision that there are no grounds for refusal of recognition as referred to in Article 45.

3. If the outcome of proceedings in a court of a Member State depends on the determination of an incidental question of refusal of recognition, that court shall have jurisdiction over that question.

Section 2 Enforcement

Article 39

A judgment given in a Member State which is enforceable in that Member State shall be enforceable in the other Member States without any declaration of enforceability being required.

? NOTES

1 In the United States, the obligation to recognize judgments rendered by the courts of sister states is mandated by an original clause of the U.S. Constitution. It thus has the highest authority, and has existed since the creation of the American Republic.

The language of the Full Faith and Credit Clause is general, and the scope of the obligation is not limited to certain fields of the law. The only exception is workers' compensation. In *Thomas v. Washington Gas Light Co.*,[2] the U.S. Supreme Court held that the decision of a Virginia tribunal granting compensation to a worker did not prevent a tribunal in another state from granting a supplemental compensation award to the same worker, and that it would be an unnecessary aggressive application of the Full Faith and Credit Clause to rule otherwise.

2 In the European Union, by contrast, the obligation was never found in any of the founding treaties, let alone in the original 1958 Rome treaties. Originally, the Member States had not granted competence to the European Communities to legislate in the field, but rather planned to conclude an international convention for that purpose. This is the reason why the obligation was first laid down 10 years after the beginning of European integration, when the Member States entered into the 1968 Brussels Convention on Jurisdiction and on the enforcement and recognition of judgments in civil and commercial matters. The Brussels Convention was to be eventually replaced by a European Regulation after the European Union was eventually granted the competence to legislate in the field in 1999 (today, the 'Brussels Ibis Regulation'). While the new Regulation did not impact significantly the grounds for denying recognition and enforcement to sister states judgments (see *infra*, 2), it has abolished the need for any prior procedure to declare them enforceable in other Member States (*exequatur*).

Another important difference with the United States is that the scope of the obligation to recognize and enforce sister states judgments has developed gradually in Europe. In 1968, it was limited to certain 'civil and commercial matters' which excluded insolvency and family matters.[3] In 2000, it was extended to insolvency[4] and, in 2003, to matrimonial matters and parental responsibility.[5] In 2015, it was extended to succession matters[6] and it is planed that it also will in matrimonial property matters.

3 Remarkably, the obligation to recognize sister states' judgments in Europe is not limited to Member States of the European Union. It extends to three European States (Iceland, Norway, Switzerland) which did not want to join the European Union, but were interested in benefiting from a simplified mechanism of recognition of judgments. This was achieved by having the European Union conclude an international convention mirroring the 2000 Brussels I Regulation with those three States.[7] The same grounds for denying recognition to foreign judgments apply. From a procedural perspective, however, a prior review procedure is still

---

2 448 U.S. 261 (1980).

3 Except maintenance. The recognition of judgments in the field of maintenance obligations is now governed by EC Regulation No 4/2009 of 18 December 2008 on jurisdiction, applicable law, recognition and enforcement of decisions and cooperations in matters relating to maintenance obligations.

4 Today, EC Regulation No. 2015/848 of 20 May 2015 on Insolvency Proceedings.

5 EC Regulation No. 2201/2003 of 27 November 2003 concerning jurisdiction and the recognition and enforcement of judgments in matrimonial matters and the matters of parental responsibility.

6 EC Regulation No. 650/2012 of 4 July 2012 on jurisdiction, applicable law, recognition and enforcement of decisions and acceptance and enforcement of authentic instruments in matters of succession and on the creation of a European Certificate of Succession.

7 Lugano Convention on jurisdiction and the recognition and enforcement of judgments in civil and commercial matters of 30 October 2007.

necessary to declare enforceable (as opposed to recognize) foreign judgments in other participating States.

It is interesting to note that the result is to consider States which are not members of the European Union as sister states. One reason is that these States share many values with the members of the European Union, since they are all parties to the European Convention on Human Rights.

2 Requirements for recognition of sister states' judgments

The essential consequence of the faith or trust in sister states is that their judgments should be easily recognized and enforced. Requirements for recognition are thus much more limited than for judgments originating from foreign nations.

2.1 Jurisdiction of the sister state's court

Please read the following cases and assess the extent to which the requirement that the foreign court has jurisdiction remains where the judgment originates from a sister state.

 CASE

U.S. Supreme Court, 2 December 1963 *Durfee v. Duke*[8]

Facts: In 1956, Durfee brought an action in a Nebraska court to contest ownership of a piece of land situated along the Missouri River on the Nebraska and Missouri border. Duke appeared in the Nebraska court and through counsel fully litigated the issues, explicitly contesting the court's jurisdiction on the ground that the land in question was not located in Nebraska. The court ruled that the land was in Nebraska and that Durfee was the owner. Two months later, Duke filed suit in Missouri, alleging that the land was in Missouri and seeking a judgment that she held title to the same land. The District Court found that the land was in Missouri, but that the Nebraska judgment was res judicata and precluded relitigation of the same issues. The Court of Appeals reversed, ruling that the full faith and credit principle did not apply in a controversy involving land. Durfee appealed to the Supreme Court.

Held: The judgment of the Nebraska Court was res judicata in Missouri and the issue could not be relitigated there. A judgment is entitled to full faith and credit, for res judicata purposes, even as to questions of jurisdiction, where the second court's inquiry disclosed that those questions have been fairly and fully litigated and finally decided in the court which rendered the original judgment.

---

8 375 U.S. 106 (1963).

JUSTICE STEWART.

(. . .) Full faith and credit thus generally requires every State to give to a judgment at least the res judicata effect which the judgment would be accorded in the State which rendered it. (. . .)

(. . .) the respondent relies upon the many decisions of this Court which have held that a judgment of a court in one State is conclusive upon the merits in a court in another State only if the court in the first State had power to pass on the merits – had jurisdiction, that is, to render the judgment. As Mr. Justice Bradley stated the doctrine in the leading case of *Thompson v. Whitman*, 18 Wall. 457, 'we think it clear that the jurisdiction of the court by which a judgment is rendered in any State may be questioned in a collateral proceeding in another State, notwithstanding the provision of the fourth article of the Constitution and the law of 1790, and notwithstanding the averments contained in the record of the judgment itself.' 18 Wall., at 469. The principle has been restated and applied in a variety of contexts.

However, while it is established that a court in one State, when asked to give effect to the judgment of a court in another State, may constitutionally inquire into the foreign court's jurisdiction to render that judgment, the modern decisions of this Court have carefully delineated the permissible scope of such an inquiry. From these decisions there emerges the general rule that a judgment is entitled to full faith and credit – even as to questions of jurisdiction – when the second court's inquiry discloses that those questions have been fully and fairly litigated and finally decided in the court which rendered the original judgment.

With respect to questions of jurisdiction over the person, this principle was unambiguously established in *Baldwin v. Iowa State Traveling Men's Assn.*, 283 U.S. 522. There it was held that a federal court in Iowa must give binding effect to the judgment of a federal court in Missouri despite the claim that the original court did not have jurisdiction over the defendant's person, once it was shown to the court in Iowa that that question had been fully litigated in the Missouri forum. 'Public policy,' said the Court, 'dictates that there be an end of litigation; that those who have contested an issue shall be bound by the result of the contest, and that matters once tried shall be considered forever settled as between the parties. We see no reason why this doctrine should not apply in every case where one voluntarily appears, presents his case and is fully heard, and why he should not, in the absence of fraud, be thereafter concluded by the judgment of the tribunal to which he has submitted his cause.' 283 U.S., at 525–526.

Following the *Baldwin* case, this Court soon made clear in a series of decisions that the general rule is no different when the claim is made that the original forum did not have jurisdiction over the subject matter. (. . .) In each of these cases the claim was made that a court, when asked to enforce the judgment of another forum, was free to retry the question of that forum's jurisdiction over the subject matter. In each case this Court held that since the question of subject-matter jurisdiction had been fully litigated in the original forum, the issue could not be retried in a subsequent action between the parties. (. . .)

The reasons for such a rule are apparent. In the words of the Court's opinion in *Stoll v. Gottlieb*,

> We see no reason why a court, in the absence of an allegation of fraud in obtaining the judgment, should examine again the question whether the court making the earlier determination on an actual contest over jurisdiction between the parties, did have jurisdiction of the subject matter of the litigation . . . Courts to determine the rights of parties are an integral part of our system of government. It is just as important that there should be a place to end as that there should be a place to begin litigation. After a party has his day in court, with opportunity to present his evidence and his view of the law, a collateral attack upon the decision as to jurisdiction there rendered merely retries the issue previously determined. There is no reason to expect that the second decision will be more satisfactory than the first.

(. . .)

It is argued that an exception to this rule of jurisdictional finality should be made with respect to cases involving real property because of this Court's emphatic expressions of the doctrine that courts of one State are completely without jurisdiction directly to affect title to land in other States. This argument is wide of the mark. Courts of one State are equally without jurisdiction to dissolve the marriages of those domiciled in other States. But the location of land, like the domicile of a party to a divorce action, is a matter 'to be resolved by judicial determination.' *Sherrer v. Sherrer*, 334 U.S., at 349. The question remains whether, once the matter has been fully litigated and judicially determined, it can be retried in another State in litigation between the same parties. Upon the reason and authority of the cases we have discussed, it is clear that the answer must be in the negative.

It is to be emphasized that all that was ultimately determined in the Nebraska litigation was title to the land in question as between the parties to the litigation there. Nothing there decided, and nothing that could be decided in litigation between the same parties or their privies in Missouri, could bind either Missouri or Nebraska with respect to any controversy they might have, now or in the future, as to the location of the boundary between them, or as to their respective sovereignty over the land in question. Either State may at any time protect its interest by initiating independent judicial proceedings here.

For the reasons stated, we hold in this case that the federal court in Missouri had the power and, upon proper averments, the duty to inquire into the jurisdiction of the Nebraska courts to render the decree quieting title to the land in the petitioners. We further hold that when that inquiry disclosed, as it did, that the jurisdictional issues had been fully and fairly litigated by the parties and finally determined in the Nebraska courts, the federal court in Missouri was correct in ruling that further inquiry was precluded.

Brussels Ibis Regulation (2012)
CHAPTER III RECOGNITION AND ENFORCEMENT

Section 3 Refusal of recognition and enforcement

Sub section 1 Refusal of recognition

Article 45

1. On the application of any interested party, the recognition of a judgment shall be refused:

(...)

(e) if the judgment conflicts with:

(i)   Sections 3, 4 or 5 of Chapter II where the policyholder, the insured, a beneficiary of the insurance contract, the injured party, the consumer or the employee was the defendant; or

(ii) Section 6 of Chapter II. See *supra*, p. 182.

2. In its examination of the grounds of jurisdiction referred to in point (e) of paragraph 1, the court to which the application was submitted shall be bound by the findings of fact on which the court of origin based its jurisdiction.

3. Without prejudice to point (e) of paragraph 1, the jurisdiction of the court of origin may not be reviewed. The test of public policy referred to in point (a) of paragraph 1 may not be applied to the rules relating to jurisdiction.

4. The application for refusal of recognition shall be made in accordance with the procedures provided for in Subsection 2 and, where appropriate, Section 4.

Sub section 2 Refusal of enforcement

Article 46

On the application of the person against whom enforcement is sought, the enforcement of a judgment shall be refused where one of the grounds referred to in Article 45 is found to exist.

 CASE

European Court of Justice, 28 March 2000 *Dieter Krombach v. André Bamberski* (Case C-7/98)[9]

Facts: Mr Krombach was the subject of a preliminary investigation in Germany following the death in Germany of a 14-year-old girl of French nationality. That preliminary investigation was subsequently discontinued. In response to a complaint by Mr Bamberski, the father of the young girl, a preliminary investigation was then opened in France, the French courts declaring that they had jurisdiction by virtue of the fact that the victim was a French national. At the conclusion of that investigation, Mr Krombach was committed for trial before the Cour d'Assises de Paris. That judgment and notice of the introduction of a civil claim by the victim's father were served on Mr Krombach. Although Mr Krombach was ordered to appear in person, he did not attend the hearing. The Cour d'Assises de Paris thereupon applied the contempt procedure governed by Article 627 et seq. of the French Code of Criminal Procedure. Pursuant to Article 630 of that Code, under which no defence counsel may appear on behalf of the person in contempt, the Cour d'Assises reached its decision without hearing the defence counsel instructed by Mr Krombach and sentenced him to 15 years imprisonment after finding him guilty of violence resulting in involuntary manslaughter. By judgment of 13 March 1995, the Cour d'Assises, ruling on the civil claim, ordered Mr Krombach, again as being in contempt, to pay compensation to Mr Bamberski in the amount of FRF 350,000. Mr Bamberski sought to enforce the French civil judgment in Germany.

Held: While German courts may not review French courts' jurisdiction, the civil judgment is contrary to public policy for refusing to allow the defendant to have his defence presented unless he appeared in person.

Judgment:

Preliminary observations

18 By its questions, the national court is essentially asking the Court how the term public policy in the State in which recognition is sought in point 1 of Article 27 of the Convention should be interpreted.

19 The Convention is intended to facilitate, to the greatest possible extent, the

---

9 ECLI:EU:C:2000:164, [2000] E.C.R. I-01935.

free movement of judgments by providing for a simple and rapid enforcement procedure (see, inter alia, Case C-414/92 *Solo Kleinmotoren v. Boch* [1994] ECR I-2237, paragraph 20, and . . .).

20 It follows from the Court's case-law that this procedure constitutes an autonomous and complete system independent of the legal systems of the Contracting States and that the principle of legal certainty in the Community legal system and the objectives of the Convention in accordance with Article 220 of the EC Treaty (now Article 293 EC), on which it is founded, require a uniform application in all Contracting States of the Convention rules and the relevant case-law of the Court (see, in particular, Case C-432/93 *SISRO v. Ampersand* [1995] ECR I-2269, paragraph 39).

21 So far as Article 27 of the Convention [*now art. 45*] is concerned, the Court has held that this provision must be interpreted strictly inasmuch as it constitutes an obstacle to the attainment of one of the fundamental objectives of the Convention (*Solo Kleinmotoren*, cited above, paragraph 20). With regard, more specifically, to recourse to the public-policy clause in Article 27, point 1, of the Convention, the Court has made it clear that such recourse is to be had only in exceptional cases (Case 145/86 *Hoffmann v. Krieg* [1988] ECR 645, paragraph 21 . . .).

22 It follows that, while the Contracting States in principle remain free, by virtue of the proviso in Article 27, point 1, of the Convention, to determine, according to their own conceptions, what public policy requires, the limits of that concept are a matter for interpretation of the Convention.

23 Consequently, while it is not for the Court to define the content of the public policy of a Contracting State, it is none the less required to review the limits within which the courts of a Contracting State may have recourse to that concept for the purpose of refusing recognition to a judgment emanating from a court in another Contracting State.

24 It should be noted in this regard that, since the Convention was concluded on the basis of Article 220 of the Treaty and within the framework which it defines, its provisions are linked to the Treaty (Case C-398/92 *Mund & Fester v. Hatrex Internationaal Transport* [1994] ECR I-467, paragraph 12).

25 The Court has consistently held that fundamental rights form an integral part of the general principles of law whose observance the Court ensures (see, in particular, Opinion 2/94 [1996] ECR I-1759, paragraph 33). For that purpose, the Court draws inspiration from the constitutional traditions common to the Member States and from the guidelines supplied by international treaties for the protection of human rights on which the Member States have collaborated or of which they are signatories. In that regard, the European Convention for the Protection of Human Rights and Fundamental Freedoms (hereinafter the ECHR) has particular significance (see, inter alia, Case 222/84 *Johnston v. Chief Constable of the Royal Ulster Constabulary* [1986] ECR 1651, paragraph 18).

26 The Court has thus expressly recognised the general principle of Community law that everyone is entitled to fair legal process, which is inspired by those fundamental rights (Case C-185/95 P *Baustahlgewebe v. Commission* [1998] ECR I-8417, paragraphs 20 and 21, and judgment of 11 January 2000 in Joined Cases C-174/98 P and C-189/98 P *Netherlands and Van der Wal v. Commission* [2000] ECR I-0000, paragraph 17).

27 Article F(2) of the Treaty on European Union (now, after amendment, Article 6(2) EU) embodies that case-law. It provides: The Union shall respect fundamental rights, as guaranteed by the European Convention for the Protection of Human Rights and Fundamental Freedoms signed in Rome on 4 November 1950 and as they result from the constitutional traditions common to the Member States, as general principles of Community law.

28 It is in the light of those considerations that the questions submitted for a preliminary ruling fail to be answered.

The first question

29 By this question, the national court is essentially asking whether, regard being had to the public-policy clause contained in Article 27, point 1, of the Convention, the court of the State in which enforcement is sought can, with respect to a defendant domiciled in that State, take into account the fact that the court of the State of origin based its jurisdiction on the nationality of the victim of an offence.

30 It should be noted at the outset that it follows from the specific terms of the first paragraph of Article 1 of the Convention that the Convention applies to decisions given in civil matters by a criminal court (Case C-172/91 *Sonntag v. Waidmann and Others* [1993] ECR I-1963, paragraph 16).

31 Under the system of the Convention, with the exception of certain cases exhaustively listed in the first paragraph of Article 28, none of which corresponds to the facts of the case in the main proceedings, the court before which enforcement is sought cannot review the jurisdiction of the court of the State of origin. This fundamental principle, which is set out in the first phrase of the third paragraph of Article 28 of the Convention, is reinforced by the specific statement, in the second phrase of the same paragraph, that the test of public policy referred to in point 1 of Article 27 may not be applied to the rules relating to jurisdiction.

32 It follows that the public policy of the State in which enforcement is sought cannot be raised as a bar to recognition or enforcement of a judgment given in another Contracting State solely on the ground that the court of origin failed to comply with the rules of the Convention which relate to jurisdiction.

33 Having regard to the generality of the wording of the third paragraph of Article 28 of the Convention, that statement of the law must be regarded as being, in principle, applicable even where the court of the State of origin wrongly founded

its jurisdiction, in regard to a defendant domiciled in the territory of the State in which enforcement is sought, on a rule which has recourse to a criterion of nationality.

34 The answer to the first question must therefore be that the court of the State in which enforcement is sought cannot, with respect to a defendant domiciled in that State, take account, for the purposes of the public-policy clause in Article 27, point 1, of the Convention, of the fact, without more, that the court of the State of origin based its jurisdiction on the nationality of the victim of an offence.

 NOTES AND QUESTIONS

1 The principle in the United States is that enforcing courts may review the jurisdiction of sister states' courts. The principle in the European Union is opposite: as underlined by the European Court of Justice in *Krombach*, the Brussels Regulation (then Convention) prevents enforcing courts from reviewing the jurisdiction of courts of other Member States.

There is an important difference between the United States and the European Union in the field of jurisdiction. The Brussels Regulation does not only govern recognition of foreign judgments but also lays down uniform rules of international jurisdiction. By contrast, U.S. states remain free to determine the international jurisdiction, as long as they comply with the requirements of the Due Process Clause.[10] Do you think this difference explains the apparent liberalism of E.U. law on this point?

2 The difference between the U.S. and E.U. regimes is not as sharp as it seems, however, since enforcing courts in the United States may only review the jurisdiction of sister states' courts when the issue was not fully litigated before the foreign court. The U.S. Supreme Court has also held that enforcing courts may not review the jurisdiction of a sister state's court so long as there was an opportunity to raise a jurisdictional challenge.[11] Matters which were actually presented to the first court, but also those which might have been, may not be relitigated in other states. The result is thus that the scope of the power to review the jurisdiction of the foreign court is, in effect, limited to default judgments.

Should the conduct of the parties in the first proceedings matter for the purpose of assessing the jurisdiction of the first court?

3 Both in Europe and in the United States, there are subject matters where enforcing courts exceptionally have full power to review the jurisdiction of sister states' courts. In the European Union, these exceptions concern weaker parties (consumers, employee, insured) for whom protective jurisdictional rules apply, and five subject matters for which one single court in Europe is deemed to have exclusive jurisdiction. The first of them is 'rights *in rem* in immovable property or tenancies of immovable property' (Brussels Ibis Reg., Art. 24, *supra* p. 182).

In the United States, there is only one such exception: a foreign judgment cannot operate directly on land.[12] This is the 'land taboo'. The limit, however, only applies to *in rem* jurisdiction:

---

10 *Supra*, Part II.
11 *Chicot County Drainage Dist. v. Baxter State Park* 308 U.S. 371 (1940).
12 *Fall v. Eastin* 215 U.S. 1 (1909).

The territorial limitation of the jurisdiction of courts of a state over property in another state has a limited exception in the jurisdiction of a court of equity, but it is an exception well defined. A court of equity, having authority to act upon the person, may indirectly act upon real estate in another state, through the instrumentality of this authority over the person. Whatever it may do through the party, it may do to give effect to its decree respecting property, whether it goes to the entire disposition of it or only to affect it with liens or burdens.[13]

The United States and the European Union share a common exception: the land taboo. What is the rationale for it? Does it, and should it apply to actions by landlords against tenants? Does it make a difference if the property was rented for private use for a few weeks or months (vacation)? Why are there so many more exceptions in the European Union than in the United States? Is it because the degree of integration is different?

2.2   Public policy

 CASE

U.S. Supreme Court, 13 January 1998 *Baker v. General Motors Corp.*[14]

JUSTICE GINSBURG

(...) A court may be guided by the forum State's 'public policy' in determining the *law* applicable to a controversy. See *Nevada* v. *Hall*, 440 U. S. 410, 421–424 (1979). But our decisions support no roving 'public policy exception' to the full faith and credit due *judgments*. See *Estin*, 334 U.S., at 546 (Full Faith and Credit Clause 'ordered submission . . . even to hostile policies reflected in the judgment of another State, because the practical operation of the federal system, which the Constitution designed, demanded it.'); *Fauntleroy* v. *Lum*, 210 U.S. 230, 237 (1908) (judgment of Missouri court entitled to full faith and credit in Mississippi even if Missouri judgment rested on a misapprehension of Mississippi law). In assuming the existence of a ubiquitous 'public policy exception' permitting one State to resist recognition of another State's judgment, the District Court in the Bakers' wrongful-death action, see *supra*, at 230, misread our precedent. 'The full faith and credit clause is one of the provisions incorporated into the Constitution by its framers for the purpose of transforming an aggregation of independent,

---

13 *Fall v. Eastin*, 8.
14 522 U.S. 222 (1998).

sovereign States into a nation.' *Sherrer v. Sherrer, 334* U. S. 343, 355 (1948). We are 'aware of [no] considerations of local policy or law which could rightly be deemed to impair the force and effect which the full faith and credit clause and the Act of Congress require to be given to [a money] judgment outside the state of its rendition.' *Magnolia Petroleum Co. v. Hunt*, 320 U.S. 430, 438 (1943).

Brussels Ibis Regulation (2012)

Section 3 Refusal of recognition and enforcement

Sub section 1 Refusal of recognition

Article 45

1. On the application of any interested party, the recognition of a judgment shall be refused:

(a) if such recognition is manifestly contrary to public policy (*ordre public*) in the Member State addressed;

(b) where the judgment was given in default of appearance, if the defendant was not served with the document which instituted the proceedings or with an equivalent document in sufficient time and in such a way as to enable him to arrange for his defence, unless the defendant failed to commence proceedings to challenge the judgment when it was possible for him to do so;

(. . .)

3. Without prejudice to point (e) of paragraph 1, the jurisdiction of the court of origin may not be reviewed. The test of public policy referred to in point (a) of paragraph 1 may not be applied to the rules relating to jurisdiction.

4. The application for refusal of recognition shall be made in accordance with the procedures provided for in Subsection 2 and, where appropriate, Section 4.

Subsection 2 Refusal of enforcement

Article 46

On the application of the person against whom enforcement is sought, the enforcement of a judgment shall be refused where one of the grounds referred to in Article 45 is found to exist.

Section 4 Common provisions

Article 52

Under no circumstances may a judgment given in a Member State be reviewed as to its substance in the Member State addressed.

CASE

European Court of Justice, 28 March 2000 *Dieter Krombach v. André Bamberski* (Case C-7/98)[15]

Facts and held: see above 2.1.

Judgment

The second question

35 By this question, the national court is essentially asking whether, in relation to the public-policy clause in Article 27, point 1, of the Convention [*now art. 45(1) (a)*], the court of the State in which enforcement is sought can, with respect to a defendant domiciled in its territory and charged with an intentional offence, take into account the fact that the court of the State of origin refused to allow that defendant to have his defence presented unless he appeared in person.

36 By disallowing any review of a foreign judgment as to its substance, Article 29 and the third paragraph of Article 34 of the Convention prohibit the court of the State in which enforcement is sought from refusing to recognise or enforce that judgment solely on the ground that there is a discrepancy between the legal rule applied by the court of the State of origin and that which would have been applied by the court of the State in which enforcement is sought had it been seised of the dispute. Similarly, the court of the State in which enforcement is sought cannot review the accuracy of the findings of law or fact made by the court of the State of origin.

37 Recourse to the public-policy clause in Article 27, point 1, of the Convention can be envisaged only where recognition or enforcement of the judgment delivered in another Contracting State would be at variance to an unacceptable degree with the legal order of the State in which enforcement is sought inasmuch as it infringes a fundamental principle. In order for the prohibition of any review of the foreign judgment as to its substance to be observed, the infringement would have to constitute a manifest breach of a rule of law regarded as essential in the legal order of the State in which enforcement is sought or of a right recognised as being fundamental within that legal order.

38 With regard to the right to be defended, to which the question submitted to the Court refers, this occupies a prominent position in the organisation and conduct of a fair trial and is one of the fundamental rights deriving from the constitutional traditions common to the Member States.

39 More specifically still, the European Court of Human Rights has on several occasions ruled in cases relating to criminal proceedings that, although not abso-

---

15 ECLI:EU:C:2000:164, [2000] E.C.R. I-01935.

lute, the right of every person charged with an offence to be effectively defended by a lawyer, if need be one appointed by the court, is one of the fundamental elements in a fair trial and an accused person does not forfeit entitlement to such a right simply because he is not present at the hearing (see the following judgments of the European Court of Human Rights . . .).

40 It follows from that case-law that a national court of a Contracting State is entitled to hold that a refusal to hear the defence of an accused person who is not present at the hearing constitutes a manifest breach of a fundamental right. (. . .)

44 It follows from the foregoing developments in the case-law that recourse to the public-policy clause must be regarded as being possible in exceptional cases where the guarantees laid down in the legislation of the State of origin and in the Convention itself have been insufficient to protect the defendant from a manifest breach of his right to defend himself before the court of origin, as recognised by the ECHR. Consequently, Article II of the Protocol cannot be construed as precluding the court of the State in which enforcement is sought from being entitled to take account, in relation to public policy, as referred to in Article 27, point 1, of the Convention, of the fact that, in an action for damages based on an offence, the court of the State of origin refused to hear the defence of the accused person, who was being prosecuted for an intentional offence, solely on the ground that that person was not present at the hearing.

45 The answer to the second question must therefore be that the court of the State in which enforcement is sought can, with respect to a defendant domiciled in that State and prosecuted for an intentional offence, take account, in relation to the public-policy clause in Article 27, point 1, of the Convention, of the fact that the court of the State of origin refused to allow that person to have his defence presented unless he appeared in person. (. . .)

QUESTIONS

1   The public policy exception enables the forum to deny recognition to foreign judgments when they violate its most fundamental values. Is this compatible with the establishment of a community of states? If this community is based on shared values, why would you need to verify that they are respected by other sister states? Precisely because they might not always respect them?

In the European Union, most of the values defining public policy are expressed in the European Convention on Human Rights, to which all members of the European Union are parties. Why would you need a public policy exception to deny recognition to judgments made in violation of the Convention? Does it matter that European States are regularly found to be in violation with the Convention by the European Court of Human Rights?

2   The Brussels Ibis Regulation has retained the public policy exception. But the European Court of Justice has attempted to constrain the discretion of Member States to use it. How?

2.3   Abolishing all requirements?

Sovereign States may join together and transfer powers to a common entity to various degrees. They can remain independent entities with significant powers or, to the contrary, achieve advanced integration. If they reach a certain level of integration, the issue will arise as to whether they should still regard each other as foreign or whether they should simply acknowledge that they have become a single entity. From the perspective of the law of judgments, the debate may translate into a debate on whether judgments rendered by sister states should circulate as freely as judgments do in a single state, that is, without any review.

Remarkably, the idea of fully abolishing the review procedure (exequatur) of sister states' judgments was promoted in the European Union from 1999 until 2012 by European institutions.

> *Report from the Commission to the European Parliament, the Council and the European Economic and Social Committee on the application of Council Regulation (EC) No 44/2001 on jurisdiction and the recognition and enforcement of judgments in civil and commercial matters*[16]
>
> **3.1. The abolition of exequatur**
>
> Following the political mandate by the European Council in the Tampere (1999) and The Hague (2004) programs, the main objective of the revision of the Regulation should be the abolition of the *exequatur* procedure in all matters covered by the Regulation.
>
> As regards the existing *exequatur* procedure, the general study shows that, when the application is complete, first instance proceedings before the courts in the Member States tend to last, on average, from 7 days to 4 months. When, however, the application is incomplete, proceedings last longer. Applications are often incomplete and judicial authorities ask for additional information, in particular translations. Most applications for a declaration of enforceability are successful (between 90% and 100%). Only between 1 and 5% of the decisions are appealed. Appeal proceedings may last between one month and three years, depending on the different procedural cultures in the Member States and the workload of the courts.
>
> In cases where the declaration of enforceability is challenged, the ground of refusal of recognition and enforcement most frequently invoked is the lack of appropriate service pursuant to Article 34(2). However, the general study shows that such challenges are rarely successful today. As to public policy, the study shows that this ground is frequently invoked but rarely accepted. If it is accepted, this mostly occurs in exceptional cases with the aim of safeguarding the procedural rights of

---

16 COM(2009) 174 final.

the defendant. It seems extremely rare, in civil and commercial matters, that courts would apply the public policy exception with respect to the substantive ruling by the foreign court. The other grounds for refusal are rarely invoked. (. . .)

As for the control of certain jurisdiction rules, it should be considered whether this still fits with the prohibition of review of a foreign court's jurisdiction; in addition, the practical importance of the rule is limited in that the court is bound in any event by the findings of fact by the court of origin. (. . .)

European Regulation (EC) No 2201/2003 of 27 November 2003 concerning jurisdiction and the recognition and enforcement of judgments in matrimonial matters and the matters of parental responsibility (Brussels IIbis)

Section 4 Enforceability of certain judgments concerning rights of access and of certain judgments which require the return of the child

Article 40 *Scope*

1. This Section shall apply to:

(a)   rights of access; and
(b)   the return of a child entailed by a judgment given pursuant to Article 11(8).

2. The provisions of this Section shall not prevent a holder of parental responsibility from seeking recognition and enforcement of a judgment in accordance with the provisions in Sections 1 and 2 of this Chapter.

Article 41 *Rights of access*

1. The rights of access referred to in Article 40(1)(a) granted in an enforceable judgment given in a Member State shall be recognised and enforceable in another Member State without the need for a declaration of enforceability and without any possibility of opposing its recognition if the judgment has been certified in the Member State of origin in accordance with paragraph 2.

Even if national law does not provide for enforceability by operation of law of a judgment granting access rights, the court of origin may declare that the judgment shall be enforceable, notwithstanding any appeal.

2. The judge of origin shall issue the certificate referred to in paragraph 1 using the standard form in Annex III (certificate concerning rights of access) only if:

(a)   where the judgment was given in default, the person defaulting was served with the document which instituted the proceedings or with an equivalent document in sufficient time and in such a way as to enable that person to arrange for his or her defense, or, the person has been served with the document but not in compliance with these conditions, it is nevertheless established that he or she accepted the decision unequivocally;
(b)   all parties concerned were given an opportunity to be heard; and
(c)   the child was given an opportunity to be heard, unless a hearing was

considered inappropriate having regard to his or her age or degree of maturity.

The certificate shall be completed in the language of the judgment.

3. Where the rights of access involve a cross-border situation at the time of the delivery of the judgment, the certificate shall be issued ex officio when the judgment becomes enforceable, even if only provisionally. If the situation subsequently acquires a cross-border character, the certificate shall be issued at the request of one of the parties.

Article 42 *Return of the child*

1. The return of a child referred to in Article 40(1)(b) entailed by an enforceable judgment given in a Member State shall be recognised and enforceable in another Member State without the need for a declaration of enforceability and without any possibility of opposing its recognition if the judgment has been certified in the Member State of origin in accordance with paragraph 2.

Even if national law does not provide for enforceability by operation of law, notwithstanding any appeal, of a judgment requiring the return of the child mentioned in Article 11(b)(8), the court of origin may declare the judgment enforceable.

2. The judge of origin who delivered the judgment referred to in Article 40(1)(b) shall issue the certificate referred to in paragraph 1 only if:

(a)   the child was given an opportunity to be heard, unless a hearing was considered inappropriate having regard to his or her age or degree of maturity;

(b)   the parties were given an opportunity to be heard; and

(c)   the court has taken into account in issuing its judgment the reasons for and evidence underlying the order issued pursuant to Article 13 of the 1980 Hague Convention.

In the event that the court or any other authority takes measures to ensure the protection of the child after its return to the State of habitual residence, the certificate shall contain details of such measures.

The judge of origin shall of his or her own motion issue that certificate using the standard form in Annex IV (certificate concerning return of the child(ren)).

The certificate shall be completed in the language of the judgment.

If the public policy exception is abolished, can a foreign judgment be denied recognition on the grounds that the foreign court did not comply with human rights?

CASE

European Court of Justice, 22 December 2010 *Aguirre Zarraga v. Simone Pelz* (Case C-491/10 PPU)[17]

Facts: Mr Aguirre Zarraga, of Spanish nationality, and Ms Pelz, of German nationality, married in 1998 in Spain. Their daughter, Andrea, was born in 2000 in Spain where they lived until 2007. The parents then separated and were divorced by a Spanish court. Both parents sought sole rights of custody of Andrea. In May 2008, a Spanish court provisionally awarded rights of custody to Mr Zarraga, while Ms Pelz was granted rights of access. Andrea thus went to live with her father and Ms Pelz moved to Germany and settled there. In August 2008, at the end of the summer holidays which she had spent with her mother, Andrea was not returned to her father in Spain and remained in Germany. An order ordering the return of the child to Spain was issued by a Spanish court. Ms Pelz challenged its enforcement in Germany on the ground that the child had not been heard.

Held: the German court cannot oppose the enforcement of a judgment ordering the return of a child who has been wrongfully removed, on the ground that the court of the Member State of origin which handed down that judgment may have infringed the right of the child to be heard, since the assessment of whether there is such an infringement falls exclusively within the jurisdiction of the courts of the Member State of origin.

42 By the questions referred for a preliminary ruling, which should be dealt with together, the referring court asks, in essence, whether, in circumstances such as those in the main proceedings, the court with jurisdiction in the Member State of enforcement can exceptionally oppose the enforcement of a judgment ordering the return of a child, which has been certified on the basis of Article 42 of Regulation No 2201/2003 by the court of the Member State of origin, on the ground that the latter court stated, in the certificate, that it had fulfilled its obligation to hear the child before handing down its judgment, in the context of divorce proceedings, on the award of rights of custody in respect of that child, although that hearing did not take place, which is contrary to the said Article 42, interpreted in accordance with Article 24 of the Charter of Fundamental Rights.

43 In order to answer those questions, it must first be recognised that what is at issue, in a context such as that of the main proceedings, is wrongful retention of a child within the meaning of Article 2(11) of Regulation No 2201/2003.

44 As observed by the Advocate General in points 120 and 121 of his view, Regulation No 2201/2003 starts from the assumption that the wrongful removal

---

17 ECLI:EU:C:2010:828, [2010] E.C.R. I-14247.

or retention of a child in breach of a court judgment handed down in another Member State is seriously prejudicial to the interests of that child and it therefore lays down measures to enable the return of the child to the place where he or she is habitually resident as quickly as possible. In that regard, that regulation set up a system whereby, in the event that there is a difference of opinion between the court where the child is habitually resident and the court where the child is wrongfully present, the former retains exclusive jurisdiction to decide whether the child is to be returned.

45 The result of the requirement of rapid action which underlies such a system is that, in such circumstances, the national courts seised of an application for return of the child must make their decision expeditiously. It is moreover to that end that Article 11(3) of Regulation No 2201/2003 requires those courts to use the most expeditious procedures available in national law and, except where exceptional circumstances make it impossible, to issue their judgments no later than six weeks after the application is lodged.

46 It should also be added that, in order to achieve that objective, the system established by Regulation No 2201/2003 is based on the allocation of a central role to the court which has jurisdiction to rule on the substance of the case pursuant to the provisions of that regulation and that, as distinct from recital 21 in the preamble to the regulation, in accordance with which the recognition and enforcement of judgments given in a Member State should be based on the principle of mutual trust and grounds for non-recognition should be kept to the minimum required, recital 17 in the preamble to the regulation provides that, in a case of wrongful retention of a child, the execution of a judgment entailing the return of the child must take place without any special procedure being required for the recognition or enforcement of that judgment in the Member State where the child is to be found.

47 With the aim therefore of ensuring expeditious enforcement of judgments, Articles 40 to 45 of Regulation No 2201/2003 provide for specific procedures to ensure that those judgments are enforceable in the Member State where they are to take effect, in particular where the judgments concerned order the return of a child and are handed down, as in the main proceedings, in the circumstances specified in Article 11(8) of that regulation.

48 Accordingly, it is apparent from Articles 42(1) and 43(2) of Regulation No 2201/2003, interpreted in the light of recitals 17 and 24 in the preamble to that regulation, that a judgment ordering the return of a child handed down by the court with jurisdiction pursuant to that regulation, where it is enforceable and has given rise to the issue of the certificate referred to in the said Article 42(1) in the Member State of origin, is to be recognised and is to be automatically enforceable in another Member State, there being no possibility of opposing its recognition (see, to that effect, Rinau, paragraph 84, and Povse, paragraph 70).

49 Consequently, the court of the Member State of enforcement can do no more than declare that a judgment thus certified is enforceable. (. . .)

69 However, as stated in paragraph 51 of this judgment, it is solely for the national courts of the Member State of origin to examine the lawfulness of that judgment with reference to the requirements imposed, in particular, by Article 24 of the Charter of Fundamental Rights and Article 42 of Regulation No 2201/2003.

70 As was emphasised in paragraph 46 of this judgment, the systems for recognition and enforcement of judgments handed down in a Member State which are established by that regulation are based on the principle of mutual trust between Member States in the fact that their respective national legal systems are capable of providing an equivalent and effective protection of fundamental rights, recognised at European Union level, in particular, in the Charter of Fundamental Rights.

71 That being the case, as stated by the Advocate General in point 135 of his view, it is therefore within the legal system of the Member State of origin that the parties concerned must pursue legal remedies which allow the lawfulness of a judgment certified pursuant to Article 42 of Regulation No 2201/2003 to be challenged.

72 As regards the dispute in the main proceedings, it is apparent from the documents submitted to the Court that appeal proceedings are still pending before the Audiencia Provincial de Bizkaya. Further, the Spanish Government stated at the oral hearing that the judgment of the Audiencia Provincial will itself be open to appeal under domestic law, namely, at the very least, a 'recurso de amparo' before the Constitutional Court, the grounds of which appeal may include any infringements of fundamental rights, including the child's right to be heard.

73 It is therefore for those courts of the Member State of origin to determine whether the judgment certified pursuant to Article 42 of Regulation No 2201/2003 is vitiated by an infringement of the child's right to be heard.

74 It follows from all of the foregoing that, in circumstances such as those of the main proceedings, the issue of whether the court of the Member State of origin which handed down the certified judgment may have infringed Article 42(2)(a) of Regulation No 2201/2003 falls solely within the jurisdiction of the courts of that Member State and that the court with jurisdiction in the Member State of enforcement cannot oppose the recognition and enforcement of that judgment, having regard to the certificate issued by the court concerned of the Member State of origin.

75 Taking all of the foregoing considerations into account, the answer to the questions referred is that, in circumstances such as those of the main proceedings, the court with jurisdiction in the Member State of enforcement cannot oppose the enforcement of a certified judgment, ordering the return of a child who has been wrongfully removed, on the ground that the court of the Member State of origin which handed down that judgment may have infringed Article 42 of Regulation No 2201/2003, interpreted in accordance with Article 24 of the Charter of Fundamental Rights, since the assessment of whether there is such an infringement falls exclusively within the jurisdiction of the courts of the Member State of origin.

? **NOTES AND QUESTIONS**

1 In 1999, the highest authority in the European Union announced at the Tampere Summit its plan to gradually abolish the review procedure of sister states' judgments (exequatur). The European lawmaker started implementing this policy with Regulation No 2201/2003 for matters of rights of access and return of children (in other fields, the Regulation maintained exequatur). At that time, the goal was not only to abolish the formal review procedure of sister states' judgments, but also the grounds for reviewing them. Thus, and most importantly, this entailed abolishing the public policy exception. Between 2004 and 2007, the European lawmaker also adopted regulations establishing a new European title for uncontested claims and two new European procedures which resulted in judgments which could freely circulate throughout the Union without any review procedure.

   What is the impact of the evolution on the protection of human rights in the European Union? The public policy exception is a remedy against human rights violations. After the abolition of exequatur, would there be any remedy to deny enforcement to a judgment rendered in violation of European fundamental rights?

2 The policy underlying the abolition of the exequatur procedure is that all challenges and recourses against the judgment should be made in the State of origin. In a federal, or quasi-federal system, there should be no difference between the courts of the different Member States, which are all to be trusted. For instance, all courts should be trusted when they apply European rules of jurisdiction. Are you convinced? Would it be different for challenges of domestic rules on the ground that they do not comport with European fundamental rights? Can you equally expect courts of other Member States to apply properly European rules and to rule that some of their rules of civil procedure violate the right to a fair trial as afforded by Art. 6 of the European Convention on Human Rights? (For an example, see *Krombach v. Bamberski*).[18]

3 In 2010, the European Commission proposed to move to the second stage of the abolition of exequatur, and to extend its scope to most civil and commercial matters. The Member States eventually rejected the proposal. The resulting Brussels Ibis Regulation retains all the previously available grounds for review of sister states' judgments, including the public policy exception. Exequatur is only suppressed as a mandatory review procedure: judgments are now automatically and immediately enforceable throughout the European Union, but defendants may apply for a refusal of enforcement if they believe that one of the available grounds exists. It seems that the momentum for the full abolition of exequatur has passed.

2.4 Other requirements

Under both E.U. and U.S. law, the existence of a conflicting judgment is a ground for denying recognition to a judgment rendered by the court of a sister state. Under E.U. law, the judgment which was given first is preferred, unless the second judgment was rendered by a court of the forum.[19] By contrast, in the United States, the second judgment will be preferred, but

---

18 *Supra*, 2.2.
19 See Brussels Ibis Regulation, Art. 45 (1)(c) and (d).

only if the earlier judgment is superseded by the later judgment under the local law of the state where the later judgment was rendered.[20]

Furthermore, in the United States, sister states judgments may also be denied recognition on the ground of fraud.

---

20 See Restatement (Second) of Conflict of Laws § 114 (1971).

Part IV

Contracts

8

Jurisdiction in contractual matters

As already pointed out in Chapter 3, the law of jurisdiction varies widely between civil law and common law countries. Civil law countries rely on simple and rigid rules. In contractual matters, jurisdiction typically lies with the court of the place of performance of the contract (1). Common law jurisdictions rely on more sophisticated tests which not only require certain minimum contacts between the dispute and the forum, but also take into consideration the acceptability of asserting jurisdiction in a given case (2).

Parties to international contracts may also wish to agree on the court having jurisdiction by including a jurisdiction clause: see *supra* Ch. 5.

1 Place of performance

European Regulation (EU) No 1215/2012 of 12 December 2012 on jurisdiction and on the enforcement and recognition of judgments in civil and commercial matters (Brussels Ibis)

SECTION 1 General provisions
Article 4
1. Subject to this Regulation, persons domiciled in a Member State shall, whatever their nationality, be sued in the courts of that Member State. (. . .)
SECTION 2 Special jurisdiction
Article 7
A person domiciled in a Member State may be sued in another Member State:
(1)(a) in matters relating to a contract, in the courts for the place of performance of the obligation in question;
(b) for the purpose of this provision and unless otherwise agreed, the place of performance of the obligation in question shall be:

— in the case of the sale of goods, the place in a Member State where, under the contract, the goods were delivered or should have been delivered,

— in the case of the provision of services, the place in a Member State where, under the contract, the services were provided or should have been provided;

(c) if point (b) does not apply then point (a) applies;

NOTES

1. In contractual matters, Article 7(1) grants jurisdiction to the courts for the place of performance of the obligation in question. Yet, the general rule of Art. 4 remains applicable: the court of the domicile of the defendant also has jurisdiction.

2. Article 7(1)(b) was introduced in 2000 when the 1968 Brussels Convention became a European Regulation (known as the Brussels I Regulation, or Regulation 44/2001). Before the 2000 reform, then Art. 5(1) of the 1968 Brussels Convention only provided for the jurisdiction of the courts of the place of performance of the obligation in question (see today Art. 7(1)(a)). Article 7(1)(b) adds a specification of the place of performance of the obligation in question for two special contracts: sale of goods and provision of services. As a result, an important distinction is in order:

   – for sale of goods or provision of services, Art. 7(1)(b) directly provides where the place of performance is, and thus which court has jurisdiction. For a sale of goods, it is the court of the place of delivery of the goods.

   – for other contracts, it is still necessary to determine the place of performance. In *Falco Privatstiftung* (Case C-533/07),[1] the European Court of Justice made clear that it would be necessary to apply the rules that it had laid down for that purpose in the context of the 1968 Brussels Convention

Read the following case and explain (1) what is the obligation 'in question' and (2) how its place of performance should be determined.

CASE

European Court of Justice, 5 October 1999 *Leathertex Divisione Sintetici v. Bodetex* (Case C-420/97)[2]

The main proceedings

8 For a number of years Bodetex acted as commercial agent for Leathertex in the Belgian and Netherlands markets under a long-term arrangement. It received 5% commission by way of remuneration.

9 After asking Leathertex to no avail during 1987 for payment of commission which it considered to be owing to it, Bodetex regarded its commercial agency agreement as terminated and, by letter of 9 March 1988, took formal note of the

---

1 Case C-533/07 *Falco Privatstiftung and Thomas Rabitsch v. Gisela Weller-Lindhorst* ECLI:EU:C:2009:257, [2009] E.C.R. I-03327.
2 ECLI:EU:C:1999:483, [1999] E.C.R. I-06747.

termination and demanded from Leathertex payment of arrears of commission and compensation in lieu of notice.

10 Since Leathertex did not reply to that letter, on 2 November 1988 Bodetex sued it for payment in the Rechtbank van Koophandel (Commercial Court), Courtrai.

11 By judgment of 1 October 1991, the Rechtbank van Koophandel found that two separate obligations formed the basis of the action. It held that the first, namely the obligation to give a reasonable period of notice on termination of a commercial agency agreement and, in the event of failure to give such notice, to pay compensation in lieu, was to be performed in Belgium, whereas the second, namely the obligation to pay commission, was to be performed in Italy under the principle that debts are payable where the debtor is resident. The Rechtbank van Koophandel accordingly found that it had jurisdiction in respect of the obligation to pay compensation in lieu of notice, by virtue of Article 5(1) of the Convention, and then declared that it had jurisdiction over the whole proceedings given the connection between that obligation and the obligation to pay commission. It ordered Leathertex to pay Bodetex arrears of commission and compensation in lieu of notice. (. . .)

Consideration of the question submitted

19 By its question, the national court is essentially asking whether, on a proper construction of Articles 2 and 5(1) of the Convention [*now Arts. 4 and 7(1)(a)*], the same court has jurisdiction to hear the whole of an action founded on two obligations of equal rank arising from the same contract even though, according to the conflict rules of the State where that court is situated, one of those obligations is to be performed in that State and the other in another Contracting State. (. . .)

31 It should be noted first of all that, in paragraphs 8, 9 and 10 of the judgment in Case 14/76 *De Bloos v. Bouyer* [1976] ECR 1497, after observing that the Convention was intended to determine the international jurisdiction of the courts of the Contracting States, to facilitate the recognition of judgments and to introduce an expeditious procedure for securing their enforcement, the Court held that those objectives implied the need to avoid, so far as possible, creating a situation in which a number of courts had jurisdiction in respect of one and the same contract and that Article 5(1) of the Convention could not therefore be interpreted as referring to any obligation whatsoever arising under the contract in question. The Court concluded, in paragraphs 11 and 13 of the same judgment, that, for the purposes of determining the place of performance within the meaning of Article 5(1), the obligation to be taken into account was that which corresponded to the contractual right on which the plaintiff's action was based. It stated in paragraph 14 that, in a case where the plaintiff asserted the right to be paid damages or sought dissolution of the contract on the ground of the wrongful conduct of the other party, that obligation was still that which arose under the contract and the non-performance of which was relied upon to support such claims. (. . .)

33 Also, the Court has held on several occasions that the place of performance of the obligation in question is to be determined by the law governing that obligation according to the conflict rules of the court seised (Case 12/76 *Tessili v. Dunlop* [1976] ECR 1473, paragraph 13, (...)).

34 In the present case, the Belgian courts have held, in accordance with the case-law cited above, that the obligation to pay compensation in lieu of notice was to be performed in Belgium while the obligation to pay commission was to be performed in Italy.

35 Furthermore, it is apparent from the order for reference and the file forwarded by the national court that the contract at issue in the main proceedings, under which the claims for payment of commission and of compensation in lieu of notice have been brought, does not constitute a contract of employment.

36 When the specific features of a contract of employment do not exist, it is neither necessary nor appropriate to identify the obligation which characterises the contract and to centralise at its place of performance all jurisdiction, based on place of performance, over disputes concerning all the obligations under the contract (Shenavai, cited above, paragraph 17).

37 Therefore, the obligation which characterises the agency agreement is not to be taken into account in the main proceedings in order to determine jurisdiction based on place of performance.

38 Nor can the court which has jurisdiction to hear the claim for payment of compensation in lieu of notice found its jurisdiction in respect of the claim for payment of commission on any relation between those two claims. As the Court has made clear, Article 22 of the Convention is intended to establish how related actions which have been brought before courts of different Contracting States are to be dealt with. It does not confer jurisdiction. In particular, it does not accord jurisdiction to a court of a Contracting State to try an action which is related to another action of which that court is seised pursuant to the rules of the Convention (see Case 150/80 *Elefanten Schuh v. Jacqmain* [1981] ECR 1671, paragraph 19, and Case C-51/97 *Réunion Européenne and Others v. Spliethoff's Bevrachtingskantor and Another* [1998] ECR I-6511, paragraph 39).

39 Finally, when a dispute relates to a number of obligations of equal rank arising from the same contract, the court before which the matter is brought cannot, when determining whether it has jurisdiction, be guided by the maxim *accessorium sequitur principale* referred to by the Court in paragraph 19 of the judgment in Shenavai, cited above.

40 The same court does not therefore have jurisdiction to hear the whole of an action founded on two obligations of equal rank arising from the same contract when, according to the conflict rules of the State where that court is situated, one of those obligations is to be performed in that State and the other in another Contracting State.

41 It should be remembered that, while there are disadvantages in having different courts ruling on different aspects of the same dispute, the plaintiff always has the

option, under Article 2 of the Convention, of bringing his entire claim before the courts for the place where the defendant is domiciled.

42 The answer to be given to the question referred for a preliminary ruling must therefore be that, on a proper construction of Article 5(1) of the Convention, the same court does not have jurisdiction to hear the whole of an action founded on two obligations of equal rank arising from the same contract when, according to the conflict rules of the State where that court is situated, one of those obligations is to be performed in that State and the other in another Contracting State.

 NOTES AND QUESTIONS

1 The characteristic obligation of a contract is the obligation which makes it different from others. The obligation in question is the one on the basis of which the plaintiff actually sues the defendant (in most cases, for lack of performance). If the plaintiff founds his action on the breach of several obligations, there are several obligations in question. In *Leathertex*, what is the consequence of this on the number of courts having jurisdiction to decide the case?

2 Once the obligation(s) in question has been identified, it is necessary to find its place of performance. In certain cases, it will be provided by the contract itself. In other cases, a default rule will be provided by the applicable law. While many European scholars would have preferred that the European Court of Justice develop an autonomous concept of place of performance, the Court has instead always insisted that the rule would be provided by the applicable national law. This law must be determined by application of the choice of law rule applicable in contractual matters. This will typically be the Rome I Regulation. The purpose of the determination of the applicable law in the *Definitely Maybe* case (*supra*, p. 10) was to determine the place of performance of the obligation in question:

> 4 In order to resolve the jurisdiction issue the court must, initially, turn to the Brussels Convention (. . .). Under that Convention, the normal rule is that a person, including, of course, a corporate entity, should be sued in the place where he is domiciled; in other words, Germany. But the normal rule is displaced if the place of performance of the obligation in question, namely the duty to pay, is England. But the place of performance of an obligation such as this may, and in this case does, depend upon which system of law governs the contract. Under German law the place of performance of an obligation to pay is the domicile of the debtor, namely Germany. Under English law the place of performance of the Defendant's obligation to pay is England, the place where the money is to be received. Thus, the question as to whether these proceedings can continue in this jurisdiction is dependent upon the answer to the question: what is the governing law of the contract? If the answer is English law, then the proceedings can continue here and the appeal must be allowed. Conversely, if the answer is German law then the appeal must be dismissed and the stay of proceedings in this jurisdiction continued.

Since the 2000 reform, the key issue has become whether the contract under consideration can fall within one of the two categories identified by Art. 7(1)(b). Read the following case and explain which court has jurisdiction to hear disputes related to an exclusive distribution agreement and why.

CASE

European Court of Justice, 19 March 2013 *Corman-Collins SA v. La Maison du Whisky SA* (Case C-9/12)[3]

32 The Court also observed, regarding the place of performance of the obligations arising from contracts for the sale of goods, that the Regulation, in the first indent of Article 5(1)(b) [*now Art. 7*], defines that criterion of a link autonomously, in order to reinforce the objectives of unifying of the rules of jurisdiction and predictability (*Wood Floor Solutions Andreas Domberger*, paragraph 23 and the case-law cited). Those objectives are also those of the second indent of Article 5(1)(b), since the rules of special jurisdiction provided for by the regulation for contracts for the sale of goods and the provision of services have the same origin, pursue the same objectives and occupy the same place in the scheme established by that regulation (*Wood Floor Solutions Andreas Domberger*, paragraph 26 and the case-law cited).

33 It is by taking account of those objectives that it must be examined whether a distribution agreement falls into one of those two categories of contracts referred to in Article 5(1)(b) of the Regulation.

34 In that connection, the Court has stated that, in order to classify a contract in the light of that provision, the classification must be based on the obligations which characterise the contract at issue (Case C-381/08 *Car Trim* [2010] ECR I-1255, paragraphs 31 and 32).

35 Thus, the Court has held that a contract which has as its characteristic obligation the supply of a good will be classified as a 'sale of goods' within the meaning of the first indent of Article 5(1)(b) of Regulation No 44/2001 (*Car Trim*, paragraph 32).

36 That a classification may be applied to a long-term commercial relationship between two economic operators, where that relationship is limited to successive agreements, each having the object of the delivery and collection of goods. However, it does not correspond to the general scheme of a typical distribution agreement, characterised by a framework agreement, the aim of which is an undertaking for supply and provision concluded for the future by two economic operators, including specific contractual provisions regarding the distribution by the distributor of goods sold by the grantor.

---

3 ECLI:EU:C:2013:860.

37 As to whether an exclusive distribution agreement may be classified as a contract for the 'supply of services' within the meaning of the second indent of Article 5(1)(b) of the Regulation, it must be recalled that, according to the definition given by the Court, the concept of 'services' within the meaning of that provision requires at least that the party who provides the service carries out a particular activity in return for remuneration (Case C-533/07 *Falco Privatstiftung and Rabitsch* [2009] ECR I-3327, paragraph 29).

38 As far as the first criterion in that definition, namely, the existence of an activity, it is clear from the case-law of the Court that it requires the performance of positive acts, rather than mere omissions (see, to that effect, *Falco Privatstiftung and Rabitsch*, paragraphs 29 to 31). That criterion corresponds, in the case of an exclusive distribution agreement, to the characteristic service provided by the distributor which, by distributing the grantor's products, is involved in increasing their distribution. As a result of the supply guarantee it enjoys under the exclusive distribution agreement and, as the case may be, its involvement in the grantor's commercial planning, in particular with respect to marketing operations, factors in respect of which the national court has jurisdiction to make a ruling, the distributor is able to offer clients services and benefits that a mere reseller cannot and thereby acquire, for the benefit of the grantor's products, a larger share of the local market.

39 As to the second criterion, namely the remuneration paid as consideration for an activity, it must be stated that it is not to be understood strictly as the payment of a sum of money. Such a restriction is neither stipulated by the very general wording of the second indent of Article 5(1)(b) of the Regulation nor consistent with the objectives of proximity and standardisation, set out in paragraphs 30 to 32 of the present judgment, pursued by that provision.

40 In that connection, account must be taken of the fact that the distribution agreement is based on a selection of the distributor by the grantor. That selection, which is a characteristic element of that type of agreement, confers a competitive advantage on the distributor in that the latter has the sole right to sell the grantor's products in a particular territory or, at the very least, that a limited number of distributors enjoy that right. Moreover, the distribution agreement often provides assistance to the distributor regarding access to advertising, communicating know-how by means of training or yet even payment facilities. All those advantages, whose existence it is for the court adjudicating on the substantive action to ascertain, represent an economic value for the distributor that may be regarded as constituting remuneration.

41 It follows that a distribution agreement containing the typical obligations set out in paragraphs 27 and 28 above may be classified as a contract for the supply of services for the purpose of applying the rule of jurisdiction in the second indent of Article 5(1)(b) of the Regulation.

42 That classification excludes the application to a distribution agreement of the rule of jurisdiction laid down in Article 5(1)(a) of the Regulation. Taking account

of the hierarchy established between points (a) and (b) by point (c) of that provision, the rules of jurisdiction laid down in Article 5(1)(a) of the Regulation is intended to apply only in the alternative and by default with respect to the other rules of jurisdiction in Article 5(1)(b) thereof.

43 In the light of all the foregoing considerations, the answer to the second and third questions is that on a proper constitution of Article 5(1)(b) of the Regulation, the rule of jurisdiction laid down in the second indent of that provision for disputes relating to contracts for the supply of services is applicable in the case of a legal action by which a plaintiff established in one Member State claims, against a defendant established in another Member State, rights arising from an exclusive distribution agreement, which requires the contract binding the parties to contain specific terms concerning the distribution by the distributor of goods sold by the grantor. It is for the national court to ascertain whether that is so in the proceedings before it.

 NOTES AND QUESTIONS

1 The innovation introduced by Art. 7(1)(b) is that, although the provision still refers to the 'obligation in question', this obligation is always the same for sales of goods or provision of services, and does not change depending on the foundation of the action of the defendant. In truth, Art. 7(1)(b) relies on characteristic obligations, rather than obligations in question. Can a situation where several courts have jurisdiction to decide different aspects of a contractual dispute arise under Art. 7(1)(b)?

2 What are the criteria to identify whether a contract can be characterized as a contract for the supply of services? In *Falco Privatstiftung* (Case C-533/07), the court held that a contract under which the owner of an intellectual property right grants its contractual partner the right to use that right in return for remuneration is not a contract for the provision of services, because the owner does not have to perform any positive act under the contract.

3 Under Art. 7(1)(b) as interpreted by the European Court of Justice, which court would have jurisdiction in the *Definitely Maybe* case? In the *Leathertex* case?

Japanese Code of Civil Procedure

Article 3-3 *Jurisdiction over Actions Relating to, inter alia, Contractual Obligations*
The actions set out in each sub-paragraph below may be filed with the courts of Japan in the circumstances described in each of them.
(i) An action for the enforcement of a contractual obligation, an action arising from negotiorum gestio (management of another's affairs without mandate) performed in connection with a contractual obligation, an action relating to unjust enrichment arising in connection with a contractual obligation, an action seeking damages for the breach of a contractual obligation, or any other action relating to a contractual obligation: in the circumstances where the place of performance of the obligation as specified in the contract is located in Japan or where the place of performance of the obligation is located in Japan according to the governing law chosen in the contract.

QUESTIONS

In Japan, is jurisdiction based on the characteristic obligation of the relevant contract, or on the obligation in question? How is the place of performance of the obligation to be determined?

Chinese Law on Civil Procedure (1991, as amended)

Article 265

A lawsuit brought against a defendant who has no domicile in the People's Republic of China concerning a contract dispute or other disputes over property rights and interests, if the contract is signed or performed within the territory of the People's Republic of China, or the object of the action is within the territory of the People's Republic of China, or the defendant has detainable property within the territory of the People's Republic of China, or the defendant has its representative agency, branch, or business agent within the territory of the People's Republic of China, may be under the jurisdiction of the people's court located in the place where the contract is signed or performed, the subject of the action is located, the defendant's detainable property is located, the infringing act takes place, or the representative agency, branch or business agent is located

Article 266

Lawsuits brought for disputes arising from the performance of contracts for Chinese-foreign equity joint ventures, Chinese-foreign contractual joint ventures, or Chinese-foreign cooperative exploration and development of the natural resources in the People's Republic of China shall be under the jurisdiction of the people's courts of the People's Republic of China.

 NOTES

1 Article 265 grants jurisdiction not only to the court of the place of performance of the contract, but also to the court of the place where the contract was signed. Chinese courts also have jurisdiction over defendants domiciled in China.

2 In 2007, the Supreme Court adopted rules imposing the application of Chinese law to each of the contracts listed in Article 266.[4] The purpose of Art. 266 is thus to make the jurisdiction of Chinese courts over such contracts exclusive.

2 Sophisticated tests

English and U.S. courts have developed more sophisticated jurisdictional tests insisting not only that there be a nexus between the dispute and the forum, but also that the assertion of jurisdiction be otherwise reasonable or appropriate.

---

4 Rules on the Related Issues concerning the Application of Law in Hearing Foreign-Related Contractual Dispute Cases in Civil and Commercial Matters of 11 June 2007, Art. 8.

2.1 Nexus and reasonableness

Read the following case and assess which connection is required between the contract or the dispute and the U.S forum, and which other factors are considered.

 CASE

U.S. Court of Appeals for the First Circuit, 12 November 2014 *C.W. Downer & Co. v. Bioriginal Food & Science Corporation*[5]

LYNCH, Chief Judge.

The Due Process Clause of the Fourteenth Amendment allows a state's courts to exercise jurisdiction over a nonresident defendant only when doing so 'does not offend "traditional notions of fair play and substantial justice."' *Int'l Shoe Co. v. Washington*, 326 U.S. 310, 316 (1945). This contract case presents these issues where the parties' contacts were not first-hand and involved no physical presence in Massachusetts, but were by phone, e-mail, and internet over an international border. The district court concluded that it could not exercise personal jurisdiction over the defendant consistently with the Due Process Clause. We conclude to the contrary that the Massachusetts courts do have long-arm jurisdiction over the Canadian defendant.

In 2009, the defendant Bioriginal Food & Science Corporation, a Canadian company, contracted with C.W. Downer & Co., a Massachusetts investment bank, to be its exclusive financial advisor for the sale of its business. The parties negotiated and executed the agreement remotely, and subsequently spent four years collaborating from their respective home offices. Downer later sued in state court in Massachusetts for breach of contract, and Bioriginal removed the case to federal court. (. . .)

II.

(. . .) To establish personal jurisdiction in a diversity case, a plaintiff must satisfy both the forum state's long-arm statute and the Due Process Clause of the Fourteenth Amendment. *Ticketmaster–New York, Inc. v. Alioto*, 26 F.3d 201, 204 (1st Cir.1994). The district court and the parties each proceed directly to the constitutional analysis, and we will do so as well.

---

5 771 F.3d 59.

Downer asserts only that Massachusetts has *specific* in personam jurisdiction over Bioriginal, not general jurisdiction. That is, the jurisdictional basis for Downer's suit arises from and is limited to Bioriginal's suit-related conduct. *See Walden v. Fiore*, 134 S.Ct. 1115, 1121 (2014). To evaluate whether Bioriginal's suit-related conduct creates the necessary minimum contacts with Massachusetts, courts consider (1) whether the claim 'directly arise[s] out of, or relate[s] to, the defendant's forum state activities;' (2) whether the defendant's in-state contacts 'represent a purposeful availment of the privilege of conducting activities in the forum state, thereby invoking the benefits and protections of that state's laws and making the defendant's involuntary presence before the state's courts foreseeable;' and (3) whether the exercise of jurisdiction is reasonable. *Daynard v. Ness, Motley, Loadholt, Richardson, & Poole, P.A.*, 290 F.3d 42, 60 (1st Cir.2002).

There is one fact about this case which has not been recognized in the briefing. It is that a state's long-arm jurisdiction is being asserted against a defendant who is in a foreign country, and not in a sister state. In *Asahi Metal Industry Co. v. Superior Court*, 480 U.S. 102, 107 (1987), the Court applied the usual three part analysis in a foreign-defendant case. *Id.* at 109–16. As to the reasonableness prong, in Part II.B of its opinion, the Court noted that the reasonableness of the exercise of jurisdiction depends on different factors, including the 'burden on the defendant, the interests of the forum State, and the plaintiff's interest in obtaining relief.' *Id.* at 113. A court 'must also weigh in its determination "the interstate judicial system's interest in obtaining the most efficient resolution of controversies[ ] and the shared interests of the several States in furthering fundamental substantive social policies."' *Id.*. The Court applied those considerations with special emphasis in light of that case's factual context, including the defendant's international home forum. We return to *Asahi* when we discuss reasonableness.

Downer must succeed on all three prongs in order to establish personal jurisdiction. We hold that it has.

A. *Relatedness*

Bioriginal did not contest relatedness in the district court and spends less than three pages of its brief here on the issue. We discuss it because the district court found no relatedness, as it found no purposeful availment. *Downer*, at *3.

The relatedness prong requires the plaintiff to show 'a demonstrable nexus between [its] claims and [the defendant's] forum-based activities, such . . . [that] the litigation itself is founded directly on those activities.' *Adelson v. Hananel*, 652 F.3d 75, 81 (1st Cir.2011). This test is a 'flexible, relaxed standard.' *Id.* In a contract case, we focus on 'the parties' "prior negotiations and contemplated future consequences, along with the terms of the contract and the parties' actual course of dealing."' *Daynard*, at 52. We conduct this analysis with reference to the contacts the defendant creates with the forum state, though those contacts may be 'intertwined' with the activities of the plaintiff. *Walden*, at 1122–23; *see Adams v. Adams*, 601 F.3d 1, 6 (1st Cir.2010) (discussing 'whether the defendant's activity in the forum state was instrumental either in the formation of the contract or its breach' or whether the defendant was 'subject to substantial control and ongoing connection to [the forum state] in the performance of th[e] contract').

In this case, the evidence of contacts during the course of dealing is powerful. Bioriginal had an ongoing connection with Massachusetts in the performance under the contract. Downer's claims arise from the alleged breach of that contract. That is enough to establish relatedness. *See Adelson*, at 81–82.

B. *Purposeful Availment*

We now turn to the 'purposeful availment' prong. The purposeful availment prong 'represents a rough quid pro quo: when a defendant deliberately targets its behavior toward the society or economy of a particular forum, the forum should have the power to subject the defendant to judgment regarding that behavior.' *Carreras v. PMG Collins, LLC*, 660 F.3d 549, 555 (1st Cir.2011). The cornerstones of this inquiry are voluntariness and foreseeability. *Daynard*, at 61. This places the emphasis on the defendant's intentions and prohibits jurisdiction based on 'random, fortuitous, or attenuated contacts.' *Carreras*, 660 F.3d at 555. Purposeful availment is an equally important factor when foreign defendants are involved. *See J. McIntyre Mach., Ltd. v. Nicastro*, 131 S.Ct. 2780, 2790–91 (2011) (plurality opinion).

The contacts here clearly were not random, fortuitous, or attenuated. First, the genesis of the Downer engagement strongly supports the case for purposeful availment. After all, Downer first learned of Bioriginal's sale from Johnson, Bioriginal's de facto chairman, in Downer's Boston office. *Cf.*, e.g., *Adelson*, at 82–83 (relying in part on solicitation); *Phillips*, at 29 (emphasizing the absence of solicitation when finding no purposeful availment). Johnson's statement was certainly voluntary, and there is nothing to indicate Bioriginal lacked foreseeability as to it. Downer, in response, then contacted Bioriginal's headquarters to negotiate the agreement. Downer's call to Bioriginal was not a cold call: it was with reference from Johnson.

Second, the contract was not of a short duration or quickly accomplished. Bioriginal had a four-year working relationship with Downer, including intense periods with many exchanges. Bioriginal knew or should have expected Downer's Boston office—its only North American office, and the one with which Bioriginal negotiated the Letter Agreement—to be the site of its partner team. This was no small project: according to the Letter Agreement, Downer was Bioriginal's 'exclusive financial adviser' on the sale of the entire firm. To that end, Bioriginal personnel (including its CEO and Board) and Downer's Boston office collaborated intensively. The record includes statements from Downer personnel detailing contacts, eleven e-mails and documents traded between the two firms, and eleven iterations on one document. Moreover, many of those e-mails refer to other e-mails or to phone calls and teleconferences involving Bioriginal and Downer's Boston office. Bioriginal and Downer worked together on significant documents, and Bioriginal provided its input on many items, including individual slides. As part of that work, Downer asserts it contacted hundreds of potential buyers on Bioriginal's behalf. At least once, Downer arranged and hosted a conference call with Bioriginal and a potential buyer. And Bioriginal sent three payments to Downer in Boston.

To be sure, the purposeful availment inquiry is focused on contacts between the defendant and the forum state, not between the defendant and the plaintiff. *Walden*, at 1122. The contacts here, however, are hardly the 'random,' 'fortuitous,' 'attenuated,' or 'isolated' contacts inadequate to give rise to jurisdiction. *Burger King*, 471 U.S. at 475 & n. 18. Rather, Bioriginal 'reach[ed] out beyond' Canada and into Massachusetts by 'entering a contractual relationship that "envisioned continuing and wide-reaching contacts" in the forum state.' *Walden*, at 1122.

True, many of the e-mails, phone calls, and other activities were originated by Downer in Massachusetts and directed to Bioriginal and third parties elsewhere (although others were directed by Bioriginal to Downer in Massachusetts). But it makes little sense to focus too much on who initiated a particular contact in exploring a lengthy course of dealing in a services contract. By retaining Downer, Bioriginal actively caused Downer to undertake extensive activities on Bioriginal's behalf within Massachusetts. Part of what Bioriginal was paying for was for Downer to take initiative on its behalf. And so, while a plaintiff's 'unilateral activity' cannot constitute a jurisdictional contact, *World–Wide Volkswagen*, 444 U.S. at 298 (internal quotation marks omitted), Downer's extensive Massachusetts activities in this case, given the context, were not 'unilateral.' They were undertaken at Bioriginal's request and are attributable to Bioriginal.

The district court's rejection of jurisdiction was based on reasoning that 'interstate communications by phone and mail are insufficient to demonstrate purposeful availment' absent other contacts. *Downer*, at *4. The district court then concluded that Bioriginal negotiated the agreement from Canada, felt the benefit of the agreement in Canada, and was in breach of the agreement by failing to act in Canada. *Id.* at *3–6. Bioriginal urges the same on appeal.

That reasoning does not support rejection of jurisdiction. '[I]t is an inescapable fact of modern commercial life that a substantial amount of business is transacted solely by mail and wire communications across state lines . . .' *Burger King*, at 476. In light of this reality, the Supreme Court has 'consistently rejected' a physical contact test for personal jurisdiction. *Id.* Before *Burger King*, in *International Shoe*, the Court had already said that a nonresident's physical presence within the territorial jurisdiction of the court is not required.

It is not true that interstate remote communications are, by their nature, per se insufficient to constitute contacts that sustain personal jurisdiction. *See Daynard*, at 61 n. 11 ('The transmission of facts or information into Massachusetts via telephone or mail would of course constitute evidence of a jurisdictional contact directed into the forum state.' A nonresident defendant purposefully avails itself of the forum state when the defendant's actions 'create a "substantial connection" with the forum State.' *Burger King*, at 475. A 'substantial connection' can arise whenever the defendant deliberately directs its efforts toward the forum state. *Id.* at 476. Jurisdiction has been upheld where the defendant purposefully reached out 'beyond [its] State and into another by, for example, entering a contractual relationship that envisioned continuing and wide-reaching contacts in the forum State.' *Walden*, at 1122. The number and duration of the remote contacts are significant to the analysis.

The district court's reasoning drew on two different categories of cases. First, the district court analogized to 'passive purchaser' cases, in which the nonresident defendant merely purchases and receives goods from the forum state. *See R & B Splicer Sys., Inc. v. Woodland Indus., Inc.*, No. 12–11081–GAO, 2013 WL 1222410 (D.Mass. Mar. 26, 2013); *cf. Telford Aviation, Inc. v. Raycom Nat'l, Inc.*, 122 F.Supp.2d 44, 47 (D.Me.2000) (finding no purposeful availment where nonforum resident exchanged communications with forum resident only to schedule delivery of services). Bioriginal was not passive. It actively negotiated the contract and the contract required interactive communications between the two companies for an extended period of time. Nor is this like cases where the defendant passively puts an item in the stream of commerce. See, e.g., *J. McIntyre Mach.*, at 2788.

Second, the district court analogized to cases in which clients sue their non-resident lawyers for legal malpractice. See, e.g., *Kowalski v. Doherty, Wallace, Pillsbury, & Murphy*, 787 F.2d 7 (1st Cir.1986). These cases are inapt for multiple reasons. Most significant, they present the reverse scenario from this case: in those cases, a client sought to sue a service provider at the client's home. Unlike this case, they do not involve a defendant who procured the performance of extensive services in the very forum in which the defendant would be subject to jurisdiction.

C. *Reasonableness*

Though Downer has satisfied the first two prongs of the analysis, we must nonetheless assure ourselves that Massachusetts's assertion of jurisdiction is fair and reasonable. We do so with reference to five 'gestalt' factors:

(1) the defendant's burden of appearing [in the forum state], (2) the forum state's interest in adjudicating the dispute, (3) the plaintiff's interest in obtaining convenient and effective relief, (4) the judicial system's interest in obtaining the most effective resolution of the controversy, and (5) the common interests of all sovereigns in promoting substantive social policies. *Ticketmaster*, at 209.

These factors typically 'play a larger role in cases'—unlike this one—'where the minimum contacts question is very close.' *Adelson* at 51; *see Ticketmaster*, at 210 ('[T]he weaker the plaintiff's showing on the first two prongs . . . the less a defendant need show in terms of unreasonableness to defeat jurisdiction.') We do not consider the minimum contacts issue to be very close.

Nor is the fact that a foreign defendant is involved of much moment here. Those concerns are of far less weight in this case than in *Asahi*. Bioriginal identifies no special burden imposed by requiring it to litigate across the Canada–United States border, nor any international policy burdened by Massachusetts's exercise of jurisdiction. Massachusetts, Saskatchewan, and all individuals involved transact business in a common language, English. Indeed, even in the Massachusetts forum, Saskatchewan will have its laws govern the substantive issues in the case, and Bioriginal itself has emphasized the similarities between Saskatchewan and Massachusetts law. The international dimensions of the case do not create 'unique burdens' for Bioriginal. *Asahi*, at 114. Indeed, Bioriginal makes no claim to that effect. *See United Elec.*

Radio & Mach. Workers of Am. v. 163 Pleasant St. Corp., 987 F.2d 39, 46–47 (1st Cir.1993).

We compare *Asahi*'s facts to those of this case. The dispute in *Asahi* was whether 'a Japanese corporation should indemnify a Taiwanese corporation on the basis of a sale made in Taiwan and a shipment of goods from Japan to Taiwan.' 480 U.S. at 115. Jurisdiction over the defendant would have required the defendant, from a civil law country, to litigate in California. See, e.g., Shishido, *Japanese Corporate Governance*, 25 Del. J. Corp. L. 189, 195 (2000). The defendant also would have had to litigate across the Pacific Ocean. And the burden of litigating at such a distance was greater given that the transaction underlying the claim took place entirely in Asia. *Asahi*, at 114. None of these burdens are present in this case.

Bioriginal does emphasize the inconvenience imposed on any witnesses who will be required to travel from Saskatoon to Boston. This is a far milder complaint than in *Asahi*, which concerned the burden of conducting the entire course of litigation at substantial distance from the defendant's normal forum. This inconvenience does not determine the outcome of our jurisdiction analysis. '[M]ounting an out-of-state defense most always means added trouble and cost,' *BlueTarp Fin., Inc. v. Matrix Constr. Co.*, 709 F.3d 72, 83 (1st Cir.2013), and modern travel 'creates no especially ponderous burden for business travelers,' *Pritzker v. Yari*, 42 F.3d 53, 64 (1st Cir.1994). For this type of burden to affect the analysis, the defendant must show that it is 'special or unusual.' *BlueTarp Fin.*, at 83. Bioriginal has not done so. And we suspect that the merits issues may come down to a question of contract interpretation for the court. Most logistical challenges can be resolved through the use of affidavits and video devices.

In this case, the gestalt factors do not overcome the earlier showing. The parties have identified few burdens, interests, or inefficiencies that cut strongly in favor of or against jurisdiction. In our view, a particularly weighty factor is Massachusetts's interest in adjudicating the dispute. *Cf. Asahi*, at 115–16 (identifying California's 'minimal' interest in the validity of the indemnification claim, a loss allocation question between two foreign corporations). Massachusetts has 'significant' interests in providing a convenient forum for disputes involving its citizens and in ensuring that its companies have easy access to a forum when their commercial contracts are said to be breached by out-of-state defendants. *Champion Exposition Servs., Inc. v. Hi–Tech Elec., LLC*, 273 F.Supp.2d 172, 179 (D.Mass.2003); *see BlueTarp Fin.*, at 83 (recognizing Maine's 'stake in being able to provide a convenient forum for its slighted residents' and in 'redressing harms committed against its companies by out-of-state companies'); *Sawtelle v. Farrell*, 70 F.3d 1381, 1395 (1st Cir.1995) (noting that these interests have 'added importance in our age of advanced telecommunications' in which parties contract without meeting in person); *C & M Mgmt., Inc. v. Cunningham–Warren Props., LLC*, No. 12–P–1944, 3 N.E.3d 1119, at *4 (Mass.App.Ct. Feb. 27, 2014) (unpublished) (explaining that Massachusetts 'has a manifest interest in providing a convenient forum to residents asserting good faith and objectively reasonable claims for relief').

In opposition to this interest, Bioriginal marshals the choice-of-law provision in favor of Saskatchewan law, and it argues that the contractual transaction fee provision is non-standard, 'presenting a matter of first impression under Saskatchewan law.' We see no injustice in having a Massachusetts court interpret the contract. As the district court noted, 'federal district courts are in the regular practice of applying laws of other' fora. *Downer*, at *8.

We conclude where we began. Downer's showing on the first two prongs of the inquiry is strong, so Bioriginal carries the burden of defeating jurisdiction with a similarly strong showing of unfairness. To the limited extent that the gestalt factors are meaningful, they weigh in favor of jurisdiction even considering the international context. Bioriginal has not met its burden.

? NOTES AND QUESTIONS

1 Under the relatedness prong of the analysis, the court does not focus on one particular contact with the forum (such as the place of performance of one particular obligation), but considers all possible contacts. Recall, however, that under the Due Process clause, the focus should be on the defendant, and that the relevant contacts should therefore be between the activities of the defendant and the forum.

2 Under the Brussels Ibis Regulation, which court would have jurisdiction? Would the contract be characterized as a provision of services?

3 The jurisdictional test does not only require that there be a nexus, but also that the assertion of jurisdiction be acceptable from a dual perspective. First, the defendant should have deliberately availed himself of the forum by directing its efforts to it. Interestingly, the court insists that the place of performance of the services is important in order to assess whether this prong is met. Could a service provider seriously deny that he deliberately availed himself of the state where he provides services? Secondly, the assertion of jurisdiction should be fair and reasonable under five factors. Some relate to procedural fairness. Others have a substantive dimension. However, their role is limited where there are strong contacts with the forum. Will this be typically the case where the services will be provided in the forum?

4 The distinction between the nexus between the activities of the defendant and the forum and the reasonableness of the assertion jurisdiction originates in the case law of the Supreme Court prior to 2011. In *J. McIntyre Mach., Ltd. v. Nicastro*, however, the Supreme Court focused on the nexus prong and did not mention the evaluation of the reasonableness of the jurisdiction of the forum, so that it is unclear whether the reasonableness prong will remain: see *supra* Ch. 3.

5 In contractual matters, is the jurisdiction of U.S. courts broader than the jurisdiction of European courts?

2.2 Nexus and appropriateness

The jurisdictional test in contractual matters is also sophisticated in England and the countries which follow its lead. As we have seen in Part II, jurisdiction is linked to service, and English courts will only permit service outside of the jurisdiction if three requirements are met. First, the plaintiff should demonstrate that there is a serious issue to be tried on the merits. Second, he should demonstrate that it is likely that there exists one of the contacts listed in Practice Direction 6B. Contrary to the U.S. test, the existence of one of the recognized contacts is enough.

English Practice Direction 6B Service Out of the Jurisdiction

Service out of the jurisdiction where permission is required

3.1 The claimant may serve a claim form out of the jurisdiction with the permission of the court under rule 6.36 where –

General Grounds

(1) A claim is made for a remedy against a person domiciled within the jurisdiction.

(. . .)

Claims in relation to contracts

(6) A claim is made in respect of a contract where the contract –

(a)   was made within the jurisdiction;

(b)   was made by or through an agent trading or residing within the jurisdiction;

(c)   is governed by English law; or

(d)   contains a term to the effect that the court shall have jurisdiction to determine any claim in respect of the contract.

(7) A claim is made in respect of a breach of contract committed within the jurisdiction.

(8) A claim is made for a declaration that no contract exists where, if the contract was found to exist, it would comply with the conditions set out in paragraph (6).

? **QUESTION**

How does ground (7) compare with Article 7 of the Brussels Ibis Regulation?

Third, the plaintiff should show that England is clearly or distinctly the appropriate forum for the trial of the dispute. As already underscored, the appropriateness of the forum will be assessed by considering factors focusing on the interests of the parties, but excluding public interests. It is therefore different from the U.S. prong of fairness and reasonableness which not only considers fairness to the parties, but also the interests of the forum to resolve the dispute.

? QUESTIONS

Do grounds (6)(a) and (c) reveal a strong connection between England and the dispute? How legitimate is the jurisdiction of an English court relying on such a connection?

9

Choice of law in contractual matters

Remarkably, the choice of law rule in contractual matters affords to the parties the freedom to choose the law governing their contract (1). While this power is widely used in international commercial transactions, there are still many instances where the parties fail to provide for the law governing their contract. It is then necessary to apply a default choice of law rule (2).

1 Freedom of choice

In private international law as in contract law, freedom of contract is generally favoured because it enables the parties to frame a legal regime which best fits their needs (1.1). Abuse is possible, however. The clearest case is where one of the parties has a much lower bargaining power than the other. Certain legal systems afford special choice of law rules aimed at protecting weaker parties (1.2).

1.1 General rules

1.1.1 *Freedom to choose mandatory rules?*

Contract laws are composed of two different types of rules. Certain rules are mandatory: the parties may not derogate from them by agreement. If they try, their contractual term, and possibly the entire contract, will be illegal and void. Other rules are only defaults. They only apply to supplement the contract when the parties have not specifically included a contractual term on the relevant issue.

The power to choose the applicable law is uncontroversial for default rules. The parties could have displaced such rules by including an express contractual provision. By choosing a foreign law as the law governing their contract, they would displace all default rules of the law which would have otherwise applied, and replace them with the default rules of the chosen law. They could have done so anyway by expressly stipulating terms with a similar content to that of the foreign rules.

By contrast, the power to choose the applicable law is much more remarkable with respect to mandatory rules. Such power amounts to allowing the parties to indirectly displace the mandatory rules of the law which would have otherwise applied and to replace them by the rules of the chosen law.

The U.S. Restatement distinguishes between the two types of rules. Can you identify the legal consequences of the distinction?

> *American Restatement (Second) of Conflict of Laws (1971)*
> **Section 187.** LAW OF THE STATE CHOSEN BY THE PARTIES
> (1) The law of the state chosen by the parties to govern their contractual rights and duties will be applied if the particular issue is one which the parties could have resolved by an explicit provision in their agreement directed to that issue.
> (2) The law of the state chosen by the parties to govern their contractual rights and duties will be applied, even if the particular issue is one which the parties could not have resolved by an explicit provision in their agreement directed to that issue, unless either
>
> (a) the chosen state has no substantial relationship to the parties or the transaction and there is no other reasonable basis for the parties' choice, or
> (b) application of the law of the chosen state would be contrary to a fundamental policy of a state which has a materially greater interest than the chosen state in the determination of the particular issue and which, under the rule of s 188, would be the state of the applicable law in the absence of an effective choice of law by the parties.

Most countries do not distinguish between mandatory and default rules and simply give freedom of choice in international transactions.

In effect, this means that the parties may shop around and choose mandatory rules of their liking. Whereas the very concept of mandatory rules is that they trump the agreement of the parties, in an international setting, they apply as a consequence of a choice of the parties.

Is it acceptable?

1. To answer this difficult question, it is useful to recall that international contracts involve several parties typically coming from different jurisdictions. If one accepts that the solution cannot be the cumulative application of the laws of all parties, a choice has to be made, and the law of

at least one party will not apply. This means that the mandatory rules of the law of origin of that party will be ignored. In other words, in international transactions, no solution could possibly satisfy all laws connected to the relevant transaction. One law will have to be chosen, and the others excluded. Note that, in the absence of choice by the parties, a choice would have to be made anyway, with the same consequences, on the basis of the applicable choice of law rule.[1]

2. Additionally, a practical dimension of international contractual negotiations has an important impact on the issue. Parties to international contracts typically fear that, if the law of the other party is chosen, they will have conceded an important advantage. This would be especially true if they had also conceded the jurisdiction of the other party's courts. Thus, it often happens that the parties are unable to agree on either of their laws, and that the only way forward is to agree on a 'neutral law', that is, the law of a third state. Swiss law (and Switzerland as an arbitration venue) is extremely often chosen as a neutral law by parties with no connection to Switzerland.[2] This means that parties to international contracts will often choose a law which is unconnected to their dispute without caring for its mandatory rules.

3. This does not change the fact that, in some cases, parties could use their freedom of choice to choose a law for the sole purpose of avoiding a mandatory rule of their law of origin. In the worst case scenario, they would choose a law for the sole purpose of avoiding a rule which would be common to the law of origin of both parties. There are a certain number of devices to sanction such a behaviour. The most important is the doctrine of *international* mandatory rules, which will trump choice of law.[3] The efficacy of the doctrine in the context of international contracts, however, is directly related to the rules on enforcement of choice of court agreements.[4] A more radical way to resolve the issue is to prohibit choosing a law which is not connected to the transaction: see below, 1.1.2.

EU Regulation No 593/2008 of 17 June 2008 on the law applicable to contractual obligations (Rome I)

Article 3 *Freedom of choice*

1. A contract shall be governed by the law chosen by the parties. (. . .)

---

1 *Infra*, 2.
2 Christiana Fountoulakis, 'The Parties' Choice of "Neutral Law" in International Sales Contracts' (2005) 7 European J.L. Reform 303.
3 *Supra*, Ch. 1.
4 *Supra*, Ch. 5.

3. Where all other elements relevant to the situation at the time of the choice are located in a country other than the country whose law has been chosen, the choice of the parties shall not prejudice the application of provisions of the law of that other country which cannot be derogated from by agreement.

4. Where all other elements relevant to the situation at the time of the choice are located in one or more Member States, the parties' choice of applicable law other than that of a Member State shall not prejudice the application of provisions of Community law, where appropriate as implemented in the Member State of the forum, which cannot be derogated from by agreement. (. . .)

Quebec Civil Code

Article 3111

A juridical act, whether or not it contains any foreign element, is governed by the law expressly designated in the act or whose designation may be inferred with certainty from the terms of the act.

Where a juridical act contains no foreign element, it remains nevertheless subject to the mandatory provisions of the law of the State which would apply in the absence of a designation. (. . .)

? NOTES AND QUESTIONS

1 Is it possible to choose the applicable law in domestic contracts? The Rome I Regulation, the Quebec Civil Code and Art. 1210(5) of the Russian Civil Code allow it. However, the consequence of a choice in this context is very different. What is its impact on mandatory rules?

2 The power to choose the law governing a contract raises the issue of the relationship between the private will of the parties and the law. Is the law superior to the will of the parties, or is the will of the parties superior to the law? Art. 3(1) of the Rome I Regulation and Art. 3111 of the Quebec Civil Code both provide that the law chosen by the parties *governs* the contract. This means that, although the parties have the power to choose the applicable law, the chosen law remains superior to the contract and to the will of the parties. Its mandatory rules (whether domestic or international) apply and, as the case may be, might invalidate any clause contradicting them.[5]

A lawmaker could decide to give private parties a more limited power, however. It might wish to allow them to provide for the application of a foreign law, but only to the extent that its mandatory rules (whether domestic or international) would remain applicable. The choice of law would only displace the default rules of the otherwise applicable law, but not its mandatory rules. As already discussed, this would not be very controversial. The parties could have reached the same result by expressly providing for contractual terms having the same content as the foreign law. This kind of choice of law with limited effect is called *incorporation*. The chosen law is incorporated in the contract, as express contractual terms would, and it thus has the same status as contractual clauses. The contract remains governed by the mandatory rules of the otherwise applicable law. The chosen law is incorporated in the contract and will only displace the default rules of the otherwise applicable law.

---

5 On this issue, see *infra* 1.1.5.

3 In certain jurisdictions, the parties may only choose the applicable law in international contracts: see for example, American Uniform Commercial Code, s. 1-105 (infra, 1.1.2). But what if the parties do provide for the application of a foreign law in a domestic contract? Are they allowed to stipulate however they wish when a given issue is not governed by a mandatory rule? In effect, therefore, they may always incorporate any rule in their contract, including foreign rules.
If the parties do incorporate a foreign law in their contract, can they add express contractual terms which would not be aligned with, and thus would in effect derogate from the foreign law? Would it matter whether the particular rule of foreign law would be mandatory in the foreign legal system?

4 Is it possible for the parties to freeze the chosen law?

Institut de droit international, Session de Bâle (1991) Resolution on the Autonomy of the Parties in International Contracts Between Private Persons or Entities
Article 8
If the parties agree that the chosen law is to be applied as it is in force at the time when the contract was concluded, the provisions of that law shall be applied as substantive provisions incorporated in the contract; if, however, the chosen law has been amended or repealed by mandatory rules which are intended to govern existing contracts, effect shall be given to those rules.

5 Is it possible to choose a non-national law?

Rome I Regulation (2008)
Preamble
(13) This Regulation does not preclude parties from incorporating by reference into their contract a non-State body of law or an international convention.

6 Which law governs the contract in cases covered by Art. 3(4) of the Rome I Regulation? On Art. 3(4), see also *supra*, p. 25.

1.1.2   May the parties choose a law unconnected to the contract?

Rome I Regulation (2008)
Article 3 *Freedom of choice*
1. A contract shall be governed by the law chosen by the parties. (. . .)

Law of the People's Republic of China on the Laws Applicable to Foreign-Related Civil Relations (2010)
Article 41
(1) The parties may by agreement choose the law applicable to their contract. (. . .).

Interpretation of the Supreme People's Court on Issues regarding the Application of the Law of the PRC on the Laws Applicable to Foreign-Related Civil Relations (Part 1, 2012)

Article 7

If one of the parties claims that the choice of law is invalid, on the ground that no genuine connection exists between the law chosen by mutual agreement and the disputed foreign-related civil relation, the People's Courts shall not uphold the claim.[6]

American Uniform Commercial Code

§ 1-105. *Territorial Application of the Act; Parties' Power to Choose Applicable Law.*

(1) Except as provided hereafter in this section, when a transaction bears a reasonable relation to this state and also to another state or nation the parties may agree that the law either of this state or of such other state or nation shall govern their rights and duties. Failing such agreement this Act applies to transactions bearing an appropriate relation to this state.

(2) Where one of the following provisions of this Act specifies the applicable law, that provision governs and a contrary agreement is effective only to the extent permitted by the law (including the conflict of laws rules) so specified: Rights of creditors against sold goods. Section 2-402. Applicability of the Article on Leases. Sections 2A-105 and 2A-106. Applicability of the Article on Bank Deposits and Collections. Section 4-102. Governing law in the Article on Funds Transfers. Section 4A-507. Bulk sales subject to the Article on Bulk Sales. Section 6-103.

Restatement (Second) of Conflict of Laws (1971)

Section 187. LAW OF THE STATE CHOSEN BY THE PARTIES

(2) The law of the state chosen by the parties to govern their contractual rights and duties will be applied, even if the particular issue is one which the parties could not have resolved by an explicit provision in their agreement directed to that issue, unless either

(a) the chosen state has no substantial relationship to the parties or the transaction and there is no other reasonable basis for the parties' choice, or (. . .)

❓ NOTES

1   It is widely accepted in Europe and in many other parts of the world (China for instance) that parties to an international contract may provide for the application of the law of any nation. There is no requirement that the law chosen by parties be connected to the parties or the transaction in any way whatsoever.

The rule is opposite in the United States: both the Uniform Commercial Code and the Restatement require that there be a reasonable relation, or a substantial relationship between the law chosen and the parties or the transaction.

---

6   Translation Ilaria Aquironi (2013) Diritto del Commercio Internazionale 891.

2 An alternative for the substantial relationship in s. 187 is the existence of a 'reasonable basis' for the choice. U.S. courts have accepted that this includes the choice of a law which is widely used in a given industry such as English law in maritime matters. However, they have not accepted that the need for a neutral law is a reasonable basis.

3 In 2001, the Uniform Law Commission (also known as the National Conference of Commissioners of Uniform State Laws) proposed to abandon the traditional requirement for commercial transactions and to maintain it only for transactions involving consumers. A choice of the law of a state or a country was effective 'whether or not the transaction bears a relation to the State or country designated' (Proposed Section 1-301(c)(2)). However, the proposed reform did not convince American state lawmakers, as only the Virgin Islands adopted it in the following years. The Uniform Law Commission eventually withdrew it and reverted to the original rule in 2008.

4 The requirement that the chosen law be connected to the transaction largely prevents the parties from using their freedom of choice to bypass mandatory rules. The options are limited to choosing between the mandatory rules of the few laws which are connected to the transaction. In the absence of a choice by the parties, one of them only would have applied anyway, excluding the application of mandatory rules of all others.

5 Note that the European lawmaker has limited the power of parties to European contracts to choose the law of a non-European state: see Art. 3(4) of the Rome I Regulation *supra* 1.1.1.

New York General Obligations Law

§ 5-1401. *Choice of law.*

1. The parties to any contract, agreement or undertaking, contingent or otherwise, in consideration of, or relating to any obligation arising out of a transaction covering in the aggregate not less than two hundred and fifty thousand dollars, including a transaction otherwise covered by subsection one of section 1-105 of the uniform commercial code, may agree that the law of this state shall govern their rights and duties in whole or in part, whether or not such contract, agreement or undertaking bears a reasonable relation to this state. This section shall not apply to any contract, agreement or undertaking (a) for labor or personal services, (b) relating to any transaction for personal, family or household services, or (c) to the extent provided to the contrary in subsection two of section 1-105 of the uniform commercial code.

2. Nothing contained in this section shall be construed to limit or deny the enforcement of any provision respecting choice of law in any other contract, agreement or undertaking.

❓ NOTE AND QUESTION

The rule that parties to international contracts may not choose a law unconnected to the parties or the transaction is not good for business. It means that, if foreign parties were willing to provide for the application of the law of a U.S. state, and thus bring business to American attorneys, such a choice of law clause would not be enforceable in a U.S. court. In order to enable the lawyers based in their jurisdiction to compete on the international market for contracts,[7] a number of U.S. states

---

7 See Gilles Cuniberti, 'The International Market for Contracts – The Most Attractive Contracts Laws', (2014) 34 Northwestern J. Int'l L. and Business 455.

have passed special legislation to displace the general rule and allow foreign parties to choose the law of their state.[8]

Why do you think the New York lawmaker only allowed such a choice for transactions above a certain limit? Does § 5-1401 allow for the choice of Swiss law as a neutral law?

1.1.3   Form and timing of choice

Rome I Regulation (2008)

Preamble

12. An agreement between the parties to confer on one or more courts or tribunals of a Member State exclusive jurisdiction to determine disputes under the contract should be one of the factors to be taken into account in determining whether a choice of law has been clearly demonstrated. (. . .)

20. Where the contract is manifestly more closely connected with a country other than that indicated in Article 4(1) or (2), an escape clause should provide that the law of that other country is to apply. In order to determine that country, account should be taken, *inter alia*, of whether the contract in question has a very close relationship with another contract or contracts.

Article 3 *Freedom of choice*

1. A contract shall be governed by the law chosen by the parties. The choice shall be made expressly or clearly demonstrated by the terms of the contract or the circumstances of the case. (. . .)

2. The parties may at any time agree to subject the contract to a law other than that which previously governed it, whether as a result of an earlier choice made under this Article or of other provisions of this Regulation. Any change in the law to be applied that is made after the conclusion of the contract shall not prejudice its formal validity under Article 11 or adversely affect the rights of third parties. (. . .)

Swiss Federal Code on Private International Law (1987)

Article 116 *II. Applicable law 1. In general a. Choice of law by the parties*

1 The contract shall be governed by the law chosen by the parties.

2 The choice of law must be express or clearly evident from the terms of the contract or the circumstances. In all other respects it shall be governed by the law chosen.

3 The choice of law may be made or modified at any time. If made or modified following the conclusion of the contract, it shall be retroactive to the time the contract was concluded. The rights of third parties shall take precedence.

---

8   See Geoffrey Miller & Theodore Eisenberg, 'The Market for Contracts' (2009) 30 Cardozo L.R. 2073.

Japanese Act on the General Rules of Application of Laws (2006)
Article 9 *Variation of Applicable Law by the Parties*
The parties may vary the law otherwise applicable to the formation and effect of a juristic act. However, such variation shall not be asserted against third parties where it would be prejudicial to their rights.

? NOTES AND QUESTIONS

1 Choice of law needs not be express. It can be implicit from the terms of the contract or the circumstances of the case. What could be a choice which would not be express, but would be demonstrated by the terms of the contract?
2 Should a choice of law made in a related contract be relevant? Could that be relevant circumstances to assess the existence of an implied choice of law? Is Recital 20 of the Rome I Regulation useful to answer this question?
3 Could a forum selection clause be relevant? Does an agreement on jurisdiction entail an agreement on the applicable law? Is it possible to provide for the jurisdiction of the courts of one country, and the application of the court of another country?
4 In most cases, parties will choose the applicable law at the time of conclusion of the contract by stipulating a choice of law clause. It is widely accepted, however, that the parties may make such choice at a later stage. If so, which law governed the contract in the meantime?
5 Should a choice of law made after the conclusion of the contract apply retroactively? Compare the Rome I Regulation and the Swiss Law.

1.1.4   Dépeçage

Rome I Regulation (2008)

Article 3 *Freedom of choice*
1. A contract shall be governed by the law chosen by the parties. The choice shall be made expressly or clearly demonstrated by the terms of the contract or the circumstances of the case. By their choice the parties can select the law applicable to the whole or to part only of the contract.
(. . .)

Quebec Civil Code

Article 3111
A juridical act, whether or not it contains any foreign element, is governed by the law expressly designated in the act or whose designation may be inferred with certainty from the terms of the act.
(. . .)
The law may be expressly designated as applicable to the whole or to only part of a juridical act.

NOTES AND QUESTIONS

1 The Rome I Regulation, the Quebec Civil Code and Art. 1210(4) of the Russian Civil Code give the power to the parties not only to choose any law they wish, but also to choose a law applicable to part only of their contract.[9] Which law will govern the other part?

2 Although Art. 3 of the Rome I Regulation does not expressly provide so, it is widely accepted that it gives the power to choose two laws to govern respectively two different parts of the contract. The application of two laws to the same legal relationship is known as '*dépeçage*', from the French dismemberment. It can be the result of the will of the parties, but it is also often the result of the existence of different choice of law rules for the purpose of determining the applicable law to different aspects of a given legal relationship.[10]

3 Is it acceptable to allow the parties to choose a law for partial application? Are there any limits to such power? Would it be possible to choose law A to govern the entirety of the contract, and law B to govern one clause only, which is prohibited by a mandatory rule of law A? Could the parties choose to subject different parts of the contract to three, four or five different laws? By so doing, could they eventually avoid being subjected to any mandatory rule?

CASE

European Court of Justice, 6 October 2009 *Intercontainer Interfrigo SC (ICF) v. Balkenende Oosthuizen BV* (Case C-133/08)[11]

41 By the second part of its second question and the third and fourth questions, the national court in essence asks in which circumstances it is possible, under the second sentence of Article 4(1) of the Convention [on the law applicable to contractual obligations, opened for signature in Rome on 19 June 1980], to apply different national laws to the same contractual relationship, in particular as regards the limitation of the rights under a contract such as that at issue in the main proceedings. The Hoge Raad der Nederlanden asks, inter alia, whether, if the connecting criterion provided for in Article 4(4) of the Convention applies to a charter-party, that criterion relates only to the part of the contract concerning the carriage of goods.

42 In that regard, it must be borne in mind that, under the second sentence of Article 4(1) of the Convention,[12] a part of the contract may, by way of exception, be made subject to a law other than that applied to the rest of the contract, where it

---

9 In the United States, the drafters of the *Restatement (Second)* also accepted this power: see § 187, cmt i.

10 Marriage is one of the most remarkable examples. Different choice of law rules apply to determine the law governing the formation and the effects of marriage, and often to determine the law governing different aspects of the formation of marriage, and different aspects of the effects of marriage: see *infra* Ch. 11.

11 ECLI:EU:C:2009:617, [2009] E.C.R. I-09687.

12 Art 4(1) of the Rome Convention provided: 'To the extent that the law applicable to the contract has not been chosen in accordance with Article 3, the contract shall be governed by the law of the country with which it is most closely connected. Nevertheless, a severable part of the contract which has a closer connection with another country may by way of exception be governed by the law of that other country.'

has a closer connection with a country other than that with which the other parts of the contract are connected.

43 It is apparent from the wording of that provision that the rule providing for the severance of a contract is of an exceptional nature. In that regard, the Giuliano and Lagarde report states that the words 'by way of exception' in the last sentence of Article 4(1) 'are . . . to be interpreted in the sense that the court must have recourse to severance as seldom as possible'.

44 In order to ascertain the conditions in which the court may sever the contract, it is necessary to consider that the objective of the Convention, as was stated in the preliminary observations in paragraphs 22 to 23 of this judgment, is to raise the level of legal certainty by fortifying confidence in the stability of the relationships between the parties to the contract. Such an objective cannot be attained if the system for determining the applicable law is unclear and that law cannot be predicted with some degree of certainty.

45 As the Advocate General pointed out in paragraphs 83 and 84 of his Opinion, the possibility of separating a contract into a number of parts in order to make it subject to a number of laws runs counter to the objectives of the Convention and must be allowed only where there are a number of parts to the contract who may be regarded as independent of each other.

46 Consequently, in order to determine whether a part of a contract may be made subject to a different law it is necessary to ascertain whether the object of that part is independent in relation to the purpose of the rest of the contract.

47 If that is the case, each part of a contract must be made subject to one single law. In particular, therefore, the rules relating to the prescription of a right must fall under the same legal system as that applied to the corresponding obligation. In that regard, it must be borne in mind that, under Article 10(1)(d) of the Convention, the law applicable to a contract governs in particular the prescription of obligations.

48 In the light of those considerations, the answer to the second part of the second question and the third and fourth questions is that the second sentence of Article 4(1) of the Convention must be interpreted as meaning that a part of a contract may be governed by a law other than that applied to the rest of the contract only where the object of that part is independent.

49 Where the connecting criterion applied to a charter-party is that set out in Article 4(4) of the Convention, that criterion must be applied to the whole of the contract, unless the part of the contract relating to carriage is independent of the rest of the contract.

? NOTES AND QUESTIONS

1 The *ICF* case was concerned with Art. 4(1) of the Rome Convention, which related to the applicable law in the absence of choice. Article 4 of the Rome Regulation is now silent on *dépeçage*. Does this mean that *dépeçage* is no longer possible in this context?

2 To which extent is the *ICF* case relevant for the purpose of interpreting Art. 3 of the Rome Regulation?

3 Could you think of examples of parts of a contract which have independent objects? Is a non-liability clause a part of a contract having an independent object? Does a contract for the sale of a car, including a set of winter tyres (in addition to the summer tyres) have separate parts with independent objects? How many?

1.1.5 Law governing choice of law agreement

Parties will typically choose the applicable law by providing to that effect in a clause of their contract. Which law governs the validity of such clause?

Rome I Regulation (2008)

Article 3 *Freedom of choice*

1. A contract shall be governed by the law chosen by the parties. (. . .)

5. The existence and validity of the consent of the parties as to the choice of the applicable law shall be determined in accordance with the provisions of Articles 10, 11 and 13.

Article 10 *Consent and material validity*

1. The existence and validity of a contract, or of any term of a contract, shall be determined by the law which would govern it under this Regulation if the contract or term were valid.

2. Nevertheless, a party, in order to establish that he did not consent, may rely upon the law of the country in which he has his habitual residence if it appears from the circumstances that it would not be reasonable to determine the effect of his conduct in accordance with the law specified in paragraph 1.

 CASE

Supreme Court of Georgia, 28 March 2008 *CS-Lakeview at Gwinnett v. Simon Property Group, Inc.*[13]

Carley, Justice.

CS-Lakeview at Gwinnett, Inc. (CS-Lakeview) and related entities entered into a joint venture concerning commercial property with Simon Property Group, Inc. and related entities (Simon). Many of the entities involved in the joint venture are Delaware corporations and, when a complex dispute arose, Simon sued CS-Lakeview in Delaware. In a subsequent settlement agreement, the joint venture assets were divided, including a 133-acre tract of land located in Georgia, which was received by Simon. The agreement purported

---

13 283 Ga. 426.

to give CS-Lakeview a right of first refusal with respect to that property. The agreement further provided that it was to be 'subject to and construed in accordance with the laws of the state of Delaware.'

When Simon received a third-party offer for the Georgia property, the parties differed as to the required procedures, and Simon eventually sold the land to the third party. CS-Lakeview sued Simon in Georgia, alleging that Simon had not allowed CS-Lakeview to exercise its right of first refusal. The trial court granted summary judgment in favor of Simon on the ground that CS-Lakeview's right of first refusal was invalid under Delaware's rule against perpetuities.

On appeal, the Court of Appeals affirmed, holding that Delaware law governed the validity of CS-Lakeview's right of first refusal and that such provision of the settlement agreement was invalid under that state's rule against perpetuities. *CS-Lakeview at Gwinnett v. Simon Property Group*, 283 Ga.App. 686, 688(1), 642 S.E.2d 393 (2007). The Court of Appeals further ruled that the trial court correctly refused to reform the agreement so as to remedy the parties' mutual mistake in choosing Delaware law, which invalidates the right of first refusal, in favor of Georgia law, which authorizes such a provision. Having granted certiorari to review this latter ruling, we conclude that mutual mistake is not a valid basis upon which to nullify the parties' choice of Delaware law in order to uphold the right of first refusal.

The Court of Appeals mistakenly relied on OCGA § 23-2-27, which states that, where the facts are all known and there is no misplaced confidence or fraudulent conduct inducing the mistake or preventing its correction, 'ignorance of the law by *a* party (not a mutual mistake by both) shall not authorize the intervention of equity . . . [T]his Code section has no application to a mutual mistake of law by both parties.' (Emphasis in original.) *Superior Ins. Co. v. Dawkins*, 229 Ga.App. 45, 48(1), fn. 2 (1997). See also *A.J. Concrete Pumping v. Richard O'Brien Equip. Sales*, 256 Ga. 795, 796(1) (1987) ('"(E) quity will reform a written instrument for the unilateral mistake of one party accompanied by fraud or inequitable conduct on behalf of the other party."').

An alleged mutual mistake of law is governed by OCGA § 23-2-22, which applies to '[a]n honest mistake of the law as to the effect of an instrument on the part of both contracting parties, when the mistake operates as a gross injustice to one and gives an unconscionable advantage to the other . . .' 'A mistake relievable in equity is some unintentional act, omission, or error arising from ignorance, surprise, imposition, or misplaced confidence.' OCGA § 23-2-21(a). 'Where reformation is sought on the ground of mutual mistake, it must, of course, be proved to be the mistake of both parties.' *A.J. Concrete Pumping v. Richard O'Brien Equip. Sales.* 'The power to relieve mistakes shall be exercised with caution; to justify it, the evidence shall be clear, unequivocal, and decisive as to the mistake.' OCGA § 23-2-21(c). See also *Fulghum v. Kelly*, 255 Ga. 652, 654 (1986).

Relying on the Restatement (Second) of Conflict of Laws § 187(2) cmt. e and several cases, CS-Lakeview contends that, in choosing a governing law which rendered the right of first refusal invalid, the parties made a mutual mistake and would have chosen Georgia law if they had considered the issue. However, this Court has declined to adopt § 187(2) of the Restatement (Second) of Conflict of Laws, and continues to adhere to traditional conflicts of law rules. *Convergys Corp. v. Keener*, 276 Ga. 808, 812, (2003). Compare *Kipin Indus. v. Van Deilen Intl.*, 182 F.3d 490, 493(II) (6th Cir.1999) (applying law of Michigan, which follows §§ 187 and 188 of the Second Restatement of Conflict of Laws); Russell J. Weintraub, *Commentary on the Conflict of Laws*, § 7.3C, p. 495 (5th ed. 2006) (advocating adherence to the Second Restatement).

In light of OCGA § 1-3-9, the law of the jurisdiction chosen by parties to a contract to govern their contractual rights will be enforced unless application of the chosen law would be contrary to the public policy or prejudicial to the interests of this state. *Convergys Corp. v. Keener*, at 810.

'"[A] contract should not be held unenforceable as being in contravention of public policy except in cases free from substantial doubt where the prejudice to the public interest clearly appears."' (Cit.) . . . "Enforcement of a contract or a contract provision which is valid by the law governing the contract will not be denied on the ground of public policy, unless a 'strong case' for such action is presented; mere dissimilarity of law is not sufficient for application of the public policy doctrine . . ." *Nationwide General Ins. Co. v. Parnham*, 182 Ga.App. 823, 825(4) (1987).

'The fact that the law of the forum state is different than the law of the foreign state does not mean that the foreign state's law necessarily is against the public policy of the forum state.' *Punzi v. Shaker Advertising Agency*, 601 So.2d 599, 600 (Fla.App.1992).

'The policy of giving effect to the parties' intent to have a binding contract and the general policy of contract validation come into conflict when the law that the parties have chosen would invalidate the *whole* contract.' (Emphasis in original.) Scoles, Hay, Borchers & Symeonides, *Conflict of Laws* § 18.11,

p. 982 (4th ed. 2000). However, under either the traditional approach or the Restatement, where, as here, the law chosen by the parties invalidates *only a part* of the contract, the parties' expectations of having a binding contract are satisfied. Consequently, in the absence of special circumstances, there is little reason to allow one party to pick the favorable and discard the unfavorable provisions of the chosen law. [Even] [t]he Second Restatement does not support this type of private eclecticism, and most cases have expressly rejected it. [Cits.] (Emphasis in original.) Scoles, at p. 983. See also Symeon C. Symeonides, 'Choice of Law in the American Courts,' 48 Am. J. Comp. L. 143, 162(IV)(1)(d) (2000) (Restatement (Second) of Conflict of Laws § 187(2) cmt. e 'contemplates the analytically and practically different situation in which the chosen law invalidates the entire contract rather than merely a provision thereof').

It matters not that the parties may not have been actually aware of the [invalidating effect of Delaware's rule against perpetuities] when they signed the [settlement agreement]. They agreed to be bound by [Delaware] substantive law, of which the [rule against perpetuities] is a part. *Boatland v. Brunswick Corp.*, 558 F.2d 818, 822(II) (6th Cir.1977).

In reviewing the foregoing Georgia law on mutual mistake, as well as commentary and foreign authority with respect to contractual choice-of-law provisions, we conclude that the type of conflict that arose in the present case is not relievable in equity as a mutual mistake in this state. Again, the equitable power to relieve mistakes must be 'exercised with caution,' and the evidence regarding the mistake must be 'clear, unequivocal, and decisive.' OCGA § 23-2-21(c). Furthermore, to reform a contract based upon mutual mistake, it must be shown that the alleged mistake resulted in a contract which fails to express accurately the intention of the parties. *Zaimis v. Sharis*, 275 Ga. 532, 533(1) (2002); *Fox v. Washburn*, 264 Ga. 617, 618(1) (1994). It is clear that the parties expressly selected the choice-of-law provision of their contract. CS-Lakeview has proved that such provision invalidates a single other contractual term. However, it does not invalidate the entire contract, and a choice of Georgia law may have had its own undesirable implications for the multiple entities and properties involved in the settlement agreement. It is not possible to conclude that the parties clearly and unequivocally intended the choice-of-law provision to fall whenever it would invalidate any provision of the contract. To assume that the parties intended for the right of first refusal to be effective instead of their choice of law is not any more justifiable than the converse assumption. Application of the doctrine of mutual mistake in this case would erroneously be based upon a mere dissimilarity of law.

The dissent's desire to apply the doctrine based upon 'special circumstances' other than the ground of public policy is contrary to this state's continued adherence to traditional conflicts of law rules. *Convergys Corp. v. Keener*; *Nationwide General Ins. Co. v. Parnham*. Furthermore, the dissent remarkably discounts the choice-of-law provision as mere 'boilerplate' based solely on a commentator's general observation and the absence of evidence that the parties gave it any special consideration. Actually, that provision, like almost all others in the settlement agreement, cannot properly be viewed as 'boilerplate.' Before it was drafted and inserted, the parties to the agreement first had to select and agree to the law of a particular state. Moreover, in the very next paragraph, the parties specifically contemplated and provided for the possible invalidity of any provision of the contract, not by limiting the effect of their choice of law, but rather by means of a severability clause. See *Boatland, Inc. v. Brunswick Corp.*, at 823(II). Thus, the dissent's effort to find an implied intent that the right of first refusal prevail must fail.

Accordingly, we hold, as a matter of law, that the parties' settlement agreement is not subject to the reformation sought by CS-Lakeview under the doctrine of mutual mistake.

Judgment affirmed.

All the Justices concur, except SEARS, C.J., and MELTON, J., who dissent.

SEARS, Chief Justice, dissenting.

Because I conclude that the parties labored under a mutual mistake when they chose Delaware law to control their settlement agreement, I dissent to the majority opinion.

CS-Lakeview contends that the parties made a mutual mistake in choosing Delaware law to govern their contract, as it rendered CS-Lakeview's right of first refusal invalid,[FN1] and that, if the parties had considered the issue, they would have chosen Georgia law to apply to the right of first refusal. CS-Lakeview relies on several cases to support its position. For example, in *Kipin Indus. v. Van Deilen Intl.*,[FN2] the parties had an agreement for certain work to be performed in Kentucky, and a provision in their contract prohibited the filing of liens. The parties also chose Michigan to govern their contract. Under Michigan law, lien-waiver provisions were invalid, but, under Kentucky law, they were valid. A dispute arose between the parties, and a lien was filed. On appeal, the court held that Kentucky law should govern the validity of the lien-waiver provision on the ground that it should be assumed that the parties made a mistake in choosing a law—Michigan—that would invalidate that portion of their contract. In so ruling, the court relied on Comment e of § 187 of the Restatement, Second, Conflict of Laws. That comment states, in relevant part, as follows:

> On occasion, the parties may choose a law that would declare the contract invalid. In such situations, the chosen law will not be applied by reason of the parties' choice. To do so would defeat the expectations of the parties which it is the purpose of the present rule to protect. The parties can be assumed to have intended that the provisions of the contract would be binding upon them (cf. § 188, Comment b). If the parties have chosen a law that would invalidate the contract, it can be assumed that they did so by mistake. [FN4]

FN1. Under Delaware law, CS-Lakeview's right of first refusal violates the rule against perpetuities and is considered void ab initio. *Stuart Kingston, Inc. v. Robinson*, 596 A.2d 1378, 1383-1384 (Del.1991).

FN2. 182 F.3d 490 (6th Cir.1999).

FN4. The majority criticizes CS-Lakeview's reliance on *Kipin* on the ground that this Court has not adopted § 187 of the Restatement, Second, Conflict of Laws. *Kipin*, however, simply adopted the principle of mistake of law noted in Comment e of § 187. We need not adopt § 187 in order to rely on that principle.

The rationale of *Kipin* has been followed by other courts. Moreover, the rule established in *Kipin* has been cited with approval by Russell J. Weintraub, a leading commentator on conflict of laws.[FN6] Weintraub notes that choice-of-law clauses are 'becoming ubiquitous boilerplate in commercial contracts' and that parties may inadvertently choose a law that invalidates 'the contract in whole or in part.' [FN7] Weintraub concludes that '[t]his problem of the inadvertent stipulation of invalidating law is easily resolved. A court should disregard a stipulation of invalidating law as an obvious mistake and choose the proper law by some other means . . . Commercial convenience and upholding of expectations are served whenever the validating rule is applied and disserved whenever invalidating law is invoked.' [FN8]

FN6. Russell Weintraub, Commentary on the Conflict of Laws § 7.3C, pp. 494-495 (5th ed. 2006).

FN7. *Id.* at 494. Contrary to the majority's statement, Weintraub does address the situation where the parties choose a law that invalidates the contract in part.

FN8. *Id.* at 495.

On the other hand, as the majority correctly notes, the ruling in the *Kipin* case has been criticized for applying the doctrine from Comment e of § 187 of the Restatement, Second, Conflict of Laws, to a single provision of a contract.[FN9] Even that criticism, however, leaves open the possibility of disregarding an invalidating law even when only a part of a contract is at issue if 'special circumstances' are present.[FN10]

FN9. Scoles, Hay, Borchers, & Symeonides, Conflict of Laws § 18.11, p. 983 (4th ed. 2000).

FN10. *Id.*

I find the rationale of cases such as *Kipin* and the commentary expressed in Weintraub persuasive and conclude that, under that rationale, the parties made a mutual mistake in choosing Delaware law to govern their contract. Moreover, even under the more restrictive rule espoused by Scoles, I would find the presence of special circumstances in this case. In this regard, Simon's attorney conducted the negotiations for Simon, and he testified that there were five or six terms of the settlement agreement that were material and that, without them, the agreement 'wouldn't have been done.' He added that the right of first refusal was one of those material terms. In addition, there is no evidence in the record that the parties gave any special consideration to the choice-of-law provision, much less the same consideration that they attached to the right of first refusal. As noted by Weintraub, the choice-of-law provision in this case seems to have been 'boilerplate.' Given that the parties clearly intended to create a valid right of first refusal for CS-Lakeview and that the parties' complex dispute would not have been settled without that right, it is reasonable to conclude that the parties assumed that the choice of Delaware law would not invalidate that critical provision of the contract. Because of the critical nature of the right of first refusal compared to the 'boilerplate' choice-of-law provision, I conclude that this is a special circumstance in which the choice-of-law should not be applied to invalidate the right of first refusal.

In addition, this conclusion is consistent with Georgia law on mutual mistake. The parties made an 'honest mistake of law as to the effect' of the written contract they entered [FN12] when they chose Delaware law to govern their agreement. Stated differently, the parties "'labored under the same misconception'" as to the terms of the settlement agreement, "'intending at the time of the execution of the instrument'" to make the right of first refusal valid and enforceable, but "'by mistake'" rendering it invalid, so that the settlement agreement did not express the intent of the parties to give CS-Lakeview a valid right of first refusal.[FN13] Finally, given the testimony of Simon's counsel that the right of first refusal would either make or break the parties' agreement, I conclude that the evidence shows unequivocally and decisively that the parties made a mistake in choosing a law that would invalidate that provision.[FN14]

FN12. OCGA § 23-2-22.

FN13. *Fox v. Washburn*, 264 Ga. 617, 618, 449 S.E.2d 513 (1994).

FN14. OCGA § 23-2-21; *Fulghum v. Kelly*, 255 Ga. 652, 654, 340 S.E.2d 589 (1986).

For the foregoing reasons, I conclude that, even though the parties' chosen law invalidates only a part of the parties' contract, the choice of an invalidating law should be considered a mutual mistake. Accordingly, I dissent to the majority opinion. I am authorized to state that Justice MELTON joins in this dissent.

? QUESTIONS

1 A choice of law clause is an agreement which will only be valid if it meets the traditional requirements of contract law. But which one? In *CS-Lakeview*, the Justices argued over the content of Georgia law to decide whether the choice of law clause could be invalidated. But why was Georgia law to be applied to determine this issue? The parties had chosen Delaware law to govern their contract, and the law governing a contract is applicable to both formation and effects of the contract and its clauses. What would a European court have held under the Rome I Regulation?

2 Would the application of the law chosen by the parties be more sensible? The issue is whether the choice of law was valid. Is it possible to apply the chosen law to determine whether it was validly chosen? If the chosen law provides that it was not, this means that the choice of law was never effective. But if it was never effective, how could it apply to decide this issue in the first place?

3 Is foreign law ever applicable to choice of law issues?

Quebec Civil Code

Article 3112

If no law is designated in the act or if the law designated invalidates the juridical act, the courts apply the law of the State with which the act is most closely connected in view of its nature and the attendant circumstances.

[?] QUESTIONS

What should happen if the law designated by the parties invalidates the contract or one of its clauses? Quite clearly, that is not what the parties wanted. However, if the chosen law is superior to the will of the parties, should the contract not be invalidated? Would a U.S. court handle the issue differently than a Quebec court?

1.2 Protecting weaker parties

The freedom to choose the applicable law creates the risk that a party with a stronger bargaining power might want to impose the application of a law which would only favour his interests. The laws of many jurisdictions afford special regimes protecting parties deemed to have a lower bargaining power, such as employees, consumers or commercial agents. However, stronger parties could take advantage of an unlimited freedom to choose the law governing their contract to bypass the application of these laws.

1.2.1 Special choice of law rules

In many jurisdictions, special choice of law rules were adopted to protect certain categories of parties deemed weaker against risks of abuse.

The most radical solution is to prohibit choice of the applicable law.

Uniform Consumer Credit Code

§ **1.201.** [Territorial Application]

(8) Each of the following agreements or provisions of an agreement by a consumer who is a resident of this State at the time of a consumer credit transaction is invalid with respect to the transaction:

(a) that the law of another jurisdiction apply;

Note: the Uniform Consumer Credit Code was adopted by 11 U.S. states.

The E.U. lawmaker has adopted a more nuanced solution to protect not only consumers, but also employees.

Rome I Regulation (2008)

Preamble

(23) As regards contracts concluded with parties regarded as being weaker, those parties should be protected by conflict-of-law rules that are more favourable to their interests than the general rules. (. . .)

(34) The rule on individual employment contracts should not prejudice the application of the overriding mandatory provisions of the country to which a worker is posted in accordance with Directive 96/71/EC of the European Parliament and of the Council of 16 December 1996 concerning the posting of workers in the framework of the provision of services.

(35) Employees should not be deprived of the protection afforded to them by provisions which cannot be derogated from by agreement or which can only be derogated from to their benefit.

(36) As regards individual employment contracts, work carried out in another country should be regarded as temporary if the employee is expected to resume working in the country of origin after carrying out his tasks abroad. The conclusion of a new contract of employment with the original employer or an employer belonging to the same group of companies as the original employer should not preclude the employee from being regarded as carrying out his work in another country temporarily.

Article 8 *Individual employment contracts*

1. An individual employment contract shall be governed by the law chosen by the parties in accordance with Article 3. Such a choice of law may not, however, have the result of depriving the employee of the protection afforded to him by provisions that cannot be derogated from by agreement under the law that, in the absence of choice, would have been applicable pursuant to paragraphs 2, 3 and 4 of this Article.

2. To the extent that the law applicable to the individual employment contract has not been chosen by the parties, the contract shall be governed by the law of the country in which or, failing that, from which the employee habitually carries out his work in performance of the contract. The country where the work is habitually carried out shall not be deemed to have changed if he is temporarily employed in another country.

3. Where the law applicable cannot be determined pursuant to paragraph 2, the contract shall be governed by the law of the country where the place of business through which the employee was engaged is situated.

4. Where it appears from the circumstances as a whole that the contract is more closely connected with a country other than that indicated in paragraphs 2 or 3, the law of that other country shall apply.

? NOTES AND QUESTIONS

1 Under Art. 8(1), is a choice of law clause valid in an employment contract? Is it possible to choose a law with no connection with the contract?

2 What are 'provisions that cannot be derogated by agreement'? Overriding mandatory provisions? Mere domestic mandatory rules?

3 For the special rule protecting consumers, see *infra* 1.2.2.

Japanese Act on the General Rules of Application of Laws (2006)

Section 2 Juristic Acts

Article 7 *Choice of Applicable Law by the Parties*
The formation and effect of a juristic act shall be governed by the law of the place chosen by the parties at the time of the act.

Article 12 *Special Rules for Labor Contracts*
(1) Even where by choice under Article 7 or variation under Article 9, the applicable law to the formation and effect of a labor contract is a law other than the law with which the contract is most closely connected, when the employee indicates to the employer his or her intention that a particular mandatory rule from within the law of the place with which the employee is most closely connected should apply, this mandatory rule shall apply to the matters covered by the rule concerning the labor contract's formation and effect.

(2) For the purpose of the preceding paragraph, it shall be presumed that a labor contract is most closely connected with the law of the place where the work should be carried out under the contract (i.e., the law of the place of business through which the employee was engaged, where the work is not to be carried out in a particular place. The same applies for the next paragraph).

(3) Notwithstanding Article 8, paragraph 2, where no choice under the provision of Article 7 has been made with regards to the formation and effect of a labor contract, it shall be presumed that regarding its formation and effect the contract is most closely connected with the law of the place where the work should be carried out under the contract.

? NOTES AND QUESTIONS

1 E.U. private international law has been quite influential. Art. 3118 of the Quebec Civil Code is clearly inspired by Art. 6 of the Rome Convention (now Art. 8 of the Rome I Regulation).
2 How does Art. 12 of the Japanese Act compare with Art. 8 of the Rome I Regulation?

1.2.2 *Application of general doctrines of choice of law*

Weaker parties could also be protected against risks of abuse of the freedom to choose the applicable by relying on general doctrines of choice of law theory.

The clearest example is the rule limiting the freedom of choice to laws connected to the contract. Such limitation prevents stronger parties from imposing the application of most laws, and thus from evading the application of the laws which could legitimately want to apply.

The protection of weaker parties could also be considered as a fundamental policy of the forum, and thus trigger the application of the public policy exception and international mandatory rules. Read the following case and identify under which basis the court decides to disregard the choice of law provision contained in the employment contract.

CASE

Court of Appeal, First District, Division 3, California, 23 February 1998 *The Application Group, Inc. v. The Hunter Group, Inc.*[14]

PHELAN, Presiding Justice.

The Hunter Group, Inc. timely appeals from a judgment by which the San Francisco Superior Court declared that covenants not to compete contained in the employment contracts of Hunter consultants who do not reside in California are illegal in the circumstances of this case, and cannot be enforced against respondents The Application Group, Inc. (AGI), a California-based corporation, and Dianne Pike (Pike), a resident of Maryland and former Hunter consultant who was recruited to work for AGI in California in 1992. The trial court's judgment was based on sections 16600 and 17200 of the California Business and Professions Code.

In relevant part, section 16600 provides: '[E]very contract by which anyone is restrained from engaging in a lawful profession, trade, or business of any kind is to that extent void.' (. . .)

This appeal raises one of the many interesting and difficult legal questions created by the rapid expansion of computer technology. It involves what might be called the 'virtual employer,' one whose employees work out of their homes, or from branch offices scattered throughout the country, or at customer sites in various states, as necessary to provide 'consulting' services with respect to the customers' computerized human resources systems. Competition among such employers is fierce, both for customers and for qualified employees. The situation gives rise to potential conflicts among the laws governing solicitation, recruitment, and employment in the various states where the employees, employers and customers can be said to 'reside.'

In this case, we must decide whether California law may be applied to determine the enforceability of a covenant not to compete, in an employment agreement between an employee who is not a resident of California and an

---

14 61 Cal.App.4th 881.

employer whose business is based outside of California, when a California-based employer seeks to recruit or hire the nonresident for employment in California. (. . .)

1. *California Choice-of-Law Principles.*

California will apply the substantive law designated by the contract unless the transaction falls into either of two exceptions: 1) the chosen state has no substantial relationship to the parties or the transaction, or 2) application of the law of the chosen state would be contrary to a fundamental policy of the state. Under the second exception, where application of a choice-of-law provision would result in the contravention of California's public policy, the provision will be ignored to the extent necessary to preserve public policy. (. . .)

The *Nedlloyd* court elaborated: '[T]he proper approach under Restatement section 187, subdivision (2) is for the court first to determine either: (1) whether the chosen state has a substantial relationship to the parties or their transaction, or (2) whether there is any other reasonable basis for the parties' choice of law. If neither of these tests is met, that is the end of the inquiry, and the court need not enforce the parties' choice of law . . . If, however, either test is met, the court must next determine whether the chosen state's law is contrary to a *fundamental* policy of California . . . If there is no such conflict, the court shall enforce the parties' choice of law. If, however, there is a fundamental conflict with California law, the court must then determine whether California has a 'materially greater interest than the chosen state in the determination of the particular issue . . .' (Rest., § 187, subd. (2).) If California has a materially greater interest than the chosen state, the choice of law shall not be enforced, for the obvious reason that in such circumstances we will decline to enforce a law contrary to this state's fundamental policy.' (*Nedlloyd Lines B.V. v. Superior Court* (1992) 3 Cal.4th 459, at p. 466)

2. *Application of California Choice-of-Law Rules to This Case.*

There is no dispute that the chosen state—Maryland—has a 'substantial relationship' to the parties and their transaction. There is also no dispute that there is a 'reasonable basis' for the parties' contractual choice-of-law provision. Indeed, the mere fact that one of the parties to the contract is incorporated in the chosen state is sufficient to support a finding of 'substantial relationship,' and the mere fact that one of the parties resides in the chosen state provides a 'reasonable basis' for the parties' choice of law. (*Nedlloyd*, at pp. 467–468)

The parties also agree that California and Maryland are 'potentially concerned' states with diametrically opposed laws regarding the enforceability of Hunter's noncompetition clause.[FN14] As we have noted, with certain limited exceptions, California law renders void such provisions (§ 16600), while Maryland law permits them so long as they are reasonable in scope and duration (*Holloway v. Faw, Casson & Co.*, 572 A.2d at p. 515). Furthermore, as we will discuss, each state purports to have significant interests in having its law applied. Thus, the real issues for decision are whether Maryland's law is contrary to a *fundamental* policy of California and, if so, which state has a 'materially greater interest' in the determination of the issue and which state's interests would be more seriously impaired if its policy were subordinated to the policy of the other state. (*Bernhard v. Harrah's Club*, 16 Cal.3d at p. 320) As our Supreme Court has instructed, 'careful consideration' of California policy and Maryland's interests is required in order to resolve these issues. (*Nedlloyd*, at p. 466, fn. 6)

> FN14. Thus, this is a '"true" conflict' case. (See *Sommer v. Gabor*, 40 Cal.App.4th at p. 1467) There are other 'potentially concerned' states including, for example, the ones in which other nonresident Hunter employees may reside, which may have interests, like Maryland's, in the enforceability of covenants not to compete, valid where made, and the competitive advantages of such provisions. On the other hand, other 'potentially concerned' states may broadly prohibit covenants not to compete, as does California, with the result being no real 'choice-of-law' issue. Or the 'other' states might allow 'reasonable' restrictions on the Hunter employee's freedom to compete after termination, but may find one year too long a period or the geographical reach of the covenant too broad. However, the parties focus their choice of laws arguments on California and Maryland as the two 'potentially concerned states' with respect to the enforceability of Pike's covenant not to compete, and agree that these laws call for diametrically opposite results on that issue. For that reason, our discussion will maintain the same focus.

AGI is correct when it argues that section 16600 reflects a 'strong public policy' of the State of California. As the Second Appellate District recently observed: 'California courts have consistently declared this provision an expression of public policy to ensure that every citizen shall retain the right to pursue any lawful employment and enterprise of their choice. Section 16600 has specifically been held to invalidate employment contracts which prohibit an employee from working for a competitor when the employment has terminated, unless necessary to protect the employer's trade secrets. The corollary to this proposition is that [a competitor] may solicit another's employees if they do not use unlawful means or engage in acts of unfair competition.' (*Metro Traffic Control, Inc. v. Shadow Traffic Network*, 22 Cal. App.4th at p.859) In *Diodes, Inc. v. Franzen* (1968) 260 Cal.App.2d 244, the court further explained the policy underpinnings of section 16600, as follows: 'The interests of the employee in his own mobility and betterment are deemed paramount to the competitive business interests of the employers, where neither the employee nor his new employer has committed any illegal act accompanying the employment change.' It follows that California has a strong interest in protecting the freedom of movement of persons whom California-based employers (such as AGI) wish to employ to provide services in California, regardless of the person's state of residence or precise degree of involvement in California projects, and we see no reason why these employees' interests should not be 'deemed paramount to the competitive business interests' of out-of-state as well as in-state employers.

To the extent it is invoked by a California *employer* to protect itself from 'unfair competition,' moreover, section 16600 is all the more important as a statement of California public policy which ensures that California employers will be able to compete effectively for the most talented, skilled employees in their industries, wherever they may reside. In this day and age—with the advent of computer technology and the concomitant ability of many types of employees in many industries to work from their homes, or to 'telecommute' to work from anywhere a telephone link reaches—an employee need not reside in the same city, county, or state in which the employer can be said to physically reside. California employers in such sectors of the economy have a strong and legitimate interest in having broad freedom to choose from a much larger, indeed a 'national,' applicant pool in order to maximize the quality of the product or services they provide, as well as the reach of their 'market.' California has a correlative interest in protecting its employers and their employees from anti-competitive conduct by out-of-state employers such as Hunter—including litigation based on a covenant not to compete to which the California employer is not a party—who would interfere with or restrict these freedoms.

Hunter suggests, however, that Maryland has an equally strong public policy favoring the use and enforcement of its noncompetition covenants, insofar as they serve the interests of Maryland employers in preventing recruitment of employees who provide 'unique services,' and the misuse of trade secrets, routes, or lists of clients, or solicitation of customers. However, there is nothing in the record of this case to support a finding that failure to enforce Hunter's noncompetition covenant would significantly impair either of the asserted interests. We have no reason to doubt the parties' showing that highly skilled consultants such as Pike are a scarce resource. But, with all due respect to Ms. Pike, there is no showing that she performed 'unique services' for Hunter.[FN15] There is also no showing that Pike was attempting to exploit Hunter's trade secrets or other protected information about its customers. In any event, should such concerns arise with respect to the recruitment of other Hunter consultants for employment in California, Hunter has recourse under both Maryland and California law. (See, e.g., *Morlife, Inc. v. Perry* (1997) 56 Cal.App.4th 1514.)

> FN15. It appears that Hunter's *real* concern about Pike's recruitment was that it would have to pay more for a replacement than it was paying her. But, in light of the 'no damages' judgment in the Maryland court, even that concern did not materialize.

We are, therefore, convinced that California has a materially greater interest than does Maryland in the application of its law to the parties' dispute, and that California's interests would be more seriously impaired if its policy were subordinated to the policy of Maryland. Accordingly, the trial court did not err when it declined to enforce the contractual conflict of law provision in Hunter's employment agreements. To have done so would have been to allow an out-of-state employer/competitor to limit employment and business opportunities in California. As the *Nedlloyd* court held, California courts are not bound to enforce a contractual conflict of law provision which would thus be 'contrary to this state's fundamental policy.' (*Nedlloyd*, at p. 466)

NOTES

1 Weaker parties can be protected by applying general rules of choice of law. In this case, the California court simply applies the public policy exception.
2 Note that, although it does benefit employees, the court makes clear that California's fundamental policy aims at protecting California employers. The protection of employees has not been cause for concern in the American conflict of laws. This reveals that the protection of weaker parties is a substantive policy, and that it will logically translate into special choice of law rules only in States interested in advancing such policy.

General doctrines of choice of law are not only used in the United States. They can also be used in the European Union. One reason is that the application of general doctrines is not limited to certain pre-defined categories of weaker parties, and therefore can be used to protect other parties.

Read again the *Ingmar* case (*supra* p. 22) and identify the category of parties that the court intended to protect, and the general doctrine used for that purpose.

One interesting question is whether, where lawmakers have adopted special choice of law rules affording some protection to a certain category of weaker parties, such protection could be supplemented through the use of general doctrines.

Rome I Regulation (2008)

Article 6 *Consumer contracts*

1. Without prejudice to Articles 5 and 7, a contract concluded by a natural person for a purpose which can be regarded as being outside his trade or profession (the consumer) with another person acting in the exercise of his trade or profession (the professional) shall be governed by the law of the country where the consumer has his habitual residence, provided that the professional:

(a)   pursues his commercial or professional activities in the country where the consumer has his habitual residence, or

(b)   by any means, directs such activities to that country or to several countries including that country,

and the contract falls within the scope of such activities.

2. Notwithstanding paragraph 1, the parties may choose the law applicable to a contract which fulfils the requirements of paragraph 1, in accordance with Article 3. Such a choice may not, however, have the result of depriving the consumer of the protection afforded to him by provisions that cannot be derogated from by agreement by virtue of the law which, in the absence of choice, would have been applicable on the basis of paragraph 1.

3. If the requirements in points (a) or (b) of paragraph 1 are not fulfilled, the law applicable to a contract between a consumer and a professional shall be determined pursuant to Articles 3 and 4.

4. Paragraphs 1 and 2 shall not apply to: (. . .)

? NOTES AND QUESTIONS

1   Article 6 uses the same technique as Art. 8 (*supra*, 1.2.1) to protect consumers. The parties may choose the applicable law to their contract, but such choice cannot result in depriving the consumer from the protection of the otherwise applicable mandatory rules.

2   Article 6, however, does not protect all consumers. It only protects consumers residing in countries where the professional directed his activities. These consumers are passive consumers, insofar as they would not have transacted with a foreign professional if he had not marketed his services or products in their country of residence. By contrast, active consumers, who will on their own motion go abroad to find better deals, are not protected: see Art. 6(3).

3   Should active consumers be protected through the use of general techniques of choice of law such as overriding mandatory provisions? In 1997, the German federal court held that the special provision on consumers (today Art. 6) should be regarded as the only protection afforded to this category of parties, and that the application of the general

provision on overriding mandatory provisions (today Art. 9) could not be used to supplement it.[15]

In 2006, however, the French Supreme Court applied French consumer law in a case where a couple residing in France near the German border had contracted a loan with a German bank in Germany without being approached first by the bank. The consumers were active and thus could not benefit from the special rule in Art. 6. The court applied the relevant French consumer law as an overriding mandatory provision in the meaning of Art. 9.[16]

What is the right solution?

2 Applicable law in absence of a choice

While parties may choose the law governing their contract in most jurisdictions, they do not always do so. It is therefore necessary to have a default choice of law rule for cases where parties have not made such choice.

Under the traditional choice of law methodology, it has been difficult to find a wholly satisfactory connecting factor. One reason is that contracts raise different issues (validity, performance) which arise at different times and thus potentially point to different places. Another reason is that contracts are very varied and that scholars and lawmakers were unable to find a single factor fitting for all.

While certain jurisdictions still rely on one single connecting factor, most lawmakers have adopted flexible choice of law rules or approaches.

2.1 Place of conclusion of the contract

Read the following case and identify the reasons offered by the court for the application of the law of the place where the parties entered into the contract.

 CASE

Supreme Court of Florida, 24 March 1988 *Josephine Sturiano v. Martin Brooks*[17]

Kogan, Justice.

The petitioner, Mrs. Sturiano, was injured when the car in which she was a passenger, struck a tree. Her husband, Vito Sturiano, the driver of the car,

---

15 BGH, 19 March 1997, case VIII ZR 316/96.
16 Cass. Civ. 1, 23 May 2006, case no 03-15637.
17 523 So.2d 1126, 13 Fla. L. Weekly 224.

was killed in the collision, and Mrs. Sturiano brought an action against his estate alleging negligence on the part of Mr. Sturiano. Because Mrs. Sturiano was also the personal representative of her husband's estate, a guardian ad litem was appointed to represent the interests of the estate. Other than Mrs. Sturiano, Vito Sturiano was survived by no heirs or lineal descendents.

Following a jury verdict for Mrs. Sturiano and a reduction to the amount of applicable insurance coverage, Brooks, the guardian ad litem, appealed to the fourth district. That court held the doctrine of interspousal immunity did not bar the action, reasoning that the traditional policy reasons for maintaining the doctrine simply did not apply. However, the court reversed the verdict, holding the doctrine of lex loci contractus required that New York law apply because the contract was executed there. Under a New York statute, the action is barred unless the insurance policy specifically includes coverage for claims between spouses. Absent such a provision, no coverage exists. The fourth district then certified questions regarding both issues to this Court.

Both certified questions involve challenges to established common law doctrines followed in Florida. The first question, which we will answer last, involves the conflict of laws doctrine known as lex loci contractus. The other question, which we shall address first, requires this Court to again examine the doctrine of interspousal tort immunity. (. . .)

The other question posed by the fourth district requires us to address the doctrine of lex loci contractus. Specifically, we must examine whether the rule requiring that the laws of the jurisdiction where the contract was executed should apply. The fourth district has certified the following question:

DOES THE *LEX LOCI CONTRACTUS* RULE GOVERN THE RIGHTS AND LIABILITIES OF THE PARTIES IN DETERMINING THE APPLICABLE LAW ON AN ISSUE OF INSURANCE COVERAGE, PRECLUDING CONSIDERATION BY THE FLORIDA COURTS OF OTHER RELEVANT FACTORS, SUCH AS THE SIGNIFICANT RELATIONSHIP BETWEEN FLORIDA AND THE PARTIES AND/OR THE TRANSACTION?

We answer the certified question in the affirmative, limiting this answer to contracts for automobile insurance, and approve the decision of the district court.

The Sturianos, lifelong residents of New York, purchased automobile insurance in New York six years prior to the accident which took the life of Vito

Sturiano and injured Josephine Sturiano. Subsequently, the couple moved to Florida each year for the winter months. They did not notify the insurance company of this migration, and the insurance company had no way of knowing that such a move had taken place.

Under the doctrine of lex loci contractus, it is clear that New York law must apply. That rule specifies that the law of the jurisdiction where the contract was executed should control. However, in recent years this doctrine has been criticized and, in several jurisdictions, discarded in favor of the more flexible 'significant relationships' test.

That test, as stated in the Restatement (Second) of Conflict of Laws § 188 (1971), provides:

> § 188. Law Governing in Absence of Effective Choice by the Parties
> (1) The rights and duties of the parties with respect to an issue in contract are determined by the local law of the state which, with respect to that issue, has the most significant relationship to the transaction and the parties under the principles stated in § 6.
> (2) In the absence of an effective choice of law by the parties (see § 187), the contacts to be taken into account in applying the principles of § 6 to determine the law applicable to an issue include: (. . .)

Thus, under the Restatement view, and seemingly the trend of courts around the nation, the place the contract is executed is only one of five factors used in determining which jurisdiction's law should control.

Sturiano argues that in this modern, migratory society, choice of law rules must be flexible to allow courts to apply the laws which best accommodate the parties and the host jurisdiction. She contends that the archaic and inflexible rule of lex loci contractus does not address modern issues or problems in the area of conflict of laws. While it is true that lex loci contractus is an inflexible rule, we believe that this inflexibility is necessary to ensure stability in contract arrangements. When parties come to terms in an agreement, they do so with the implied acknowledgment that the laws of that jurisdiction will control absent some provision to the contrary. This benefits both parties, not merely an insurance company. The view espoused in the Restatement fails, in our opinion, to adequately provide security to the parties to a contract.

Although lex loci contractus is old, it is not yet outdated. The very reason Sturiano gives as support for discarding lex loci contractus, namely that we live in a migratory, transitory society, provides support for upholding that doctrine. Parties have a right to know what the agreement they have executed provides. To allow one party to modify the contract simply by moving to another state would substantially restrict the power to enter into valid, binding, and stable contracts. There can be no doubt that the parties to insurance contracts bargained and paid for the provisions in the agreement, including those provisions that apply the statutory law of that state.

We recognize that this Court has discarded the analogous doctrine of *lex loci delicti* with respect to tort actions and limitations of actions. However, we believe that the reasoning controlling those decisions does not apply in the instant case. With tort law, there is no agreement, no foreseen set of rules and statutes which the parties had recognized would control the litigation. In the case of an insurance contract, the parties enter into that contract with the acknowledgment that the laws of that jurisdiction control their actions. In essence, that jurisdiction's laws are incorporated by implication into the agreement. The parties to this contract did not bargain for Florida or any other state's laws to control. We must presume that the parties did bargain for, or at least expected, New York law to apply.

For these reasons, we answer the certified question concerning conflict of laws in the affirmative, limiting that answer to situations involving automobile insurance policies. (...)

❓ NOTES AND QUESTIONS

1 The law of the place of conclusion of the contract was the traditional choice of law rule in the United States before the American Revolution in choice of law. It was consistent with the vested rights theory, according to which the applicable law should be the law of the place where rights 'vest', i.e. arose. Today, the rule is still followed in a dozen U.S. states.

2 Is the place of contracting an appropriate criteria for determining the applicable law? In this case, a party referred to a modern, migratory society. Imagine two commercial parties who decide to meet and negotiate their contract at one of the numerous fairs in the world where they travel each year to promote their products. Should the place of contracting be relevant?

3 The court insists on the expectations of the parties. Is this genuinely a case about the determination of the applicable law absent a choice? When the parties think of the contract they are negotiating, do they contemplate its formation or its performance? If they have no legal training, do they have any expectations with respect to the applicable law?

4 What is the most important in the contracting process: formation or performance? In 1934, the first Restatement of the Conflict of Laws (1934) referred to the place of contracting for questions of validity (§ 332), but provided that a number of questions concerning performance be governed by the law of the place of performance (§ 358). In this case, was the issue one of validity or performance?

2.2   Habitual residence of a party

Rome I Regulation (2008)

Article 4 *Applicable law in the absence of choice*

1. To the extent that the law applicable to the contract has not been chosen in accordance with Article 3 and without prejudice to Articles 5 to 8, the law governing the contract shall be determined as follows:

(a)   a contract for the sale of goods shall be governed by the law of the country where the seller has his habitual residence;

(b)   a contract for the provision of services shall be governed by the law of the country where the service provider has his habitual residence;

(c)   a contract relating to a right in rem in immovable property or to a tenancy of immovable property shall be governed by the law of the country where the property is situated;

(d)   notwithstanding point (c), a tenancy of immovable property concluded for temporary private use for a period of no more than six consecutive months shall be governed by the law of the country where the landlord has his habitual residence, provided that the tenant is a natural person and has his habitual residence in the same country;

(e)   a franchise contract shall be governed by the law of the country where the franchisee has his habitual residence;

(f)   a distribution contract shall be governed by the law of the country where the distributor has his habitual residence;

(. . .)

2. Where the contract is not covered by paragraph 1 or where the elements of the contract would be covered by more than one of points (a) to (h) of paragraph 1, the contract shall be governed by the law of the country where the party required to effect the characteristic performance of the contract has his habitual residence.

3. Where it is clear from all the circumstances of the case that the contract is manifestly more closely connected with a country other than that indicated in paragraphs 1 or 2, the law of that other country shall apply.

4. Where the law applicable cannot be determined pursuant to paragraphs 1 or 2, the contract shall be governed by the law of the country with which it is most closely connected.

? NOTES AND QUESTIONS

1   The Rome I Regulation focuses on the place of the habitual residence of one of the parties, with the traditional exception of contracts relating to immovable property. Is this an appropriate connecting factor to locate a contract which, by definition, involves at least two parties? Why would the location of one party be more meaningful than the location of the other(s)?

Most importantly, why would the location of one party be more meaningful than the place of contracting or the place of performance of the contract? The main answer is that the drafters of the Rome Convention (which inspired the Rome I Regulation) recognized that the place of performance was the best connecting factor, but thought it would sometimes be hard to identify. In the light of Art. 7(1) of the Brussels Ibis Regulation, what do you think of this argument?

2   Article 4(3) provides for an exception clause. If the habitual residence of one of the parties is not a strong connecting factor, this means that there will often be another law which will be manifestly more closely connected to the contract, and thus will apply. In effect, is the true choice of law rule that the law of the place of performance applies? See the *Definitely Maybe* case *supra* at p. 10.

Are there lessons to be drawn from Quebec?

Quebec Civil Code
Chapter III Status of Obligations
Section I General Provisions § 2 Content of Juridical Acts

Article 3112.

If no law is designated in the act or if the law designated invalidates the juridical act, the courts apply the law of the State with which the act is most closely connected in view of its nature and the attendant circumstances.

Article 3113.

A juridical act is presumed to be most closely connected with the law of the State where the party who is to perform the prestation which is characteristic of the act has his residence or, if the act is concluded in the ordinary course of business of an enterprise, has his establishment.

Section II Special Provisions § 1 Sale

Article 3114.

In the absence of a designation by the parties, the sale of a corporeal movable is governed by the law of the State where the seller had his residence or, if the sale is concluded in the ordinary course of business of an enterprise, his establishment, at the time the contract was concluded. However, the sale is governed by the law of the State in which the buyer had his residence or his establishment at the time the contract was concluded in any of the following cases:

(1) negotiations have taken place and the contract has been concluded in that State;

(2) the contract provides expressly that delivery shall be performed in that State;

(3) the contract is concluded on terms determined mainly by the buyer, in response to a call for tenders.

In the absence of a designation by the parties, the sale of immovable property is governed by the law of the State where it is situated.

3   Article 4(1) provides different choice of law rules for a number of specific contracts. The Rome Convention only provided for a general principle, which is found in Art. 4(2) of the Regulation.

The applicable law is the law of the habitual residence of the party required to effect the characteristic performance of the contract. The concept of characteristic performance was originally developed by Swiss scholars. It refers to the obligation which is characteristic of a given kind of contract, and thus allows it to be distinguished from other kinds of contracts. A contract of sale is characteristic insofar as it transfers the ownership of the purchase. The characteristic performance is thus effected by the seller. Typically, payment of a price or a fee is not the characteristic performance of a contract.

4 A second argument supporting the choice of the habitual residence of one party is that it leads to the application of the law of origin of the product or the service (where the manufacturer or the service provider is based). The European Union is a federal system, and one of its most fundamental principles is the four freedoms of movement: persons, products, services and capital. Like any other rule, a choice of law rule could restrict a freedom of movement.[18] By providing in effect for the application of the law of origin of products and services, Art. 4 prevents the issue from arising.

Japanese Act on the General Rules of Application of Laws (2006)

Section 2 Juristic Acts

Article 8 *In the Absence of a Choice of Applicable Law by the Parties*

(1) Where there is no choice under the preceding Article, the formation and effect of a juristic act shall be governed by the law of the place with which the act is most closely connected at the time of the act.

(2) For the purpose of the preceding paragraph, where only one party is to effect the characteristic performance of the juristic act, it shall be presumed that the juristic act is most closely connected with the law of his or her habitual residence (i.e., the law of his or her place of business where that place of business is related to the act, or the law of his or her principal place of business where he or she has two or more places of business related to the act and where those laws differ).

(3) For the purpose of the first paragraph of this Article, where the subject matter of the juristic act is immovables, notwithstanding the preceding paragraph, it shall be presumed that the act is most closely connected with the law of the place where the immovables are situated. (...)

? NOTE AND QUESTION

Article 8 (1) and (2) are based on Art. 4 of the 1980 Rome Convention which also expressed the choice of law rule in terms of presumptions. Article 4(5) of the Rome Convention eventually added an exception clause (such as Art. 4(3) of the Rome Regulation). Article 8 does not. Does it make a difference?

---

18 *Supra*, p. 68.

Law of the People's Republic of China
on the Laws Applicable to Foreign-Related Civil Relations (2010)

Article 41

(2) Absent any choice by the parties, the law of the habitual residence of a party whose performance of obligation is most characteristic of the contract or the law that most closely connected with the contract shall be applied.

 NOTES AND QUESTIONS

1 Article 41(2) offers an alternative between two laws, but gives no guidance as to which is to prevail over the other. In practice, courts tend to blur the distinction between the two rules by referring to both.[19]

2 Although it is not expressed in terms of presumptions, the rule seems to be inspired from Art. 4 of the 1980 Rome Convention. Is the last part of Art. 41(2) an exception clause? In 2007, the Supreme Court had issued a rule modelled on Art. 4 of the Rome I Regulation (as opposed to the Rome Convention),[20] but it has now been abolished.

2.3 Proper law

 CASE

Supreme Court of Canada, 23 May 1967 *Imperial Life Insurance Co. of Canada v. Colmenares*[21]

RITCHIE J.: --This is an appeal brought with leave of this Court from a judgment of the Court of Appeal for Ontario, (Porter C.J., dissenting) dismissing an appeal from a judgment of Mr. Justice Stewart whereby he awarded the respondent the sum of $ 8,744.22, being the equivalent in Canadian currency of the cash surrender value, payable in American dollars, of two policies of insurance on the life of the respondent which were issued through the appellant's branch office in Havana, Cuba, in 1942 and 1947 at a time when the respondent was resident and domiciled in that country.

The sole question at issue in this appeal is whether the proper law of the contracts of life insurance is the law of Ontario or the law of Cuba. In this regard the parties are agreed that if the proper law of the contracts is found to be that of Ontario, the respondent is entitled to succeed, but that if the law of Cuba

---

19 See Yongping Xiao and Wenwen Liang, 'Mainland China', in Alejandro Carballo Leyda (ed.), *Asian Conflict of Laws: East and South East Asia* (Wolters Kluwer 2015) 17.

20 Rules on the Related Issues concerning the Application of Law in Hearing Foreign-Related Contractual Dispute Cases in Civil and Commercial Matters of 11 June 2007, Art. 5.

21 [1967] S.C.R. 443.

applies, unless permission has been granted by the National Bank of Cuba, the payment of the cash surrender value in dollars to a person resident in the United States, as the respondent is and was in September 1961 when he surrendered the policies, would be an offence contrary to the Foreign Exchange Contraband Law of Cuba.

The circumstances giving rise to this litigation have been thoroughly reviewed in the Courts below and they are not in dispute, but a brief resume of the essential facts is, in my opinion, necessary to any intelligible discussion of the law applicable thereto.

The two policies here in question were in identical terms and they were both written in Spanish, which is the language of Cuba, for delivery by the appellant's Cuban agent to the respondent who was then a Cuban national and who had made application for the policies in Cuba pursuant to an application form by which he agreed, inter alia:

> That any policy granted pursuant hereto shall take effect only upon its delivery and upon payment of the first premium thereon in full, to be vouched for by the Company's printed official receipt duly countersigned and provided that upon such delivery and payment there shall have been no material change in my health or insurability since the completion of part 2 of my application.

The respondent's offers as contained in his applications for these policies were by their terms irrevocable and he specifically agreed to accept the policies if any when they were issued. Before delivery the policies were duly authenticated before a Notary in accordance with the law of Cuba.

It is contended on behalf of the appellant, on the basis of these facts, that the contracts were made in Cuba and are governed by the law of that country.

On the other hand, it is pointed out by the respondent that the applications were addressed to 'The Imperial Life Assurance Company of Canada, Head Office, Toronto, Canada' and were prepared at that office, where the policies were also prepared and that, although these policies were written in Spanish, they were drawn in the common, standard form as used in the Province of Ontario and in conformity with the laws of that Province. These policies stipulated that they could not be varied except by writing thereon signed at the head office of the company by two of its executive officers and that any interlineations, additions or alterations had to be attested by two of the said officers. It is also to be noted that all payments under the policies, whether to or by the company, were required to be made 'by bank draft drawn on New York payable in legal currency of the United States of America' and although it is true that many of the premiums were paid in pesos in Cuba, I think it to be apparent that at the time when the contracts were made it was contemplated that the cash surrender value would be payable in American dollars and it is made clear in the policies themselves that the request for such payment was required to be made in writing to the head office of the company at Toronto.

It is submitted on behalf of the appellant that the determination of the proper law applicable to these contracts is governed by the fact that they were made in Cuba, but I am by no means satisfied that they were so made. I am, on the other hand, of opinion that the time of the making of the contracts was when the initial irrevocable offers contained in the respondent's applications were accepted by the mailing of the policies from the appellant's head office in Toronto. (See *North American Life Assurance Co. v. Elson* (1903), 33 S.C.R. 383 at p. 392 and *Milinkovich v. Canadian Mercantile Insurance Co.* [1960] S.C.R. 830 at pp. 835 and 836). (. . .)

I am, however, in agreement with Mr. Justice MacKay who observed in the course of the reasons for judgment which he delivered on behalf of the majority of the Court of Appeal that:

> The place where the contract was made is not by any means decisive in determining the question of what law is applicable to the contract.

It now appears to have been accepted by the highest Courts in England that the problem of determining the proper law of a contract is to be solved by considering the contract as a whole in light of all the circumstances which surround it and applying the law with which it appears to have the closest and most substantial connection.

This test was adopted by the Privy Council in *Bonython v. Commonwealth of Australia* [1951] A.C. 201, where Lord Simonds said at p. 219:

> . . . the substance of the obligation must be determined by the proper law of the contract, i.e., the system of law by reference to which the contract was made or that with which the transaction had its closest and most real connexion.

This approach to the problem was restated in the House of Lords in *Tomkinson v. First Pennsylvania Banking and Trust Co.* [1961] A.C. 1007, per Lord Denning at p. 1068 and Lord Morris of Borth-y-Gest at p. 1081.

The many factors which have been taken into consideration in various decided cases in determining the proper law to be applied, are described in the following passage from *Cheshire on Private International Law*, 7th ed., p. 190:

> The court must take into account, for instance, the following matters: the domicil
> and even the residence of the parties; the national character of a corporation and
> the place where its principal place of business is situated; the place where the con-
> tract is made and the place where it is to be performed; the style in which the con-
> tract is drafted, as, for instance, whether the language is appropriate to one system
> of law, but inappropriate to another; the fact that a certain stipulation is valid under
> one law but void under another; . . . the economic connexion of the contract with
> some other transaction; . . . the nature of the subject matter or its situs; the head
> office of an insurance company, whose activities range over many countries; and, in
> short, any other fact which serves to localize the contract.

In referring to the location of the 'head office of an insurance company
whose activities range over many countries' as a factor to be taken into
account in determining the proper law of a life insurance contract, the
learned author cites as his authority the cases of *Pick v. Manufacturers' Life
Insurance Company* [1958] 2 Lloyd's Rep. 93, and *Rossano v. Manufacturers'
Life Insurance Company* [1963] 2 Q.B. 352, both of which have been extensively reviewed in the Courts below, but he expresses doubts, which I share,
as to whether they afford justification for the general proposition that the
proper law of a contract of life insurance is necessarily the country in which
the head office of the insurer is situated.

In the present case, however, in my view, the significance of the location of the
head office of the appellant company is underscored by the fact that the evidence makes it quite plain that the actual decision to 'go on the risk' was made
there and could not have been made in Havana. In this regard, in the course
of his cross-examination, the appellant's general manager gave the following
answers:

> Q. We are clear that when the application was made in Havana it was a head office
> decision whether it could go on the risk?
> A. Yes.
> Q. And that decision could not be made in Havana?
> A. No.

While it is clear that all relevant circumstances surrounding the making of a
contract are to be given due weight in determining the locality with which
it is most closely associated, I am of opinion that in the present case the
fact that both the applications and the policies were prepared in Ontario in
a common, standard form which complied with the law of that Province,
is to be regarded as of preponderating importance in determining the law
governing the contracts.

I think it to be a reasonable inference that a person applying for insurance on a form prepared at the head office of an Ontario company would anticipate that the policies which he was to receive would be governed by the law of that Province, and I think that the form of the policies which were issued in the present case evidences the fact that the insurer intended to be governed by that law.

For these reasons, as well as for those which have been so fully stated in the reasons for judgment of Mr. Justice MacKay, I am of opinion that the proper law of these contracts is the law of Ontario.

? NOTES AND QUESTIONS

1 The proper law of the contract was the traditional English choice of law rule before the United Kingdom ratified the Rome Convention. However, a number of jurisdictions of the Commonwealth continue to follow the traditional rule. They include Canada, but also Australia and Singapore.

2 The proper law of the contract applies absent a choice of law made by the parties. The purpose of the rule is to determine which law has objectively the closest connection with the dispute. The Canadian Supreme Court insists that the fact that the policy insurance was prepared in Ontario should have made the person applying anticipate that Ontario law would govern, and that the form of the policy evidences the intent of the insurer. Is the court trying to establish the intent of the parties, or the law having the closest connection with the contract? Parties' choice can be expressed or inferred from the circumstances.[22] Is it important to clearly distinguish between the assessment of the implied will of the parties and the determination of the proper law of the contract?

3 Reread *Hillcrest Media v. Fisher Communications, Inc., supra* p. 61. How different is the analysis conducted by the Court of Appeals of Washington from the proper law rule?

2.4   Governmental interests

 CASE

Court of Appeals of Washington, 1 May 1978 *Nelson v. Kaanapali Properties*[23]

Ringold, J

Nelson is a specialty subcontractor, doing business as Nordic Tile Company, residing in the state of Washington. Nordic Tile at all relevant times was a registered contractor in the state of Washington under the contractor's registration act, RCW 18.27.

---

22 *Supra*, 1.1.3.
23 19 Wn. App. 893.

The defendant, Kaanapali Properties, is a joint venture between Kaanapali Realty, Inc., a Washington corporation, and West Maui Properties, Inc., a Hawaiian corporation. Both corporations are controlled by Richard Hadley, a Seattle resident involved in land development and construction business. Kaanapali, as owner and general contractor, commenced construction of a 360-unit condominium project in Maui, Hawaii, consisting of two multi-story towers.

In November 1974, Nordic Tile was requested to provide a quotation for installation of teak parquet flooring in the condominium units. Agreement was reached and work commenced, the formal subcontract being signed by Nelson and Hadley in December 1974. After conclusion of the installation, a dispute arose regarding which of the parties should bear the cost of extra workers required by an accelerated work schedule and of extra expenditures allegedly required as a result of Kaanapali's failure to maintain work schedules and to coordinate the progress of the work.

Nordic Tile's complaint seeks to recover damages for breach of contract and misrepresentation. Kaanapali counterclaimed for its cost of completing Nordic Tile's work in excess of the contract price. As an affirmative defense to Nordic Tile's complaint for damages, Kaanapali alleges that Nordic Tile, unlicensed in Hawaii as a contractor, is thereby barred from bringing suit on the contract by virtue of the applicability of Hawaii law. (. . .)

ISSUE

Was the trial court correct in holding that a subcontractor residing and registered under the Washington contractor's act was precluded by the contractor's licensing act of the state of Hawaii from maintaining a cause of action for breach of contract in the state of Washington?

STATUTES

Hawaii Revised Statute:

> 444-9 Licenses required. No person within the purview of this chapter shall act, or assume to act, or advertise, as general engineering contractor, general building contractor, or specialty contractor without a license previously obtained under and in compliance with this chapter and the rules and regulations of the contractors license board.
> 444-22 Civil action. The failure of any person to comply with any provision of this chapter shall prevent such person from recovering for work done, or materials or

supplies furnished, or both on a contract or on the basis of the reasonable value thereof, in a civil action, if such person failed to obtain a license under this chapter prior to contracting for such work.

Revised Code of Washington:

RCW 18.27.020 Registration required – Partnerships, joint ventures – Penalties. (1) It shall be unlawful for any person to submit any bid or do any work as a contractor until such person shall have been issued a certificate of registration by the state department of labor and industries.

RCW 18.27.080 Registration prerequisite to suit.

No person engaged in the business or acting in the capacity of a contractor may bring or maintain any action in any court of this state for the collection of compensation for the performance of any work or for breach of any contract for which registration is required under this chapter without alleging and proving that he was a duly registered contractor and held a current and valid certificate of registration at the time he contracted for the performance of such work or entered into such contract.

THE SIGNIFICANT RELATIONSHIP TEST

The trial court determined that the most significant contact in the instant case was the factor of performance in Hawaii, and that, therefore, the Hawaii law should apply. Our resolution of the significant contacts analysis indicates that Washington law should apply.

The controlling authority in this state is *BAFFIN LAND CORP. v. MONTICELLO MOTOR INN, INC.*, 70 Wn.2d 893 (1967), where the court abandoned the lex loci contractus rule.

In BAFFIN the court, drawing on the work of the drafters of the Restatement (Second) of Conflicts, adopts the significant relationship test, saying: 'The basic rule is that the validity and effect of a contract are governed by the local law of the state which has the most significant relationship to the contract'. BAFFIN, at 900.

The factors which are to be considered as significant, the court listed as follows:

(1) In the absence of an effective choice of law by the parties, consideration will be given to the following factors, among others, in determining the state with which

the contract has its most significant relationship: (a) the place of contracting, (b) the place of negotiation of the contract, (c) the place of performance, (d) the situs of the subject matter of the contract, (e) the domicile, residence, nationality, place of incorporation and place of business of the parties, (f) the place under whose local law the contract will be most effective. *BAFFIN LAND CORP. v. MONTICELLO MOTOR INN, supra* at 901. The trial court held that Hawaii law should govern because that is where the work was done.

In determining the weight to be given the various factors in BAFFIN, the court said '[t]he approach is NOT to count contacts, but rather to consider which contacts are most significant'. The court indicates that the most significant contact in a contract for the rendition of services is that state where the contract requires that the services be performed. Looking to the Restatement (Second) of Conflicts 196 (1969), where the importance of the place of performance is discussed, it appears that in personal service contracts the local law of the place of performance should be applied 'unless, with respect to a particular issue, some other state has a more significant relationship . . . in which event the local law of the other state will be applied.' Comment D, following section 196, delineates the circumstances wherein the local law of the state where services are to be rendered should not be applied:

> On occasion, a state which is not the place where the contract requires that the services, or a major portion of the services, should be rendered will nevertheless, with respect to the particular issue, be the state of most significant relationship to the transaction and the parties and hence the state of the applicable law. This may be so, for example, when the contract would be invalid under the local law of the state where the services are to be rendered but valid under the local law of another state with a close relationship to the transaction and the parties. In such a situation, the local law of the other state should be applied unless the value of protecting the expectation of the parties by upholding the contract is outweighed in the particular case by the interest of the state where the services are to be performed in having its invalidating rule applied.

In personal service contracts the Restatement rule appears to be that when the expectation interest of the parties outweighs the policy of the performance state in applying its invalidating rule, the local law of the place of performance should not apply. Washington law not only supports this position, but requires consideration of the public policies of both Hawaii and Washington. In *POTLATCH FED. CREDIT UNION v. KENNEDY*, 76 Wn.2d 806, 810 (1969) the court states:

> Certainly an identification of contacts is meaningless without consideration of the interests and public policies of potentially concerned states and a regard as to the

manner and extent of such policies as they relate to the transaction in issue. These competing policies must also be weighed against the justified expectations of the parties.

The desire of the parties at the time of contracting was to create an enforceable contract. Kaanapali expected the work to be performed and Nordic Tile expected to be paid and to make a profit. Consideration of the expectation interest of the parties would weigh heavily in upholding the validity of the contract against the interests and public policy of Hawaii.

The policy interest of Hawaii is expressed by the Department of Regulatory Agencies, rules and regulations for the Contractor's License Board, Title 7, ch. 8, 1.2:

> The Board interprets the primary intent of the Legislature in creating the Contractors License Board to be the protection of the public health, safety and general welfare, in dealing with persons engaged in the construction industry, and the affording to the public of an effective and practical protection against the incompetent, inexperienced, unlawful and unfair practices of contractors with whom they contract.
> All rules, regulations or orders adopted by the Board shall be interpreted and construed in light of the policies announced herein.

The public policy of the State of Washington is set forth in RCW 18.27.140: '[T]o afford protection to the public from unreliable, fraudulent, financially irresponsible, or incompetent contractors.' The policy interest of both states is substantially the same. In *ANDREWS FIXTURE CO. v. OLIN*, 472 P.2d 420, 423 (1970), the court expanded upon this state's policy:

> Courts have not insisted on literal compliance with a contractor registration law where the party seeking to escape his obligation has received the full protection which the statute contemplates . . .
> . . . To deny plaintiff a recovery would transform this socially desirable registration act, designed primarily to protect the public from irresponsible contractors, into an unwarranted shield for the avoidance of a just obligation.

Thus a policy consideration is that of providing Washington residents a forum for the resolution of an adjudicable issue. The Hawaii statute, if applied, would deny to Nordic Tile access to any court for resolution of this question. While Hawaii can control access to its courts, it should not as a matter of policy be able to control access to Washington courts, which have jurisdiction, for resolution of a dispute primarily between Washington domiciliaries.

DECISION

The significance of the place of contracting, the domicile and residence of the parties (except one member of the Kaanapali joint venture), the expectation interests of the parties, and the policy of Washington in providing a forum far outweigh the significance of the place of performance and the public policy of Hawaii in applying its rule. Washington law applies.

? NOTES AND QUESTIONS

1 What is the relevance of the reference to the place of contracting, or the place of performance, under the Restatement? What is the difference between the proper law of the contract (*supra*, 2.3) and the most significant relationship?

2 The court considers that the policy of each of the States is to control access to their respective courts. Is this really the reason why the lawmakers of both Hawaii and Washington passed these laws? Wasn't the policy rather to protect a certain category of persons? If so, who are these persons in the present case? Were they contemplated by the Washington lawmaker? Would the policy of Washington be advanced by applying its law in this case?

Part V

Torts

10
Choice of law in tort matters

International tort cases also raise issues of jurisdiction. These issues are discussed in depth in Chapter 3 which presents general jurisdictional rules applicable in tort matters and special rules applicable in product liability cases in the United States, the European Union and the British Commonwealth.

1   General rules

Unlike contract law, it was traditionally inconceivable for the parties to choose the law governing torts. Recent legislation, however, has granted freedom of choice to the parties in certain limited circumstances.

1.1   Applicable law in the absence of a choice

The traditional choice of law rule in tort matters has been the *lex loci delicti*: the application of the law of the place where the tort occurred. The rule, however, raises an issue where the act giving rise to the damage (that is, the wrongful act, such as a fault in the meaning of Article 1382 [now 1240] of the French *Code Civil* or the breach of a duty of care in the English tort of negligence) occurred in one jurisdiction, but the damage was sustained in another. While it is possible to grant jurisdiction to the courts of each jurisdiction, it is not possible to provide for the cumulative application of both laws.

In many jurisdictions, the issue was resolved by deciding to apply the law of the place of the damage. The Supreme Court of Alabama famously decided so in *Alabama Great Southern Railroad v. Carroll* in 1892.[1] Carroll, who worked on a train running from Alabama to Mississippi, was injured in Mississippi as a result of negligence committed on the train in Alabama. The court held that Mississippi law governed, as the law of the place of the injury. The main rationale given by the court was that the right had vested after all requirements for liability were met, and was to be recognized in other states: 'the

---

1 97 Ala. 126.

negligent infliction of an injury here, under statutory circumstances, creates a right of action here, which, being transitory, may be enforced in any other state or country the comity of which admits of it'. Around ten U.S. states, including Alabama, still follow *Carroll*.

Without relying on the idea that the right vested in the place where the last requirement was fulfilled, many other States have adopted the same solution. We have already seen that this is the general rule under Art. 4 of the Rome II Regulation, which makes clear that the law of the place of the damage applies 'irrespective of the country in which the event giving rise to the damage occurred' (*supra* p. 4).

Both Japan and Quebec would also apply the law of the place of the damage, but subject to one qualification.

Japanese Act on the General Rules of Application of Laws (2006)
Article 17 *Tort*
The formation and effect of claims arising from tort shall be governed by the law of the place where the results of the acts causing the damage arose. However, where the occurrence of the results in such place would usually be unforeseeable, the law of the place where the acts causing the damage occurred shall govern.

Quebec Civil Code
Article 3126 (first paragraph)
The obligation to make reparation for injury caused to another is governed by the law of the State where the injurious act occurred. However, if the injury appeared in another State, the law of the latter State is applicable if the person who committed the injurious act should have foreseen that the injury would manifest itself there. (. . .)

[?] NOTES AND QUESTIONS

1 Japan and Quebec apply the law of the place of the damage only in cases where such damage was foreseeable. If it were not, which law would apply?
2 There is no comparable qualification under Art. 4 of the Rome II Regulation. However, Art. 4 insists that the law of the place of the damage applies 'irrespective of the country or countries in which the indirect consequences of that event occur'. Is indirect damage foreseeable?

***

Another law than the law of the place of the damage could be more closely connected to the tort, and thus more appropriate. Should it be applied?

Japanese Act on the General Rules of Application of Laws (2006)

Article 20 *Exception for Cases with a Clearly Closer Connection to Another Place*

Notwithstanding Articles 17, 18, and 19, the formation and effect of claims arising from tort shall be governed by the law of the place with which they are clearly more closely connected in light of the circumstances such as where at the time of the tort both of the parties had their habitual residence in a place under the same law, or where the tort occurred by breaching obligations in a contract between the parties.

Quebec Civil Code

Article 3082

Exceptionally, the law designated by this Book [on Private International Law] is not applicable if, in the light of all attendant circumstances, it is clear that the situation is only remotely connected with that law and is much more closely connected with the law of another State. This provision does not apply where the law is designated in a juridical act.

Article 3126 (second paragraph)

In any case where the person who committed the injurious act and the victim have their domiciles or residences in the same State, the law of that State applies.

 **QUESTIONS**

Like Quebec, Art. 4(2) of the Rome II Regulation provides for the application of the law of the common domicile of the litigants. Like Japan, Art. 4(3) of the same Regulation provides for an exception clause, but only suggests one instance of operation of the clause: 'a pre-existing relationship between the parties, such as a contract, that is closely connected with the tort/delict in question'. How different is the law under the three sets of rules?

Is the Chinese choice of law rule inspired from Art 4 of the Rome II Regulation? Can you identify differences?

Law of the People's Republic of China on the Laws Applicable to Foreign-Related Civil Relations (2010)

Article 44

Tortious liability is governed by the law of the place of tortious act. Where the parties have common habitual residence, the law of their common habitual residence shall be applied. Where the parties have chosen by agreement an applicable law after the tortious act occurs, the agreement shall be followed.

 NOTE

In 1988, the Chinese Supreme Court had issued an Opinion providing that, where the place of conduct and the place of injury were different, Chinese courts had the power to choose the law of either country.[2] The Opinion, however, did not provide guidance as to how such discretion should be exercised.

---

2 Supreme People's Court Opinion on Several Issues concerning the Implementation of the General Principles of Civil Law of the PRC of 2 April 1988, Art. 187.

***

Traditionally, English courts applied the double actionability rule with respect to torts committed abroad.[3] A plaintiff would have to demonstrate not only that the conduct was actionable under the applicable foreign law, but also under the law of the forum. The rule was largely superseded in England by the Rome II Regulation, and was abrogated in Canada and Australia, but it remains applicable in some Commonwealth jurisdictions (India, Singapore, New Zealand).[4]

Has Japan also indirectly introduced a double actionability rule?

> *Japanese Act on the General Rules of Application of Laws (2006)*
> **Article 22** *Public Policy Limits in Tort*
> (1) Where events that should otherwise be governed by the foreign law applicable in tort do not constitute a tort under Japanese law, recovery of damages or any other remedy under the foreign law may not be demanded.
> (2) Even where the events that should otherwise be governed by the foreign law applicable in tort constitute a tort both under the foreign law and under Japanese law, the injured person may not demand recovery of damages or any other remedy not recognized under Japanese law.

Note: some Japanese scholars are highly critical of this provision.[5]

***

Today, the vast majority of U.S. states have abandoned the traditional choice of law methodology in the field of torts as exemplified by *Carroll*. The approach in terms of governmental interest analysis is essentially different, but has it resulted in different outcomes?

---

3 *Boys v. Chaplin* [1971] A.C. 356 (HL).
4 And in about 15 countries, mostly from the Middle East and the former Soviet Union: Symeonides, *Codifying*, 83.
5 See, calling for the deletion of Art 22, Toshiyuki Kono, 'Critical and Comparative Analysis of the Rome II Regulation on Applicable Laws to Non-contractual Obligations and the New Private International Law in Japan', in Jürgen Basedow, Harald Baum and Yuko Nishitani (eds), *Japanese and European Private International Law in Comparative Perspective* (Mohr Siebeck 2008) 232.

CASE

New York Court of Appeals, 23 April 1969 *Tooker v. Lopez*

See *supra*, p. 34.

Symeon C. Symeonides, Territoriality and Personality in Tort Conflicts[6]

[A]t least in tort conflicts, the American choice-of-law revolution did not bring about a complete dislodging of the principle of territoriality, which was the basis of the traditional *lex loci delicti* rule. This is not surprising because, as *Babcock* indicated, the revolution's goal was not to banish the *lex loci* rule from being used in tort conflicts, but rather to define the circumstances under which one should continue to employ that rule. Four decades after *Babcock*, 41 other jurisdictions have followed New York's lead and have abandoned the *lex loci* rule as the rule by which to resolve all tort conflicts. In fact, one might argue that in most of these jurisdictions the rule as such has ceased to exist, in that the courts now rely on multiple contacts, factors, and policies which are antithetical to the single-mindedness of the lex loci rule.

Nevertheless, when one looks at the results that these multifaceted flexible approaches have produced since the *Babcock* days, one realizes that, in many categories and patterns of tort conflicts, these approaches have produced the same results as the *lex loci* rule would have produced: they applied the law of a state of injury, even if that state had additional contacts and even if the rationale for applying that law was partly based on those additional contacts or other factors.

In some other categories of cases, the courts applied the law of the place of conduct (rather than the place of injury) and thus produced a different result than the American version of the *lex loci* rule would produce. However, because the place of conduct is a territorial rather than a personal conduct, these cases remain in the territorialist column.

This means that, in terms of the results of actual cases (rather than in terms of underlying rationale or methodology), territoriality has lost relatively little ground as a result of the American choice-of-law revolution (. . .)

The preceding discussion supports the following conclusions, (. . .):

(1) Territoriality continues to reign supreme in conflicts between conduct-regulating rules. In these conflicts, the courts disregard the parties' domiciles and focus on the two territorial contacts–the place of conduct and the place of injury. When both of these contacts are in the same state, the courts invariably apply the

---

6 In Thalia Einhorn and Kurt Siehr (eds) *Intercontinental Cooperation Through Private International Law: Essays in Memory of Peter Nygh* (T.M.C. Asser Press, 2004) 432–3.

law of that state. When these contacts are in different states, the courts choose one of those states, as explained above. When they choose the law of the place of conduct, the result deviates from the *lex loci* rule as applied in the United States, but it is still a territorial result.

(2) Territoriality has lost significant ground to personality in conflicts between loss-distribution rules. However, the ground lost is confined to one category of cases–cases in which both the tortfeasor and the victim are domiciled or have significant affiliations with the same state (common-domicile cases), and are involved in a tort which occurred in another state or states. In these cases, the courts have almost unanimously applied the law of the parties' common domicile. Thus, one can say that the principle of personality reigns supreme in loss-distribution conflicts of the common-domicile pattern.

(3) This leaves the middle ground of loss-distribution conflicts of the split-domicile pattern. This is the arena in which territoriality and personality continue to challenge each other (. . .). Although the courts that have abandoned the *lex loci* rule consider both the personal and the territorial contacts, the majority of courts end up applying the law of the state that has the territorial contacts (even if that state also has a personal contact) rather than the state that has only a personal contact. In that sense, one can say that, at least for now, territoriality continues to carry the day in these middle conflicts.

If one assumes that the goal of the American choice-of-law revolution was to banish territoriality from tort conflicts, one would have to conclude that the revolution has scored only a partial victory. However, as noted earlier, such an assumption would be incorrect. The revolution's goals were neither as deliberate nor as narrow. The chief goal was to free American choice-of-law from the shackles of a mechanical rule that inexorably required the application of the law of a state that had a single contact–which happened to be territorial–regardless of any other contacts or factors, and regardless of the issue involved in the conflict or the content of the conflicting laws. Judged in this light, the revolution has succeeded in demolishing not only this particular rule, but also the system that gave birth to it. Along the way, the revolution has brought about a new accommodation or equilibrium between territoriality and personality.

QUESTIONS

1. The fundamental distinction in the United States is between conduct regulating and loss allocating rules, for which different choice of law rules apply. How different is the articulation of these choice of law rules from Art. 4 of the Rome II Regulation?

2. How do the following provisions compare with American new choice of law rules?

Rome II Regulation (2007)

Preamble

(33) According to the current national rules on compensation awarded to victims of road traffic accidents, when quantifying damages for personal injury in cases in which the accident takes place in a State other than that of the habitual residence of the victim, the court seised should take into account all the relevant actual circumstances of the specific victim, including in particular the actual losses and costs of after-care and medical attention.

(34) In order to strike a reasonable balance between the parties, account must be taken, in so far as appropriate, of the rules of safety and conduct in operation in the country in which the harmful act was committed, even where the non-contractual obligation is governed by the law of another country. The term 'rules of safety and conduct' should be interpreted as referring to all regulations having any relation to safety and conduct, including, for example, road safety rules in the case of an accident.

Article 17 *Rules of safety and conduct*

In assessing the conduct of the person claimed to be liable, account shall be taken, as a matter of fact and in so far as is appropriate, of the rules of safety and conduct which were in force at the place and time of the event giving rise to the liability.

1.2   Freedom of choice

The freedom to choose the law governing a tort is a recent innovation. It is, however, much more limited than in contract matters.

Japanese Act on the General Rules for Application of Laws (2006)

Article 21 *Variation of Applicable Law by the Parties*

After a tort occurs, the parties to the tort may vary the law that would otherwise be applicable to the formation and effect of claims. However, such variation shall not be asserted against third parties where it would be prejudicial to their rights.

 NOTES AND QUESTIONS

1   Under Japanese law and under Chinese law,[7] the parties may only vary the law governing the tort after it occurred. A similar limitation is often found in contract matters to protect weaker parties. What is the rationale for resorting to this limitation in the context of torts? Are victims of torts weaker parties?

---

7 See Art. 44 of the 2010 Law on the Laws Applicable to Foreign Related Civil Relations, above 1.1.

2   Reread Art. 20 of the Japanese law above: does Japanese law allow indirectly the choice of the applicable law to torts arising in connection with a contract?

Rome II Regulation (2007)

Article 14 *Freedom of choice*

1. The parties may agree to submit non-contractual obligations to the law of their choice:

(a)   by an agreement entered into after the event giving rise to the damage occurred; or

(b)   where all the parties are pursuing a commercial activity, also by an agreement freely negotiated before the event giving rise to the damage occurred.

The choice shall be expressed or demonstrated with reasonable certainty by the circumstances of the case and shall not prejudice the rights of third parties.

2. Where all the elements relevant to the situation at the time when the event giving rise to the damage occurs are located in a country other than the country whose law has been chosen, the choice of the parties shall not prejudice the application of provisions of the law of that other country which cannot be derogated from by agreement.

3. Where all the elements relevant to the situation at the time when the event giving rise to the damage occurs are located in one or more of the Member States, the parties' choice of the law applicable other than that of a Member State shall not prejudice the application of provisions of Community law, where appropriate as implemented in the Member State of the forum, which cannot be derogated from by agreement.

?   **NOTES AND QUESTIONS**

1   Like Japanese law, Art. 14 grants the parties with the power to vary the law governing the tort after it occurred. A wider power is only granted to commercial parties. What does this say about the rationale for limiting the power of all other parties?

2   The more innovative rule is to enable commercial parties to choose the applicable law before the tort occurred. Of course, torts typically involve parties who did not know each other before one injured the other. They therefore had no possibility to enter into any agreement. Yet, torts can also occur between parties who had entered into a contractual relationship. Despite the existence of this contract, tort claims might arise in the context of this contractual relationship. The parties might thus have the opportunity to provide not only for the law governing their contract, but also for the law governing any tort claim arising in this context. This may be done by drafting wide, all-encompassing, choice of law clauses in international commercial contracts. This issue is the same as for jurisdiction clauses: see *supra* p. 279.

3   Suppose an international commercial contract providing for the law governing disputes 'arising out of' the contract. This would not seem to reveal the intention of the parties to choose the law governing any tort action that might arise 'in connection with' the contract. But what would

be the result of the operation of the exception clause in Art. 4(3) of the Rome II Regulation: which law would govern the tort claim?

4   Article 14(2) and (3) are borrowed from Art. 3 of the Rome I Regulation. See *supra* p. 383 and 25.

2   Special rules for product liability

In many legal systems, victims of defective products are entitled to seek compensation from manufacturers and suppliers of such products. Today, products can be manufactured in one country, sold in another, and finally used in a third, and possibly many others where the customer might travel to. From the perspective of the manufacturer, the application of the law of the place of the damage raises an issue, because it is entirely unpredictable where customers might take products which can be easily carried in a suitcase. Should manufacturers be ready to compensate customers under the laws of any place in the world where a given customer might choose to travel and suffer a damage? Or, by contrast, should manufacturers and suppliers be allowed to foresee the applicable law and thus to manage risks?

In the European Union, two choices of law regimes coexist. Certain Member States (France, Spain) still apply the 1973 Hague Convention, while others (United Kingdom, Germany) apply the special provision of the Rome II Regulation.

Read Art. 5(1) of the Regulation and explain why each of the three options refers to the law of the place of marketing of the product.

Rome II Regulation (2007)

Preamble

(20) The conflict-of-law rule in matters of product liability should meet the objectives of fairly spreading the risks inherent in a modern high-technology society, protecting consumers' health, stimulating innovation, securing undistorted competition and facilitating trade. Creation of a cascade system of connecting factors, together with a foreseeability clause, is a balanced solution in regard to these objectives. (...)

Article 5 *Product liability*

1. Without prejudice to Article 4(2), the law applicable to a non-contractual obligation arising out of damage caused by a product shall be:

(a)   the law of the country in which the person sustaining the damage had his or her habitual residence when the damage occurred, if the product was marketed in that country; or, failing that,

(b) the law of the country in which the product was acquired, if the product was marketed in that country; or, failing that,

(c) the law of the country in which the damage occurred, if the product was marketed in that country.

However, the law applicable shall be the law of the country in which the person claimed to be liable is habitually resident if he or she could not reasonably foresee the marketing of the product, or a product of the same type, in the country the law of which is applicable under (a), (b) or (c).

2. Where it is clear from all the circumstances of the case that the tort/delict is manifestly more closely connected with a country other than that indicated in paragraph 1, the law of that other country shall apply. A manifestly closer connection with another country might be based in particular on a pre-existing relationship between the parties, such as a contract, that is closely connected with the tort/delict in question.

QUESTIONS

1 Under Art. 5(1), the applicable law can only be the law of the place where the product was marketed. The last paragraph of Art. 5(1), however, is a foreseeability clause which provides that this law will not be applied if the defendant (the alleged tortfeasor) could not reasonably foresee that the product would be marketed in this country. How could the defendant not know where his products are being marketed? Should a distinction be made between the manufacturer and the various distributors or retailers of the product, who could all be liable under the applicable product liability regime?

2 Article 5(1) refers to the place where the product was marketed. But only (b) refers to the place where the product was actually acquired. This means that under Art. 5(1)(a), a customer could buy a product in State A, and then suffer a damage in State B where he lives. Is it foreseeable for the manufacturer to apply the law of State B?

3 Article 5(1) applies without prejudice to Art. 4(2), which provides for the application of the law of the common habitual residence of the victim and the tortfeasor. Is it foreseeable for a manufacturer that the law of his home State might apply irrespective of whether he markets any of his products there? What if he had decided not to market his products in his home state because the local law is too strict? Compare with Art. 45 of the Chinese 2010 Law below.

4 If a product which is marketed Europe-wide causes a damage, Art. 5(1)(a) provides for the application of the law of the residence of the victim rather than the law of the place where the product was acquired (b) or the law of the place of the damage (c). Why does the law of the place of the damage rank so low?

5 Contrary to the Hague Convention, Art. 5 does not offer a subsidiary solution where none of the rules in Art. 5(1) apply. Should the general rule under Art. 4(1) apply? But that would mean that the law of the place of the injury could apply irrespective of whether the product was marketed there, and would thus contradict Art. 5(1)(c). Could Art. 5(2) apply?

6 Article 5 only determines the law applicable to non-contractual obligations. If the customer sues the retailer from whom he purchased the product, his action will be contractual. The concepts of tort and contract have been given autonomous definitions by the European Court of Justice under the European law of jurisdiction, which should also be relevant for choice of law purposes.

The 1973 Hague Convention is applicable in only 11 countries, all European, including Spain, France, the Netherlands and Luxembourg. Because it also binds states which are not Member States of the European Union, it was left untouched by the Rome II Regulation, and prevails in participating Member States. Contrary to the Rome Regulation, the scope of the 1973 Hague Convention is not limited to tort actions, and also includes contractual actions. The goal was to make the issue irrelevant.

Hague Convention on the Law Applicable to Products Liability (1973)

Article 4

The applicable law shall be the internal law of the State of the place of injury, if that State is also –

a)   the place of the habitual residence of the person directly suffering damage, or

b)   the principal place of business of the person claimed to be liable, or

c)   the place where the product was acquired by the person directly suffering damage.

Article 5

Notwithstanding the provisions of Article 4, the applicable law shall be the internal law of the State of the habitual residence of the person directly suffering damage, if that State is also –

a)   the principal place of business of the person claimed to be liable, or

b)   the place where the product was acquired by the person directly suffering damage.

Article 6

Where neither of the laws designated in Articles 4 and 5 applies, the applicable law shall be the internal law of the State of the principal place of business of the person claimed to be liable, unless the claimant bases his claim upon the internal law of the State of the place of injury.

Article 7

Neither the law of the State of the place of injury nor the law of the State of the habitual residence of the person directly suffering damage shall be applicable by virtue of Articles 4, 5 and 6 if the person claimed to be liable establishes that he could not reasonably have foreseen that the product or his own products of the same type would be made available in that State through commercial channels.

QUESTIONS

1 Article 5 prevails over Art. 4, and should thus be read first. Does Art. 5(a) have an equivalent under the Rome II Regulation?
2 Art. 5(b) provides for the application of the law of the place of habitual residence of the victim *and* acquisition of the product. After reading Art. 7, do you think that marketing of the product in that same State is relevant

In case Arts. 4 and 5 fail to designate the applicable law, Art. 6 gives an option to the claimant. In China and Quebec, the victim may also choose between several laws.

Law of the People's Republic of China on the Laws Applicable to Foreign-Related Civil Relations (2010)

Article 45

Products liability is governed by the law of the habitual residence of the victim. Where the victim chooses the law of the tortfeasor's principal place of business or the law where the damage occurs, or the tortfeasor does not engage in any business activity in the victim's habitual residence, the law of the tortfeasor's principal place of business or the place where the damage occurs shall be applied.

Quebec Civil Code

Article 3128

Whatever its source, the liability of the manufacturer of a movable is governed, at the choice of the victim,

(1) by the law of the State where the manufacturer has his establishment or, failing that, his residence, or

(2) by the law of the State where the movable was acquired.

Article 3129

The application of the rules of this Code is mandatory with respect to civil liability for any injury suffered in or outside Québec as a result of exposure to or the use of raw materials, whether processed or not, originating in Québec.

 NOTES AND QUESTIONS

1 Contrary to Art. 6 of the Hague Convention, Art. 45 and Art. 3128 do not apply subsidiarily. The Chinese and Quebec lawmakers have thus made the policy choice to favour victims. Which lawmaker is the most generous?
2 Art. 3129 provides that Quebec rules regarding liability arising out of exposure to or use of raw materials are international mandatory rules. The issue, however, was not so much to ensure that Quebec courts would enforce Quebec rules, but also to resist enforcement in Quebec of foreign judgments finding Quebec asbestos producers liable of damage suffered abroad. For that purpose, Art. 3151 provides for the exclusive jurisdiction of Quebec courts for any disputes contemplated by Art. 3129, knowing that under Art. 3165, foreign judgments violating the exclusive jurisdiction of Quebec authorities will be denied enforcement.

Japanese Act on the General Rules of Application of Laws (2006)
Article 18 *Special Rules for Product Liability*
Notwithstanding the preceding Article, where a claim against a producer (i.e., a person who produces, processes, imports, exports, distributes, or sells a product in the course of trade) or a person who makes a representation that leads others to believe he or she is a producer of a product (hereinafter referred to jointly in this Article as 'producer or similar person') arises from a tort injuring the life, body, or property of others caused by the defect of a delivered product (i.e., a produced or processed thing), the formation and effect of those claims shall be governed by the law of the place where the injured person has been delivered the product. However, where the delivery of the product to that place could not usually be foreseen, the law of the principal place of business of the producer or similar person (or the law of his or her habitual residence where he or she has no place of business) shall govern.

 QUESTIONS

1 Article 18 provides for the application of the law of the place of delivery of the product. What is the impact of the qualification that this place should have been foreseeable?
2 Recall that Art. 20 provides for an exception clause applicable in tort matters (*supra*, 1.1). Do you think that, in the case scenario envisaged by Art. 5(1)(a) of the Rome II Regulation, Art. 20 would lead to the application of the law of the place of the injury?

***

The drafters of the Rome II Regulation and the Hague Convention cared very much about the foreseeability of the determination of the applicable law for the potential tortfeasors. Instead of relying on a simple connecting factor such as the place of the injury, they crafted sophisticated choice of law rules to favour one category of parties. But what about the interest of victims? Under U.S. governmental interest analysis, the substantive policies pursued by lawmakers are central to the determination of the applicable law. In the following case, the court assessed the policies pursued by the various interested states in order to decide which law to apply. Did the court find that product liability laws are intended to favour victims or manufacturers?

 CASE

Supreme Court of Montana, March 7, 2000 *Phillips v. General Motors Corporation*

See *supra*, p. 47.

? QUESTIONS

1 At § 61, the court addresses the expectations of the parties. How does it address the foreseeability of the determination of the applicable law for the manufacturer?

2 In this case, the law of the residence of the victims was applied although the product was acquired in another state and the injuries were suffered in a third state. Which law would apply under Art. 5(1)(a) of the Rome II Regulation? Under Art. 6 of the Hague Convention? Under Art. 18 of the Japanese law?

Part VI

Marriage

11

Validity of marriage

The issue of the validity of marriage is primarily an issue of choice of law. While a party could initiate an action to set aside the marriage immediately after its celebration, this rarely happens. Instead, the issue is generally litigated years after, for the purpose of defending divorce proceedings or asserting rights of inheritance in the estate of one of the spouses.[1] However, as the law of the place of celebration often applies at least in part, it is necessary to discuss briefly the jurisdiction to celebrate the marriage.

1 Jurisdiction to celebrate marriage

In most legal systems, marriages are celebrated by non-judicial authorities. In certain jurisdictions, they must nevertheless be public authorities. As such, the territorial scope of their power must be determined just as the power of courts. Certain States have therefore expressly defined the international jurisdiction of their authorities to celebrate marriages.

Belgian Code of Private International Law (2004)
Article 44 *Jurisdiction of the Belgian authorities to celebrate the marriage*
The marriage can be celebrated in Belgium if one of the prospective spouses has the Belgian nationality or has his domicile in Belgium or has since more than three months his habitual residence in Belgium when the marriage is celebrated.

Swiss Law of Private International Law (1987)
Chapter 3 Section 1 Celebration of marriage
Article 43 *Jurisdiction*
1 Swiss authorities have jurisdiction to perform the celebration of marriage if one of the future spouses is domiciled in Switzerland or is a Swiss citizen.
2 Foreign couples without Swiss domicile may also be permitted to marry in Switzerland by the competent authority if the marriage is recognized in the State of the domicile or citizenship of the future spouses.

---

1 See, e.g., the *Udny v. Udny* and *In the Matter of Daoud Farraj* cases below.

3 Permission may not be refused solely because a divorce granted or recognized in Switzerland is not recognized abroad.

 NOTES AND QUESTIONS

1 Pursuant to public international law, public authorities may not act physically on the territory of other States. These two provisions only define the power of local authorities to celebrate a marriage on the territory of the States which established them. An accepted exception to the rule is the power of consuls to celebrate marriage within the consulate or the embassy of their State.

2 In Japan and Belgium, the law of the place of celebration only governs the formalities regarding the celebration of the marriage, but not the more important substantive requirements which are governed by the law of the nationality of the spouses (see below, 2.2). The relevance of the place of celebration is minimal. Why does the Belgian lawmaker limit the jurisdiction of its authorities? By contrast, Japanese authorities will accept to register any marriage as long as the spouses are present in Japan, and the Japanese official is satisfied that the marriage would be valid under the law applicable pursuant to Japanese choice of law rules.

3 A limping marriage is a marriage valid in one country, but not in another. How does the Swiss lawmaker address the issue?

4 It is in the United States that the place of celebration has the biggest impact on the applicable law, but there is no similar limitation on the power of local authorities to celebrate marriages: *infra*, 2.3.

2 Choice of law

Marriage is one of the fields of the conflict of laws where choice of law rules have been the most varied. The field is not harmonized in the European Union, and the Hague Convention on Celebration and Recognition of the Validity of Marriages, of 14 March 1978 was only ratified by three States: Australia, the Netherlands and Luxembourg.

2.1 Law of domicile

In England, the status and capacity of persons have traditionally been governed by the law of their domicile. The same rule is followed in many Commonwealth jurisdictions, including Ghana and Kenya.[2]

---

2 See *Davis v. Randall* (1962) 1 GLR 1 (Ghana) and *In re. an Application by Barbara Simpson Howison* [1959] EA 568, 572-3 (Kenya). In both jurisdictions, the law of the domicile only applies to the essential validity of marriage.

High Court of England and Wales, 9 July 1970 *Szechter v. Szechter*[3]

The wife, Nina, was born in Poland in 1940. When very young, she was dispatched by the Germans with her mother to an extermination camp. On the way there her mother threw her out of the railway-train into the snow, thereby saving the child's life but at the cost of permanent injury and ill-health. She was rescued and brought up in Warsaw by a Mrs. Karsov. In August 1966 she was arrested, together with the respondent whose secretary she then was, and the respondent's wife. Her arrest was followed by 10 months' detention under interrogation. At the end of that time, although she remained in custody, she was allowed to see a lawyer, who had been instructed by the respondent. The lawyer put to Nina a plan that the respondent and his wife had devised to help her. The plan was that the respondent and his wife should be divorced, that the respondent should marry Nina and take her to Israel as his wife, there to join the respondent's wife, whom the respondent would then re-marry. Nina agreed to this plan and, pursuant to it, the respondent and his wife were secretly divorced in April 1967. In October 1967, Nina was tried on a charge of 'anti-state activities,' convicted and sentenced to three years' imprisonment. Her health continued to deteriorate and she came to the conclusion that she would not be able to survive three years' imprisonment. On February 2, 1968, Nina and the respondent went through a ceremony of marriage in Mokotow Prison. In September 1968 Nina was released from prison. In November 1968 she and the respondent left Poland and went first to Austria and, in December 1968, they reached England, where they had resided ever since, with the intention of remaining permanently in England, although their permission to reside in England was limited to December 1969, later extended to December 1970. On August 15, 1969, Nina petitioned for a decree declaring that the marriage between her and the respondent was void for duress.

The second preliminary question is what is the proper law to apply in order to determine whether an ostensible marriage is defective by reason of duress. There is little direct authority on this matter. But the effect of duress goes to reality of consent and I respectfully agree with the suggestion in rule 32 of Dicey and Morris, *Conflict of Laws*, 8th ed. (1967), p. 271, that no marriage is valid if by the law of either party's domicile one party does not consent to marry the other. This accords with the old distinction between, on the one

---

3 Probate, Divorce and Admiralty Division [1971] P. 286.

hand, 'forms and ceremonies,' the validity of which is referable to the lex loci contractus, and, on the other hand, 'essential validity,' by which is meant (even though by, as the editors of *Rayden on Divorce*, 10th ed. (1967) p. 121, remark, 'not a happy terminology') all requirements for a valid marriage other than those relating to forms and ceremonies, for the validity of which reference is made to the lex domicilii of the parties: ... So far as capacity (also a matter of 'essential validity') is concerned, there can be no doubt that no marriage is valid if by the law of either party's domicile one of the parties is incapable of marrying the other. (...)

Both Nina and the respondent were domiciled in Poland at the time of the ceremony of marriage on February 2, 1968. It is therefore for Polish law to answer whether, on the facts as I have found them, the marriage was invalid by reason of duress. (...)

 QUESTION

Does the law of the domicile govern all issues regarding the validity of marriage?

The concept of domicile in English law is very peculiar. In the following case, the issue was whether the effect of the second marriage of Colonel Udny in 1854 was to legitimate the child he had a year before with Ann Allat and whether, as a consequence, the child could inherit from him. The law of his domicile governed. But where was his domicile?

 CASE

House of Lords, 3 June 1869 *Udny v. Udny*[4]

Facts: John Udny, the father of Colonel Udny, and the grandfather of the defender, was born at Aberdeen, in 1727, of Scottish parents, and his domicil of origin was undoubtedly Scotch. He went to Italy, at what time the evidence did not shew, and for several years prior to 1760 lived at Venice, and was engaged in some kind of business there. In 1761 he was appointed British Consul at Venice, and he held that office till 1777. In that year he was appointed British Consul at Leghorn (*Livorno*), which office he continued to hold until his death, which took place in London, while he was there on leave of absence from Leghorn in 1800. In 1777 he was married to an English lady, Selina Shore Cleveland. There were two children of this marriage, John Robert Udny, the defender's father, who was born in 1770, and a daughter. They were both born at Leghorn. Mrs Udny continued to live at Leghorn with the Consul till 1784, when she went to London, accompanied by her children.

---

4 (1869) 7 M. (H.L.) 89.

John Robert Udny, the Consul's son, lived with his mother in London from 1784 till 1794, when he was sent to Edinburgh University. He remained there from 1794 to 1797. He entered the army in 1797, and continued in it till 1812. In 1802 (his father having died in 1800) he succeeded to Udny. In 1812 he married Miss Emily Fitzhugh, an Englishwoman, and in the same year retired from the army. From 1812 to 1845 he lived in a house in Grosvenor Street, London, which he rented. That was the sole residence which he had during these thirty-three years, except occasional country houses in England. His wife and family lived with him in that house. There was no house on the Udny estate. He, however, came to Scotland nearly every year to look after his estate, and he exercised his rights and discharged his duties as a landowner. He was a freeholder in the county of Aberdeen from 1802, and a justice of the peace, a deputy-lieutenant, and a member of various clubs and associations in that county. He had no employment or occupation in London beyond what a taste for the turf gave him. In 1845, in consequence of pecuniary embarrassments, he went to reside at Boulogne, and while there, his wife being dead, he lived with Ann Allat, the defender's mother. In May 1853 the defender was born, and the Colonel and Ann Allat left Boulogne, and came to Scotland in the month of November in that year, and after residing in Ormiston, in Haddingtonshire, for about six weeks, they were married on 2nd January 1854. After that date the Colonel continued to reside in Scotland till 1861, when he died in Edinburgh. (. . .)

Lord Westbury—

The law of England, and of almost all civilised countries ascribes to each individual at his birth two distinct legal states or conditions; one by virtue of which he becomes the subject of some particular country, binding him by the tie of natural allegiance, which may be called his political status; another by virtue of which he has ascribed to him the character of a citizen of some particular country, and as such possessed of certain municipal rights, and subject to certain obligations, which latter character is the civil status or condition of the individual, and may be quite different from his political status, for the political status may depend upon different laws in different countries, whereas the civil status is governed universally by one specific principle. Domicil or the place of settled residence of an individual is the criterion established by law for the purpose of determining the civil condition of the person, for it is on this basis that the personal rights of the parties,—that is, the law which determines his majority or his minority, marriage, succession, testacy or intestacy,—must depend. Every man has ascribed to him by law a domicil, which is a fiction or creation of inter-national law, and depends on rules which, being mainly derived from the Roman law, are common to the jurisprudence of all civilised nations. It is a settled principle that no man shall be without a domicil, and to secure this result the law attributes to every individual as soon as he is born the domicil of the father if the child be legitimate, or the domicil of the mother if illegitimate. This has been called the domicil of origin, and it is involuntary. Other domicils are domicils of choice, for as soon as the individual is *sui juris*, it is competent to him to elect and assume another domicil, the continuance of which depends upon his will and act. When another domicil is put on, the domicil of origin is for that purpose relinquished, and remains in abeyance during the continuance of the domicil. But as the domicil of origin is the creature of law, and independent of the will of the party, it would be inconsistent with the principles on which it is by law created and ascribed to suppose that it is capable of being, by the mere act of the party, entirely obliterated and extinguished. It revives and exists whenever there is no other domicil, and it does not require to be regained or reconstituted *animo at facto* in the manner which is necessary for the acquisition of a new domicil of choice.

Domicil of choice is a conclusion or inference which the law derives from the fact of a man fixing voluntarily his sole or chief residence in a particular place, with the unlimited intention of continuing to reside there. This is a description of the circumstances which create or constitute a domicil, and not a definition of the term. There must be a residence freely chosen, and not prescribed or dictated by any external necessity, such as the duties of office, the demands of creditors, or the relief of illness. And it must be residence fixed not for any defined period or particular purpose, but general and indefinite in its future duration. It is true that residence, originally temporary, or intended only for a limited period, may afterwards become general and unlimited, and in such a case, so soon as the change of purpose or the *animus manendi* can be inferred, the fact of domicil is established.

The domicil of origin may be extinguished by act of law, as, for example, by sentence of death, exile, and perhaps outlawry, but it cannot be destroyed by the act of the party. (. . .)

The application of these general rules to the circumstances of the present case is very simple. My Lords, I concur with my noble and learned friend that the father of Colonel Udny, the Consul at Leghorn and afterwards at Venice, and again at Leghorn, did not, by his residence there in that capacity, lose his Scotch domicil. Colonel Udny was therefore a Scotchman by birth. But I am certainly inclined to think that when Colonel Udny, to use the ordinary phrase, settled in life, and took a long lease of a house in Grosvenor Street, and made that the place of abode of himself and his wife and children, becoming in point of fact subject to the municipal duties of a resident in that locality, and remained there for a period, I think, of thirty-two years, there being no impediment, in point of occupation or duty, to prevent his going to reside in his native country—under these circumstances, I should come to the conclusion, if it were necessary to decide the point, that Colonel Udny undoubtedly acquired an English domicil. But if he did so he eventually relinquished that English domicil in the most effectual way by selling or surrendering the lease of his house, selling his furniture, discharging his servants, and leaving London in a manner which would leave not the least doubt that he never intended to return there for the purpose of residence. If, therefore, he acquired an English domicil, he abandoned it absolutely *animo et facto*. Its acquisition being a thing of choice, was equally put an end to by choice. He lost it the moment he set foot on the steamer to go to Boulogne, and he reacquired his domicil of origin. The rest is plain. The marriage, and the consequences of that marriage, must be determined by the law of the country of his domicil.

? NOTES AND QUESTIONS

1 Under English law, a person may only have one domicile: it can be either the domicile of origin or the domicile of choice.
2 In this case, where was the domicile of the father of Colonel Udny when he lived in Italy? Where was the domicile of Colonel Udny when he lived in London after 1812? When he left London to go to France? Did he acquire a domicile of choice when he lived in France from 1845 until 1853? Are the reasons why Colonel Udny left for France relevant?
3 The English concept of domicile was developed in Victorian times, when many Englishmen lived abroad to govern the Empire. Is it still suited to modern times? Attempts were made to abolish the presumption of the continuance of the domicile of origin, but none of them succeeded.[5]
4 How different are the concepts of domicile of origin and nationality?

***

A few civil law jurisdictions also apply the law of the domicile to the 'essential validity' of marriage and the law of the place of celebration to the formal validity of marriage: see, e.g., Art. 3083 and 3088 of the Quebec Civil Code. However, they do not rely on such a peculiar concept of domicile. Indeed, China has a similar rule, but it relies on the common habitual residence of the spouses.

---

5 Rogerson, p. 27.

Law of the People's Republic of China on the Laws Applicable to Foreign-Related Civil Relations (2010)

Article 21 Conditions of marriage are governed by the law of the parties' common habitual residence. Absent common habitual residence, the law of their common nationality shall be applied. Absent common nationality, the law of the place where the marriage is concluded shall be applied, if the marriage is concluded in a party's habitual residence or in the country of a party's nationality.

Article 22 Formalities of marriage are valid if they conform to the law of the place where the marriage is concluded, or the law of a party's habitual residence or nationality.

2.2 Law of nationality

In the civil law tradition, the status and capacity of persons have traditionally been governed by the law of their nationality.

Belgian Code of Private International Law (2004)

Article 46. *Law applicable to the formation of marriage*

Subject to article 47, the conditions regarding the validity of the marriage are governed, for each spouse, by the law of the State of the spouse's nationality when the marriage is celebrated. (. . .)

Article 47. *Law applicable to the formal validity of the marriage*

§ 1. The formalities regarding the celebration of the marriage are governed by the law of the State on the territory of which the marriage is celebrated.

§ 2. That law determines if and according to which specific rules:

1. that State requires a declaration and publicity in advance of the marriage;
2. that State requires the determination and registration of the deed of marriage;
3. a marriage celebrated before a religious authority has legal effect;
4. a marriage can take place by proxy.

 NOTES

1   As in England, the law of the nationality only governs the essential validity of marriage. The law of the place of celebration governs the formal validity of marriage. The same distinction and rules are found in France and Japan.[6]
2   Characterizing particular requirements as belonging to substantive or formal validity is not always easy. Article 47 §2 expressly identifies issues belonging to formal validity. In most jurisdictions, however, characterization is left to courts, as in France: see the *Caraslanis* case *supra* p. 80.

---

6 See Arts. 202-1 and 202-2 of the French Civil Code, Art. 24 of the Japanese Act on the General Rules of Application of Laws.

3 In many jurisdictions, the application of the law of the place of celebration is perceived as a convenient rule allowing the parties to comport with local requirements where it might not be possible to comply with the requirements of their national law. This explains why it might be expressly allowed to apply, with respect to formal requirements, either the local law or the law of the nationality of the parties,[7] and that certain jurisdictions expressly allow foreigners to marry on their territory pursuant to foreign formal requirements.[8]

4 If the future spouses hold different nationalities, the substantive validity of the marriage is governed by two different laws. For requirements which are personal to each spouse such as minimum age, the two laws can be applied distributively, i.e. respectively to each spouse. By contrast, for requirements which are concerned with the relationship itself such as the maximum number of spouses or difference of sex, the two laws must be applied cumulatively, which means that, in effect, the more conservative law prevails.

***

The application of the law of the nationality raises an issue where the relevant persons hold several nationalities. How does German law resolve this issue?

Introductory Act to the German Civil Code

Article 5 *Personal status*

(1) If referral is made to the law of a country of which a person is a national and where this person is a bi- or multinational, the law applicable shall be that of the country with which the person has the closest connection, especially through his or her habitual residence or through the course of his or her life. If such person is also a German national, that legal status shall prevail.

(2) If a person is stateless or if his nationality cannot be identified, the law of that country is applicable in which the person has his or her habitual residence or, in the absence thereof, his or her residence.

(3) If referral is made to the law of a country in which a person has his or her residence or habitual residence and a person without or under restricted capacity to contract changes his or her residence without the consent of his or her legal representative, the application of another law does not ensue from this change alone.

 NOTE

The distinction between persons holding several foreign nationalities and persons holding the nationality of the forum and a foreign nationality is widely accepted, and so are the two solutions offered by Art. 5(1).[9]

---

7 See Art. 28 of the Italian PIL Act (1995); Art. 46 of the Tunisian Code of PIL (1998). See also Art. 49 of the Polish PIL Act (2011), allowing also the celebration of the marriage according to the law of the common residence of the spouses.

8 See Art. 13(3) of the Introductory Act to the German Civil Code; Art. 10:30 of the Dutch Civil Code.

9 See Art. 38 of the Japanese Act on the General Rules of Application of Laws; Art. 3 of the Belgian Code of PIL (2004); Art. 2 of the Polish PIL Act (2011).

***

One of the consequences of the application of the law of the nationality is that immigrants remain governed by their law of origin (as long as they do not acquire local nationality). As a result, those immigrants might have the right to marry in circumstances unknown to the local law, or conversely be forbidden to contract certain kinds of marriages which are allowed under the local law.

Compare the four following provisions and explain which problem was identified by the relevant lawmaker, and how it was resolved:

Dutch Civil Code

Article 10:28 *Recognition of the contracting of a marriage*

A marriage is contracted:

a. if each of the prospective spouses meets the requirements for entering into a marriage set by Dutch law and one of them is exclusively or also of Dutch nationality or has his habitual residence in the Netherlands, or;

b. if each of the prospective spouses meets the requirements for entering into a marriage of the State of his nationality.

Introductory Act to the German Civil Code

Article 13 *Marriage*

(1) The conditions for the conclusion of marriage are, as regards each person engaged to be married, governed by the law of the country of which he or she is a national.

(2) If under this law, a requirement is not fulfilled, German law shall apply to that extent, if:

1.   the habitual residence of one of the persons engaged to be married is within the country or one of them is a German national;
2.   the persons engaged to be married have taken reasonable steps to fulfill the requirement; and
3.   it is incompatible with the freedom of marriage to refuse the conclusion of the marriage; in particular, the previous marriage of a person engaged to be married shall not be held against him or her if it is nullified by a decision issued or recognized here or the spouse of the person engaged to be married has been declared dead. (. . .)

Japanese Act on the General Rules of Application of Laws (2006)

Article 24 *Formation and Formalities of Marriage*

(1) For each party, the formation of a marriage shall be governed by his or her national law.

(2) The formalities of a marriage shall be governed by the law of the place of the ceremony (*lex loci celebrationis*).

(3) Notwithstanding the preceding paragraph, formalities that satisfy the requirements of either of the parties' national law shall be effective, unless the marriage is celebrated in Japan and one of the parties is a Japanese national.

Belgian Code of Private International Law (2004)

Article 46. *Law applicable to the formation of marriage*

(. . .) A provision of the law designated by para 1, which prohibits the marriage between two natural persons of the same sex, is not applicable if one of the natural persons has the nationality of a State of which the law allows such marriage or has his habitual residence on the territory of such State.

? NOTES AND QUESTIONS

1 Article 10:28 of the Dutch Civil Code originates from the 1978 Hague Convention on Celebration and Recognition of the Validity of Marriages. It is also found in Art. 171 of the Luxembourg Civil Code.
2 Is the choice of law rule in the Netherlands and Germany really that the law of nationality governs the substantive validity of marriage? Can you reformulate the rule more accurately?
3 What is the goal of the Japanese lawmaker? Is it different from the goal of the Dutch and German lawmakers?
4 What is the goal of the Belgian lawmaker? France has adopted a similar rule in Art. 202-1 §2 of the Civil Code. A constitutional challenge that it violated equality before the law was rejected by French courts. Do you agree?

All those statutory provisions aim at validating marriages which might not comply with the law of the nationality of one of the spouses. However, application of foreign law can also lead to the opposite problem.

Dutch Civil Code

Article 10:29 *Contracting of a marriage in conflict with public order*

- 1. Irrespective of what is provided for in Article 10:28, no marriage can be contracted if the contracting of that marriage could not be accepted on the basis of Article 10:6 (i.e. incompatible with Dutch public order), and in any case if:

a.   the prospective spouses have not reached the age of fifteen years;
b.   the prospective spouses are related to each other by blood or by adoption in the direct line or, by blood, as brother and sister;
c.   the free consent of one of the prospective spouses is missing or the mental capacity of one of them is so disturbed that he is unable to determine his own will or to understand the significance of his declarations;
d.   the marriage would be in conflict with the rule that a person may only be united in marriage with one other person at the same time;

> e. the marriage would be in conflict with the rule that a person who wants to enter into a marriage may not simultaneously be registered as a partner in a registered partnership.

> - 2. The contracting of a marriage cannot be refused on the ground that there is an impediment to this marriage under the law of the State of which one of the prospective spouses has the nationality, if that impediment cannot be accepted on the basis of Article 10:6 (i.e. if the impediment itself is contrary to Dutch public order).

 NOTES

1 Article 10:29 defines the content of Dutch public policy with respect to marriage. In many countries, this will be left to courts, as in France (see *supra* p. 141).
2 The Dutch lawmaker has defined Dutch public order in absolute terms. Other jurisdictions limit the operation of their public policy exception to cases with a strong connection with the forum (see *supra* p. 141).

2.3   Law of place of celebration

The traditional choice of law rule in the United States is that the law of the place of celebration of marriage governs all aspects of the validity of marriage. Contrary to the rest of the world, the rule does not distinguish between formal and substantive validity: one single law governs both.

CASE

Court of Appeals of New York, 14 July 1953 *In the Matter of the Estate of Fanny May, Deceased*[10]

Lewis, C.J.

In this proceeding, involving the administration of the estate of Fannie May, deceased, we are to determine whether the marriage in 1913 between the respondent Sam May and the decedent, who was his niece by the half blood — which marriage was celebrated in Rhode Island, where concededly such marriage is valid — is to be given legal effect in New York where statute law declares incestuous and void a marriage between uncle and niece.

The question thus presented arises from proof of the following facts: The petitioner Alice May Greenberg, one of six children born of the Rhode Island marriage of Sam and Fannie May, petitioned in 1951 for letters of administration of the estate of her mother Fannie May, who had died in 1945.

---

10 305 N.Y. 486 (1953).

Thereupon, the respondent Sam May, who asserts the validity of his marriage to the decedent, filed an objection to the issuance to petitioner of such letters of administration upon the ground that he is the surviving husband of the decedent and accordingly, under section 118 of the Surrogate's Court Act, he has the paramount right to administer her estate. Contemporaneously with, and in support of the objection filed by Sam May, his daughter Sirel Lenrow and his sons Harry May and Morris B. May — who are children of the challenged marriage — filed objections to the issuance of letters of administration to their sister, the petitioner, and by such objections consented that letters of administration be issued to their father Sam May.

The petitioner, supported by her sisters Ruth Weisbrout and Evelyn May, contended throughout this proceeding that her father is not the surviving spouse of her mother because, although their marriage was valid in Rhode Island, the marriage never had validity in New York where they were then resident and where they retained their residence until the decedent's death.

The record shows that for a period of more than five years prior to his marriage to decedent the respondent Sam May had resided in Portage, Wisconsin; that he came to New York in December, 1912, and within a month thereafter he and the decedent — both of whom were adherents of the Jewish faith — went to Providence, Rhode Island, where, on January 21, 1913, they entered into a ceremonial marriage performed by and at the home of a Jewish rabbi. The certificate issued upon that marriage gave the age of each party as twenty-six years and the residence of each as 'New York, N. Y.' Two weeks after their marriage in Rhode Island the respondent May and the decedent returned to Ulster County, New York, where they lived as man and wife for thirty-two years until the decedent's death in 1945. Meantime the six children were born who are parties to this proceeding.

A further significant item of proof — to which more particular reference will be made — was the fact that in Rhode Island on January 21, 1913, the date of the marriage here involved, there were effective statutes which prohibited the marriage of an uncle and a niece, excluding, however, those instances — of which the present case is one — where the marriage solemnized is between persons of the Jewish faith within the degrees of affinity and consanguinity allowed by their religion.

In Surrogate's Court, where letters of administration were granted to the petitioner, the Surrogate ruled that although the marriage of Sam May and the decedent in Rhode Island in 1913 was valid in that State, such marriage was not only void in New York as opposed to natural law but is contrary to the provisions of subdivision 3 of section 5 of the Domestic Relations Law. Accordingly the Surrogate concluded that Sam May did not qualify in this jurisdiction for letters of administration as the surviving spouse of the decedent.

At the Appellate Division the order of the Surrogate was reversed on the law and the proceeding was remitted to Surrogate's Court with direction that letters of administration upon decedent's estate be granted to Sam May who was held to be the surviving spouse of the decedent. In reaching that decision the Appellate Division concluded that the 1913 marriage of Sam May and the decedent in Rhode Island, being concededly valid in that State, is valid in New York where the degree of consanguinity of uncle and niece is not so close as to be repugnant to our concept of natural law, and that the statute (Domestic Relations Law, § 5, subd. 3) — which declares such a marriage to be incestuous and void — lacks express language which gives it extraterritorial force. The case comes to us upon appeal as of right by the petitioner and her two sisters Ruth Weisbrout and Evelyn May.

We regard the law as settled that, subject to two exceptions presently to be considered, and in the absence of a statute expressly regulating within the domiciliary State marriages solemnized abroad, the legality of a marriage between persons sui juris is to be determined by the law of the place where it is celebrated. (*Van Voorhis v. Brintnall*, 86 N. Y. 18, 24; Restatement, Conflict of Laws, §§ 121, 131, 132; Story on Conflict of Laws [7th ed.], § 113; 2 Beale. Conflict of Laws, pp. 669–670)

In *Van Voorhis v. Brintnall* (*supra*) the decision turned upon the civil status in this State of a divorced husband and his second wife whom he had married in Connecticut to evade the prohibition of a judgment of divorce which, pursuant to New York law then prevailing, forbade his remarriage until the death of his former wife. In reaching its decision, which held valid the Connecticut marriage there involved, this court noted the fact that in the much earlier case of *Decouche v. Savetier* (3 Johns. Ch. 190, 211 [1817]), Chancellor KENT had recognized the general principle 'that the rights dependent upon nuptial contracts, are to be determined by the lex loci.' Incidental to the decision in *Van Voorhis v. Brintnall* (*supra*) which followed the general rule that 'recognizes as valid a marriage considered valid in the place where celebrated' (id., p. 25), this court gave careful consideration to, and held against the application of two exceptions to that rule — viz., cases within the prohibition of positive law; and cases involving polygamy or incest in a degree regarded generally as within the prohibition of natural law.

We think the Appellate Division in the case at bar rightly held that the principle of law which ruled *Van Voorhis v. Brintnall* and kindred cases cited (*supra*) was decisive of the present case and that neither of the two exceptions to that general rule is here applicable.

The statute of New York upon which the appellants rely is subdivision 3 of section 5 of the Domestic Relations Law which, insofar as relevant to our problem, provides:

> **§ 5. Incestuous and void marriages.**
> A marriage is incestuous and void whether the relatives are legitimate or illegitimate between either:
> 3. An uncle and niece or an aunt and nephew.
> If a marriage prohibited by the foregoing provisions of this section be solemnized it shall be void, and the parties thereto shall each be fined not less than fifty nor more than one hundred dollars and may, in the discretion of the court in addition to said fine, be imprisoned for a term not exceeding six months. Any person who shall knowingly and wilfully solemnize such marriage, or procure or aid in the solemnization of the same, shall be deemed guilty of a misdemeanor and shall be fined or imprisoned in like manner.

Although the New York statute quoted above declares to be incestuous and void a marriage between an uncle and a niece and imposes penal measures upon the parties thereto, it is important to note that the statute does not by express terms regulate a marriage solemnized in another State where, as in our present case, the marriage was concededly legal. In the case at hand, as we have seen, the parties to the challenged marriage were adherents of the Jewish faith which, according to Biblical law and Jewish tradition — made the subject of proof in this case — permits a marriage between an uncle and a niece; they were married by a Jewish rabbi in the State of Rhode Island where, on the date of such marriage in 1913 and ever since, a statute forbidding the marriage of an uncle and a niece was expressly qualified by the following statutory exceptions appearing in 1913 in Rhode Island General Laws:

> § 4. The provisions of the preceding sections shall not extend to, or in any way affect, any marriage which shall be solemnized among the Jews, within the degrees of affinity or consanguinity allowed by their religion. . . .
> § 9. Any marriage which may be had and solemnized among the people called Quakers, or Friends, in the manner and form used or practised in their societies, or among persons professing the Jewish religion, according to their rites and ceremonies, shall be good and valid in law; and wherever the words 'minister' and 'elder' are used in this chapter, they shall be held to include all of the persons

connected with the society of Friends, or Quakers, and with the Jewish religion, who perform or have charge of the marriage ceremony according to their rites and ceremonies.

As section 5 of the New York Domestic Relations Law (quoted, *supra*) does not expressly declare void a marriage of its domiciliaries solemnized in a foreign State where such marriage is valid, the statute's scope should not be extended by judicial construction. (*Van Voorhis v. Brintnall, supra*, p. 33.) Indeed, had the Legislature been so disposed it could have declared by appropriate enactment that marriages contracted in another State — which if entered into here would be void — shall have no force in this State. (*Putnam v. Putnam*, 25 Mass. 433, 435.) Although examples of such legislation are not wanting, we find none in New York which serve to give subdivision 3 of section 5 of the Domestic Relations Law extraterritorial effectiveness. (*Van Voorhis v. Brintnall, supra*, pp. 25–37.) Accordingly, as to the first exception to the general rule that a marriage valid where performed is valid everywhere, we conclude that, absent any New York statute expressing clearly the Legislature's intent to regulate within this State marriages of its domiciliaries solemnized abroad, there is no 'positive law' in this jurisdiction which serves to interdict the 1913 marriage in Rhode Island of the respondent Sam May and the decedent.

As to the application of the second exception to the marriage here involved — between persons of the Jewish faith whose kinship was not in the direct ascending or descending line of consanguinity and who were not brother and sister — we conclude that such marriage, solemnized, as it was, in accord with the ritual of the Jewish faith in a State whose legislative body has declared such a marriage to be 'good and valid in law', was not offensive to the public sense of morality to a degree regarded generally with abhorrence and thus was not within the inhibitions of natural law.

? NOTES AND QUESTIONS

1 The origin of the application of the law of the place of celebration is to be found in an analogy between marriage and contract. The traditional rule in contractual matters was the application of the law of the place of contracting (*supra*, p. 408). The rule was applied to marriage contracts, and led to the application of the law of the place of celebration. In a country of immigrants, it had the great virtue of enabling new immigrants, and later settlers travelling west, to marry freely unencumbered by restrictions of the law of their previous communities.[11]

---

11 Peter M. North, 'Development of Rules of Private International Law in the Field of Family Law' (1980) 166 Collected Courses of the Hague Academy of International Law 22.

2   Does the rule indirectly give freedom of choice to the parties? It all depends on the jurisdictional rule that the local authority will apply for assessing in which situations it can celebrate a marriage. If American authorities, as Swiss or Belgian authorities, would only celebrate marriage for couples of residents or nationals (*supra*, 1), they would refuse to marry parties with no connection with the forum. But this is not the case in the United States. Local authorities will typically celebrate the marriage of any couple requesting it; indeed, in some states, marriage can validly be celebrated in presence of a clergyman only.[12] In effect, therefore, the American choice of law rule enables couples to freely choose the law governing the validity of marriage: they can 'vote with their feet', that is, designate the applicable law by travelling to a state whose law they prefer.

3   Logically, couples living in states where they could not marry have looked for more liberal states and travelled to get married there. The states of their common domicile (often both before and after the celebration of the marriage) have sometimes developed tools to sanction what they perceived as an evasion of their law. A few states adopted the *Uniform Marriage Evasion Act* 1913.[13] Sometimes, the different rule applied by the state of celebration of the marriage was regarded as contrary to public policy. But, in most cases, the state of the common domicile has accepted the marriage celebrated out of state as valid.[14]

4   The freedom which the choice of law rule in effect affords to the parties is puzzling. Why would the state of the common domicile accept that its law be so easily circumvented? Is it that courts are more liberal than the lawmakers, and welcome a narrowing of the scope of the local mandatory rules?[15] One problem with the rule is that, although all residents of conservative states may travel to other states, in practice only rich and affluent people might take advantage of the rule.[16]

5   Is the rule generating a healthy legislative competition? Where conservative states see high numbers of residents travelling abroad to get married, is this creating an incentive to change the law? Is it to be welcomed? Are conservative rules always worse than liberal rules?

Could states change their law for the purpose of attracting out-of-state couples who may spend significant sums of money locally? When New York introduced same-sex marriage in 2011, the New York Senate's Independent Democratic Conference calculated that it would bring US$ 311 million in revenues to the local economy and to the state, including marriage license fees (3m), sales tax (22m), wedding revenue and tourism (283m) and hotel occupancy taxes (259,000). The rule has long had the potential of creating a legal market for marriage in the United States.[17]

6   The rule is consistent with the old American choice of law doctrine of vested rights. As the marriage was constituted by its celebration, it seemed logical to apply the law of the place of marriage to the formation of this relationship. What would be the result of a governmental interest analysis?

---

12   See *infra* the *Daoud Farraj* case.
13   See *supra*, p. 87.
14   Weintraub, § 5.1.A.
15   Weintraub, § 5.1.C.
16   Id.
17   Erin A. O'Hara and Larry Ribstein, *The Law Market* (OUP 2009) Ch. 8.

CASE

Supreme Court, Appellate Division, New York, 27 April 2010 *In the Matter of Daoud Farraj*[18]

In May 2003 the petitioner, Rabaa M. Hanash, and Daoud Farraj, a/k/a David I. Farraj (hereinafter the decedent), participated in a formal marriage ceremony in accordance with Islamic law, at the home of the petitioner's brother in Clifton, New Jersey. Prior to the marriage ceremony, the decedent was a resident of New York and the petitioner lived at her brother's residence in New Jersey. An Imam (Islamic clergyman) came from New York to New Jersey to solemnize the marriage. However, a marriage license was not obtained. Immediately after the marriage ceremony, the petitioner and the decedent returned to Brooklyn, where they had a wedding celebration. The decedent and the petitioner lived together in New York until the decedent's death in July 2007.

The decedent died intestate and Letters of Administration were issued to the appellant, the decedent's son from a prior marriage. Subsequently, the petitioner filed a petition to compel an accounting of the decedent's estate. The appellant moved to dismiss the petition pursuant to CPLR 3211(a)(3) on the ground that the petitioner lacked standing as a surviving spouse, since her marriage to the decedent was invalid under New Jersey Law.

Under the law of the State of New Jersey, the failure to obtain a marriage license renders a purported marriage absolutely void (*see* N.J. Stat. Ann. § 37:1–10). In New York, while the Domestic Relations Law deems it necessary for all persons intending to be married to obtain a marriage license (*see* Domestic Relations Law § 13), a marriage is not void for the failure to obtain a marriage license if the marriage is solemnized (*see* Domestic Relations Law § 25). A marriage is solemnized where the parties 'solemnly declare in the presence of a clergyman or magistrate and the attending witness or witnesses that they take each other as husband and wife' (Domestic Relations Law § 12). Therefore, if New Jersey law is applied to determine the validity of the marriage between the petitioner and the decedent, the marriage is void. If New York law is applied, the marriage is valid. The Surrogate's Court applied New York law and denied the appellant's motion. We affirm.

The general rule is that the legality of a marriage 'is to be determined by the law of the place where it is celebrated' (*Matter of May*, 305 N.Y. 486, 490, 114 N.E.2d 4). The Restatement (Second) of Conflict of Laws § 283, however,

---

18 72 A.D.3d 1082, 900 N.Y.S.2d 340.

provides a more flexible approach, whereby '[t]he validity of a marriage will be determined by the local law of the state which, with respect to the particular issue, has the most significant relationship to the spouses and the marriage'. We look to the Restatement (Second) of Conflict of Laws § 283 for guidance in determining which law should govern the validity of the marriage at issue here.

The petitioner and the decedent had a justified expectation that they were married, since they participated in a formal marriage ceremony in accordance with Islamic law (*see* Restatement [Second] of Conflict of Laws § 6). The only reason the petitioner and the decedent had their marriage ceremony in New Jersey was because, under Islamic law, the marriage ceremony was to be conducted in the residence of the bride's eldest male relative, which was the petitioner's brother. In addition, the intended and actual matrimonial domicile was New York, and the petitioner and the decedent held themselves out as a married couple in New York. Therefore, New York has a significant interest in the marriage between the petitioner and the decedent. While New Jersey has an interest in enforcing its marriage requirements, this interest is not particularly strong here, since the petitioner and the decedent left New Jersey immediately after the marriage ceremony, and lived in New York for the entirety of their marriage.

Therefore, the Surrogate's Court properly determined that New York had the 'most significant relationship to the spouses and the marriage' and that New York law should apply to determine the validity of the marriage. Under New York law, the marriage between the petitioner and the decedent was valid, even without a marriage license, since it was solemnized (*see* Domestic Relations Law §§ 12, 25). Accordingly, the appellant's motion to dismiss the proceeding was properly denied.

? | NOTES AND QUESTIONS

1 What is the reason for concluding that New York is strongly interested in the marriage? In effect, will this approach lead to the application of the law of the place of celebration?
2 The court also insists that the parties' expectations should be respected. But what are these expectations when they marry abroad? A comment to § 283 states:

> Parties enter into marriage with forethought. To the extent that they think about the matter, they would usually expect that the validity of their marriage would be determined by the local law of the state where it was contracted. In situations where the parties did not give advance thought to the question of which should be the state of the applicable law, or where their intentions in this regard cannot be ascertained, it may at least be said that they expected the marriage to be valid.

In 2014, the New York Supreme Court distinguished *Farraj* as follows:

> The reasons for the parties here having had their wedding in Mexico stand in stark contrast to the reasons Mr. Farraj and Ms. Hanash traveled to New Jersey. Without a doubt, plaintiff and defendant were under no obligation, religious or otherwise, to travel to Mexico for their wedding ceremony. The only impetus for having the wedding in Mexico was the sentimental value of the beach town of Tulum, where defendant had proposed to plaintiff on vacation a year earlier, along with their desire to have a wedding at a Mexican beach resort in February. They chose the site of their wedding completely of their own volition, and once there did not make any attempt to follow the local laws. In a very real sense, the parties availed themselves of the facilities, services and hospitality of Mexico to hold a destination wedding and then completely disregarded the rules and customs of the host country.
>
> (. . .) no finding can be made here that the parties either jointly or justifiably had an expectation that they were legally married as result of the Mexican ceremony. The record clearly establishes that defendant unequivocally knew both before and after the wedding that it did not constitute a valid marriage. The record also strongly indicates that plaintiff knew, or at least should have known, this as well; after all, the very same wedding guide from the Dreams Tulum Resort that plaintiff admits she used to select the food to be served at the reception stated in no uncertain terms that the type of wedding ceremony the parties planned would only be symbolic and would not give rise to a legal marriage. Plainly, if plaintiff did not know about the legal infirmities of the purported marriage, it was because she chose not to know.
>
> (. . .) it is clear that neither defendant nor plaintiff expected, or could have expected, that their marriage was valid in Mexico. Nothing in their papers supports a reasonable inference that they contemporaneously or subsequently expected their marriage to be valid in New York. The Restatement's formulation, which, again, is merely persuasive authority and goes against longstanding Court of Appeals precedent, appears to have been adopted to protect people like the couple in *Farraj*: people who fully and reasonably believed together as a couple that they were marrying officially and had every reason to justifiably expect that their marriage was valid. Inasmuch as the parties in this case cannot be found to have had the same reasonable beliefs and justifiable expectations concerning their marriage, there is no basis to apply either the holding in *Farraj* or Restatement § 283 to circumvent the general rule of comity. Accordingly, the validity of their marriage must be determined by applicable Mexican law (. . .).[19]

What is the law in New York after these two cases?

---

19 *Ponorovskaya v. Stecklow*, 987 N.Y.S.2d 543 (N.Y. Supr. 2014).

12
Divorce

1 Jurisdiction

Under the laws of most countries, divorce must be granted judicially. In some Asian jurisdictions such as Japan, however, divorce is typically obtained from administrative authorities upon request of the parties.

1.1 United States

 CASE

Superior Court of Connecticut, Judicial District of New London, 13 September 2012 *Chamberlin v. Chamberlin*[1]

Generally, in Connecticut, 'personal jurisdiction over the other party [to a marriage dissolution] is not necessary for actions involving the marriage itself . . . [the] domicile of at least one [party] for the twelve month period preceding the actual issuance of a dissolution decree is necessary.' *Pavlick v. Pavlick*, Superior Court, judicial district of New London, Docket No. 523485 (February 4, 1993, Mihalakos, J.); see General Statutes § 46b–44(c); *Keefe v. Keefe*, Superior Court, judicial district of Hartford, Docket No. FA 00 0723938 (May 31, 2000, Gruendel, J.) ('[b]ecause any state where the parties to a marriage may be domiciled has an interest in their marital status, a state has the power to exercise judicial jurisdiction to dissolve the marriage even if only one of the spouses resides in that state'). Although the court has the power to exercise jurisdiction over the defendant to dissolve the marriage, it does not, automatically follow that the court has the power to exercise jurisdiction over the defendant 'to entertain or make orders for alimony, child support, custody, or property.' *Keefe v. Keefe, supra.* '[Personal jurisdiction] over a nonresident requires statutory authorization.' *Cato v. Cato*, 27 Conn.App. 142, 144 (1992).

---

1 54 Conn. L. Rptr. 623.

The 'statutory basis for [personal] jurisdiction is mandatory, and . . . the concept of due process cannot take the place of statutory compliance.' *Id.*

 CASE

Superior Court of Connecticut, Judicial District of New Haven, July 28, 1989 *Babouder v. Abdennur*[2]

Fuller, Judge.

This action for dissolution of marriage commenced when the defendant was served with a copy of the complaint on May 10, 1989. The defendant has filed a motion to dismiss the complaint on five grounds: (1) personal service upon the defendant was accomplished by trick, fraud or artifice; (2) the plaintiff is not a resident of Connecticut now or when this action was commenced, and therefore has no standing to bring or to maintain this action under General Statutes § 46b-44; (3) there is pending in the Family Court, Patriarchy of Catholics, in Beirut, Lebanon, a prior claim commenced by the plaintiff claiming similar relief; (4) the plaintiff failed to file a custody statement as required by General Statutes § 46b-99; (5) the plaintiff allegedly violated the clean hands doctrine by her unauthorized removal of the parties' minor child from Lebanon in violation of a court order, by the method she used to serve the complaint on the defendant, and by her misrepresentation as to her residence. (. . .)

The defendant claims that personal jurisdiction was obtained over him by trick, fraud and artifice by the plaintiff and her attorney because of the method used to obtain service of process. The defendant's affidavit, which the court accepts for the factual basis of this claim, particularly since it was not contradicted by the plaintiff's testimony or affidavit, is as follows: The defendant, after determining that his wife was living with a man in New Haven, came to the United States from the United Arab Emirates. After the defendant contacted the plaintiff by telephone, the plaintiff told him that if he wanted to see their daughter, he would have to arrange it through the plaintiff's attorney, Elizabeth Curry. When the attorney was contacted, the defendant was told that he had to come to the attorney's office that afternoon at 5:30 to make arrangements. When the defendant arrived, the attorney had the sheriff serve him with this action and other legal papers. In Connecticut, as in other states, the court will not exercise jurisdiction in a civil case which is based upon

---

2 41 Conn.Supp. 258.

service of process on a defendant who has been decoyed, enticed or induced to come within the court's jurisdiction by any false representation, deceitful contrivance or wrongful device for which the plaintiff is responsible. *Siro v. American Express Co.,* 99 Conn. 95, 98 (1923); *Hill v. Goodrich,* 32 Conn. 588 (1865). This also applies to conduct by a plaintiff's agents and attorneys. *Hill v. Goodrich,* at 590. This rule does not apply, however, when the defendant enters the state on his own, even if the plaintiff and his agents then engage in trickery to make service of process. (. . .). In the present case, the defendant came to Connecticut voluntarily, and the attempt to serve him did not occur until after he had arrived. The action will not, under these circumstances, be dismissed for abuse of process. (. . .)

The final claim is that the plaintiff does not have standing to bring this action since she is not a resident of this state, but a citizen and domiciliary of Lebanon, where she was born, married and resided before entering the United States on September 4, 1988. At the hearing on this motion there was testimony from the plaintiff and Sheila Brent, an attorney specializing in immigration law, as to the plaintiff's immigration status. The complaint alleges that the plaintiff had been a resident of this state for nine months when the action was started on May 10, 1989. Where a motion to dismiss is accompanied by supporting affidavits containing undisputed facts, those facts may be accepted on jurisdictional issues, and the court does not have to presume the validity of the allegations of the complaint. *Barde v. Board of Trustees,* 207 Conn. at 62. Where there is testimony on a motion to dismiss, it can be given more weight than statements in affidavits. *Rosenblit v. Danaher,* 206 Conn. 125, 136 (1988).

The plaintiff applied for and obtained a B-1 Business Visa from the United States consulate in Lebanon, which allowed her to come to the United States. To obtain this type of visa she was required to swear that she was a resident of Lebanon and intended to return there when the visa expired. Upon arriving in the United States, and in order to enter, she was issued an I-94 form which governs the length of the authorized stay under the visa and is issued for six months. One six month extension is allowed for a B-1 Business Visa, and one has been granted to the plaintiff until September 3, 1989. Since this is a temporary visa, for immigration law purposes a person cannot establish residence here while in a B-1 status, because it is issued on the basis that the applicant is a resident of another country and will return there when the visa expires; it does not establish any legal status in this country. The plaintiff has no relatives here and has not applied for a change in her status or type of visa, and remains a nonimmigrant visitor to this country. Even a change in status, if applied for, cannot establish residence retroactively. The defendant claims that the plaintiff's temporary status here also cannot give her residency status for purposes of satisfying the statutory requirements for a dissolution action under the laws of this state. The plaintiff claims that she intends to remain in Connecticut, eventually hopes to marry the man with whom she is residing in New Haven, and that the intent to remain, if possible, gives her standing to bring this action.

The pertinent statute is § 46b-44, which provides in part: '(a) A complaint for dissolution of a marriage or for legal separation may be filed at any time after either party has established residence in this state. (b) Temporary relief pursuant to the complaint may be granted in accordance with sections 46b-56 and 46b-83 at any time after either party has established residence in this state. (c) Decree dissolving a marriage or granting a legal separation may be entered if: (1) One of the parties to the marriage has been a resident of this state for at least twelve months next preceding the date of the filing of the complaint or next preceding the date of the decree . . .' While the court has personal jurisdiction over the defendant because of the personal service of the complaint on him, the court can enter a dissolution of the marriage without personal jurisdiction over the defendant; *Fernandez v. Fernandez*, 208 Conn. 329, 334 (1988); if the plaintiff meets the residency requirement in the statute. A dissolution can be filed and the court has subject matter jurisdiction if the plaintiff is a resident of the state at the time the action was started. *Cugini v. Cugini*, 13 Conn.App. 632, 635 (1988). Residency of one party without a showing of domicil is sufficient to give the court jurisdiction for the purposes of filing a complaint or for the granting of alimony and support pendente lite. *LaBow v. LaBow*, 171 Conn. at 439. A party can have more than one residence, and residence with intent to remain in Connecticut is the foundation for jurisdiction. *Cugini*, at 636. A dissolution decree cannot be granted until twelve months after the plaintiff has established residence in this state. General Statutes § 46b-44(c)(1); *LaBow v. LaBow*, at 438. Jurisdiction for filing the action and jurisdiction to grant a dissolution have different requirements. The court finds that the plaintiff intended to reside here permanently when she filed this action even if she may not be able to accomplish that objective without a future change in her status under the immigration laws.

The key question is whether the plaintiff can be a resident for purposes of § 46b-44 when she intends to reside here permanently when the action is filed but is not a resident and is in a nonimmigrant status, under a temporary visa, for immigration law purposes. In *Torlonia v. Torlonia*, 108 Conn. 292, 142 A. 843 (1928), the plaintiff was born in the United States but was apparently a citizen of Italy who came to the United States under a nonimmigrant visitor's visa. Despite her entry into this country on a temporary basis, she was not precluded from establishing her domicil in this state for purposes of maintaining a divorce action. A similar result has been reached in other states where the plaintiff is in this country only on a temporary visa. The fact that the plaintiff entered the country with intent at that time to return to the foreign country did not prevent the plaintiff from acquiring residence status to bring a dissolution action in *Williams v. Williams*, 328 F.Supp. 1380 (D. St. Croix 1971); or prevent 'dual intent,' namely intent to remain if that could be accomplished, or intent to leave if required by law, which conferred standing to file the action. *Bustamante v. Bustamante, supra.* In *Alves v. Alves*, 262 A.2d 111 (D.C.1970), where the plaintiff had the present intent to reside in the District of Columbia, the court held that the absence of a visa giving the legal right to remain in the United States did not prevent jurisdiction for a divorce action. In *Santangelo v. Santangelo*, 137 Conn. 404, 408 (1951), the fact that the plaintiff was a nonresident of the state did not prevent a collateral attack on a prior divorce decree rendered in another state obtained by the defendant, and the court stated that an alien was in the same position as a nonresident. The plaintiff in the present case sufficiently meets the residency requirement in § 46b-44(a). This court, therefore, has subject matter jurisdiction.

The motion to dismiss is denied.

 NOTES AND QUESTIONS

1   The vast majority of American states share the same jurisdictional rule: domicile, or residence, of one of the parties in the forum suffices to give jurisdiction to its courts to rule on divorce. The judgments of the Supreme Court in *Williams* are considered to be authority for that proposition,[3] although they were concerned with the recognition of a foreign divorce decree. The Court explained:

> Domicil implies a nexus between person and place of such permanence as to control the creation of legal relations and responsibilities of the utmost significance. The domicil of one spouse within a State gives power to that State, we have held, to dissolve a marriage wheresoever contracted. (. . .) Divorce, like marriage, is of concern not merely to the immediate parties. It affects personal rights of the deepest significance. It also touches basic interests of society. Since divorce like marriage, creates a new status, every consideration of policy makes it desirable that the effect should be the same wherever the question arises.[4]

3   *Williams v. North Carolina I* 317 U.S. 287 (1942); *Williams v. North Carolina (II)*, 325 U.S. 226 (1945).
4   *Williams II*, at 229–30.

2   In many jurisdictions, granting jurisdiction to the courts of the domicile of the plaintiff (*forum actoris*) is considered as unfair to the defendant. One would have expected U.S. courts to find that such jurisdiction violates the Due Process clause for lack of nexus between the court and the defendant (*supra* Chapter 3). But, as the previous quote exemplifies, the foundation of the jurisdiction of the court of the domicile has been understood in public law terms. Some federal courts have held that relying on other criteria such as a six weeks' residence would actually violate the Due Process clause.[5] Would the Connecticut statute (§ 46b-44) resist a constitutional challenge?

3   As shall be shortly explained, American courts apply the law of the forum to divorce actions. The jurisdictional rule is thus indirectly the choice of law rule in American divorce actions. Can plaintiffs freely choose the law governing their action? Which steps do they have to take in order to secure the jurisdiction of their preferred court?

1.2   European Union

EU Regulation No 2201/2003 of 27 November 2003 concerning jurisdiction and the recognition and enforcement of judgments in matrimonial matters and the matters of parental responsibility (Brussels IIbis)

CHAPTER II JURISDICTION

SECTION 1 Divorce, legal separation and marriage annulment

Article 3 *General jurisdiction*

1. In matters relating to divorce, legal separation or marriage annulment, jurisdiction shall lie with the courts of the Member State

(a) in whose territory:

- the spouses are habitually resident, or
- the spouses were last habitually resident, insofar as one of them still resides there, or
- the respondent is habitually resident, or
- in the event of a joint application, either of the spouses is habitually resident, or
- the applicant is habitually resident if he or she resided there for at least a year immediately before the application was made, or
- the applicant is habitually resident if he or she resided there for at least six months immediately before the application was made and is either a national of the Member State in question or, in the case of the United Kingdom and Ireland, has his or her 'domicile' there;

(b) of the nationality of both spouses or, in the case of the United Kingdom and Ireland, of the 'domicile' of both spouses.

2. For the purpose of this Regulation, 'domicile' shall have the same meaning as it has under the legal systems of the United Kingdom and Ireland.

---

5   See eg *Alton v. Alton*, 207 F.2d 667 (3 Cir. 1953).

Article 6 *Exclusive nature of jurisdiction under Articles 3, 4 and 5*

A spouse who:

(a) is habitually resident in the territory of a Member State; or

(b) is a national of a Member State, or, in the case of the United Kingdom and Ireland, has his or her 'domicile' in the territory of one of the latter Member States, may be sued in another Member State only in accordance with Articles 3, 4 and 5.

Article 7 *Residual jurisdiction*

1. Where no court of a Member State has jurisdiction pursuant to Articles 3, 4 and 5, jurisdiction shall be determined, in each Member State, by the laws of that State.

2. As against a respondent who is not habitually resident and is not either a national of a Member State or, in the case of the United Kingdom and Ireland, does not have his 'domicile' within the territory of one of the latter Member States, any national of a Member State who is habitually resident within the territory of another Member State may, like the nationals of that State, avail himself of the rules of jurisdiction applicable in that State.

 NOTES AND QUESTIONS

1. Contrary to the Rome III Regulation for choice of law (*infra*, 2.2), the Brussels IIbis Regulation is applicable in all Member States of the European Union, with the exception of Denmark. There is no mirror convention applicable to Switzerland, Norway and Iceland.

2. The jurisdictional rules of the Brussels IIbis Regulation are exclusive of the application of national rules of jurisdiction of the Member States where the defendant has his habitual residence within the European Union or is a national of a Member State (Art. 6). Where the defendant resides habitually outside of the European Union and is a national of a third State, national rules of jurisdiction apply (Art. 7), including available exorbitant heads of jurisdiction.

3. Article 3 grants jurisdiction to seven courts without establishing any hierarchy among them. A strict *lis pendens* rule applies.[6] Will this result in a rush to the courts that each spouse will perceive as more favourable to his/her interests, whether for legal and psychological reasons? Suppose spouses of different nationalities separate and go back to their respective country of origin. They then consider initiating divorce proceedings and would like to secure the jurisdiction of their home court by suing first there. Does Art. 3 allow it?

1.3   China

Under Art. 22 of the Chinese Civil Procedure Act of 1991, Chinese courts will entertain divorce proceedings if the defendant is domiciled or resides within the jurisdiction of the court.

However, in an Opinion on Some Issues relating to the Application of the Civil Procedure Act issued on 14 July 1992, the Chinese Supreme Court decided that Chinese courts should also retain jurisdiction in cases involving overseas Chinese:

---

6 Art. 19. The rule is similar to the rule found in the Brussels Ibis Regulation: see *supra* p. 202.

1. where the marriage was celebrated in China, or
2. where both spouses live abroad, but the foreign court declined jurisdiction on the ground that the dispute should be decided by the court of the common nationality of the spouses, or
3. where a spouse living in China wishes to initiate proceedings against a spouse living abroad.[7]

1.4 Japan

There is no express provision in Japanese legislation on jurisdiction in divorce matters, but the Japanese parliament was considering a bill on international jurisdiction in personal matters in 2016. The Japanese Supreme Court has rarely ruled on the issue,[8] because judicial divorce is rarely granted by Japanese courts, and spouses typically divorce by filing a joint declaration with a family registration official.

There is no rule of jurisdiction limiting the power of registration officials to accept a joint filing for divorce: one of the spouses must simply be 'present' in Japan. However, while the official might accept to issue a 'certificate attesting the official acceptance of a filing for divorce' absent any other connection with Japan, he will only do so if the applicable law pursuant to the Japanese choice of law rule allows divorce by agreement. Article 27 of the Application of Laws Act (*infra*, 2.2) allows him to apply Japanese law if one spouse is both a national of and resident in Japan.

2 Choice of law

2.1 Law of the forum

In the common law tradition, courts have traditionally applied the law of the forum in divorce cases.

---

7 See Weidong Zhu, 'The New Conflicts Rules for Family and Inheritance Matters in China' (2012–2013) 14 Yearbook Pr. Int. L. 369.

8 Yasuhiro Okuda, 'Divorce, Protection of Minors, and Child Abduction in Japan's Private International Law', in Jürgen Basedow, Harald Baum and Yuko Nishitani (eds), *Japanese and European Private International Law in Comparative Perspective* (Mohr Siebeck 2008) 305.

CASE

UK Supreme Court, 20 October 2010 *Radmacher v. Granatino*[9]

103. In England, when the court exercises its jurisdiction to make an order for financial relief under the Matrimonial Causes Act 1973, it will normally apply English law, irrespective of the domicile of the parties, or any foreign connection: *Dicey, Morris & Collins, The Conflict of Laws*, 14th ed (2006), vol 2, rule 91(7), and e.g. *C v. C (Ancillary Relief: Nuptial Settlement)* [2005] Fam 250, para 31.

104. The United Kingdom has made a policy decision not to participate in the results of the work done by the European Community and the Hague Conference on Private International Law to apply uniform rules of private international law in relation to maintenance obligations. Although the United Kingdom Government has opted in to Council Regulation (EC) No 4/2009 of 18 December 2008 on jurisdiction, applicable law, recognition and enforcement of decisions and cooperation in matters relating to maintenance obligations, the rules relating to applicable law will not apply in the United Kingdom. That is because the effect of article 15 of the Council Regulation is that the law applicable to maintenance obligations is to be determined in accordance with the 2007 Hague Protocol on the law applicable to maintenance obligations, but only in the member states bound by the Hague Protocol.

105. The United Kingdom will not be bound by the Hague Protocol, because it agreed to participate in the Council Regulation only on the basis that it would not be obliged to join in accession to the Hague Protocol by the EU. The United Kingdom Government's position was that there was very little application of foreign law in family matters within the United Kingdom, and in maintenance cases in particular the expense of proving the content of that law would be disproportionate to the low value of the vast majority of maintenance claims.

NOTES AND QUESTIONS

1   This case was concerned with an application for financial relief made by a husband against his wife in the context of divorce proceedings. While English courts have rarely ruled on the issue of the applicable law to other aspects of divorce, nullity of marriage or legal separation, the proposition that English courts normally apply English law in divorce proceedings is widely accepted. It was long expressed in s. 46(2) of the Matrimonial Causes Act 1973. This provision was repealed, but it is understood that the law has remained the same.[10]

2   The rule has long been the same in the United States, where courts have almost always applied forum's law to determine grounds for divorce.[11]

---

9 [2010] UKSC 42.

10 Dicey, Morris and Collins, § 18-029.

11 Richman and Reynolds, § 120.

3 As the U.K. Supreme Court underscores, a major advantage of forum's law is that it needs not be proven. The resolution of the dispute is thus less costly. However, the argument could be made for all disputes, and would militate for the application of forum's law in all cases.[12]

4 Forty years ago, English[13] and American[14] scholars made the more interesting argument that the rationale for the application of the law of the forum would be that divorce law is mandatory in character, and that the forum should thus necessarily apply its own law. While divorce might have been allowed in a few defined cases in the past, it is more broadly available in many countries today. Is the argument that divorce law should be internationally mandatory convincing in jurisdictions where divorce by consent is widely available?

5 Choice of law rules may only be applied by courts which retain jurisdiction. They should thus be read in conjunction with jurisdictional rules. If common law courts only retained jurisdiction on the basis of the domicile of the parties, the application of the law of forum would be uncontroversial, as it would in truth amount to the application of the personal law of the parties, that is, the law of their domicile.[15] Is it the case, however?

6 The application of the law of the forum creates an incentive for forum shopping. One way to address the issue is to limit the cases in which the court would retain jurisdiction. How broad is the jurisdiction of American courts in divorce proceedings (*supra*, 1.1)? Does it significantly limit the possibilities of out-of-state residents to shop around for their preferred law?

7 London has the reputation for being the world's divorce capital. English courts will apply English law, but are the doors of English courts open to any interested customer? Where the defendant habitually resides in the European Union or is a national of a Member State, their jurisdiction is defined by the Brussels IIbis Regulation: can you determine which steps a plaintiff wishing to sue in London will have to take for jurisdiction to lie with an English court (*supra*, 1.2)?

In other cases, it is defined by s. 5(2)(b) of the Domicile and Matrimonial Proceedings Act 1973:

Section 5. *Jurisdiction of High Court and county courts*

(2) The [High court or divorce county court] shall have jurisdiction to entertain proceedings for divorce and judicial separation if (and only if):

(a) The court has jurisdiction under the Council Regulation; or

(b) No court of a Contracting State has jurisdiction under the Council Regulation and either of the parties to the marriage is domiciled in England and Wales on the date when the proceedings are begun.

Is jurisdiction wide enough to promote London as the world's divorce capital?

---

12 Peter M. North, 'Development of Rules of Private International Law in the Field of Family Law' (1980) 166 Collected Courses of the Hague Academy of International Law 82.

13 North, n. 12, p. 83.

14 David Cavers, 'Contemporary Conflicts Law in American Perspective' (1970) 131 Collected Courses of the Hague Academy of International Law 245.

15 North, n. 12, p. 83.

Chinese choice of law rules also provided for the application of the law of the forum. In 2010, an exception was made for consensual divorce, but the traditional rule remains with respect to non-consensual divorce.

Law of the People's Republic of China on the Laws Applicable to Foreign-Related Civil Relations (2010)

Article 26 In respect of consented divorce, the parties may by agreement choose to apply the law of a party's habitual residence or nationality. Absent any choice by the parties, the law of their common habitual residence shall be applied; absent common habitual residence, the law of their common nationality shall be applied; absent common nationality, the law of the place where the agency responsible for completing the divorce formalities is located shall be applied.

Article 27 Divorce decided by a court is governed by the law of the forum.

2.2   Law of common nationality

In the civil law tradition, personal status in general and the substantive validity of marriage in particular have traditionally been governed by the law of nationality. The effects of marriage were logically subjected to the law of the common nationality of the spouses, and divorce was analysed as an effect of marriage.

Japanese Act on the General Rules of Application of Laws (1989)

Article 25 *Effect of Marriage*

The effect of a marriage shall be governed by the spouses' national law when it is the same, or where that is not the case, by the law of the spouses' habitual residence when that is the same, or where neither of these is the case, by the law of the place with which the spouses are most closely connected.

Article 27 *Divorce*

Article 25 shall apply mutatis mutandis to divorce. However, divorce shall be governed by Japanese law where one of the spouses is a Japanese national with habitual residence in Japan.

Tunisian Code of Private International Law (1998)

Article 49

Divorce and separation are governed by the law of the common nationality of the spouses in force when the proceedings are initiated. Failing a common nationality, the applicable law is the law of the last common domicile of the parties or, failing that, the law of the forum. Provisional measures granted during the proceedings are governed by Tunisian law.

? NOTES

1 Article 49 of the Tunisian Code reflects the choice of law rule laid down by the French Supreme Court in 1953 and codified in Luxembourg in 1990. In both countries, however, the Rome III Regulation (*infra*, 2.3) has superseded these rules.
2 The obvious issue raised by common nationality is that the spouses can hold different nationalities. A default choice of law rule is thus necessary. Civil law jurisdictions have typically relied on common domicile or residence, or to a more flexible criterion such as the country to which the spouses are the most closely connected.

2.3 Law of common habitual residence

Regulation (EU) No 1259/2010 of 20 December 2010 implementing enhanced cooperation in the area of the law applicable to divorce and legal separation (Rome III Regulation)

Article 8 *Applicable law in the absence of a choice by the parties*

In the absence of a choice pursuant to Article 5, divorce and legal separation shall be subject to the law of the State:

(a) where the spouses are habitually resident at the time the court is seized; or, failing that

(b) where the spouses were last habitually resident, provided that the period of residence did not end more than 1 year before the court was seized, in so far as one of the spouses still resides in that State at the time the court is seized; or, failing that

(c) of which both spouses are nationals at the time the court is seized; or, failing that

(d) where the court is seized.

? NOTES

1 The Rome III Regulation only applies in 14 Member States, which include Germany, Spain, Italy, France and Luxembourg. Others, including the United Kingdom, apply their national choice of law rules. In the participating Member States, the Regulation entirely supersedes the previous legal regime, as their courts must apply the regulation in all disputes, irrespective of the applicable law and their connection with Europe.
2 Article 8 provides primarily for the application of the last common habitual residence of the spouses. It is only if divorce proceedings are initiated more than a year after the spouses separated that another law will apply, or if both spouses have left the place of their last common habitual residence. This law will be the law of the common nationality of the spouses, or, failing that, the law of the forum. This last possibility must be read in conjunction with the jurisdictional rules of the Brussels IIbis Regulation: jurisdiction will lie with the court of either the residence of the defendant, or, under certain conditions, the residence of the plaintiff (*supra*, 1.2).
3 In the majority of the participating Member States, the law of the common nationality of the spouses governed divorce. The priority given by Art. 8 to the common habitual residence over common nationality is thus an important innovation. The European lawmaker considered that

Europe being an immigration destination, the application of the law of the place of residence would strengthen internal cohesion and ease the administration of justice. More generally, relying on nationality is increasingly perceived as incompatible with the European project of building a common area of justice.

2.4   Choice of applicable law by the parties

Rome III Regulation (2010)

Preamble

(15) Increasing the mobility of citizens calls for more flexibility and greater legal certainty. In order to achieve that objective, this Regulation should enhance the parties' autonomy in the areas of divorce and legal separation by giving them a limited possibility to choose the law applicable to their divorce or legal separation. (16) Spouses should be able to choose the law of a country with which they have a special connection or the law of the forum as the law applicable to divorce and legal separation. The law chosen by the spouses must be consonant with the fundamental rights recognised by the Treaties and the Charter of Fundamental Rights of the European Union. (17) Before designating the applicable law, it is important for spouses to have access to up-to-date information concerning the essential aspects of national and Union law and of the procedures governing divorce and legal separation. To guarantee such access to appropriate, good-quality information, the Commission regularly updates it in the Internet-based public information system set up by Council Decision 2001/470/EC. (18) The informed choice of both spouses is a basic principle of this Regulation. Each spouse should know exactly what are the legal and social implications of the choice of applicable law. The possibility of choosing the applicable law by common agreement should be without prejudice to the rights of, and equal opportunities for, the two spouses. Hence judges in the participating Member States should be aware of the importance of an informed choice on the part of the two spouses concerning the legal implications of the choice-of-law agreement concluded.

Chapter II – Uniform Rules on the Law Applicable to Divorce and Legal Separation

Article 5 *Choice of applicable law by the parties*
1. The spouses may agree to designate the law applicable to divorce and legal separation provided that it is one of the following laws:

(a)   the law of the State where the spouses are habitually resident at the time the agreement is concluded; or

(b)   the law of the State where the spouses were last habitually resident, in so far as one of them still resides there at the time the agreement is concluded; or

(c)   the law of the State of nationality of either spouse at the time the agreement is concluded; or

(d)   the law of the *forum*.

2. Without prejudice to paragraph 3, an agreement designating the applicable law may be concluded and modified at any time, but at the latest at the time the court is seized.

3. If the law of the *forum* so provides, the spouses may also designate the law applicable before the court during the course of the proceeding. In that event, such designation shall be recorded in court in accordance with the law of the *forum*.

Article 6 *Consent and material validity*

1. The existence and validity of an agreement on choice of law or of any term thereof, shall be determined by the law which would govern it under this Regulation if the agreement or term were valid.

2. Nevertheless, a spouse, in order to establish that he did not consent, may rely upon the law of the country in which he has his habitual residence at the time the court is seized if it appears from the circumstances that it would not be reasonable to determine the effect of his conduct in accordance with the law specified in paragraph 1.

Article 7 *Formal validity*

1. The agreement referred to in Article 5(1) and (2), shall be expressed in writing, dated and signed by both spouses. Any communication by electronic means which provides a durable record of the agreement shall be deemed equivalent to writing.

2. However, if the law of the participating Member State in which the two spouses have their habitual residence at the time the agreement is concluded lays down additional formal requirements for this type of agreement, those requirements shall apply.

3. If the spouses are habitually resident in different participating Member States at the time the agreement is concluded and the laws of those States provide for different formal requirements, the agreement shall be formally valid if it satisfies the requirements of either of those laws.

4. If only one of the spouses is habitually resident in a participating Member State at the time the agreement is concluded and that State lays down additional formal requirements for this type of agreement, those requirements shall apply.

? NOTES AND QUESTIONS

1   Contrary to the rule found in contractual matters, Art. 5 does not grant unlimited freedom of choice. It allows the parties to choose between a number of laws which are all reasonably connected to the dispute. Recall that the law of the forum will indirectly be determined by the Brussels IIbis Regulation.

2 Recital 18 of the Preamble explains that the informed choice of both spouses is a basic principle of the Regulation. The choice could indeed have dramatic consequences. How does the Regulation ensure that the choice be indeed informed? Pursuant to Art. 7, the spouses may enter into an agreement on the applicable law on their own. Will the website announced by Recital 17 suffice for that purpose? If a national law requires the involvement of a lawyer (for instance a notary), does this requirement apply?

3 When should it be possible to designate the law applicable to divorce? Article 5 allows for a choice of law at the time of marriage, but also shortly before the initiation of the proceedings. While the spouses should be able to agree easily at the earliest stage of their relationship, their choice might produce consequences decades later. The chosen law might have changed dramatically. Agreements might be harder to reach shortly before separation, but spouses contemplating a consensual divorce may be able to agree on a law and a jurisdiction where such divorce can be obtained at the lowest cost. Recall that Art. 3 of the Brussels IIbis Regulation grants jurisdiction to seven courts where the parties could freely decide to initiate jointly the proceedings.

Law of the People's Republic of China on the Laws Applicable to Foreign-Related Civil Relations (2010)

Article 26 In respect of consensual divorce, the parties may by agreement choose to apply the law of a party's habitual residence or nationality. Absent any choice by the parties, (. . .)

Article 27 Divorce decided by a court is governed by the law of the forum.

 NOTES

1 As Art. 5 of the EU Regulation, Art. 26 grants a limited freedom of choice to choose the law governing divorce. The rule allows overseas Chinese married in China to displace the application of the law of their residence and to choose the application of Chinese law.

2 Unlike the EU Regulation, Art. 26 limits the scope of such freedom to consensual divorce.

Short bibliography

Comparative conflict of laws

Basedow, J., F. Ferrari, G. Rühl and P. de Miguel Asensio (eds.), *Encyclopedia of Private International Law* (Edward Elgar 2016).

Hartley, T., *International Commercial Litigation – Texts, Cases and Materials on Private International Law*, 2nd edn (Cambridge University Press 2015).

Hay, P., R. Weintraub and P.J. Borchers, *Comparative Conflict of Laws: Conventions, Regulations and Codes* (Thomson Reuters 2009).

Symeonides, S., *Codifying Choice of Law Around the World* (Oxford University Press 2014).

Asia

Carballo Leyda, A. (ed.), *Asian Conflict of Laws: East and South East Asia* (Wolters Kluwer 2015).

Commonwealth Africa

Frimpong Oppong, R., *Private International Law in Commonwealth Africa* (Cambridge University Press 2013).

England and Wales

Briggs, A., *The Conflict of Laws*, 3rd edn (Oxford University Press 2013).

Collins, L. et al., *Dicey, Morris and Collins on the Conflict of Laws*, 15th edn (Sweet & Maxwell 2015).

Rogerson, P., *Collier's Conflict of Laws*, 4th edn (Cambridge University Press 2013).

France

Batiffol, H. and P. Lagarde, *Droit international privé* (Sirey, Vol. I 1993, Vol. II 1983).

Mayer, P. and V. Heuzé, *Droit international privé*, 11th edn (Lextenso 2014).

Muir Watt, H. and D. Bureau, *Droit international privé*, 3rd edn (PUF, 2 vol., 2014).

Germany

von Bar, Ch. and P. Mankowski, *Internationales Privatrecht* (Beck, Vol. I 2003, Vol. II 1991).

von Hoffmann, B. and K. Thorn, *Internationales Privatrecht*, 10th edn (Beck 2016).

Italy

Ballarino, T. and D. Milan, *Corso di diritto internazionale private* (CEDAM 2008).
Barel, S. and B. Armellini, *Manuele breve de diritto internazionale private* (Giuffre 2012).

USA

Brilmayer, L., J. Goldsmith and E. O'Hara O'Connor, *Conflict of Laws: Cases and Materials*, 7th edn (Aspen 2015).
Currie, D., H. Kay, L. Kramer and K. Roosevelt, *Conflict of Laws: Cases, Comments, Questions*, 9th edn (West 2013).
Hay, P., P. Borchers and S. Symeonides, *Conflict of Laws*, 5th edn (West 2010).
Little, L., *Conflict of Laws: Cases, Materials and Problems* (Aspen 2013).
Richman, W. and W. Reynolds, *Understanding Conflict of Laws*, 4th edn (Carolina Academic Press 2013).
Weintraub, R., *Commentary on the Conflict of Laws*, 6th edn (Foundation Press 2010).

Index